The Supervisor
and the Job

McGraw-Hill Series in Management

Keith Davis and Fred Luthans, *Consulting Editors*

The Supervisor and the Job

Third Edition

Aaron Q. Sartain
Alton W. Baker
Southern Methodist University

McGraw-Hill Book Company

New York   St. Louis   San Francisco   Auckland   Bogotá   Düsseldorf
Johannesburg   London   Madrid   Mexico   Montreal   New Delhi   Panama
Paris   São Paulo   Singapore   Sydney   Tokyo   Toronto

To Our Wives
Thelma and Mary

Library of Congress Cataloging in Publication Data

Sartain, Aaron Quinn   date
    The supervisor and the job.

    (McGraw-Hill series in management)
    Published in 1965 and 1972 under title: The supervisor and his job.
    Bibliography: p.
    Includes index.
    1. Supervisors.   2.   Supervision of employees.
I.   Baker, Alton Wesley   date   joint author.
II.   Title.
HF5549.S175   1978   658.3'02   77-24624
ISBN 0-07-054756-4

THE SUPERVISOR AND THE JOB

3 4 5 6 7 8 9 0 F G R F G R 7 8 3 2 1 0 9

This book was set in Times Roman by National ShareGraphics, Inc.
The editors were William J. Kane and Barry Benjamin;
the cover was designed by John Hite;
the production supervisor was Dennis J. Conroy.
The drawings were done by Fine Line Illustrations, Inc.
Fairfield Graphics was printer and binder.

Contents

Preface

In looking backward over the last few years since our second edition it becomes more and more clear, from the vantage point of our experience, that one of the most important—though sometimes the most difficult—things that the supervisor of today can do is to learn to bend constantly with the winds of change. Generally speaking, managing people will never be the same as in the past, even the very recent past.

Employees increasingly have more rights, and supervisors have had added to their world new forces—many *external to their firms*—that have profoundly changed their jobs. For example, as we discuss in a new chapter concerned with OSHA, a federal agent called a compliance officer from the Occupational Safety and Health Administration, sometimes colorfully referred to as "The Man from OSHA," armed with the capability of enforcing sweeping legislative changes, can enter the supervisors' workplaces at will (indeed it is a violation of federal law to give advance notice to anybody), interview their employees, and monitor their health and safety performance.

In another new chapter, which deals with civil rights, we note that much of the literature in recent years has been directed at the responsibilities of higher management for developing and installing affirmative action programs. In our experiences, many supervisors of firms where affirmative action programs have been installed have little or no concept of what such a program means to them. For one thing, there is often little recognition that after the initial phase of recruitment and hiring of minorities, a variety of supervisory decisions must be made; for example, how much remedial training and development should be given and how should this be handled? Will standards of performance, promotion, and discipline need to be relaxed until minority employees are fully productive? How should regular employees be handled, who may in some instances resent what appears to them to be pampering and perhaps reverse discrimination?

In reviewing managerial practices in the planning and decision-making process and in operating under a management systems program, we note that the fundamental decision-making skills of the individual supervisor (especially the career-minded individual with ambition and drive toward higher levels of management) are still of critical importance, despite progress made in the application of the systems-management approach in some well-defined areas such as accounting, inventory control, production scheduling and control, and purchasing.

In such areas especially, management often has greatly helped supervisors to develop *decision alternatives,* narrowing the range from which informed supervisory judgment must come. However, it is clear that in many instances, supervisors—and especially higher-level managers—are confronted with poorly structured *problems* concerning such areas as training and development, motivation, and disciplining of employees. Finding and clearly defining *problems* is, of course, the first and indispensable step in the decision-making process.

In our experience, the intelligent use of computers, PERT, and the various kinds of flow-process charts and other tools and techniques of systems management we discuss is more likely to extend, rather than replace, the competent supervisor's capacities, relieving him or her of much routine and structured work. Certainly we are at present far from achieving the total management systems mentioned in management literature so often in recent years.

A hard look at Management by Objectives and/or Management by Results in action over the past few years—another new chapter in this edition—reveals that this technique has many inherent problems which have accounted for its spotty record of success througout industry, academia, business, and government. Management by Objectives and/or Results programs have very frequently had, and will continue to have, only limited success unless they are supported by a number of more sophisticated management techniques than are now being widely applied (including measures for identifying at the outset some of the individual's personal goals, more sophisticated performance evaluation, job design, compensation, training and development, and similar techniques) and more dedication, capability, and commitment than many supervisors have. Though we note that enthusiasm for MBO and/or Results is still quite high throughout the country, it is obvious that such approaches are not for all organizations or for all supervisors.

In this edition we place special emphasis on the point that all institutions are accountable for the quality of life; that since our society is increasingly becoming one of business organizations, supervisors more and more will have to make fulfillment of basic social values, beliefs, and purposes a major objective of their continuing activities rather than a social responsibility that restrains or lies outside their primary functions.

This is because our society as a whole is changing. For an individual, the most important motivational factors are social concerns. We may not welcome—but must expect—such happenings as increasing involvement of the government in supervisory affairs. Social and environmental factors will each, for different but in some cases associated reasons, encourage greater governmental intervention.

Finally, it is worth noting that in this edition we spend relatively little time on the history of management, with its well-catalogued "schools of thought," disciplinary contributions, achievements (and jealousies), and so on. This is not because we consider such data unimportant, for they are, especially to the advanced student; one has to acknowledge that the ways of the past are often compelling and can be of invaluable aid to us in improving our very difficult task of prediction. However, a comprehensive history of management requires much more space than we have at our disposal. Also, there are a number of outstanding books on the history of management.

We have preferred to restrict our discussion to what we shall refer to simply as modern management theories and practices, including a sampling of theories, concepts, and practices (without labeling them as "behavioral," "traditional," and so forth), which we consider to be of value to those who aspire to be supervisors, or teach supervision, or manage supervisors, or simply those interested in knowing something of what we consider to be a very fascinating and significant facet of organization life.

We would like to acknowledge the assistance of our colleagues who read the manuscript in its various stages and offered many helpful suggestions. They are: Keith Davis, Arizona State University; Winston E. Wallace, North Dakota State University; John W. Lloyd, Monroe Community College; and William Wright, Sante Fe Community College. To these and the many others who contributed to this work, our heartfelt thanks.

Aaron Q. Sartain
Alton W. Baker

Part One

Introduction

In every work situation where one person has responsibility for overseeing the work of another or others, the supervisor-subordinate relationship has been set up. Naturally our first tendency was, and perhaps still is, to take such a relationship for granted and, as supervisors, merely "to do what comes naturally." In some instances this has proved to be a satisfactory course of action. In many others it has left much to be desired. It is inevitable therefore that people have developed theories about what constitutes good supervision.

One of these theories allowed great leeway to the supervisor. Those under his or her direction were to do as they were told—or alternatively "to get off the ship." Valuable as this point of view was—and under certain circumstances may continue to be—it had limitations. What happened, for example, if the subordinate fails to do as told and also fails to resign? Or what is the proper outcome if the demand of the supervisor is unreasonable or his/her manner of giving orders is so offensive as to demotivate the subordinate?

Another approach has been to talk to supervisors about highsounding virtues like honesty, fairness, decisiveness, drive, consideration, and the like. One can hardly come out against these but, on the other hand, even an extended discussion of one or all of them is seldom of any real aid to the supervisor faced by an important employee problem.

Still another attack on this situation stressed the "how-to-do-it" approach. Here the advice is often a set of apparently obvious directions supposed to solve, or maybe prevent, most or all problems. Thus the supervisor is encouraged to call the person by his first name; to reprimand in private but to praise generously in public; or to plant suggestions in the minds of employees and, when these are later offered by the employee, to greet

1

them as most significant, worthwhile, and even original courses of action. Needless to say these bits of advice do not always produce desired results, however useful they prove to be at times. More than that, in some instances they may lead employees to believe they are being manipulated or hoodwinked by a person who has no interest at all in their welfare as such.

Evidently, then, what it takes to be a good supervisor is more complex than at first it appears to be, and it is in no sense true that almost everyone is an expert at it. On the other hand it requires study, investigation, experimentation, reflection, and dedication, as well as a realization that no matter how well one does, there is always an opportunity to do better.

This book is about the supervisor's job, and this section, consisting entirely of Chapter 1, is about his or her place in the organization. It will soon be evident that, complicated as our subject is, real progress has been made in understanding it and in what it takes to function as a supervisor. It is to that improved understanding and functioning that this book is dedicated.

Supervision—The Gateway to Management

This text is about supervision, its challenges, problems, opportunities, and its social significance. It is also about modern management theories and the relationship of supervision to middle management and top management. The place of the job of supervision in the management hierarchy is shown in Figure 1-1. In this illustration we equate the term supervision with first-level management.

This figure shows why the job of supervision is often called the gateway through which everyone must pass to a career in higher-level management.

SUPERVISION IS INDISPENSABLE

The job of supervisor evolved from the realization that we accomplish very little alone. John Donne's "No man is an island" is prophetic as well as poetic. But then neither can we accomplish much by simply grouping together. A group does not become a fraternity, a restaurant, or a football team simply by the act of grouping together. For any kind of group to hold together, to survive, to avoid disintegration, something else is needed.

First, there must be a *common objective* that the members of the group are *committed* to strive for. Second, when this has been accomplished, we soon become acutely aware that *direction* is needed to channel the diverse and often disorganized efforts of individuals (no matter how committed) into a purposeful stream of productivity to achieve the common objective. Third, out of this awareness, and to satisfy this need, *managing*—which we define as the process of designing and operating an environment where people, working together in groups, contribute as individuals toward the attainment of group purposes—

3

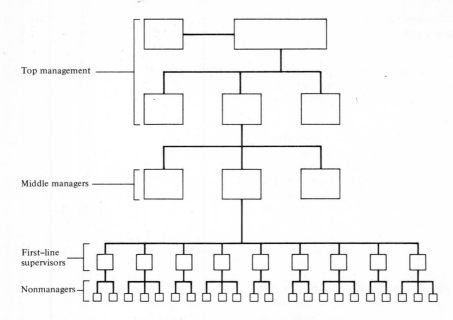

Figure 1-1 The place of supervision in the management hierarchy.

was created and management theory evolved. This book is dedicated to that evolution and seeks to assist those who would aspire to play the managerial role.

SUPERVISORS MUST "PUT IT ALL TOGETHER"

One objective of this book is to present selected information designed to help the supervisor or would-be supervisor develop a philosophy of management. A philosophy is a definite way of thinking about the duties and responsibilities that make up the position of a supervisor. It is concerned with answering questions such as: What differentiates me from my subordinates? What prerogatives, rights, or authority do I have that my subordinates do not? Equally important, what prerogatives do my subordinates have? How should I go about communicating with, or evaluating, or disciplining or motivating my subordinates? What should be my relationship to other and especially to higher managers in the organization?

Good supervisors develop good answers to questions such as these and apply them in their jobs. Importantly, they become aware that such answers are all interrelated. They "put it all together" then, and that is what a philosophy of management is all about.

WHAT DIFFERENTIATES A SUPERVISOR FROM SUBORDINATES?

At this point we shall attempt to answer a question posed above: What differentiates me—as a supervisor—from my subordinates (assuming the latter have had no supervisory experience)? Newly appointed supervisors do not usually bring management skills with them when they are promoted. This is true even if they were the most skilled workers in their departments before their promotion. The reason is that the work of supervising is completely different from the things they have done before.

Major *kinds* of work, or functions, that must be acquired by a new supervisor are summarized next.

Planning

First, the new supervisors have to *plan* the work that subordinates must do. As nonsupervisors they had only to plan and make decisions regarding themselves. Skills involved in planning and decision making are discussed in Chapter 2.

Organizing

Second, new supervisors have to *organize* the work of others. That is, they have to decide which of their subordinates will do what specific work and where and how it should be done. They have to assure that means for performing such work are available, such as space, materials, equipment, established procedures and methods, and budgets. Also, they have to decide when and how long it should take. Time is money, and has to be budgeted.

As nonsupervisors, on the other hand, they were responsible only for performing work assigned to them. They were told how, when, and where—as necessary—this should be done.

Theories, concepts, and practices involved in organizing are discussed in Chapter 3.

Directing

Third, new supervisors have to *direct* subordinates, usually on a face-to-face basis. They have to use authority and leadership judiciously to motivate subordinates to *want* to do their assigned work. Sometimes even the best leadership fails, for we all have our bad hours, days, or even months. Some subordinates simply cannot be motivated positively, even in the long run. When this happens, supervisors have to *order* such subordinates to perform their assigned tasks. This requires a great deal of skill because few of us like to be ordered.

During their nonsupervisory careers, the new supervisors probably had only the responsibility for motivating themselves to do their jobs. Commonly they had little conception of the nature and complexity of directing individuals and groups in a formal organization. For example, they probably had never had experience in saying no to "logical" requests (such as an unscheduled free day) from trusted friends—and especially when the requests were presented as being for the "good of the organization."

Throughout this text principles of directing (or of face-to-face leadership) are discussed. For example, concepts of motivation and leadership style are included in Chapter 5.

Controlling

Fourth, the new supervisor has to *control* the work of subordinates, to ensure that plans are properly carried out. He or she* must make sure that each subordinate knows what standards of performance apply, and understands these standards. Supervisors must appraise all work performed, and make sure that subordinates perform the right amount of work, of the right quality, and the right time. If things are not going according to plans supervisors have to take whatever corrective action is necessary. This can mean disciplining subordinates. A most compelling difference between supervisors and subordinates

---

*One problem the authors have encountered in writing this book is to avoid "sexist" language as well as any expressions that tend to "put down" females, blacks, or other members of "disadvantaged" groups. Thus we do not often use the term *foreman* because of its obvious male reference, preferring on the other hand *supervisor*, which is of course sexually—as well as racially—neutral. From time to time in referring to the supervisor we shall say "he or she," "his or hers," or "him or her," but sometimes we do not, for such an expression often repeated tends to become tiresome. When we do not use it, however, we *mean to imply it.* We are fully committed to the notion that *good supervisors* (and middle managers and executives also) can be and often are females as well as males.

derives from the fact that supervisors are forced to accomplish work through others rather than doing it personally. This can mean that to a degree they lose some control over their future. As a worker they can, given the chance, control their output through their own personal efforts. As supervisors they have the difficult and delicate task of controlling the output of the department essentially by motivating others to produce. Personal success as a supervisor depends almost entirely upon an ability to get things done through others.

Supervision often requires endless attention and the most delicate sort of guidance. The supervisor must concern herself or himself perpetually with learning, as contrasted with nonsupervisory jobs which, once learned, often require relatively little or no additional education and training. Of course, not all work done by those in supervisory positions is concerned with the supervision of others. Some of the work is nonsupervisory even though it is concerned with the organization. For example, a supervisor of salespeople who sells to, or listens to complaints of, customers is not doing supervisory work. Often the nonsupervisory tasks are as important as the supervisory work.

However, if the organization above the level of supervision is defective in conception or maintenance, the amount of nonsupervisory work is likely to be excessive to the extent that it leaves too little time for supervision. For example, subordinates may be ill-chosen and ill-trained, or the supervisor may lack the authority to command. Often the failure of supervisory self-discipline rather than uncontrollable factors results in an inordinate amount of time being spent on nonsupervisory tasks; supervisors often find it extremely difficult to delegate, to let go of, nonsupervisory functions. Nonsupervisors do not do any of these things. They only have to control themselves. The function of controlling is discussed in Chapter 4.

Summary

The *kinds* of work presented above that supervisors must perform, that is, *Planning, Directing, Organizing* and *Controlling,* are generally identified as comprising the *process of management.* Among writers in the field of management there is rather wide agreement regarding the nature of the basic functions of all supervisors, as distinguished from the functions performed by their subordinate nonsupervisors.

Readers may be quite confused, however, unless they know that authors of management texts *classify* the basic functions of management in a wide variety of ways, probably based principally on individual preference. For example, some authors classify these kinds of activities as coordinating, communicating, and/or staffing. However, the above classification does not overlook such important functions. We consider that coordinating and communicating are involved in all the four functions specified above. Staffing we consider as an element of the organizing function. Our classification is presented solely for teaching purposes. We do not imply that these kinds of functions are performed in the sequence given, nor performed separately from another, for they are not. All inextricably overlap in practice.

Successful supervisory management is not a body of theoretical and practical knowledge, not a set of techniques and practices, not a set of traits, not ethical behavior. It is not any of these things—alone. It is all of them plus another extremely important thing: a way of approaching problems, many of which involve a consideration of human behavior. Successful supervision, then, is a frame of mind, an attitude, a way of asking questions and looking for answers. Furthermore, the successful supervisor cannot wait for researchers and others to study each of his problems and work out precise, everlasting solutions. Most problems demand working solutions of some sort *now.*

PRINCIPLES CAN HELP SOLVE PROBLEMS

Fundamental to a supervisor's development of a philosophy, or way of thinking, about supervisory management is an accumulation of a working knowledge of some of the more significant *principles of management.*[1] Principles provide insights or considerations that might be profitable and useful to the supervisor in deciding how to perform on a day-to-day basis the major functions of planning, organizing, directing, and controlling. Over the centuries, and at an increasing rate in the last few decades, we have been provided with a seemingly infinite number of principles of management. To this complicated situation must be added the fact that those principles are defined in a great many ways. Thus in this text it is necessary not only to be selective in presenting a sampling of what we consider to be some of the more important principles, but also to carefully define *principle* as we shall use it.

We arbitrarily define a principle as a *relatively widely* accepted statement or explanation of possible *alternative ways* of solving particular kinds of problems. The key point in our definition is that principles are at best possible alternative approaches to solving problems in a particular situation. They are not universal truths. No principle could be *the one best way* to solve any problem.

A knowledge of principles can be of value in problem solving provided it is recognized that the principles are generalizations and that they must be adapted or modified to be useful—and that none may apply in a particular situation.

DEFINITION AND OBJECTIVE OF SUPERVISION

Definition

A famous philosopher of several centuries ago is credited with having said, "If you would talk with me, first define your terms." This advice is of first-rate importance in the study of supervision. In the theory and practice of supervision there is almost no standardization of terms, and such is the potency of words that some of the greatest misunderstandings and errors made in the study and practice of supervision are due to failures to define terms strictly and to use them according to such definitions.

Thus, to avoid misunderstanding over terms we shall usually employ the term supervision to designate the fundamental duties of the job at the very bottom or first level of the management hierarchy, the job that bears the formally assigned authority and responsibility for planning and controlling the activities of subordinate, nonsupervisory employees usually on a direct, face-to-face basis. Of course, managers at all levels have a responsibility for direct (as well as indirect) face-to-face leadership of subordinates. Thus, to a degree, the concepts in this book are equally applicable to all.

Supervision Is Situational

The above discussion of the nature of principles now leads us to discuss an interrelated point of fundamental importance: that is, supervision is situational in nature. Put another way, the successful supervisor views principles as useful *depending on* a great many things in the work environment at a particular point in time (some things might change tomorrow). We know there is an almost infinite number of things that might be important. All of them probably can be included under these three very broad classifications: (1) *the supervisor* himself, *and his characteristics.* For example, a supervisor may be unable to apply successfully some principles because he or she is not trained or educated adequately to understand them, or because of other factors in his frame of reference (see Figure 1-2);

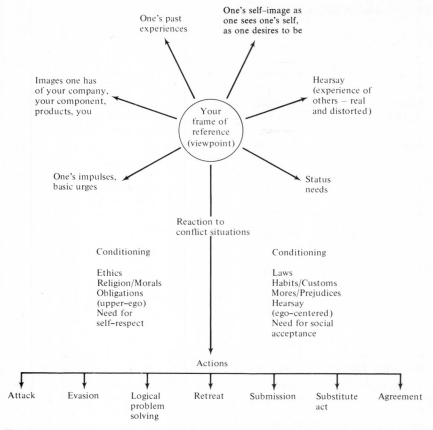

Figure 1-2 Frame of reference chart: Individuals will usually act from their own frame of reference, a way of seeing things, that is conditioned by many things: status needs, past experience, and so on. Most important of these, however, is their self-image, which changes as they mature and grow.

(2) *the led, or subordinates, and their characteristics.* For example, certain laudable principles of management—that is, participation, freedom of choice, relaxed supervision—may be quite ineffective because subordinates may lack commitment and may determinedly abuse such freedom; (3) *the situation and its characteristics.* Here the philosophy of higher management (democratic or autocratic), the policies, procedures, organization structure, and so on, can strongly influence the supervisor's choice of principles to use in planning and decision making. (See Table 1-1.)

The concept that supervision is situational in nature has been recognized by many for a long time. Only recently have attempts been made to build a theory (for example, a "contingency theory") around it.[2]

Objective

An analysis of supervision is sometimes restricted to what it takes to secure the satisfaction, happiness, or acceptance of the supervisor's subordinates. But we know that employee happiness is not a valid criterion of effective supervision; a happy employee is not necessarily an effective one.

Table 1-1 Situational Management

Three of the most critically important variables involved in determining the kind of supervision needed in any particular organization

Every supervision problem — including the problem of organization — has three interacting primary factors:

1 **The supervisor and his characteristics.** The supervisor may be the dynamic force in the actual work of organization and operation. He may or may not have a strong effect over everything in the organization. He is also, in turn, affected by everything in the organization insofar as his characteristics and activities are concerned.

A main point to be emphasized is that a supervisor, in order to effectively organize and direct and control a team under him, must make a self-analysis and become aware of his actual capabilities and potentialities. He cannot successfully simply copy a leader he admires, for example, or pick out a character from a textbook. He must tailor his organization and his controls, first, on the basis of careful evaluation of his own assets and liabilities.

2 **The "led" (subordinates) and their characteristics.** The characteristics (needs, wants, capabilities) of the people to be led have a direct bearing on the type of organization and leadership required. For example, a group of unskilled workers will require one type; a group of technicians and technical specialists will require a different type. Also, the amount of skill each has in his job duties must be taken into consideration. (For example, a relatively highly skilled group of employees, other things held constant, may call for an organization structure with a greater span of control, greater delegation of authority and responsibility, and so forth.)

Finally, the personality needs of the led must be considered. Some prefer an autocratic structure, some do not, for example. And individual needs, and wants, and capabilities are dynamic, that is, changing from day to day.

3 **The situation and its characteristics.** The kind of organization, direction, and control that a supervisor can establish is determined by the situation, or environment, that surrounds him. (One hears frequently that a real supervisor can create his own situation, but this concept has its limitations. Mostly he inherits a situation.)

The kind of organization structure the supervisor can create is controlled greatly by the characteristics and requirements of the organization's objectives and policies. Other important factors are the kind of equipment, buildings, and layout that make up the present situation, or environment. The present stage of development of the organization, or its success, can be critical factors. An emergency situation, for example, can demand an authoritarian organization structure and leadership, in order to keep a group from disintegrating.

Conversely, a description of the supervisory job is often limited to an analysis of what it takes to please top management. This approach often results in expressions of oversimplified and overidealized principles of supervision which may bear a resemblance to the Boy Scout Oath (Be Respectful, Be Sincere, and so forth) and which have aptly been termed "votes for virtue." Such ideal, and static, performance requirements may have little meaning to the real-life supervisor whose world of work is dynamic, who deals intimately and on a day-to-day basis with subordinates, and who possesses essentially the same fears, wants, needs, and imperfections as those supervised.

While it will not be practicable in this book to adopt and follow exclusively a single perspective on the supervisor's job—it is too complicated for that—the primary goal or objective emphasized will be that of getting effective results through people. The effective results will be thought of primarily in terms of the proper and legitimate work goals of an organization, whether this is for example, a business, a hospital, a university, or a government agency.

Two major objectives of supervision that have been popular for some years now relate to (1) productivity and (2) worker satisfaction (though as just indicated there may be little or no correlation between these two). Thus supervision plays an essential role in our economy because one of the primary goals is causing individuals to work cooperatively, not only as individuals but also as members of groups, to create most efficiently and effectively, with the aid of financial and physical resources, the specified products or services of organizations. While doing this, the supervisor must also have due regard for the personal interests of employees.

THE SUPERVISOR AS THE KEY PERSON—MYTH OR REALITY?

Frequently Encountered Views

A major problem one commonly encounters in analyzing the literature on supervision is that the importance of supervisors may be described in a number of ways. At one extreme, they quite naively are almost deified as the "key person" or even more sweepingly referred to, at least to subordinates, as *the* organization. If their superiors accept this view supervisors may then be held responsible for all human-relations failures. Thus it is sometimes said with a straight face that if supervisory leadership were as effective as that of top management, there would be no problems!

On the other hand, the supervisor is described by some as becoming more and more closely identified with higher management, while others describe the supervisor as being helplessly trapped between workers and management, and as having the uneasy status of being an accepted member of neither management nor the worker group.

Many supervisors feel they exist in a managerial "never-never land." While deprived of the comaraderie of hourly workers, they are not truly admitted to the inner sanctum of the management club. This denial of clear identity within the company can be a distressing force.

A finding turned up as a by-product of an attitude survey of certain American companies lends credence to what many management authorities suspect, namely, that supervisors often, and perhaps usually, feel less secure in their jobs than subordinates. Blain Britton, president, Management Surveys, Inc., reports that 78 percent of salesmen rate sales work as being favorable while sales supervisors rate their own work as 56 percent favorable. This survey also indicates that supervisors feel in their jobs they have fewer opportunities for personal growth and development.

Another factor contributing to the supervisor's insecurity, according to Britton, may be management's system of appraising employee performance. "In most cases, the salesman's work can be measured by production figures (his sales). This is much harder to do in the case of the supervisor. Production data relate to his group, not to him personally. In one sense, the supervisor is off the hook, but in a subtle way he is left hanging."

Because they generally do not have exact and personal production goals, supervisors are often left frustrated and unchallenged. This may not be good for the supervisor, since most people like definite goals and respond favorably to challenge. This lack of direct personal pressure may account to a large degree for the supervisors' occasional poor attitude toward their own supervisory role and the general dissatisfaction with trying to get things done through others.

Thus, supervisors, existing as they do between the workers at the performance level and the rest of the superstructure of management, do play a unique and difficult role. However, their position is most significant because, as discussed previously, regardless of how good the plans of higher management are in theory, they are worthless in practice unless the supervisors and their associates are effective in their performance.

However, many factors in the worker's environment in addition to the individual supervisors and their social skills may have a more decided impact on productivity. Thus too frequently the supervisor's influence is enthusiastically overstated. Such an overidealization of the supervisor's role may have inspirational value, but, it clearly has real dangers. It may result in the formation of unrealistic premises that provide the basis for shallow, misleading, and even dangerous conclusions about supervision. The authors feel that the reader should be provided at the outset with an appraisal of some of the more critical or limiting factors in the situation surrounding the supervisor, in order to understand better the problems facing him or her and some possible solutions that are presented subsequently in this book.

Supervisory Prerogatives

First, whether or not the supervisor is a key person depends to a great extent on whether certain traditional principles of management are adhered to. If they are, an unbroken chain of command or power or authority must flow from the top management level to the bottom, or supervisory, level. This power or authority is called supervisory prerogatives. The implication is that the supervisor has the power, influence, and resources to effect some kind of reconciliation of conflicts between company demands for more goods or services at lowest cost and worker demands for such things as pay, status, and freedom of choice. However, in actual practice many deviations from this norm obviously occur and must be recognized. The supervisor's formally delegated authority (that is, prerogatives) is usually limited in varying degrees by numerous situations, such as for example, the existence of an open-door policy by higher management. Also power over subordinates may be challenged, first, by a great number of governmental codes and regulations; second, by a new generation of increasingly educated and informed citizens and employees, differing greatly from those of previous generations, most of whom were governed by traditional social ethics, and many of whom were poor, uneducated immigrants; and third, by the labor unions, either directly or indirectly.

The supervisor may face a problem of quite a different nature, however. Though workers and other groups in the business environment may be pressuring for changes in the way subordinates are supervised, higher management may judge supervisory performance in the same old way. In other words, in spite of pious public pronouncements, supervisory training programs, personnel devices, and a parade of other provisions, top management may present the supervisor with the reality that raises and promotions are based on achieving the same old results in the same old way.

Status Symbols

In order for the supervisor to represent the company to subordinates, he or she should have an adequate amount of prestige or a "commanding position." However, in practice, the supervisor frequently has insufficient status symbols to be identified as a member of the management team. Frequently the trappings of office, such as adequate office space, special dining or parking facilities, or paid membership in trade or professional and civic organizations that higher management takes for granted, are lacking. Also, a supervisor's pay may differ very little from that of subordinates. (A few hours' overtime pay may actually put the latter in a higher pay bracket.) Thus, the supervisor may be considered economically and otherwise closer to the workers than to higher-level managers. Actually, the status gulf between supervisor and higher management is one that is most difficult to bridge. Regardless of all efforts to upgrade the status of supervisors, the difference in power between levels of management is always in the background. Consciously or unconsciously, supervisors and their subordinates react to such factors.

Recognition, Promotion, and Security

The opportunity for maximum utilization of the supervisor's talent and also for his or her promotion and security is very important. Higher management frequently has failed to provide these things. Studies reveal that only rarely is there a sufficient delegation of responsibility and authority down through management for best accomplishment of the necessary tasks of supervisors and even middle managers. Supervisors are thus likely to be frustrated and resentful and to withhold their maximum efforts on the job in those organizations where top management either does not trust them or doubts their willingness to take on added responsibilities. Many authorities deplore a practice of stockpiling supervisors for future promotions and future corporate expansion. It is reasoned that under such conditions supervisors, instead of playing a "key person" role, deteriorate rapidly because they are denied the stimulus of accomplishment and growth.

The desire for security is frequently deplored as a supervisory trait and considered inferior as a motivating force to competitiveness and creativity. However, the desire to have the opportunity to earn security can certainly be said to be a fundamental human want. Supervisors commonly know, as do their subordinates, that their position is uncertain, subject to constant pressures, and frequently less secure than that of subordinates. To a great extent subordinates' regard depends upon the supervisor's security and influence with superiors, a point we discuss later in this book.

Time and Competitive Pressures

Much of the "key person" theory of supervisory leadership is based on the premise that the supervisor has or should take adequate time to perform the management functions. However, time and competitive pressures in an organization constantly interfere with the supervisor's desire to do what is needed and what he or she wants to do. Supervisors are commonly in competition for advancement with other supervisors and are struggling to meet a budget that is deliberately "set tight" so as to demand best efforts. They work with people in budgetary, cost, quality, or personnel control, persons who often gain their successes through discovering and reporting failures. Faced with rising material costs and wages, the supervisor must spur his or her organization to greater efficiency, so that the department produces greater output and still keeps costs down and profits up. Supervisors have many kinds of specialists such as design engineers, industrial engineers, and personnel people to help accomplish the goals, and yet much time and energy is devoted to untangling the snarls that arise among the people who make up the complex and sensitive organization that the supervisor directs.

In addition to pressures from above, the supervisor is expected to respond to a commonly held ideal of the successful American manager. That ideal demands that he or she not be content with today's achievement but be constantly pushing to increase productivity. The impact of internal forces on the supervisor's time is illustrated by one minute-to-minute observations study of production foremen on an automobile assembly line. The study revealed that many supervisors were performing actual supervisory tasks as few as three hours in the eight-hour working day. A number of things beyond the control of the supervisors frequently required them to perform tasks that either were not properly a part of their jobs or that they would not have to do if the organization were functioning properly.

Unionization

Unionization of the supervisor's subordinates, whether in shop or office, tends to limit considerably the supervisor's authority in making decisions regarding employees. This is especially true in large organizations, where he or she is considered the representative of management, particularly with respect to management policy and grievance procedure. But the real issues involved in negotiating the union contract and in living with it are settled between union representatives and higher management. The supervisor is expected to conform to the joint decisions of these representatives and thus is placed in the position of being the recipient of rather than a contributor to either agreement or conflict between the union and higher-management representatives. Such a passive role is in sharp contrast with the concept of the supervisor as a "key person" in union-management relations.[3]

Informal Organization

It is frequently said that the effectiveness of human relations in an organization depends primarily on the human-relations skill of the supervisor and others in leadership positions (see particularly Chapters 4 to 7). The supervisor, however, is frequently in a very nonstrategic position for changing human relations in the organization. For one thing, it must be recognized that certain forces operating in informal organizations are often more powerful than the human-relations techniques of individual supervisors. For example, studies show that workers do not necessarily form well-organized informal work groups with definite and stable structures, but on the other hand, informal organizational patterns vary widely from very stable organizations to groups that are so disorganized as to make it difficult to speak of them as groups.[4] Besides, supervisors of large departments may have to deal with several informal work groups. Such groups are dynamic in nature; at any particular time one may be in competition with another. The supervisor thus may face the problem of handling relations between groups as well as relations within each separate group.

Communications

A fundamental requirement of leadership, and of management at any level, is being informed, having current and authoritative information to use and to impart.[5] By virtue of its position, higher management typically has extensive information-getting and information-processing networks, but supervisors' positions at the bottom of the chain of command make them largely dependent upon one formal source of information, or upon very few sources at best. To the extent that this is true, their authority, power, and function as members of management suffer. The result is that much information regarding company plans and policies, for example, is likely to reach the supervisor formally, if at all, in sterile form after filtering through various management levels. Under such circumstances, the supervisor's subordinates soon learn to get much of the information regarding the company through informal channels rather than through the supervisor. The supervisor similarly feels compelled to use the communication network of the informal organization. In all fairness, it must be said that the desires and efforts of higher-level management to improve communications may be quite sincere, but the problems of time pressures and spatial distances are difficult to solve.

It is apparent that the supervisor's job is by no means as simple as it is often described to be. Perhaps it never was, but its complexity has certainly increased in recent years.

A RESEARCH APPROACH TO SUPERVISING

The Supervisor as Skeptic

An exceptionally important part of the philosophy of successful supervisors concerns the way they approach problem-finding and problem-solving situations, the proper one being what we shall refer to as the *research approach*. Fundamental to the research approach is possession on the part of the supervisor of a *healthy skepticism*, as opposed to cynicism. Cynicism, as we define the term, is dangerous to successful supervision. It implies a sourness of outlook. It is a dissatisfaction with *everything*. The cynic, like the thorough-going radical, is in favor of tossing out all the traditional answers, all established procedures, and sometimes even all existing concepts, theories, and practices, no matter what their source. Cynics often offer little or nothing to fill the vacuum created by their wholesale "cleaning jobs." The simple act of destructive criticism of everything seems to spell fulfillment to the cynic. Their predominant social skill may be that of "bitching," at the coffee break, at lunch, after work, between jobs or wherever. Their natural habitat may be any organization.

Skepticism, on the other hand, is the tendency to look before leaping to conclusions, and it is one of the outstanding traits of the successful supervisor. It is a trait that is often "trained out" of people in an environment that commonly prevails—where knowing and believing are generally more highly regarded than is questioning. But it is a trait that can be learned by anybody who wants to work at it. Skeptical supervisors strive to view things more rationally than otherwise. They want to look in the mouth of every gift horse of tradition and authority, to accept and apply as working truths those that are supported by evidence adequate to the situation, and to modify or even toss out those that do not stand up under hardheaded, situational examination.

Popular notions to the contrary, successful supervisors know relatively little, if anything, for *sure*. Their central characteristic is not one of knowing for sure, but of questioning. They are alternative-gatherers, in other words. And they also have a willingness to *act* when action is called for.

On the average, people commonly feel that they know a great deal. The influence of family, education, personal experiences, and so on, all contribute to teaching them answers. They tend to bring these answers to the world of work. To word it differently, they tend to bring a *frame of reference* to the workplace. (See Figure 1-2.) (A frame of reference may be loosely defined as comprising everything that has happened to individuals that causes them to be ready to have a certain attitude [for example, a bias].) Often their frames of references get in the way of good supervision.

By way of contrast, successful supervisors have come to a healthy suspicion even of "the everlasting verities." They have learned that many of them are not so everlasting after all. They have also found that many of the ready-made answers so readily handed to them will not stand up under clearheaded scrutiny. They thus establish the habit of asking questions such as "What is the evidence?" "Are these real facts or counterfeit ones?" and the like.

Counterfeit Facts

We all are exposed to some degree or other to facts that turn out to be counterfeit. The following are illustrative:

Traditional Answers   Efficient supervisors cast a suspicious eye on many of the "of courses" we live by. They do not want to be taken in by any assumption that may be hidden in traditional beliefs handed down through the centuries, free of charge. Supervisors do not have, nor should they have, an antipathy to traditional wisdom itself. But they do not want to be misled by alleged wisdom that turns out to be not very wise.

There are plenty of "of courses" about discipline, morale, motivation, learning, and other aspects of human behavior that supervisors will encounter. The skillful supervisors evaluate them, consider them as possible alternative approaches to problem solving in a specific situation, and then possibly reject them.

Fact by Authority   The supervisor should be wary of accepting concepts as facts because they have "kept good company." If widely known researchers, politicians, and so on, believe something, the reasoning goes, that something is probably very worthy of believing. Again, it must be kept in mind—even if the famous, widely known individual did not—that there is seldom *one best way* of doing anything in any situation. However, the thoughtless habit can become compelling. Even some well-known individuals who preach that there is *no one best way* become so attached to their own concepts over the years that implicitly or not, and knowingly or not, they push their concepts as *the one best way*. This situation may become apparent later as we discuss some of the various theories and concepts.

Facts Based on Our Own Observations   Supervisors should be skeptical not only of traditional answers and facts by authority, but of their own observations. They should know something about the infallibility of human thought and remember that they themselves are human—and fallible. Such self-suspicion may be hard on individuals who may need to carry with them a feeling of certainty or even a delusion of omniscience. However, it can on many occasions keep individuals from making fools of themselves.

Supervisors should suspect their initial observations because such observations have been filtered through their frames of reference, and may be unduly influenced by their biases and assumptions. They should check with other observers—subordinates, superiors, peers—and make every possible effort to ensure that what they see is really there.

For example, a supervisor may well "see" a subordinate as being insubordinate for refusing to paint a window three stories above a street. After another look at the employee, and striving to *understand rather than judge* that employee, the supervisor may "see" an entirely different thing. The employee may have a phobia for heights and be ashamed to admit it to supervisors and even peers.

To cite an even more unfortunate illustration, a supervisor may "see" a subordinate as behaving indifferently and conclude that the employee is lazy. What if the employee is behaving apathetically because to behave with initiative would immediately incur the wrath of the supervisor? The supervisor in this illustration may never "see" real events—only events he wants to see. In such a case some subordinates may be truly victims of their supervisor's influence and suffer emotional scars that last a lifetime. Such, in not a few instances, can be the importance of the supervisor's social influence on people.

Opinions   Several kinds of opinions can be artificial facts, an opinion being a personal relation between an observer and what that person observes. "Facts" that are based on a single observation or even repeated observations are really opinions. They may be good opinions if the observer is free of bias or emotion. But it is an opinion, because it is a relation between only one individual and the thing that individual observes.

Opinions are commonly charged with some degree of emotion in spite of our best efforts—because none of us is perfect. Emotional opinions are sometimes easy to spot. But the important point to be emphasized is that too often they still frequently manage to get themselves accepted as fact and lead to more feeling than thinking.

More will be said on this subject at several points later in this book. In particular, it is closely related to the concept of *autism,* discussed in Chapter 7. It is hard for those who are inexperienced in research or critical approach to human behavior to realize the role of opinion and other forms of "feeling" in influencing what every one does.

Abstractions   An abstraction disguised as a fact can also turn out to be counterfeit and confuse the problem-solving process. We continuously talk and think about people in terms of abstractions, that is, some attributes or characteristics or "need" of people that cannot be immediately seen. To illustrate, we cannot see a person's *need* for hunger, or praise, or self-fulfillment, nor can we see intelligence, or motivation, or human nature. We can see people behaving, say, in such a way that we guess that they are hungry. They may be restless around noon and make stomach noises. However, they may not be hungry. They may simply be bored and nervous because they wish our lecture would end.

Actually, we cannot get along without abstractions. The content of any science is comprised of organized schemes of abstractions. An abstract term is often a handy—and maybe a most useful—way to summarize and represent a lot of complicated facts. But to really get at facts in the specific supervisory situations we have to observe, we must think and talk in terms of how people actually behave. It is relatively easier to get agreement on how people behave or what they *do* than on *why* they do it or on what traits or characteristics they have.

While abstractions are useful and necessary, they should not be confused with their factual ancestors. The relative impreciseness of our abstractions of management is understandable. Any worthwhile endeavor emerges first as an art. People succeed before they know why. The practice of engineering or medicine did not begin with an intensive study of the science, but as an exercise in judgment based on experiences. The need to understand better the foundations on which an art rests motivates the development of its underlying science. Management is no exception to this generalization.

THE SUPERVISOR'S PLACE IN MANAGEMENT

A generalization to the effect that all levels of management perform essentially the same basic functions, such as planning, organizing, directing, and controlling, while true, has only limited value to supervisors who wish to understand better the differences between their positions and the position that is organizationally the next higher step in the power structure, and possibly the next higher step in their future career plans.

Distinction Among Management Levels

Levels of management are customarily divided into three: (1) supervision, or first-level management; (2) middle management, or all levels of management from supervisory management up to the vice president or equivalent level; and (3) top management, comprising the president, vice presidents, and sometimes the board of directors.[6]

Supervisory versus Middle Management   The first level of management differs in an important way from all higher-level management positions in terms of who is supervised. Higher levels of management are responsible for giving orders to and managing people most of whom are at least in theory identified with management. An essential characteristic of the supervisor's job is that it is concerned with the transmission of orders to employees who clearly are not part of management. Methods employed in getting work done by supervisors and in getting work done by nonsupervisory workers are often by no means the same. The direction of supervisors by middle management involves a relationship among people who all, presumably, have common managerial objectives and speak a common language. At the supervisory level, two quite different philosophies, that of the manager and that of the worker, often come into contact with each other. Thus, the supervision of workers frequently involves different relationships and the use of different approaches.

A second difference between levels of management exists in the *number of persons supervised,* referred to commonly as the *span of control.* Supervisors, who are by far the most numerous segment of the management hierarchy, directly supervise more subordinates than all higher levels of management. Generally, higher levels of management tend to have progressively smaller spans of control, or number of people reporting directly to them, than do supervisors, due to the fact that work becomes more complex and diverse in nature at each higher level of management. It is important to note, too, that higher levels of management differ from the supervisory level in that the higher levels not only directly supervise employees but indirectly manage employees through their subordinate managers. Supervisors are limited to direct, face-to-face management of subordinates.

Still another difference exists in the extent of *specialization.* Supervisors are usually in charge of one generally cohesive or specialized function, while middle management typically is in charge of directing and coordinating dissimilar functions. The higher the level of middle management generally, the greater is the number of dissimilar kinds of work that must be integrated and coordinated by the manager. As a consequence, at each higher level of management, managers must progressively become less specialized and more "generalized" as managers. A very apt cliché is the advice, "If one wants to climb the management hierarchy one must fight against specialization." In other words, the ambitious supervisor will resist being content with merely mastering his or her specialized area. He or she will seek to learn other related, specialized areas so as to be technically equipped to advance to the next higher level of management charged with coordinating various specialized functions.

Finally, supervision differs from middle management in the kinds of decisions made. The supervisor directs the work of individual employees and may accomplish much detailed work himself. A great deal of decision making is concerned with interpreting, applying, and distributing the instructions or general requirements of superiors. A superior must also make decisions of this type. However, the superior can lessen the difficulty of making such decisions by delegating responsibility to subordinate supervisors. The first-line supervisor can seldom delegate responsibility of this kind to nonsupervisory subordinates. He or she is responsible for achieving excellence in the specialized area to the greatest extent possible with the workers assigned. Therefore, the supervisor is greatly concerned with and involved in handling the details of technique and execution. Middle managers are also concerned with what is to be done, but with general rather than specific ways of doing it. Their job is to establish objectives, to develop plans for their accomplishment, to determine tactics, and to integrate the various functions of subordinate managers or supervisors so as to create an efficient and effective combination.

The Status of Top Management

Most supervisors solve problems by thinking along specialized, departmental lines. They tend to think about higher-management jobs in the same way. For example, a supervisor might well think of a top manager's job as dealing with sales problems, or accounting problems, or finance problems, or other departmental problems. However, the chief executive's job and those of his or her immediate subordinates involve handling problems of a complexity and scope that extend beyond the level of even the top specialists. Top management cannot deal with top-level problems by making them fit departmental categories. Each problem, regardless of how it is worded, commonly has to be thought about in terms of its impact on all the departments in the firm. For example, though the problem of whether to try to increase the company's share of a certain market may arise in the sales department, it must be considered by the president in terms of finance ("Can we afford it?"), of Personnel ("Can we get or train enough salesmen?"), of Accounting ("What will it do to our budget?"), and so on. Thus top managers transmit to their subordinate middle managers the objectives of *top* management, they develop plans for achieving at least a portion of the objectives, and they direct and control progress. The immediate objective is to see to it that their team of subordinate middle managers and supervisors turns out the right quantity and quality of output at the right time and cost, but it must be harmonized with the longer-range objective of developing and improving their team of subordinate managers. Top management is continuously concerned with analyzing and appraising results, with current performance of middle management, and with taking corrective action. Thus middle management operates under financial and manpower considerations that are determined by top management.

Obviously then, top management, often referred to as administrative management, differs markedly from other sorts. As has been said, the major differences between top management and lower levels of management are (1) that the functions and problems handled are broader in scope and more diverse, dealing with major divisions or segments of the company, and in the case of the chief executive, the entire company; and (2) that major planning responsibility concerns the development of long-range projections and objectives, frequently dealing with five or ten years in the future, and with the development of major policies, plans, strategies, and programs for accomplishing these objectives. Middle management is responsible for converting these into specific short-range objectives, plans, tactics, and procedures, and for directing, coordinating, and controlling activities to achieve specific results that harmonize with and lead toward the broad objectives.

Social-science theory has tended to view management in terms of a "closed system."[7] That is, the firm or the agency is often regarded as sufficiently independent to allow most of its problems to be analyzed with reference to its own internal structure and without reference to its external environment. However, top management is especially concerned with managing both an internal system and an external environment. Its tasks center on problems in which there is a continuously high level of uncertainty, and complex value decisions are inevitably involved. This has a direct bearing on the kinds of skills, traits, and personalities required of persons occupying positions on the top-management level. The chief executive needs depth of understanding and the ability to think conceptually. That is, he or she must always be thinking about the organization as a whole in relation to its external environment (the community, the government, the customers, and so on). The chief executive must constantly plan and reorganize the resources of the firm to take advantage of opportunities. Things that the chief executive takes into consideration almost as a way of life are often novel and surprising to lower-level managers and supervisors. Top management must be aware of environmental opportunities and must reshape the organization to take advantage of these opportunities. By creating new objectives or redefining existing ones, top management directs the work of the next level of managers who, in attempting to meet the new objectives, are in turn consciously reshaping the environment. Thus, an important responsibility of top management is the *management of change.*

Additional Responsibilities of Top Management   However, top management cannot rest with being a part of a changing environment; it must attempt to *shape* the environment. To cite one illustration, a vice president of engineering has the responsibility for helping the designer of a packaging machine visualize design criteria as involving much more than merely specifications setting design limits. On the other hand, the designer has to visualize his task as that of attempting to meet a kind of packaging need. Once the machine has been designed, its introduction on the market and its use reshapes a portion of the packaging industry.

Both the change itself and the timing of the change are important. The company that is first to attempt to change the environment with the new design may be too early. On the other hand, the company that is second or third may be too late.

Top management is usually concerned with the details of how middle managers and supervisors work only to the extent that they are meeting company objectives and/or making a profit. When they are not, top management does not typically attempt to handle the detailed procedures and techniques of lower-level work. It attempts to determine whether the failure is caused by poor performance of middle or supervisory management or some other source, either external or internal. For example, top management must determine whether its own objectives, policies, or methods of selecting and developing its management team are at fault, and act accordingly.

RESPONSIBILITY OF MIDDLE MANAGEMENT FOR TRAINING AND DEVELOPMENT OF SUPERVISORS

Obviously, a subject as important and complicated as supervision cannot dependably be learned by mere trial and error, by hit-and-miss methods. The major responsibility for the training and development of supervisors rests, in the final analysis, on middle management.

Time and money spent on supervisory training and development should be considered an investment and not an expense. It is an investment in the future of the organization, recognizing that people are an organization's most important asset. Benefits should be viewed as a return on the investment. We shall discuss four significant reasons why supervisory training and development are worth the time and money they cost.[8]

Improvement in Present Job Requirements

First of all, the main thrust of supervisory training and development should be to improve performance on the present jobs. If present performance is not as good as it can be, present attitudes, knowledges, and skills may be improved and an immediate payoff may be obtained in improved performance and productivity of the workers they supervise.

Changes in Present Job

A second need for training and development exists if the present job of the supervisor is changing along with changes in the organization.

In the technical area, supervisors may need to learn more about the nature and potential of computers, the preparation and administering of budgets, laws relating to the work environment (such as the Occupational Safety and Health Act) and other technical subjects related to their jobs and their departments. Managerial aspects that may need to be learned may include the latest and best approaches in supervisory planning and decision making, controlling, motivation, and so on.

Promotions to Middle Management

Third, technical and managerial training and development is prerequisite, both from the standpoint of the individual and of the organization, to promotions of supervisors to the ranks of middle management.

New technical training needs emerge such as increased understanding of the computer, linear programming, PERT (program evaluation and review technique), and budgeting. New managerial needs might include a more in-depth understanding of organization development, manpower planning, delegation, styles of leadership, decision making, long-range planning, motivation, communication, and the development of subordinates. Training replacements who can immediately occupy their positions is sometimes a prerequisite for middle management promotions.

Improvements in Supervisory Attitudes

Fourth, middle managers often are faced with a general feeling of frustration and low morale on the part of their subordinate supervisors. These negative attitudes of supervisors are commonly reflected in the attitudes and performance of their subordinates. Obviously, until improvements are made in the attitudes of subordinate supervisors, attempts to improve the productivity and satisfaction of workers on the performance level are likely to be unsuccessful.

There is a substantial amount of research data available that may be of value in training and development programs designed to improve the attitudes of supervisory personnel. However, in all fairness to middle managers it must be acknowledged that in certain kinds of situations it may be beyond their capabilities to improve supervisors attitudes. More is said on the subject of training and development in Chapter 11 of this book.

QUESTIONS

1 Studies frequently show little or no correlation between productivity and employee satisfaction. Why do you think this might be true in some situations?
2 Essentially the same traits are required for effective supervision regardless of the situations in which supervisors find themselves. Discuss why this is true or not true.
3 What pressures on the supervisor might you expect to result from the fact that he or she is the only member of the management team whose subordinates are "workers," that is nonsupervisors?
4 Explain the statement, "When a person is promoted to a supervisor he or she loses a great deal of freedom."
5 Do you believe that the universality of the supervisory management process enables managers to move from one organization to another with no real problems?
6 What part does personal integrity play in effective supervision?
7 Why do you think that supervisory styles have changed so drastically over the years?
8 If a supervisor concentrates upon personally performing directly the work of subordinates, how may this affect the performance of the whole section?

NOTES

1 For a good appraisal of principles of management see Dalton E. McFarland, *Management Principles and Practices,* 3d ed. (New York: Macmillan, 1970), pp. 12–14.
2 A comprehensive coverage of this approach is contained in John W. Newstrom, William E. Reif, and Robert M. Monizka, *A Contingency Approach to Management: Readings* (New York: McGraw-Hill, 1975).
3 For a good discussion of this subject see Edwin B. Flippo, *Management, a Behavioral Approach,* 2d ed. (Boston: Allyn and Bacon, 1970), pp. 513–533.
4 For a comprehensive coverage of the problems of informal organizations see Keith Davis, *Human Behavior at Work* (New York: McGraw-Hill, 1972), pp. 273–451.
5 For further information on communications see John B. Miner, *The Management Process: Theory, Research and Practice* (New York, Macmillan 1973), pp. 368–377.
6 For a further distinction between the levels of management see Jerome Kantnee, *Management—Oriented Management Information Systems* (Englewood Cliffs, N.J.: Prentice-Hall, 1972), pp. 2–9.
7 For a good comparison of open versus closed systems see Howard M. Carlisle, *Situational Management* (New York, AMACOM, 1973).

8 For example, see Theo Haiman and William Scott, *Management in the Modern Organization* (Boston: Houghton Mifflin, 1970), pp. 370–375.

CASES

At this point it might be well to call attention to the cases that are found at the end of the chapters of this book. Real-life instances of situations actually faced by supervisors and other managers can do a great deal to provide insight into the supervisory situation as well as to aid in the development of needed skills. To that end some two or three such cases are included with each chapter.

Selecting *which* case to go with *which chapter* was not easy because cases so frequently involve all or many parts of the supervisor's job, including attitudes and skills, and we try in each chapter to concentrate on only one or a few. But that in no way detracts from the possibility of real learning from a study of such cases.

For this chapter we have chosen three widely different incidents, partly to indicate the complexity of the supervisor's job, but more particularly to emphasize the much greater willingness these days for "ordinary workers" to challenge decisions by supervisors and other managers. Thus Hank Hester (the names in all cases are fictitious but *the events were real*) challenged what he thought was an improper order by refusing to carry it out. Anthony Fairfax, though sincerely maintaining his innocence, defied management in its attempt to administer a polygraph examination. And Trina Gonzalez, a Spanish-surnamed American (SSA) or a Chicana, was entirely unwilling to accept what she thought was an improper discharge.

As you examine these cases and those found in other chapters we hope you will give serious thought to how the existing situation should be handled by management—or in some cases perhaps, by a labor arbitrator. It may also be worthwhile to try to decide how certain developments could have been prevented, though one should never let this second question interfere with answering the first and more immediate one.

CASE 1-1

Hank Hester is an operator of the Janesville plant of the corporation. He has been an employee of the Company for seventeen years and an operator (under the supervision of a foreman in charge of a particular unit of the plant) for more than five. His personnel folder contains no record of written reprimand, disciplinary demotion, layoff, or other penalty.

Operators in the Janesville plant have long had the habit of coming to work early and usually relieving the employee on the preceding shift considerably ahead of the stated time for shift change. When the relieved operator has passed the necessary information along to the oncoming one, he or she clocks out and goes home. Thus some days the operator may work considerably less than eight hours, depending on when the time of starting and when relieved, while on others it may be quite a bit more. In all such cases, however, the pay is for just eight hours.

Certain government agencies have an interest in such situations, among them the Wage and Hour Division of the Department of Labor. After a visit by representatives of this division, the Management of the plant decided the workers would have to change these ways of relieving and it issued orders to that effect. According to the rules, a man would have to be on his unit at 7 A.M. if he was on the day shift and he would not leave until 3 P.M. In other words, the time at which he clocked in or out at clock house did not govern his hours of work.

The workers were very unhappy about this. For one thing, it took away a certain amount of their freedom and self-determination concerning what they did. For another, it removed a valuable "cushion." Under the old system, for example, if one started from home with the idea of relieving at 6:15 A.M. instead of 7 A.M. he still had a leeway of forty-five minutes to take care of unanticipated delays before he would be penalized for being late. Under the new system the "cushion" was completely gone.

The problem of this case may very well have come primarily from Hester's feelings about this matter, for he had not been reluctant to express his opposition. Indeed, he had gone far enough to try to "get the straight of things" from the Wage and Hour Division, and he concluded, properly or improperly, that the company was completely arbitrary in the new rules.

On the day in question Hester was on the evening shift. He appeared on the unit just before 3 P.M., as the rules required. Shortly thereafter Stanley Jacobsen, his foreman, came to the control house where he was working, and approximately the following conversation took place between them:

Jacobsen: "Hank, when the shift is over (at 11 P.M.) I want you to take these IBM cards to the desk in the room where you clock out."

Hester: "Stan, you know that's not my job. That's the job of the operator helper. Besides, my time stops at 11 P.M. straight up, and I have to be on the unit till then. I'm sorry. I can't take the cards."

Jacobsen: "I'm sorry you feel that way about it. You tell Joe (the operator helper) to take them."

Hester: "I'm telling Joe nothin'. I'm not a supervisor. If you want him told somethin', you tell him. I may suggest that he take the cards. I'm not ordering him to do anything."

Jacobsen: "Hank, if that's the way you feel about it, I'll make it a direct order. As you leave this unit at 11 P.M. you are to take these cards to the desk where they are usually left."

The walk to the clock house takes five minutes or less.

At this point Jacobsen left the control house and later he went home early since his wife was to have an operation the next morning. The IBM cards from Hank's unit were not delivered to the clock house, nor were they delivered that night from six out of the other eight units in the plant.

Jacobsen was absent from the plant the next two days on account of his wife's illness and these two days also happened to be Hester's regular days off. Upon return, Jacobsen was asked to come in early and go directly to the office of the plant manager. There he found the plant manager and also the superintendent, and the two of them then informed him of Hester's failure to deliver the cards and asked him what he thought should be done. After some deliberation Jacobsen recommended a written reprimand and a layoff of two weeks without pay. The plant manager and the superintendent agreed on this penalty, and Hester was promptly notified. Five days later the company received a grievance signed by Hester, alleging that the disciplinary penalty was arbitrary and without merit and demanding pay for all the time lost.

Was the case properly handled by the company? What are the fundamental considerations involved in the handling of this case? Was a reprimand justified? What about the layoff without pay?

CASE 1-2

Anthony Fairfax is a shipping clerk for the Company. He has worked for it two years and has been a satisfactory employee.

For some time the Company has suspected that theft and pilferage are occurring among its employees in either the warehouse or the delivery department. Catching one of the drivers in a suspicious set of circumstances, the Company required him to take a lie detector test (as he and all other FHJ employees at the time of employment agreed in writing to do). The test indicated his guilt and he subsequently confessed to theft, worked out arrangements to make restitution, and implicated several other employees, including Fairfax. He was then discharged.

The same thing happened to five other employees, including another driver and four employees of the warehouse. They, too, confessed, either after taking the lie detector test or being told they would have to take it. They were also discharged, some after implicating other employees.

Tony Fairfax was the next suspect. Rod Harney, the personnel director, asked him to come to the personnel office for a conference. Fairfax asked whether he might bring a union representative, and Harney said, "No, not unless and until you file a grievance. This is just going to be a conference between you and me." When Fairfax got to Harney's office, however, he found Jasper Johnson, the plant manager, there also. Both Harney and Johnson questioned him closely, and each man appeared to be taking careful notes.

Fairfax denied any wrongdoing and also insisted that he neither had seen nor known of any employees who were guilty. He was asked to sign a statement to that effect, and this he did. He was then told that he must take a lie detector test and was shown the application blank he filled out at the time of his employment. On it was his written promise to take such a test if required.

Fairfax protested against taking the test but finally agreed to do so. He was then asked to sign a document entitled "Release" in which he voluntarily agreed to submit to the polygraph test. It also said, "I hereby release, absolve and forever hold harmless the FHJ Company (and the testing agency) from any and all claims of any nature whatsoever. . . . I request that any apparatus necessary to conduct the examination be placed on my person."

When Fairfax refused to sign the release, he was discharged by the Company. Does his action justify this penalty? Suppose he had refused to take the test even if no release were required? What difference did it make that he had earlier promised upon hiring to take the test if required?

CASE 1-3

Trina Gonzales is a fifty-eight-year-old employee of the Company. She completed the fifth grade before dropping out of school to go to work. She and her husband have seven children. She has worked for the company for twenty years. Most of her time has been spent in the parts department, where at present she is, as she has been for a number of years, an inspector-packer. Her record reveals no negative factors except for several industrial injuries, all minor. Some two years ago she was disqualified from her job and from company employment on medical grounds, but was eventually put back to work after an arbitration hearing.

Late last year Ms. Gonzales learned that her oldest daughter, living in Japan with her Air Force husband, was to have a baby, and plans were made for her to visit them soon after the baby was born. It was decided that April or May would be the best time, and plans were made accordingly.

Ms. Gonzales was entitled to three weeks of vacation, and with no difficulty arranged to have it scheduled for the first three weeks in April. She then requested personal leave for two additional weeks.

There is disagreement about this request. Juan Lopez, her foreman, says he never encouraged her to believe he could grant it (April through May is the busiest season of the year for the parts department), but she says he at first said he didn't see any problems with her taking it and only on the day before she was to leave was she told (she says) that she could have only one week of personal leave. At the same time, she insists, Raul Martinez, the long-time Union president and a person widely respected by both the employees and the Company, told her she had five weeks in all and under the circumstances could take any additional time she actually needed.

Not only did Gonzales take all five weeks she had requested but upon her return to Los Angeles on Monday, the beginning of the sixth week, had denture problems, went to see her dentist on Tuesday, and returned to work—with a written "excuse" from her dentist—on Wednesday of the sixth week. It is agreed that at no time after she left some 5½ weeks before did she make any effort to contact anyone at the Company. It is also agreed that she made the round trip of more than 10,000 miles by military planes rather than on regularly scheduled airlines.

The Company takes the position that by overstaying her vacation plus leave by some 1½ weeks she forfeited her job with the Company and hence is no longer an employee of it.

How should one rule on her grievance, which alleges an unjust discharge and asks for reinstatement to her job with back pay, full seniority, and fringe benefits? What important considerations should be taken into account? How should Management respond if a Title-VII violation is charged, on either sex or national-origin grounds? (See Chapter 18 in connection with the reference to Title VII.)

Part Two

The Basis for Effective Supervision

We have chosen to divide the major or central section of this book into three main parts: (1) the fundamental requirements for successful first-level leadership, (2) the day-to-day problems that supervisors encounter, and (3) those factors from the past that have made the supervisor's job—including opportunities, challenges, and threats—what it is.

In this part of the book our major concerns are three in number. First, in the light of our Chapter 1 investigation of the role of the supervisor, we examine his or her chief functions (in Chapters 2, 3, and 4). These we have classified under headings like planning, organizing, and controlling, but it is apparent that each function is an involved one. We also stress the importance of recognizing that the division of management responsibility into three functions is in a way artificial or arbitrary and that a basic obligation of the supervisor is to see to it that his organization is a functioning, systematic whole.

The second section (Chapters 5, 6, and 7) involves both what the supervisor needs to know and needs to be. Here stress is put on *knowing* (for example, on a critique of motivation theories), *character,* and *emotional maturity.* Then some attention is given to the nature of the present-day American worker and also to the kind of work—or organization—in which he functions.

The third section stresses methods useful to the supervisor. At first it may seem inconsistent with the implication of the Introduction to Part I to the effect that techniques are not our primary concern, but two observations are in order: First, the chapter on methods is only *one* in the several chapters of this part and this book; and, second, even more than stressing methods as such, we emphasize employing them with understanding and with dedication to basic values.

All this sets the stage for Part III, where we look at the concerns of the supervisor in particular areas of his job.

Chapter 2

Planning and Decision Making

A factor that plays a major part in determining pay, status, and, hopefully, satisfaction of supervisors is the frequency, complexity, and diversity of planning and decision-making tasks for which they are responsible. We stated in Chapter 1 that the authority and responsibility for planning the work of others is one of the major distinctions between the work of supervisors and their nonsupervisory associates who do not have such authority and responsibility.[1]

The job of supervisors in turn is distinguished from middle-management and top-management jobs to a great extent on the basis of the degree of depth, scope, and diversity of the planning and decision-making duties that are required. These increase in difficulty in proportion at each level in the management hierarchy.

SOME ASPECTS OF A PHILOSOPHY OF PLANNING

Successful supervisors consciously or unconsciously form a pattern of thinking in solving problems. This thought pattern is called the decision process. Closely related to it is the creative process. This is because successful decisions on important matters cannot usually be made without creative thought. A lack of skill in the latter can permanently inhibit any supervisor's progress and advancement and may prevent him from progressing beyond the world of the routine.

But it is not enough that supervisors use orderly thought processes or think creatively. There is a particular characteristic of supervisors that makes them successful. Not all supervisors fit into one specific supervisory mold. However, certain kinds of characteristics and abilities are common to all.

In short, though they seldom are able to verbalize it, successful supervisors have a system of thought, or way of thinking about how to plan and solve problems.

In the past few years we have seen an increasing emphasis placed on developing a "scientific approach" to the planning and decision-making process. There is every indication that such efforts will continue to be intensified in the future, and probably at an increasing rate.

Such an understanding, coupled with advances made especially in the last two decades in theories of organization, human behavior, leadership, economic analysis, market research, and so on, are decidedly altering and improving our skill and preformance.

We now have available for use a great number of techniques for coping with planning and decision-making processes, including quantitative decision-making concepts, made possible by advances in computer technology. But any supervisor can learn the most important things about planning and decision making without using any of the quantitative techniques. That is, supervisors can understand that planning and decision making is, or should be, a rational and systematic process, and that it consists of a definite sequence of steps. In the opinion of highly respected theorists and practicing businessmen, the ability to make such decisions is one that can be taught and learned and constantly improved.

THE UNCERTAIN WORLD OF THE PLANNER

All planning involves change and risk taking to some degree or other.[2] We cannot eliminate unpredictability and risk in decision making, but we can improve our ability to lessen them. As the supervisor moves further forward in time from the present to the future we know that unpredictability becomes an increasing problem. Effective planning certainly is not dependent upon the existence of ideal conditions, or even upon conditions that are known in advance. Obviously, plans must always be based upon unknown factors to a greater or lesser extent. In the supervisor's workaday world unexpected developments are almost certain to occur—changes in programs, processes, and procedures; changes in organization structure; changes in competitive conditions both internal and external to the organization; loss of key superiors or subordinates—all these and other developments are possible.

Unexpected events such as these do not, however, reduce the need for planning. On the contrary, they forcefully point to the need for carefully thought-out plans to take advantage of opportunities or to soften a blow that might otherwise prove disastrous.

It is precisely because supervisors operate in an environment of uncertainty and change that they should not rely on fate or chance. This is not to say that future events can always be made to happen or that outside interferences can be completely controlled. However, without plans involving such matters as sales, budgets, expansion, personnel, and finances, future events would necessarily be left entirely to fate.

COMPONENT PARTS OF PLANS

Major kinds, or component parts, of plans which we shall next discuss are: (1) objectives, (2) policies, (3) procedures, (4) methods, (5) rules.

Objectives

All planning and all other managerial actions, that is, organizing, directing, and controlling, begin with objectives.[3] First, there must be a clear understanding of the overall objectives of an organization, such as, "We shall manufacture and sell electronic components for X products." Or, "We shall develop and administer programs for the health, education, and general welfare of all citizens."

We define an objective as a general statement of our mission or what we intend to do. After overall objectives are established they set the stage for, and serve as a point of departure for, establishing a hierarchy of objectives for each kind of function at each level in an organization. For example, the overall objective of manufacturing and selling electrical components would occasion the development of such supporting objectives as, "We shall purchase supplies, store, and manufacture parts," and "We shall market products manufactured."

Policies

Since objectives are broad statements of our mission, they can be merely dreams unless supported by ways and means of accomplishing them. A policy goes a step further by providing information on *how* we shall accomplish our goals. It is defined as a *broad guide for accomplishing an objective* or objectives. For example, a policy of considerable importance concerning an objective to purchase supplies might be: "We shall purchase all supplies from one dealer." A policy of significance concerning an objective of selecting and maintaining manpower resources might be: "We shall promote from within the organization."

Procedures

Since policies are only broad guides for accomplishing our objectives they are seldom if ever adequate. They must be supported by procedures, which we define as *detailed steps describing how to accomplish policies.* For example, the policy of promoting from within leaves much unsaid. A procedure might explain how we go about identifying promising talent as early as possible, how we develop such talent, how we go about promoting such talent, and so on.

Methods

Frequently procedures do not provide enough detail. So we must proceed to develop methods, which we (arbitrarily) define as a detailed description of one step in a procedure. Methods can, and in fact do, become as specific as specifying the positioning and movement of each hand in performing a manual operation (see Chapter 17).

Rules

We shall define rules as restrictions concerning the personal behavior of employees. Though their preparation might seem to involve simple planning, the process of rule making can be difficult. People change, job content changes, even standards of ethical conduct change. Poorly developed rules, as with all kinds of plans summarized above, can be disastrous.

It is to be noted that the kinds of planning summarized above, proceeding from the development of objectives, all tend progressively to limit the freedom of choice of employees (see Table 2-1). Obviously a balanced approach must be taken in developing such kinds of plans. Not enough objectives, policies, procedures, methods, and rules can create a chaotic condition, with some people completely lost, some happily "doing their own thing" in conflict with actions of others, and so on. On the other hand, an overabundance of such kinds of plans can stifle initiative and create a creeping paralysis in an organization. Skill in constantly reading the current situation is a supervisory and higher-level management 'must'.

CONCEPT OF PLANNING TRADE-OFFS

The survival of a supervisor as a planner necessitates maintaining a delicate balance between factors such as quality of output, quantity of output, time, and cost. It may be necessary to put less emphasis on any one of these in order to accomplish another one

Table 2-1   Kinds of Plans That Progressively Become More Specific and Reduce Freedom of Choice of Employees

Kinds of plans	Definition	Illustration
Overall objectives	Statement of the overall missions or goals of the organization; its reason for existing	To manufacture and sell electronic computer parts
Hierarchy of objectives, for each activity at each level in the organization	Statement of overall missions or goals that support the overall missions, e.g., Manufacturing, Building and Grounds, Personnel, etc.	Personnel: "Select and maintain employees for entire organization"
Policies for overall organization and for each activity at each level	Broad guides for accomplishing all objectives	Personnel: "We shall promote from within"
Procedures for all policies of all activities at all levels	Step-by-step description of how to accomplish specific policies	Personnel: SOP (Standard Operating Procedures) for above policy "SOP for early identification of potentially promotable talent."
Methods	Detailed description of one step in a procedure	Personnel: "method for filing identification data on individuals"— a step in the above procedure
Rules	Descriptions of standards for personal behavior of individuals and of penalties for violations	Rules governing dress, tardiness, absences, and so on

more important at a particular time. For example, it may be necessary to "trade off" (or put up with) some inefficiencies in some subordinates at a particular point in time in order to achieve greater total productivity of the whole group. The inefficient employees can be dealt with at a more propitious time.

As another example, it may be necessary to "trade off" some quality of output if the supervisor receives an ultimatum to "finish that job by (a particular time) tomorrow, *regardless*." Or, on the other hand, the supervisor may "trade off" a *time* and/or *cost* deadline if he or she knows that a certain *quantity* of work of a certain *quality* must be produced regardless of time or cost.

The supervisor may encounter many instances of this kind in which a gain in one variable (quality, quantity, time, and cost) may have to be achieved by a loss in one or more of the other variables. The successful supervisor is skilled in the art of deciding which set of outcomes will be most advantageous to his or her organization and in the art of keeping the outcomes in favorable balance.

THE IMPORTANCE OF PLANNING STRATEGY

An integral part of planning is *strategy*. Strategy is the use of persuasion to gain or keep power. Unless the supervisor takes the initiative in persuading others to do what he or she feels should be done, others are likely to take over through persuasion to gain control. For example, in the planning function, considering the critical factor of the "right time" can be a valuable form of strategy. Assume you have a well-thought-through idea that will lead to work simplification and cost reduction. Your proper timing in the presentation to your superior can affect greatly its acceptance. Everyone, even top managers, is somewhat skeptical of any kind of change at first; thus, your presentation must be adequately prepared to anticipate any questions asked in testing your theory. Choosing the proper time to present the idea is paramount. To interrupt your boss when you know he is very busy with other problems, or to present the idea when you know he is burdened with a personal problem, could mean disaster to your plan. So, your strategy in anticipating all angles of the proposal as well as picking the right time of presentation can add greatly to its chances of acceptance.

MAKING A PLAN ACCEPTABLE

Of course planning, by its very nature, involves changing the way things are being done. Consequently, an important limiting factor in planning is that of resistance to change. A major problem facing managers at all levels is that those employees directly affected by plans may not be the only ones who resist changes. The supervisor himself may consciously or unconsciously resist them. Nevertheless, the objective of planning is improvement, and this means that change often *must* take place. So, in order for planning to be effective, there must be created an environment of acceptance of change. Unless such an environment is deliberately developed and continuously fostered, a persistent resistance to plans may be expected from employees.

Observations and experiences over the years have resulted in the development of several principles to aid supervisors in creating a better environment for the acceptance of change. *First*, it has been found that change may be more acceptable to persons new on the job than to veterans. New employees may be more anxious to please, while employees with considerable seniority may be deeply entrenched in informal groups that have developed resisting changes as a major objective. *Second*, change may be more acceptable to employees who have been trained in the philosophy of work simplification or methods improvement discussed in Chapter 17. A widely used slogan for work simplification is to "work smarter, not harder." *Third*, change may be more acceptable to employees who clearly understand the nature of the change and the reasons for it. Certainly a program of informing employees of important changes that may be forthcoming should be considered a must. *Fourth*, and perhaps to a degree repetitious, change may be more acceptable to those who do not see a threat in it than to those who do. (At this point it is not relevant whether the change *is* threatening. The only short-term consideration is whether it *is felt* to be.) More is said on this point in later chapters.

A word of caution may be in order at this point, however: The task of creating a change-acceptance environment should not be considered an easy one. A supervisor can hardly expect to describe and completely communicate in a few minutes a plan that he has thought about and worked on for hours, perhaps days. The amount of time spent in explaining a plan should bear some relationship to the complexity of the plan, the number of problems encountered in developing it, and the extent to which the plan contains changes of vital significance to the lives of those affected by it.

Fifth, the principle of participation is important in planning. This principle, which we of course shall mention in other connections in this book, holds that employees tend to be more receptive to changes affecting them when they have participated in the planning that creates such changes. By being thus identified with the plan, the employees may strive to assure the success of the changes involved (see Chapter 17). *Finally,* changes may be more acceptable to employees after previous changes have been completed and are operating smoothly. In other words, proposed changes are more likely to be acceptable when previous changes have been successful than when they have resulted in failure. This suggests to the supervisor that changes might best be made first in areas where employee acceptance is judged to be best.

FLEXIBILITY IN PLANNING

Not only is the need for employees to accept change essential; the plan itself must be subject to change when conditions dictate. Just as no successful organization can remain static (it is properly said that "a firm must go forward or it will surely go backward"),[4] no useful plan can be established once and for all in a final form. Unless there is periodic evaluation and revision of a plan to adapt it to conditions that are constantly changing, the organization is in danger of becoming hidebound and unable to keep pace with its more flexible competitors and/or public demand.

In this respect, business planning by a supervisor may appear to differ from planning of a relatively static nature such as that concerned with the construction of a highway or a house. Such projects are usually thought of as complete in themselves at the time of construction. Nevertheless, these things too are dynamic when considered from the overall viewpoint. Highways must be constantly widened, straightened, or abandoned entirely in favor of more up-to-date routes; houses must be modified, enlarged, remodeled, or even moved to accommodate more modern structures. Likewise, planning in business must be adaptable to change; it must be a continuous process, since dynamic enterprises simply cannot be planned once and for all. While planning may be relatively constant in terms of standards such as goals and objectives, qualities and quantities, or methods of accomplishment, these standards are by no means the plan in its entirety. They are but steps in the plan, and even they are subject to revision and replacement as more efficient standards are discovered.

Many times adequate flexibility in planning is not reflected in a single plan, but rather in *alternative ones,* which may be put into effect once it becomes apparent that the original, even with modifications, is not adaptable to the situation. The existence of such alternative plans is usually essential as a practical tool of management. Obviously, the premises upon which planning is based tend to narrow as the time for action approaches. The day arrives when, for example, a decision must be made whether or not to adopt a new process or to install a new technique. At this time, a certain amount of inflexibility attaches itself to the plan. The die is cast; the supervisor is committed to a definite course of action. Now, the supervisor may find himself or herself in the position of standing firm in the face of pressures to alter some portion of the plan, to reconsider a basic assumption, or even to abandon the entire project. Therefore, not only must the plan be adaptable to change and flexible in execution, it must also be rigid enough to withstand pressures when the going is rough and the future may not be perfectly clear.

TIME CONSIDERATIONS

One of the most important variables in planning, as mentioned earlier, is that of time. Among the many aspects of the time element that must be considered in order to plan efficiently are (1) the amount of time available for planning; (2) deadlines or schedules for accomplishing plans; (3) the "right" time; and (4) the time span that will be covered by the plan, that is, whether it will be a long-range or a short-range plan.

Time Available

The time available for planning is of primary importance, for it will determine the nature and extent of the study, research, and discussion that can be undertaken. Developing the "perfect plan" in business and government is seldom possible, due to time limitations. In fact, the planning "perfectionist" may actually be a liability to an enterprise. He or she may still be struggling to achieve a "perfect" plan long after the deadline for a workable decision has passed. At this point, the perfectionist may be confronted with the fact that there is no further need for a plan because the issue is dead; the customer has cancelled the order, the employee with a grievance has quit, or the obsolete equipment has caused a fire.

Rather, supervisors should strive to develop the *best plan possible within the time limits set*. When they arrive at work in the morning, supervisors may be presented with a problem that requires a solution by noon. They may recognize that a six-week study should ideally be made to develop the most efficient plan. However, they have to accept the fact that their responsibility is to make the best decision possible before the noon deadline. Spending more time on the plan becomes a luxury that cannot be afforded at the moment. In such cases, prompt action is more desirable than lengthy, detailed planning; and the ability to recognize and the willingness to accept such situations is one measure of capable supervisors.

Deadlines and Schedules

Deadlines and schedules are integral parts of all plans. A plan cannot become operational until specific dates and times of accomplishment are written into it. For example, the objective of "getting a million dollars of additional sales" or "reducing poverty in a community" has no significance whatsoever until it is expressed in terms of time, such as "in the next six months" or "in the next five years." Deadlines and schedules are also essential to plans because they serve as disciplinary restrictions on people in getting work accomplished. Few supervisors have all the time they desire; most of them need to budget their time or have their time budgeted for them. Deadlines and schedules serve as motivations, or "starters," to get work done. Also, they are essential in coordinating the component part of a plan, and in coordinating one plan with another.

The "Right" Time   Another critical factor in many plans is whether or not the time is "right" for the plan under consideration. Is the time right insofar as competition is concerned? Insofar as employees are concerned? Insofar as the public is concerned? The best-prepared plans may fail if competition is introducing a better or cheaper competitive product, if the employees who must carry out the plans are not prepared because of lack of training, or if either the employees affected by the plan, or the public, solidly opposes it. Probably no other aspect of the time element in planning is more important than the responsibility for determining the right time for introducing a plan. Not only does it call for good judgment and considerable experience; it also demands the exercise of imagination and intuition and the ability to assign correct values to the different aspects of the operational atmosphere.

It is for these reasons that decisions about the right time for instituting major plans are generally vested in top management. We have only to glance around to find examples of success and failure in judging the right time for introducing new plans: the Edsel's unfortunate entry into the automotive market, American Motors' successful entry into the small-car field, Montgomery Ward's mistaken decision to restrict its retail operations after World War II, and Lorillard's bonanza in the filter-cigarette race.

The Time Span   Finally, the span of time covered by plans is of great importance. As we have seen, all planning involves some degree of futurity. The time span may vary from a matter of days to several years, depending upon such factors as the organizational level at which the plan is made, the capital outlay required, the effect upon the organization's identification with a particular field, or the extent of change from current practices. Supervisors at the lowest management levels and often middle management levels are generally concerned with planning involving a minimum of futurity, as compared with top management whose planning may involve a time span of several years. Present indications are, however, that the supervisory level and middle management may, as time goes by, be increasingly called upon to participate significantly in planning covering increasingly longer time spans, as we shall illustrate later in this chapter. This may especially be true in the case of supervisory positions that involve dealing directly with customers.

The number of types of plans available to supervisors and higher management in terms of span of time, although seemingly large, is in reality quite limited. In fact, types of plans may be loosely grouped into only two broad classifications: (1) short-range plans and (2) long-range plans.

Any attempt to evaluate the relative merits of the two types would be pointless. Each has its place in the organization's attempts to reach its objectives in the most efficient manner. While each must obviously bear a close relationship to the other and both must be concerned with identical overall goals, each type has a specific use. Short-range plans are used to prepare for the rises and falls in the business cycle in the immediate future, while long-range plans indicate the direction of progress aspired to by the organization. There is a tendency to classify short-range or long-range plans and to assign them a relative importance according to the company's accounting periods. For example, short-range plans (those conforming to fiscal quarters, in many cases) are considered to be more accurate and reliable simply because they are identified with a more familiar period, the near future. Long-range plans may be arbitrarily classed as those unlikely of fulfillment within one year and continuing for any period of time up to five or—an increasingly common practice—ten years.

Plans concerned with periods of time longer than five years tend to shade off into basic policy; they often become too nebulous to support definite short-range programs. Shorter periods of time, say, three months, on the other hand, may be entirely consumed by operating problems, with the danger that planning may be neglected or relegated to a spot which is subsidiary to operations.

A capable manager will make sure that there is an adequate balance between long-range and short-range plans at all levels in the organization. A principle that may prove useful to the supervisor assigned the responsibility for participating in the development of short- and long-range plans is as follows: Short-range plans should be viewed as steps in achieving long-range plans. If a short-range plan is evaluated as making no contribution to any long-range plan, it should be carefully appraised to be sure that it is justified. Long-range plans, on the other hand, have little meaning unless they are supported by an adequate number of short-range plans with specified target dates.

PLANNING FORECASTS

While the two terms are often used interchangeably, *planning* and *forecasting* are by no means synonymous. Planning connotes a proposed course of action. It involves not only procedures but also methods of control, possible alternatives, and continuous evaluation to meet agreed objectives or goals. Simple forecasting, on the other hand, generally refers to present estimates of future events or of the behavior of people. Forecasts can be made without planning, but it is difficult to conceive of a sound plan that does not involve some forecasting.

While there is a need for forecasting in some degree, in all planning, it must be recognized that all forecasts contain a certain amount of pure guesswork and that they are subject to varying degrees of error as a result. For this reason, it is essential to recognize the limitations of forecasting as they affect planning. If the assumptions upon which a forecast is based are carefully examined and fully understood, the impossibility of prophesying the future with perfect accuracy need not restrict the usefulness of the plan. It is through the analysis of the basic assumptions, the reasonableness of the estimates, and the interpretation of the supporting facts that a supervisor is able to incorporate the uncontrollable factors of the forecast into the controllable outline of the plan.

MANAGEMENT BY OBJECTIVES

As stated above, a concept that has been popular, especially in the last few years, is that planning should be pushed as far down the organizational hierarchy as managers are capable of handling it. The concept of *Management by Objectives* (MBO)[5] is in one way a manifestation of this philosophy. This, like many other management approaches and techniques, first originated in managerial practice and then was further refined and extended by various researchers and management writers. Peter Drucker is held to be responsible for first publicizing the MBO approach in his *Practice of Management,* written in 1954. The MBO approach has fluctuated in popularity over the years, with a recent somewhat spectacular resurgence in popularity—including, somewhat surprisingly, its current wide use in middle- and smaller-size organizations.

Definition[5]

Management by Objectives (for our purposes loosely equated with *Results Management*) is basically a philosophy and a set of techniques for planning, organizing, directing, and controlling in such a way that encourages (in fact requires) everyone in an organization (for example, a government agency, bank, university, and so on)[6] knowingly to work toward achieving specific objectives and results that are a part and parcel of the total result that is expected of the organization.

To be successful in operating by MBO it is imperative that usual or traditional ways of supervising be changed—in some cases revolutionary changes are necessary—as we shall discuss next. It will become obvious that MBO is not for every organization, or for that matter, for all supervisors.

Develop an Overall Favorable Working Environment

It is the job of supervisors and all higher levels of management to develop an overall working climate such that each individual in the organization—from workers on up—can assume responsibility for a recognized part of the total objectives of the organization. This should be based, though, on an understanding approach to employees—their motivations, interests, and desires—rather than on ways they *should* act.

The Content of Jobs Shoud Be Designed in Terms of Results

A basic requirement of work simplication is that the content of all jobs should be based on the results that are expected (see Chapter 17). If the results expected cannot be defined, then it is not a job. This is counter to the common trend in management of designing jobs by activity. For example, the requirement that a person work at something—supervise a crew, handle a territory, research a product, prepare statements—all of these focus on activity. There is no final accomplishment stated that in itself advances the enterprise. This focus has been heightened by the emphasis on individualized, specialized activities suggested by the development of more and more knowledge in smaller and smaller areas of professional management. This trend has often made it difficult to obtain sound accountability, and therefore direct people effectively toward the overall results of the enterprise. By emphasizing overall results and component subordinate results that are expected of each employee, it is hypothesized that each person will be more apt to work in the right direction and with the right emphasis.

All Levels of the Organization Must Participate Cooperatively

A major responsibility to a great extent beyond the scope of the supervisor's authority, however, is that all managers at all levels of the organization must participate cooperatively in striving to achieve their own objectives and at the same time further the related objectives of others. There is little or no room for jurisdictional jealousy, destructive competition, or selfishness. The skill involved here is that of attempting to predict and minimize the areas of personal strife that may develop between individuals, each of whom is attempting to reach given and usually interrelated objectives. The problem of design of job content enters at this point again. The objectives and results that have been defined for each job must be analyzed as necessary to make sure they are harmonious with those of other related jobs in the organization. Simply issuing strong directives or admonitions to cooperate certainly cannot always be relied on to accomplish cooperativeness.

Staff Should Be Accountable for Results

A common feature of many MBO programs is the requirement that all staff jobs should be designed to include responsibility for specific objectives and results. Commonly, staff employees are charged with providing an advisory, suggestive, or consultative service. Too frequently this leads staff personnel to feel that they have no responsibility or accountability for accomplishing specific results. Whether their advice is good or bad may have relatively little effect upon their performance rating. Staff ideally should not accept assignments that do not include a clear statement of the results expected, and preferably identification of the part those results contribute to the overall goal. To accomplish this, the content of line and staff jobs must be different from those in common use, and new concepts of responsibility accounting should emerge.

Committees Should Be Accountable for Results

One major problem in defining harmonious objectives and results for individuals is the feeling that, in a broad sense, all results of an enterprise may be viewed as group results and the tendency to favor operation by committee. This tendency has been heightened by the emphasis often placed on employee participation and a warped concept of group effectiveness in an enterprise. But the fact is that a man or woman accomplishes a result, and if groups are involved, there may be as many as two or three persons who are still *individually* accomplishing a part of the total result. This should be recognized so that the sense of personal accountability is established in any type of group endeavor. To do otherwise loses the accountability and direction that is so vital to the accomplishment of results.

Firm Time Periods for Accomplishing Results Should Be Set

In order to get results accomplished cooperatively and harmoniously from all members of a complex organization, obviously a specific period of time for accomplishment must be established as part of the target. There is frequently an optimum value at any one time beyond which a result is of little value. This means that controls must be installed to actually prevent accomplishment of an objective beyond the point where it is currently valuable. For example, an extreme emphasis on quality may lead to excessive waste. Or a single-minded drive for total sales volume may lead to poorly balanced, and therefore costly, operation. Failure to recognize this principle in stating goals for each position is often a major reason for imbalance. The resultant difficulties lead to tighter policy and procedure restrictions, with the danger of a consequent withering of individual initiative and increased frustration.

Authority for Results Must Include the Right To Make Mistakes

In order to attain an enlightened approach with the full development of each man and woman at every level, it is important for managers to take a broader view of authority. The traditional approach of stating authority in general terms of job description, or of setting dollar limits, is inconsistent with management by objectives and results. Authority must be the stimulating catalyst to unleash creative endeavor and it must leave leeway to make mistakes. As an organization becomes large and diversified, there is danger that, in fact, mistakes are not permitted down the line. As a consequence, people do not grow and develop and produce to the fullest of their capacity. There is a fear of trying anything new, and the NIH factor—"Not Invented Here"—begins to multiply. Improvements may be welcomed, but fiercely opposed, even by management at all levels. The status quo can reign with the stagnation of creative initiative. This often occurs because authority is not developed in relation to the objectives set. The true concept of decentralizing accountability for results incorporates this understanding of authority as basic, if we wish to capitalize on the drive and the ingenuity of everyone in the enterprise.

Present Economic Compensation Plans Are Inadequate for MBO

Simply establishing objectives and results and accountability and authority for accomplishing them is clearly not sufficient for an effective MBO program. In fact, these alone can produce chaos. Unfortunately we have a lot to learn in relating employee and management compensation philosophies (discussed in Chapter 10) to sound accountability for results. There has been a tendency to overweigh such items as education, experience, effort, and even prevailing wage rates. Compensation should be looked at as a reward for achievement of the results expected and an incentive for improvement. There should be adequate economic incentives at every level of an organization to encourage each person to accomplish the results expected.

Presently Used Concepts of Performance Evaluation Are Inadequate for MBO

One of the most important factors in results accountability is an adequate plan for evaluating employee performance. Present performance appraisal plans, as is true of present pay plans in use, have many shortcomings. In an MBO program, managers must think beyond the usual, and vague, performance factors of judgment, initiative, cooperativeness, and so on, to an appraisal based on accomplishment of the objectives and results of particular people on particular jobs. Chapter 13 discusses an MBO approach to employee appraisal.

Summary From our brief sampling of characteristics of MBO, it can be seen that MBO, which often seems deceptively simple even to those who have installed it, actually can be exceptionally demanding in terms of sophisticated techniques and capabilities on the part of all employees involved. In spite of its wide popularity, our experience is that it has probably failed more often than not. Still, readers may find themselves participants in MBO programs and need to know more than our brief summary provides.

METHODOLOGY OF PLANNING AND DECISION MAKING

As we have said, the capable supervisor consciously or unconsciously forms a pattern or habit of thinking in solving problems. A basic, continuing requirement is that supervisors should discipline themselves to engage in logical thinking. The supervisor who thinks logically, for example, can look at a list of ten events that are out of sequence and see the order in which these events should be planned. For example, a good production supervisor may recognize that the arrival of raw materials must precede their use by three days so quality control can check them.

Logical thinking requires emotional stability. It does not require total objectivity, free of all emotional content, for this would be an impossible ideal. However, supervisors must have the ability to think clearly and sort out irrelevant facts. Those who do not plan logically are likely to create delays in the processes in their departments or make it necessary to bring material back to an area for further processing. An advertising supervisor may finish all at once several projects sheduled for completion at various earlier and later times. Equally as inefficient, an illogical planner may adhere rigidly to a schedule when all parts of a project are not ready for processing. Such inflexibility frequently results from a supervisor's preference for following an established order rather than for thinking and planning. The inevitable result of illogical planning is usually a wide fluctuation in costs, quality, volume, or personnel behavior.

Supervisors may develop their logical thinking and planning processes by many approaches. Courses in network techniques, such as PERT or CPM, discussed in Chapter 17, present valuable lessons in logic to anyone connected with planning in any way. In some cases the "J" course of World War II on Job Methods Training (JMT), consisting of step-by-step procedures, may be a useful starting point.

In the day-to-day press of activities, of course, a combination of circumstances may force immediate action. In such cases, intuitive reactions or hunches are sometimes substituted for careful planning, regardless of how much the latter may be needed, but often a supervisor may simply neglect to provide the necessary time for proper planning. A principle of planned action, therefore, is that *planning should be as complete as circumstances allow before any action is taken.* A corollary to this principle is that, whenever feasible, plans should be put into writing before execution, especially those of major significance. To do so helps to assure that the plan has been carefully thought through and that all "whats, hows, whens, whos, wheres and whys" have been considered, sometimes called a "planning formula" (see Table 2-2).

Steps in the Planning Process[7]

We shall now discuss a sequence of planning steps which is generally recognized as helpful in efficient and effective planning, though admittedly terminology in the field varies. A logical approach, such as we *now* present, might well be consciously used by supervisors when time permits until it has become programmed into their memories.

Table 2-2   The Planning Formula

1   What is to be done?
Get a clear understanding of what your unit is expected to do in relation to the work assigned to it. Break the unit's work into separate jobs in terms of the economical use of the workers, equipment, space, materials, and money you have at your disposal. Think each job through.

2   Why is it necessary?
When breaking the unit's work into separate jobs, think of the objective of each job. This may suggest alternate methods, or the possibility of eliminating parts of jobs or whole jobs. The best way to improve any job is to eliminate unnecessary motion, material, etc.

3   How is it to be done?
In relation to each job, look for better ways of doing it in terms of the utilization of workers, materials, equipment, and money.

4   Where is it to be done?
Study the flow of work and the availability of the workers, materials, and equipment best suited to doing the job.

5   When is it to be done?
Fit the job into a time schedule that will permit the maximum utilization of workers, materials, equipment, and money; and the completion of the job at the wanted time. Provisions must be made for possible delays and emergencies.

6   Who should do the job?
Determine what skills are needed to do the job successfully. Select or train the person best fitted for the job.

Need Determination   Before any plan is formulated, there is a need. In the case of a large corporation there is a need to know what the future of the business is. It is important to prepare new tools, new products, or new financial arrangements. In the case of the housewife, she needs to know what her family wants or should have for dinner. Regardless of the circumstances, there is always some need that has prompted the formulation of a plan.

Supervisors are in a position where they must work with needs that arise from both above and below their level. They may get orders from above requesting that they keep a continuous inventory count, or get word from below that a machine has broken and six employees have nothing to do. In either case the need has been determined for the supervisors. Sometimes realization that a need exists may not be so easy. Constant and careful examination of existing conditions is the only way to determine what some needs are.

Regardless of whether the need comes from above or below, or whether it is evident or hidden, the need must be determined before effective action can be taken. Often in planning and decision making it is valuable to state a need in the form of a question. Next, an evaluation of the importance of this need can be useful (as on a scale of 1 to 10). How much does it cost? What would be its impact on employee morale? What is the possibility of unintended consequences? *Unanticipated consequences* commonly result when supervisors become so preoccupied with what they are doing at the moment that they fail to see future effects that they will ultimately regret.

Objective   Once the need has been determined, an objective must be set. Knowing that departmental output is low does not accomplish any action. Obviously, the supervisor must establish an objective to find out why it is low and correct it.

The objective is what, in general terms, the supervisor hopes to do about the need. Using the earlier illustration of the broken machine and six employees out of work the supervisor has determined the need or problem, namely, six employees out of work and a broken machine. He or she may then decide the objective is to find something for those employees to do and get that machine fixed. The supervisor has set some sort of a goal. This is an essential step in planning, the determination of what one is trying to do.

People Involved   When the need is realized and an objective set, the people involved in developing the plan must be considered. Several questions must be answered:

1   Who will authorize the plan?
2   What people need to coordinate in the plan?
3   Who will develop the plan?
4   Who will approve the plan?

For example, a supervisor with assigned authority in this type of situation may then assign another person to handle the situation, or may handle it personally.

Next the supervisor may have to coordinate with different people. In the above illustration the supervisor may talk with the maintenance department about fixing the machine, or order a part through purchasing. The idle employees might be used in some other department while the machine is being fixed, in which case the supervisor would have to talk with some other supervisor. Now the supervisor develops a plan of action, to talk with various people and get them to fix the machine and find temporary work for subordinates. Once the plan is approved, the supervisor can set it in motion.

The next step is to take it to someone for approval. In this case it might be the plant engineering department head since it might be cheaper to get a new machine. Approval can come after two final steps are taken, obtaining and evaluating necessary data and finally testing the plan, which we discuss next.

Obtaining and Evaluating Necessary Data   Obtaining and evaluating data are essential, since this is what will determine how well information stands up under testing and ultimately whether the plan should be accepted or rejected. (The term *data* can refer to a variety of things, such as production costs, employee morale, or feasibility studies.) The important things to consider are that accurate and necessary data be collected and that the data be interpreted correctly.

Continuing with the earlier example, the supervisor may find that approval of his or her plan can come only after some data have been gathered and evaluated and the plan tested. It may be necessary to find out how long it would take to get the new part and also how long it would take to get a new machine. The employees might have other skills that would be useful somewhere else in the company. Other data might, of course, be collected. It will then be necessary that the plan be evaluated as to accuracy and applicability.

Testing the Plan   The planner has now arrived at the point where a plan has been formulated.

Returning to the earlier example, when the supervisor has collected and evaluated his data, the next step is to test the plan. Assuming that the plan is to replace the machine with a new type of machine, the supervisor can test the plan by comparing it with a similar plan used by some other organization. Perhaps the company down the street did this same thing six months ago and is now producing larger quantities of output with less expense.

The supervisor has now arrived at a plan, which, it is hoped, will be accepted. The basic steps in arriving at his plan have been taken. First, becoming aware of the need; second, establishing an objective; third, contacting the necessary people; fourth, obtaining and evaluating the necessary data; and, fifth, testing the plan. The supervisor who may have done many of these things unconsciously went through the steps nonetheless. These steps do not need to be written down and checked off; the supervisor needs only from time to time to be aware of them.

Decision Making within the Plan

Definition of a Decision   A decision, simply stated, is the resolution of conflicting alternative choices involved in solving a problem or problems.

Obviously, if there are no possible alternative choices of ways of solving a problem (not even whether an action should be taken or not taken) a decision is not involved. For example, sometimes a supervisor may be asked by a superior for an opinion regarding the superior's way of solving a problem. The supervisor may know that regardless of his or her opinion the solution proposed by the superior will be applied—that is, no alternative way will be accepted. Though the supervisor's response may serve some purpose, it does not involve a decision regarding the stated problem.

The increasing complexity of business decisions during the past century has brought an emphasis on the study of the nature of a decision, on the process of searching for a more scientific way of choosing among a group of alternatives. Attempts have been made to divide the decision-making process into a series of component parts that can be analyzed both quantitatively and qualitatively. All the newer branches of management science, such as operations research and industrial dynamics, can trace their objective to a search for a more rational or quantitative basis for making a decision.

Interrelationship of Decision Making and Planning   Decisions are used at every step in the planning process and are, therefore, inextricably interrelated with planning. Conversely, it is possible to use a plan to arrive at a decision, but decisions and plans are not the same, and decision theory and planning theory are quite different bodies of thought.

Responsible authorities have warned about viewing decision making as the romantic center of supervision, rather than in the context of the total supervisory job. That is, unless the supervisor recognizes decision making as part of the much more complicated and rational process of planning, there is a danger that decision making will be considered as an end in itself. In the latter case, the supervisor may be tempted prematurely to get rid of a problem or reach a conclusion. The process of making a decision should be regarded as only one of the critical steps in the process of planning.

Basic Concepts of Decision Making   Though we have now in development a great number of advanced techniques for decision making, stimulated especially by the widespread use of computers, any supervisor can learn the most fundamental things about decision making by using at most only a few of these new techniques. That is, the supervisor can understand that it should be, insofar as the supervisor can manage, a rational and systematic process and that it consists of a definite sequence of steps. The ability to plan and make decisions is one that can be taught and learned and constantly improved. We cannot eliminate unpredictability and risk, but we can improve our ability to lessen them.

Many of the decisions that the supervisor faces in everyday operations involve very simple choices and the collection of relatively small amounts of information. That is, the supervisor may establish objectives, and weigh their importance and assess ways of doing a job, all in a matter of moments and without bothering to write anything down. This is quite appropriate. But when major decisions arise that involve complicated information, the supervisor often does not bother to put down and assess all the factors involved. This is a mistake, for no manager is able to hold in his or her head all the various assessments and factors that may go into making a major decision.

The process of decision making is difficult because it involves not only experience, knowledge, common sense, and judgment, but also a great many future uncertainties that may threaten the action decided upon.

Analysis of a problem: The first task supervisors will encounter in decision making is that of how to go about preparing an analysis of a problem so that investigation of the data is thorough and conclusions reasonable and supported by existing evidence. To a certain extent a method of proper problem analysis can be outlined here. However, the following are only suggestions. Supervisors should experiment with the suggestions made here in order to arrive at a method of analysis which yields the most satisfactory results.

One method that is widely accepted has these steps:

1 *Acquire an understanding of the overall problem situation and its components.* In this preliminary study, the supervisors may find that projecting themselves into the time and atmosphere of the situation surrounding the problem will help them take a realistic approach to the specific situation. Moreover, such a procedure may aid in eliminating irrelevant influences, such as hindsight or other factors that have no immediate effect on the situation.

2 *Establish objectives.* Objectives are derived from two general areas: the *results* expected to come from a decision, and the *resources* (people, budgets, space, equipment, and so on) available for expenditure in carrying out a decision. Supervisors must ask: What is to be accomplished? What are the resource limits within which we must stay? Both of the questions must be answered in a definitive way, which can be measured.

3 *Classify objectives according to importance.* All the objectives that have been listed will exert some degree of influence on the course of action that is elected. But some will be of absolute and overriding importance, some will be quite important but not mandatory, others will be nice to accomplish as a bonus but probably will not affect the situation a great deal one way or another. All the objectives should be listed under two headings: MUSTS and WANTS. The MUSTS set the limits that cannot be violated by any alternatives. Objectives that are WANTS do not set absolute limits but express relative desirability.

By distinguishing between MUSTS and WANTS in setting objectives, supervisors avoid the mistake of settling for an alternative action, only to find later that it is not satisfactory because some essential requirement in making the decision was forgotten.

Some WANT objectives will always be far more important than others, and supervisors must weigh each one carefully. They can rank or weigh each WANT objective by giving it a numerical weight of importance such as 1 to 10.

4 *Develop alternatives from which to choose.* The set of MUST and WANT objectives becomes a set of specifications by which to develop alternative courses of action. The objectives spelled out are individual statements of functions to be performed or fulfilled by the course of action.

5 *Evaluate the alternatives against the objectives to make a choice.* To evaluate an alternative, supervisors test it against the objectives, measuring it to see how good a job it will do. Each alternative is first assessed against the MUST objectives on a GO/NO-GO basis. If an alternative fails to perform what a MUST objective requires, it must be immediately discarded. Alternatives that satisfy all the MUST objectives can then be evaluated further against the WANT objectives; each of them should be scored against one of the objectives separately. A supervisor can use a scoring scale for this, say 1 to 10, with the best alternative receiving the top score. To get an overall judgment of the relative worths of each alternative, the supervisor must multiply the score of each alternative by the weight assigned to each objective. The weighted scores can now be added up to give totals for each of the alternatives. These total figures give the relative positions of each of the alternatives on those items of performance considered in the specific objectives.

   6 *Choose the best alternative as a tentative decision.* The alternative that receives the highest weighted score on performance against the objective is presumably the best course of action to take. However, regardless of the scores the supervisor must assess the consequences of his or her choice as completely as possible.

   7 *Assess the adverse consequences of the tentative decision.* Supervisors should now take the best alternatives and consider them independently, visualizing each as though it were already in operation. They should question the effect the alternative will have on other things and the effect that other events will have on it. They are not reconsidering the attainment of objectives, but estimating the future possible effects of the action necessary to attain them. In doing this a supervisor is looking for trouble, trying to find the potential breakdowns and shortcomings that have escaped his or her notice so far. These will be hidden and obscure. They will lie primarily along the lines of contact between the proposed course of action and other activities going on in the organization.

   8 *Control effects of the final decisions by preventing adverse consequences and by follow-up.* Once supervisors start to implement the final decision, every adverse consequence considered earlier becomes a potential problem. Now, before it is too late, the supervisor has the opportunity of preventing these consequences from ever coming to pass. He or she can analyze them for possible causes and then take preventive actions to remove those causes. Or failing to remove a possible cause, he or she can decide on a *contingency* action to be taken if and when the potential problem actually occurs.

QUESTIONS

 1 The decision-making steps discussed in this chapter imply that they are made logically and by an individual. What would you add to the steps if a group decision was involved?

 2 Why are objectives vital in any set of managerial plans?

 3 What are some of the best ways in which a supervisor can gain his or her subordinates' acceptance for a crucial change in the subordinates' job?

 4 Do you think that the authoritarian type of supervisor could encourage and stimulate creativity? Why or why not?

 5 What are some advantages and disadvantages of supervisors allowing their subordinates to participate in planning?

 6 What are the major characteristics of a good decision?

 7 How does a forecast differ in nature and importance from a plan?

 8 Should freedom to make mistakes be granted along with authority delegated to a supervisor?

NOTES

 1 For a good discussion of planning read David I. Cleland and William R. King, *Management: A Systems Approach* (New York: McGraw-Hill, 1972), pp. 197–219.

 2 Harold A. Leavitt, William R. Dill, and Henry B. Eyring, *The Organizational World* (New York: Harcourt, Brace, 1973), pp. 3–15.

 3 A good discussion of goal setting in a factual setting is contained in Alfred P. Sloan, *My Years With General Motors* (Garden City, N.Y.: Doubleday, 1964).

4 Robert A. Townsend, *Up the Organization* (New York: Knopf, 1970).

5 For a good discussion of the scope of applicability of the technique of Management by Objectives see Arthur C. Beck, Jr., and Ellis D. Hillmar, "OD to MBO or MBO to OD: DOES IT MAKE A DIFFERENCE?" *Personnel Journal,* vol. 51, no. 11, pp. 827–834, November 1972.
   Also see an extensively researched book by Stephen J. Carrol and Henry Tosi, Jr., *Management By Objectives* (New York: Macmillan, 1973), pp. 1–16.

6 For a discussion of the applicability of the technique of Management by Objectives to universities and colleges see Y. Krishna Shetty and Howard M. Carlisle, "Organizational Correlates of A Management by Objectives Program," *Academy of Management Journal,* vol. 15, no. 1, pp. 155–157, 1972.

7 For a good description of the planning process see Harry R. Knudson, Robert T. Woodworth, and Cecil H. Bell, *Management An Experiential Approach* (New York: McGraw-Hill, 1973), pp. 119–133.

CASES

A word about the cases we have selected for this chapter. One, that of Bill Nelson, deals with a supervisor who is, on the whole, an effective manager but who is developing, if he has not already developed, a serious problem. Another, that of Jack Bohannon, concerns a worker who participated in what was apparently a contract violation and yet later filed a grievance against the company concerning it.

   The third case is that of Angus McClelland, a foreman dedicated to Company objectives, who may be too dedicated—if that is possible—to them.

CASE 2-1

Bill Nelson has been with the Company for five years. For the last two years he has been the supervisor of a clerical group of twelve employees. Prior to being made supervisor he had been a worker in a similar group; indeed, a majority of his present subordinates were once his fellow workers before he was made supervisor. Bill is thirty-five years of age, is married, and has one child. He has three years of college and was in the Navy for four years.

   Bill was a good worker before he was made supervisor. He was interested in his work, tried hard, and caught on quickly. Management soon noticed his performance and made him a supervisor in an unusually short time. At the time he seemed to be well pleased with his progress and took the new job without hesitation.

   As a supervisor Bill has been successful though not outstanding. His subordinates respect him, and things usually go well for the work group. He does have a tendency to concentrate on getting out the work and to forget the feelings of his people, but on the whole management is pleased with his performance—except in one respect.

   Bill has developed a habit of being tardy. This did not start until after he had been supervisor for several months and at first was only once a month, or less. Now, however, it has become more frequent, averaging almost three times a month for the last three months. The worst part of this is that Bill's group usually does not really get started to work until he arrives, and, furthermore, they are beginning to come in late also.

Jerry Slocum, Bill's supervisor and the office manager, has talked with him on occasion about the problem, and each time Bill has promised to do better, though Jerry feels that he has never really "gotten through" to Bill. At any rate, the promises have made little if any difference, and Jerry has decided that the time has come for a further and more thorough examination of the problem with Bill.

How should Jerry conduct this interview?

CASE 2-2

Jack Bohannon is a maintenance mechanic for the Company. He has been in this position for about fifteen years and does a good job.

Last week Bohannon was assigned to the rework of a sump pump. Since the needed repairs were fairly minor, he was able to do them in just under four hours, and thus plenty of time was left before the end of the shift for the reinstallation of the pump.

However, a problem had arisen. When sump pumps are removed for repairs, the sump pits in which they are placed are nearly always cleaned out and reconditioned, an operation carried out not by the maintenance group to which Bohannon belongs but by the operating people, represented by another international union.

In the past when this particular pit has been cleaned out, only about half a day was needed, but this time complications arose, and the pit was still being worked on at the end of Bohannon's shift. Bohannon was "kept over" to install the pump, being assigned other duties while the pit was being readied. Two other mechanics were also held over, assigned to other tasks while they waited to assist in the installation of the pump.

Actually the installation of the pump is a one-person job except for two periods of about 15 to 20 minutes each, during which three are needed. In addition the work is quite unpleasant, being hot and extremely dirty and requiring boots as one works in the sludge from the pit.

An unexpected development occurred in connection with the installation where three people were needed. The two operators who were cleaning out the pit assisted Bohannon on each occasion, the other mechanics not being called though they were only 15 or 20 feet away. They undoubtedly saw the operators assisting Bohannon and offered no protest, in part at least because their tasks were much easier and more pleasant than installing the pump. Both the maintenance foreman and the operations foreman were also in the area and neither they nor Bohannon made any protest. The pump was installed without further difficulty, and Bohannon and the other two mechanics were sent home after four hours of overtime work.

Two days later Bohannon and the other two mechanics filed a grievance which contended that Management violated the agreement in permitting operators rather than mechanics to assist Bohannon, and asked as a penalty that Bohannon be paid for one hour at time-and-a-half.

How should Management answer this grievance?

CASE 2-3

Angus McClelland is a foreman in the repair shop of a plant of the Company. He is fifty years of age and "has come up the hard way," that is, until some three or four years ago he was a pipefitter in the shop. His work as a craftsman was always good, and his promotion to foreman came after twenty-five years of work for the company. He started as a laborer and later completed the apprentice program for pipefitters.

One of McClelland's problems since he has been foreman has been to "keep his hands off the work." Partly because of his great desire to get the work done satisfactorily and to an extent because of his twenty-five and more years of work "on the tools," he is tempted not only to give direct orders to his workers about what they are to do but to do a good deal of the actual work himself.

For some time, the Union has been watching Angus closely on this matter, and union members have told him of their disapproval of his doing what they consider to be bargaining-unit work. Angus has typically shrugged these matters off and denied that he has violated the labor contract in any way. (The contract contains the usual provisions allowing managers to "work" in emergencies or for purposes of instruction, and in the local situation there is an oral agreement that fifteen minutes of work by a foreman will not be protested.)

The cause for concern is a series of events that took place less than a week ago. Angus was in charge of the "graveyard" shift when a conveyor broke down. He summoned a pipefitter helper and a laborer, and the three of them fixed the conveyor. The operation took thirty-five to forty minutes, during which time McClelland not only handled a big Stillson wrench for some minutes and made two trips to a nearby storeroom, but also worked long and hard enough so that he was wet with perspiration.

This was too much for the Union. The next morning a grievance was filed, charging that McClelland not only had done bargaining-unit work, thus depriving Union members of work properly theirs, but had avoided calling out a pipefitter. Such a call-out seemed expensive to McClelland, since minimum call-out pay was four hours at time-and-a-half.

When Bill Morgan, McClelland's zone foreman, investigated the matter, he found that Angus was convinced he was entirely in the right. An emergency had arisen, he said, and he had taken care of it; besides, he had taken advantage of the situation to save the company the cost of a call-out. He stated that he certainly did not mind hard work and would do it any time Bill wanted him to.

Bill had serious reservations about the Company's case. He knows that the conveyor did not have to be fixed that night, since another was working well. Indeed, the day shift could easily have done the job. Besides if the work was to be done that night, only a real emergency would justify failure to call out a pipefitter.

Angus has already told Bill he intends to deny the grievance. What does Bill do now? After this grievance is disposed of, how does he handle Angus's tendency to "work"? How much success is he likely to have? What are the hazards he faces with Angus? With the employees?

Chapter 3

Organizing

WHY PEOPLE ORGANIZE IN GROUPS

As a point of departure for presenting some of the more important principles of organizing, we shall first discuss *why people organize in groups.* Of course we know from personal experience that the chief reason is to achieve what they could not accomplish as individuals. And it is well known that according to generally accepted economic theory, people in the aggregate have "unlimited wants or needs." We shall discuss two major kinds of organizational arrangements of fundamental importance to supervisors: formal organizations, and informal organizations.

Formal and Informal Organizations

First, we define broadly a formal organization, sometimes called a *formal social system,* as one in which resources of men/women, materials, money, machines, management, and methods—the six M's—are *deliberately* utilized in the (hopefully) most effective manner so that the *explicit* purpose of an organization is attained. Examples are not only business corporations, but also universities, the armed services, the Mafia, labor unions, religious organizations, welfare departments, and a great many more.[1]

A second major kind of organization is an informal organization, or *informal social system.* Probably each of us belongs to a great many more informal than formal organizations. These informal, as distinguished from formal, organizations typically do not arise as a result of design or deliberation, but evolve naturally whenever people interact with each other, especially over extended periods of time. For example, in a business establishment

47

informal organizations such as a lunch-break clique emerge spontaneously because of personal preferences of people to group together.

Needs Satisfied in Joining Groups The organizing process from the viewpoint of need satisfaction necessarily encompasses, among others, both psychological theories of individual behavior and sociological theories of group behavior.[2] Groups are, of course, composed of individuals, but a significant point for a supervisor is that once in a group, a collection of individuals takes on group properties. Individuals do not stop behaving like individuals, but groups have properties of their own that influence the ways each member in a group behaves.

Individuals join groups, both formal and informal, in order to satisfy usually not one but a pattern of needs. Further, the overall pattern may be different for each group one joins, and the pattern of needs may differ somewhat from day to day in the same group. The following are some illustrative "needs satisfiers" or rewards an individual seeks to satisfy by becoming a member of either a formal or informal group.

First, a definite, satisfying relationship. Gregariousness is not enough. Individuals commonly need the security of having a set relationship with others over an extended time period, a definite role to play.

Second, status within the group. Individuals also commonly need to "be somebody." They need social status among others. Status is often a matter of personal value judgment. How much status an individual *feels* he needs depends unfortunately upon his level of aspiration and of course is influenced by many other factors.

Third, status because of the group. This is another kind of ego reward. An individual's impression of himself may be elevated simply because he is a member of a group that is well thought of in the community, or is exclusive; that accomplishes much; or that is looked up to by nonmembers. (Level of aspiration is a strong factor here, too. From a formal-organization standpoint, for example, job specifications that help screen out people with low levels of aspiration may markedly affect the character of the organization.)

Most of us work and live much of our lives under the influence of many organization forces, both formal and informal. Everyone's conduct is dominated or qualified or conditioned in some way by these organizational relationships. It is not necessary that we participate or possibly even consciously be aware of many of the countless organizations which in some way or other influence our lives. However, it is important that not only supervisors but managers at all levels be keenly aware of the forces, both formal and informal, that do directly affect their own lives. And they must also be aware of the impact of such forces on the workers they manage.

We shall now discuss in more detail some of the more important principles of, first, formal organization and, second, informal organization.

CHARACTERISTICS OF FORMAL ORGANIZATIONS

At the outset it is important to note that there are a number of fundamental characteristics common to both formal organizations and informal organizations. (See Table 3-1.) First, as stated above, we summarize some of the more important concepts, principles, and practices regarding formal organizations.

Organizing is a process, or kind of work, that must be done to some degree by managers at all levels.[3] A more apt term would be reorganizing, especially in a large

Table 3-1 Characteristics Common to Both Formal and Informal Organizations

	Characteristic	Formal organization	Informal organization
1	Objective(s) (why the organization exists)	There must be an overall objective(s) and a hierarchy of supporting objectives	An objective(s) is essential. E.g., "provide a rapid communication network"; or perpetuate work methods found to be satisfying; or "get even with the supervisor"; or "help the supervisor"
2	Norms ("musts" that are essential to accomplish the objective(s))	Must have policies, procedures, methods, rules, etc. Even the organization chart is a norm	E.g., if objective is to "get even with the supervisor": Norms. might be "do not speak to supervisor unless latter requests it"; "do *only* the work specifically given"; "work leisurely—especially when supervisor is not looking"
3	Reward and penalty system	Must be present to enforce the norms (i.e., policies, procedures, rules, etc. Rewards may be intrinsic or extrinsic (see Chapter 5). Penalties might be suspension, demotion, firing, etc.	Necessary to enforce norms. Rewards might be more status, etc. Penalties might be less status in the group, outright expulsion, etc.
4	Power structure	As indicated in organization charts, organization manuals, etc.	There is *always* a leader. Members occupy various levels of status
5	Rituals and symbols (e.g., customary ways of behaving, etc.)	Dress and behavior, etc., strongly influenced by custom, current values, e.g., rolled up shirtsleeves and no ties for the executive suite	Also codes of behavior and dress; though not written or spoken, e.g., must be observed

organization, since the process is almost always a continuing one. Almost never do we have the opportunity to start from scratch and develop a completely new organization. This is true no matter what level of management we achieve, even the top management levels.

For practical purposes managers at all levels inherit an organization structure. Making *significant* changes in an inherited organization structure often is exceptionally difficult and even impossible, especially in the short run.[4] This point is significant in studying supervisory management, and especially for the reason that there exists an abundance of publications devoted almost exclusively to utopian descriptions of how organizations *in toto should be* structured and/or restructured. We certainly endorse many of these "should be's." Their central focus commonly is on the dignity of people, including workers. However, such concepts must be kept in perspective by the supervisor. The achievement of major changes in organization structures is generally beyond the capabilities of the supervisor and even middle management (where "cost-effectiveness" is a major criterion)[5] and must start with efforts of top management. But even top management may be unable to effect such changes even if they agree with them. Thus such managers may be overruled by boards of directors. The latter in turn may be overruled by stockholders, especially if such changes in the short run negatively affect profits.

Let us look at the formal organization from the standpoint of (1) objectives, (2) division of work, and (3) authority.

Objectives: The First Step in Supervision

A discussion of formal organization theory must begin with a consideration of objectives or goals. We establish, rearrange, or utilize an organization structure to accomplish objectives. Objectives are an organization's reason for existing. They are therefore a supervisor's reason for existing.

Objectives may or may not be clearly stated. They may be of relatively little value to anyone except members of the organization, but they must be there, consciously or unconsciously, or the organization will disintegrate. And of course if the objectives change at the supervisory or any other level of management, the people involved should usually be informed and the organization structure analyzed to determine whether people in the work force (along with budgetary and other resources) need to be rearranged to best accomplish the changed mission.

Objectives

Kinds of Objectives   A significant point, insofar as supervisors are concerned, is that they, along with managers at all levels, must cope with three kinds of objectives. First, and obviously, attention must be directed at all times to the *common objectives* of the organization. Second, they must cope with objectives (wants and needs) *of subordinate individuals,* many of whom may have little or no interest in the common objectives. For example, individuals motivated to belong to an organization that manufactures washing machines may have little or no interest in washing machine output or other economic motives of their organization. An employee may want financial security, an adequate retirement plan, a job title that sounds important, or merely to be working with friends.

The supervisor's challenging problem of dealing with, and attempting to reconcile, the formal organization's objectives with the goals of individuals is further complicated by a third and distinctly different type of objective with which he must cope. This is the objective of *informal groups.* Individuals do not necessarily change their personal goals and values when they join informal groups. However, in order to belong to the latter they may sometimes have to alter their predispositions to behave in certain ways. This is so that they can conform to certain common group objectives and norms of informal organizations in order to be accepted. Of course these objectives of informal groups may result in behavior that interferes with, or contributes to, the achievement by the supervisor of formal organization objectives.

An exceptionally important principle that supervisors should keep in mind is this: *objectives and norms of informal groups may be more compelling for their subordinates than the authority* of their managers.

Objectives of the Formal Organization   In the final analysis, the effectiveness and efficiency of a supervisor's department must be judged on the basis of how well it contributes to attaining the overall objectives of the enterprise.

Thus, a supervisor's organizing, or reorganizing, must be preceded by, and based upon, a clear understanding of what his department is expected to do to achieve the organization objectives. Success is achieved by planning ahead, and a serviceable plan of organization cannot be formulated unless the purpose for which it is made has first been established. Though company objectives are the responsibility of top management, a basic organizational concept, often referred to as the hierarchy of objectives, discussed in Chapter 2, directly involves the supervisor in the function of objective-setting and objective-coordination. The principle that objectives must be clearly established and defined not only for the organization as a whole, but for each department, division, section, and other organizational unit in the company is best illustrated by the concept of *results management* and/or *Management by Objectives,* which we discussed in Chapter 2. It advocates participation by a supervisor and his or her immediate superior periodically, for example every six months, in setting the department's short-range objectives, or "results," for that period of time. These short-range results, of course, should be designed to contribute to better achievement of the long-range objective of the larger group. At the end of the six-month period (the period may vary), the supervisor is again scheduled to meet with his or her superior and discuss the extent to which the results were achieved, and why or why not. Objectives, or results, are then planned for the next six months, and the cycle begins again.

Long-Range Objectives   The establishment of departmental objectives by the supervisor may be based on his or her present organization structure, or it may be the basis for reorganizing. In the short run, the supervisor looks to his or her existing personnel and must plan the immediate goals on the basis of their capabilities. However, objectives cannot always be established exclusively on this basis. Changes in objectives, or results, that are seen as necessary by the supervisor may be beyond the capability of present personnel, and reorganization may be necessary. A practice that seems to be gaining increasing acceptance is for the supervisor, as is commonly true of higher management, to plan organization needs in terms of both long-range objectives and short-range objectives.

All of us are concerned to some degree with both long-range objectives as well as short-range objectives. For example, we may be concerned with a short-range objective of getting a college degree. The kind of degree we plan (for example, business administration) should logically be based on a long-term objective such as practicing as a Certified Public Accountant.

It must be pointed out that long-range objectives are not entirely dependent upon the extent and degree to which they may be achieved: for a knowledge of them is important even if we never accomplish them. Not only a business, but every organization of a *permanent* kind is vitally concerned with setting long-range objectives. An organization must disintegrate if it cannot accomplish its long-range purpose at least to a satisfactory degree. A large number of otherwise successful organizations come into being and then disappear for this reason. Hence most continuous organizations must repeatedly adopt new purposes, often including long-range ones.

Short-Range Objectives   Short-range objectives are those goals that the supervisor hopes to accomplish within a definite period of time in the immediate future, within a few days, weeks, or months. Two major principles dealing with immediate objectives are: First, they should, insofar as possible, be capable of expression in definite, tangible, quantitative terms, such as completion dates of projects. Second, they should represent logical stages in the accomplishment of long-range objectives. Looked at from another angle, there may be very little value in developing long-range objectives unless definite short-range objectives that represent steps in achieving them, with target dates for each, are also developed.

It is not enough that objectives be established and an organization constructed to achieve them. Insofar as possible, the supervisor constantly must attempt to insure that they are known, understood, and accepted by his or her personnel. For example, communications believed by subordinates to be incompatible with the organization's objectives, as they understand them, may not be accepted. Further, insofar as possible, the objectives must be such as to command the confidence of subordinates (as well as of the public), or effectiveness is likely to suffer. Finally, the supervisor must exercise care that unwarranted personal objectives of employees do not come before the organizational objectives. Continued attempts by important individuals or groups of individuals to satisfy personal goals at the expense of the common goals may lead to the breakdown of supervision, and even the entire organization.

At all times supervisors must keep in mind a fundamental principle of organizational balance. That is, the expenditures (in time, salaries, space, equipment, cost) for the operation and maintenance of the supervisor's department should be no greater than is warranted by the values the supervisor's department or unit contributes to the achievement of the objectives of the larger organizational unit of which it is a part.

Division of Work

Once short- and long-range objectives are clearly established, the first step supervisors must take in appraising their departments is to determine whether the sum total of work for which they are responsible is divided in the best possible ways into jobs that will accomplish the purpose. Next, they should define the duties, authority, and responsibility of each job in such a way that employees clearly understand what is expected of them, what limits of authority and responsibility are imposed by their jobs, and what relationships their jobs bear to other jobs in the department.

Work Division and Specialization   The division of work into specialized jobs is generally accepted as an inevitable characteristic of all group effort. The purpose is to overcome individual limitations. Few individuals are capable of doing everything well. Each must become specialized through training and experience in performing particular kinds of tasks. The fact is obvious not only in business but also, for example, in football, where the total effort is divided into positions of defensive backs, offensive backs, offensive linemen of various specialized kinds, and so on. The reader may speculate that a football team whose backs were *all* capable of passing exceptionally well might indeed be awesome, at least in terms of passing capability. Division of work and specialization are especially pronounced in the medical, legal, and other professions, but appear everywhere. Put perhaps more succinctly, a jack-of-all trades is very apt to be a master of none, while a specialist may become an expert.

The job of supervision owes its very existence to the practice in business and industry of dividing the work into specialized positions. The supervisor is charged with providing the leadership and communication among the various experts to make it possible for them to work cooperatively toward the organization's goals. *The organization structure must do its part in creating a situation in which the supervisor can most effectively provide this leadership. In this sense, organizing is a technique that can facilitate leadership.* If the division of duties and authority creates a situation in which the supervisor's task of leadership is facilitated, the organization has accomplished an essential task. But if supervisors are buried in detail or if the authority they need in carrying out their responsibilities is delegated to someone else, the organization has overshadowed and thwarted them.

The importance of specialization was emphasized several centuries ago by Plato, who said:

> No two persons are born alike but each differs from the other in individual endowments, one being suited for one thing and another for another, and all things will be provided in superior quality and quantity and with greatest ease when each man works at a single occupation with his natural gifts.

Specialization promises to become progressively more significant as technological and other developments make business organizations more and more dependent upon the skill of experts. This trend cannot be stopped, because no single individual today would be capable of knowing more than a small fraction of the factual knowledge at our disposal in many fields. Further, many seriously doubt that it should be stopped, because such an attempt would probably signify a reduction in the rate of increase in knowledge.

Principles of Work Division A large part of organization theory is devoted to the problem of how to go about dividing the work of an organization most effectively. Most of it derives from a few elementary principles. First, and possibly basic to all principles of organization, is the *exception principle.* As applied to the division of work in a supervisor's section, this principle holds that all work and all decisions to the extent possible should be divided among subordinates, leaving only the exceptional work and decisions to be handled by the supervisor.

Too frequently for a variety of reasons to be discussed later, supervisors feel they must either do all the work or closely supervise all the work of subordinates in order to be sure it is well done. However, some situations hopefully of short term, may demand that this be done. This can be unfortunate, for supervisors usually have time only for the exceptional problems in their departments. It is their obligation, therefore, so to give directions and so to train their subordinates that the latter can handle the constantly recurring problems and refer only the exceptions to their supervisors. In fact, one of the most challenging problems of supervision is how supervisors may free themselves of the unnecessary burden of detail by delegating the duties as well as the authority to make decisions to subordinates capable of handling them.

A second elementary principle of the division of work is that, insofar as practicable, work should be divided into simple, routine, repetitive tasks. Continuous effort is, and always has been, required to do this, for the division of work into its elements that represent the "one best way" is an elusive goal that is seldom, if ever, completely achieved. The technique of work simplification, referred to in Chapter 17, is designed to assist in accomplishing this.

Having divided work of a department into simple, repetitive tasks as much as possible, a third elementary principle may be applicable: Tasks may be grouped together, insofar as possible, into positions on the basis of similarity of work. This principle, called the *principle of functional homogeneity* or *task similarity,* holds that wherever possible each position should contain work tasks that are not different in kind and degree of skill required, for if they are too different, the advantage of specialization is lost. The division and grouping of work on the basis of its similarity is, of course, relatively easier at the worker level, below that of supervisor, where work tends to be routine and limited compared to the more varied work of middle- and top-level managers.

The same principle of dividing work on the basis of its similarity may be applied as a basis for grouping jobs into sections, each suitable for control by a supervisor, for grouping supervisors and their subordinates into higher organizational units such as departments, and so on until all levels are organized. For example, all purchasing and related work such as traffic management may be grouped into a purchasing department; and all product design, style design, and process design may be grouped into an engineering department. The process of grouping together organization units rather than grouping tasks into jobs, is often called *departmentation.*

Obviously not all work by any means can be grouped on the basis of similarity. Depending upon the situation, organization units may be grouped by any one, and usually several, of the following: by type of customer (as industrial customers or residential customers); by region (as sales for the northwest part of a state, or the whole country); by nature of the function (as production or office services); by process (as engine lathe operators or milling machine operators); and by product (as by subassembly or by final assembly of electronic components for a computer).

A final principle is concerned with how the supervisor should go about organizing or reorganizing to cope with short- or long-range changes in overall organization, objectives, and policies. Of course in the short run (day-to-day or week-to-week), the supervisor has limited choices in reorganizing, and usually must simply make the best use of the existing organization. That is, supervisors *must plan and assign and control work on the basis of both the positions that presently exist in their departments and of the capabilities of specific subordinates that presently occupy these positions.* These existing positions and the capabilities of the subordinates who hold them set a limit on the overall capability of the supervisor's department.

Hopefully, managers at all levels can anticipate changes and prepare for them. However, in the short run, changes in overall organizational objectives and policies can occur and drastically and immediately change the nature of the work that must be performed in a supervisor's department. As one illustration, we have witnessed a situation in which a corporation concentrated all its human, financial and other resources toward achieving a government contract, only to learn that it was just barely too large to meet the government criteria for being classified as a small business. Naturally organizational objectives had to be immediately and drastically changed. When situations like this occur, the supervisory and nonsupervisory levels frequently take the major brunt of the shock of such changes.

However, most organizations (especially large ones) attempt to plan as far in the future as feasible and cope with anticipated changes such as changes in needs of consumers, changes in administration, and changes in allocated budgets in governmental organization. Long-range changes, if and when they filter down from top management to the supervisory level, can offer the opportunity for a different approach to reorganizing. An important *principle of long-range planning is that positions should be organized on the basis of overall objectives and work to be done rather than on the basis of people who happen to be currently employed.* Existing personnel, of course, must be appraised and trained as necessary in advance to meet future requirements. This is a major developmental responsibility of the supervisor. Sometimes training may not be feasible, however, because some present employees have reached their highest level of aspiration or capability, or ambition and drive, among other variables. Consequently, it may become necessary for the supervisor to recommend that such subordinates be replaced with personnel who have the necessary capability or potential. Unless this is done, positions and people occupying them can become obsolete and hamper the growth of the organization.

Shortcomings of Work Specialization The efficiency gained through the extreme specialization of jobs is, of course, not without unwanted consequences. There are likely to be, for example, unfortunate social-psychological effects on workers. Among the many opponents of extreme specialization back through the years were Marx and Engels, who said that the worker was simply an appendage of the machine, and it is only the most simple, most monotonous, and most easily acquired knack that is required of him. Earlier, in 1776, Adam Smith, while praising the marvelous economies of specialization, viewed this feature of economic development as a "producer of idiots." Many research studies indicate that the following characteristics of extreme job specialization can adversely affect worker satisfaction and motivation: mechanical pacing of work, repetitiveness, minimum of skill requirements, predetermination in the use of tools and techniques, minute subdivision of product worked on, and superficial mental attention required. A generalization resulting from these research findings is that extremely specialized jobs, that is, jobs that are routine and repetitive, are boring and excessively fatiguing to a significantly large sample of the working population. Where this premise is correct, and it is not always correct, extreme specialization should be avoided if possible.

In order to reduce the physical and mental ill effects that may result from performing highly simplified jobs, a variety of methods have been tried, such as the introduction of rest periods, training, competition between groups, the introduction of music, and so on. Another is a process known as job enlargement.

Job enlargement can be defined as increasing the responsibility and number of tasks performed by an employee along the flow of work. Its objective is to aid in increasing productivity and employee satisfaction.

The premise of job enlargement is so general that most would agree with it: in spite of the economies gained by job specialization, there is a point of diminishing returns in the subdivision of work. It is further assumed that when this point is reached, employees are bored and dissatisfied because they see no future in terms of self-development. To the extent that this is true, job enlargement becomes a real possibility. A major problem, of course, is that exactly where the point of diminishing returns occurs depends on the situation—the physical and social environment, the way employees are managed, and so on.

As a matter of fact the process of job enlargement is often reversed. In the experience of one of the authors it was helpful to break down an involved or complex job into two jobs. Previously lathe operators were required to do two things, set up their machines and operate them. Machine set-up was a complicated activity requiring very considerable skill and knowledge (for example, of shop math and blueprints) but occupying less than 10 percent of the total time. Machine operation, on the other hand, could be done satisfactorily with very limited education and experience. An obvious improvement was to establish two jobs, a set-up operator, who would be highly paid and responsible for setting up—and keeping properly set up—a dozen machines, and a machine operator, who simply ran what the other operator set up. The result was not only a significant saving in wages but it more genuinely challenged set-up operators and produced fewer frustrated or overwhelmed machine operators.

Thus increasing technological developments in equipment and facilities can in some cases increase and in others decrease the degree of job specialization. It also has obvious implications for the complexity of operations the supervisor may be called upon to supervise.

Job Enlargement Versus Participation Some theorists contend that the concept of job enlargement as defined above is not broad enough to be effective. For example, Argyris maintains that satisfactions do not increase as tasks along the work flow become more complex or numerous, but concludes that a broader form of the concept must be utilized in order to obtain maximum results. The concept Argyris advocates is one in which the employees not only use their "doing" abilities but also have an opportunity to employ their "knowing" abilities. Such an opportunity should be provided in instances where employees participate in the making of decisions that affect their immediate working environment.

It can readily be seen that Argyris's concept of job enlargement is actually one of *participative management,* wherein subordinates are encouraged to participate with their superiors in the making of decisions that directly affect their working environment.

A great deal of research supports the principle of participation as a useful consideration in supervising. At the present time, however, we can conclude from research studies only that (1) there does exist a need for participation in the solving of job problems on the part of many employees, and (2) the satisfaction of these needs will in many cases result in greater effectiveness on the job. How generally the technique is likely to be used in the future is discussed below, particularly in Chapter 8.

Clearly Specified Duties, Authority, and Responsibility

A common practice in large organizations is to attempt to *formally establish, standardize, and make known the duties, authority, and responsibility of each individual.* For example, it is believed that supervisors and their subordinates should know exactly what their positions are, what they are authorized to do, and the relationship of their positions to other positions. A number of reasons are commonly given for formally establishing a standardized network of positions, rather than allowing employees to set their own job boundaries.

First, it is held that individual employees are incapable of working out relations among their positions because each sees only a part of the big picture. Individual employees would be unable to interweave all the work and other aspects of an organization into an efficient network of duties, authorities, and responsibilities.

A second reason for formally established positions is that in every organization employees vary in their degree of aggressiveness. The more aggressive employees, unless restrained by a formally established structure, may tend to dominate the others and establish informal centers of power, or "empires." It might be argued that the "survival of the fittest" should be encouraged. A counterargument, however, is that too often superiors equate the "most aggressive" with "the fittest," and the overly aggressive employees are not necessarily the most competent or conscientious. In the absence of formally established positions of power the stage may be set for constant conflict. A continuous maneuvering for status through power could displace concern for the objectives of the company.

A third reason is that certain kinds of work cannot be made palatable to certain kinds of people over a continuous and predictable period of time no matter what means are employed. Some employees may not really want to work or do not want responsibilities, or cannot be positively motivated to do this work. Specific and well-known job duties at least help in dealing with such people. Also, it must be recognized that a hopefully small percentage of individuals may not be mentally or emotionally capable, regardless of how motivated, to work except under prescribed and supervised conditions.

Fourth, many people prefer the security that accompanies formally prescribed duties and authorities. There are many reasons why this attitude may exist. It may be difficult, if not impossible, to evaluate employees who occupy positions that are vaguely defined. Where duties blur and fuse together, some employees may be given credit for something they did not do, giving rise to charges of favoritism; others may be blamed for not doing work that they may have presumed should be done by others.

Authority

We have discussed the importance to the process of organizing of a group of principles that relate to the division of work. Keeping in mind the needs of the supervisor, we now turn to the concept of authority and describe its significance as another major facet of the organizing process.[6]

Definition of Authority   We shall very broadly equate the term *authority* with *power.* There tend to be two kinds of power or authority, that of position and that of personality, to utilize a concept advanced by Henri Fayol. A supervisor who is able to influence the behavior of subordinates because of his or her position in the formal organization structure has *authority of position,* while a supervisor who derives his or her influence from personality or behavior has *personal* authority (often referred to as leadership). This leads us to a very fundamental point: The supervisor's *authority is the sum of his or her authority of position and personal authority.*

Authority of Position   Authority of position we define, following prevailing practice in business and industry, as power delegated by top management to middle management and subsequently to supervisory positions. (A conflicting concept, the "acceptance theory of authority" is discussed later.) To differentiate authority of position from personal authority, the former might be termed semipermanent in most large organizations. It remains relatively unchanged over some degree of time. People, on the other hand, move from one position to another as they compete for better positions, are transferred, or step out of the organization and leave room for new recruits. When workers are promoted to the position of supervisor, they assume the authority and power—often referred to as *management rights* or prerogatives—that are formally placed in that position.

The policy of an organization regarding the delegation of authority to its supervisory personnel is important to the success of both the organization and the supervisors. How much authority should a supervisor have? A fundamental principle is that, insofar as possible, adequate authority should be delegated to enable supervisors to carry out the duties for which they are held responsible. Obviously, such an ideal can probably never be achieved completely.

The source of authority of position, according to the most prevalent view, is the chain of command extending to the chief executive, who may reserve to himself or herself the right to hire, fire, and transfer employees, to set their wages, to rate their performance or to take other actions. Senior management, in turn, delegates to middle management and to supervisors those rights that it deems necessary and wise for them to have. If supervisors are not fully informed regarding their authority, as well as the duties for which they are responsible, they may be reluctant to make decisions, or they may overstep their authority. Either result is likely to lead to inefficiency. They will rarely command the respect of subordinates if they are reluctant to make decisions or if their decisions are often over-ruled.

A common complaint of many supervisors is that supervisors in a large organization today have lost too many of their rights or prerogatives, or authority, and thus control over their subordinates. Certainly it is common practice for higher-level management to withhold from supervisors authority for making certain critical decisions. The authority to hire and especially to fire subordinates is most frequently limited. Often the supervisor can only recommend discharge of a worker. Approval from superiors, personnel specialists, or others may be necessary before final action can be taken. The authority to hire is often similarly limited. For example, the supervisor may participate in the selection of candidates, who may be prescreened first by others. Often supervisors do not participate in the hiring process at all. Such limitations on authority are based on a generalized premise that supervisors cannot be trusted with complete control of such critical functions as hiring and firing because of inadequate skill, knowledge, or emotional control, or because they may use such power to further their own ends.

The limitations on supervisory authority are designed to protect the interests both of the organization and of the employees as a whole. Any gains from such limitations must of course be balanced against possible losses from weakening of the supervisor's position.

In spite of complaints often heard that supervisors have lost too many of their prerogatives, most of them probably do not use all the authority that is delegated to their positions. Reasons for this may be good or bad. A bad reason, assuming that the use of delegated authority is necessary in a situation, may be indifference, but probably more often it is fear. Supervisors often fail to use authority because of fear of reprisals by subordinates either as individuals, or perhaps more importantly, as members of informal groups. Certainly one of the most difficult, unpleasant, and potentially dangerous tasks of supervision is the use of authority of position *to say no* to workers' requests. Saying yes to all of the employee wants or demands, of course, may appear to be the easiest part of supervision, and for the new supervisor may pave the way for a pleasant, if brief, honeymoon with his subordinates.

Of course, there are innumerable other *bad* reasons why supervisors do not use the authority of their positions even though such use is needed. Many reasons are not the supervisors' fault. They may not *know* exactly what the scope of their authority is, or their superiors may arbitrarily and without reason refuse to allow the supervisors to exercise adequately their authority of position.

Personal Authority   A *good* reason why supervisors may use little, if any, of their authority of position is that they are so respected by their subordinates because of their personal qualities (or leadership) that they can induce subordinates to perform work capably without having to fall back on the use of authority delegated to their positions. This discussion points up the value of another very fundamental principle. *To the extent that supervisors can do it and still perform efficiently and effectively they should never use their authority of position.* It should be kept in reserve, to fall back on only when it becomes necessary. Most of us resent the use of raw power of position.

Personal authority (leadership) as contrasted with authority of position, then, may be quite flexible and unlimited, whereas the latter may be quite rigidly limited.

The supervisor may develop and expand his or her personal authority so that it extends even beyond his subordinates, and may do so in many ways. First, he may acquire so much knowledge and respect regarding the work of not only his section or department but other sections and departments that he can strongly influence people's actions and thinking in these areas without giving orders. Second, he may be so proficient with respect to job evaluation or training, or organizational strategy, for example, that subordinates and perhaps peers and even superiors may become so accustomed to looking to him for answers that they are soon accepting the supervisor's authority of knowledge. Third, supervisors may have the respect of higher management which, many modern research studies show, tends greatly to increase their influence over subordinates. It may equally increase the supervisor's influence over peers and even immediate superiors. Supervisor's suggestions and implied preferences may sometimes take on the characteristics of an order because superiors know that the suggestions and recommendations carry great weight with higher management.

As a final example, a supervisor's code of ethics and judgment may be such as to win a great deal of respect and resulting personal power. More is said on this point in Chapter 6. Meanwhile we need to remember that it is the authority formally delegated to the supervisory position, plus the additional power that incumbent supervisors assume by means of their personal leadership that is critical to success.

Barnard cited four conditions that must be met before a person will decide to accept a communication as being authoritative:

1   He can and does understand the communication.

2   At the time of his decision he believes that it is not inconsistent with the purpose of the organization.

3   At the time of his decision he believes it to be compatible with his personal interest as a whole.

4   He is able mentally and physically to comply with it.

Barnard recognized that not every executive order can be consciously analyzed, judged, and either accepted or rejected. Rather, most types of orders fall within a person's "zone of indifference." If an order falls within the zone, the person will respond without question, but if it falls outside the zone, he will question and accept or reject it. The width of the zone depends upon the degree to which the inducements exceed the burdens and sacrifices. The main difference between the two views presented above regarding the source of authority may lie in its definition. "Downward flowing" authority, or the power to make decisions, is defined as *"power."* "Bottom-up" authority is best thought of as a *set of behaviors.* The latter concept may be considered to add perspective, rather than to invalidate, the concept of downward flowing authority. It is just another way of viewing authority, which we earlier defined as the total of authority of position plus personal authority.

Situational Nature of Authority   The important point is that the effective use of power is situational. In some instances people follow the supervisor's orders or even his wishes, because they *want* to, because of anticipated extrinsic rewards (such as money), or because of some dedication or some other intrinsic motive. (Intrinsic and extrinsic motivation is discussed further in Chapters 6 and 7.) On the other hand, workers and even work groups may be unwilling to work unless they have to. Here delegated authority is almost always required.

Principles of Authority: Unity of Command   A number of principles of organization deal with the concept of authority. One of the more venerable ones is that of unity of command.

Unity of command is one of the most pervasive in day-to-day operations throughout business, industry, and government. The principle of unity of command is expressed most simply by the proverb, "No man can serve two masters." Each employee in the organization should receive orders from, and report to, only one manager. This manager, in turn, should receive orders from, and report to, only one superior, and so on, up through a chain of command, or line of control, that ends with the head of the organization.

The purpose of having unity of command in an organization is to establish well-defined channels of authority and communication. The orders, policies, and instructions of top management are transmitted through middle management and through the supervisory level to the workers. Progress reports and other communications are returned through these same channels to top management.

The advantages cited for unity of command are many. With it, each supervisor is likely to know what he is responsible for and whom he directs. Unity helps avoid conflicting orders and confusion over priority of assignments. It provides a single channel of appeal or responsibility for each employee's training, development, and promotion. Thus unity of command is usually given formal recognition, and organization charts rarely show any violations of this principle. In practice, however, unity of command is frequently violated. A common example is the practice of skipping a link in the chain, or bypassing supervisors in communication. This is considered to have the following disadvantages: (1) the supervisor who is bypassed has lost control in some degree over part of his work force, and (2) the employees who receive instructions from someone other than their immediate supervisor may be uncertain about to whom they should report. Such bypassing of supervisors is often due to impatience with the slowness of the formal chain of command in getting action. Sometimes it results from a mistaken concept of authority and ability, or of what constitutes efficiency, sometimes from a dislike of restrictions imposed by formal channels. If the principle of unity of command is violated by someone who assumes authority over a supervisor's workers, this can mean that the supervisor is relieved of part of his authority and left only with the responsibility. This violates another principle, that *authority and responsibility should be equal,* a principle however, that is also often violated because of situational demands.

On the other hand, the principle of unity of command was never meant to apply without exception. For example, it would make no sense to require that all communications go all the way to top management and be cleared before action is taken. The chain of command simply becomes too lengthy in a large organization to provide for speedy action. So in circumstances where quick action is necessary, strict adherence to the flow of authority up through the management channels is modified by providing for informal cross-contacts to expedite the exchange of information. The chain of command may be safeguarded if in exchanging information through cross-contacts one employee does not assume the authority that belongs to another. In other words, supervisors may be able to cope with this principle by following this procedure: If subordinates of Supervisor A must deal directly because of time pressures, for example, with subordinates of Supervisor B, unity of command is still maintained if subordinates of Supervisor A report both to their own supervisor and to Supervisor B what action was done and why. This enables both supervisors to maintain control by keeping informed of what their subordinates are doing. Thus, operating within the concept of unity of command and still maintaining effective and speedy channels of communication involves two principles of organization: *Authority and responsibility must be kept equal,* as stated above, *and everyone must be kept adequately informed.*

Obviously not all improper violations of the chain of command are due to the perversity of subordinates. Many workers violate it because supervisors fail as leaders. Frequently they are a bottleneck. They may fail to give clear, adequate orders; they may fail to explain why or how work should be performed; they may fail to give authority necessary to carry out responsibility; or they may fail to keep their subordinates informed of what is going on. Subordinates can be expected to bypass them to correct such situations. Of course, supervisors may bypass their own superiors for the same reasons, and the process may be repeated in all levels of management.

There are times when it is not wise to follow rigidly the principle, but it should not be rejected. It often has real utility. For example, the final location of power and authority should be generally known and understood throughout an organization. Even though decisions may frequently be made through a consensus of opinion, an organization can be effective only when everyone understands that in the last analysis the supervisor, or other formally designated member of management involved, makes the decision when necessary and resolves the issues in case of conflict. For example, a supervisor's decisions may be unduly influenced by some informal leader or by group opinion. But even if a supervisor's authority must be exercised by a degree of group action, it must be orderly group action, because the supervisor must assume the responsibility for decisions made. Responsibility is a fundamental part of the principle of unity of command.

INFORMAL ORGANIZATION

Our discussion of the nature of the formal organization has covered only one of two major aspects of organization theory. Equally important is the concept of the informal organization.[7] As we have said, the purpose of the formally established organization is to aid in achieving a logical, orderly, and predictable means of accomplishing the objectives and plans of the company.

The Nature of Informal Organization

However, a formally prescribed organization structure neither can nor should be expected to provide for all the relationships that do or should exist between employees. In fact, it would be impossible to secure absolute compliance with, or conformity to all aspects of the formally established organization structure. Throughout the company, from chief executive down to workers, the authority and prestige of positions established by the formal organization must give way in varying degrees to esteem for *persons,* thus paving the way for the spontaneous development of the informal organization. The latter consists of employees who through face-to-face encounters associate with each other, typically in small groups, because of personal preferences. These voluntary and spontaneous clusters of congenial associates, friendship and gossip groups, cliques and grapevines constitute a network of relationships around which powerful sentiments are mobilized. Collectively they exert a powerful influence on the organization climate.

Although it is seldom, if ever, apparent to a supervisor, each of these informal groups emerges and exists in order to achieve one or more objectives, as is true of formal organizations (refer again to Table 3-1). Even members of such informal groups may typically be consciously unaware of the group objectives. However, they exist; in fact, an informal group, as is true of formal organizations, would disintegrate if objectives did not exist.

Objectives of informal groups may differ with each such group. And, of course, an individual employee may belong to many such groups, each with a different objective. Even though objectives of informal groups that exist within a supervisor's jurisdiction typically defy precise definition, it may be of critical importance for him to be sensitive to such goals, for they often influence the group's productivity and work satisfaction. Obviously, the major goals of informal groups frequently are simply of a social nature, a common liking for a sport or simply the company of others. However, in a great many cases they derive from the nature of the work being performed.

Illustrative of work-related objectives of informal groups are these: to provide a rapid communication network to compensate for inadequate communications through formal channels; to perpetuate what members find satisfying, and to resist work changes; to support a well-liked supervisor; or to displace a supervisor who is disliked.

Thus depending upon its objective, an informal organization can easily impede or support the formal organization represented by the supervisor. For example, informal groups may be supportive to supervisors by favorably propagandizing policies, procedures, and rules; helping newcomers get adjusted; and enhancing the objectives of work quotas or contests by bringing forth extra effort. They also may be one mechanism through which the formal organization might increase its cohesiveness by, for example, bringing together employees from across departments and levels to meet face-to-face in informal gatherings such as parties, outings, and athletic activities.

On the other hand, the informal organization may be nonsupportive or harmful to supervision, for example, by undermining a new incentive plan; mobilizing discontent to unseat an unpopular supervisor; or demoralizing trainees by spreading false rumors. It may act as a protection or evasion device for disaffected personnel and as a rallying point for opposition to supervision.

Development of Informal Groups

Among the more important factors that cause or facilitate informal group development, one is the physical settings or arrangements of space in which people perform work. This is because face-to-face interaction is an important element in the formation of social groups, and individuals must, of course, be together at the same time in the same place for face-to-face interaction to occur. Too, the characteristics of the space they share influence group formations; it is easier for people to talk to each other when they are close together in space; walls and other physical barriers tend to prevent interaction. Noise can be a barrier to personal interaction.

Even the location of work in relation to aisles and doorways affects opportunities for workers to interact with others walking through or coming into a work area. As a final example, the direction a worker faces or his position in a work area, if uniform, may be a significant factor in social grouping. This point will be illustrated in a discussion of the Bank Wiring Observation Room of the Western Electric studies (see Chapter 19) where there existed a clear social differentiation between the *front* of the room and the *back* of the room. Two distinct subgroups developed in the room. The "group in front" was considered to be "better" or to have higher status than the "group in back."

A second major factor in informal organization is that of time. Not only does nearness of work positions facilitate social interaction patterns, but workers must also be present at the same time. For example, workers on one shift would be unlikely to interact with workers on other shifts even though they work at the same workplaces. Also, the amount of time workers spend together per day or week is an important factor in social group formation. For example, factory work groups may normally be together over an entire forty-hour working week, while certain management groups such as task groups or committees may be together only a few hours each week. Further, the latter may have a limited time-span expectancy, as is often true of a temporarily formed group of workers drawn from diverse locations to handle an emergency.

This factor of time span of group life can in itself be an important factor in group behavior. For example, some studies show that the more transient a group in the life of its members, the less it may command involvement in the group. However, transient groups with important purposes may create a sense of urgency in members and a high degree of emotional commitment.

Space and time are, of course, only two of innumerable factors that stimulate informal group formation. Controlling factors may be age (older workers may group together, sometimes defensively, because younger workers prefer companions of similar age and youthful interests), sex, color, religion, nationality, and so on. As we have said, a worker normally belongs to many informal groups, each with a different objective. This may create a conflict situation for the individual, depending upon the frequency with which he meets with each group, the different amounts of time he spends with each, and the sequence in which he encounters them. Where technological organization of work creates spatial or temporal conditions that restrain employees from beneficial social interactions, the burden for developing an effective group falls heavily upon supervisors. Supervisors in such cases must effectively become centers of communication and exercise considerable skill in relating workers to each other. In technical settings where such constraints do not exist, workers are better able to develop their relationships on their own initiative.

Valuable as is our knowledge of the informal organization, practicing managers generally consider that it does not lessen the value of the principles of formal organization. The formal organization must still exist to accomplish a firm's objectives and establish the limits within which these spontaneous forces operate.

A Theory about the Use of Informal Groups The above view is not completely acceptable to some researchers working on the frontier of organization behavior theory.[8] They reason that formal objectives of a firm can be achieved as well, and perhaps even better, when employees establish their own work relationships without formal design, that is, when they create their own work groups. This viewpoint advocates the need for principles ranging from an extreme of simply altering the prevailing kinds of organization structures (for example, emphasizing large spans of control, decentralization, and job enlargement as mentioned earlier) so as to permit more permissive, democratic manager-worker relationships, to that of eliminating formal organization altogether in some cases.

Changes such as these, it is argued, will encourage "natural" or "live" informal organization "systems" to evolve by individual preferences; being more motivated thereby, the systems may more efficiently and effectively handle the decision-making process.

Fundamental to this view is the basic premise previously described, that in the aggregate people *inherently want to work* and *under proper conditions will work* more effectively if given adequate opportunity and freedom to form work groups of their own preferences.

However, even though human beings do inherently want to work and do display self-motivated organizing tendencies, informal social organizations evolve slowly, by trial and error processes. Too, these relationships are usually more unstable than those established by the formal organization, since authority and power are conferred by associates based on human sentiments, rather than delegated by superiors as in a formal organization. Informal social organization might be adequate for accomplishing a firm's objectives if resources were unlimited and there were no variables present such as illness, ignorance, and unpredictable developments in a firm's various environments. However, a business manager cannot wait until his or her employees become organized. While they are going through a trial and error process of developing an optimum informal organization (and the organizing process is a continuing one), the businessman must bear the losses coincident with the unwise use of resources, and in the meantime, in the words of one author, he "may be clobbered in the market place by his competitors."

Thus, management after setting goals or objectives, usually establishes or modifies a formal organization designed so as to best achieve them. The process of formal organizing is a complex, highly skilled task because it inevitably involves compromises and trade-offs which must be determined by managements at the various levels that have the perspective for considering the good of the entire system. This is true because every organization is always, at any one point in time, limited by a fixed amount of resources (money, management know-how, materials, machine capacity, and so on). Obviously it cannot take advantage of all the possible opportunities available to it. When it applies all its resources to achieve one purpose, the attainment of other possible goals is prevented.

ORGANIZATION CHARTS AND MANUALS

A discussion of the process of organizing would be incomplete without at least mention of the technique of preparing organization charts and manuals. Both of the latter have, of course, been used extensively for decades by large, and less often by smaller, organizations.

Organizing is at times thought of as a process simply of drawing up an organization chart. Nothing could be further from the truth. The chart does nothing more than reflect the results of the organizing process. It is limited to representing graphically the formal lines of authority and responsibility and communications of supervisory and higher-level management positions, at the particular point in time that they are published.

An organization manual, on the other hand, may be thought of as an extension of the organization chart. It typically includes job description or specifications that spell out in detail not possible for a chart the duties, responsibilities, and authority limits of each position, and the interrelationships between positions.

A major limitation of the organization chart (as well as the organizational manual) is that obviously it represents only the formally or officially sanctioned structure. It does not reflect informal relationships not sanctioned by management that emerge in *all* formal organizations. A cliché sometimes heard is, "A new organization chart is 100 percent effective only up to the instant that it is published." One reason for this, in terms of informal organizations, is that even the publication of an organization chart can in itself cause the spontaneous development of informal social organizations of employees who group together if for no other reason than to protect themselves from, and possibly resist, the official power structure.

To expand upon this point somewhat, the organizing process may be viewed as comprising three major sets of relationships. The first set of relationships is the one of formally established positions, titles, and channels of communication. These are indicated on the organization chart. A second set of relationships is concerned with status, which is not necessarily indicated by the organization chart. Status is commonly inferred from the formal organization chart, however, because it might seem obvious that it should indicate the prestige of individuals in the organization structure. This is, of course, frequently far from the actual situation encountered. For example, a highly aggressive individual who may or may not possess great personal competence may act as the "power behind the throne" regardless of his official title. As another example, an individual to whom others have learned to turn for help may exercise the widest influence without ever being fully aware of it himself. To be efficient and effective a supervisor must be aware of such kinds of status relationships, often complex and in a constant state of change, of which the organization chart gives no hint.

A third set of relationships is the *informal lines of communication,* which must be followed by the supervisor as well as other managers to avoid the red tape of the formal lines. These informal lines obviously are not usually indicated on the organization chart. There are many reasons for this. Their inclusion, along with formal lines of authority and communications, could create a confusion of lines in any graphic presentation; but more common reasons are, first, that top management commonly is unaware of these informal lines and, second, that it does not wish to recognize them. Regardless, these informal contacts, which are often infinite in number, are tolerated as an alternative to unwieldly lines of formal communication.

Such relationships as the three just described occur in a variety of patterns, determined, as stated above, by need, convenience, status, sociability, and individual preference. One writer contributes graphic illustrations of the problem. He suggests the supervisor might think of the formal organization chart as a basic guide to action. However, over this we must superimpose a "system of overlays" in order to reflect realistically any actual situation. Three examples of such overlay charts are illustrated in Figure 3-1. One is the *special friendships* (or sociometric) overlay. Another is the *functional* overlay, which concerns the manner in which staff specialists interact with live or operating departments. A third is the *power overlay,* which shows diagrammatically the impact of power on decisions. Many other kinds of overlays could depict informal relationships, such as a decision-making overlay, which could graph the way decisions are actually made, and a communications overlay, which could reflect the actual informal communications network.

Though most large organizations accept the concept of organization charts, the charts have limited value in day-to-day operations because, as stated above, from the moment of their publication they tend to progressively become obsolete. Revisions in charts are not always timely. Their preparation is a major undertaking in a large firm since positions and incumbents are constantly changing and the resulting preparation, printing, and distribution costs can strain manpower time and budgetary resources.

In the face of such limitations why do most large, and some small, organizations develop organization charts? Two major reasons frequently advanced are, first, that there is often an inequitable division of responsibilities within a firm. This can occur so gradually as to be generally unnoticed. Constructing or periodically revising a chart may reveal this fact. Second, the chart provides a clear definition of responsibilities and authority among supervisors and higher management, enabling each to know how he formally stands relative to everyone else. The same reasons apply to the technique of preparing an organization manual. Like the chart, its major advantage is to stimulate thinking and planning about the organization structure, as well as to facilitate the allocation of definite responsibility.

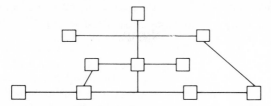

Special Friendships Overlay: "I'll talk to my friend George in Purchasing. He'll know what to do."

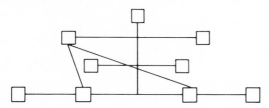

Functional Overlay: Direct relationships between specialist assistants and operating departments. "You have to see Personnel for approval to take that training course."

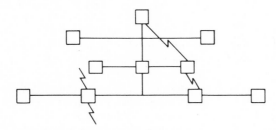

Power Overlay: "Before you go further, you had better check that with Jack in Production Planning."

Figure 3-1 Examples of overlay charts.

QUESTIONS

1 An efficiently and effectively developed formal organization structure would obviate the need for informal organization structures. Is this true or false? Explain why.
2 "The average person prefers a job with clearly defined duties, responsibilities, and authority that are known by all concerned." Do you agree or disagree with this statement? Why?
3 Are leaders of informal groups generally likely to be good prospects for promotion to supervisory positions? Why or why not?
4 What are some of the benefits that informal organizations provide for the formal organizations of which they are a part?
5 Can "authority" be considered as the key to the management job? Why?
6 If formal authority is being increasingly questioned, what can the supervisor do to accomplish his job? What alternatives can he develop to supplement his questioned formal authority?
7 What factors affect the power over supervisors that subordinates may have in the organization structure?

8 People join formal organizations because they want to satisfy their needs or wants. Does this mean people in general like to work? Explain.

NOTES

1 The variety of kinds of organizations is matched by a wide variety in effectiveness of their organizational structures. For example, for a description of organization structures (universities) being characterized as "organized anarchies," see Michael D. Cohen, James C. Marsh, and John Johan Olsen, "A Garbage Can Model of Organizational Choice," *Administrative Science Quarterly,* vol. 17, no. 1, pp. 1–23, March 1972.
2 The subject of needs, purpose, and organization is discussed in Charles L. Hughes, *Goal Setting* (American Management Association, 1965), pp. 19–23.
3 Organizing from a public administration viewpoint is discussed in Marshall Dimock and Gladys Dimock, *Public Administration* (New York: Holt, 1969), pp. 331–347.
4 For an interesting discussion of how "techniques" bring change: see Harold Leavitt, William R. Dill, and Henry B. Eyring, *The Organizational World* (New York: Harcourt Brace, 1973), pp. 320–329.
5 Studies of the impact of cost control on employees: see William F. Whyte, *Organizational Behavior* (Homewood, Ill.: Richard Irwin, 1969), pp. 368–377.
6 Edwin B. Flippo, *Management a Behavioral Approach,* 2d ed.(Boston: Allyn and Bacon, 1970), contains a good discussion of authority, pp. 156–161.
7 A psychologist evaluates informal organization in Edgar H. Schein, *Organizational Psychology,* 2d ed. (Englewood Cliffs, N.J.: Prentice-Hall, 1970), pp. 80–104.
8 For a constructive critique of prevailing organization theory: see David R. Hampton, *Modern Management* (Belmont, Calif.: Dickenson, 1969), pp. 61–71.

CASES

Again in this chapter we are selecting cases that may not be uniquely relevant to it and certainly do not relate to it alone. They do, however, involve supervisory problems. The first, that of Mary Davidson, concerns a worker who is superior in performance—or at least who has been and can be—but who, due partly to limitations in the way she has been supervised, has developed some seriously adverse characteristics.

The second case illustrates how difficult it is to cover all possible situations with predetermined procedures, how managers often have no way of knowing all that goes on in the organization, and how the feelings of people influence how they work—or do not—as workers and how they supervise as supervisors. It may also represent an informal group, about which this chapter has made comments.

The third case involves a situation where the management admits it made not one but three successive errors, and the workers involved took offense at what had happened. Why do you suppose they cared so much?

CASE 3-1

Mary Davidson is a proof-machine operator at the Bank, a medium-sized one in a large city. She is twenty-six years of age and is the mother of a seven-year-old boy by a previous husband, whom she divorced shortly after the child's birth. Her present husband works as a parts man in the repair shop of a local automobile dealer.

Mrs. Davidson was employed by the Bank 3½ years ago, at the minimum rate for her job. In addition to all of the general increases since then, she has received two small merit increases.

Mrs. Davidson's personal characteristics are a real liability. She dresses in a slovenly and unattractive manner. Her speech is loud and coarse, and at times even uncouth or vulgar. From the first she was rather uncooperative and not infrequently disregarded general policies of the Bank and of the proof department. Thus, she frequently made appointments for as early as 1:30 in the afternoon and left as soon as her work was completed. (When she first came to the Bank, this was not a violation of written policy or rules though it was discouraged.) Besides all this, she was almost always heavily in debt.

In her work Mary has been outstanding. Her speed and accuracy have consistently been far above average, and she is able to finish her work much earlier than any other person in the department. Even here she is uncooperative, however, and has made herself more unpopular with fellow workers by bragging about her clearly outstanding work.

To understand the situation that eventually developed, it is necessary to describe the proof department as it was when she was employed and its subsequent very rapid development and expansion. When Mary was first employed, there were only two proof-machine operators, and they reported directly to Jack Johnson, the department head, who also supervised the bookkeeping department. At present, in addition to Mr. Johnson, there are two supervisors in the department, one each for bookkeeping and proof. As the department has grown, Management has insisted that the proof operators observe more regular hours, starting (as they always have) at 7:00 A.M. and staying until *all* the work in the department is completed.

Mary's conduct under these circumstances has created at least three problems. For one thing, in spite of Management pressure to the contrary, she not infrequently leaves the Bank when she has finished her own work, which continues to be very rapid and the most accurate of any of the operators. In the second place, she usually disregards her immediate supervisor and goes directly to Johnson with her problems and complaints. Furthermore, she makes occasional remarks that reflect on the ability of her supervisor. Finally, with every change in or addition to the department, she complains about the lack of ability of the new people and continues to brag about her own superior work.

These developments have led Johnson to the conclusion that the situation requires action on his part. What should he do?

CASE 3-2

The incidents of this case grew out of a Company-Union safety meeting held in Jonesboro, some 60 miles from Pleasantville, the city in which the three affected employees worked. These three persons, John Smith, assembler and local Union president; Dave Wilkins, also an assembler; and Ms. Janet Brown, a plant clerk, left Pleasantville around 8 A.M. that day and arrived in Jonesboro shortly after 9 A.M. Between that time and the 10 A.M. safety meeting, they got coffee and visited with friends, most of whom did in Jonesboro the same sort of work they did in Pleasantville.

The safety meeting broke up about 2 P.M. but Horace King, a district manager and chairman of the meeting, suggested an inspection of some new equipment and also the examination of some records discussed during the meeting. Employees Smith, Wilkins, and Brown left Jonesboro about 3 P.M. and arrived in Pleasantville about 4 P.M., going directly to their homes instead of the plant. (Their regular hours of work are 8:30 A.M. to 5 P.M.)

When Smith arrived at home he found a message asking him to call a fellow-assembler who was at work in the plant. The latter reported that the Company was threatening to reopen a matter that had been resolved between the Union and the Company and that could lead to serious discipline for him, and requested that Smith come at once to the plant. This he did, arriving at or shortly after 4:30 P.M. and immediately going into conference with one or more Company representatives. This conference continued informally through some drinks and dinner until about 7:30 P.M.

When Wilkins got home he changed into his work clothes but found that his wife had taken his pick-up on a shopping trip. She arrived back home about 4:40 P.M., too late for Wilkins to get to the plant and do even five minutes of work; consequently he did not go in.

Brown is the secretary of the safety committee and as such is required to prepare minutes of the safety meetings, which are later signed by her and the chairman. She had long had permission to prepare these on Company time, and testified that on this occasion she at once began work on them but did not get them into final, typed form until almost 7:30 P.M.

When these three employees came to work the next day, each was instructed by his foreman to report to the department head. The latter informed all three that they were receiving a written reprimand for not coming to the plant on their return from Jonesboro and that Smith and Wilkins were also being laid off five days without pay. (Brown was not given a layoff because of the work she did on the safety meeting minutes.)

The grievance that followed was signed by all three and demanded removal of the reprimand and, for Smith and Wilkins, rescinding of the layoff and payment for lost wages.

The Company contends that the grievants actually got back to Pleasantville sometime after 3 P.M. (or at least they should have if they did not deliberately delay their return). In any case they were under obligation to return to work, or at a minimum to notify their foremen and secure permission not to do so. Furthermore, before they left work the day before these incidents, each filled out his or her time card for eight hours for the day of the safety meeting, but no one of them made any effort to correct this false claim for a full day of pay when they came in the next day.

Actually, Smith's coming into the plant allegedly on Union business is a "made-up story." He came in, it is true, but he got no permission from his foreman to do so, that is, to be away from his work. Additionally, he knew full well that there was no important pending issue between the employee in question and the Company and even if there had been it could have been attended to just as well the next day.

In the case of Wilkins, there is no legitimate excuse for his not coming in. It is his responsibility to provide transportation to work and he did not. Likewise Brown did not have and did not attempt to get permission to be away from her job. Even though preparation of the minutes is extenuating, she, as well as Smith and Wilkins, is guilty of deliberately failing to follow long-standing and proper work rules. Thus the Company's action is proper and should be sustained.

The Union contends that there is no justification for any kind of penalty for any of the grievants. It is long-established practice to fill out one's time card the day before a safety committee meeting, and the Company has never instructed them to the contrary. Indeed similar situations, including return an hour before quitting time, have occurred in the past, and the Company has not expressed any disapproval.

Penalizing Smith is entirely unreasonable. He was conducting legitimate Union business, as he has every right to do under the contract and for which the Company cannot refuse him permission. Brown's situation is equally justifiable. As a matter of fact, she missed at most one hour of work at the plant, but at home she did at least three hours of work for which she would have been paid if it had been done on the job. And in Wilkins' case, the circumstances were beyond his control. He tried to come in but could not, and the resulting reprimand and layoff are unfair and unreasonable. Thus the grievance clearly should be sustained.

What is the proper resolution of this situation—and why?

CASE 3-3

In three different instances the Company called the wrong employee for an overtime assignment. The Company admitted its errors and in each case gave the bypassed employee the opportunity to work the next available overtime. However all three maintained that they should have been paid for the lost overtime, that an opportunity to make up the lost time is insufficient.

The general provision for overtime assignment is that an employee's name appears on the overtime list in accordance with the overtime he *has worked* or *turned down,* and the person with the fewest such hours is at the head of the list. Thus those who were incorrectly assigned the overtime dropped to—or close to—the bottom of the list, and those incorrectly passed by got a chance at the next overtime. The Company maintained that thus in the long run no one was hurt by its error, since everyone got a chance at his share of the total overtime available. The Union, on the other hand, contended that the errors must be compensated for; that otherwise the Company could continue its careless ways and even effectively bypass the overtime provisions of the contract; and that especially three such mistakes in rapid succession indicated an attitude of carelessness if not of disregard of the negotiated provision.

It should also be noted that in the negotiations leading to the present labor contract the Union proposed that overtime missed by improper Company assignment should be "paid up, not made up," but that no such provision was included in the agreement.

What is the proper disposition of this case?

Chapter 4

Controlling

The function of controlling is an essential link that ties together the three previously mentioned functions of planning, organizing, and directing. The objective of control is to provide feedback on performance. If we operate an automobile without some sort of feedback on its speed, such as a speedometer, or if the feedback mechanism is defective, we may be in trouble.

The best kind of supervisory control corrects deviations before they occur. The *next best* method is to detect them as they are occurring.

Throughout history we have accumulated ample evidence that human beings, in spite of their best intentions, are far from perfect. We all make mistakes, not only in planning and organizing but also in predicting and influencing the behavior of those we must work with (superiors, peers, subordinates, public, and so on). The same, of course, is true of our own behavior.

Thus the process of control is critical universally, for all managers and for all levels of management. Various interlocking control systems and subsystems must be established throughout an organization to achieve the best results. At the top management level, certain production goals are established for a product or service based on the market potential, personnel are hired and assigned to tasks, production equipment is purchased and placed in operation, storage facilities are made available, and so on. All these functions in an organization contribute to and are dependent upon the amount of product or service that can be turned out over a given time at a predetermined cost. Should market or budgets change, up or down, a control system must quickly indicate this so that proper adjustments can be made in all areas involved.

THE SUPERVISOR AND CONTROL SYSTEMS

Supervisors are an integral part of this control system because they are closest to functional operations, such as sales or personnel, established to create or facilitate production. If production supervisors, for example, find that because of machine problems, inferior or inadequate supply of materials, or shortages or inadequate performance of personnel they cannot meet their goals, they and the control system at their level must quickly bring the problem to light so that timely, effective steps can be taken to remedy the situation. Corrective action may involve, for example, making any of an infinite number of decisions to alter performance within their area of jurisdiction. On the other hand, it may involve alerting higher-level control systems to take corrective action, as for example, making adjustments to increase production or alerting sales staffs to alter the target dates or reduce the volume of commitments.

Thus, the primary control seeks to compel events to conform to plans. Its object is to determine digressions from plans, to correct such digressions, and to prevent their recurrence. The very fact that a supervisor is known to apply effective controls may in itself contribute markedly to successful operations. It helps keep his subordinates on their toes. Perhaps most important, however, controls tell the supervisor in what direction his operation is headed and how effective his decisions have become. They tell him when to change his course. They may be compared to the brake and the accelerator of the automobile.

ELEMENTS OF CONTROL

All control systems have the same essential and minimum elements. This is true whether, for example, a supervisor is controlling the quality of a product (quality control), or the performance (or "merit" or "efficiency") of personnel, or personal behavior of employees (disciplinary control), or the control of funds (financial control).

The basic elements of control are, first, *standards* of required performance. Second, there must be a means for measuring day-to-day (even minute-to-minute) performance in order to compare it with the established standards and determine if any deviations occur. Finally, there must be methods for correcting deviations from standards.

The last element listed, corrective action, may often be thought of at the supervisory level as primarily involving retraining, disciplining, or discharging subordinate employees. However, few standards and few measurement techniques for which the subordinate may have responsibility are sacrosanct and infallibly accurate or fair. Thus, supervisors must recognize that corrective action sometimes more realistically involves revising the first two control elements listed—standards and measuring techniques—in order to restore stability to a system being controlled. The problem may be the supervisor or his boss, not a subordinate.

It is worth repeating that unless each of these three elements, which we shall now discuss, is present, it is impossible for the supervisor to perform adequately his function of controlling.

Standards

Standards are established criteria against which actual results can be measured. The need for standards is fundamental to all human behavior. For example, in the world of work everyone is concerned, sometimes desperately so, with where he stands in relation to his peers. "What am I expected to do?" and "What do others think of my performance?" are questions that constantly tend to influence our behavior to some extent, either consciously or otherwise. Finding the answer to questions such as these is just as important to the supervisor who wants to keep his superior satisfied as it is to his subordinates, and to the president of the company, who must equate his performance with the performance expected of the company.

Thus, we are always comparing things to see how they measure up against each other. Whether we are conscious of it or not—and usually we are not—such comparisons are always based on some standards. For example, whether or not we think the weather is good today depends upon our comparison of the actual weather with a standard that we have established and carry around with us. Standards directly affect our thinking and approach to the daily happenings in our lives, and without them our lives would become indecisive and confused.

In the supervisor's world of work, if standards of performance do not exist or are not known by those concerned, there can be no answers to such questions as these, many of which are of deep personal concern to us. A predictable result is a supervisory operation out of control, with low employee satisfaction and productivity.

Thus we can begin to visualize the tremendous importance and scope of the problem of standards. Theoretically, standards are an indispensable prerequisite to all efficient work performance, for without such standards we have no way of determining whether such performance is meaningful or not.

A factor that contributed significantly to early attempts to launch the *scientific management* theory in the United States (around 1880) was the lack of techniques for establishing standards of work performance. Consequently attempts to establish fair standards for workers occupy a central position in the history of management.

Basis for Standards   Since standards must be established to cover all kinds of performance throughout an organization, they are expressed in a multitude of ways: for example, policies, procedures, methods, rules, and other techniques established to achieve work objectives constitute standards. An organization structure serves as a standard for authority and responsibility given to specific employees.

Standards may be physical, in the sense that they represent quantities of products, units of service, person-hours, speed, volume of rejections, noise, sound, illumination, and countless other items of physical measurements. They may also be stated in monetary terms, such as costs, revenues, or investments. Standards should, of course, be stated in terms of specific, quantitative units whenever possible. However, it is important to remember that they also must be established for a great many intangibles concerned with customer, employee, and public-opinion factors which may be difficult or impossible to quantify.

Supervisors and Standards   In the business world the product or service turned out must meet acceptable quality standards in order to realize a profit, or in the case of a nonprofit organization for it to successfully accomplish its objectives. Generally speaking, supervisors have little to do with formulating standards, even though they are universally considered ultimately responsible for meeting them. Standards are set by upper management and often simply filter down through layer after organizational layer until they reach supervisors and workers, who constitute the heart of the system. Supervisors must then produce within the guidelines given them (or on occasion, when they are highly inaccurate, in spite of them).

However, standards received from higher management levels are very seldom if ever detailed or complete enough to enable supervisors to accomplish their missions without formulating additional standards of their own. They are constantly compelled to juggle their given and available resources of people, materials, equipment, supplies, and time to compensate for an infinite number of intrusive problems. Thus, they frequently find that meeting all standards imposed on them is impossible and are faced with making trade-offs of, for example, less quantity for more time expended, or more cost incurred in order to meet standards of quality.

Too, the supervisors find themselves constantly struggling to cope with many kinds of standards deriving not only from the formal organization that they represent but also from informal organizations that are unique with respect to them and their particular levels in the organization. A problem of significant proportions is that supervisors' established formal standards, the "norms" or "musts" of informal groups and the values (or "oughts") of individual subordinates represent kinds of criteria that may be in conflict at any one point in time with respect to an infinite number of problem areas. Productivity, dress, behavior, attendance, discipline, tardiness, and methods of work are all illustrative problem areas as will be noted again in our subsequent discussion of the Hawthorne studies and other experimental researches (see Chapters 19, 20, and 21).

Behavioral-scientist researchers have contributed data that reinforce many principles handed down through the centuries from bosses to supervisors through on-the-job training. Some of the more important, to cite research studies just mentioned, are, first, that standards should be developed that present a challenge to workers, that are difficult to attain, but that are attainable without undue hardship. Second, standards established on a competitive basis, as between individuals and groups, are often effective. Third, standards should be such that they can be accepted by all concerned as being fair. Other characteristics useful as guides to setting standards abound. For example, they should be as simple as possible, known and clearly understood by all concerned, and, as mentioned above, stated quantitatively whenever possible.

An area that justifies considerable emphasis concerns how widely a standard of performance can be applied among a supervisor's subordinates. *It is clear that the same standard of performance can be applied to more than one subordinate provided,* first, that work tasks are identical among all workers involved, in terms of scope and complexity; second, that all factors in the physical and social environment are identical and standardized; third, that there exists a continuous, identical flow of work to each of the individuals; and, finally, that it is within the power of each of the individuals to control his or her output. To the extent that any one of these conditions does not exist for any one or more individuals, however, a single standard designed to cover a group is not applicable. To illustrate, two salespeople assigned to different geographical regions of a state, each having different numbers and kinds of customers (different income groups, and so on), each operating under different expense accounts, one supervised closely and autocratically and the other working under decentralized, democratic supervision, could obviously not be assigned the same standards of performance.

Finally, it must be recognized that standards may become established simply by default, by inertia, or by precedent. Though it may never have been intended that such would happen, this fact may be quite incidental. The supervisor may simply be faced with the reality, and changing such standards may be much more difficult than establishing new standards.

Measurement and Comparison of Performance

A second essential element of control is a means of measuring and comparing actual performance against standards. If standards are appropriately developed and if means are available for measuring exactly the performance of employees, machines, or other resources involved, appraisal is fairly easy. However, just as there are many activities for which it is extremely difficult to develop sound standards, there are also many that are hard to measure.

As the accomplishment of tasks moves from the locale of the assembly line and of continuous operations to job shop or intermittent operations (both office and factory), the job of control becomes more complex, as concrete and meaningful measurement becomes more difficult. Measurement is *relatively* easier where conditions exist in which systematic techniques such as time and motion analyses can be used to establish standards (that is, where there is a continuous volume of work flow, a worker can control his output, and physical conditions can be standardized).

However, such work conditions commonly do not exist in offices and often not in shops today. Increasingly, especially due to the tremendous increase in the service type of occupation, work is for custom orders, and each order requires that it be unique because of a different combination of skills, materials, or patterns. In such situations, measurement techniques obviously must be devised that allow for more deviations than those in routine production lines.

Use of Strategic Points   It is important for the supervisor to establish measurement points at strategic or significant stages of a work process, a principle discussed more fully later in this chapter. A strategic point in a process is one where something highly important to the process has just occurred. The earlier in a work process a supervisor has established strategic measurement points, the better the opportunity afforded for detecting deviations from standards before the attainment of goals is affected. Another important point is that the supervisor not only must be able to measure whether a deviation exists, but the measurement scale must be fine enough so that the deviation can be detected at an early stage before the work process is entirely out of control, or before any actions on his or her part to correct the process become relatively ineffective.

A common illustration of a measuring technique for a physical process is a room thermostat, which is placed at a strategic point in a work space. This instrument normally has a fine measuring scale. If it did not, the temperature in a room would fluctuate widely around an established standard, for example, 65 degrees. As an illustration, if the thermostat detected only deviations of plus or minus 10 degrees, when the temperature reached 75 degrees, the heat would go off. When it fell to 55 degrees, the heat would turn on again. The temperature in the room would fluctuate widely around the standard of 65 degrees. Thus, even though the average temperature would be 65 degrees, the actual temperature would seldom be at this standard.

This example also illustrates the importance to the control process of having accurate measurement techniques. If the thermostat were not used and judgments of occupants were substituted as the measuring element, an established standard such as 65 degrees would probably seldom be met. That is, there would be no reliable means of measuring deviations from standard; some employees would likely be satisfied, some would feel too hot, and some too cold at any one point in time. The heat might not be turned on or off until the temperature became generally intolerable and the system temporarily out of control.

Thus, not only is it desirable that the supervisor be able to measure whether a deviation exists at an important point of work, but the measurement criterion must be sensitive enough so that a deviation can be detected before the process is entirely out of control and corrective actions become ineffective. The needs of a specific task will, of course, determine the degree of accuracy necessary.

Selecting Units of Measurement   It is important that measurements be in units similar to those of the predetermined standards. If this is not done, too much time can be consumed in trying to utilize measurement information that has been collected, time that may be critical in correcting a serious situation.

Some variation can be expected in all activities; therefore, a critical question facing the supervisor is, When is a variation from a standard large enough to be significant and worth attention? If variation limits are not clearly established, he or she may spend excessive time in evaluation of a particular measurement or be overly concerned in one area while overlooking critical happenings elsewhere.

It is important that comparisons of standards with actual performance be presented in the best way known at a current point in time. Generally, the simplest and most direct method is the *best*. The supervisor must be able to visualize important relationships and not be confused or misled by insignificant or unnecessary details. The graphic method is a frequently used approach that satisfies these requirements.

Another aspect of the comparison phase is important to the supervisor. In addition to revealing mistakes it should also aid in predicting future problems. Too, the measurement/comparison phase should be designed to present information clearly and quickly so that trouble can be prevented. A good supervisor is alert to process data that indicate a specific action is needed both to return the desired stability to his or her work process and to eliminate potential future problems before they develop.

Correction of Deviations

The final element of the control process as we have defined it is the action phase of making necessary corrections, when there are deviations from established standards. A decision to take no corrective action at all, even though deviations from standard occur, is always, however, a possibility. Any number of variables may intrude in this decision-making step. An all-too-obvious, but sometimes ignored, fact bears repeating: no one, including ourselves, is perfect. We have bad hours, bad days in spite of ourselves. This leads to a fundamental point that inefficiencies should be put in perspective, in term of the whole picture. Sometimes it is *strategic to ignore or overlook minor inefficiencies in order to achieve or maintain a greater overall effectiveness in the supervisor's department.* The costs of corrective action in terms of time, money, decreased employee morale, and innumerable other considerations may overbalance the gains of taking such corrective action at any one point in time.

As is true of the decision-making process in general, it is imperative that the supervisor carefully analyze all available information possible in the time available prior to instituting corrective action, in order to determine the *cause:* who, what, and where, and when, and why? This step has the highest order of priority. The actual cause of a problem may, for example, be an office or shop machine, located in a bottleneck position, that needs to be replaced and placed in a new layout. Instant accusation of an operator as the cause, a predictable "reflex action" by a poor breed of supervisors one sometimes encounters, obviously creates possible serious personnel problems that further compound and complicate the original problem.

A common supervisory pitfall derives from a situation in which the various segments of a work process are actually performing efficiently, but the supervisor's plan of operation is defective. An attempt may be made to force an efficient performance to conform to a defective plan rather than to apply corrective action to the plan. The result can be described in terms of "efficient" and "effective." In this case worker performance may be efficient, but due to causes external to the worker, it is probably not effective.

Sometimes corrective action requires reexamining all the steps in the management process of planning, organizing, directing, and controlling to determine the best way of solving a problem. Corrective action, for example, may necessitate the supervisor's conferring with others in the management chain to correct deviations from standards that at the outset may have appeared to have roots only in his or her own area of responsibility. A "total picture" awareness is thus often of critical importance. To state it in different terms, we have "closed the loop" in describing the basic functions of supervision; the corrective action in the function of controlling may involve reexamination of the effectiveness with which the function of planning and of organization has been performed.

MAJOR KINDS OF CONTROL

Controls are commonly grouped into four major classifications: those controls of quantity, quality, time, and cost.[1] The importance of these classifications lies in their value as a guide to the supervisor in doing a complete job of planning and administering controls. Every situation to be controlled always involves one or more of these kinds of controls, sometimes all of them.

Quantity

The supervisor, of course, plays a vital role in the control of quantity of output, whether it is, for example, the number of airline reservations made "over the counter" at an airport, the number of requisitions filled, the number of pages typed, the quantity of parts machined, or the volume of sales calls made. It is not uncommon for the supervisor to place undue importance on this kind of control relative to the others; frequently his or her reason may be somewhat justifiable, or at least understandable.

The supervisor's superiors and their superiors up through the hierarchy sometimes exert pressure on their subordinates to meet standards of quantity even at the expense of, for example, quality standards required and expected by top management. Where such relatively few, it is hoped, instances occur, it is possibly because quantity of output is visible whereas quality may more easily be concealed.

Certainly the possibility of such a practice is to some degree responsible, for example, for the quality-control function in manufacturing firms commonly being one of the first activities to be separated from the line function of production as a company grows, and organized as a separate staff department responsible directly to the chief executive for exercising an independent check on the quality of production.

The reasons for the severe pressures commonly exerted on the supervisor to control the quantity of output are easily explained by the competitive characteristics of an enterprise. The typical manufacturing or service organization purchases materials from a large variety of suppliers, processes them to a desired state, and sells the completed or partially completed products or services to customers.

Ideally the entire operation flows in an orderly fashion from start to finish, utilizing the entire capacity of the processing system of which the supervisor is a part. Of course, for many reasons this is usually difficult if not impossible to attain. The typical process may utilize many different kinds of materials and a variety of machines, workplace layouts, physical environments, and personnel of various ages, skills, and so on. In conjunction with these factors, sales probably fluctuate constantly by type and amount of products and services. The list of variables that make optimal quantity controlling complex and difficult to achieve is almost infinite.

Suppose the first-line supervisor is directed by upper management to produce within specified target dates a certain amount of product with his or her unit. The amount is based on and directly related to factors such as those mentioned above, especially that of consumer demand. The supervisor is then obligated to organize his or her schedule and operating procedures to meet the requirements; if this is not possible, the supervisor must advise his or her superior of the problem and recommend alternative solutions. Not only are both line and staff supervisors responsible for producing a required *quantity*, but it must of course be of a certain *quality*, available within a certain *time* frame, and not exceed established *cost* parameters.

Quality

Achieving a specified quality of output is, in the final analysis, the responsibility of all supervisors in all functional areas. This is true, for example, even though, as just mentioned, in all large manufacturing firms quality control is organized as a separate staff agency, responsible for monitoring quality of product. But when quality-control inspectors detect substandard work, the ultimate responsibility is placed on the supervisor in charge of the operation involved.

Today's products and services tend to be increasingly more highly sophisticated, and the demand from increasingly discriminating consumers is for reliable, trouble-free products and services. The question may be asked, What level of quality is necessary? The answer by no means is, "The *highest* quality." The problem is much more complicated than this and involves consideration of many, frequently highly complex, variables. A more appropriate answer might be, "That quality that best accomplishes the intended purpose of the product or service, at a price the consumer is willing to pay, and at a feasible cost to the organization."

All levels of management must share in solving the problems of quality. Such control can be effective only if information relative to the "goodness" or "badness" of the product or service is quickly fed back to the supervisors, to aid them in evaluating the effectiveness of their planning, organizing, and controlling. If, because of the nature of the output, a supervisor cannot evaluate its quality, it is his obligation to attempt to secure the information necessary from applicable sources. It is, to repeat, at the supervisory level that the greatest potential exists for maintaining quality standards.

Time

Controlling through the effective use of *time* is a distinguishing mark of truly competent supervisors. Of critical importance is not only the efficient management of subordinates' time, but also of their own. Time is a consumable; thus consuming it efficiently becomes imperative.

The amount of output required of supervisors is often a "given." However, they may be granted considerable latitude in the utilization of time to achieve it. It is, of course, imperative that they determine at the outset whether a given set of goals is within the realistic capabilities of their present workers, machines, materials, and supplies. The *time available* then becomes a major criterion; they must determine what are the best people, work procedures, equipment, and schedules and deadlines for best accomplishing the mission within the established time frame. It is their obligation to inform superiors if the workload is excessive or adequate, or if less than the expected or required output is possible.

Cost

Last but certainly not the least of supervisors' control functions discussed in this chapter is *cost*. To ignore this control function is a luxury relatively few practicing supervisors can afford. Unfortunately, many utopian theories of how supervisory controls "should be" can have little or no value because they include no hint of a price tag. In competitive enterprises, if total costs over an appropriate period of time are not equalled or exceeded by total income, an organization or one or more of its units will suffer or even cease to exist. Even in nonprofit organizations, if supervisors too often exceed their budgets, either the supervisors or their units may be in the same situation, simply because the kinds of activities we are concerned with herein cannot normally exist without funds.

There are obviously many kinds of costs (depreciation, property taxes, and so on) over which supervisors have no control. However, in many ways they may influence many organization costs. For example, allocated costs of material, labor, selling, and overhead originate at a much higher organization level than that of supervisors. However, supervisors play a critical role in the successful allocation of them through their control of work assignments, personnel, machine utilization, idle time, waste, materials, supplies, and many other obvious factors. The success of an organization's overall cost-reduction and cost-control programs often rests in the final analysis on the supervisor's performance.

One must keep in mind that the above types of control may actually be incompatible. In order to maintain a specified operating schedule, overtime labor may be required, a development that causes the cost standard to be exceeded. Elaborate inspection procedures to ensure that quality standards are met can increase costs considerably and even reduce output (quantity). When management is establishing standards, managers at all levels must take into account these various factors, balance them out, and arrive at procedures compatible with the overall objective of the enterprise. On occasion any one factor may be deemphasized in order to meet the overall objective. For example, the production of a particular *amount* of output, such as a certain amount of client information, or a given number of repaired parts, or a specific number of items of a product, may be more compelling within a certain *time* frame than either *quality* or *cost*.

MAJOR PRINCIPLES OF CONTROL

As is true of planning and organizing, the process of controlling is fundamentally a state of mind and depends, generally speaking, upon a philosophy rather than a mastery of mathematical, scientific, technological, or behavioral methods. Such a philosophy is based on a belief that the supervisor's world of work can be stabilized, even in an environment of erratic, frequently almost unpredictable variables, a condition faced not only by the supervisor but by the entire business environment.

Each of us, of course, should develop our own philosophy, composed of concepts or principles which we personally support as a basis for controlling. Ideally, we should derive such principles from experience, but "starting from scratch" is usually unwise. Rather, we can profitably begin by examining past and prevailing practices. Certainly centuries of recorded experiences in controlling a wide variety of organizations cannot be dismissed as valueless; rather they provide us with data useful in developing our own individual philosophies of controlling. A more practical approach is to view these data as resource possibilities. Some of these principles may be essentially correct; some principles may need to be discarded completely; others may carry some elements of truth that have been hidden in too general a formulation; still others may need more specification and flexibility in application; and sometimes new principles may need to be formulated.

We shall summarize at this point some of the more important principles of control widely accepted by managers (and in some cases supported by responsible research) as constituting alternative possibilities that might profitably be considered in solving control problems.

Exception Principle of Control

First, the exception principle of control, discussed earlier, is one of the most basic of all concepts. It applies to the control of both people and things. The exception principle recognizes that controls are always expensive to some degree, and if not carefully developed and installed, can quickly mushroom to the point where the cost in maintaining them far exceeds their value to the organization.

The exception principle specifically holds that at least major controls over quality, quantity, time, and cost should be restricted to the relatively few, exceptionally important work tasks or things. Stated in another way, in any series of elements to be controlled, a selected small fraction, in terms of numbers of elements, always accounts for a large fraction, in terms of effect. (Obviously this does not mean the "trivial many" should be completely ignored.) For example, as applied to *people* the principle holds that a small percentage of the total employees on the payroll usually account for the bulk of the personnel headaches, accidents, and so on. Also relatively few of a large number of workers are accident prone, generally speaking. Similarly, on the positive side, relatively few are highly creative or are the informal leaders. The supervisor's attention to these out-of-the-ordinary people and things is likely to pay large dividends.

An example relating to the control of *things* is the concept that a relatively few exceptional items out of an inventory of thousands of items can justify having the most concentrated controls. In an assembly plant a great many items such as bolts, nuts, and rivets may receive only minimal control. They may be placed at the point of use; and even though a considerable amount of pilferage or destruction may be predicted, this may be less expensive in terms of total cost than extensive control of such items would be. On the other hand, "exceptional" items of inventory, such as metal hardness testers and expensive tools and dies, may justify extensive controls. However, these controls may be expensive, involving perhaps floor space, an enclosed structure, storage shelves and other equipment, a requisition clerk, and requisition paperwork. Not least among many other costs is the time of staff personnel who must process such paperwork and the time of workers who must requisition such inventory and return it after use. Thus the exception principle is to be applied carefully and "exceptional" things controlled no more than necessary.

Principle of Strategic Control Points

An important aspect of the exception principle, also mentioned earlier, is worth special attention: the concept of *strategic control points*. A 100 percent control over all operations (for example, typing, filing, selling, or designing) is seldom possible or justified; thus a supervisor is usually concerned with establishing limited-sample, optimum controls. One approach to achieving optimum controls is to establish major control efforts at only the most important key, or limiting, points in a process—where important changes occur—sometimes termed strategic control points.

A useful assumption in some situations is that people will concentrate their efforts on the parts of their job that they know will be inspected. This provides the supervisor with a very important tool for control. Where one puts his or her attention in the presence of subordinates is where they will tend to focus their efforts. If a supervisor concentrates on the *key-result area of their jobs,* they may do the same. If on the other hand, he or she is concerned with trivia, to the neglect of the key areas of the job, the people may do the same. Inspection of work should be, in part, systematic and periodic. Some things the supervisor may want to set up to check every two hours, or every day, or three times a week, and the workers should know that this is what is going to be done. At the same time, the supervisor needs to take into account the Principle of Random Sampling, discussed below.

If the points selected for control are in fact the most strategic to the operation, either in the sense that they are the limiting factors or that they, better than any others, show whether activities are occurring as projected, the supervisor may be able to exercise his talents over a larger group of subordinates and thereby possibly increase his span of management, with resulting benefits in cost savings and improvement of communication.

There are no universal rules for the actual selection of such points because of the peculiarities of enterprise and department functions, the variety of products and services to be measured, and the infinite number of policies and plans. There are, of course, many rules of thumb. For example, strategic control points should be located at points in a process or operation where the cost of a failure is significantly more than the cost of the control. Thus, in aircraft production, a critical control point is inspection of internal riveting in an outer-wing panel at that point in assembly prior to installation of the metal skin covering. A similar approach can be applied to selection of strategic control points in the process of preparing a purchase order, that of designing dresses or mechanical products, or of controlling incoming inventory and/or inventory-in-process.

Fail-Safe Principle of Control

A third fundamental principle might be termed the *fail-safe principle of control,* defined in this way: If there is danger that any part of an important plan might fail, then it should be assumed, for control purposes, that the failure will occur. Consequently, one or more duplicate or alternative ways of performing that part of the plan should be built into the plan. Put more simply, some points are sufficiently vulnerable that they should be checked twice or more. In case of a failure an alternative plan should (sometimes instantly) be available. A riot-control plan of a police department provides a dramatic illustration of the importance of this principle.

Principle of Random Sampling

A fourth principle is really a supplement to the principle of strategic control points. Along with periodic inspections, the supervisor should pay *random personal attention* to what is going on in his or her department. Otherwise, as stated above, employees may spend a disproportionate amount of time and effort in work designated as strategic control points.

Presuming a supervisor has an understanding with subordinates as to exactly what is expected, this kind of random checking can consist in a large number of short conversations with each individual. This approach may be as simple as asking questions such as, Is everything OK? Any problems? Are you going to finish on time? Of course at other times it may have to be carried out more formally.

Principle of Control Choices

A fifth principle is concerned with the corrective-action phase of control. It elaborates on one phase of the logical decision-making process: that an effort should be made to consider *several alternative kinds* of correction before action is taken. This principle stresses a critical point, that one of the choices is better administration of the existing ways in which things are being done. For example, before expensive replanning or reorganizing or establishing a new control system, an analysis may reveal that present plans, organization, and control systems are quite adequate if properly administered. It is commonly cited that we as individuals, whether workers or supervisors, may frequently perform at no more than 35 percent to 60 percent of our actual capacity. If such a situation exists, the most promising alternative action might be better administration of present supervisory systems (for example, better employee motivation) rather than developing and installing an expensive new control system—or trying to find new employees.

Principle of Economy in Control

Sixth, controls should be as *economical* as possible. Too often an analysis of the costs of controls is neglected. Controls have no value to a bankrupt organization. A constantly increasing expenditure of people and money is often a lazy manager's way of trying to counterbalance an inherent inefficiency. Many supervisors fail to realize that affluence in terms of dollars and people may be a millstone around their necks rather than a contribution to success. Improved supervision of persons composing an existing payroll may result in more financial success than an increased budget would provide, for if supervisory control is weak, each increment in labor will add to the inefficiency.

Accountability Principle of Control

A seventh and exceptionally important concept, the *accountability principle of control,* cautions that in taking corrective action many deviations from standards may very well not be the fault of a specific worker involved in the deviation. We can define this principle as follows: An individual can be held responsible for deviations from standards only provided the following conditions are met: First, he must know what he is supposed to do. Second, he must know how to accomplish what he is assigned to do. Third, it must be within his personal control to regulate what he is doing.

To illustrate, workers can be held responsible for costs only if they know what their costs should be, according to a budget or some cost standard. Further, they must know what their costs are; there must be available a means of informing them of the costs as they are actually incurred. Finally, they must be able to regulate costs. For example, they alone should have the authority to requisition materials, or utilize services and facilities if they have the sole cost responsibility for such factors.

If all these conditions are present simultaneously, then a supervisor might be warranted in holding subordinates responsible. If any one of them is absent, the subordinates cannot be held fully responsible.

Gresham's Law of Controls

Equally important to supervisors is an eighth principle we shall call *Gresham's law of controls* (derived from Gresham's law of money: bad money drives out good money). The point to be made here is that bad controls tend to drive out good controls. If supervisors establish employee controls that are unrealistic or unethical or are not being enforced, the result can be the abandonment of all reality in meeting standards. Unless such "bad" controls are corrected, they may drive out all controls, including the "good" ones. It is especially important that a control be established in such a manner that if the activity it monitors ceases, the control becomes inoperative. Obviously, if a control continues to function beyond the life of the activity, costs increase, the accuracy of total input data is sometimes questionable, and confusion may be expected to arise.

Principle of Accuracy and Timeliness

Ninth, an obvious but frequently neglected principle is that critical control information must be gathered by the supervisor and relayed upward with optimum *accuracy and timeliness.* A properly devised control system filters out unimportant information and reports only significant items. This reporting or feedback must accurately report deviations. Of course, in attempting to attain a high degree of accuracy, more time may be necessary to get adequate data. On the other hand, unless controls provide data on a timely basis, results may be nothing more than a historical record of events. If time and accuracy come into conflict, the supervisor is, of course, faced with the important responsibility of determining which is more critical. His or her decisions, which call for considerable supervisory expertise, will depend upon such factors as the magnitude of the decision, the time pressure involved, and the amount of additional information necessary to make a better decision.

Social Problems

Finally, it is apparent that often the greatest problem that arises in controlling is not a technical problem but one of *human relations and communications.* For example, a new control form, issued by a supervisor without a detailed explanation of its purpose and how the information to be collected will aid the workers or the section, may not only be filled out improperly, but may not be filled out at all.

Ultimately the success of a control system is determined by its effectiveness in getting people to make necessary modifications in their own performance. Supervisors and subordinates alike tend to resist controls for many reasons. Some of the more common reasons are: First, a person usually rates high in his own mind the quality of performance he produces in relation to the performance of others. Since control reports highlight those things a person does poorly, obviously a person's self-image is constantly in danger of getting damaged.

Second, a person who fails to accept organizational goals or considers standards unnecessary or not applicable to personal or organizational goals may reject such controls.

Third, employees cannot be expected to expend their best efforts if standards are too high or too low. It is to be repeated that research data reveal that high-producing supervisors tend to set standards or goals that are challenging but attainable. If performance standards are too low, employees' interest in their jobs and the incentive to meet or exceed standards may wane, especially after the operations become familiar and easy. On the other hand, standards that are too high and unattainable may greatly dampen their efforts. Instead of experiencing the satisfaction that accompanies achievement, subordinates may feel the nagging sense of guilt that comes with repeated failure.

Controls—And Confidence in Employees

Additionally, it is not rare to find people basically accepting controls themselves, but resisting conformity to them because of a personal conflict with the person or persons assigned to enforce them. A supervisor's lack of *trust and confidence* in subordinates, for example, may create over a period of time insurmountable control problems (see Chapter 6).

Douglas McGregor says that conventional managerial control systems tend to generate and accent the very behavior they seek to prevent, namely, noncompliance. He views the actions and reactions of management controls and the "measured" employees as a vicious circle. In a climate lacking trust and confidence, the "measured" employees frequently view the controls as a threat against which they develop hostile, defensive behavior. Attempts to correct the system may disrupt results creating more measurement and tighter controls, further decreasing trust and confidence.

Supervisors who as a way of life lack confidence in the abilities of subordinates will constantly be fretting about them and trying to prevent them from hurting the operation. In so doing, they are likely to fall into the habit of sheltering employees from the risk and challenge necessary to growth. As a consequence, to forestall their mistakes they may set up controls that give the subordinates very little freedom and responsibility. By cultivating this dependency on the part of subordinates, supervisors can hamstring them to the point of insecurity, incapacity for decisive action, and even hostility. The result is a downward spiral. Because supervisors see their subordinates as not very competent or strongly motivated, they adjust the control system to compensate for these failings. Thus subordinates' failings become real, forcing supervisors, or so they think, to make further adjustments, continuing the spiral.

Eventually, if the process continues, at the bottom of the spiral the supervisors will have eliminated all opportunity for subordinates to manifest any spark of initiative, responsibility, and achievement. Their subordinates no longer have any meaningful involvement in, or commitment to, the job. The company may simply become a means for them to pick up a paycheck and a place to put in a minimum of time and effort. Even too much emphasis by supervisors on a seemingly very positive quality, loyalty, may paradoxically create a negative control climate. It is not uncommon to encounter supervisors who prize loyalty on the part of their subordinates far more than competence. Obviously, one quality is of little avail without the other. However, supervisors' insistence on unswerving loyalty can completely stunt subordinates' growth.

Research studies have indicated that control systems grounded on trust and confidence in subordinates may have many advantages in certain kinds of situations and with certain kinds of employees. However, no matter how well meaning supervisors' intentions, a too-rapid switch from very negatively oriented controls to this mode can be fraught with dangers. Certainly, only employees who have had experience in solving problems and making decisions on their own are likely to withstand the anxiety involved in any action where there is a risk of failure. Subordinates whose experience has primarily consisted simply of doing things the way the supervisor thought they should be done can seldom work effectively when assigned to perform assignments where they have to think and act independently to some degree. Thus a successful change in supervisory style usually takes much time, patience, and effort.

Even controls by supervisors over socializing with subordinates can be significant. It can be stated as a *principle that supervisors must exercise care that their socializing with subordinates is not too close to cause loss of respect* and thus their capability to control them. Such decisions must, of course, be made on an individual basis, in terms of specific situations. However, characteristics of specific supervisors, subordinates, and work situations, all are critical factors in determining the optimum "social distance" that supervisors should establish between their workers and themselves.

Controls and Empathy

It is especially true that performance of the control function, which concerns a high-risk, ego-involvement situation, should be keyed to consistent, unemotional, calm behavior on the part of the supervisor. Judgments should be based as much as possible on facts, not personalities. In situations where personality conflicts do exist, restraint must be used to balance personal dislikes against the rational changes necessary to maintain effective control and accomplishment of objectives.

A supervisory attribute that makes control more palatable is empathy (see Chapter 7). The first-line supervisor must understand and anticipate how subordinates will react to the pressures of control and be flexible in his or her interpretation of control data. The supervisor must allow subordinates a certain amount of tolerance in how they use their skills; however, he or she cannot permit this flexibility to interfere with making corrections if substandard performance continues beyond a reasonable period of time. Empathy allows a supervisor to understand and appreciate why deviations happen, and it can provide a basis for permitting unusual circumstances to subvert the system for a short period of time. This line of thought, however, must not be used to release the supervisor from accountability while the workers are held to the mark. Empathy provides the supervisor with an assist to the implementation of control system, but it too must be exercised with considerable constraint.

Summary

Our discussion of the process of controlling concludes our description of the basic functions of management. It is worth repeating that the division of managerial work into the functions of planning, organizing, directing, and controlling is simply one widely used breakdown of management into its assessable and understandable parts to facilitate the teaching and analysis of the supervisory job. In practice, management actions typically involve most or all of these functions simultaneously.

THE SYSTEMS CONCEPT

At this point it is pertinent to introduce another approach to describing the management job, an approach that stresses the importance of considering the *interrelationships* between the basic functions of management *throughout all levels of an organization,* and both vertically and horizontally. This approach is known as the *systems concept.*[2]

The systems approach to managing has grown so extensively in the past decade or so that a book on supervision without some discussion of it would be incomplete. However, the subject is so complex (indeed, volumes have been written about it) that we can only briefly summarize the philosophy of systems and relate it specifically to the job of the supervisor.

The systems concept is primarily a way of thinking, a frame of reference, that may be utilized by management at all levels in planning, organizing, directing, and controlling operations.

Though the systems approach utilizes principles espoused by modern theorists, its emphasis is on a distinctly different dimension. It originated in response to a compelling need for a means of coping with a world of work that was becoming more and more complex because of the accelerated rate of technological and social changes faced by large organizations. Today a supervisor may control an operation that comprises technical, social, and financial problems of a degree of complexity that was undreamed of a few decades ago.

The systems approach corrects approaches that prevailed widely in the past and to some extent still occur today. They tended to view an enterprise as composed of a multitude of entities acting separately (broadly termed a *closed system*). The systems approach, termed an *open system* sees the organization as a system composed of many subsystems internal to the company, subsystems that must be combined properly to achieve goals. Further, managements of the various organizational levels are viewed as being forced to cope with many systems outside the company, such as labor, government, customers, and so on.

What Is a System?

The broad concept of systems is certainly not new to our society even though it is relatively new to management theory. The solar system, the nervous system, the utility system, and the system some aspire to "beat," for example, are terms and phrases quite familiar to us all.

Those who write about systems usually define the term in the light of their own interests. Thus, the biologist may relate his definition to the central nervous system, the anthropologist to the value system, the behavioral scientist to the social system, and so on. Some authors define a system in such a way as to make a subsequent discussion of its characteristics more obvious. For example, one definition is: "A system is an established arrangement of components which leads to the attainment of particular objectives according to plan." Here we might expect effective planning, organizing, and controlling to be stressed, along with goal attainment. One writer says, "A system is a group of components—at least some of which are pieces of equipment—designed to work together for some common purpose."[3] It should come as no surprise to learn that the title of this writer's book is *Man-Machine Engineering.*

Why operating management and management education are, relatively speaking, just "beginning to come around" to a systems approach is hard to say, because managing at all levels is basically a matter of dealing with complex systems. We have just traditionally called them by their more common names: *people, equipment, machine, section, customer, boss, company, society,* and so on.

We could pursue definitions of a system at length, but we shall simply say that *a system is anything that consists of interdependent elements or parts acting (or forced to act) together to reach a goal.* The behavior or state of each element or part is dependent upon the behavior or state of the other elements in achieving the overall goal. For example, the cooling system, the electrical system, the power system, and other systems of an automobile must operate not only efficiently as separate systems, but interdependently; a failure of any part of any one system will likely render the automobile inoperable. Obviously, systems may be virtually any size and are usually part of a larger system; when viewed as parts of a whole, they are identified as component *subsystems.*

Though the systems concept has developed primarily in response to the compelling needs of managerially coping with large, complex organizations, its value is not limited to such situations. It is equally applicable to organizations of all sizes, both business and industry, and both office and shop. It is also applicable to all levels of management, from chief executive to supervisor. Furthermore, the systems concept is not limited in applicability to any one or more functional activities; the breakdown of an organization into operations, sales, finance, accounting, and personnel, for example, is an arbitrary and artificial division that at times has been considered necessary by practically all organizations up to, and including, the present. This and many other current approaches to organizing, however, may be rendered obsolete by the systems approach. The same can be said of the process of planning and controlling, as we shall briefly explain later.

It is important for the supervisor of today to be familiar with the implications of the systems approach especially as this approach is employed by upper echelons of management. Certainly to one "on the way up," especially in large establishments, it may be imperative for him to be so informed. On the other hand, a supervisor of today may find himself directing a subsystem that is intimately intercorrelated with other subsystems and that involves him in reporting to several superiors, as we shall discuss.

Basic Systems Facing the First-line Supervisor

In directing our discussion of systems to the supervisor and his job, we view the system which he controls as composed of such subsystems as workers, equipment (these two working together constitute man-machine systems), materials, and work habits which he causes to act together, through his supervisory expertise, effectively and efficiently within his budgeted person hours, to reach goals set for his section. Indeed, what we have termed the subsystem of supervisory expertise has a firm basis in the self-reliance, humility, and empathy of the supervisor. His acceptance of "the way he is" goes a long way in influencing his effectiveness.

A smooth-functioning team effort with the supervisor effectively converting the disorganized resources of employees and material into a useful and efficient enterprise is a worthwhile endeavor. It is especially important, in this sophisticated age of highly complex technology, for the supervisor to recognize the manner in which his section relates to others in solving a problem of achieving desired company results. Outside the formal organization, labor unions, customers, and suppliers may, depending upon the supervisory job, also bear heavily as subsystems affecting him.

It is this *interrelationship* of the parts that makes the whole. It is certainly usually true that the person who sees the parts and their relationships with one another within the framework of the whole system will usually be the best supervisor. While merely "seeing" is not sufficient in itself, this overall view can greatly aid in increasing a supervisor's effectiveness and empathy for coworkers and codepartments, and in increasing his or her potential for development and promotion.

For example, the systems approach means that specific problems must be solved *optimally* (rather than *maximally*) in some cases, even though this may violate some time-honored principles. For example, a certain amount of inefficiency on the part of one or more specific workers may have to be overlooked at a specific point in time in order to avoid widespread discontent that could be a threat to achieving an overall goal on a specific target date. Stated in the language of the systems world, *subsystems* (that is, the specific workers) *should not always be maximized. Rather, all subsystems should be optimized; failure to do this results in total system suboptimization.*

The supervisor is involved in a network of systems, some of which he controls and some of which control him. We shall now discuss some of the techniques that are commonly used to aid in coping with problems of managing systems.

Techniques Utilized in the Systems Approach

While we stated at the outset that the systems approach was basically a philosophy or a way of thinking about supervising, there are several trademarks of the concept that set it apart from more traditional supervisory approaches. Illustrations of systems techniques are operations research, project management, program monitor, PERT (Program Evaluation and Review Technique), and CPM (Critical Path Method). Some first-level supervisors will never need any detailed information concerning these techniques. Others may use them quite routinely on a daily basis. Some theorists may quarrel with the implication that these techniques are uniquely applicable to the systems approach. It is not our intention to leave that impression, but rather to call attention to their peculiar relevance to this concept.

Operations Research   Typically, *operations research* is a mathematical technique used to provide a quantitative basis for decision making.[4] Commonly it involves only a very limited part of the *planning* process as we have defined it for the supervisory job. It is not concerned with establishing problems or deciding on a solution. It is, stated simply, a technique for quantifying or putting in terms of numbers (costs, profits, and so on) possible alternative solutions to a problem.

Of the techniques mentioned, this one has a more unique affinity for systems. This technique works best in clearly defined and quantified decision areas. If a problem can be stated in mathematical terms, it can be set up in an "objective function" equation with accompanying equations specifying the limits or constraints of the variables affecting the objectives. A prime characteristic of operations research is this consideration of the way subsystems interact, an activity that precedes the search for possible solutions to a problem. Then presentation of a significant number of alternative solutions, and in terms of costs, is often a real contribution to management. Operations research obviously has wider applicability among higher echelons of management because of the multisystem flavor that it brings to the task of decision making. However, a developing trend in some industries is the breaking up and decentralization of operations research staffs and the assignment of operations research individuals to divisions and departments.

Project Managers and Program Monitors   Project managers and program monitors are terms describing techniques that have become more prominent since the advent of the systems approach. "Program management" usually means substantially the same as "functional authority," which may be defined as "authority delegated to an activity which gives members of that activity the right to command . . . those not their subordinates." A project manager or program monitor is an individual inserted into the normal chain of command to supervise or control a particular system development. For example, using a manufacturing illustration, a project manager would be placed in charge of a particular program or contract item such as a pocket-sized computer, beginning with the design stage; progressing through production, quality control, and so on; and ending with final inspection and shipping, when the project or contract item moves out the firm's doors.

We see this form of control not only in business but frequently in military or space programs when someone outside the normal chain of command is brought in to supervise a complex weapons or space system. In fact, many defense contracts now require the use of program management in the development of highly technical, "problematical" systems. Large police departments may use the systems concept to a degree. For example, in a homicide investigation one detective may at the outset be placed in charge of coordinating the efforts of all groups involved until the case is solved or marked "unsolved." After completion of the project, the project manager returns to his regular, full-time job or is assigned to another special project.

The impact of all this on the first-line supervisor is rather clear: he may find himself working for two or more direct superiors, the manager on the organizational chart and one or more project managers, or he may find some of his very own people working for other bosses. This overlap frequently causes friction in an organization. The supervisor must clearly understand the delineation of areas of mutual concern held by his "competing" superiors. (While the word "competing" is perhaps inappropriate in the light of the systems viewpoint, it serves to illustrate the strong opinions held by some for program management.) A systems attitude can aid the supervisor and his workers in living more comfortably within the dichotomous picture just painted.

PERT and CPM   PERT, an acronym for Program Evaluation and Review Technique, and CPM (Critical Path Method) are somewhat similar in their relationship to the systems concept. Both are planning and controlling techniques developed at about the same time, and both have as their basis the project network diagram.

PERT was originally conceived in 1958 when the U.S. Navy and Lockheed Aircraft Corporation found themselves faced with inadequate control methods in the development of the Polaris missile system.[5] Du Pont developed the CPM technique in a construction project to reduce downtime for periodic maintenance. Some call CPM the "civilian counterpart of PERT." Both techniques are primarily slanted toward obtaining better managerial control of time. An essential difference between the two techniques is that PERT uses three time estimates of component activities that compose a system: best possible, most probable, and least likely, while CPM uses only anticipated time.

As in the case in program management, most of the complicated defense contracts now require the use of PERT in planning and controlling contract performance. Many benefits accrue through the correlation of diversified activities into a visible network diagram with time estimates for the completion of each activity. Not only is management provided with on-the-spot control at any given time and at any organizational level, but the resulting visual display also serves suppliers and customers as well as others in the broad context of the firm.

In summary, the likelihood of a first-line supervisor becoming intimately involved with PERT and/or CPM depends greatly upon the nature and scope of his or her firm's operations. These methods are most applicable to complex systems where failure to promptly determine interdepartmental problems may cause serious mission impairment. There is increasing evidence, however, that they are being used more and more by smaller companies for shorter, less complex operations. As the experiments and refinements of these methods continue, these smaller projects increasingly may also find a commonplace helpmate in PERT and CPM.

Figure 4-1 is a modified version of a PERT chart used by one of the authors as an aid in controlling research activities concerned with large, semiautomated postal installations.

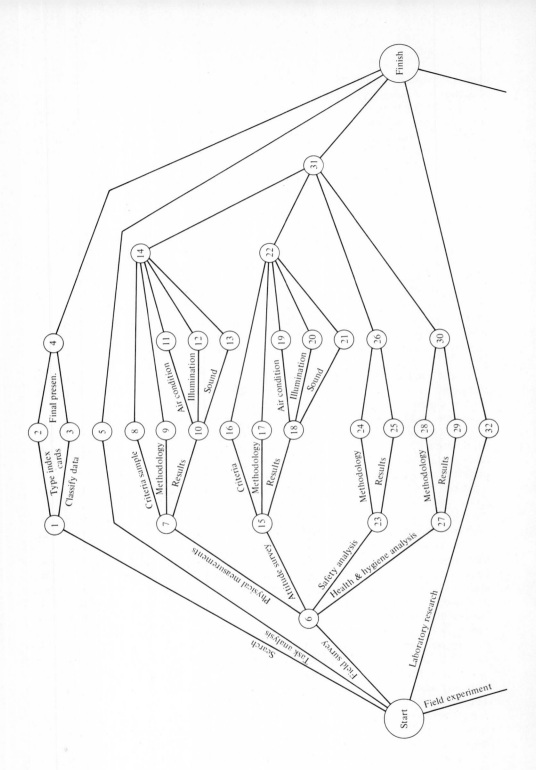

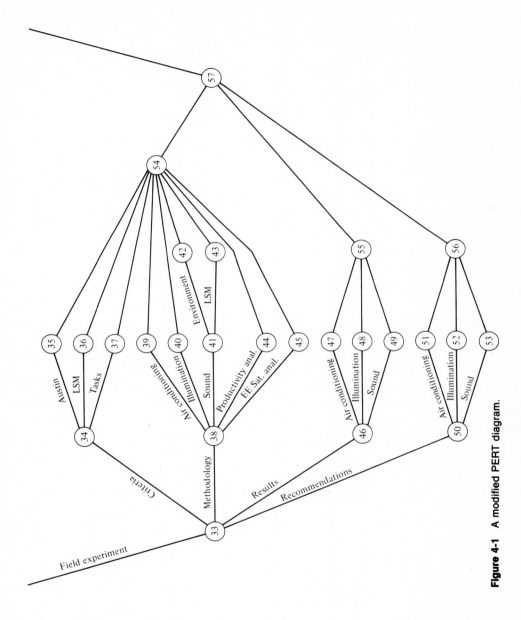

Figure 4-1 A modified PERT diagram.

The lines represent a search of the literature, an analysis of tasks to be studied, a field survey, a laboratory research, and a field experiment. The circles represent completion times (not shown), and in this case, a sequence of activities, to help assure that the tasks were completed in the proper order (as well as time).

When the number of tasks to be controlled is in terms of hundreds or thousands, the services of a computer are necessary. However, any supervisor responsible for controlling several tasks more or less simultaneously may profitably prepare by himself a simple PERT chart such as illustrated above.[6]

Can It Help?

After all this discussion of the systems way of looking at the supervisor and his job, the question naturally arises, Can it help supervisors? The answer is that the systems approach may very well help first-level supervisors, even though it is most applicable to higher management. If superiors are using the systems concept, that is reason enough for supervisors to become capable of applying some of its principles. They may be in a firm where newer management techniques are applied at the top level for a while before bringing them down to the supervisor level. If so, supervisors will not be completely baffled when superiors start trying out some of the terms and techniques of the systems approach on them. And if the system concept is adopted company-wide, supervisors and their sections may be far ahead of the "power curve" through a rudimentary understanding of the basics.

We conclude that the systems approach is a valuable tool for ensuring that company objectives and supervisory and higher-level goals are compatible and integrated for optimum productivity. The provision of a means for establishing proper relationships with codepartments is a facet of the approach that can provide supervisors with a common ground for discussing conflicting actions with peer supervisors.

The systems approach is not a panacea, some of its apostles notwithstanding. Used in conjunction with traditional and behavioral approaches, it can be a valuable aid. Whether we like it or not, the technical advances being made by our society leave too little time for comprehending all the ramifications of the "better life." The systems approach is a development that aids in coping with this knowledge explosion and will logically impinge more and more on first-level supervisors.[7]

QUESTIONS

1 Why is our so-called Gresham's law of control so important? Can you give an illustration?

2 Briefly discuss the importance of control throughout all the basic functions of supervision.

3 Can control be viewed as an aspect of the problem of motivation? Discuss.

4 Why should a supervisor carefully analyze how well a poorly operating control system is being supervised before redesigning it?

5 Control techniques are frequently not noticed at all when they are operating well. Discuss.

6 Controlling and planning are often said to be two sides of the same coin. Why and how is this true?

7 The stage of taking corrective action in the process of control might well begin with a supervisory self-examination. Explain.

8 What are the limitations a supervisor will encounter if he or she operates the department as a closed system?

NOTES

1 For a further discussion of the interdependence of quality, quantity, time, and cost standards see Robert E. McGarrah, *Production and Logistics Management* (New York: Wiley, 1963), pp. 4–14.
2 The nature and potential of systems theory is discussed by Richard Farmer in *Management of the Future* (Belmont, Calif.: Wadsworth, 1967), pp. 55–70.
3 Alphonse Chamanis, *Man-Machine Engineering* (Belmont, Calif.: Wadsworth, 1965), pp. 13, 14.
4 R. J. Thierauf and R. A. Grosse, *Decision Making through Operations Research* (New York: Wiley, 1970), p. 14.
5 Thomas Haiman and William G. Scott, *Management in the Modern Organization* (Boston: Houghton Mifflin, 1970), p. 231.
6 Henry Sisk, *Principles of Management* (Dallas, Texas: Southwestern, 1969), p. 643.
7 Max Wortman and Fred Luthans, *Emerging Concepts in Management* (New York: Macmillan, 1969), pp. 293–300.

CASES

One problem often encountered by management is the unusually good employee who has one or more serious limitations. That is true of Helen Brown. She has been with the Bank 35 years and, many would say, is quite unlikely to change. Is there a way in which improvement might be brought about or should her boss "just leave well enough alone"?

The Louis Jones case involves what the employee and his friends see as undue provocation. They do not attempt to say that Jones was correct in his response but insist that the Company made a great error in what it did.

Finally, the Gleason case represents a bypassed, disappointed employee thoroughly convinced that he can do the disputed job a lot better than the person selected. Maybe he is correct in his contention—but then maybe he isn't!

CASE 4-1

Helen Brown is fifty-four years old. She has worked for the Bank for thirty-five years, since her employment in 1927. (*It is now 1962.*) She came to the Bank directly from the local high school, where she was valedictorian.

Mrs. Brown has done every sort of "women's work" in the Bank—bookkeeping, transit, filing, typing, serving as teller, and so forth. For a while she was informally in charge of transit and bookkeeping, and supervised the three office girls who did this work. She has done secretarial work principally for the last fifteen years, and for the last ten has been secretary to William King, the president, who has just retired after more than fifty years with the Bank. Mr. & Mrs. King have just left for a three-months' trip around the world.

Mr. King was succeeded as president by Jim McNulty, who came from a smaller bank some 300 miles away. He is fifty years of age and a graduate of the College of Business of the State University.

McNulty has now been president of the Bank for forty-five days. His relations with Mrs. Brown have been friendly and he has felt quite comfortable in working with her. During the six weeks he has known her, he has come to three conclusions: First, as an executive secretary her abilities and performance leave nothing to be desired. She takes and transcribes dictation as rapidly as anyone McNulty has ever seen. She handles telephone calls and visitors in an excellent fashion, and she displays a great deal of initiative in carrying out her responsibilities. She meets regularly with the board of directors, apparently at their suggestion, to take notes on the meetings.

Second, McNulty has developed some questions concerning her relationships with small customers of the Bank. Several times he has seen a maid, a yardman, or a truckdriver stop by Helen's office with a cheery "Hello," and he has no evidence that Helen has responded in any way.

Third, he knows that Mrs. Brown has and freely expresses a poor opinion of the motivation and accomplishment of most, if not all, of the other employees of the Bank. She thinks they come in unduly late, go home too early, overstay lunch and rest breaks, and in general do not work hard for it. In addition, there is a loan officer to whom she has never spoken (except on business) since he was employed. He once tried to give her dictation, and she haughtily refused. McNulty does not know the source of these feelings on Helen's part.

Does McNulty have an "actionable" problem in this case? That is, should he plan to have an interview with Mrs. Brown in the next few days? If so, how about (a) his objectives, (b) his strategies, and (c) his tactics for the interview?

CASE 4-2

This case involves the discharge of a food clerk in a supermarket, the labor agreement containing a "just cause" clause relative to discharge, and the grievance alleging the lack of such just cause. The agreement also recognizes the propriety of certain shop rules, covering among other topics reporting to work as scheduled or notifying Management when unable to do so, proper use of work time, and prohibition of abusive language and of insubordination.

Louis Jones started with the Company as a stocker; later he was made a food clerk. During the six months of his employment he had been warned in writing three times, once for reporting to work ahead of schedule and without permission; once for "leaving for lunch ten minutes early and returning ten minutes late"; and finally for "(a) failure to sign in and sign out, (b) loafing on the job, and (c) interrupting other employees while they were working." The last letter carried a one week's layoff without pay and the notation that it was a "final warning," and warned of discharge unless "you correct your attitude and conduct."

Jones's discharge by Wm. Johnson, the store manager, occurred after the latter found a great deal of incorrectly marked merchandise in a section of the store for which Jones had responsibility. There was also merchandise that had not been properly "rotated," that is, the new goods put at the back and the older pulled to the front. Johnson took all that he could find out of the shelves and threw it on the floor in front of the space it had occupied. When he confronted Jones the latter denied both charges whereupon Johnson said, "I'll kiss your ass if you've rotated and properly marked these goods!"

When he was ordered to start rotating and marking some boxes of cake-mix Jones took off his vest and apron, and threw them and his price-stamper on the floor. With a loud burst of profanity as he went down the aisle from near the back, where the incident took place, to the front, Jones left the store. There were a number of customers, both men and women, in the store at the time, including some at the check-out counter in the front. "Goddamn" and "fuck you" were included in his profanity, each more than once.

The Company admits that Johnson made a mistake in the way he gave his order but insists that this in no way justified Jones's outburst. Especially in view of his prior record and the written warning, it holds that Jones's discharge was fully merited.

The Union asserts provocation on Johnson's part, not only that day but on a continuing basis ever since Jones was first hired. Besides profanity is a "way of life" in this store, and Management can expect no better when it is the chief offender. Jones should be restored to his job with full back pay. Alternatively, at the very most he deserved nothing more than a reprimand and a short layoff.

Was this discharge for just cause? If not, what is the proper remedy?

CASE 4-3

A significant clause in the labor agreement between these parties provided, in case of a job vacancy, that the Company would post a bid for it "for three working days"; that "any full-time employee in the Bargaining Unit who wishes to do so shall affix his signature to the posted bid"; but that "the award of the posted bid shall be at the sole discretion of Management in good faith, taking into account seniority and qualifications."

Chad Gleason is a bread twister in the large bakery in which this case arose. He has been employed by the Company for twenty-two years, during which time he has worked in most of the bargaining-unit jobs in the plant, though for many his assignment was as a vacation—or illness—relief and not a permanent occupant of the job. This was true, for example, of the job of dough mixer, a position in which cumulatively he has put in a number of weeks through the years but always for only at the most a few days at a time.

Gleason, along with a number of other employees, signed a bid for an oven operator vacancy. The bid was put up at about 11 A.M. on a Monday and taken down about 9 A.M. the following Friday. Sometime around 6 A.M. on Friday the bid sheet was signed by Jack Horn, who was subsequently picked to fill the vacancy. Horn had previously worked several months as a dough mixer, though his years of Company service were less than Gleason's. Parenthetically, it might be noted that both Gleason and Horn had also worked some on a temporary basis as oven operator.

Gleason grieved this action on two grounds: (1) that Horn's bid should not have been considered, since he did not sign within the three-day period; and (2) that in any case he should be awarded the job rather than Horn since he has qualified (as he has frequently demonstrated) and has greater seniority. (It should be noted that the plant operated seven days a week, though most production employees were off on Tuesdays. Unofficially Tuesday was referred to as a "down day" by most people in the plant.) The grievance also asked that Gleason be immediately transferred to the job and made whole for lost wages and benefits.

The Union contends that when the labor agreement says "three days" it means *three days* and not four or five or some other number. Virtually a whole crew of service, mechanical, and clerical personnel work regularly on Tuesday, as do about 25 percent of the production crew. Tuesday must therefore be considered a "working day" and hence any bid entered after 11 A.M. on Thursday may not be considered.

The Company's assertion that filling vacancies was at its "sole discretion" overlooks the "good-faith" aspect of the same provision. It knew that Gleason was qualified; he undoubtedly had more seniority; and hence, even if Horn's bid is considered Gleason should be awarded the job opening.

The Company contends that "three working days" means "not less than three working days." Prior to inclusion of this phrase there were protests that job bids were not left up long enough. And any contention that the Company could keep the job open indefinitely and not fill it is negated by another provision that any opening must be filled within fourteen days of initial posting.

The Company would have been in real trouble, it contends, had it taken the posting down on Thursday, for someone likely would have grieved that only two "working days" (and one "down day") had elapsed. Besides, since no harm can be done by keeping a notice up longer than three days, the Company was justified in doing so.

On the matter of Gleason's qualifications for the opening, the Company contends that it made a reasonable, good-faith decision. While one can successfully serve as an interim oven operator a few days at a time when he is surrounded by other oven operators who can assist if needed, to be really qualified for the position an employee must have had a considerable amount of experience on a continuing basis in dough-mixing. Though repeatedly given the opportunity to be assigned to it, Gleason had turned it down.

How should this grievance be disposed of?

Chapter 5

Theories of Worker Motivation

In this chapter we summarize some of the leading theories of motivation. Motivation is a central factor in the function of *directing*, the last of the basic functions of supervising. Most of the remainder of this text is concerned with directing, which deals with problems of face-to-face leadership of subordinates.

THE NATURE OF MOTIVATION

Motivation we define as a state of mind that induces subordinates to *want* to do what the supervisor wants them to do. Little probably needs to be said to emphasize the importance of motivation. If subordinates cannot be induced to *want* to do tasks assigned them, the supervisor may feel the need to use "raw power." If indeed the supervisor is forced to use such power and if he or she is successful in its use, subordinates will be led to *want* to do what is commanded, for they are brought to a situation where they want to do this rather than to suffer the consequences of a failure to do it.

Leadership is often distinguished from supervision or management by a similar kind of definition. Leadership is the act of inducing people to *want* to do what you what them to do (or to do it voluntarily). It is to be noted that a manager does not positively *motivate* people in a direct sense; rather, the manager may behave in such a way or set up working conditions in such a fashion that, hopefully, people *become* motivated by themselves.

Since motivation is central to managing, any complete discussion of the subject would encompass a discussion of all basic functions of management.[1] To illustrate the scope of the problem, a a supervisor or manager at any level in the organization can best motivate employees by *planning*, by *organizing*, by *directing or leading*, and finally, by *controlling* in such a way as to provide optimal employee motivation.

Do we ever apply principles or generalizations regarding motivation directly to solving problems? Sometimes we do. However, we do not do so very much at the supervisory level, because supervisors deal *primarily* with *individuals*. But as we ascend the management ladder we increasingly and directly use principles of generalizations regarding needs of people, both employees and those outside of the organization, such as customers. At the chief executive level, most objectives and policies, and even procedures, methods, and rules, are based on some assumptions regarding the motivations, or *needs* and *wants* of a significantly large number of people.

For example, at the top management level, *objectives* regarding products or services are based on assumptions that people outside the organization (customers) will be motivated to want or need such products or services.

As another example, *policies* established at the chief executive level are based on generalizations regarding the needs of a significant number of people, both inside and outside the organization. For example, a policy such as, "Our organization will establish credit for customers" is based on the assumption that as a result a significant number of *responsible* customers will be motivated to trade with us.

A concept discussed in the preceding chapter illustrates this point. This is the concept of *job enrichment*, which is based on the generalization that what employees very much want or perhaps want most of all (and thus what may motivate them most) is jobs that give them a feeling of continually increasing achievement or self-fulfillment. However true this may or may not be, supervisors usually have relatively little opportunity to create such kinds of jobs, since they are located at the lowest management level where the content of their subordinates' jobs as well as of their own is largely fixed. Thus if the concept of job enrichment is to have much influence on the world of work, that will be very largely because it has become a reality because it is accepted and implemented by higher-level management. It will be interesting to see, as we have more and more experience with the application of the idea, how realistic it is in motivating the average worker.

Characteristics of Motivators

Some characteristics of motivators are generally accepted among behavioral scientists. Among the more important are, first, that motivation is psychological rather than logical; it is primarily an emotional process rather than a "thinking" process.

Second, motivation is fundamentally an unconscious process or at least very important parts of it are. This is hard for many people to believe. However, very often employees do not know the real reasons why they act as they do and what it is that they seek simply because many of their basic motives are hidden and intangible. The behavior others see in them may appear to be illogical, but somehow inside them what they are doing likely makes sense. It is significant to note that employees cannot always give a sound reason for doing what they do, or wanting what they want; even if they can, the reason may actually be a rationalization (see Chapter 7).

Third, not only do motives differ from person to person, but in any individual they vary from time to time. There is a constantly shifting group (and perhaps hierarchy) of needs within people. Some one of all the things they want is at the top of their list at any given moment. Once it is achieved or the situation changes, it tends to drop out so far as potency is concerned and another need takes its place.

Fourth, motivation is a social process. Our actions and needs are influenced from the moment of birth by the people around us. Some of this influence comes through the broad general society in which we live, some through the smaller groupings of which we find ourselves a part, and some through the impact of the specific individuals with whom our life is intertwined. We must depend on others for satisfaction of many of our needs.

Fifth, in most of our daily actions we are guided by habits established by motivational processes that were active many years earlier. It is often hypothesized that 95 percent of what we do involves no conscious selection, judgment, or decision making. Whether the 95 figure is the correct one or not, we very often simply follow patterns that we have learned are the "right" ones for us.

Finally, motivation is individual in nature. A knowledge of needs common to *people in general* may be used only as a point of departure in dealing with an *individual.* How do we determine what the needs of a specific individual are? Generalizations regarding needs cannot be relied upon, and motivation theories may be of little use. We cannot tell from textbooks, surveys, and opinions of others what a *specific person's needs* are. There is only one way to do so: a supervisor must observe the individual's behavior, analyze it, and use his best judgment in estimating what the situation is.

It is important to remember that we do not observe *needs*; we observe *behavior.* Needs as we know them are what we judge to be explanations or causes of behavior. For example, we do not observe a person needing security. We may observe him behaving in such a way that we conclude that he needs security. On the other hand, our analysis of his behavior may be quite wrong, and he may actually need something else. Thus we may state an important principle of motivation: *If our assumptions regarding a person's needs are wrong, our actions to satisfy such needs will probably be wrong.*

THEORIES OF MOTIVATION AND LEADERSHIP STYLE

We shall now summarize theories of motivation and leadership styles developed by several of the best-known behavioral scientists (see Table 5-1).

Table 5-1 Some Theories of Motivation and Supervisory Styles

Name of author	Ineffective	Effective
Abraham Maslow	Lower-need fixation: halted growth	Self-actualization Realizing potential
Frederick Herzberg	Environmental comfort "hygiene seeking"	Meaningful work Motivation seeking
Chris Argyris	Autocratic relationships; conflict and conformity, alienation	Authentic relationships Interpersonal and technical competence, commitment
Douglas McGregor	Theory X Reductive assumptions	Theory Y Development assumptions
Robert Blake	1,1 Neutrality and indecision 1,9 Inadequate concern for production 5,5 Compromise, middle of the road 9,1 Inadequate concern for people	9,9 Integration of resources

Name of author				
Rensis Likert	System 1 Exploitive authoritative	System 2 Benevolent authoritative	System 3 Consultative	System 4 Participative group

Note: While such a table as this oversimplifies the theories involved, it helps somewhat in understanding the concepts involved in the respective views and indicates some significant comparisons between them.

Abraham Maslow

Abraham H. Maslow[2] has developed a theory of human motivation which has been widely acclaimed and accepted. He postulates that all of us are subject to a definite rank order in the priority of our needs, as shown in Figure 5-1.

The Five Kinds of Motives   Maslow theorizes that all of us are subject to five sets of basic needs. Central to his theory is the concept that these five basic needs are related to one another and constitute a hierarchy in terms of motivation, starting with (1) physiological or physical needs, and progressing through (2) safety and security needs, (3) affectional or belonging needs, (4) ego or self-esteem needs, and finally, (5) self-fulfillment needs.

Maslow assumes what might be termed two principles of hierarchical needs: first, that the satisfaction of needs at any one level in this hierarchy will motivate a subordinate's behavior only if needs at all lower levels have been at least reasonably satisfied, and second, that satisfied needs cease to be motivators (as long as they are satisfied). This implies, of course, that once optimal satisfaction has been achieved at any one level, further satisfaction of that need by the supervisor will not further motivate an individual. We shall briefly identify each of these basic needs.

Physiological Needs   Of first importance to an individual are the physiological or physical needs, those at the base of the pyramid in Figure 5-1. These are the compelling needs for food, liquids, air, rest, shelter, and other factors concerned with maintenance of the human body. If people have barely enough food, shelter, and water to exist, all their energies are devoted to eking out an existence. The theory holds that until these needs are generally satisfied, individuals cannot usually be motivated through promised satisfaction of any higher level needs. For example, a supervisor's announcement of an attractive retirement system would have no motivational value to an employee working in a basement room filled with water up to the waist, and gasping for air in order to cope with a dwindling supply of oxygen. However, when individuals' physiological needs have been optimally (or at least minimally) satisfied, only then will the satisfaction of their next higher level needs—safety or security—motivate them to better work performance.

Safety or Security Needs   The safety needs involve one's concern for being protected from dangers inherent in the environment. Illustrations of needs in this level are protec-

Figure 5-1   Maslow's hierarchy of needs.

tion from physical injury, and especially in the world of work, financial security, freedom from arbitrary and harmful decisions of management, and protection from a number of other physical as well as imaginary dangers that tend to haunt employees and keep them from feeling that "all is right with the world." To illustrate the hierarchical concept, satisfying the next-level need (belonging) by providing an employee with the opportunity for greater socialization with others may have little or no motivational value if that employee constantly feels insecure in his or her relationship with the supervisor. However, when needs at the safety level have been satisfied, a higher-level need may come into play.

Affection and Belonging Needs   Affection and belonging needs, which constitute the third level in the pyramid, are defined as the need to be with others, to have friends, acceptance, and respect, and to socialize with a group on a continuing basis. These needs, along with those at higher levels, are more nebulous and less concrete than those at lower levels, and individuals are seldom able to fully satisfy them.

Ego and Self-esteem Needs   At the fourth level are the ego needs. These differ from lower-level socialization needs in that they comprise an individual's internal and personal needs for respect, recognition, and status, as for example in a friendship group. However, Maslow believes that, both as individuals or as members of a group, we have a pronounced need for independence, self-confidence, self-esteem, and appreciation.

Self-fulfillment Needs   At the top of the hierarchy are the self-fulfillment or self-actualization needs. This need is almost as difficult to describe as to satisfy. It is variously referred to as the need to attain one's full growth and potential, to utilize to the fullest one's abilities, experience, interests, education, and so on. Defined in such terms, this is an open-ended need that is never capable of complete fulfillment. No matter what measure of success a person achieves financially or otherwise, he or she may still experience, either consciously or otherwise, a feeling of lack of complete self-fulfillment.

Maslow believed that physiological and safety needs (and possibly social needs) of employees are relatively well satisfied by business and industry in the United States today. Ego needs, on the other hand, he thought, are only moderately satisfied, and self-actualization needs are hardly satisfied at all, at least for the rank-and-file worker. Thus it was his belief that as we move up in the hierarchy of needs, each successively higher level is possibly less susceptible to optimal satisfaction by most employees in business and industry.

Critique   To begin with, it is well to recognize that Maslow's hierarchy theory is at best only a broad generalization and cannot be applied by the supervisor to all individuals at all times. Thus an individual's job may not as a matter of fact satisfy most of his or her lower-level needs—or at best do so very poorly—and yet the worker may be loyal, dedicated, and hard-working, abundantly satisfied and still fail or even refuse to take advantage of opportunities to satisfy the higher-level ones. Maslow may be generally correct, but he surely is not always so.

At the same time, there is no doubt but that he made real contributions to our understanding of human motives, if in no other way than by emphasizing that "man does not live by bread alone." At the same time he left a number of unanswered questions. Among these are: (1) Are there just five kinds of motives? (2) Do fulfilled motives really cease to motivate, that is, though we may not be hungry now, may we not take steps to guard against future hunger? (3) Are lower-level motives always fulfilled before the person has any interest in a higher-level one; that is, might not a parent who is safe and sound outside a burning building still rush in to save a child who is trapped by the fire? And (4) which of a person's many potentials, including possibly those for outstanding skill in some field of crime, should he try to realize, and why? These are possibly difficult questions for anyone who believes Maslow to have the last word in motivation theory. As a matter of fact, he obviously does not.

Frederick Herzberg

Basic Motives   Herzberg[3] holds, as Table 5-1 suggests, that there are two separate processes of motivation, one of which is composed of what he calls *motivation* factors and concerns high-level needs that, when fulfilled, can really "satisfy."

The second consists of what he terms *hygiene* factors, which concern lower-level needs (he includes pay), which even when fulfilled cannot really "satisfy." At best their fulfillment can only provide a "neutral" state, whereas at worst, their nonfulfillment can be "dissatisfiers" that can create serious problems.

Motivation Factors   The process that Herzberg terms *motivation* factors involves the so-called rich and potent high-level needs, often called *self-fulfillment* or *self-actualization needs*, which he believes to be the key to superior work performance. When they are entirely fulfilled, an employee's performance can be expected to soar from neutral to high productivity. Herzberg describes these "needs" as being directly imbedded in the actual doing of work itself. They include achievement in a task; recognition for task achievement; the challenging nature of the task; responsibility for the task; and professional growth or advancement in task responsibility. The last three tend to be most important in terms of lasting change of attitudes. All are concerned with work itself, rather than its surrounding physical or social environment. For example, a skilled toolmaker can be richly motivated by the pride he feels in his craftsmanship. A similar feeling can be experienced by an engineer or a salesman cited in a company magazine for an exceptional contribution.

Hygiene Factors   Herzberg's second process of motivation is composed of what he terms *hygiene* factors, which serve primarily to *prevent job dissatisfaction,* while having little effect on positive job attitudes. This process (variously referred to as *maintenance* or *housekeeping motivation*) involves the "lower-order" needs such as the physiological ones and some of the simpler elements of the psychological. These can be depicted on a continuum ranging from "neutral" to "dissatisfiers."

Many of these are the sort which every worker in an organization *expects* will be fulfilled. Indeed fulfilling them is simply good housekeeping (or good *hygiene*, a term used by Herzberg in analogy with the medical use of this term as preventative and environmental), and they refer primarily to the job context or job environment. For example, the major negative motivators, that is, the common ones that tend to decrease job satisfaction, are (1) less than satisfactory money and other forms of remuneration, (2) less than fair treatment, (3) inadequate or inequitable company policy and administration, (4) lack of job security, (5) less than satisfactory work conditions, such as inadequate lighting, improper facilities for food, inadequate eating facilities, lack of any kind of recreational or rest facilities for women, and so on, and (6) even status, that Herzberg says, "defines job context."

Thus by failing to satisfy these "housekeeping" needs supervision can create dissatisfaction with resulting serious problems. At the other extreme, however, even though the supervisor fulfills these needs lavishly, Herzberg believes he cannot thereby raise the motivational level beyond neutral.

To elaborate on this point briefly, an older theory contended that salary and wages, for example, are very frequently at the top of the list of factors that really motivate workers. However, Herzberg believes that money typically is a dissatisfier, especially if an employee feels he is unfairly paid in comparison to other employees. On the other hand money *can* be a true motivator when, for example, it is viewed as a direct reward for outstanding individual performance and thus contributes to a sense of "recognition" and/ or "achievement." As an affector of job attitudes, though, Herzberg holds that salary typically has more potency as a job dissatisfier than as a job satisfier.

Additional Assumptions   Thus, a basic assumption of Herzberg is that if the worker is to be truly motivated, the job itself is the major source of that motivation. All that the hygienic factors can do is serve as a basis for "cleaning up" the environment and preventing dissatisfaction.

Furthermore, Herzberg's approach to employee satisfaction rests on another assumption regarding the nature of the individual: that he has a need to avoid pain and a need to grow. Motivation factors may provide an opportunity for creativity, growth, and movement toward some degree of self-actualization. On the other hand, hygiene factors may prevent dissatisfaction and pain by providing fair treatment and a good work environment. For example, the factor of salary meets two kinds of avoidance needs of the employee. First is the avoidance of the economic deprivation that is felt when actual income is insufficient. Second is the need to avoid feelings of being treated unfairly. Both sets of needs should be met in the business organization.

Supervisory training that emphasizes security and stability in the work surroundings is probably essential to the maintenance of good hygiene at work. This is particularly true for the many jobs, both at rank-and-file and managerial levels, in which modern industry offers little chance for the operation of the "motivators." Hygienic efforts can produce a great deal if a supervisor wants cooperation, reasonable compliance, and "constructive apathy," but under such circumstances he would expect little or no enthusiasm. A significant principle involved here is that *the fewer the opportunities for the "motivators" to appear, the greater must be the hygiene offered* in order to make the work tolerable.

Recommendations to the Supervisor   Herzberg believes that a meaningful approach to positive motivation of employees is through the heretofore-mentioned process of "job enrichment." This is not to be confused with job enlargement, the latter simply making a job structurally larger. Job enrichment, as we have previously pointed out, is concerned with providing an opportunity for an employee to accomplish psychological growth.

Herzberg contends that if the dissatisfiers are eliminated, good hygiene will result and conditions will be produced under which job enrichment, if present, may lead to self-motivation. The process of enriching jobs may be approached by such supervisory actions as (1) removing some controls while retraining supervision, (2) increasing the accountability of individuals for their own work, (3) giving a person a complete "natural unit" of work (module, division, area, and so on), (4) making periodic reports directly available to the worker himself rather than to the supervisor, (5) introducing new and more difficult tasks not previously handled, (6) providing opportunities for greater decision-making responsibilities, and (7) putting people in jobs they like and in groups they enjoy.

Critique of the Two-factor Theory   Herzberg's work is both well known and quite controversial. It undoubtedly contains some valuable insights, some being similar to those of Maslow. But at the same time it undoubtedly has limitations. One criticism concerns his original research approach, which included securing data through an interviewing technique. For example, respondents were asked to tell stories related to their work about which they felt exceptionally good or bad. From these stories it was felt that the situations leading to negative or positive job attitudes and their effects could be discovered. However, a direct study of people actually then responding to various work situations might well have been much superior. Another criticism is that his groups consisted very largely of white-collar employees, including chiefly professional employees; but those familiar with the characteristics of blue-collar workers realize that their motivation is usually quite different from that of accountants, engineers, and similar professional employees.

Also, the rewards promised through job enrichment may involve risks that many employees in many kinds of situations refuse to take. Further, the motivation of an employee to achieve high-quality performance and rich productivity typically requires a democratic supervisory style. The supervisor must stay in the background and can provide an employee only the *opportunity* to perform tasks that in themselves will be rewarding.

One of the questions asked of Maslow can also be asked of Herzberg: How does he know there are just two kinds of influences, "satisfiers" and "motivators"? As a matter of fact, do good working conditions, including congenial bosses and fellow workers, only "satisfy" and never "motivate"?

Finally, there is the simple fact that in worker motivation it is often not so much what is "out there"—the money or the recognition, for example—as it is how this appears and appeals to the worker. Thus low pay from an employer who can afford no better may be motivating, while high pay from one who is considered arbitrary or unfair in his handling of money may thoroughly "turn one off." Again, Herzberg, like Maslow, has a theory that has made contributions but also has serious limitations.

Chris Argyris

One of Argyris's[4] contributions to motivation theory has been the development of a systematic framework for analyzing the nature of the relationship between the demands of formal organization and the needs of individuals. Using this approach, he has derived hypotheses regarding their mutual impact. His objective has been to identify factors that may serve as criteria for an organization that wishes to move in a direction that releases much of the psychological energy available but presently is underutilized in the work force.

Individual's Organization Needs　　Basically, Argyris hypothesizes, there is a *fundamental opposition* between the *needs of the individual and those of the formal organization* in which he works. He sees the problems of management, if not of our whole industrial civilization, in terms of the way people react to this dichotomy. His major findings from research appear to him to tend to validate this hypothesis. His approach may be divided into three major facets, which we shall now describe.

Interdependence of Individuals and Organizations　　Argyris presents three major propositions concerning the relationship between individuals and organizations. First, he stresses the point that individuals and organizations are interdependent. Both are organized, dynamic systems. Both the individual and the organization exist for some purpose or, usually, purposes. The major purpose of an individual is to fulfill his needs and achieve his goals. The purpose of the organization is to achieve the objectives for which it is created, as, for example, to produce a product or provide a service. In order for both the individual and the organization to exist they must maintain their "internal organization" and adapt to their external environment. Neither the individual nor the organization can satisfy needs and wants alone; they require each other's aid. Individuals cannot exist and continuously develop without social organization. On the other hand, a social organization by its very definition requires individuals.

Needs of a Mature Individual　　Second, Argyris analyses the individual's growth cycle from immaturity to maturity, or the direction of the development of an individual's personality today, if permitted as much freedom for expression as desired. He finds the following trends in personality development to be characteristic of people in today's environment: they tend to develop (1) from receiving and incorporating aspects of culture as infants, to controlling, using, redefining, and helping others incorporate these aspects of culture as an adult; (2) from a state of being passive as infants (having other people initiate action for them), to a state of being increasingly active as adults (initiating action as much or more than other people do toward them); (3) from being capable of behaving only in a few ways and in a rigid manner as infants, to being capable of behaving in many different ways and in a flexible manner as adults; (4) from being in a subordinate position in the family and society as infants, to occupying a more equal and/or superordinate position in the family and society as adults; (5) from a state of high dependence on others as infants to a state of independence, and finally to a state of interdependence in society as adults.

Demands of Formal Organizations   Third, Argyris analyzes the characteristics of formal organizations in terms of their impact on the individual. His analyses have led to the conclusion that if the organization were able to express itself freely without interference, then most workers would be assigned to jobs (1) that would tend to permit them little control over their workaday world; (2) that would tend to place them in a situation where passivity rather than initiative would frequently be expected; (3) that would tend to force them to occupy subordinate positions; (4) that would tend to permit them a minimum degree of fluidity and tend to emphasize the expression of one (or perhaps a few) of the workers' relatively minor abilities; and (5) that would tend to make them feel dependent upon others, such as the bosses.

Some Other Assumptions   Based on his comparison of the characteristics of individuals and of organizations, Argyris has derived some major propositions. First, he states that "there is a lack of congruity between the needs of healthy individuals and the demands of the formal organization." Such principles as chain of command, unity of command, task specialization, (limited) span of control, and so on, are more likely to satisfy the needs of infants (passivity, dependency, and so on) than those of mature healthy adults. In fact, Argyris seems to believe that organizations might find that immature and even mentally retarded individuals would make excellent employees in certain jobs, and concludes that a continual disturbance can be expected when the needs of individuals are not congruent with characteristics of the organization.

His second proposition follows logically: "The results of this disturbance are frustration, failure, short-time perspective, and conflict." Drawing upon many research studies, as is characteristic of Argyris, he supplements this proposition with several reasons why healthy and mature individuals would experience such results as, for example, inability to satisfy self-actualization needs, and inability to participate in individual short-range as well as long-range goal setting and goal achieving.

Argyris's third and final major proposition is that "the nature of the formal principles of organization cause the subordinate, at any given level, to experience competition, rivalry, intersubordinate hostility, and to develop a focus toward the parts rather than the whole." This proposition is based on personality studies that indicate that one of the primary characteristics of the human personality is that it is a dynamic, integrated, or "whole" entity. Consequently, it will tend to express itself in an integrated, "whole" manner. That is, it will require that it be assigned to a job that provides it with an opportunity to express itself in as many of its abilities, needs, and sentiments as require expression.

However, this is not the existing state of affairs. Rather, subordinates are made dependent upon a leader. Too, they are rewarded for performing a task (or part of a whole) well and as instructed to do. This increases the subordinates' degree of dependence, creating a circular process: dependence and rivalry and competition for the leader's favor. Finally, because the number of positions above any given level always tends to decrease, there tends to be constant rivalry and hostility and competitiveness among subordinates.

The Concept of "Fusion"　Thus, the wants and needs of individuals and of organizations are, at crucial points, fundamentally different and even antagonistic. In order for them to live and work together, as they must, Argyris advocates a *fusion* of the individual with the organization. The objective of this *fusion* is to aid the individual to obtain the maximal expression of his personality and achievement of his needs. Simultaneously, the organization should be aided in fulfilling its needs at the highest possible level.

Argyris's fusion model of organization has two basic elements: (1) the personalizing process by which the individual actualizes himself and makes organization an agency for the individual, and (2) the socializing process by which the organization accomplishes its goals. The fusion process is operative only when these two elements are simultaneously actualized. Argyris's contribution to research using this approach is in the determination of the varying relationship between the individual and the organization.

Argyris has used an analogy to aid in clarifying his term fusion. Automotive engineers must create a maximum fusion process where the amount of gas and the amount of spark that ignites the gas are "just right" to enable the car to move forward with the maximum thrust, while at the same time there is an optimum use of gas, without excessive burning out of the points on the spark plug.

Critique　A major contribution of Argyris is methodological.[5] He has developed data-gathering methods that comprise intensive interviews with employees throughout an organization hierarchy and clinical assessment of data gathered. Undoubtedly, his conclusions are often insightful and at a minimum they point out serious problem areas in today's work situation. He has also been described as an "organizational clinician." His approach has been likened to a physician's diagnosis of a patient in a clinic. Argyris has established questions to ask, symptoms to search for, and behavioral manifestations that are presumed to be related to various organizational conditions. His theoretical model is considered by many to be a good beginning to analysis of (1) the role of the individual in the organization, and (2) the possibilities for most effectively coping with differences between needs of the two.

At the same time many of us are far less pessimistic than he about the meshing of individual and organizational goals. Much more will be said on this later (see especially Chapters 19 and 20). Here let us simply ask, Are there not times when it is a lot of fun to be part of an organization that is "going somewhere" and making notable, worthwhile progress? Maybe individuals are not always as *individual* as Argyris thinks, and maybe organizations are not always *anti-individual*.

Douglas McGregor

Theory X and Theory Y[6]　The late Douglas McGregor, one of the most widely acclaimed behavioral scientists, produced the now classic Theory X and Theory Y conceptions of motivation. His view was one that challenged traditional management's basic premises about human nature and human beings at the work place. The faulty premises of Theory X, he said, in turn serve as the basis for unrealistic planning, organizing, directing, and controlling. The logic behind such premises and the management practices on which they are based constitute what he called an "elaborate unrealistic game."

Theory X and Theory Y are believed by some to have derived at least partially from (1) the work of Mayo and the conclusions reached in the Hawthorne study (see Chapter 19), and (2) Maslow's notion that men and women need to use their talents to the utmost, an opportunity that industry presently seldom allows. Thus an interchange of ideas between McGregor and Maslow is obvious.

Premises of Theory X   McGregor felt that behind most managerial decisions are the following *erroneous* assumptions about human nature and behavior:

First, the average human being has an inherent dislike of work and will avoid it if possible. McGregor holds that this assumption has roots so deep that they extend back historically to the banishment of Adam and Eve from Eden into the first world of work where they *had* to work for a living. Today, management's stress on productivity, "a fair day's work," and rewards for performance are decisions based on this "fallacious" assumption.

Second, because of this human characteristic of dislike of work, most people must be coerced, controlled, directed, and threatened with punishment to get them to put forth adequate effort toward the achievement of organizational objectives. Even rewards such as pay are not motivators; employees will simply take wages and demand higher ones. Examples of current managerial attitudes and practices derived from this premise are a trend toward recentralization of authority, a criticism of "human relations," and autocratic leadership.

Third, the average human being prefers to be directed, wishes to avoid responsibility, has relatively little ambition, and wants security above all. McGregor equates this assumption with the "mediocrity of the masses" concept. He believes that a great many managers privately support this assumption as a basis for decision making even though they give lip service to the ideal of the worth and dignity of the individual. They pretend to believe in the latter concept simply because it is demanded by our political and social values.

Accepting "fallacious" premises, management has no option other than to manage employees closely. Actually, if managers continually treat their employees as if these premises are true, this system of management can be self-validating. Subordinates who are treated by an authoritarian management as though they are lazy, dishonest, and primarily materialistic will tend to behave that way.

Premises of Theory Y   McGregor believes his Theory Y reflects much better the "sociotechnical system" that exists in the world of work than do theories and practices of the vast majority of today's managers. Theory Y motivation is based on assumptions regarding human nature and behavior that are often diametrically opposed to those of Theory X. Theory Y postulates that people on the average do not inherently dislike work or lack ambition but like and want to work, *under proper conditions.* Incidentally, the last limiting phrase should carefully be noted, as it is very significant. (If *conditions of work* are not considered "proper" by an individual or group, we must conclude that the premise does not hold [see Chapter 17]).

Obviously, the process of planning, organizing, directing, and controlling based upon this and related assumptions may be dramatically different from a management style based upon Theory X assumptions. Let us quote McGregor's major premises and philosophy regarding the nature and behavior of the individual at the workplace:[7]

   1   The expenditure of physical and mental effort in work is as natural as play or rest. The average human being does not inherently dislike work. Depending upon controllable conditions, work may be a source of satisfaction (and will be voluntarily performed) or a source of punishment (and will be avoided if possible).

   2   External control and the threat of punishment are not the only means for bringing about effort toward organizational objectives. Man will exercise self-direction and self-control in the service of objectives to which he is committed.

3 Commitment to objectives is a function of the rewards associated with their achievement. The most significant of such rewards, for example, the satisfaction of ego and self-actualization needs, can be direct products of effort directed toward organizational objectives.

4 The average human being learns, under proper conditions, not only to accept but to seek responsibility. Avoidance of responsibility, lack of ambition, and emphasis on security are generally consequences of experience, not inherent human characteristics.

5 The capacity to exercise a relatively high degree of imagination, ingenuity, and creativity in the solution of organizational problems is widely, not narrowly distributed in the population.

6 Under the conditions of modern industrial life, the intellectual potentialities of the average human being are only partially utilized.

Extrinsic and Intrinsic Rewards   Much light is thrown on McGregor's views if one examines carefully the difference between intrinsic and extrinsic rewards (and punishments).

Extrinsic rewards (and punishments) may be directly related to worker behavior and can be controlled by management. The most obvious example involves money in its various forms, such as pay resulting from merit increases and promotions. Other examples are granting or withholding a wide variety of fringe benefits, including individual praise, recognition, and even social acceptance.

Intrinsic rewards, on the other hand, consist of such things as achieving knowledge, skill, and self-respect, and are best described as being inherent in the work itself. Thus they cannot be directly controlled by management. However, management can influence characteristics of the work environment in such a way as to enhance or limit a worker's opportunities to obtain intrinsic rewards.

McGregor theorizes that a major shortcoming of management is that it pays inadequate attention to intrinsic rewards and for two reasons. *First*, it is obviously difficult for management to establish a direct link between performance and intrinsic rewards. As McGregor states, an employee can be *given* money, an extrinsic reward, in terms of a pay raise or a promotion for superior performance. The relationship between performance and reward is clear to the employee. However, an employee cannot be *given* a sense of accomplishment and self-fulfillment, an intrinsic reward, by the manager. Thus management cannot easily or directly control intrinsic rewards.

While management cannot *give* an intrinsic reward to an employee, it can behave so as to prevent that employee from obtaining such rewards. Behavior of this type is illustrated by close supervision that eliminates any opportunity for the employee to make decisions independently and perhaps creatively. McGregor finds that even under such circumstances, however, employees may obtain this reward by "ingenious solutions that involve a kind of sabotage of management's control systems." That is to say, "beating the system" may become a game in which the intrinsic rewards are high.

The second reason for management's inadequate attention to intrinsic rewards derives from management's premises regarding the Theory X nature and behavior of people at work. In a word, management is pessimistic, and McGregor believes unduly so, about the real influence of intrinsic motives.

McGregor's "strategy" for motivation centers around ways to motivate employees through intrinsic rewards. His framework for achieving this is similar to the assumptions of Maslow and Herzberg. He postulates that if employees are freed from the necessity of satisfying lower-level needs, they will by nature pursue goals associated with higher-level needs. In a word, the motivation of employees is best achieved when management creates an environment that encourages members of an organization at all levels to best achieve their own individual goals (involving both intrinsic and extrinsic rewards) by directing their efforts toward the goals of the organization.

His formula for achieving this situation involves attention to both lower-level needs and higher-level needs in creating the proper organizational environment. With respect to lower-level needs, management should provide equitable extrinsic rewards for all contributions to productivity. It is significant that McGregor also includes management's responsibility for equitably administering extrinsic punishment for negative contributions to productivity. It is with respect to higher-level needs that McGregor feels that too often management has neglected to take into account the implications for strategically satisfying such needs.

Critique　　One asset in McGregor's theory of motivation is that it concentrates on the importance of planning, organizing, directing, and controlling to provide an appropriate environment that will permit and encourage employees to seek intrinsic rewards at work. Another is that, like the theories of Maslow and Herzberg, it makes abundantly clear that we generally overemphasize extrinsic factors and underemphasize intrinsic ones when we deal with workers.

On the other hand, McGregor's theory is widely criticized because often the provision of opportunities for intrinsic rewards becomes a matter of removing restraints. For example, the theory suggests an organization climate characterized by: less restrictive policies and planning; less emphasis on a hierarchical, authoritarian, organization structure, and more emphasis on having short spans of control along with more democratic leadership and few controls over individuals; open communications at all levels; the creation of a climate of genuine mutual trust; and the development of mutual respect for the individual and for individual differences. Critics hold that these courses of action can easily be carried too far—and that carried any more than a little way they will lead to loss of efficiency. If thoroughly adopted and practiced, these critics believe, the destruction of the organization will be the result.

In fairness, however, it must be recognized that more than most theorists McGregor was a realist. He did not advocate eliminating all controls over employees, nor did he believe that his major premises fit all employees. He recognized that some percentage of any group of employees would not respond at all or would take advantage of a Theory Y management. He specifically stated that the limits imposed by planning, organizing, and controlling at times had to be firmly enforced, and if necessary, such enforcement should be followed by dismissal of certain persons. Otherwise, he stated, there is a danger that indulgence toward such employees will adversely affect the entire organization.[7]

Robert Blake

Robert Blake and Jane Mouton[8] have developed a theory of motivation, called the *grid theory*, that is concerned with identifying the optimum style of management that would "integrate creativity, high productivity, and high morale through concerted team action."

Basic Approach　　Their approach, which comprises a group-learning program, attempts to aid a person first, in conducting a preassessment to determine what he *perceives* his managerial style to be; and second, to determine what his managerial style *really is* through a self-examination in group interaction sessions. It is hoped he will thus discover any discrepancy between what he thinks is his impact on others and what in fact it really is.

The grid program is also designed to aid participants in constructively changing their leadership styles as necessary. A number of alternative managerial styles available to a manager are defined, as are requirements of shifting from any one style to another.

The Managerial Grid program is typically administered by Blake or his representatives to businessmen arranged in groups which undergo intensive training sessions day and night over a continuous period of several days. There are several phases of the program. We shall briefly summarize only one.

The Managerial Grid A fundamental feature of the Managerial Grid is the identification of five theories of managerial behavior, based on two variables common to organizations (see Table 5-2). One variable (shown on the horizontal axis) reflects a concern for production or output. The second variable (shown on vertical axis) reflects a concern for *people*. (A word about the term "concern for" is in order: it does *not* represent real production or the extent to which human relationship needs are actually met. It *does* indicate managerial interest in or feeling about production and/or people and for how these influence each other.)

Table 5-2   The Managerial Grid

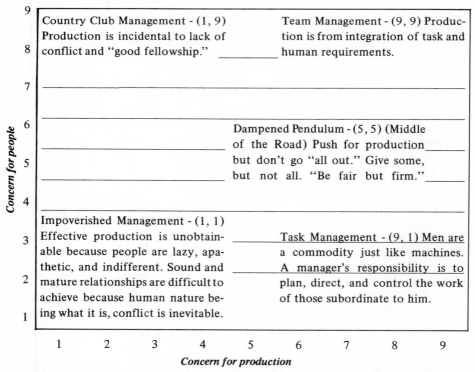

(*Source*: R. E. Blake & Jane S. Mouton, *The Managerial Grid*, Houston: Gulf Publishing Company, 1964)

Each of the two variables, or dimensions, represented as coordinates on the graph, is given a range of intensity from 1 to 9. For example, on the vertical dimension a rating of 1 represents a minimum degree of concern by a boss for *people* while 9 represents a maximum concern. This framework makes it possible to chart a wide array of managerial styles (at least eighty-one possible combinations). However, for training purposes, emphasis is placed on only five managerial styles. These are shown at the four corners and in the middle of the chart.

These five leadership styles summarized in Table 5-2 are (1, 1) the "bureaucrat" type of manager or "impoverished manager," who is not concerned with either dimension; (1, 9) the "country club" manager, who has a high concern for people and a low concern for task; (9, 1) the "taskmaster," who has a high concern for the task but a low concern for people; (9, 9) the "ideal" or "team" manager, who has a high concern for *both* tasks and people; and finally (5, 5) the firm but fair compromiser, who fluctuates expeditiously (the "dampened pendulum").

An advantage cited for this approach is that it avoids a limitation imposed by theories of many behavioral scientists: the division of leadership styles into a dichotomy (two classifications). While a dichotomy, or a division into extremes of "good" and "bad" leadership styles, has merit for accomplishing certain purposes, it misses an infinite number of styles in between these extremes.

Arguments abound regarding the advantages of one extreme versus another. Examples of such "either/or" styles of leadership are (1) scientific management versus human relations, (2) autocratic versus democratic, (3) authoritarian versus participative, (4) production-centered versus people-centered, and (5) Theory X versus Theory Y. In the preface to the *Managerial Grid*, Blake states:

> These labels have been admittedly inadequate and confusing. The stress on terms which present extremes has placed many managers in a position where they felt they could not accept *either* alternative. It placed researchers in a position of trying to prove the benefits of one system over the other, when they rarely could locate behavior which was clearly either one of these extremes. It led many teachers of management theory to overemphasis of the human relations side of the dichotomy, and thus their efforts were seen by many managers as promoting "soft" leadership.

Managerial-grid learning groups perform exercises that typically involve ranking given courses of managerial behavior according to how participants would behave in certain situations. The situations cover such areas as planning, execution, and follow-up and involve circumstances in which the mode of dealing with other people varies. A respondent's rankings are then scored on the two-dimensional grid which describes the manager's style preference. We shall now define each of the five leadership styles that constitute criteria for evaluating behavior. In each case we reflect the opinions of Blake and Mouton without at this point attempting any evaluation of them.

The 9,1 "Taskmaster" Style   In the lower right-hand corner of the grid is 9,1. At this position a high concern for production, 9, is coupled with a low concern for people, 1. In the 9, 1 managerial style, the assumption is made that, somehow, there is an inevitable contradiction between organizational needs of production and personal needs of people. If one is met, the other must be sacrificed. Yet people must be used to attain the production for which the manager feels responsible. If he acts from a 9, 1 orientation, he seeks to resolve the dilemma by arranging conditions of work that minimize the importance of feelings and attitudes. He does so in a way that prevents the "human elements" from interfering with efficiency and output.

A manager using the 9, 1 leadership style is characterized as being a "no-nonsense boss" type of manager, interested primarily in getting things done—mostly from a short-range approach—and in *his* way, even though he steps on some toes. He emphasizes tight controls, meeting target dates, and taking corrective action. He attempts to smother conflicts that arise; emotionally he is defensive and resistant; he uses hard-hitting humor, and he drives himself and others. He, according to his theory, personifies the "entrepreneurial spirit." His motto is, "Nice guys finish last."

The 1,9 "Country Club" Style   In the upper left-hand corner of the grid is the 1,9 managerial orientation. Here a low functional concern for production, 1, is coupled with a high concern for people, 9. As with 9,1, the 1,9 managerial orientation also is rooted in the assumption that production requirements are contrary to the needs of people. To a manager with a 1,9 style, however, the attitudes and feelings of people are important. They are valuable in their own right. They come first. Within this context, conditions are arranged so that personal, social, and welfare needs can be met.

The 1,9 type of manager is characterized by attempts to minimize friction, be complimentary, emphasize noneconomic motivations, be pleasant, please, and get along with individuals and groups. He prefers opinions, attitudes, and ideas of others to his own. He copes with conflict by attempting to avoid causing it. Emotionally, he reacts in a warm and friendly way to problem-solving situations in order to avoid tension. His humor is designed to further friendly relations, or to shift attention from serious problems. He rarely leads, rigidly defined. His motto is, "Nice guys don't fight."

The 1,1 "Bureaucrat" Style   Low concern for production is coupled with low concern for the people in the lower left-hand corner of the grid, where the 1,1 managerial pattern is located. Like 9,1 or 1,9, an incompatibility is assumed to exist between production requirements and needs of people. However, since concern for both is low, the manager with 1,1 orientation experiences little or no dilemma between production and people—he is more or less "out of it," while remaining in the organization. Little is expected of him, and little is given by him in return. As an approach to motivation 1,1 is rare in organization situations of nonrepetitive action where each situation presents a different set of problems to be solved. It is far more common in routine operations and various staff functions.

The manager using the 1,1 leadership style is characterized by using no initiative, not contributing, desirous of being left alone, exerting minimal effort, ignoring problems, doing one thing at a time as it arises without planning, not evaluating effort of subordinates, and communicating minimally, attaching no weight to costs or profits. He goes along with the ideas, attitudes, and convictions of others to avoid taking sides. When conflict arises, he is neutral or stays out of it. Emotionally he remains neutral so as to rarely get stirred up. His humor is pointless, and he expends only enough effort to get by. His motto is, "Ignore it and maybe it will go away."

The phrase "1,1 management of people" is an anomaly. A person who has adopted a 1,1 orientation might better be described as "lost among," rather than "managing," people. Anomalous though it may seem, there are, today, many persons in managerial ranks whose supervision is best pictured as 1,1.

The 1,1 approach is unnatural. It comes to those who have accepted defeat. To permit oneself again to become involved and concerned over what happens in the work situation can only lead to deeper frustration and discouragement. It is an approach characterized, then, by low involvement with people and the contribution of minimum effort toward organization purpose.

The 5,5 "Compromiser" Style   In the center of the grid is the 5,5 approach to motivation. It is the "middle of the road" or "fence-straddling" approach. In this style, the manager attempts to trade off concern for production for a satisfactory level of morale among his people.

The 5,5 type of leader is characterized by utilizing tried and true methods, following clear guidelines, performing only expected work, being satisfied with "good enough," going halfway, following past performance criteria, spot-checking, conducting post mortems, being concerned with the majority. His philosophy is to initiate middle-ground positions, handle conflicts fairly but firmly, and achieve equitable solutions. Emotionally he is under considerable tension and unsure which way to shift or turn to avoid further pressure. His humor is geared to selling himself or a position. He maintains a good steady pace. His motto is, "Fluctuate expeditiously."

The 9,9 "Ideal Leadership" Style   In the upper right-hand corner is located 9,9 where a high concern for production, 9, is coupled with a 9 of high concern for people. Unlike the other basic approaches, it is assumed in the 9,9 managerial style that there is no necessary and inherent conflict between organization purpose of production requirements and the needs of people. Under 9,9, effective integration of people with production is possible by involving them and their ideas in determining the conditions and strategies of work. Needs of people to think, to apply mental effort in productive work, and to establish sound and mature relationships on a hierarchical plane and with one another are utilized to accomplish organizational requirements. A basic aim of 9,9 management, then, is to promote the conditions that integrate creativity, high productivity, and high morale through concerted team action.

The 9,9 orientation views the integration of people into work from a perspective different from other approaches. In contrast to 9,1, the solution for a given problem is not necessarily defined by the boss's authority. Unlike 5,5, the 9,9 approach is oriented toward discovering the best and most effective solution in a given situation, not the one defined by tradition. By utilizing both the mental and execution skills of people, this approach aims at the highest attainable level of production. The highest level is possible only through work situations that meet mature needs of people. Sociability for the sake of togetherness, status based on aspects unrelated to work, or power exercised for its own sake or out of frustration are not viewed as mature needs. Rather, accomplishment and contribution are seen as the critical aspect of organization performance and individual motivation. When one is met, the other is gratified automatically.

The 9,9 approach to motivation and managing conflict is clear. The solution to the problem is that of direct confrontation. Direct confrontation means facing up to the conflict, getting it out on the table where it can be examined and evaluated by all who are a party to it. In this way, the reasons for it can be examined and assessed. The conditions for its resolution then can be discussed by those who are involved.

The 9,9 type of leader attempts to make sound, creative decisions in such a way that there is understanding and agreement. He listens for and seeks out attitudes, opinions, and ideas. He has sound convictions but the capability of changing his mind, when convinced differently. He handles conflict by trying to identify reasons for it and resolving underlying causes. Emotionally he generally contains himself. However, his impatience may be visible. His humor fits situations and gives perspective; he retains a sense of humor even under pressure. He applies vigorous effort personally and attempts to induce others to join in.

Critique   Among critics of the grid theory is McGregor[9] (who is indirectly criticized in Blake's book). As an example, McGregor questions one of its fundamental propositions, that the two major variables (concern for production and concern for people), and only these two, affect managerial style. His view is, first, that the position 9,9 on the grid representing maximum concern for both people and production does not accurately represent an ideal style (called the "team theory of management" by Blake). McGregor contends that a team theory "does not evolve simply from the maximization of the two variables represented on the grid . . . managerial style is the result of complex interaction among *many* variables."

McGregor also contends that the grid theory is a useful but "oversimplified view of a variety of managerial styles which are commonly recognized today." However, these styles rely primarily on "*extrinsic* rewards and punishments." Thus they "are not as successful as they might be because they . . . largely ignore the existence of *intrinsic* rewards and punishments . . . and fail to recognize the interweaving of man's rational and emotional characteristics and his social human nature."

McGregor further depreciates "conventional forms of management training . . . [which] attempt to get managers to adopt a certain managerial style that is felt by training directors or higher levels of management to be desirable." He feels this may create a threatening and even unfortunate situation for many participants in a training program because it challenges deep-rooted beliefs and convictions associated with an existing managerial style.

Such a challenge could, of course, produce constructive results. On the other hand, participants may merely take a "relatively easy way out." This is simply to change their *perception* of their own managerial styles without actually changing their basic beliefs and values. This may not necessarily involve a deliberate attempt to deceive; it may simply be a protective device involving unconscious forces.

Thus, we see that this approach also has limitations. By now it must be apparent that this is a fact about all current theories of motivation.

Rensis Likert

Likert's contribution to motivation theory is primarily the development and utilization of what he thinks of as a professional, "science-based" *research approach*[10] to developing fundamental principles applicable to the effective and efficient management of people. His two major criteria for evaluating administrative "effectiveness" are (1) productivity per man-hour or some similar measure of the organization's success in achieving its productivity goals and (2) the job satisfaction and other satisfaction derived by employees or members of the group. The work of Likert and his colleagues at the Institute for Social Research at the University of Michigan is unique in that few, if any, other behavioral-science programs are grounded on such a rigorous research methodology (see Chapter 20).

Universal Principles of Management It is to be noted that Likert has at least one thing in common with "traditional" organization theorists. His basic premise is in agreement with that of the latter: There are common fundamental principles applicable to the effective organization of human activity ("traditionalists" use the phrase *universal principles*). Also his two major performance criteria, productivity and worker satisfaction, are identical with those employed by "traditionalists."

The similarity between Likert's concepts and those of the "traditionalists" ends here; he rejects most, if not all, of the principles of the latter. Further, he contends that currently managers fail because they adhere too tightly to classical organization theories, which he considers to be obsolete. His objective is to develop scientifically valid principles, that is, based on careful empirical investigations and verified when tested again and again. Presently, he feels that his work constitutes only a beginning, acknowledging that the development of scientifically valid data adequate to support a generally acceptable theory is something that we can only look forward to in the years ahead. Nevertheless he and his followers believe that progress has already been made toward achieving this goal.

Characteristics of High-productivity Supervisors Specifically, Likert has been well known for the last two decades and more for his studies concerning the relations between (1) the organizational structure and (2) the principles and methods of leadership and management that characterize high-productivity work groups and supervisors, as compared with those that characterize low-productivity groups of workers and supervisors. He has, for example, generally found that a supervisor's style of operating and his attitudes, values, and sentiments have a fairly consistent relationship to the productivity of his group. This topic is covered in some detail later in this book (see Chapter 20) as we discuss empirical or experimental investigations of effective supervision.

A Systems Approach to Supervising At this point we are concerned about Likert's views concerning possible styles of supervising leadership and his conclusion as to the best of these. He refers to these as *systems*, thinks of them as aspects of an integrated whole, and recognizes that management styles might be best depicted on a continuum, rather than described as a dichotomy. He then proceeds to describe a continuum from "System 1" through "System 4."[11]

The system he recommends (System 4) appears designed to aid organizations, to use Maslow's terms, in moving from Theory X assumptions to Theory Y assumptions. That is, he recommends moving from a supervisory style that fosters infantile, immature behavior to one that encourages and aids in developing mature behavior. (Note that Argyris makes a similar recommendation expressed in much the same terms.) Stated in other words, he advocates the utilization of a supervisory style that, to use Herzberg's terminology, concentrates on recognizing and helping workers to satisfy the "motivators" rather than a style that emphasizes concern only for *hygiene* factors. But let us now briefly identify the major characteristics of his four systems.

System 1 might be termed *exploitive-authoritative*.[11] This is essentially a task-oriented system based on the premise (McGregor's Theory X) that subordinates cannot be trusted by management. Administrators of this kind of system seldom involve workers in any part of the decision-making process. Authority, decision making, and controls are centralized. Employees are negatively motivated or rewarded through satisfaction of lower-level needs. Supervision is mostly autocratic. Informal organizations tend to develop with goals that oppose those of the formal organization.

System 2 might be termed *benevolent-authoritative*. This management style is characterized by a condescending confidence and trust in subordinates, as in the master-to-servant relationship. Goal setting, decision making, and control are primarily centralized, though there is some decentralization of authority within rigidly defined limits, to middle management and lower levels. The supervisory style is characterized by condescension, creating an atmosphere of caution and fear. Informal organizations tend to develop with goals that do not necessarily oppose those of the formal organization.

System 3 might be termed *consultative*. This management style is based on the premise that subordinates can be substantially, but not completely, trusted. The top level makes policies and general decisions, but specific decision making is cautiously delegated to lower levels. There exists a communications network throughout the hierarchy. The motivation process comprises some punishment and some rewards, such as involvement opportunities. In this system, an informal organization develops that may either support or partially resist the goals of the organization.

System 4 might be termed *democratic-participative*. This management style is based on the premise that complete confidence and trust can be placed in subordinates (similar to Theory Y assumptions). Planning and controlling are widely decentralized throughout the organization. There is a rapid and efficient vertical and horizontal flow of communications. Motivation is by participation and involvement in goal setting, economic and other rewards, and methods improvement. In this system the informal and formal organizations may often be the same. Likert's research program is directed to developing valid principles that would constitute a science-based System 4 approach to managing.

Evaluating Organizations   Likert's method for analyzing organizations in terms of his systems theory includes an instrument, basically a sort of attitude survey designed to gather data about a number of operating characteristics (such as leadership, motivation, and so on) of an organization. For example, hundreds of managers from many different types of organizations have been asked to indicate, first, where the *most* productive department or other organization unit they have known would fall on the scale between System 1 and System 4; second, where the *least* productive organization unit would fall on the scale.

Likert has arrived at a number of tentative conclusions deriving from his research studies and regarding the relative productivity of the four systems. For example, firms having practices falling on the continuum toward System 4 appear to be more productive and have lower costs and more favorable attitudes. Firms where System 4 is used apparently show higher productivity, low scrap loss, low costs, favorable attitudes, and "excellent" labor relations. The converse seems true for firms whose approach falls more toward System 1 on the continuum.

Another interesting conclusion derived from his research studies is the discouraging finding that although System 4 is felt by most managers to be the most appropriate, few see their companies presently utilizing this approach.

Supervisors might well ask what fate awaits them if their companies should at some future date embrace Likert's "science-based management." Likert, while recognizing the massive reeducation job of all concerned from top management to hourly workers, provides an answer that is reassuring:

> The results of research, as well as general experience, are providing ample evidence that no manager need fear that the introduction of a new management system will make his managerial skills obsolete. Any manager who really wishes to do so can learn to shift the system of management he uses from System 2 to 4 or to any other science-based systems. No one can do it overnight, but it can be done gradually over a few years.

Critique   It will be apparent from succeeding chapters that the authors believe that Likert's research has been outstanding. Indeed, it has thrown more light on supervision than has any other research of its sort. But to endorse his research is not necessarily to approve his interpretation of it.

In a way the rest of this book (and in particular the next few chapters) is an exploration of his fundamental idea that a certain management style is always and almost uniformly the best. Without in any sense condemning System 4 where appropriate—and it is often most useful—the authors of this book have reservations about whether this is indeed our best insight to date in supervision. We shall try later to make clear our reasons for believing that motivation of workers is more influenced by *why* they think and feel managers follow certain courses of action (for example, System 4) than *whether* they do. If this is an adequate conclusion, Likert's position must be modified before being accepted.

While we have now presented in some detail the motivational theories of five prominent individuals, it must not be overlooked that there are many, many more that we have not had space to discuss. A few of these are mentioned later in this section and others in other parts of the book. But this is not a book on motivation as such; we cannot expect to cover all of them or even all of the important ones.

One other motivational approach probably ought to be mentioned at this time, though it is to be discussed later—in Chapter 21. It is usually called "Organizational Development," is not associated by any means exclusively or even frequently with a single individual, and has grown directly out of the work of particularly Maslow, McGregor, and Likert. It seems important enough to resume its discussion in the concluding portions of the book.

A CONCLUDING STATEMENT[12]

In this chapter we have summarized some need-satisfaction concepts of motivation by prominent behavioral theorists. All of these tend to emphasize the notion of participation in organizations. Maslow conceived of a hierarchy of needs culminating in the need for self-actualization. He hypothesized that man needs to use his talents to the utmost in the world of work; however, industry seldom allows this to happen.

Likert, elaborating on the latter point, contended that currently managers fail because they adhere too tightly to classical organization theories, which he considered to be obsolete. He engaged in developing "scientifically valid" theories to replace the latter.

McGregor developed Maslow's concepts further in his comparisons of Theory X and Theory Y. Blake's descriptive system, the Managerial Grid, which identifies styles of leadership in numerical terms, may have drawn some of its inspiration from McGregor.

An ever-increasing emphasis on values of the workplace, such as self-actualization, finding meaning in one's work, and the identification of an individual within a significant group, have motivated other behavioral scientists to develop similar conceptions.

For example, Argyris presented the theory that mature individuals search for meaning in their work; organizations, however, present job opportunities that usually appeal to persons who are mentally immature or infantile. Argyris feels that when meaningful work is not provided mature adults, they will go to great lengths to develop it, sometimes in ways deleterious to management.

Herzberg can be classed with this group: he compared job factors that are motivators to those that are hygienic or dissatisfiers. If hygiene factors (which usually include pay) are lacking, the individual may be dissatisfied; if met, the result is at best only neutral. However, it takes motivators (self-fulfillment need, achievement) to get good productivity and worker satisfaction.

There is no general agreement among behavioral scientists regarding which needs, if any, are "universal" or common to all persons,[12] nor is there general agreement regarding the relative potency of certain needs as motivators to productivity and worker satisfaction. The theories discussed in this chapter most closely agree regarding the widespread existence in mature individuals (and the high potency) of the self-actualization or self-fulfillment needs as motivators at the workplace.

However, even this hypothesis is challenged by other behavioral scientists. For example, Strauss indicates that need-oriented theories of motivation, such as those discussed in this chapter, are more indicative of the highly educated behavioral theorists themselves than they are of the rank and file of blue-collar workers. The latter may place a much higher value on security, and the freedom of thought made possible by a structured, repetitive, simple task, which might be boring to the educated professional.

One research study conducted by Strauss in an industrial setting indicated that the need to self-actualize may not be so widely spread in the population as indicated by Maslow, McGregor, and Argyris. The study revealed a positive correlation between need satisfaction and job structure. That is, the higher the structure, the greater was the need satisfaction in such areas as achievement, affiliation, autonomy, and recognition.

Many behavioralists support this position. Still others cite such findings as a good example of a point not to be overlooked (see Chapter 17), that man has a fantastic capacity for adapting (or perhaps being conditioned to adapt?) not only to physical conditions that are without question injurious to his health but to tightly regimented work situations which Argyris contends would demand immature, infantile behavior.

Finally, it is worth repeating that not all the forces at work within business organizations are under the control of the supervisor. In many instances the supervisor can do no more than slightly influence the motivational atmosphere that surrounds a business environment. Therefore, it is every supervisor's responsibility to consider how he, as an "influence," is affecting his subordinates. Every supervisor who recognizes this fact will wish to ask himself: What are the consequences of my influence? What changes in my ideas, attitudes, and behavior might be more beneficial for this organization?

No supervisor who can answer these questions and is aware of his influence over subordinates is likely to underestimate the importance either of incentives or controls, including financial incentives and controls that are externally imposed. However, a supervisor with a bit of background in the behavioral sciences is aware that studies have indicated that incentive pay and technical controls can be most effective when used as part of a managerial system that stimulates inner motivation and self-control by employees. Moreover, research findings show that while there is a constantly shifting hierarchy of needs within a person (see Table 5-2), the higher-level needs when currently felt can generate the strongest motivation. It makes sense, therefore, for supervisors to develop policies, procedures, and practices that can liberate such drives as those for achievement and self-actualization.

An effective supervisor must know his people well and must have insight into and knowledge about why people behave as they do. Human beings, as we have seen, are motivated by many factors. One of these is the quality of leadership they get and the attitudes of management toward them. By making it possible for employees to find true satisfaction in their work and by stimulating them to merge their efforts without submerging their personalities, a supervisor is likely to increase the productivity and the profitability of the entire enterprise.

QUESTIONS

1 It has been said that "People don't appreciate what you have done for them; they only appreciate what you are going to do for them." Can you relate this statement to Herzberg's theory of motivation and/or hygiene needs?

2 To what extent have assumptions regarding Theory X, Theory Y, and self-actualizing people been adequately enough proven to be called scientific facts?

3 Do you think that job enrichment would make more or less work for the workers, supervisors, and upper management?

4 The conflict that Argyris describes between an individual and an organization is based on the assumption that employees generally are "mature." Do you agree? Explain.

5 How do you think (1) intrinsic and (2) extrinsic motivation might be accomplished with students? With clerk typists? With waitresses? With design engineers?

6 To what extent can we determine what an individual subordinate's needs are by using generalizations developed by behavioral scientists?

7 Do you think conflict is characteristic of a Theory Y type of organization, and if so can you justify your answer?

8 What is a major advantage of Blake and Mouton's approach compared with theories of leadership style of McGregor?

NOTES

1 See John B. Miner for a study on motivation: *The Management Process* (New York: Macmillan, 1973), pp. 297–326.

2 A. Maslow, *Motivation and Personality* (New York: Harper, 1954).

3 For a detailed discussion see Frederick Herzberg, *Work and the Nature of Man* (Cleveland: World, 1966); and Frederick Herzberg et al., *The Motivation to Work* (New York: Wiley, 1959).

4 See Chris Argyris, *Executive Leadership* (New York: Harper, 1953). References).

5 For a good summary of Argyris's research approach to motivation, see Maneck Wadis, *Management and the Behavioral Sciences* (Boston: Allyn and Bacon, 1968), pp. 275–292.

6 See Douglas McGregor, *The Human Side of Enterprise* (New York: McGraw-Hill, 1960), and a text published posthumously: Douglas McGregor, *The Professional Manager* (McGraw-Hill, 1967).

7 McGregor, *The Human Side of Enterprise*, pp. 47, 48.

8 For a comprehensive discussion of the Managerial Grid, see R. E. Blake and Jane S. Mouton, *The Managerial Grid* (Houston: Gulf, 1964).

9 See McGregor, *The Professional Manager*, pp. 61–65.

10 Details of research findings are described in Rensis Likert, *New Patterns of Management* (New York: McGraw-Hill, 1961).

11 The systems approach is described in Rensis Likert, *The Human Organization* (New York: McGraw-Hill, 1967), p. 191.

12 For an interesting discussion of the restraints comprised in utilizing the universality of needs concept, see Robert A. Sutermeister, *People and Productivity*, 2d ed. (New York: McGraw-Hill, 1969), pp. 13–22.

CASES

There is obviously no way in which one can select cases that uniquely illustrate all the theories of worker motivation. What we have done in this chapter, therefore, is to select three cases where motives (or motivation) play a central role. (Of course there are many other cases that would have served equally well.)

In one of these cases, that of Ed Meredith, we have a hard-working, reasonably effective supervisor. What do you suppose makes him hard-working? Why are not all supervisors like him? If you had to appraise him and give him the results, how would you conduct the interview? Could you praise him too much? Should you suggest ways of improvement? Which ones?

Jim Nulty has his feelings hurt, and the Company is about to lose him. If you had been one of the Engineering managers *would* (not could) you likely have prevented this situation from arising? What do you do now?

The Harry Jones case well illustrates how mixed our motivation may be and how rapidly it can change. How does the Company handle the pending grievance? Should it take other action as well?

CASE 5-1

Ed Meredith is a job supervisor in the Barrow refinery of the Company. A job supervisor is a first-level manager over maintenance mechanics and laborers in the mechanical division of the plant. Job supervisors report to zone foremen. They in turn report to the general foreman of the division.

Ed is forty-five years old and has been with the Company twenty-one years, including three years in the Navy after World War II. He started as a machinist's helper and after some years was promoted to machinist. He has been a job supervisor for four years. Except for summer employment and odd jobs, all his work experience has been in the Barrow refinery. He dropped out of a small-town high school in his senior year.

Ed generally does his job well, but under pressure he does exhibit some lack of thoroughness. Especially when he feels that time is short for the completion of a task, he may allow his people to turn out some work that is not up to standard. On the whole, however, he and his people do a good job and also come up with more than their share of new ideas about the work.

Ed is quite dependable, and when something is delegated to him, his supervisor can usually depend on him to follow through until the job is completed. His people generally get from him the decision they need, and he allows them considerable freedom in doing their jobs. He is cooperative, and his attitudes toward the Company, its policies, and his fellow workers are excellent. He does not become disheartened because one of his pet projects is turned down, but often has an alternate plan ready. He is able to adapt to a changed proposal quickly and easily.

Perhaps because he tries too hard, Meredith's analysis of some situations is not always as good as it should be. Sometimes he makes decisions and recommendations without the proper amount of careful consideration, and he occasionally has preconceived ideas which tend to hamper his ability to analyze correctly the suggestions of others. This, however, is not a serious problem.

The people with whom he works like him and respect him, but he has on occasion become upset with the operations or process people who disagreed with some of his ideas about how certain maintenance work should be done. On many other occasions when there was a disagreement, a friendly solution has been worked out. He also has a fault that a great many people possess to some degree; he does not always give credit to others for a job well done. This is most likely due to thoughtlessness rather than to intent.

On the whole Ed Meredith is thought of by his bosses as a job supervisor whom they are glad to have but who would be more valuable to the plant if some of his limitations could be overcome.

How should an interview for review of performance be handled with Ed? How realistic is it to expect decided improvement in Ed?

CASE 5-2

John Smith is the head of the engineering department in a manufacturing plant in the Southeast. About one hundred professional people are in the department. They are responsible for the planning and design of new facilities in the plant, for evaluation of machines and materials including the appraisal of possible new equipment, for cost studies on current and projected contracts, and for technical advice on operating and maintenance problems.

One of the engineers is Jim Nulty. He is a mechanical-engineering graduate of the State University with better-than-average grades and came with good recommendations from his professors and others. He joined the firm four years ago and has received normal increases in pay since that time. Most of his work has been in the design division. In fact, he has been moved from this work only on a temporary and short-term basis. He is twenty-eight years of age, is married, and has two children.

Jim is an employee concerning whom there is real disagreement among managers. Dick Wilson, his section head for the first 3½ years, had a low opinion of his competence and effort and went so far on two occasions as to recommend to John Smith that Jim be encouraged to seek employment elsewhere. Smith, on the other hand, has concluded that Jim is at least average and perhaps better in his achievement. He thinks of Jim as a "late bloomer" and believes he will become, if he is not already, a valuable technical employee.

Six months ago a new section head, Bob Taylor, was put over Jim's section. Bob studied Jim's situation carefully and concluded that John Smith's estimate of Jim was accurate and that Jim was an engineer who would be increasingly valuable as time went along.

Meantime Jim has become disturbed. To have been continued for four years on the same kind of assignment is a bad sign so far as an engineer's future in this Company is concerned, and to have received no more than the usual salary increases is another. Furthermore, Dick Wilson's unfavorable opinions inevitably became known to Jim, though he never suspected that Dick really wanted to encourage him to leave.

Even though Bob Taylor has been section leader for six months, Jim sees no indication that his situation is improving. Bob has been friendly in his relations with Jim, but has not directly complimented him, secured a raise for him, or moved him to other work.

Yesterday Jim put on Bob's desk a letter of resignation and sent a carbon to John Smith. Bob and John now have the problem of what to do with this letter and how to handle the situation.

CASE 5-3

The Company manufactures heavy machinery, particularly for use in earth-moving. It has a large machine shop, including a group of eight machinists who report to Louie Klopsteg, foreman of the section. These men operate lathes, grinders, and other machines, with about one-fourth their total time spent on grinders. All are classified as machinists, all do good work, and they are all paid the same hourly rate.

It is in connection with the grinders that the present difficulty arose. Traditionally the Company had assigned two machinists to the grinders on a full-time basis, with the other six men each assigned to a certain lathe or other machine. The work load varies, of course, and from time to time it is necessary for a man to work on something other than his regular assignment. However, at least 75 percent and perhaps as much as 90 percent of a man's time on the average was spent on "his" machine or machines.

Some six months ago Jim Sutherland and Bill Driver, the grinders, complained about their assignments. They claimed that grinding was hot, dirty work and that it was unhealthy to do it on a full-time basis. The Company checked on working conditions in the grinding room and found no evidence to support the complaint. True, there was somewhat more dust in the area, but neither the physician nor the industrial hygienist, in independent investigations, found it anywhere close to a dangerous level. The temperature in the grinding room was the same as it was in the rest of the machine shop, and it seemed apparent that grinding was no more tiring than operating a lathe. Nevertheless, Sutherland and Driver continued to complain to Klopsteg.

Actually Klopsteg and Tom Smith, his general foreman, preferred to continue the existing arrangement. They felt there was a bit greater efficiency when each employee had his regular duties, and besides, rotating all eight of them would require unnecessary effort and record keeping. However, all of them were qualified to do any of the work in the department, each was apparently willing to do his share of the grinding, and the two grinders very much wanted a change. Klopsteg decided to put the employees on a rotating basis, with each one to spend a period of two months in the grinding room and six months on other tasks. He told them, however, that management reserved the right, if it wished, to return to permanent assignments. Klopsteg did make one exception to the rotation. Thomas Wheeler, one of the machinists, was seventy years old, and Klopsteg did not feel he should be called upon to do grinding work even though he always did a good job. No one in the work crew objected to the new arrangement, including the provisions about Wheeler.

The first problem arose two months later when it was time for the first rotation. Harry Jones, one of two placed in the grinding room for the first two months, asked to be assigned permanently to grinding. Klopsteg was pleased with this request, since Jones was a good grinder and besides, as pointed out earlier, the company really preferred permanent assignments for all. Klopsteg agreed at once to the arrangement.

Things appeared to go smoothly for a few days, but Klopsteg gradually began to realize that things were not going well in the section. As he observed the situation more closely, it became apparent that the trouble centered about Jones. At first his conduct was quite satisfactory, but gradually he developed habits of loud talk and horseplay, the latter of a mild sort, but evidently designed to irritate those who were not in the grinding room. He also began to brag about his job, insinuating that it was easy work and that he "had a home back there (in the grinding room)." The situation was compounded by two other factors. First, Jones had never been a Union member nor had he displayed any interest in the Union. Now he began to deprecate and make disparaging remarks about it, especially in the presence of the other machinists, who, with the possible exception of Wheeler, were strong Union members.

The second factor concerned his relationship with Klopsteg. The two had been friends before they joined the Company and had started at about the same time as machinist's helpers. They were known to play golf and to fish together, and they and their families visited one another frequently.

The matter came to a head during the third week after Jones's permanent assignment. Early in the week Klopsteg received a grievance signed by six machinists (Wheeler and Jones being the two who did not sign), charging Klopsteg in particular and the Company in general with discriminatory treatment in favor of Jones. It alleged that he was being given special favors by being left in a permanent assignment and that this was in part a reward for opposition to the union. It asked that Jones be required to take his turn of rotation outside the grinding room and that "management be required to treat all machinists fairly and alike." The situation of Wheeler was not referred to in the grievance.

What action should Klopsteg take in this situation? Within forty-eight hours he must answer the grievance in writing. What should he say?

Chapter 6

The Critical Role of Trust and Confidence

In this section, which concerns the basis for effective supervision, we have so far looked at two different subjects, the fundamental processes of planning, organizing, and controlling as they affect supervision, and certain theories of worker motivation. We have seen how these three processes are essential to every supervisor and indeed that they influence directly or indirectly virtually all of his or her actions. And we have also concluded that while there is truth in many of the theories proposed to account for the motivation (or lack thereof) of today's workers, all of them have limitations. *The* theory of motivation, that is, the ultimately correct one, still has to be discovered (if indeed it ever is).[1]

But to conclude that a theory is less than perfect is not necessarily to say that it is worthless. Even if a particular one is not universally true (that is, true without exceptions), it may still represent one or more profitable generalizations, which is another way of saying that it may contain significant insights the lack of which would leave us with less understanding of those with whom we deal. This point of view, namely that while there are few universal truths in our field there are still many valid generalizations, is appropriate, particularly for the next three chapters.

As we have just indicated, the distinction between the *generalization* and the *universal* is a fundamental one. Table 6-1 should help to make this clear:

Table 6-1   The Conclusions We Draw

Kind	Accuracy	Example	Usefulness
Universal	Always true	"Two plus two equals four"	Valuable in logical analysis (formal logic); is seldom or never found in world of observation
Generalization			
Based on observation and reflection	Frequently accurate	"More effective supervisors are more critical"	Has good batting average
Based on "common sense"	Often false or at best half true	"Workers inherently resist change"	To be accepted with caution if at all

IMPORTANCE OF TRUST AND CONFIDENCE

The authors of this book have concluded that the most important single factor in effective supervision is the *trust and confidence* that those who are supervised have in their supervisors. And the fundamental factor here is the extent to which they believe them to be basically deserving of their confidence. If they feel that the managers are sound individuals, committed to worthwhile goals and dedicated in their efforts to attain them, they can and do go with them a long way. If, on the other hand, they feel they are less than admirable in their actions and particularly in their intentions, they have a great deal of difficulty in following them no matter how clever, pleasant, or knowledgeable they may be.[2]

Illustrations of Importance

Examples are easy to find. Our first is by way of contrast. One worker, upon being asked about his supervisor, said, "Oh, you mean this little old area foreman. Why, he's no boss; he's a politician."

And it is interesting what he added after a pause: "Now don't get me wrong. He's not a 'yes man,' for he's learned that around here they don't like 'yes men.' But he always says 'No' to just the right people on just the right subjects at just the right time."

Then he repeated, "Hell, he's no boss; he's a politician."

It needs no extensive experience or great perceptiveness to see that this foreman, if his other people share these views, is probably restricted, so far as methods of supervision are concerned, to the use of force or enticement (see Chapter 8) as a means of getting people to work. A term like "inspiration" would have little relevance under such circumstances.

Another illustration is a positive one. It concerns the attitude of workers toward an owner-manager (let us call him Joe Jones) for whom they have great regard. Among the other things unusual about this Company is a weekly meeting, at which attendance is voluntary but to which virtually every one of the 400 employees goes, regardless of position in the Company. At this meeting the health of sick employees is discussed, there is group singing, the financial progress—or lack thereof—of the firm is covered, with questions from the floor invited, frequently asked, and always frankly answered. The performance of Company products is also covered in detail if there are any new developments, and prospects for the Company discussed in an open fashion. (It is also significant that the employees get the bad news, financial and also as concerns products, right along with the good, no effort being made to conceal or even minimize the former.)

Two of Mr. Jones's policies may help. One is that he not only rejects the notion that it is bad to hire two members from the same family, but he seeks out additional members. His logic is that if a good employee comes from a certain family, that fact increases the likelihood of finding another like him in that family. Regardless of the general propriety of *nepotism* (hiring of relatives), the practice works well for Mr. Jones, for it is interpreted by employees in the light of the perceived character of Mr. Jones and of his genuine concern for his people.

The other policy of the Jones Company is that after one has become a permanent employee, his or her job—no matter how high or how low—is as good as Mr. Jones's, that is, Mr. Jones will take in percentage terms at least as much cut in salary as he asks employees to take, and no permanent employee will be laid off as long as it is possible for the business to continue. Incidentally, Mr. Jones's sincerity was thoroughly tested during the Depression and to an extent in more minor periods of business reversals since that time. No permanent employee of the Company has ever been laid off for lack of work, though hours of work were once greatly reduced. There have also been disciplinary discharges, and Mr. Jones makes no secret of the fact that he plans to keep the right to execute these.[3]

It is interesting, incidentally, how completely these attitudes are a two-way street, for not only do the employees trust Mr. Jones, but he respects them, too. The confidence of employees in their bosses nearly always goes with the confidence of bosses in their subordinates, and it is difficult to say in such cases which is the chicken and which is the egg.

The Case of Don Davis   Our third illustration involves a plant manager whom we call Don Davis. About 4000 people report to him directly and indirectly, somewhat more than half being hourly or blue-collar employees. Most of the latter are represented by a large, independent union.

Relations between Management and the workers have been good through the years. While there have been many differences of opinion and a few minor crises, no one can remember even one major work stoppage by the employees. Pay is above average and so are fringe benefits. There has never been any kind of extensive layoff of employees, and the plant has long had an outstanding production record.

Mr. Davis has spent his entire working life in this plant. Though an engineer by training, he was hired as a laborer and has held management positions at every level, including that of first-line supervisor. He has been plant manager for a number of years.

We are concerned primarily with Mr. Davis and his handling of grievances that are appealed to his level, the last one before arbitration (if the Union elects to arbitrate). This is known as Step IV in the grievance procedure. (See Chapter 15 for more on grievance procedures.)

It is interesting what employees say about Mr. Davis and his handling of Step IV grievances. Perhaps a comment by a pipefitter summarizes it best:

"You take it to Mr. Don," he said. "He will probably tell you you're wrong, and if he thinks you're wrong he damned sure tells you so. But if he thinks you're right he'll tell anybody so. You can depend on Mr. Don."

And it is instructive to find what sentiments and beliefs lie behind these statements. To put the matter briefly, Mr. Davis has convinced a great majority of the workers (a) that they are always heard if they persist and (b) that after hearing them "he calls it as he sees it," regardless of what New York headquarters or his own subordinate managers or the affected employees wish him to do. Relatively few managers have been able to convince blue-collar workers that this is true of them, but then there are not many Don Davises!

On one other point we need to be careful. The workers do not believe that Mr.

Davis's decisions are always correct. (Asked if the plant manager ever makes mistakes, one operator said: "Make mistakes, hell! He's human, ain't he?") In fact most can and do cite instances of what they judge to be mistakes on his part. But it is noteworthy that with few, if any exceptions these are said to be "honest mistakes," a phrase that means they judge the decision to have been based on the facts as Davis saw them, on what he honestly believed was right, and not on "political" considerations.

Mr. Davis is an unusual manager. He is very near to compulsory retirement from his job. How difficult will it be to replace him?

Particularly this and the succeeding chapter will deal with some of the reasons for the success of Mr. Jones and Mr. Davis. We may not be able to account for all of it—after all, human beings and human situations are complex and many factors, including unknown ones, are often influential—but we can discover valuable insights nevertheless.[4]

THE BASIS FOR TRUST AND CONFIDENCE

A fundamental question in the supervision of people is how trust and confidence are started and how they grow. While others might give different and equally adequate answers, we have chosen to deal with the subject by discussing three fundamental characteristics of supervisors: their ethical and moral beliefs and practices, their emotional maturity, and their wisdom and understanding. The first two of these we shall cover in this chapter. The third is discussed in the one to follow. Only after these three points are covered will we turn to his methods (in Chapter 8).

Devotion to Ethical and Moral Values

In attempting to answer the question, What is the basis for effective supervision? the authors of this book are emphasizing what is often dealt with superficially or not at all, namely, that the *fundamental* problems of any manager who has responsibility for motivating others are *ethical and moral* problems. They concern what is right and what is wrong and the relations between these and one's own personal goals and behavior.

We have just implied that this is not a popular position. Certainly that is true if we take the written and spoken words of management theorists, for they either fail to discuss the matter or make general statements about it in an almost offhanded way. We do not question that they believe that ethical and moral values and conduct are important. We only wish that they were more explicit on this point.

Questions about Ethical Values   One sees a great deal in the management literature these days about the duty of the manager to maximize productivity, efficiency, and profit. Indeed, there are those who insist that this is his or her only real goal (unless another is to advance the manager's own personal welfare). In pursuing it, he or she is of course not to violate the law, nor to alienate workers, customers, or the public—all this not because it is wrong, but because it will prove to be unprofitable to do so. Likewise, the supervisor donates to charity and supports worthy causes not basically out of generous motives but because this practice is, or at least is thought to be, "good for business."

Proponents of this point of view have little need for ethics as such. They will be interested only if ethical behavior can be used to increase net return—or in the case of a government agency, maximum efficiency. Otherwise, ethical matters are to be left to the minister, the priest, the rabbi, the educator, or the social worker; the manager is to concentrate on making a profit.[5]

It must be confessed that this point of view is an attractive one. It does make sense to look out for oneself and one's organization, for if one does not, who will? Besides, are not people selfish by nature? Is there really any other practical way to proceed?

Then, too, there is the problem of what is ethical. Just what is the standard for separating right from wrong? What is the difference between being ethical and being religious? Can we talk seriously of being ethical without becoming involved in the morass of different moral and religious beliefs and practices? Is this a place for the manager? Are there not enough problems without adding these?

Even if these questions can be answered, others remain. People often differ in their judgment about what is right and what is wrong, and these differences may be as far apart as the poles. What is the manager to do under these circumstances? Suppose he or she makes what he or she considers to be an ethically good decision, and the workers or customers or the stockholders believe it to be morally wrong. Would the manager not be well advised to stay on the familiar ground of profitability and efficiency?

A Conception of Ethics Regardless of the difficulties that our position carries with it, we do not feel that the supervisor can afford to disregard or neglect the nature and the place of the ethical. We shall therefore have to face the question of the basis for such decisions, whatever one decides it should be. We cannot hope to solve the problem completely, especially in a book like this, and yet some comments must be made.

To begin with, religion and ethics are not the same. The former concerns man's beliefs and practices with regard to the nature of the universe, including its relationship to man and the powers that control it; the latter concerns man's relationships to man. It cannot be denied that the two are related. The fact is that religion is at times a powerful motivator to ethical behavior, and modern religions, with few if any exceptions, emphasize the necessity for ethical behavior. But the point that needs to be emphasized here is that regardless of theological differences, the orthodox Jew, the practicing Catholic, and the devout Baptist can be and usually are ethical, that is, sensitive and devoted to the needs of their fellows. Oddly enough, while they may be far apart in doctrine, they will usually differ much less on important ethical issues. The authors of this book certainly do not believe the working place should become a religious forum or theological debating society, but the manager can be be committed to doing what is ethically and morally right and can devote real effort to accomplishing this, and seldom or never get into an argument involving religion.

Even in spite of genuine differences of opinion as to what constitutes ethical and moral practices and the varying conclusions about this over time and from one culture to another, one fact stands out in all the apparent confusion. It is that every continuing human group demands devotion to the common good (or the welfare of the group) before it bestows truly first-class, top-drawer membership on an individual.

Examples of the Common Good As an example, suppose a person joins a service club for one purpose and one purpose only, namely, for what he or she personally can get out of the club, and is resolved to make no net sacrifices for it. No matter how much that person supports the club, no matter how much money he raises for its charitable projects or what he does to aid in membership or programs, if these feelings are known (as they are likely to be) and as long as they persist, people will have their reservations about him. Even though he may be elected club president, he never enjoys the status of being the best kind of member.

The number of such illustrations is almost limitless, for the same principle applies to alumni associations, athletic teams, professional organizations, church boards, and family groups. This, of course, is not at all strange since the basic teachings of both the Judeo-Christian tradition and the American way of life join to condemn the unbridled pursuit of self-interest. It should be noted that it also applies to the careful, calculated, and clever following of one's own welfare in disregard of the good of the group. And while this may not be of great significance to the American manager, it is also true that groups all over the world join in this opinion, even though they may be far removed from the influence of either the Bible or the Declaration of Independence.[6]

A topic which we do not have space to discuss in this book is the foundation for standards of right and wrong. Table 6-2 gives some views of this subject.

Implications for the Supervisor That this point has the greatest significance for the effectiveness of the supervisor's personal influence is immediately apparent. If he or she follows these percepts, there will be no attempt to "use" the people, that is, to profit by their efforts without considering their welfare. Furthermore, the supervisor will not knowingly sacrifice the interests of subordinates to gain for himself. He will not "step on their necks" in order to get ahead.

This ethical standard also demands that the supervisor be not simply a "politician," using every known device to appear in a favorable light to the boss and upper management and doing so at the sacrifice of principles and even integrity. (It is distressing how many workers believe that bosses are guilty here and are trying to get ahead by using any means they can find.) The supervisor is under obligation to give credit where credit is due, and even to give the other person the benefit of the doubt so far as credit is concerned.

Certainly this position also requires that a supervisor "stand up for" the workers when judgment indicates that they are right and the boss and perhaps the big bosses are wrong. It is frequently desirable even on ethical grounds that this position be taken diplomatically and efforts be made to avoid giving offense to anyone, including the bosses. Unfortunately there may be situations where the diplomatic approach does not work. Under these circumstances the supervisor has a significant *personal* moral problem: How far should he or she go in standing for what he thinks is right? How important is the principle involved? What will be the effects, both long-run and short-run, if one does not stand by it? Here the supervisor will find use for all of his or her experience and very best judgment, for only *he* or *she* can ultimately answer such a question.

Table 6-2　Basis for Ethical Judgment

Kind	Example	Meaning	Consequences of acceptance
Absolute	The Bible; Kant's Categorical Imperative	Right because it is right; divinely revealed or an inherent part of nature	Rigidity; does not change with conditions; even divinely revealed standards must be interpreted
Relative Subjectivism	"There's nothing either good or bad, but thinking makes it so"	One's own standards are all there are for him	Eliminates or at least weakens serious devotion to or concern about the ethical
Cultural Relativism	It's totally a matter of the mores of the group	Whatever the culture says is right is right for every member	Works well in a totally isolated group; obviously incorrect at times (e.g., human sacrifice)
Devotion to "the common good"	It's wrong to further pollute Lake Erie	What is right is what ultimately contributes to human welfare	Conclusions based on it are often hotly debated—but where is the alternative?

The point of the above is obviously not that the supervisors should do what is right because it will be profitable to them. Rather it is that they should do what is right because it is *right* to do so, because it is their best judgment that in this way they can make their greatest contribution to human welfare. To be good in order to gain is to be selfish and self-centered. To be good because one is committed to certain values that are bigger than one's own interests is what our ethical teachings demand and what subordinates expect of the boss (or at least, what they think he or she should do).

It is also worth noting that this kind of action also usually works best for the supervisor so far as the opinion of the big bosses are concerned. After all, executives do not usually have any more admiration for the "yes-man" than the rest of us do and are not likely to reward him in the long run for that kind of conformity. Management certainly should reward, and not punish, *healthy* dissent and it does that more often than subordinates usually recognize. Dissent can be overdone—of that there can be no doubt—but the greater danger is not encouraging it sufficiently.

Thus if there is a *key* to effective personal influence, it rests on mutual trust and confidence, and the only substantial basis for such trust and confidence is an understanding and acceptance of ethical principles and values and the practice of them on a realistic, day-to-day basis.[7]

EMOTIONAL MATURITY

We remarked earlier that the trust and confidence of which we speak rest on three characteristics of the leader: ethical and moral beliefs and practices, emotional maturity, and wisdom and understanding. In this section of this chapter we shall explain the meaning and importance of emotional maturity. The last of these three basic characteristics will be examined in the next chapter.

Meaning of Emotional Maturity

What we mean by emotional maturity is the ability to live *comfortably in the world as it is, with oneself as one is and with people as they are.* It implies an understanding of oneself and others, but even more vital, the acceptance of oneself and one's associates as they are, as the facts of the situation dictate, and doing this without emotional upset, recriminations, or regret. We are talking about understanding and living satisfactorily or even enthusiastically with people (including oneself) as one finds them.

One word of caution: This point of view counsels neither contentment nor resignation. We may be quite unhappy with ourselves as we find ourselves to be, and also with the others with whom we deal. If so, there is nothing to be said against and much to be said for the starting of a program of reconstruction. What is being emphasized here, however, is starting the program realistically, beginning with the *actual* situation one faces, and not fighting "straw people" or jousting with windmills. Certainly there is an element of the latter in any endeavors based on a magnified or distorted picture of the people with whom one deals.

The Role of High Expectations

Feelings about the Nature of People One way in which supervisors differ is the greater amount of confidence which the better supervisors are likely to have in their associates. Certainly, this confidence applies to the members of their work groups, that is, their subordinates, but seldom is it restricted to them. After all, people need confidence in their boss, their boss's boss, and top management; in staff people, with whom they often have close contact and who are at least supposed to help supervisors do their job; in suppliers, whether these are outsiders to the company or other work groups on whom their group depends for important materials or services; in customers, again whether these are the ultimate users of the product or service or merely other company people who depend on the group for their "raw material"; and even in people in general, for one's attitudes toward people in general no doubt have a strong influence upon one's attitudes toward particular individuals.

There is at least one other person, unmentioned in the above list, in whom the supervisor needs confidence, and that is the supervisor himself or herself. Oddly enough, self-confidence usually comes first and confidence in others follows from it, or in the unfortunate cases where self-confidence is lacking, confidence in others is not likely to be high.

This is a point easily overlooked, that our attitudes toward others are to an appreciable degree dependent on our attitudes toward ourselves. Indeed, the best "projective" material in the world is probably not the Rorschach ink blots or the unstructured pictures or other such devices, but human beings and their thoughts, motives, and reactions. After all, by looking closely—and sometimes by merely looking—we can usually find in others almost any kind of person we wish to find. In other words, the human knowing and perceiving mechanism is such that we can very often see in people what we want or need to see, and this we all do to an appreciable degree. Thus, self-confidence (or its opposite) begets confidence in others (or a lack of such feelings).

It is hardly necessary to point out that the confidence of which we are speaking is not of an unlimited or naive sort. There is nothing in either research or practical experience to lead to the conclusion that, without limit and without exception, the more confidence the supervisor has the more successful he will be. Unrealistic confidence, either in oneself or in others, is certainly no basis for firm cooperation. Neither, on the other hand, are pessimism, cynicism, or even undue anxiety about success.

A point often overlooked but quickly accepted when one stops to think about it is that true self-confidence, instead of leading to braggadocio, ostentation, and "show," in fact almost never does so. The person who is good and who knows, both consciously and unconsciously, that he is good, does not feel under compulsion to inform others about or to emphasize that fact. Bragging about one's abilities is almost always evidence of either recognized or unrecognized feelings of inferiority.

Expectations about Performance   A second point concerns one's expectations about the performance of one's associates and is very close to the one just discussed. Of course, one can have confidence that the work group will not perform satisfactorily, but that is pretty clearly not the sort of confidence we seek. Rather it is the confidence that expects a great deal and not infrequently gets a great deal more.

At this juncture one thing needs to be clear regarding both expectations and confidence: The sort of attitudes and values we are seeking are real and not feigned ones. We are not referring, in other words, to what a supervisor tells his associates he expects of them, nor even, strangely enough, to what he tells himself he expects of them. Rather, we are referring to what he really and truly does expect. It seems odd, but it is true, that one may believe he has high confidence and expectations when in reality that is not the case. Likewise, one can seriously underestimate the amount of these feelings. What we are saying, at any rate, is that the confidence a supervisor actually has in his crew and the expectations he has about how they will perform are quite significant influences on how they do perform.

After all, there is nothing strange or mysterious about this. We often get from people about what we give, and we are frequently repaid with attitudes we ourselves display. Perhaps a couple of illustrations would be in order. A young high school teacher enters her classroom each day fearful that her pupils will create a disturbance and actually expecting them to do so. As a general rule not many days pass under these circumstances until a disturbance is created—and the teacher has what she expects. Years pass, however, and this teacher develops skill, confidence, and high expectations. It would be too much to suppose that all her problems disappear and her pupils always behave perfectly, but they do behave better, study better, and probably find the situation generally more satisfying. Other factors may be operating, but the attitudes and values of the teacher must not be overlooked.

A second illustration: Whenever one finds himself with a group of managers, whether executives, supervisors, or people in between, one is very likely to find many who believe that today's workers are out for themselves, to get as much as they can for as little effort as possible. These managers often assert that the success of the company means nothing to the average worker except as a means to his own pay, and that he or she is not really concerned about it, knowing jobs are available elsewhere.

Whether or not this is an accurate opinion might be debated at length, for who is "the average worker" and what is one really like? The authors of this book do not happen to agree that these statements fit the majority of workers, but that is not the point. It is rather that to the extent that workers are that way, at least a part of the responsibility for the situation depends on managers who have these beliefs, for here as elsewhere people tend to repay us in kind of coin we use in paying them. After all, nothing is much more discouraging than to find that one's boss, or one's boss's boss, holds one in low esteem. This is not, to say the least, the basis for great enthusiasm in one's work.

A closely related, damaging conception reflects not so much on the worker's morality as on that person's intelligence. All too many managers assert and believe that workers are not very bright, that they understand little about even the elementary facts of business life, and hence must be dealt with much as though they were children. This is also far from the opinion of the authors, but that again is hardly relevant. The real point is that if managers feel this way and show it (and show it they almost certainly will, even if they try to conceal it), the effect is definitely adverse. One wonders how some workers work as enthusiastically and well as they do, considering the atmosphere of disapproval in which they work and the vote of no confidence they receive every hour of every day from some supervisors. Under the circumstances it is a tribute to the American workers that they let these things influence them as little as they do.

Comfortableness in Dealing with Associates

An observation closely related to the one we have been making is that effective supervisors typically feel comfortable in the presence of their associates, including their subordinates. They are not embarrassed when they are with them; they do not have "to keep their guard up"; they do not find it necessary to pretend to be something other than what they are or to believe something other than what they really believe. On the positive side, they enjoy being with them, are interested in their problems and aspirations, know them well, and talk freely with them.

Many persons in leadership positions, including some successful ones, lack these feelings. For example, one of the authors knows a plant manager who is not comfortable except within the four walls of his office (if indeed he is really comfortable then). Even his immediate subordinates, the assistant plant manager and the superintendents, are nearly always called to *his* office when he wishes to see one of them, and it is rare indeed to see him in one of their offices. He has two secretaries, an important part of whose duties it is "to keep people out," and they do this quite well. He almost never visits the work areas except on some item of specific business, and then makes it a point to return to his office as soon as possible, rationalizing to himself that he is too busy to do otherwise.

This man has the necessary technical competence to do his job very well indeed, in spite of these attitudes that are real handicaps. It is tragic, however, that even his close associates as well as the vast majority of the workers have misjudged him. They think of him as callous, production-minded, unsympathetic, and little interested in, if not contemptuous of, the feelings of others. Actually, he is a shy person, greatly desirous of warm, sympathetic contacts with other people. He is vaguely aware of how people feel about him and this causes him discomfort, though again he has rationalized that this is one of the prices one has to pay for being a manager and for doing his job well. Actually, his problem is that he is not comfortable in the presence of others, and especially of his subordinates.

Unfortunately, to recognize this man's problem and even to bring him to recognize it is not to solve it. It would really do no good to tell him to be comfortable in the presence of other people, for these feelings are seldom amenable to resolution, no matter how weak or strong. However, it is helpful to understand what is happening. It should certainly be useful in selecting other managers, and it might eventually be used to help this man improve. Obviously, however, this sort of improvement is a complicated, slow, subtle, and not too promising affair.

By way of contrast, we have all known managers who are the exact opposite of this manager. (Incidentally, some of them are quite successful, as this man is, and some are failures, for no one characteristic typically either makes, or breaks, the performance of the manager's functions.) Here, for example, is a manager who almost literally has never seen a stranger. He is open and friendly with all whom he meets, though he can be "tough" when the occasion warrants. He is on a first-name basis with all his associates, a situation that arises naturally for most of them, but one which he openly encourages. He never drinks coffee alone, nor has his lunch sent into his office. He has a lively interest in almost anything of concern to his people and seldom hesitates to express his opinions. It is an interesting experience to attend a meeting with him and his immediate subordinates. So free is the give-and-take that it is difficult to tell who is the boss and who the subordinates.

Let us note again that these attitudes and practices do not guarantee success in leadership. In fact, used unwisely they may do more harm than good. But is it not evident that the odds are with the manager who has them and practices them wisely?

Attitudinal Requirements of Supervision

All this puts us in a strange situation: Some managers are unsuited to be managers by virtue of their attitudes and values. If they can and do change, they may become efficient. If they do not, they become expensive luxuries for their employers. All this is said in spite of the fact that it is easy to understand, in view of what has happened to certain managers, why they may lack confidence in workers and have low expectations about how they will work. This background, however, in no way alters the effects of such attitudes and values.

Thus the evidence indicates that the best supervisors do have real confidence in their subordinates, including confidence that a merely mediocre performance will not be forthcoming. Really and truly, consciously and unconsciously, they expect much from their people—and their expectations help them to get it.[8]

The wheel has now made a full revolution and we are back to the starting point: Confidence, high expectations, and employee-centeredness come primarily *from within the supervisor*. In the high supervisor, in other words, we see an emotionally mature and emotionally secure person. He is not afraid of people and is not dismayed by criticism, even that directed toward him and his actions. We have already made the point that confidence in others comes from within, that is, from self-confidence. Now we see that most successful leadership of workers has the same source.

Willingness to Admit One's Limitations

One mark of the inadequate supervisor, as of the inadequate teacher or athlete, is an inability to acknowledge errors. All of us know people who in their own eyes are without fault. They are sure that they are generous, well informed, unprejudiced, and expert in human relations. Furthermore, they appear to have no serious question about their superiority to the average supervisor, teacher, athlete, or other person.

Actually, the appearance they make is usually a front or a veneer hiding feelings quite different from those that an outsider can observe. Inwardly, there is nothing like the self-assurance that meets the eye, although the point must be stressed that they themselves are often unaware of their own psychological processes. One may feel inferior or insecure, in other words, and refuse to admit the fact either to himself or to others. One may believe himself generous, secure, superior, and objective when none of these characteristics can be properly applied to him. Self-understanding is hard for any of us to come by and especially so for those whose self-understanding would damage their exaggerated conceptions of themselves.

Ability to Recognize That One Makes Mistakes   On the other hand, emotionally mature individuals have few (or at least many fewer) problems along this line. They not only know that they make mistakes, but they also know that everyone else, including bosses, do also. They recognize that they have limitations in many respects—that they may be prejudiced against a certain employee or group of employees, for example—and not only admit this possibility but take steps to guard against these possible shortcomings.

Likewise, they feel no compulsion to prove that the top management or the company or even they themselves are always right. While they certainly do not spread dissension, they feel no need to be "yes-men" and would seldom be thought to be that. Since they know that no one is perfect, they can usually live more comfortably with their own or their bosses' mistakes, even when these affect them adversely.

It goes without saying that the contemporary American worker can usually work well with such a supervisor. They, too, know bosses are not perfect. (Indeed, it is often shocking how imperfect they frequently take them to be.) Those who do not pretend or even expect to attain perfection are "their kind of people," and given anything like a reasonable situation, they get along with such people. But they have great difficulty with the perfect kind.

What we have been saying is that supervisors need a certain measure and kind of humility, one that enables them to see some of their limitations and to realize they share the common lot of all men in this respect. Certainly we are not talking about a kind of humility that robs them of all assurance and hence of achievement, but the kind that enables them to see that in reality they are in many ways the servants of the workers, doing their jobs primarily so that the workers can do theirs better, and thus very decidedly contributing to the accomplishment of the real goals of the enterprise. Is this not close to what the Declaration of Independence means when it talks about the equality of all men? Is it not also closely related to the fundamentals of the Judeo-Christian tradition?

Willingness to Do Anything One Asks   Tied in very closely with the topic just discussed is a willingness on the part of supervisors to do anything they ask or expect subordinates to do. This point is one that is easy to misunderstand. We are not saying that supervisors should *do* anything they ask of another or even that they must necessarily be able to do it as well as the person to whom it is assigned. What we are saying is that they should be *willing* to do it if it is feasible and appropriate for them to do it.

Naturally, there are many reasons why it may not be appropriate for supervisors to do what they ask of a worker. They may not be qualified to do it, they may have more pressing duties to perform, it might (as it frequently does) undermine self-development and self-reliance on the part of the worker, and it might be a clear-cut violation of a labor contract. The conclusion is not that the supervisors should do anything they expect of a worker but they they should not be "too good" to do it, no matter how high the status of the supervisor or how low that of the worker or the work. American workers know, respect, and admire this attitude. They have no patience with a "holier than thou" attitude.

Humility and Self-Confidence   It is interesting how we often misconceive even simple human experiences. There are those who would immediately assert that self-confidence and humility are exact opposites, that if one is truly self-confident he or she is not humble in any real sense. It often takes half a lifetime to realize how erroneous this position is and to appreciate one of the fine insights of human history, namely, that it is only the truly self-confident who can be truly humble. Little people have to be perfect in their own eyes and, it is hoped, in those of others. The truly self-confident know they have limitations and can live comfortably with them.

"Toughness" In Decision Making

One place where managers' attitudes reveal themselves very clearly is in their reaction to the sort of situation in which they have to make decisions. There are at least three often unrecognized characteristics of this situation.

Difficulties in Decision Making   For one thing, the supervisor typically has to decide on the basis of incomplete information. It is all very well to tell people to withhold judgment until all the facts are in, but the plain truth is that many choices have to be made on the basis of incomplete evidence and not infrequently with only sketchy information at hand. Obviously, it requires a certain sort of person to be emotionally comfortable in such cases.

For another, managers are often faced with circumstances involving compromises. Typically, they do not have the luxury of choosing between the obviously right and wrong, or between black and white. Their choices are typically between shades of grey (and how close together they frequently are!). Thus, when a salaried employee asks for an hour or a day off with pay and the supervisor feels he must say no, it is quite likely that on an earlier occasion another worker was allowed the privilege under circumstances not unlike those of the denied employee. Furthermore, even people whom one must discharge are seldom without their virtues, and sometimes these are considerable. And it is certainly true that the people one does not see fit to fire fall short of perfection. Unfortunately, people seldom come in clear-cut classes or divisions. Adjacent employees that are most alike usually differ from each other only by small degrees, and yet no one can be fired or even promoted only to a degree. Thus compromise, which comes hard for many, is an inevitable way of life for the supervisor.

In the third place, there is the unpopular decision. Unfortunately, even the best of managers exerting his or her very best efforts will from time to time encounter situations where agreement simply cannot be secured. What is worse, they will on occasion be called upon to make decisions with which not a single worker (and maybe not even the boss) will agree. In other words, they will find it necessary to take actions that offend the conclusions and the opinions of the entire group. An example is often found in the discharge. No matter how much dissatisfaction people may express about a fellow worker who completely fails to carry his share of the load, when it comes to firing him, they disapprove almost without exception and at least in their own minds condemn the manager who takes the action. Of course, illustrations of unpopular decisions are by no means restricted to discharges.

Decision Making and Emotional Maturity   Granted that the supervisors should do all that they honorably and feasibly can to avoid these circumstances, they still inevitably arise. Here is a situation that tests the emotional security of managers. If they have the necessary maturity, they can "step up and make" the decision when it is called for, and having made it, they can "turn it off." This does not mean that they lose concern about their action. It is hoped they never do that as long as it is operative. But it does mean that they do not even *begin* to worry about that which cannot be avoided. Incidentally, there are no circumstances where trust and confidence, earned through years of ethical, devoted conduct, can be of more use than in situations such as these.

Even at that, the subject is more complicated than it appears to be. Certainly the ability to put one's best into carrying out a selected course of action is desirable, but it is also necessary to be sufficiently flexible and open-minded so that if it becomes apparent that the decision needs to be altered or reversed, the action too can be taken promptly. At the same time the loss in face that one is likely to sustain must be taken in (emotional) stride, and, above all, the mistakes must not be allowed to undermine one's own self-regard and self-esteem. It takes quite a human being to be a good supervisor!

Incidentally, one weakness of the present-day emphasis on decision making is its frequent failure to realize that making a good decision is only half the story. How one implements it, the maturity with which one enforces it, and the flexibility with which one examines and reexamines it are at least equally significant. A mediocre decision, well sold and well carried out, is usually superior to the best of decisions implemented in a blind or emotionally immature way.

THE SUPERVISOR AND TRUST AND CONFIDENCE

Thus what the supervisor's subordinates (and bosses) think and feel about his or her motives and desires are the most important things about him or her so far as they are concerned. And they simply cannot trust very far a supervisor unwilling to stand for what is right when such a stand is costly.

At this point it is tempting to emphasize "what people think and feel the supervisor is" and to conclude that therefore the basic goal should be to bring people to feel so, regardless of what the facts are. Our theory supports such a conclusion except for one thing: It is a rare manager who can long pretend along this line without being found out, particularly by people who see him or her every day and almost every hour of every day. In other words, the only way the average one of us has any chance of being accepted as ethical *is to be ethical*.[9]

While one can, by "taking thought," do something about one's values and conduct, it is doubtful whether the same is true of emotional maturity. After all, a great deal of this is required before one can even begin to be realistic in self-perception or the perception of others. And many a manager simply lacks this to the degree that he or she can never really get started. There is not much advantage in moralizing about how managers should be more emotionally mature. About all that can be done realistically is to help them see the nature of the characteristic and then hope they can use such information effectively.

A summary of the basic philosophy of this book is found in Table 6-3:

Table 6-3 Factors in Effective Personal Leadership

Characteristic	Meaning	Use and Importance
Ethical character	Doing right even when costly	Willingness to "stick one's neck out" for subordinates
Emotional maturity	Genuine acceptance of one's limitations	Desire to admit and correct errors
Knowledge	Knowing the facts	Unemotional and often unimaginative interpretation of observations
Wisdom	Appraisal based on background of developments and effects on society.	Considers history, fundamental assumptions, and consequences of "knowledge"
Empathy	"Putting oneself in another's shoes"	Taking account of feelings of others

Before concluding this chapter an additional comment should be made about Joe Jones and Don Davis, referred to in the beginning. Enough was said above to indicate that they meet most of the requirements we have set forth, but personal experience with each resolves any doubt. Mr. Jones and Mr. Davis are *ethical* persons; that is, they have beliefs or standards or principles (the exact word is not important) on which they stand and which they do not compromise for their own personal gain. To them, in other words, some things are right and some are wrong, and they openly strive to achieve the former and avoid the latter.

And their attitudes toward themselves personally and toward their associates are in line with what we have expressed. They do believe in their people; they do expect a lot from them (and get more than the usual manager); each knows he is not perfect and is quite willing to acknowledge a mistake if convinced that one has been made (and anxious to correct it and remedy its effects as quickly and completely as feasible). And yet each is relatively "tough-minded" in the sense that he does not avoid problems or delay endlessly in decision making.

Mr. Davis and Mr. Jones are unusual and unusually effective managers. Their attitudes, beliefs, and accomplishments have had a significant influence on this book and especially on this chapter.

QUESTIONS

1 Why do the authors conclude that the trust and confidence a supervisor's associates have in him or her constitute the greatest and best measure of the likely success of the supervisor and the work crew?

2 Just what is meant by the ethical and/or moral? Are there conceptions of the meaning of these terms other than the one presented in this chapter? Explain.

3 What would workers mean if they said that a certain mistake of the boss was a "mistake of the head and not of the heart"? Why is it usually better if a boss makes a mistake for it to be "of the head and not of the heart"? (Note that "of the heart" is often used to refer to one's motives or intentions.)

4 What is the justification for saying that only the truly self-confident can be truly humble?

5 Why do workers dislike the "perfect supervisor," that is, one who gives the impression he is perfect, almost as much as they do the unethical one?
6 What would be meant by saying that one's expectations as to the performance of another person often become a self-fulfilling prophecy?
7 In what ways do "tough" decisions test the ethical character and emotional maturity of the supervisor?
8 Is it guaranteed that all ethical, emotionally mature supervisors will succeed in supervision? Why?

NOTES

1 Dorothy Emmet, " 'Motivation' in Sociology and Social Anthropology," *Journal of the Theory of Social Behavior*, vol. 6, no. 1, pp. 85–104, April 1976.
    A thoughtful treatment of many modern theories of worker motivation; critical appraisal of each including the role of everyday experience in contributing to our understanding.
2 Studs Terkel, *Working* (New York: Avon, 1974).
    A remarkable book containing many valuable insights into work and workers in America.
3 John E. Mitchell, Jr., *The Christian in Business* (Westwood, N.J.: Fleming H. Revell Co., 1967).
4 Malcolm P. McNair, "What Price Human Relations?" *Harvard Business Review*, vol. 35, no. 2, pp. 15–23, March–April 1957.
5 Paul T. Heyne, *Private Keepers of the Public Interest* (New York: McGraw-Hill, 1967).
    The author contends that the businessman *is fulfilling* his ethical obligations as and when he pursues his long-run self-interest.
6 Alvar O. Elbing Jr. and Carol J. Elbing, *The Value Issue of Business* (New York: McGraw-Hill, 1967).
7 Arthur L. Svenson, "Whose Social Responsibility?" *SAM Advanced Management Journal*, vol. 35, no. 3, pp. 14–19, July 1970.
8 Rensis Likert, *The Human Organization* (New York: McGraw-Hill, 1967).
    An influential book that lends support to this point as well as others in this section of this book. Likert's findings and his theories concerning worker motivation are discussed later in some detail (see especially Chapters 19 and 20).
9 Robt. L. Heilbroner and Paul London (eds.), *Corporate Social Policy* (Reading, Mass.: Addison-Wesley, 1975).
    While this book should ordinarily have more implications for the executive than for the first-level manager, the latter should by all odds familiarize himself as far as feasible with the general subject. One certainly does not have to agree with all the conclusions of the authors to find them provocative of additional inquiry and study.

CASES

One question faced by a management that operates under a labor agreement is how to get modifications made in the agreement during the time when it is in effect. Particularly, how does it do this if the Union will not agree? Suppose the proposed change would clearly save the Company money and at the same time do no harm to any employee. Is the Union ever justified in refusing to go along? The Aubrey Innes case raises this and some other questions.

The Nancy Newcomb case poses a very different question: What should you do if an employee who is young and inexperienced becomes openly critical of you and the Company when you attempt a corrective interview? Does it make any difference if the employee is female (and thus more likely to file "an EEOC charge")? if she is the daughter of one of your most important customers?

The day-to-day personnel problems of supervisors and other managers are not always easy to solve.

CASE 6-1

Aubrey Innes is a pipefitter for the Company. He has twenty years of service and is considered a fine, dependable employee. Shop employees of the Company had been represented by an independent union until about ten years ago, at which time the International Union made an effort to secure the bargaining rights. Innes was one of the biggest reasons why it was successful, and he has been a leader in the Union ever since. Five years ago he was elected president of the local and has been reelected each time since, virtually without opposition.

While not belligerent in his attitudes toward Management, Innes is somewhat suspicious of it and is committed to preventing it "from getting by with anything."

A few days ago Bill Kieffer, the personnel director, proposed to the Executive Committee of the Union a plan that caught Aubrey by surprise. At the present time the contract provides for an assembler mechanic job in Labor Grade 6. This assembler mechanic does both assembly and machinist work, some of which is elementary and requires little skill and some of which necessitates the knowledge and experience of a first-class machinist. The company proposed to split the duties of this job into two jobs, an assembler mechanic A, with the more complex duties, and an assembler mechanic B to take care of more routine matters. The A job would stay in Labor Grade 6, and the B one would be put in Labor Grade 4.

The contract provides that if Management proposes a new job it will submit the proposed duties to the Union for its approval. Union approval of the proposed rate is not required, but if the Union thinks the proposal inappropriate for any reason it may file a grievance to that effect. Furthermore, this grievance begins at the third step, omitting both the foreman and the department-head level.

In the past the Union has usually gone along with Management on these matters, but on this one Innes became convinced that it must not do so. He persuaded both the Workmen's Committee and the Union membership that approval of the duties must be withheld, and has just presented Bill Kieffer with a third-step grievance protesting the rate.

Kieffer is upset by this action. Along with Herman Murphree, the plant manager, and other executives, Kieffer has made plans which he shared with the Union, to put all present assembler mechanics in the A job and to use the B job for a training slot, since there are simply not enough first-class machinists available. He feels that the Union's position is arbitrary and unreasonable, and recommends to Murphree that the grievance be denied. Almost immediately after the denial is transmitted to the Union, Kieffer receives a letter from Innes, notifying the Company that the grievances will be appealed to arbitration.

Kieffer will be the Company's advocate in the forthcoming hearing. In preparing this case, what are his strongest and most convincing arguments? What will be the Union's contentions? How and what should the arbitrator decide?

CASE 6-2

Nancy Newcomb was employed by the Jonesville National Bank soon after she completed high school with outstanding honors. She was eighteen years of age at the time and has been with the Bank a little more than a year. The Bank is in direct competition with the First National Bank, the only other bank in a town of 5000 people.

Nancy is an attractive girl who dresses neatly but who has found her choice of clothes to exceed by a considerable amount what she can afford on her salary. Thus, she has opened numerous charge accounts with local merchants and has allowed some of them to become overdue. Besides, she has been known to write checks that she knows she does not have sufficient funds to cover.

In the beginning Nancy arrived for work on time, concentrated on her duties, which she handled efficiently, and was courteous in her relatively few contacts with customers. By the time of this problem, however, she had begun to take her duties lightly and to handle them indifferently.

Nancy's father, a building contractor, is one of the prominent citizens of the community and a good customer of the Bank. He always maintains a substantial balance with the Bank and has furnished Nancy with all the material things she wants.

At the time of this problem Nancy was frequently reporting for work late, sometimes by as much as thirty minutes, and was spending unauthorized time on coffee breaks with Bertha, a close girl friend of school days, who was employed by the Bank soon after Nancy began. She also asked for days off occasionally. All these developments were brought to the attention of the cashier, Allen Johnson, who, though he was not her immediate supervisor, normally handled such problems.

Johnson realized that Nancy was inexperienced in the business world, so he decided to talk to her first about the problem of overdrawing her account and having overdue charge accounts with stores about town. He explained that persons employed in banks should set good examples for their friends or associates by paying their financial obligations promptly and being careful not to write checks that their balances will not cover.

Nancy informed Johnson that she was within her rights, because so long as she did the job asked of her at the Bank what she did after hours was her concern and not the Bank's. She pointed out that her father always took care of her overdrafts promptly and reminded Johnson that her father was one of the bank's most valuable customers.

What should Johnson say or do now?

Chapter 7

Wisdom and Empathy in Interpersonal Relations

In the previous chapter we stated and partially developed a fundamental thesis of this book: that, more than anything else, the trust and confidence that their associates have in supervisors come closest to determining the success of the latter in building motivation among the former. We also discussed two of the three bases on which trust and confidence typically rest. These were (1) one's devotion to and practice of certain fundamental ethical values, including fundamental beliefs about what is right and a willingness to do what is right even when it is not personally profitable; and (2) one's emotional maturity, the ability to live comfortably in the world as it is with people as they are, including the supervisor as he or she really is.

In this chapter we shall consider a third of the three foundations for trust and confidence, namely the wisdom, the insights, and the empathy of the manager. (*Empathy* is a term that we do not encounter very frequently. We shall explain it and its significance later in this chapter.)

ROLE OF UNDERSTANDING IN EFFECTIVE SUPERVISION

Our society has a bias in favor of understanding or knowledge. Somehow we feel that even our most pressing problems would disappear or at least materially improve if only people knew more of the facts relative to them. We also have a tendency to confuse knowledge with wisdom, when in fact one can have a great deal of knowledge and still lack wisdom in his interpretations and conclusions. One can also be wise even with a limited amount of information.

This same situation is found when we investigate effective supervision. Business and industry, as well as schools of business administration, have very often tried to teach people to supervise by "filling their heads full of facts," in other words, by trying to increase markedly their store of knowledge, especially about their jobs and their subordinates.

It would, of course, be a mistake to condemn all efforts along this line. All of us can learn more about our jobs and the people with whom we work, and we are likely to find such information valuable and even occasionally invaluable. But the endeavor can be overdone.

Limitations of Knowing

For one thing, knowledge and understanding are not everything. There is, for example, the matter of values and attitudes, discussed in the previous chapter. These are no substitute for adequate understanding, but they are at least fully as important, and supervision that fails to take them into account will most likely be unproductive.

Then there is the matter of skill. Here we are referring to the ability to *do*, whether or not understanding is present. Most people can ride a bicycle, and some can do it expertly. But it is doubtful whether anyone really *knows* or *understands* how to ride a bicycle. We should not be puzzled, then, to find some supervisors who supervise well and have little understanding of why they succeed, and others who understand people and jobs well but somehow supervise poorly. Understanding is desirable and even necessary, but it is not everything by any means.

Let us look more closely at the difference between knowledge and wisdom. Knowledge refers to "knowing what the facts are" and usually involves being informed of the latest developments in a field. Wisdom must have some knowledge as its basis, but it differs from expertness in at least two ways: First, it is historically oriented, that is, it views the knowledge in the broader perspective of where it came from and its implications for and likely effects on future actions, and hence has greater long-run utility. Second, wisdom has an implication not only for the utility of knowledge but also implies that which is good for many people and not just the individual himself. Somehow wisdom and the unalloyed pursuit of self-interest do not seem to go together.

Of these two, wisdom and knowledge, there is no doubt about which contributes more to the effectiveness of the manager. Perhaps, therefore, it might be well to stress that while in supervisory development emphasis has traditionally not only been on understanding but, more particularly, on understanding external factors (for example, the job and one's subordinates), actually many supervisors need nothing else quite so much as wisdom, self-understanding, and a deep appreciation for the actual situation of others.[1]

UNDERSTANDING THE INDIVIDUAL

Uniqueness of the Individual

It goes without saying that every person is unique, that is, different from every other person in the world. The complex facts about heredity and environment suggest this, and our everyday experience confirms it. To deal with a person effectively we must do what we can to become familiar with his or her individual reactions. Some people, for example, are hurt deeply by even mild criticism, while others expect and are challenged by it. An increase in pay will appeal to some more than to others (and may be deeply demotivating to some because it is "too little and too late"). Likewise, symbols of status may motivate certain individuals, only to be greeted with indifference by others.

Illustrations of this sort can be multiplied indefinitely. We are all individuals who are not duplicated anywhere else in the world. "What's one man's meat is another man's poison" is true now and will be as long as people are people. And supervisors are under heavy obligation to know each of their people individually, to know for each what is meat and what poison, to understand his or her attitudes, values, hopes, weaknesses, fears, frustrations, goals, and the like. Only thus will they be able to use their skill in leadership most effectively, particularly in facing unusual or critical situations.

Need for Recognition as an Individual

Another bit of advice almost universally given new supervisors is that they should do their best to recognize each subordinate individually. After all, none of us likes to be merely a name on a payroll or, even worse, only a number; no one likes to be looked upon as merely the equivalent to a machine, or maybe only a cog in the machine. People want to be known to their boss (and to some of the other bosses), to feel that he or she cares about them as persons, and to receive warmth for and acceptance of them. Furthermore they want to be dealt with similarly by other people in the work group.

We are dealing again with a truth that can be overemphasized; indeed, management has not infrequently been guilty here. Two observations are particularly relevant: First, *unearned* recognition is not really satisfying, especially in the long run. We have all had the experience of being praised highly for an achievement that we know deep down inside amounts to little or nothing. This is not rewarding; at times it can be embarrassing or even degrading. We have a hunger for recognition, but not for just any kind or even for all instances of favorable reaction by others.

Second, while recognition is a significant goal, it is not the only significant one. It is clear that wages and benefits are also important, but people are complex and are motivated by many things. In a later section of this chapter we shall talk about several other motives, but let us make the point here that it is good for a supervisor to appeal *realistically* to a desire for recognition. We must reject the notion that everyone has a deep hunger for promotions, titles, and other status symbols, and remember that for some their own personal approval of a job well done is worth more. For still others, some other goal may take on greater significance.

There is probably no area where we are more tempted to engage in manipulation than in this one involving recognition. It is so easy to praise insincerely and to pretend an interest we do not really feel. To recognize a subordinate when the supervisor knows that nothing at all unusual has been achieved is outright manipulation and is usually seen by the subordinate for what it is. Recognition, then, is a motive to which the supervisor may often appeal successfully, but like many other good things, it can easily be overdone.[2]

Individual Differences

A topic related to the uniqueness of each individual is the extent of differences within groups of people. A good deal of attention has been given to this topic in the last seventy-five or more years, and some significant findings have emerged.

For one thing, such variations are considerably greater than is ordinarily believed. It makes little difference what trait or ability one considers: the best possess it to a far greater degree than the poorest, and markedly more than the average or majority. For example, even in a group of skilled workers with years of experience it is not at all unusual to find one who can perform twice as effectively as the average and several times more so than the worker with minimum acceptable ability. This may not be appreciated by some experienced supervisors, but it would be well understood if the phenomenon of restriction of output and the values associated with "a fair day's work" could be canceled out for only a short while. Restriction of output is discussed further in Chapter 19.

Second, differences among individuals pertain to a wide range of characteristics. They are not restricted to intelligence, mechanical aptitude, or ability to perform a skilled job. They apply equally to aptitudes, values, beliefs, knowledge, skill in human relations, size, weight, strength of grip, and countless other characteristics.

A third observation concerns the persistence of these differences. There is no reason to believe that training obscures or does away with them. Indeed, the opposite is more likely—that the more capable take training more readily, and differences already present are increased rather than compressed.[3]

Supervisors have two heavy responsibilities, among others, in relation to differences between their subordinates. They need to do their best to see that work assignments are suited, as far as practicable, to the individuals involved, a matching that should consider social and emotional factors far more than has been true in the past. They also need to do what they can to overcome the tendency toward restriction of output, especially since this usually has its greatest restraining effects on their most able subordinates.

Figure 7-1 shows a so-called normal frequency curve and indicates how differences between individuals tend to be distributed.

THE THINGS WE HAVE IN COMMON

No one denies that people are individuals and must be understood and dealt with as such. This truth, however, has the possibility of serious misunderstanding and unwise use, for as surely as we differ from each other, we also have a great deal in common. Everyone is hurt by the prick of a pin, the loss of a loved one, or the defeat of a team or a highly valued cause, and we are all pleased by the team's victories and by genuine praise when no strings are attached. If supervisors adapt their approach to the uniqueness of each person, they are wise, but if this causes them to believe that there are no general motives to which they can appeal and no tried and effective ways of dealing with people in groups, they are being badly misled.

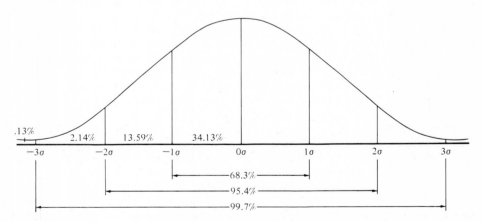

Figure 7-1   The so-called normal frequency curve represents the likely distribution of many human characteristics (e.g., IQ, height, weight, or time in running the 100-meter dash), as well as of countless other measures. It does not apply to all differences by any means but is the best bet in the absence of contrary information. The percentages above indicate the proportions of scores or other items to be found between certain points on the base line of a normal curve. (*From Sartain, North, Strange and Chapman,* Psychology: Understanding Human Behavior, *3d ed., New York: McGraw-Hill Book Company, 1967, p. 388. Used by permission.*)

The Concept of Human Nature

People have invented the concept of human nature to describe the common humanity of man. The term poses real difficulties but stresses an important point.

One of the difficulties with the concept is that some take it to imply that what people are depends solely or almost so on inheritance; this, of course, is not true. After all, heredity is essential for the production of life, but so also is environment. A person is a creature of both heredity and environment, and it must not be forgotten that the latter always has a significance fully equal to that of the former.[4]

Growing out of this mistaken belief that what we call *human nature* is due solely to heredity is the equally mistaken view that it cannot be changed or at least virtually never does change. This view is often used to express our feelings of pessimism about workers and their motivation. If, for example, a work group is indifferent and unconcerned, we may blame this condition on inheritance. Likewise, if the members are at cross-purposes with the supervisor and other managers, we often convince ourselves that by nature workers are headstrong and unreasonable. In both these situations, we overlook how cooperative, enthusiastic, and interested these same people are in some other activities of their lives. It is also worth noting that many people essentially like these may be interested and enthusiastic members of some other work group.

The concept of human nature is valuable, then, because it emphasizes the fact that especially people with a common cultural heritage have a great many things in common and may be appealed to successfully in terms of these motives. However, it does a serious disservice when it leads us to be pessimistic and discouraged and to accept undesirable attitudes, habits, and values as inherited and unchangeable.

Dealing with the Work Group

The point that needs especial stress in this connection is that there are motives that influence all the members of many groups, as well as techniques that practically all accept and admire and that are successful in influencing them. (Likewise there are techniques that all may find unpleasant and unworthy.) Furthermore there are ways of dealing effectively with people in groups, some of these being quite different from the "individual" appeals.

To explore these methods in any depth overlaps with other parts of this book and especially the following chapter, but let us at least make one comment at this point: If a supervisor wants to know how a certain worker really thinks and feels, many times he or she has a far better chance of getting this information in a small group than in an individual situation, and this especially if the thoughts and the feelings are not complimentary to the supervisor or the company. After all, most of us usually do not like to criticize another person to his face, and if the other person is the boss, we are usually quite careful.

In a group, however, a different set of forces is in operation. If supervisors invite evaluation of their own or the company's purposes and methods and if the subordinates discover that they really want to know their true feelings, the more venturesome may lead off with a mild but uncomplimentary statement. At this point, if others agree, someone is quite likely to repeat and emphasize what has been said and to speak a bit more frankly about how the workers feel. It is easy to see how this process may continue, with each person adding a bit more, until together all have said what no one would have said.

It cannot be maintained, of course, that it is always good to get complaints out in the open; furthermore, we must recognize that under these circumstances people may be stimulated to say a good deal more than they really mean and to represent their feelings as more serious than they are, facts that the understanding or perceptive supervisor bears in mind as he evaluates what is said. It is also true, however, that grudges that are harbored

and unpleasant feelings that are suppressed are often a serious source of irritation, inefficient effort, and conflict. To whatever extent managers feel it wise to discover the real
situation so far as the worker's feelings are concerned, they need to consider seriously the
use of this group technique.[5]

Group techniques may be equally useful in bringing about more enthusiasm for what
people already accept. Again, if one person makes a few rather timid or halting comments
of a favorable sort, others who agree are likely to express similar and perhaps stronger
feelings, and thus influence the goals and determination of some or even all members of
the group.

Unconscious Motives

Another area where the supervisor is prone to misjudge others relates to a person's awareness of his own motives. It is likely that no one would deny the existence of unconscious
motives in either himself or other people, but the extent and importance of motives of
which we are not aware is the subject of considerable misunderstanding and misinformation.

The most common error in this area is to underestimate the strength and influence of
unconscious motives. Even when we admit their existence, we are inclined to think of
them as having real influence only in unusual situations—typically among the maladjusted. Many supervisory practices illustrate the importance we accord man's reasoning processes and, by contrast, the small place we give to unconscious motives.[6]

Figure 7-2 illustrates a conception of the nature of unconscious motivation.

SELF-ESTEEM AND SELF-RESPECT

There is no more important concept, so far as understanding human behavior is concerned, than that of the *self*. While a discussion of it to some extent overlaps some of the
above material, and in particular that on unconscious motives, it is essential that we look
at it in some detail.

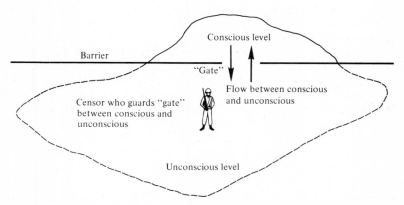

Figure 7-2 One conception of the unconscious is that it is massive and largely determines
behavior. It is represented above with a "censor" that keeps most desires repressed. The other
conception holds that wishes vary by degrees from fully unconscious to fully conscious, with
the fact of the unconsciousness of a motive in itself being a factor of no consequence.

Meaning of Self

It is important to understand clearly what is meant by *self*. There is a tendency to feel that it refers to some mysterious and intangible aspect of the individual and hence that a consideration of it should be left to those whose interest is academic or theoretical. The situation is quite different, however, in view of what we mean by the term.

The *self* is *the individual as known to and felt about by himself or herself*. In other words, it is the person as he or she appears to and is thought of and felt about by *the person* himself. In this sense, it is very significant to note the self is not the individual as he really is nor as he is conceived by anyone else. Rather it is *what he thinks and feels he is*.

Obviously, we all have many such thoughts and feelings. For one thing, I firmly believe that I am a good sport and a good citizen, and this belief would probably continue even if all who know me judge to the contrary on both points. I may also believe that I do my job in at least an acceptable (and probably a superior) fashion, and it is quite possible that no amount of objective evidence would make me feel otherwise. Likewise, I may have some strong feelings about my patriotism and my satisfactory performance as a club and church member.

Two comments are particularly in order at this juncture. First, my self is among my most valuable possessions. If something happens to enhance my own satisfactory opinion of me, I am greatly pleased. But if something is said or done that reflects discredit on me, that something is very likely to provoke my resistance, passive or active. Indeed, it is amazing how far people sometimes go in their endeavors to defend or enhance themselves. They do all sorts of otherwise completely puzzling or irrational things and may convince themselves of conclusions that no rational and objective person could possibly accept. (Strong delusions are no doubt characteristically—and some would say, always—self-defensive.) A supervisor can often be guilty of no sin worse than that of reflecting unfavorably on a worker's regard and respect for himself.

Second, the self is in no sense restricted to the physical body of the individual. It usually includes his children, his home town, and his team, and may very well also embrace his company and his union. Let us examine this point in greater detail.

Identification

By *identification* we mean the process of taking things that are not originally a part of the self and making them a part of it. At first, for example, I may care nothing about the team that represents my city in professional football. As time goes by, however, I read about the team in the newspapers and see and hear about it on television. I also talk with friends who have identified with it, and I may attend some games. Gradually, I come to identify with it also. Thus I feel disappointment when it loses and am happy when it wins, even if I have not bet on the outcome of the games and have no financial interest in its success or failure.

My children (and maybe especially my grandchildren) are a better example. Not only are they among the best-looking and most intelligent youngsters in the world, but in addition, I identify strongly with them, I rejoice in their successes, however minor, and am deeply hurt by their serious disappointments. They literally come to be a part of me, often just as much a part of me as my own right arm.

Some identifications are but lightly held, and we do not concern ourselves much about them. Some, on the other hand, may become more precious to us than anything else, including life itself, for surely parents have been known to risk, and even to lose, their lives in an effort to save their children. This may and sometimes does occur when we know full well how poor the odds are both for our success and theirs and our own survival.

Here is the vital flaw in the motivation theory of anyone who believes that self-interest, in the narrow sense of the term, is always the principal or even exclusive motivator of human beings. That the question, What is there in it for me personally? can be a powerful stimulator, no one would deny. That it is the only one, or even the only really influential one, is a position that flies in the face of identification and a multitude of human experiences.

The facts of the self and identification have at least two implications for wise supervisors. For one thing, they will do what they can do to bring workers to identify with their jobs and the objectives of the work group, their department, their plant, store, or office, or even the whole organization. If this can be done to a high degree, workers will work more willingly and enthusiastically and certainly will usually be more efficient and productive.

In the second place, wise supervisors will be thoughtful and perceptive concerning the self-esteem and self-respect of subordinates. They will leave no stone unturned to discover things that detract from or add to these feelings, will be careful not to damage them needlessly or through ineptitude, and will realize that, insofar as feasible, the best motivation comes when people are doing things that protect and enhance these feelings of self-worth.

Self-defense

It is with this background in mind that much of what has been written in the popular as well as the psychological literature about self-defense and the defense mechanisms takes on real meaning. When we find our good opinions of ourselves vulnerable and under attack, we rush to their defense. At times this defensive behavior may be as calm and rational as any we ever undertake, a likely result if the affront is not severe and has little chance of doing real damage. However, if the attack is vigorous, sustained, and based on substantial facts, we are quite likely to resort to unconscious methods of self-defense.

Many mechanisms could be introduced at this point, but the list is too long and involved to be discussed in detail. Let us illustrate with a process known as *autistic restructuring*. (*Autism* is the influence of the affective or emotional processes on the intellectual or cognitive functioning of the individual.) If I begin to lose substantially in *self*-esteem and if the usual and logical actions I take are of no avail, I am likely to begin to remake either myself or the world outside. I may, for example, succeed in convincing myself that I am more worthy than others believe or more worthy than even I have believed in the past. This restructuring, if motivated by a sufficiently strong (and often largely unconscious) need, may reach the point of a strong delusion of persecution or grandeur.

Another possibility is to remake the world and the people outside the self. If, for example, I begin to suspect my own unworthiness, it is some comfort if I can convince myself that most or all other people are unworthy too, and probably more so than I. By comparison, at least, I appear better in my own eyes.

It is very important at this point to note that such beliefs do not stem from objective evidence but from *a need to believe them*. Furthermore, they serve as a means of self-protection, usually in what the person feels is a vital area. It is unlikely, therefore, that facts, no matter how cogent or obvious, will have much influence on them, and this without regard to the intelligence or mental ability of the person involved. One gets at these problems, therefore, not through the use of logic in the usual sense of the term, but by dealing with human needs.

It is also helpful to realize that what is going on within the individual is often not understood by him at all. The processes we are describing usually are not deliberate or conscious. The person is not lying (that is, consciously or deliberately distorting). His building up of himself or degrading of others, he needs to believe and does believe, is based on fact and not on opinion or defense. In defensive behavior the degree of unconsciousness (or unawareness) may vary all the way from that which is complete to that which the individual understands *just after he has used it*. (The degree of unconsciousness, however, is at least one indication of the strength of the need to restructure.) The important point here is that not all or even most people who fail to tell the truth are hypocrites or liars. In most cases they are persons whose self-esteem and self-respect are under attack and who are doing their best to preserve them.

As indicated above, many defense mechanisms have been identified and described. Among them are *rationalization*, mentioned in Chapter 5, which is unconsciously false self-justification; *projection*, which consists in finding one's own attitudes and values in other people and objects; *regression*, which is taking refuge in the childlike, satisfactory behavior of an earlier period; *fantasy*, which is exemplified in the daydream; and as many as six to a dozen or more. Knowledge of the essentially defensive and unconscious character of these and the other mechanisms is nearly always quite useful and can be vital in understanding the behavior of workers.[7]

Table 7-1 presents the three principal ways in which human beings attempt to deal with seriously frustrating situations. In addition to these generalized responses there are a great many more specific ones such as compensation, projection, rationalization, and the like.

NEEDS WE TEND TO OVERLOOK

In our society, as in any other, certain needs of human beings receive a great deal of emphasis, and others tend to be underemphasized or overlooked. In the work situation needs like wages and fringe benefits, recognition, job security, status symbols, and opportunity for advancement are often emphasized, sometimes at the expense of other important motives of the worker.

Need for Support and Acceptance

One of the needs falling into this latter category is that for warm personal relationships with other people, including one's boss. Likewise, and particularly as relates to the boss, people want to feel that they can get support and help when needed, and that these will be offered in a spirit of concern and warmth, not in a condescending or punitive fashion.

Obviously, support and acceptance are quite different from recognition, however valuable the latter may be at times. Indeed it is easy to use recognition in a cold, impersonal way or as a form of manipulation, and thus to leave the desire for acceptance and support not only unfulfilled but even more frustrated than before.

Table 7-1   General Modes of Self Defense

Method	Meaning	Examples
By attack	Frontal assault on an impediment—or a scapegoat; may also be verbal attack	Physical aggression—or belittling one's rival
By withdrawal	Outright retreat—or retreat to realm of imagination	Complete giving up—or living in the realm of fantasy
By autistic restructuring	Emotional making over of oneself or others, typically making oneself superior or others inferior	"I am a member of the intelligensia," or "Everybody is out for himself to get as much as he can for as little as he can put out"

Need to Be Valued for What One Is Rather than for What One Does

A point that is subtle and difficult to explain but still of the greatest importance is the effect on worker motivation of a feeling that management's only interest in workers is "what it can get out of them." If this is how workers feel, they come to regard themselves as, in the eyes of management, only cogs in a machine, numbers on a payroll, or bodies occupying positions in a production-centered enterprise. They may also feel that management considers them just a necessary evil.

It is at this juncture that the *commodity conception of labor* has done irreparable damage. This theory holds that management has only one interest in the worker, namely to make a profit on his services; when a worker is no longer profitable to management, he should be unceremoniously dismissed (or "ceremoniously," if in this way one can mislead the remaining workers into believing that there is a genuine interest in them).

Strangely enough, the commodity view does not demand or even suggest arbitrary or harsh action toward workers unless this is in the long run the most profitable way to deal with them. On the contrary, it is probably wise to be "nice" to them. But one is nice not out of regard for them, but because it is more profitable. This kind of management is *manipulation*, and no amount of wages or fringe benefits will overcome the feelings that are likely to result.

What every person wants, of course, is to feel that he or she is held in esteem by the boss and the other associates not only for what he can do and does, but also for *what he is*. One is quite willing to be a means to an end for a fine, respectable management; what is resented is being *nothing more than a means to an end*.

Need to Be Needed

We have certainly already implied, if we have not specifically said, that every human being has a need to be needed, a need to feel that he or she makes a difference to at least one other person. Let us examine this need a bit more closely.

It is apparent that it is a most significant need. One can see it in children, who resent being mere playthings for adults and are often challenged by opportunities to make a contribution to the family or other group. Frustration of the motive can be seen in the middle-aged woman whose children are grown and no longer need her protection and care and whose life becomes difficult, unsatisfying, and at times neurotic. It is hard to live a rewarding life if one lives it solely for himself.

In management we have failed to make use of this motive as fully as we might. For one thing, in the minds of many supervisors it gets mixed up with a need for recognition. As we pointed out earlier, there can be no doubt that recognition is an important need, but it is not the same as being needed. One can be needed, know it, and be satisfied with his contribution, and yet never be recognized as such for it. (The mother of young, and sometimes older, children is frequently a case in point.) Likewise, one may get recognition when he feels that he has not made any real contribution, and this is not truly satisfying. Thus our conclusion that we have badly overstressed recognition and badly understressed the need to be needed.

In our overconcern with narrow self-interest and helping people to *get* instead of to *give*, we have been blind to some mistakes along this line. There is perhaps no better example than the thoughtless way in which we have dealt with the retirement of the long-service employee. All of us are familiar with the circumstances. During his working days we encourage him to identify more and more closely with the company and his job. Indeed if he follows this advice sometimes given, his job will virtually become his life. But what happens at retirement? We literally "pull the rug out from under him." One day he is a person who counts, whose instructions are followed, and for whose inner thoughts his associates try to read between the lines. The next day we turn him out to pasture with, so far as our planning is concerned, no way for him to avoid becoming a mere drone with no way to make significant contributions.

In another connection, we have all observed the effect on a member of an organization when no challenges or opportunities are put before him. In this situation his interest in the organization is usually rather low. But a challenge comes along in the form of a task for him or the group, and he finds his interest mounting as he responds to the challenge.

Of course we must not leave the impression that managers and supervisors never use or recognize this motive. Some workers at all levels do find in their jobs an opportunity to make what appears to them a real contribution. Indeed almost every plant, store, or office is blessed with a least a few such workers. They are the ones who do their best, especially when things go wrong; they act for the boss in his absence and perform as they think he would wish or in the pursuit of their common objectives. Instead of asking themselves constantly, "What is there in it for me?" they are likely to be seeking ways of getting the job done, sometimes without notice or publicity for themselves and even on occasion at their own personal risk. These are the people of whom it may properly be said that they are "the salt of the earth." Most organizations could be radically transformed in productivity if every worker and manager (or even a majority) could suddenly be brought to feel that in the work he or she had real and significant ways to satisfy this basic human need.

Perhaps every supervisor, as well as every teacher, parent, or minister, needs constantly to ask two questions: How good am I at finding opportunities for my associates to satisfy the need to be needed? and How good am I at motivating them to take advantage of these new opportunities when they come along?[8]

INDIVIDUAL AS A PART OF HIS CULTURE

One of the important limitations of the concept of human nature, discussed earlier in this chapter, is that it tends to obscure the unique contributions of the culture in which the individual grows up and in which he usually continues to function. The truth is, however, that a Japanese is different (from an American, for example) because he is Japanese, and to deal with him effectively requires more than a little knowledge of Japanese history and culture. We do not have the space in this book nor the necessary knowledge to explain in any detail as relates to most Japanese, but some words about American workers and their culture would obviously be in order. (This is a subject discussed at other places in this book, in particular in Chapters 1 and 22.)

One characteristic of today's American worker is his *expanded knowledge* of what is going on about him. Public education, TV, the automobile, and the jet plane have assured that the days of genuine ignorance are about gone.

And then there is the *growth in ego-strength*, that is, the willingness to "stand up for" what he or she thinks is right (and often particularly for his rights and those of his groups). Increasing use by workers of the grievance procedure is an example. Countless suits alleging medical malpractice or violation of civil rights are another.

Finally, there is the *growth in suspicion and disillusionment* on the part of Americans generally. Much of this increase in negative feelings has centered on politicians; not a little has been directed toward business firms; and supervisors and the other managers have received their share. Whether these feelings are justifiable is not our point. If they are present they must be taken into account, and this the wise supervisor will do.

Again, however, we emphasize our main point: attempts to understand workers without understanding their cultural background and the social order from which they come will usually swing very wide of the mark.[9]

THE ROLE OF EMPATHY

Up to this point in this chapter the emphasis has been on the significance of the understandings of supervisors. We have said that they should know about the individual, his or her needs and self-esteem; about the work group of which the worker is a part; and about the cultural background that he or she brings to the job. In the last section of the chapter we shall be concerned with a closely related concept, namely *empathy*.

Nature of Empathy

Especially noteworthy in this connection is the distinction between empathy and sympathy. In both, the supervisor attempts to put himself in the other person's place and to see the world through his or her eyes. In the case of *sympathy*, however, he adopts as his own feelings the feelings of the subordinate, for example, and comes to feel as the worker does. On the other hand, in the case of *empathy*, the supervisor understands how the subordinate feels and the reason but at the same time he or she does not allow feelings or judgment to be determined by those of the subordinate.[10]

There are many instances of the wise use of empathy in human situations. The lawyer whose client has been charged with a felony may fully understand the feelings of the latter, but he or she does not allow these feelings to interfere with his or her own good judgment and the essentials of the client's case. Likewise, the dentist may appreciate the pain caused the patient and may regret the necessity for it, but he does not allow the patient's immediate desires to overpower his responsibilities as a professional. In the same way supervisors, called upon to make decisions with which their subordinates will not agree, may fully understand the regret, unhappiness, and even spirit of rebellion their actions may induce; but while taking these into account, they do not permit them to prevent them from taking the action warranted by the situation.

It would be hard to overestimate the importance of skill in empathy on the part of the supervisor. On innumerable occasions one can behave more wisely if he or she does so with understanding of the feelings and conclusions of the worker, even though called upon to go directly contrary to them. Indeed, in many instances supervisors may be able to act ever so much more wisely if they have this understanding than if they do not.

Obviously, real skill in empathy is not a part of the native equipment of any of us. The ability to empathize well, especially with people of a background different from one's own, results from a large measure of sincere, dedicated effort (or else on occasion from sheer luck, on which the supervisor cannot afford to depend). Some managers have learned to empathize quite well, while others do it very poorly. There are few, if any, of us who could not improve decidedly.

Development of Empathy

Several methods for increasing one's ability to empathize are available. One is a knowledge acquired from some familiarity with the theories and findings of clinical psychology and psychiatry. While it is too much to expect the supervisor to become an expert in these fields, reading, study, and experience are helpful.

Another is acquaintance with significant works of literature and art. Outstanding novelists and dramatists, for example, have frequently developed a degree of insight into human feelings and motives difficult to find in a more formal work on psychiatry, motivation, or supervision. The usual writer of the latter background tries to describe how people feel or "what makes them tick," but the literary artist is often able to show what the situation really is and thus to enable the reader to live through the events with the person of the story or drama. Likewise the artist can, and sometimes does, speak clearly and dramatically of human emotions and aspirations.

It is obvious that the same remarks can be applied, even if in a different way, to treatises in the behavioral sciences and business management. These may contain insights into human behavior hard to match in the experience of a single individual. And the address, the lecture, the conference, or the film may also achieve these results to a varying but decided degree.

Another observation is the great value of personal experience along this line. Ultimately there is no substitute for it, for no matter how skillful the writer, the speaker, or the film director, some things must be experienced to be felt and really understood. Thus the supervisor's contacts with family, neighbors, fellow church or club members, and others may be invaluable along this line.

There are two great difficulties, however, in depending on experience as the means of improving ability to empathize. One is that experiences tend to be limited in scope or breadth, and the other is that they tend to be treated in an uncritical, nonevaluative, or prejudiced manner. Thus men tend to associate mostly with men, and principally men of about their own age, background, and interest—and the same kinds of remarks can be made for women and children, too. This means not only that we are limited in the kinds of contacts we have, but also that we usually interpret them in terms of our own categories, prejudices, and stereotypes. Thus, we often have opportunities to learn—and we often fail to learn.

Perhaps an illustration would be in order. In the early 1960s one of the authors had worked rather closely with a group of supervisors, all white men, who had some very definite ideas about the blacks who were members of their work crews. Two conclusions were especially prominent in this group of foremen. One was that blacks did not have the ability to move to jobs substantially higher than they were then doing, and the other was that they were content with their status, wages, living conditions, and the like. The foremen were apparently unanimous in believing that if the company ever had any "equal-employment" problems with these blacks, it would be because some outsiders "came in and stirred them up."

The author had opportunities to become acquainted with many of these black workers and found the foremen basically wrong on both counts. While it is true that many of them were, on account of background, limited in ability, education, and motivation and probably could not satisfactorily perform the duties of jobs much more demanding than their present ones, there were notable exceptions. At least one or two were college graduates, and a number had some years of education beyond high school. A few were ex-officers of World War II or the Korean crisis. Several had responsible positions in the affairs of their communities, and a number had avocations or moonlighting activities considerably above the level of the work they did in the plant. The foremen might have been correct about the ability of many of the blacks, but they were completely in error about the ability of some of them.

The foremen were even more incorrect about the basic attitudes of their black workers. Far from being content with their current assignments, they felt that they were being dealt with unfairly so far as promotional opportunities went. And it is striking how many of them who recognized that they personally were not really capable of doing more demanding jobs were resentful that the company had not promoted their fellows who were known to be capable. An outsider certainly might be required to bring these people to the place where they would make their feelings known openly, but no outsider could create these feelings; they were already present in all, or virtually all, members of the group.

The matter went at least one step further: The foremen had little or no real appreciation of what it was like to be a black in this particular work and community setting, and because of their attitudes no substantial number of them were capable of such understanding and empathy. It is easy to imagine how perplexed they were, therefore, when some "trivial incident" led to an unfavorable reaction far beyond anything they had anticipated.

Instances of this sort can be multiplied many times. How many male supervisors, for example, really empathize with their women subordinates or bosses? Again, experience in the actual work situation reveals the decidedly poor state of the insight and understanding that is frequently involved.

In general, though perhaps to a smaller extent, the same remarks can be made about union members and especially local union leaders. Many managers have a limited conception of what it is really like to be the president of a local union, or about the attitudes, values, and goals of the union representative. The result is that many of the latter's actions are viewed as self-serving, emotional, and even senseless. (Granted that some may be, it must be recognized that many are not.)

Perhaps the most unfortunate situation of all is that of the supervisor who fails or is unable to empathize with subordinates even when they are persons essentially like himself—and who is completely unaware of his limitations along this line. He usually believes that he understands them fully and that those who do not share his opinions are at fault here. This may turn out to be a situation filled with tragedy for all concerned.

It must be admitted that a good portion of what we have just been discussing is the inevitable result of being human and working with human beings. No one ever becomes truly expert at empathy no matter how long or diligently he works at the task. However, some people are much better at these activities than others are, and a few are outstanding. The latter may not make eminently successful leaders, for empathy alone is far from enough, but it is the foundation for much effective work with others. To improve in this ability should be the continuing goal of every supervisor.

One other conclusion of significance before we leave this subject: what we have been saying is *not* that we should empathize more fully so as to be able the better to please the subordinate and thus to make him happier. We have already said enough earlier in this book to make it clear that we do not endorse any such point of view. Rather, the point is that the supervisor should empathize (but not sympathize) so that he can know as much as possible about the facts of the situation (and feelings are facts, too) and handle them in the wisest, most efficient, and most ethical manner. Empathy, then, is a means to the end of effective motivation toward worthwhile goals and effective cooperation with others in the attainment of these goals.

THE SUPERVISOR AND WISDOM AND EMPATHY

It is hard to emphasize sufficiently how far we Americans have gone in idealizing knowledge and expertness and how little we have stressed what in this chapter was called *wisdom* and empathy. There is, of course, nothing bad about knowledge, wisely used, but that is just the point. Unless the knowledge is usable realistically and in the social interest it is not wisdom, and this we have not said recently as often as we should. Rather, the stress has been on, What's in the knowledge for *me*?

Unfortunately there is no easy way to acquire wisdom and empathy. They require some concerns bigger than merely one's own selfish interests, and hard work in the form of study, examination, and contemplation. And they require time and experience that come from living with and understanding unusual situations and people quite unlike oneself. Reading and listening to others can help, but what is presented must be reviewed critically and only those parts accepted that fit with what one has learned about life.

There is no easy way to become wise and empathic, but there is no substitute for trying to do so. The supervisor has no more challenging task.[11]

QUESTIONS

1 What is the difference between knowledge and wisdom? Can you put this distinction in words other than those used in the book?

2 In what way can we put too much stress on knowledge? What are some illustrations?

3 Is it true that all people are alike and all people are different? Explain.

4 Are people what they are as a result of heredity or as a result of environment? Which is more important, heredity or environment? Why do so many people, including the authors of this book, believe that the question just asked is a meaningless one?

5 What is the evidence that everyone has unconscious motives? Are unconscious motives usually more powerful than conscious ones? What is your evidence? Why is it often easier for another person to know me and my motives than it is for me to know *me*?

6 How important, so far as understanding a person is concerned, are (a) his self, (b) his self-esteem, (c) his identifications, and (d) his efforts at self-defense?

7 Why do the authors say that the work situation affords many workers little or no opportunity to satisfy the need to be needed? Why is it reasonable to believe that some part of this situation is due to limitations of the workers themselves?

8 Distinguish between *empathy* and *sympathy* and demonstrate the importance of empathy to the supervisor.

NOTES

1 Herbert E. Meyer, "Personnel Directors Are New Corporate Heroes," *Fortune*, vol. 93, no. 2, pp. 84–88, February 1976.

It is the hope of top management that professional personnel people will be able to impart a degree of wisdom that might otherwise be lacking.

2 Aaron Q. Sartain et al., *Psychology: Understanding Human Behavior*, 4th ed. (New York: McGraw-Hill, 1973), Chap. 3.

3 Ibid., Chap. 14.

4 Arnold Tannenbaum, "Rank, Clout, and Worker Satisfaction: Pecking Order—Capitalist and Communist Style," *Psychology Today*, vol. 9, no. 4, pp. 41–43, September 1975.

Though there are differences in job status between Capitalist and Communist countries, there are many similarities.

5 Maria X. Malikiosi and Richard M. Ryckman, "Occupational Stereotyping in American and Greek Cultures," *Journal of Social Psychology*, vol. 99, first half, pp. 13–20, June 1976. Even in similar cultures there are some differences in job status.

6 Greg R. Oldham, "Job Characteristics and Internal Motivation: The Moderating Effect of Interpersonal and Individual Variables," *Human Relations*, vol. 29, no. 6, pp. 559–569, 1976.

We are often in error if we depend entirely on what a person tells us his motives are. He may deliberately mislead us; more frequently he does not fully understand himself.

7   Sartain et al., op. cit., esp. pp. 64–81.

  The author had more space in another book and hence was able to develop more fully the nature and importance of the *self*, including self-defense.

8   Some research evidence that seems to support the findings of this part of the chapter may be found in Rensis Likert, *New Patterns of Management* (New York: McGraw-Hill, 1961) and *The Human Organization* (also McGraw-Hill, 1967). This evidence is reviewed briefly in Chapter 20 below.

9   The supervisor certainly needs to understand something of the feeling modern work engenders. See, for example, Louis E. Davis and Albert Chearns, (eds.), *The Quality of Working Life*, vol. 1 (New York: Free Press, 1975). These feelings along with increased ego-strength may be an integral part of the Civil Rights Movement, discussed in Chapter 18 below. For an historical view of a part of this movement see Dorothy Jongewald and Dru Scott, *Affirmation Action for Women* (Reading, Mass.: Addison-Wesley, 1974).

10 See Carl Rogers, *Client-Centered Therapy* (Boston: Houghton Mifflin, 1951), and by the same author, "Implications of Recent Advances in Prediction and Control of Behavior," *Teachers College Record*, pp. 312–322, February 1956.

11 A book that covers much of the material in this and the preceding chapter is Douglas McGregor, *The Professional Manager* (New York: McGraw-Hill, 1967).

CASES

For the cases of this chapter we have chosen two that have the same problem: Just what does the labor agreement actually provide on a point apparently not anticipated when it was negotiated? When there is disagreement on this, how does one resolve it?

  The Ruston Rogers incident involves a conflict between two seemingly desirable provisions, namely, that overtime should be equitably divided among the workers and that in many circumstances a lead person should be present when skilled work is being done. The other case represents a change in job duties that Management may or may not have had the right to make.

  Each case will call for thoughtful analysis, and even knowledgeable people may certainly disagree as to the proper outcome.

CASE 7-1

The events of this case took place in the Midwestern plant of the Company. This plant has a independent Union that is strong and enjoys the support of nearly all eligible workers.

  The plant employs both leadmen and machinists. As is often true, the leadmen are hourly rated and not considered members of Management. A partial description of their job in this plant is as follows: "They give immediate direction as to work, work methods, operations, and practices; they see that personnel and machines are properly instructed and utilized and instruct workers in current or new techniques. They may also perform the same kind of work as the workers."

  The contract between the Company and the Union also provides that overtime will, so far as possible, be distributed equally among the people in the work force.

  Ruston Rogers is a leadman in this plant. For several weeks his crew or parts of it (for he "leads" other crafts as well as machinists) has been getting a great deal of overtime. Sometimes all eight of his crew are kept over, including his four machinists, and sometimes only four or five people are selected for overtime. Indeed on one occasion only two workers were kept over. It is Company practice that a worker is not to work even on overtime without the direction of a leadman, and this means that when any of his workers are kept over, Rogers works overtime too. During overtime as during the regular shift, a great deal of his time is spent in doing the work of a machinist. This is especially true of overtime work when he has a reduced crew.

The grievance came out of this situation. Al Whaley is the machinist with least seniority in Rogers' crew, and he is the one who filed the grievance. It asserts that the Company has violated the contract in two important respects. In the first place, Rogers has spent most of his time in production work and not in "leading," this especially on overtime. His job, the grievance contends, should be combined with that of one or two more leadmen, so that the leadman would spend more than 50 percent of his time in "doing leadman's work." Any leadman not meeting this test should be "busted back" to his former classification.

In the second place, it alleges that overtime has been unfairly apportioned to Rogers, for he works every time even one of his crew does, and hence he gets much more overtime than any one of them. Furthermore, machinists in general and Whaley in particular are greatly penalized by this situation, since every time Rogers works overtime he does machinist's work and hence displaces a machinist. The grievance asks for back pay for all the time Whaley has lost as a result of the alleged improper assignment of Rogers.

What does the Company do with this grievance?

CASE 7-2

On February 20, 1976, the Company posted the following notice: "In the future the utility mechanic will hook up caustic cars, assist operators in steaming out lines and priming the pump at the Water Treatment Plant. . . . The operator will fill the tank and stop pump and steam out lines. At this point the mechanic will be called back to disconnect caustic car. The operator is to be present during the mechanic's work for safety reasons."

Prior to this date the unloading of caustic from tank cars was assigned to two mechanics, both of whom were present during the two hours that were typically needed to unload a car. This practice had been in effect for a number of years. It is agreed that on account of its viscosity caustic is difficult to unload when the temperature drops below 50° F.

The labor agreement contains the following provision: "When major changes are made in the mills which create new jobs or change the duties of existing jobs substantially, Management representatives will meet with representatives of the Union and receive from them suggestions as to size of crews and appropriate rates of pay."

The Union protested the above notice and the arrangement it put into affect and requested a return to the previous practice. It also asked for a to-be-determined amount of back pay, including any likely overtime, of which mechanics had been improperly deprived.

The Union contends that (1) the new arrangement is at least in certain circumstances highly unsafe because the operator has other duties and cannot constantly monitor the unloading and also because many operators simply do not know how to assist the mechanic in emergency situations; and (2) the Company has no right to change a long-standing, significant past practice without first negotiating the change with the Union or as a minimum notifying the Union in advance of posting such a notice, the notification to include the reasons for the change.

The Company contends that in the protested action (1) the changes in dispute are minor ones and not "major changes" as the term is used above; (2) the Company in no way discriminated against employees because of Union membership or activities, nor did it contravene any bargaining rights of the Union; (3) the prior method of unloading caustic was unnecessarily wasteful; (4) the Company has the right and the obligation to eliminate wasteful procedures; (5) the Company has agreed to furnish the mechanic and the operator with extra help when emergencies require; and (6) contrary to Union contentions and especially with the provision of emergency help, the new arrangement is in no way unsafe or dangerous to anyone.

This case raises the question of the place of past practice when such practice has not been formally negotiated and put in the Contract but has persisted for years in unchallenged form. Of course, it also raises some other issues.

Chapter 8

Useful Leadership Styles and Practices

Sooner or later in a book of this sort we get to the subject of how to supervise. It is always a good subject to discuss because that is what many people have in mind when they start reading the book. On the other hand, it is also a troublesome subject since there is no *one* *way* to supervise (nor are there three or four or even a half-dozen "sure-fire" ways).[1] In a very real sense this whole book is about how to supervise, the two chapters immediately preceding this one, for example, being as squarely on the subject as this one can be. And that is also true of most if not all the other chapters.

OVEREMPHASIS ON TECHNIQUES

A point that must not be overlooked or forgotten, especially in this chapter, is that techniques of supervision, if used without understanding and proper grounding in sound attitudes and values, may easily do a great deal more harm than good, no matter how effective they may appear to be in themselves. The really significant conclusion here is that techniques of supervision, no matter how appropriate to the situation otherwise, are likely to be seen as manipulation if they are not based solidly on intellectual, emotional, and ethical grounds. Furthermore, the chances are that if they are not so based, there will be manipulation, no matter what the user may believe or intend.[2]

In addition to the disappointments that result from expecting too much from the use of techniques, they have at least two other limitations. In the first place, however useful any method or technique may be as a general rule, it cannot be successfully applied under all circumstances. In other words, the supervisor is often faced with a unique set of facts and is required by them to adopt a solution for that situation, no matter what the usually accepted procedures may be. Techniques and methods are at best *merely good generalizations* useful in most situations, and *not universals* admitting of no exceptions.

The second limitation is inherent in the goals of this chapter. Here we are concerned with general methods and techniques, those likely to be useful under many conditions. Methods for dealing with problems that arise in particular areas of supervision will be discussed later in this book in the chapters concerned with those areas. Thus dealing with a disciplinary infraction is covered in Chapter 14, whereas handling a union grievance is one of the topics in Chapter 15.

BASIC WAYS OF MOTIVATING WORKERS

An examination of the subject will reveal that there are three basic ways of motivating persons in the work situation—and in many other situations as well. Though they may overlap at times and two or even all three may operate in any particular set of circumstances, they are distinct approaches to motivation, and their nature, along with their strengths and limitations, needs to be thoroughly understood by every manager. One of these is the use of *force,* that is, getting people to work because of the fear of some kind of punishment (we sometimes refer to it as "the stick"); another is the use of *enticement,* that is, getting people to "put out" because of some extrinsic or external reward (we sometimes call it "the carrot"); and finally, there is the endeavor to find and employ motivation that is *intrinsically* motivating, that is, rewarding in itself. Pride in one's skill as a machinist is an example; devotion to one's employer, one's family, or to one's country is another.

Table 8-1 summarizes the ways in which employees (and bosses) can be motivated.

Force as a Means of Motivating People

As just pointed out, when we speak of force in this connection we refer to the imposition on the worker of sanctions, penalties, punishment, or other unpleasant consequences.

Widespread Use of Force   Unquestionably force has been widely used historically. This is true not only in relation to workers but also to countless other groups. Slavery is, of course, a case in point but even free workers did not escape it. Thus until recently

Table 8-1   Ways of Motivating Employees

Method	Meaning	Examples
Force	Applying sanctions	Discharge, reprimand—or in-between
Enticement	Promising of (extrinsic) rewards	Dollars, recognition, status, etc.
Manipulation*	Using rewards cleverly and solely in one's own interest	Pretending a concern when one really does not have one
Intrinsic motivation	The activity or the goals of the activity are their own rewards	Pride in one's skill; enjoyment of the work; or enjoyment of the team's victory

*The term is also used at times in a *neutral* sense. Thus in the interest of accomplishment of the task, I may simply use the assets available to me without any ulterior motive. I have thus *manipulated* those assets, including any people who might be involved.

physical violence was not widely condemned, especially in dealing with the blue-collar worker, and there were many instances where the supervisor, if not encouraged to employ it, was certainly not discouraged from doing so. Under these circumstances, workers sometimes worked at least in part for fear of actual or physical pain that the supervisor might visit upon them. Discharge was also widely used.

Two additional comments before we leave this point: The use of threats and force was by no means restricted to the work situation. It was also in evidence in the military, in the schoolroom, and in the still largely patriarchal family. Children were to be seen, not heard, and the soldier had few duties other than to obey his superiors. Again, all this has changed, principally as a result of a changed social climate or public opinion.

In the second place, though we have spoken about both force and the threat, it must be remembered that the latter without a real fear of the former is all but meaningless. The threat, in other words, must occasionally be backed up by the use of force or else, no matter how common, it no longer menaces the worker. The real point here, then, is not the use of the threat; it is the use of force.

Place of Force in Motivating Subordinates   While we once used force too extensively and came to depend on it for more than was wise, there always has been and apparently always will be a proper place for this sort of motivation. This subject is discussed in some detail in the first part of Chapter 14; here we shall simply say that regardless of his or her careful study and best efforts, from time to time the supervisor will be called upon to impose disciplinary sanctions, mild at times but on occasions as severe as discharge, and he must make every effort to do this wisely and unemotionally when the occasion warrants.[3]

Enticement as a Motivator

It will be recalled that as the motivation views of Douglas McGregor were examined in Chapter 5 a distinction was made between two kinds of motivators. The first was the use of an *external* or *extrinsic* reward (or penalty), that is, something the manager, the teacher, or the coach adds to the situation as a reward. The other is the use of an *internal* or *intrinsic* reward, something that is essentially and unavoidably a part of the activity itself. Money in the form of wages, commissions, bribes, and the like, is an example of the former, whereas the exhilaration that comes to some from actually playing the game or accomplishing a task is an example of the latter.

It must be admitted that this distinction, like many other useful ones, is not always clear-cut; that is, some motivators may be difficult to classify or, perhaps even more likely, both sorts may be mixed up in the same situation. For instance, a person may work very hard in order to be promoted, and his desire to be promoted may come from a wish for more money and status. At the same time it could be that he feels he would actually enjoy much more the work of the job just ahead of his. Thus the intrinsic and the extrinsic sometimes are mixed together in the same situation.

However, the distinction is useful. Admitting that force is still a motivator at times, today a person usually participates in an activity either because he enjoys the activity and the things inherently associated with it or because he wants something people have promised him if he will do it. In this section of this chapter we shall examine external motivators and in the following section, intrinsic motivators. In discussing external motivation we shall frequently use the term *enticement,* for it describes accurately what the external reward is supposed to do, to entice the worker to work when otherwise he would not.

Widespread Use of Enticement

There is little question that many supervisors of today depend on external motivators, or enticement, in the majority of work situations. After all, they believe, very few people take a job or continue to perform it because they like the job or feel a sense of duty or an obligation to perform it well. They are thought to do it for what they can get out of it, and when the external reward stops, so do their efforts.

This view of worker motivation is considerably reinforced by a popular belief about the nature of work. According to many people, work is unpleasant and people do it only as they have to. That there may be exceptions regarding both work and workers would be admitted by most, but many have no doubt that this is true of most work and of most of the workers most of the time. This is one of the reasons for management's deep concern about wage and salary administration as well as fringe benefits. After all, if people work for what they get out of a job, compensation, both directly and in the form of benefits, is of vital importance.

Another observation that is in order is that as the use of force and threat has markedly declined, much greater emphasis has been placed on enticement. In the days when supervisors could threaten layoff, demotion, or discharge and then effectively carry out the penalty, keeping the wage plan current and competitive was not so important. It could not be entirely neglected, of course, but punishment and the threat of punishment could be relied on to a considerable degree, especially if jobs were not very plentiful.

When the use of punishment was severely restricted, however, managers who believed that work was not interesting and that workers did not really care about it or the organization turned to enticement as an alternative. This has been the prevailing note in employer-employee relationships since World War II.

Enticement and Manipulation   There was obviously a limit to how far an employer could go or was willing to go in providing wages and fringe benefits. Furthermore while various forms of recognition might be effective, they too had limitations in what they could accomplish. But an additional sort of enticement was close at hand in every work situation, and furthermore it cost little or nothing to use. It was found in the way in which a supervisor dealt with his people. After all, if he or she was very nice to a person, the latter might work hard even if he cared little for the work. Furthermore, if a boss could bring a work crew to believe that he and other managers were sincerely their friends, this ought to pay some dividends. Hence, what we might call the "charm school of supervision" began to develop.

The idea, in other words, was for the supervisors to make themselves as acceptable as possible to their employees. Relatively little was said about the supervisors' manner of dress and general appearance, but not infrequently they were given coaching to improve their voice and delivery in speech making. What was concentrated on was their behavior (not basically their attitudes and values), the effect of that behavior, and ways of changing it so it would influence people all the more in the direction of more output.

Directions given supervisors were not very profound or original, but they were often repeated: reprimand in private but praise in public; give the worker full credit (and maybe more) for his idea; display great interest in subordinates (little being said about whether or not the supervisor really *had* such interest); "plant" suggestions, wait for them to be given back by subordinates, and then treat them as the subordinates' own original ideas; give directions in such a way as to bring workers to feel they are really directing themselves; and conduct a meeting with a work group in such a fashion as to achieve a predetermined conclusion, but so as to make the group feel they worked it out. Needless to say, other such directions could be added to the list.

This point of view became popular especially after World War II and was practiced quite extensively, sometimes deliberately and sometimes without conscious planning. It was often accepted as part of the theory, discussed in Chapter 1, that the foreman is the key person in influencing workers.

What have been the effects of this theory? Certainly the positive results have been far from outstanding, in spite of the fact that many managers have extensively practiced popular psychology and human relations for a number of years. No doubt many factors were influential here, but one that cannot be overlooked is a feeling on the part of many workers that management is not sincere in its efforts and its professions, that is, that it often pretends an interest in them which it does not feel. In a word, many employees of today feel that they are being treated like machines and tools and hence simply a means of production, and at the same time management is trying to manipulate them in such fashion as to secure *more* for *less.*

There is no doubt about it: Employees are frequently in error when they so conclude about their bosses; for managers, like the rest of us, are usually interested in the well-being of other people, including their employees. At the same time, however, it must be confessed that some of the suspicions of workers are well founded. Managers have many times pretended what they did not really feel and have done this in order to secure goals which they might otherwise not be able to get, or if they did, at a much higher price. On some occasions, they have been guilty of manipulation of workers. On many others, workers have judged them to be guilty when they were not. As previously mentioned, however, in matters of this sort, the feelings of workers are critical. When they feel management has been insincere, then so far as they are concerned that is true.

The moral of the story is easy to find: It is essential to effective employer-employee (and supervisor-subordinate) relations that the worker accept the sincerity of management and believe that management has respect for his dignity, intelligence, and worth. When the supervisor pretends an interest that he or she does not feel or management shares the corporate income with workers solely in order to get more and more for proportionately less, the motivation of workers is usually decreased, and suspiciousness arises and spreads. In the light of all this, one can understand, whether in agreement or not, why many labor leaders are suspicious of management's "human relations" approach.[4]

The Role of Enticement in Employee Motivation   It would be easy, in view of the discussion just concluded, to conclude that all uses of enticement as a way of motivating workers are to be avoided. Such, however, is not the case.

One important consideration is the *necessity,* so far as most people are concerned, of external or extrinsic rewards for working. Wages and salaries are vital to us, status symbols may be extremely desirable, and if our present employer does not provide them, no matter how well we like him or our job, we are likely to seek employment elsewhere. Extrinsic rewards, then, are not only useful and important; they are necessary.

So-called "fringe" benefits have become a large part of the enticement package. It is easy to underestimate both the cost and the variety of such benefits.

Furthermore, the offer of additional income or a new title often calls forth additional effort. This is frequently seen in a sales organization, where opportunities for higher earnings have many times spurred salesmen to efforts they would not have considered otherwise. Besides, there are workers to whom no other appeal seems to have any real attraction. Try as the supervisor may, he or she cannot really interest some workers in anything except the Friday paycheck. One suspects that such employees are seldom outstanding in their contributions to the work effort; but there are such people, and they must be motivated as effectively as practicable.

Table 8-2   Fringe Benefits Often Available to Some Employees*

Pensions	Sick leave	Dental insurance
Bonuses	Leave for jury duty	Automobile insurance
Profit-sharing	Funeral leave	Credit union
Stock purchase	Leave for union	Recreation facilities
ESOP (transfer	business	Company clubs
of stock)	Personal leave	Company teams
Stock options	Tuition-refund	Child care
Savings plans	Hospitalization	Housing
Holidays	Major medical	Discounts on
Vacations	Legal insurance ·	company products

*This list is necessarily incomplete. Note that it does not include any benefits required by law such as Social Security, unemployment compensation, and workmen's compensation.

It is obvious also that we cannot put ourselves in a position where we oppose the supervisor's efforts to treat people decently and with consideration. Unquestionably, as a general rule people work more diligently and effectively for a supervisor whom they like and admire than for one whom they despise. To be genuinely concerned about the welfare of one's subordinates accords not only with our best moral teachings but also with our best judgment of what is effective in influencing people.

More will be said on this matter later in this book. Perhaps this is the best conclusion to draw now: Wisely used, enticement can be effective in motivating subordinates. Indeed without a *good* program of extrinsic rewards it is not likely that a work organization will have and sustain an outstanding or even a satisfactory record of efficiency. Likewise, treating people with respect and genuinely cooperating with them not only affords supervisors better feelings about their own jobs and their sense of integrity, but is usually rewarded by better efforts on the part of those with whom they work.

However, to be used effectively, enticement must be employed with insight and understanding. It is fine to see enticement as a way to contribute to the efficiency and hence to the profits of the firm. It is necessary at the same time to be vitally interested in the welfare and personal development of subordinates, and this interest must be such as to transcend their utility to the efficiency of the organization. One's subordinates may properly be seen as a means to achieving one's own goals, but it is never sufficient to use them *simply* as a means to these ends. To do so and to be found out is to court inefficiency and possible disaster.[5]

Intrinsic Factors in Motivation

As we have pointed out earlier, workers often work to secure something with which they can secure something else. They want money for what it will buy or status for the recognition and/or the power it brings. At other times, however, what they get from their work is not *good* for something but is its own reward. If my job is teaching and I *like to teach,* I am intrinsically motivated to do my job.

Obviously from time to time management can take advantage of these facts concerning motivation. For example, to the extent that it can place every worker in work he or she very much likes to do it has increased the odds of a productive work force. Furthermore, it can take all reasonable steps to increase such satisfaction and to build pride in accomplishment, with results which are usually good for all concerned.

There is, however, a limit to how far one can go along this way. After all there are jobs in every organization that no one "gets a kick out of doing"—and yet they have to be done. Furthermore, the position I would most enjoy may already be occupied by another person who has no intention of giving it up. Insofar as we can, of course, we should avoid "putting a round peg in a square hole," but there are serious limitations on putting every individual in his or her own unique and ideal place.

Identification and Intrinsic Motivation   It is apparent at once that the process of identification discussed in the chapter just concluded is of vital significance here. One can get people intrinsically motivated when work activities that are enjoyable are found for them. Another way to motivate intrinsically is to bring workers to *identify* with the firm or with the work that they are doing, whether or not they find pleasure in the work itself. Just as I may become greatly ego-involved in *my* team, so I may identify with *my* company or *my* department or *my* work. In a word I come to see it as valuable and worthwhile, am pleased when it goes well, and feel hurt at its shortcomings. Under these conditions it does not matter whether I like the work activity as such. What motivates me is doing something that really needs doing whether I get a kick out of the activity as such or not. Needless to say employees differ markedly with regard to the degree of their identification with their employer and their work. And employers differ equally in the amount of identification they have been able to secure from employees. But no one can deny that such identification, when secured, is likely to be an asset of great value.

There is no easy way, of course, to bring about this situation, but management really has no option except to try. The two chapters that precede this one are distinctly relevant to how to secure it, and later in this one there are some other suggestions on the subject.[6]

SKILL IN ON-THE-JOB LEADERSHIP

Another way to approach the problem of the supervisor's methods and techniques is to look at the suggestions that are often worthwhile in face-to-face, individual leadership situations. What can be said to the leader along this line?

General Supervision

In this connection one notes the effect of *general,* as opposed to close or *tight,* supervision. Research that will be presented in Chapter 20 shows what our experience has abundantly confirmed, namely, that supervisors of higher-producing groups typically supervise in a general fashion, with considerable discretion left to the subordinates, whereas the supervisors of lower-producing groups usually watch their people closely and put a great deal of pressure on them. There are exceptions to this generalization, of course, but they really are exceptional. As a general rule, general supervision and high output are found to be definitely correlated.

It should be noted in passing that what we are dealing with here is typically a difference in degree and not in kind. All supervisors supervise closely at times and generally at others, but the more effective ones usually use general supervision a great deal more.

Avoiding "Anxious" Supervision   Before we leave this phase of the subject it should be observed that nothing disturbs most workers more than "anxious" (and therefore, necessarily, close) supervision. Workers like to work for managers who have enough confidence in themselves and in them and their bosses to relax, at least to a reasonable degree. If a manager believes that things are going to turn out all right, he or she does not have to hover over associates, watching every move and fearing, if indeed not anticipating, mistakes and crises. When expectations are both high and realistic, one can supervise in a general—and relaxed—manner.

The same, or almost the same, conclusion can be made in another way: General, nonanxious supervision characteristically means less, not more, instruction in the details of a task. Indeed, perhaps the easiest way to oversupervise is to overinstruct in a situation that knowledgeable, competent workers understand quite well. Certainly the subordinate should understand the objectives of the task and be furnished any guide rules he or she does not have but will need in accomplishing these objectives. Instruction beyond this point may slow down the operation currently under way. It is quite likely to have poor long-run effects.

This sort of supervision also throws light on the notion of the span of control mentioned in Chapter 2. Much of what is believed, and has been said and written, on this subject would lead inevitably to too much and too close supervision. Indeed, one way to deal with the supervisor who has serious limitations along this line is to make his span of control so great that he cannot supervise his people as closely as he is disposed to. Admittedly this is a poorer solution than a change in attitudes and desired techniques, but it may be useful at times.[7]

In summary, then, we have said that most supervisors supervise too closely; that the proper amount of instruction and supervision will have to be different, depending on the circumstances, including the background and expectations of the workers; that the closeness of supervision will have to vary with the individuals involved; and that there is no substitute for good judgment in determining the degree of pressure, the extent of general supervision, and the amount of instruction that should be furnished to either a work group or an individual member of the group.

Proper Delegation

A point closely related to the one we have been discussing is that of delegation of duties to the subordinate. General supervision obviously demands generous delegation, whether or not this is formally discussed or even recognized, while close supervision means limited delegation. The rule here is the same as that for general supervision: Delegation should be given the benefit of the doubt.

It is certainly not difficult to make a case for this position. After all, if my boss tells me in detail what to do, watches me while I am doing it, and checks constantly on how I am doing it, this is not likely to lead to my becoming strongly ego-involved in what I am assigned to do. If he or she "calls every shot," the success or failure is more his than it is mine, and I am likely to do no more than I am instructed to do. Furthermore, as we have previously said, such action on his part is likely to strike me as a lack of confidence in me. The result is not only to impair my efficiency with regard to the task in question, but to stifle self-development and create feelings of indifference if not antagonism on my part. Millions of American workers find themselves in this situation every day they work.

Nature of Delegation   It might be well at this point to call attention to a widespread misunderstanding relative to the nature of delegation. Quite frequently it has been treated as essentially a technique or method of leadership of subordinates. It is more proper to think of wise delegation as essentially a set of beliefs and attitudes and only incidentally as a method. After all, if I have confidence in my people, their capability, and their devotion to duty, I not only will delegate to them but could hardly bring myself to adopt any system of leadership that did not provide for considerable sharing. On the other hand, if I delegate without such feelings, my actions will doubtless betray me, and the result may be loss instead of gain. Proper delegation, then, comes from the heart as well as from the head. Even if supervisors "delegate" and then go to their offices and sit there biting their nails with anxiety or a deep desire to "get their hands on the work," true, effective delegation has not occurred. This situation may be better than no delegation, but it is often worse.

One of the real difficulties of today is how little delegation is possible in many work assignments. Mass production has been responsible for some of this. Certain management philosophies have also contributed, as have the attitudes of many managers. The result is that real delegation is difficult and in many situations all but impossible. General supervision can be afforded only to a degree. In cases where delegation is limited and even general supervision can be provided only to a restricted extent, the remaining suggestions of this chapter become all the more significant.

Helping Workers to Become Informed

One way to be of real assistance to the worker doing routine, repetitive, low-status work (as well as to most other workers) is to help him or her become informed about the things that concern him or her. The matters that are significant here are as varied as the different individuals and their backgrounds and status, but there are many things of interest to all, or virtually all, members of a work group. These may involve everything from the long-range plans of the company to the details of the latest company golf contest or picnic.

It must not be thought for a moment that supervisors are the only source of information about these developments. As a matter of fact, they may be less effective here than is ordinarily believed, for workers have many sources of information. Nevertheless, supervisors should do whatever they can along this line. This will often be a real service to their people, and through them to the company and to society, for they have helped them to satisfy their desires and needs for information, including information about beliefs, attitudes, and reasons why, as well as about facts as such. When a worker's supervisor helps him or her become better informed, the worker is usually not only grateful but also feels more self-respect and importance. The process involved, in other words, is not simply a matter of knowing more or even a matter of knowing more and feeling better about one's supervisor. It also often involves feeling better about oneself and one's relation to the organization. This is the reason why this technique may have special importance to the supervisor of the worker in the low-status, unglamorous job, for such an employee gets few other opportunities for such feelings.

Limitations of Telling   There are two important qualifications, however, that need to be made. In the first place, the reader has probably noted that we have suggested *helping them become informed* rather than *keeping them informed*, the latter expression being more popular among management writers. In one way there is no distinction here, but in another there is. After all, if I am your boss and my goal is to keep you informed, I am tempted to spend a great deal of time in *telling you*. Now this may be effective at times, though the vast faith that management has in telling is hard to understand in view of the conspicuous and extensive failures of many instances of it. At other times it is not effective at all.[8]

The situation is quite different, however, when we try to help another person to become informed. Now we join in a common endeavor. We may be able to contribute to that person's knowledge, but we know and acknowledge that that person may be able to contribute to ours. Not only that, but this lays the basis for determining what he or she is really interested in rather than simply plunging ahead, secure in the belief in our own superiority as a source of dependable knowledge.

What we are suggesting, then, is a cooperative endeavor between human beings engaged in a common task, each willing to make his or her best contribution to it and each able from time to time to make a real one. This is a point of view miles away from what is often meant by "keeping them in the know."

The second qualification concerns that about which we try to help the workers become informed. Here again some contemporary writers and speakers on management problems are quite naive, for they imply, or come close to implying, that there need be no secrets in an organization, that in a well-run organization the leaders can and should share all their knowledge with all their subordinates.

Even one day in a managerial position should convince a person of the unrealism of this point of view. Certainly, there are problems, plans, accomplishments, and risks that cannot always be freely discussed with subordinates. Furthermore, we all have feelings about others, including opinions about the kind of people they are, the airing of which at times would not be helpful and might be disruptive in the extreme. It is amateurish not to recognize these realities in the supervisor's situation.

What, then, are we trying to say? That the supervisor must use good judgment in the topics on which he attempts to help his subordinates become informed; that with regard to those that are suitable it is his heavy responsibility to be of real assistance; that even here, however, he helps only to the extent that is wise and will be productive of better effort and cooperation. Thus some topics may be discussed as fully and completely as possible, some may be dealt with in general terms but without the specific details, while others are and properly should remain confidential. Examples are legion, and any topic may be first in one category and then in another.

When One Cannot "Tell"   There is yet another aspect of this subject: At times supervisors are under obligation to help their people become informed about *why they cannot help them become informed* about a particular subject. In other words, they may have to explain why they cannot explain. As a general rule, subordinates are understanding and quite content to accept the realities of the situation, if (and it is a most important *if*) the supervisors have demonstrated in the past good understanding, sincere attitudes, and real moral conviction. Of course, if these are judged to be lacking, few methods of techniques of the manager are likely to be really effective anyway.

Thus it develops that assisting people in their quest for information may involve the best skills and intelligence of the supervisor. Certainly it is no place for superficiality and uninformed, even if sincere, intentions. Effective supervision involves the best that a person can contribute to it.

Seeking Workers' Ideas

Another method of motivation which may be quite useful is that of getting the ideas of subordinates about things that concern them. It is often difficult to feel enthusiasm for a course of action that one has no voice in choosing and concerning the development of which one has no real influence. On the other hand, if the idea is mine or if I feel I made a significant contribution to it, I am more likely to work diligently to see it carried through. Thus, giving workers an opportunity to express their opinions about the work in particular or some aspect of the general working conditions may have real motivating effects.

Again, however, the method must be used with understanding. If a supervisor asks for the ideas of subordinates *after* he or she has made up his mind, and no matter what the subordinates suggest he or she has no intention of changing, this will be taken as a form of manipulation, and indeed it will be just that. (Incidentally, if this is one's real though unconscious feeling, the workers usually find it out and interpret it for what it is.) On the other hand if such ideas are sought because the supervisor has genuine respect for his associates and really expects worthwhile contributions, the method can be most useful.

Actually, for this technique to operate successfully the manager does not have to believe that the subordinate's suggestion will be of any real value as such. He may believe that, while the ideas probably will have no intrinsic merit, the subordinate will be a better person for having suggested them, that he will have higher respect for himself and the organization because they are solicited. Even under these circumstances the manager may be surprised and actually get usable methods or insights. Indeed, it is surprising how frequently good ideas do come from unexpected sources. But even if the ideas themselves are not usable, the solicitation of them may be seen as, and may be, a vote of confidence and an expression of concern for the worker. So used, the process can be most helpful.

Again, some management theorists have carried this good method too far. Some have dealt with it superficially and either have not thought out or have not pointed out its implications. Under these circumstances they have actually encouraged manipulation of workers and thus in most instances have done more harm than good.

Role of Participation in Decision Making   Some theorists are more sophisticated, however; they have interpreted seeking the ideas of subordinates to mean participation by workers in the actual decision making (as it sometimes may be, though it frequently is not, for the suggestions may simply be incorporated by the supervisor into the decision which *he or she* makes).[9] Indeed, some have even gone so far as to suggest that participation in decision making is *the* basis for effective motivation, that nothing short of this procedure will really suffice in the long run (see Chapter 5 and Chapters 21 and 22).

The authors of this book are not opposed to proper participation by workers in decisions that affect them. On the contrary, it is recognized that workers often have knowledge and experience that managers do not have, and such knowledge and experience can be most valuable. Under many conditions, in other words, participation is a very effective motivation device. But we disagree with the notion that it is *the* method of motivation and see no reason for believing that in the future all or even most important decisions will be group decisions made by all who are directly concerned with the area in question. There are several reasons for this conclusion.

One is that millions of workers have never worked under these conditions and are not intellectually or emotionally prepared to operate under them. They would be surprised and shocked if suddenly confronted with these decisions and consequently might work less well and not better.

A second reason for doubting the overriding significance of participation is the untold number of decisions that have to be made by the well informed, by persons with quite different backgrounds from that of the subordinates responsible for the work. Here we may be talking about an executive (or a manager at any level) who has access to information which must be used but which cannot be shared with subordinates; or it may be a situation in which the facts are so complex that it is not feasible to help all subordinates to become fully informed. Likewise, the circumstances may call for the judgment, based on knowledge and experience, of the true expert. Here many subordinates might be capable of contributing significantly to the decision if they had spent the years necessary to become an accountant, a lawyer, a chemical engineer, a physician, or even a wise and efficient line manager, but the point is that they are not so prepared and hence cannot be expected to decide wisely. (Of course there are many times when it would be wise to *consult* subordinates on aspects of these decisions, but consultation is not actual decision making.) With every day that passes, expert decisions loom larger in many a work situation; hence the impracticability of relying exclusively or perhaps even largely on group decisions.

A final reason for only a limited use of participation in making decisions is that many (and very likely, most) workers neither expect nor want it. American workers usually are quite willing to have management manage, though of course there are exceptions under particular circumstances. Workers know that someone has "to call the shots" and assume responsibility for the decisions; a management that is reluctant to do this soon loses their respect. They want to be consulted frequently and sincerely; of that there can be no doubt. But few of them expect or want the business to be turned over to the workers to be run as the workers wish. Workers know that management must have the right to manage, and so do the authors of this book. Any movement that further weakens this already too restricted right is certainly not to be encouraged.

What we have just said may be difficult to reconcile with some of the things workers do, especially in unionized situations. However, as we shall try to make even more clear in Chapter 15, we are here dealing with a special situation. Union leaders and union members do want a voice in the things that affect them, but they still want management to manage. The real difficulty here arises from the fact that so many decisions by management do affect workers, and hence the unions become concerned.

What is the upshot of this discussion? That under some conditions—and they are not so rare—the supervisor would be well advised to present the facts as he sees them, to his group, to help them get any other needed information, to let them make the relevant decision, and then to follow that decision resolutely. Under other circumstances, however, consultation is enough. The ideas of the workers are sought and carefully considered, with the manager having an open mind and being genuinely willing to change his present thinking if the evidence warrants. Under still other circumstances, the decision is the manager's, and it would be unwise then either to ask the subordinates to participate in the decision or even to consult with them concerning it. Only the supervisor's good judgment, based on experience and possibly consultation with other members of management, can tell him which course of action to follow under any given set of conditions.

The Special Assignment

One of the best ways to appeal to the need to be needed discussed in Chapter 7 is the special assignment to one or more of one's subordinates. When this technique is used, the employee is usually complimented and feels that he or she is not being taken for granted. Rightly approached, most people accept such tasks with some enthusiasm.

Of course, there are hazards with this as with all other supervisory techniques. The assignment must not be, and must not be accepted as being, trivial or manipulative. If it is, it will doubtless do more harm than good. Also, the employee who receives it may feel that he is being exploited, that he "gets all the dirty jobs." Needless to say, under these circumstances the outcome is seldom desirable. There is also the risk that the subordinate may take advantage of his new situation to slight or escape necessary duties in his continuing job.

All this is simply to emphasize a point already made many times, that any method of the supervisor must be used ethically and with understanding and carried out in an emotionally mature fashion. So employed, the special assignment can be quite useful.

The Art of "Visiting"

One of the authors has interviewed hundreds of workers in a variety of work situations concerning their feelings about the employer, their jobs, their bosses and fellow employees, and themselves. At the end of each such assignment, whether a hundred or a thousand people have been interviewed, it becomes necessary to report to the Management Committee of the plant or the office both what the workers have said and what they meant by what they said.

Especially for blue-collar workers it is easy to pick out the thing that such groups have emphasized most often. They send word to the "big bosses," as follows: "Why don't you come to see us more often, provided you come for the *right reason?*" There is profound wisdom in these words if the bosses properly interpret them.

For one thing, there are both proper and improper reasons for "visiting." An improper reason is a "snooping expedition." Another is to "butter them up," to pretend an interest one does not feel but which one uses to secure an unfair advantage. Examples of the first are known to everyone who has worked in a legalistic, highly restrictive climate. An example of the second is a "big boss" who had not visited the work situations for a long time but who began to do so systematically thirty days before a significant collective-bargaining election (though he never mentioned the election). Of him and his visits the employees said, "We know why he came, and it would have been better if he had not come." Unwise, unethical, "anxious" visiting does more harm than good, sometimes a great deal more.

There can be no serious question about what the workers meant by the "right reason." It was not to pass along information or to get information or even to recognize the worker as individual. (These may be judged as satisfactory goals but they are not *the* reason.) *The* reason, that is, the essential and controlling one so far as workers are concerned, was very simple: It was that managers were to visit because they *cared,* because they really and truly had an interest in the people, and furthermore an interest that transcended one aimed at inducing favorable worker attitudes and hence greater productivity.[10]

One of the writers once knew a company president (the Joe Jones of Chapter 5), who stated publicly that if one of his workers went to the hospital he (the company president) wanted always to be the *second* person to visit him or her. (Presumably the spouse would be the first.) This man was genuinely loved and admired and was an inspiration to productivity on the part of his people. However the real cause of the motivation was not that he visited people when they were ill. The real cause was that they believed he visited people for the *right* reason, namely, that he was genuinely interested in them, that he loved them. Visiting workers can be a trick and sheer manipulation. Visiting them for the right reason can be distinctly motivating.

Aside from calling on people when they are ill, supervisors do not usually get to "visit" their people, for they are already there with them, virtually all eight hours of virtually every day. Our point, however, is still essentially the same for them: Effective supervisors go out of their way to speak to their people, to "shoot the breeze with" them, to visit with them at all appropriate times. There is seldom a better way to demonstrate that one really and truly *cares.*

LEADERSHIP OF SMALL GROUPS

Earlier in this book we called attention to the fact that management is enamored of and tends to emphasize the individual approach to workers. That is, it tends to encourage motivation in terms of the uniqueness of each individual and in terms of self-interest.

It has already been agreed that there is merit in these courses of action. As acknowledged in the preceding chapter, we are all individuals and are all motivated from time to time by narrow self-interest, but as also pointed out, there is another side to the story. While we are all different, we are also all alike; that is, we have the weaknesses and the strengths, the knowing mechanisms and the emotionality of all human beings. More important, perhaps, when we grow up in the same culture and engage with others for a long period in common activities, we tend to become much like them and the similarity to others that we possess because we are all human becomes much greater. We also develop loyalties to and affections for other human beings and for groups of people. It is not at all unusual for these loyalties and affections to override self-interest, at least in the narrow sense of the term.

This brings us to another method of supervision which the manager ought to consider and to use rather often: to deal with and appeal to groups as groups rather than restrict himself to the individual approach. What sort of groups do we have in mind and what are the methods of dealing with them?

In this discussion we shall be concerned with small groups, those comprising perhaps three or twelve or—though this borders on being large—twenty or twenty-five. Thus, the small group we have in mind is typically the supervisor and his immediate subordinates.

Group Spirit   While all sorts of possibilities exist for such groups—and no doubt virtually all are real at times, for there are so many work groups—it is typical for a degree of group feeling to be present. Members of a work crew usually "stick together," respond similarly to similar treatment, and share not only many of what they take to be facts, but also similar attitudes and values. This is often seen most clearly in unionized situations, where people not infrequently band together, resist or accept the demands of the supervisor and the company, unite in the protection of weaker group members, and cooperate enthusiastically at times with other work groups and even with management. It is obvious, however, that this sort of development is by no means restricted to union members. On the contrary, the same things may happen in the absence of a formal bargaining unit and often are undertaken with equal enthusiasm.

The point that we wish to make in this section relates to the phenomena we have been describing. There is such a thing as group spirit or at least there is the possibility of it in each group. Sometimes this group spirit helps to achieve the company's objectives, and sometimes it has a contrary influence. The responsibilities of supervisors as well as their opportunities in this connection are quite clear: they should do what they can feasibly do to nurture and develop this group spirit, at the same time recognizing that it is of value only when it can be and is directed toward desirable goals. To help groups develop a "we-feeling" and employ it constructively in the interest of the company and in their own interest is at once a real challenge to and a fine opportunity for the supervisor.

Group Methods   There is, of course, no iron-clad or even easy way to accomplish this, but certain observations are pertinent. The role of the supervisors is often crucial here. If they insist on "telling," or ordering, or on openly and obviously and continuously checking up, little enthusiasm is likely. On the other hand, if they become "one of the boys" and try to make themselves indistinguishable from the rest they are not likely to gain, or retain, the respect a leader needs. The truth is that they have a rather ambiguous (or is it ambivalent?) role, for they must be of the group, that is, members of it, and yet the leader at the same time. They need the ability, wherever it is appropriate to use group techniques, to become functioning group members so far as ideas are concerned. They suggest courses of action and express opinions, but are careful not to do so as an order; they are also careful not to insist upon being the boss and not to take more than their share of the group's time. (It might be better if they would use considerably less than their proportionate part.) Furthermore, they have responsibility for permitting and encouraging others, perhaps especially the timid ones, to express their opinions.

We are again at the point where the supervisor's dealing with criticism is crucial. In a group situation, if permissiveness is created, the supervisor is really courting uncomplimentary remarks about the organization and sometimes about himself. Again, his ability to "take it," to respond meaningfully and objectively to it, and to encourage the group to express opinions freely about matters of concern—all this is as important here as in dealing with individuals, and probably considerably more so.

One reason group methods are so effective relates to this very point. If a worker has some critical feelings, in a permissive group situation, he or she is likely, as we have earlier pointed out, to express them, tentatively and mildly at first. If others disagree, they will probably let him or her know, often in a decisive way. If the others agree, those preliminary remarks are picked up and elaborated by another person, and then perhaps by others. If one really wants to know how workers feel this is probably the best, or certainly one of the best, of available methods. It can also be productive of good ideas whether or not they are related to critcism. Finally, it can set the stage for real progress, through the emotional release it furnishes the people involved, and a continuation of the process may lead to the development of considerable insight for all concerned.

Of course there are other useful courses of action. Free and complete examination of goals and objectives, and means of attaining them, may be useful at times, as may discussion of the reasons and feelings behind them. Likewise, the example of the supervisor is important. Sometimes this is a matter of "getting his hands dirty" (though it must never be forgotten that the supervisor can easily do too much production work, and indeed that this is more often a real temptation especially to the less-successful manager) or at least of demonstrating an essential community of interest with the people. Sometimes it is sincere, believable expressions of enthusiasm for the project. At still other times, use may be made of previous records or of the accomplishments of competing groups, though efforts must be made to prevent the competition with either previous records or contemporary "adversaries" from becoming *the* reason for effective work. Motivation based on these things alone is unlikely to be sustained for any long period.

Above all, the supervisor needs to believe in and expect the development of the proper sort of "we-feeling" and to demonstrate this belief in countless ways while going about his or her daily work.

In all this it must not be forgotten that in addition to his or her group responsibilities and efforts to build group spirit the supervisor continues to have responsibilities to and for individuals. Sometimes one has to "call a spade a spade." Sometimes people have to be counseled, or warned, or even laid off or discharged for disciplinary reasons. The supervisor must be able to carry out these duties too and still not let them sabotage efforts to increase the morale of the group. Combining these two kinds of functions is seldom easy, but then first-level managers do not have, and hopefully most do not want, *easy* jobs.

THE SUPERVISOR AND SUPERVISORY TECHNIQUES

At this point we must be careful not to be inconsistent with the fundamental conception that runs through this book, namely that the methods and techniques of the supervisor are secondary to the sort of individual he or she is taken to be. It is repetition to say it again, but it may nevertheless be worthwhile to do so: A supervisor who is not trusted but who uses the best methods is almost certain to be less effective than the supervisor who may be less sophisticated in methods but who still has the trust and confidence of associates. Good methods and techniques are important, but other things are often more significant in influencing achievement.[11]

It is obvious that this chapter has not involved all the many methods available to the supervisor. No attempt has been made to cover all of them; indeed such a task is an impossible one in view of the complexity of people and the varied situations they face. Perhaps the ones we have suggested are among the more generalized and widely useful ones.

Finally, we repeat an observation made earlier in the chapter. Nothing will substitute for the supervisor's own good judgment in the selection of the appropriate methods and techniques. All that we have said, particularly in the two preceding chapters, is applicable here: The methods must be selected with proper consideration given to ethical values, self-understanding, the dignity of people, and the wisdom required in making and implementing good decisions.

QUESTIONS

1 It would appear that the most important thing a supervisor could learn would be "how to supervise." What factors make it possible to spend too much time and effort on this subject?

2 In addition to "how to supervise" what else should the supervisor (or the supervisor-to-be) examine and study carefully?

3 Distinguish between motivation by (a) force, (b) enticement, and (c) intrinsic motivation. Illustrate each with examples other than those in the text.

4 If a supervisor had a choice between all three of the above motivators and could "make any or all of them work" why would intrinsic motivation be the best to choose?

5 What is meant by saying that delegation is more "a state of mind" or "a set of beliefs and attitudes" than it is a method or technique of supervision?

6 What are the strengths and weaknesses of (a) *consultation* (getting their ideas and considering them before you decide) and (b) *participation* (letting the group decide) as supervisory methods?

7 What are some of the motivation techniques that are useful with small groups but that are not useful (or at best, much less so) with individuals?

8 Understanding and wisely using "the art of visiting" gives the supervisor an unusual opportunity to demonstrate an important fact about his or her attitudes and values as these relate to the subordinates involved. What is this fact and what is its importance?

NOTES

1 Robert Townsend, *Up the Organization* (New York: Fawcett, 1971).
     Effectively attacks many of the common conceptions of the management process.

2 See Leonard R. Sayles and George Strauss, *Human Behavior in Organizations,* (Englewood Cliffs, N.J.: Prentice-Hall, 1966), especially pp. 135–154.

3 Wendell French, *The Personnel Management Process: Human Resources Administration,* 3d ed. (Boston: Houghton Mifflin, 1974), Chaps. 7 and 8.

4 Keith Davis, *Human Relations at Work,* 3d ed. (New York: McGraw-Hill, 1967), pp. 48–55, and Fremont E. Kast and James E. Rosenzweig, *Organization and Management,* by the same publisher, 1970, pp. 241–274.

5 Chas. R. Milton, *Ethics and Expediency in Personnel Management* (Columbia, S.C.: University of South Carolina Press, 1970).
     An excellent, critical history of personnel management in the U.S.

6 While they do not use the term *identification,* it is the concern of many authors. See, for example, Rensis Likert, *The Human Organization,* and Douglas McGregor, *The Professional Manager,* both published by McGraw-Hill, New York, 1967.

7 James C. Worthy, "Organizational Structure and Employee Morale," *American Sociological Review,* vol. 15, pp. 169–179, April 1950.

8 William F. Whyte, Jr., *Is Anybody Listening?* (New York: Simon and Schuster, 1951).

9 Douglas S. Sherwin, "Management of Objectives," *Harvard Business Review,* vol. 54, no. 3, pp. 149 ff, May–June 1976.
     The sum of individual goals is *not* the same as the goals of the organization; suggestions as to how to get the latter formulated and disseminated.

10   Saul W. Gellerman, "Supervision: Style and Substance," *Harvard Business Review,* vol. 54, no. 2, pp. 89 ff, March–April 1976.

The *substance* of each supervisory job and the *style* of each supervisor are different in each case and must be taken into account; the subject of a forthcoming book *Managers and Subordinates* (Dryden, 1976).

11   Roger J. Fritz, "Management Development Is *Your* Responsibility," *Personnel,* vol. 47, no. 12, pp. 857–861, 1970.

CASES

In the Bill Adams case, chosen for this chapter, we have a young man with good "connections" (his parents are friends of the president and his wife!) who has some obviously bad attitudes and habits—and the supervisor has a problem! In the Sam Cook case an insubordinate—or at least uncooperative—black has expressed himself freely in the presence of a white supervisor. (The case does not say so, but the events occurred in the very early days of the Civil Rights Act—see Chapter 17.) The supervisor has a problem here but so obviously do his bosses.

The cases help emphasize that "how to supervise" depends very significantly on the judgment of the supervisor in the particular situation, and this regardless of how many supervisory books or training courses he may be familiar with.

CASE 8-1

Bill Adams is a bookkeeper at the Bank. He is twenty-three years of age and single, and is a graduate of the local high school. He completed three years of service in the Army prior to his employment at the Bank about eighteen months ago. Bill was employed at a salary that compared favorably with that paid other bookkeepers. His subsequent increases have been about the same as those received by others in like positions.

Bill's personal characteristics work against him. He dresses in an unconventional manner, one not at all appropriate, in the opinion of Bank management, to his position. Furthermore, his hair and sideburns are much longer than the managers like. From the first he has been somewhat uncooperative. He seldom goes out of his way to do extra work and on occasion disregards some of the general policies of the Bank and bookkeeping department. Thus he has made an appointment for as early as 2:30 in the afternoon and has left as soon as his book was complete and while other bookkeepers were still working. (This practice has never been approved by the Bank, but he is not the only one who does it.) Besides all this, he is often in debt, having overdue charge accounts with local merchants. So far, however, he has eventually paid his bills.

In his work Bill has been extremely good. His speed and accuracy have consistently been above average, and he handles telephone calls from customers in a superior manner. Even in his work, however, his unpleasant personality has shown itself, for he is uncooperative with the other bookkeepers and has made himself even more unpopular by bragging about his ability and also his "drag with the boss." He has made a great deal of the fact that his parents are close friends of the Bank president, John Jones, and Mrs. Jones, and implies that Mr. Jones "will take care of him." (Actually, the Joneses and Bill's parents are good friends.) Each time a new employee comes to the department, Bill takes the first opportunity to explain that he will be with the department only for a short time since he is confident Mr. Jones will soon make him a loan officer.

About this time Hal Brown, the department head and Bill's supervisor, has learned from what he thinks is a reliable source that on at least one occasion Bill has discussed the financial standing of a customer with his brother-in-law, who is a bookkeeper in another local bank. He fears that there may have been other similar cases.

What does Mr. Brown do now?

CASE 8-2

Richard Cone is a general foreman for the Company, which is a supplier of natural gas. He is in charge of the lines between two pump stations and has four foremen under his jurisdiction. These foremen in turn supervise the pipefitters, laborers, and others who maintain the lines. Bill Gilmer is one of these foremen.

Cone is investigating an incident that has occurred within the last twenty-four hours. The principals in the story are Gilmer and Sam Cook, a black laborer. Cone's investigation, which has included conversations with both Gilmer and Cook, has developed the following facts: Gilmer is strongly recommending the discharge of Cook on the grounds of insubordination and threatened physical attack. Cook steadfastly denies both charges. Unfortunately no one else was present when the incident occurred, and Cone has no way of checking the story of either man.

The two accounts agree on certain points: Cook was cleaning up some dirt left by a ditcher and bulldozer when Gilmer walked up behind him and accused him of poor performance. There is agreement that Gilmer used profanity in addressing Cook, but wide disagreement about the circumstances of its use. Gilmer says he cursed the dirt, whereas Cook says Gilmer cursed him personally.

Some thirty minutes later Gilmer returned to the area where Cook was working and again reprimanded him for poor work. Here again there is disagreement about what happened. Gilmer admits to using profanity again. "You know you have to when you're working these people," he says, but insists that he did not curse Cook. While he was talking to Cook, the latter walked away three times (twice after being forbidden to do so) and was called back by Gilmer. The third time, Gilmer told Cone, Cook threw down his shovel and challenged Gilmer to a fight, though Cook steadfastly denies both threats and any related intentions. At any rate, when Gilmer told Cook to go back to work he did so.

By checking the records Cone found one other time when Cook had been reported for poor work. About a year before, he and another laborer were digging a ditch at an isolated location, and Dan Shaw, who had preceded Gilmer in the foreman's job, "turned them in" for "having taken four hours or more to do about an hour's work." Shaw was convinced that Cook had a poor attitude and was a poor worker. Cone knows that Gilmer had the same feeling about Cook even before he was made foreman.

Cook is forty-five years of age, has a grade school education, and has been with the Company a total of ten years. However, he was once laid off for a few weeks on account of lack of work, and once he quit only to be rehired after about a year. He has been with the Company five years since his rehiring.

What should Cone do about this case?

Part Three

Day-to-Day Problems
of the Supervisor

As useful as a *general* discussion of the supervisor's job might be, it can hardly be sufficient for one truly interested in it, if for no other reason than that the job involves many complexities—and opportunities—in certain more or less distinct aspects or areas. Without enumerating and commenting upon each chapter in this part, let us list some of the questions that this group of chapters attempts to answer, at least as well as they can be answered today:

Why is it that, though we have been saying for twenty-five or more years that *communication* is *the* problem in employer-employee (and supervisor-supervised) relations, the problem is as severe as ever? Is communication really *the* problem? Is there basis for hoping we can solve it (or even make substantial progress in doing so)? If this is not *the* problem, what is?

What can and should managers, including supervisors, do about the evaluation of employees and about providing what useful information along this line is available and is really used? How do we eliminate or minimize prejudice and personality factors in such situations? How do we lead the *evaluated* to have confidence in the system? When they are candidates for job openings, how do we appraise people wisely? How much confidence can we place in training, both formal and informal? Are there counseling assumptions and methods that contribute to success in these areas?

Another question is how much we should pay each employee, and why? Assuming that not all should receive the same amounts, how does one determine and *justify* the differences in pay? How much of what workers are paid should be diverted to what fringe benefits?

And then there is the situation of a worker who has seriously and unmistakably violated an important rule of the work organization. What do we do now, and how, and why, and how much? What if our decision is challenged? Indeed should supervisors put their weight behind appeals-mechanisms, that is, ways in which people who feel they have been unjustly disciplined may obtain a hearing before someone else?

Our three remaining concerns actually run through many of the questions just asked. One is about labor unions. Where do they come from, and why? What are their functions, duties, power, and influence? How do they affect the way the supervisor does—and should—do his or her job? What is the likely future?

And then there is the matter of civil rights. The same sort of questions can be asked in this area, one that because of its relative newness and thus the incompleteness of some answers, may require an unusual amount of the supervisor's time and effort and his best wisdom.

Finally, there is the whole matter of the design of work and carrying it out efficiently and safely. Clearly a whole text could be written on this subject alone.

There are a lot of day-to-day problems in being a supervisor.

Chapter 9

Communicating with Employees (and Bosses)

In some ways a chapter on communication is an easy one to write since the subject covers so many areas of the supervisor's job, and thus to an extent the whole field is available for conclusions and illustrations. Supervisors no doubt become involved in technical problems where the influence of communication is minimal—though probably none where it is zero—but planning, counseling, discipline, evaluation of performance, training, and work simplification all involve large elements of it and indeed would be meaningless without it.

But in other ways these facts create real difficulties. If communication is as basic as we have indicated, how can it be meaningfully discussed apart from these topics and the context of these sorts of problems? The answer to that question is that in this chapter we are attempting an overview of communication, including the situations and forces that make it difficult, some considerations that may help it along, and some applications of both the negative and the positive aspects to the situations encountered by the supervisor.

While many of the topics discussed below will be written from the standpoint of supervisors engaged in communication with their work group, it must never be forgotten that they also have other communication responsibilities—those that relate to bosses, peers, staff people, customers, suppliers, and the like. It does not seem advisable to single these out for special treatment, though remarks about some of them may be made from time to time. The important point is that the *fundamentals* of communication as they relate to subordinates also apply in many cases to these other groups as well.

WIDESPREAD INTEREST IN COMMUNICATION

There are few, if any, subjects that are of more widespread interest among managers than communication. Articles on the art of communication often appear in management periodicals, including those devoted primarily to technical fields, and there have been many books dealing with it. Whole conferences have discussed the topic, and it has been at least one item on countless other programs. Likewise it is discussed in management meetings within firms or agencies and in private conversations between managers. And while chief emphasis has been on communication with employees, other groups of people have been considered seriously—stockholders, the headquarters office, higher management, other managers at the same level, staff people, union officials, customers, suppliers, and the public. It is small wonder that many managers believe that communication is *the* problem of modern management.[1]

Some of the reasons for this conclusion are easy to discover. The increasing interest in employees and employee relations is one of them. After all, if one wishes to promote good human relationships, effective communication becomes an essential tool and the study of the subject a necessity.

Another factor has been the rapid growth of labor unions. Managers generally believe that unions have done a good job of getting across their points of view, a situation that has threatened and disturbed many. To a large number of managers nothing seems more important than to bring union members to see and accept management's situation and point of view.

Education has also been influential. A century or two ago the means of communicating with people in general and also with workers were quite limited and largely restricted to word of mouth. Now a great many devices are available, and the great reduction in illiteracy means that most of them can be used in the work situation. Furthermore, the knowledge and interests of workers have expanded decidedly, and many topics that formerly would have concerned them only slightly are now of real significance.

The increased self-confidence and feelings of independence of so many Americans also have played a part. When fewer people had the right to vote and the issues in elections were largely political in nature, it was not so important that managers keep the workers informed. Now relatively few political issues are without direct economic implications, the climate in which business operates is often decidedly influenced at the voting booth, and people feel that they have rights that must be respected. Not to communicate with people under these circumstances is to court serious trouble or even disaster.

At the same time it must also be admitted that this area has become something of a fad. After all, there are fashions in work as surely as there are in clothes, and these come and go and are altered often in unpredictable ways. Especially during the fifties and sixties it became fashionable to "communicate with workers," and managers frequently made the attempt in order not to be out of step. If the situation has changed in the seventies, it is a change in degree only.

Two movements may help illustrate our point. One was the attempt to influence the opinions of workers through films, lectures, and conferences dealing with the fundamentals of the free enterprise system. Instruction in "basic economics," as the area was often called, was frequent, and hundreds of companies made it available to thousands of employees. The feeling was that if workers could be brought to understand the essentials of the market economy, the economic climate would improve, and management could manage much more effectively (and, sometimes it was thought, to a large degree unilaterally). The other was a program to encourage employees to take part in politics. While this was directed more toward managers than to rank-and-file employees its purpose was often the same as above.[2]

Thus most managers would immediately agree that communication is a matter of real consequence, and many would insist that it is second to none in its significance for management as a group.

SOME COMMON BELIEFS ABOUT COMMUNICATION

Many people have decided opinions about a subject as significant as the one we are discussing. As is often true, some of these beliefs are quite accurate, and some swing wide of the mark. Actually, there is some truth in virtually all these beliefs, or they probably would not be widely held; but there are few if any that are entirely true and worthy of complete acceptance.

That Communication Is Transmitting of Facts

There are many who think of communication primarily in terms of ideas or facts or, as some would put it, the truth. It is held to be primarily a logical process and to have as its goal properly informing those who listen or who see and hear. It would be inaccurate to deny that communication deals with ideas, concepts, and logical propositions, but these are seldom the only things involved, and even they usually do not function in isolation. One pertinent observation is that facts must be interpreted, and in many instances the interpretation of the facts carries more weight and leads to more decided action than the facts themselves do. This is one of the difficulties in talking about making truth well understood, a goal with which few would quarrel. Truth has many facets, to an extent being the interpretation placed on available facts by the particular individual doing the interpreting. Undoubtedly, also, there are attitudinal or emotional elements here, and they often have decided effects.

Thus we are concluding that communication involves transmitting facts but that facts alone are seldom all that is involved.

That Facts Clearly Understood Secure Conviction

A similar view, or perhaps a facet of the one just discussed, is that the only effective and dependable way to secure conviction is to convey the necessary information. People are conceived of as primarily logical creatures, responding to and convinced by what is accurately and clearly presented. Again there is truth in the proposition, but again it has serious limitations.

One observation not always carefully considered is that clear communication may widen and not narrow the basic differences between two individuals or two groups. Working in ignorance, people are sometimes unaware of the differences that separate them, but when they come to understand their respective positions, they see the differences more clearly as well. Political and religious views make good illustrations, but let us choose one from the work situation.

To the naive and uninitiated it may often appear that differences between labor and management are based on ignorance and misunderstanding. Granted this is sometimes the situation, the fact remains that in other instances there is real and substantial disagreement. A tightly contested grievance, including the two cases of this chapter, is often a case in point. Each side may be thoroughly convinced of the rightness of its position, and as facts are developed each may become more thoroughly convinced. Some grievances are based on ignorance or misinformation, but many represent basic disagreements which no amount of information as such will overcome.

The same remarks may apply to issues that arise in negotiation of a labor contract, whether the concern is wages, management prerogatives, or the conditions of union recognition. Anyone who has ever tried to get a quick agreement between typical representatives of unions and management about a union-shop provision or the right to "contract out" certain kinds of work is likely to have a vivid illustration of this point.

Furthermore, in all these cases the way in which facts are presented may have a decided influence. In dealing with the individual worker, *what* we tell him may not be as important as *how* we tell him, and both what and how we tell him is usually of less consequence than the trust and confidence he has, or does not have, in us. Effective communication is a great deal more than simply the facts, no matter how clearly these are understood.[3]

That Telling Once and Clearly Is Sufficient

It is also easy to get the notion that if management has an important factual story to get across to the people, telling them once in a clear and unmistakable fashion is all that the situation requires. There are at least two limitations in this point of view. One is the inadequacies of the "telling" process itself. After all, in many situations we are little influenced by mere telling. To believe often requires that we experience what is being discussed. Also, to be *told* under some circumstances awakens resentment and leads not to acceptance or acquiescence but to outright rejection.

It should be apparent that what we are discussing here involves primarily attitudes, values, and beliefs. If you tell me the house is on fire, I will probably immediately take what I consider to be appropriate steps, and only later will I question the basis for your assertion. But if you tell me how I should vote in a forthcoming election, my response may be very different. Particularly if I suspect either your motives or your integrity or feel that you are trying to dictate to me, the result is likely to be the exact opposite of what you desire. Managements often make serious mistakes along this line.

There is also another noteworthy aspect of this situation. Even if what you tell me is relatively simple and noncontroversial, I may not understand and believe the first time. I may not be really interested. Besides, my attention span is limited, as everyone's is, and my memory is short. Our friends in the advertising field have learned and should be able to teach us a valuable lesson here: If one wants to change attitudes, secure conviction, and produce effective action, there is often no substitute for effective repetition. The advertiser's techniques, if used exactly, may not be appropriate for our "product," but the lesson is there nevertheless.

The writers know of a company that once had a ready market for its products and at a price that virtually assured a good profit. Gradually the market changed decidedly. Other firms became increasingly aggressive, and overcapacity began to plague the whole industry. What the management of this company did was to present most of the facts about the new situation to its employees, depending chiefly on one or two well-written articles in the company newspaper, and later it was shocked and disappointed when it realized that employees were almost completely in the dark about the plight of the company. Here was a situation that in the first place probably demanded more facts than the company saw fit to reveal and, in the second place, required a patient "selling program"—not simply an article or two in management periodicals and one or two meetings with employees but painstaking efforts at personal influence by every available member of the management team.

JIT, a management training program of World War II, had as one of its cornerstones that "telling alone is not enough." This is even more true in changing employee attitudes and beliefs than it is in teaching job skills.

That Communication Is Essentially Getting Management's Message Across

One of the most revealing commentaries on management's conception of communication is the content of a book, article, or conference on the topic. If it is typical, by far the largest part of it will be devoted to how management's beliefs and the justification for its actions can be made acceptable to employees. There are all sorts of discussions about what should be put in company periodicals, including consideration of how frank and open management should be in stating its case, how the human-interest aspects of the material can be increased, what level of reading difficulty is most suitable, and how frequently articles should appear. Equal consideration is often given to the contents of the president's letter, if one is to be used, or to any other materials to be put in the hands of employees. And conference leadership is often taught on the basis of how to be clever in representing the company's point of view.

We do not mean to imply at this point that there is anything wrong with giving careful attention to all the above topics, provided it is done sincerely and does not represent tricks designed to mislead employees. Indeed, every aspect of management's message needs careful planning and scrutiny if it is of real consequence. But the point is that this is not communication, or if it is, that it represents at best only a part of the process. If the purpose is a change in attitudes or values, including the winning of belief and conviction, the purpose is unlikely to be accomplished unless the process of communicating involves a measure of give-and-take. Indeed, true communication is not likely to occur, again so far as influencing attitudes, beliefs, and values is concerned, unless employees are permitted and encouraged to *say their say*. In other words, they need an opportunity to be heard, to voice uncertainties and objections, time to consider and even to reconsider, and a chance to talk back to someone other than themselves.

Naturally, this means that no matter how valuable formal means of communication are, and they often have real worth, they are frequently ineffective unless coupled with personal persuasion and contact. No department of communications, no editor of a periodical, and no set of conference leaders by themselves are likely to accomplish much, especially if there is resistance to acceptance. Personal influence is also frequently required.[4]

Even this is not enough: Communication cannot ever be as good as we have a right to expect until each party is as interested in understanding the other as he is in being understood by the other. Communication stands a chance of being really good, in other words, when managers have as much interest in really understanding workers (though not necessarily always agreeing with them) as they do in having workers "get the message." It appears that we are quite a way from that situation in most work organizations.

In a word, communication does not consist essentially in getting management's message across. It consists essentially in give-and-take between parties who have a high regard for, and something to say to, each other.

Figure 9-1 may throw light on why company house organs have been less influential than it was originally believed they would be.

That Communication Should Follow Organizational Lines

A widely accepted notion is that communication should follow the chain of command. Thus the executive tells the division head and he or she communicates with the department head, who in turn passes it along to the supervisor. It is then the job of the latter to transmit the message to the worker. Of course, in coming back up the process is reversed, and the message moves through the organization without short-circuiting.

As such, there is not much wrong with this theory other than the frequency with

THE XYZ CO. TIMES

"New and Improved Equipment To Be Put On–stream Next Friday"
"Company Sets New Records in Sales and Net Income"
"Local Management Commended for Outstanding Achievement"
"Company Product Places First in National Contest"
"Company President Addresses U. S. Chamber of Commerce"

Figure 9-1 The "news" in company house organs is nearly always favorable and often self-laudatory. Controversial issues are not discussed and union achievements nearly always remain unmentioned. Does this have an effect on employee interest in and acceptance of such publications?

which it fails to work. There are all sorts of bypasses for the line organization—the staff person, the grapevine, the union committee, the car pool, the bowling league, and perhaps a hundred more. Furthermore, "big bosses" sometimes talk to workers, at times in formal meetings and at times informally. Nearly everybody is bypassed then.

The real point to be made here is that, when time permits, when the situation is right, and when the message is suitable, the chain of command should be followed. But often these conditions cannot be met. One reason is time. We just cannot wait that long. Another is the lack of confidence on the part of workers in their immediate bosses. We are not talking here about basic mistrust or antipathy, though occasionally both exist. What we are talking about is the worker's realistic appraisal of the place of the supervisor, especially in the large organization. We must face it: In many organizations the supervisor knows no more about what is going on than the worker does (and if the latter is a union representative, the supervisor may know less). Furthermore, the worker also realizes that the supervisor frequently has no substantial influence on what is decided. Often, then, the supervisor does not know what is actually happening or why and has had no influence in making it happen. If he or she talks with the worker about it, it is necessarily as a sort of "messenger," passing on what he or she has been told.

This point can be overstated, and it is possible that it has been overstated here. Supervisors undoubtedly have important communications functions, and the company is usually the loser if they are not carried out. However, the president or the general manager or the department head often carries more weight with the worker, especially if he or she is held in esteem and believed to have "been in on" the decision. The conclusion needs to be emphasized: Top and middle management cannot turn communication over to the supervisors and expect them to carry the load even with the aid of the company newspaper, posters, and the personnel department. Supervisors can help in communication, and they can be of real help. But top and middle management can help the supervisors, and can be of real help too. Communication is not a one-person job nor even a one-person-at-a-time job. It often requires the best efforts of all who are related to the process.

Incidentally, while we have not said so explicitly, the same situation is involved, though perhaps to a lesser degree, in upward communication. Here again supervisors cannot be expected to carry the whole load, though being in contact with the employees, they may come closer to being able to do so. But their efforts can be supplemented by those of various members of the personnel department—the company nurse, the safety engineer, the labor-relations representative, for example—and also of fellow managers at various levels, to mention perhaps the most important of the helpers.

That Communication Implies No Secrets

In our anxiety to sell the need for effective communication with workers, we have at times gone far enough to imply that effectiveness along this line means full and complete disclosure, with no secrets hidden and no information held back. A moment's reflection will show that this position is, as pointed out in the preceding chapter, entirely unrealistic. Certainly there are facts that management representatives are not free to pass on to everyone in the organization, just as union plans may not always be made known to management freely and immediately.

There is nothing wrong with this situation as such. Good communication does not mean utter and complete frankness; rather it is based on using information wisely in the interests of the organization and of society as a whole. While management has apparently made more mistakes in the aggregate by withholding rather than by passing on too much information, there are times when it is wise and even necessary to withhold. What cannot be justified on moral grounds, and in the long run proves costly even on economic ones, is deliberate withholding of information in order to gain an unfair advantage over the other person.

That Communication Primarily Demands Cleverness

It is easy to get the impression from a good deal that goes on in this area that the ideal communicator is the person who figures out the motives and likely reactions of those whom he wishes to influence and then uses the latest Madison Avenue techniques or tricks to cajole people into acceptance. This would suggest that while sincerity is desirable, cleverness must not be sacrificed to any virtue. According to this point of view, a campaign must be carefully planned to exploit all areas of the worker's vulnerability, and good use must be made of any not-illegal devices to accomplish one's ends.

It would be hard to state a position more unsound than this or one with more sinister implications for the future of employer-employee relationships. Especially in the day-to-day work situation with which the worker deals, there is no substitute for sincerity. The supervisor may be clever, and he should be if he can, but he *must* be sincere.[5]

FORCES MAKING COMMUNICATION DIFFICULT

Before we turn to the subject of how to communicate, let us look briefly at some of the forces that interfere with effective communication.

Manner of Communicating

The way in which we carry out any process has a lot to do with the results we obtain, and communication is no exception. Sometimes we tell without listening, use an inappropriate vocabulary, depend on going over the story only once, attempt to be clever at the expense of sincerity—these are all examples of how we discourage progress and court failure. In the next section we shall be discussing what should be done, but it is often as important to know what should be avoided.

Lack of Knowledge or Background

One force that hampers really effective communication is lack of knowledge and understanding on the part of either those sending or those receiving the information. Some of the difficulty is due to lack of intelligence, education, and general knowledge. Thus some people have limited ability to comprehend, or they may lack exposure to or interest in a problem like the proper tax structure for the American economy.[6]

Or the ignorance of the work group may be of a more specialized nature. A firm may well face a very difficult situation with regard to its competitive position. Not only is there the problem of keeping certain information confidential, but let us suppose additionally that it manufactures hundreds of products, which go to many sorts of customers. Also, since, let us say, it operates nationally, it runs into different marketing conditions in different regions of the country. Most of the employees have little knowledge of more than a small number of its products, and there is no way for them to understand the situation faced by the company unless their knowledge is increased. Thus it can be seen that this company faces a very difficult state of affairs so far as communication goes.

Bias and Prejudice

Another force that operates to retard good communication is the bias and prejudice characteristically involved. Again, these may be the prejudices of either the communicator or those to whom the message is directed. Illustrations are virtually without limit. Thus, prejudice may be directed against an individual, and inaccurate conclusions and unfair treatment may result. In many instances workers are prejudiced against their supervisors, or they may be prejudiced against the workers, or perhaps against some of them. Union leaders may be prejudiced against management or management representatives, just as the latter may have similar feelings about the union. Blacks, foreigners, and women workers are frequent victims also. In some work situations there may be prejudice against the employee with a "practical" background as opposed to a college degree. Likewise among the college educated there may be prejudice. Thus in the opinion of others, engineers may "get all the breaks," or chemical engineers may be favored over all other sorts. Bias and prejudice characterize many important segments of the lives of all of us.

There is no better illustration of bias than the *stereotype*. This refers to "a picture in our heads" of the typical Jew or Baptist or Yankee or Democrat. Characteristics are uncritically ascribed to the members of these groups, and in most cases, if we do not belong to the group in question, a good many of the traits are uncomplimentary. However, two remarks can be made safely about stereotypes. The first is that while some of the assumed traits may apply to most members of the group, some of the traits, including usually some of the most unfavorable ones, do not. The second is that, however true the characteristics may be for most of the group members, they almost certainly do not apply to all. On the whole, blacks may be less well educated and make lower test scores than whites, but this tells us nothing about the next black we meet. He or she might be the best-educated and most capable person we have ever seen. Thus it is easy to see that stereotyped thinking is very likely to be—maybe always to a degree is—prejudiced thinking.

But what is this thing we call *bias or prejudice?* Wherein do judgments made under its influence differ from other judgments? The answer to this question lies in the essentially emotional nature of man. Man can and from time to time does make judgments based on an objective (or nonfeeling) analysis of factual situations and then decides in accordance with what these judgments suggest or require. There are other occasions, however, when a very different process operates, and the decision is based wholly or in part not on the facts but on what the individual believes, his fears, his hopes, and his feelings and attitudes. In these cases he is likely to conclude as he wants to conclude, though he tries to think objectively and usually convinces himself that he has done so.

This helps to explain why it is often difficult to get women appointed to supervisory positions when men have to make the appointments and why blacks have real difficulty in securing equal treatment in work situations under control of white managers. The point is that most managers in each case presumably try to be objective and indeed pride themselves on doing just that. Oddly enough, in this sort of area, the person who knows he or she is prejudiced and tries to allow for it is usually less prejudiced or at least less influenced by prejudice than the person who believes he is free from it.

It goes without saying that the person to whom communication is directed can be fully as prejudiced as the communicator. Employees are prejudiced, of course. Some of them are seriously prejudiced against management, as we have said. Not a few are prejudiced against communication, especially since the word carries the implication of special pleading for the management position.

There is no way, easy or otherwise, in which the effects of prejudice can be neutralized. It will be with us always, as long as we are human. Recognition of its presence and effects, however, does enable us to take steps to keep its influence to a minimum.

Filtering

One of the biggest hurdles to real understanding between people who are removed from each other by several organizational levels is the process of change through which a message goes as it moves along the line. In many work situations, to cite an example, first-line supervisors have come directly from the ranks of the workers and not only understand these people well but still think and feel like wage earners. Middle and top management may not only be ignorant of how employees think and feel, but may at the same time have seriously erroneous conceptions about them. How can this situation obtain unless the channels of communication are closed in the line organization? How can it be at times that the first-line manager knows a great deal about the workers and top management knows little about how they really think and feel?

In part this is due to the inadequacies of words when it comes to conveying especially subtle understandings. If supervisors know workers really well, how can they in a few well-chosen words tell their bosses just how employees think and especially how they feel? This they could not do very well—since much of this is difficult to verbalize—even if they had hours to talk with them directly. One reason the top manager does not become informed, then, is lack of skill and ability on the part of middle and lower management to express accurately what the situation really is.

In addition there is the process of *filtering*. This refers to the changes that a message undergoes as it passes from one person to another. Some of this filtering is done deliberately, sometimes for ulterior and sometimes for altruistic motives, but much of it is unintentional. If, for example, I have bad news that my boss or the "big bosses" ought to hear, I can remain silent or deliberately distort what I know. I may not do either, but no one likes to give the boss bad news, partly because this may hurt our standing with the boss and partly because we are sympathetic with the boss as we would probably be with any other human being. And so I may "sugarcoat" what I tell the boss or at least put as favorable a construction as possible on the facts. By the time this has happened at several levels, the initial message and particularly the subtleties of attitude and feeling have not only been lost but are likely to have been replaced by something actually misleading.

Like prejudice, filtering cannot be avoided, but also like prejudice, to know of its nature and existence permits us to take it into account and look for it in the stories we receive and pass on. We can also short-circuit the line on occasion and go directly to the source of information or to the one who ultimately has to use it. Such short-circuiting should be done wisely, but there are times when it is necessary.

It is often difficult to imagine how complex large organizations have become or even how far removed the worker is from the "big boss." Figure 9-2 shows the levels of management in a certain organization. Note that this is for a particular plant only. Part of the headquarters staff of the Company is to be put on top of the box for the General Plants Manager and no doubt is made up of several additional "layers."

"Talking Down"

Particularly during the forties and fifties there was much discussion of the kinds of words that should be used in communicating with certain groups of people, including workers. An important consideration was the difficulty of the words, that is, the degree to which they were or were not in common use and easily understood. A related concern dealt with sentence structure. Was the typical sentence in a communication long and involved, with two or more complex clauses, or was it short and direct?

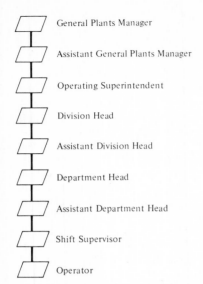

General Plants Manager

Assistant General Plants Manager

Operating Superintendent

Division Head

Assistant Division Head

Department Head

Assistant Department Head

Shift Supervisor

Operator

Figure 9-2 The above are the levels of management for the production or operating department of a large refinery. It indicates that (a) filtering can be a factor of great importance, (b) top
management often has to "short-circuit" the line, and (c) the "art of visiting" becomes an
extremely important skill.

These two factors were combined to appraise the difficulty level of reading material.
A widely used device expressed this level in terms of the grade in school where such words
and sentences of such length were commonly found. Some writing, for example, was
fourth grade in level, some eighth, and some eleventh or sixteenth, the latter representing
the equivalent of the college graduate in reading ability. One of the writers once saw an
intracompany letter that, graded on this basis, turned out to be at the forty-second grade
level! Exactly what that meant might be difficult to determine, but the sentences were
unbelievably long, cumbersome, awkward, and obscure.

Still another measurement that was applied concerned the human-interest factor,
judged primarily in terms of the use of names of people and personal pronouns. Material
could vary, of course, from lacking human interest altogether to possessing a high degree
of it.

Many people interested in communication seized upon these measures as *the* basis
for effectiveness. Why, they asked, should we write or speak in a complex fashion when a
simple way would do? Why ask people to read at the eighth-grade level if an easier level
would do just as well, and especially if some of the group had only a fourth-grade education? And why not put as much human interest in the material as possible?[7]

At first this point of view appears to be unassailable, but there are serious difficulties
connected with it. The real hazard is that it may result in "talking down" (or should we say
"writing down"?) to people. After all, if someone who is trying to communicate with me
adopts a style or a manner that reveals a low estimate of my competence and ability, I am
likely to be offended thereby. Furthermore, it is easy to see this as a form of deception and
another trick.

There is no easy answer to the question of what sort of vocabulary and style should
be used in employee communications, but it is clear that the matter is not as simple as on
the surface it appears to be. The total effect is what must be considered and not the
difficulty or human-interest level in isolation.

It is interesting, incidentally, to notice what happens when we attempt to communicate with another person and he or she refuses to accept our point of view. Especially if we judge the matter to be so plain and so evident that any normal person could not disagree and yet he or she persists in rejecting it, two results are likely. At first we attempt to simplify what we have to say and continue until it is evident that "even a fool can see it." Continued rejection here is likely to convince us that the person is a fool or at least not very bright. Of course, when he finds out that this is our opinion of him, he knows that we are talking down, and the process of change of his beliefs and attitudes most likely loses whatever chance it might have had of being successful. Talking down changes attitudes, that must be admitted, but usually in the direction exactly opposite to the desired one.

Our second course of action, assuming continued rejection of our message, will probably be to assume his or her lack of integrity and even honesty. "Surely," we tell ourselves, "no one can be so uninformed as to fail to see that. He has ulterior motives. He sees it but is willing to lie about it or merely to pretend that he does not agree." It goes without saying that only a miracle could lead to the desired change in attitude once this condition has been reached.

A recognition of the process just described helps us understand the impasse that has been reached in communication, sometimes between individuals and sometimes between groups. In some cases nations cannot communicate with other nations. Some unions and managers are also unable actually to communicate. For one party to take a certain position is to make it suspect in the eyes of the other, and each influences the other negatively, that is, by getting the response usually the opposite of the one that is desired. Trust and confidence are the basis for communication. Talking down and imputing unworthy motives to others usually make it exceedingly difficult, if not impossible.

THE SUPERVISOR AND COMMUNICATION

While much of what has been written so far applies to an understanding of communication and to the communication policies and practices of a firm or a government agency, a considerable portion is also relevant to supervisors in their relations with workers. In the concluding section of this chapter, however, we would like to look more specifically at the latter topic.

The XYZ Co. Times

Joe Jones wins trip————

Mary Smith takes vacation to

The Pat Crows have a new baby————

Helen Troy, daughter of H.B. Troy of Engineering————

Figure 9-3 Writers have urged all sorts of devices to increase the readership of company house organs, including almost interminable "personal" items. The effect of these is easily overvalued. If used as "tricks" to get people to read the publication, they usually do more harm than good.

Elements of Communication

The point has been made earlier that communication is a topic easily and frequently oversimplified. Supervisors should always bear in mind that it involves at least three components or elements: information; certain attitudes and values; and the provision of warmth, acceptance, and support for the subordinate. As we have already said, if one really expects to influence the beliefs of another, it is as important to convey sincerity and respect as it is to transmit ideas; and helping people see that they are genuinely appreciated and accepted as creatures of dignity and worth is usually essential to bringing about favorable changes in attitudes and beliefs (and very desirable even in changing behavior). In what follows, therefore, we are not talking about simply providing information.

Personal Relations

While we shall concentrate on communicating with subordinates, there are others in whom the supervisor has an interest—bosses, peers, staff representatives, and often customers—and these need to be kept in mind also.

Need for Empathy   Let us first deal with communication by means of a face-to-face relationship with an individual employee. For this discussion we shall assume that we are interested not only in informing but also in motivating and perhaps in altering opinions or attitudes of the employee. Among the suggestions that are applicable here are the obvious ones of demonstrating a genuine concern, one that goes beyond his or her mere usefulness to the organization, and cultivating as large a measure of empathy as possible. Demonstrated concern, a broadly based understanding of the person and the present situation, and a considerable measure of objectivity—these furnish the basis for such communication.[8]

Cultivating Contacts with Subordinates   A more tangible suggestion is to improve one's contact, including outside and informal contacts, with the worker. Thus, the coffee break or the bowling team may actually present greater opportunities along this line than any part of the work situation. And as pointed out in Chapter 7, visiting employees at their place of work, especially if the geography or the work situation or one's place on the organization chart removes one from them much of the time, is often quite useful.

Avoidance of Defensiveness   Since the work of a supervisor is constantly under scrutiny by his subordinates, some of the latter will on occasion disagree with what has been done and express this disapproval perhaps in rather strong terms. This poses a real difficulty for many supervisors—how to handle criticism from those they supervise. (It is hard enough to handle criticism from one's boss.) A common reaction is suppression or at least attempted suppression. The subordinate is forced to retract or at least temper his objections. Another is to pretend that the criticism does not exist and hardly admit it to oneself and never to others.

Both these ways of meeting the situation have their advantages and are useful under some conditions, but there is another alternative: The supervisor can avoid becoming unduly defensive, and can hear the worker out. (What we mean by defensive, of course, is the need, nearly always issuing in the deed, to rush to one's own defense, to show how right one is and how wrong the other person is.) Hearing the worker out is the proper way to handle such criticism much more frequently than most managers think.

It is important to realize that the supervisors in this process are not endorsing or approving subordinates' objections, but neither are they disagreeing with them. What they are encouraging is the expression of how the person really feels. "It may be regrettable that he feels that way," the supervisor might very well believe, "but if he feels that way we'll both be better off if he gets it out in the open." In the majority of cases this will lead eventually to improved communication, or at least it will lay the foundation for it.[9]

Direct and Indirect Approaches to Communication   Enough has been said earlier in this book to make it quite clear, if indeed it was not clear already, that there are two ways, among many others, to go about communicating with another person. One is to "put it on the line" directly, and the other is to engage in give-and-take in which the person has as great an opportunity as, or a greater one than, the communicator.

As an illustration, there is now considerable evidence from modern marketing practice that people often can be brought to buy the salesman's wares through encouragement to state their *objections* to his product and then to talk about them. After all, one can frequently "talk himself out of" an objection more effectively than the most persuasive salesman can. Needless to say, this has direct application to the securing of conviction that is essential in effective communication.

If the supervisor should follow such a process, this would help the worker understand that management is, after all, human, that it admits the possibility of shortcomings, and that it really cares about his opinion. Thus the *appropriate* use of the indirect method at least helps create a climate in which people come to realize that to disagree with another person is neither a cardinal sin nor a sign of failure. Disagreements can be normal, stimulating, and even pleasant.

Use of a Planned "Sales Approach"   Up to the present, we may very well have left the impression that supervisors are not to be aggressive in communication but rather that in this activity, they empathize, demonstrate concern, and encourage expression. All these things they do at times if they are wise, but they certainly also have a positive role to play. In many cases they need to demonstrate and assume positive leadership, and this must never be forgotten.

It is difficult to make very many comments on this phase of the supervisor's activity, for it varies greatly with different circumstances. A few observations are in order, however. One is that if a supervisor has a significant message to put across, he or she had better be familiar with the facts of the situation and spend considerable time in planning the "sales approach" as well as the content of the presentation. Another is that on occasion it is necessary "to call a spade a spade." Even here planning is essential; one of our biggest errors in this connection is to engage in this activity not on the basis of a well-thought-out plan, but because of strong feeling. As a general rule, following one's feelings gives a measure of emotional release, but it creates other problems, and if it secures conviction, it is often just the opposite of what is desired. Finally, one is interested in the persuasive and not necessarily the logical approach to these matters. The facts logically presented may be the persuasive approach in some instances; in others how one presents the facts, whether or not in logical sequence, and even which ones are presented are more significant.[10]

The Employee Meeting   Another communication opportunity comes to supervisors when they take part in meetings involving their people. These meetings vary greatly, of course, according to the circumstances. One meeting may be quite informal—for example, the employees may be in the change house getting ready to go to work. Another may be called for a certain time at a certain place to hear a subject covered by a person whose name is made public well in advance.

The meeting we would like to discuss particularly is one that supervisors hold with their people when all understand that it is "a meeting." Perhaps it is held on a regular basis though it may be one called for a particular purpose. What can a supervisor do to make the best use of such meetings?

One suggestion, oddly enough, is not to have too many of them. Research suggests that meetings in which people feel that nothing is accomplished usually do more harm than good.

Another good thing is to encourage participation, although before supervisors can really encourage participation they must want it. Furthermore they must be prepared for ideas they did not anticipate and opinions with which they cannot agree. An important reservation, however: Participation cannot and should not be measured solely in terms of verbal output. Some people talk a great deal in a conference and yet actually *say* very little; by their comments they may reveal that they are only remotely in touch with the goals of the meeting and events that have transpired. Other people may say little or nothing and yet be quite responsive to all that is said or done. The quality of participation is usually more significant than the quantity, and even the quality must not be judged on purely "logical" grounds.

Certainly one's leadership must be adapted to the situation. The optimum amount of participation varies, as does the amount of the supervisor's "telling." It is highly desirable to look for cues from those present about how well the meeting is going. Many of these are obvious, and most of the rest are not difficult to detect; but especially people with prepared speeches easily become blind to them. A change of pace is often greatly to be desired. Attention to those whose interest and attention are wandering can be very useful. Humor can be used very effectively at times, but it can also boomerang. A simple suggestion is not to tell stories or make remarks that hold another person or group up to ridicule (though strangely enough, skillful speakers can tell a joke about another or a group in such a way as to demonstrate that they hold it in esteem). Another suggestion for the use of humor is that if one is going to tell a story or make a remark about another and thus cause people to laugh at his expense or the expense of a group with which he identifies, it is highly desirable that one first laugh at or reflect upon oneself or one of the groups with which the speaker is clearly identified.

Needless to say, difficult points require one's best skill. These should be repeated usually in other and often in simpler terms, but again one should not underestimate the comprehension of the hearers and thus talk down to them. Likewise, it is desirable to adapt one's vocabulary and manner of speaking to the situation, taking into consideration the known background and the audience being addressed. One's manner of speaking needs to be consistent with the image that people have of him, at least to the point of not giving offense. Thus a college professor talking to boilermakers would probably be well advised not to talk like a boilermaker (for he is known not to be one and might lose their respect if he acts too much like one), but he certainly ought not to talk like a college professor either (or at least not the way college professors are often thought to talk).

It must also be remembered that in these meetings one often has something that needs to be said and should be said. The suggestions made above about the "sales approach" in the interview can be adapted a bit and applied here. And with all the recent emphasis on participation and group decision, it must still be remembered that there are times when the boss needs to "tell them." This he should do without apology to himself, or them, but in a manner calculated to secure the maximum effect. One can communicate negatively (and thus get a reaction opposite to what he wants) as easily in a public speech as in a private conversation.

Other Devices of Communication

There are a number of other ways of communicating with employees. Generally speaking, however, these do not involve the supervisor directly, and he will be concerned with them only to the extent that he can make use of them and on occasion influence the policies under which they are produced and used. They include such things as letters to employees, bulletin boards, and the company newspaper. We do not have space to comment on these individually.

THE CHALLENGE OF COMMUNICATION

It is of the greatest importance that middle managers and executives see the opportunities as well as the pitfalls of attempts to communicate and that they make the best use possible of the process. Communication also imposes many responsibilities on first-line supervisors. For them communication should become a way of living and not a detached process to be used only on certain occasions. It is essentially a philosophy and a set of values, and not a group of techniques, methods, or tricks. It is a day-by-day, hour-by-hour, minute-by-minute way of behaving that enables them to get the best results through and for their people and for their employer.

QUESTIONS

1 Is there a relationship between our present stress on *communication* in the organization and the overemphasis on *knowledge* discussed in Chapter 7? Explain.
2 If communication is more than the transmitting of facts, what more is involved? Illustrate with incidents other than those of the book.
3 Why does a management that is interested only in getting its message across usually fail to get its message across to workers?
4 In the process of communicating should top or middle management engage in short-circuiting? If not, why not? If yes, under what circumstances?
5 So far as *filtering* is concerned, discuss the role or influence of (a) concern for the boss's feelings, (b) concern for our own position and progress, and (c) prejudice.
6 When one is preparing a communication to place in the hands of employees, what is wrong with (a) using the shortest and simplest words that will express the ideas, and (b) putting in as much human interest as possible?
7 Compare and contrast the direct and the indirect approaches to communication (a) with an individual subordinate; (b) in a small-group meeting.
8 Evaluate this statement: The most important single thing to say about communication is that it must be a two-way street.

NOTES

1 The articles and books that could be cited in this connection are many in number and come from authors with widely varying backgrounds; see, for example, William H. Newman, Chas. E. Summer, and E. Kirby Warren, *The Process of Management,* 2d ed. (Englewood Cliffs, N.J.: Prentice-Hall, 1967), Chap. 10, and John M. Pfiffner and Marshal Fels, *The Supervision of Personnel,* 3d ed. (Englewood Cliffs, N.J.: Prentice-Hall, 1967), Chap. 11.
2 A critical analysis of the first of these was done by the editors of *Fortune* and their not-too-complimentary conclusions are set forth in William F. Whyte, Jr., *Is Anybody Listening?* (New York: Simon and Schuster, 1951).
3 Andrew J. DuBrin, *Fundamentals of Organizational Behavior* (New York: Pergamon, 1974), Chap. 9.
4 Paul Pigors and Charles A. Myers, *Personnel Administration: A Point of View and a Method,* 7th ed. (New York: McGraw-Hill, 1974), Chap. 5.
5 Leonard R. Sayles and Geo. Strause, *Human Behavior in Organizations* (Englewood Cliffs, N.J.: Prentice-Hall, 1966), Chap. 10.
6 This subject is discussed at many other points in this book. One area seldom explicitly considered is dealt with in Michael Argyle, *Bodily Communication* (New York: International Universities Press, 1975).

7   Rudolph F. Flesch, *The Art of Readable Writing* (New York: Harper, 1949), and *The Art of Plain Talk* (also published by Harper, 1946).

8   See the discussion of *Empathy* in Chapter 7 of this book.

9   Norman R. F. Maier and J. A. Murber, "Problems in Delegation," *Personnel Psychology,* vol. 22, no. 2, pp. 131–139, 1969.

10   Chas. Donald Porterfield, "The Effects of Emotion and Communication Skill on Message Meaning," *The Journal of Business Communication,* vol. 13, no. 3, pp. 3–14, Spring 1976. Though done on a single set of workers the effects of emotion and skill in communicating were clearly demonstrated.

CASES

It is an oversimplification to call the two cases of this chapter communication cases, though communication is a factor in both, for in each the resolution of the dispute depends on the meaning of a critical phrase or sentence.

The Henry Gagne case raises the issue of the proper pay for an employee who, while he does not work during his regular shift on a July 4 holiday, does work the eight hours from midnight to the beginning of his regular shift on that day. The other incident raises the question of whether the Company can make an overtime Saturday into a *scheduled* work day merely by scheduling work for that Saturday.

In each instance the question is how each complaint or grievance should be answered, and why?

CASE 9-1

The Company operates a chemical plant in the Southwest. The plant is a large one, and the hourly workers are covered by a contract between the Company and the International Union.

Henry Gagne, a machinist, is one of these workers. He has been active in the Union and has held one or two local offices during the approximately ten years of his employment.

The case concerns events that took place on July 3 and 4. The labor contract contains provisions for time-and-a-half for work in excess of eight hours in one day or forty hours in one week. It also provides for holiday pay at straight time for employees who do not work on the holiday and at double time rates for those who do.

Gagne reported as usual at the beginning of his shift on July 3 at 8 A.M. There was a great deal of emergency work to be done; consequently, at the end of his shift (at 4 P.M.) he was asked by Richard Mooney, his foreman, to continue work until the end of the next shift, at midnight. The emergency work had not been completed at that time, and Mooney asked Gagne to work until 8 A.M., July 4. This he did and so had worked continuously for twenty-four hours. (In this sort of shift work, employees are expected to eat during their shifts, so no time off for meals is involved.)

The question then arose of how Gagne should be compensated: There was no question about the first two shifts: from 8 A.M. to 4 P.M. he was entitled to his regular rate of $6 per hour. Likewise the second shift presented no problems. Here he was clearly entitled to eight hours pay at 1½ times his regular rate. But what about the eight hours from midnight to 8 A.M. on July 4?

Gagne argued strongly that he should be paid double time for these hours since it was holiday work and, in addition, that he was entitled to eight hours of holiday pay for

July 4, since he did not work his regular shift that day, and by contract was to be paid for the absence of work. Thus he contended that he should be paid as follows:

1st shift	8 × $6	$48
2d shift, July 3	8 × 9	72
3d shift, July 4	8 × 12	96
Holiday pay, July 4	8 × 6	48
Total		$264

The Company, through Mooney and Orville Smith, labor relations superintendent, retorted that Gagne was trying to "bleed" the Company. It insisted that Gagne did not deserve double pay for the midnight-to-8 A.M. shift and then holiday pay in addition. Since the contract called for double pay on holidays worked and provided also that there should be no compounding of overtime, the Company held that Gagne was due the following:

1st shift	8 × $6	$48
2d shift	8 × 9	72
3d shift	8 × 12	96
Total		$216

The matter was complicated considerably when Smith later sought advice from the Company's labor consultant. He recommended the following pay for Gagne:

1st shift	8 × $6	$48
2d shift	8 × 9	72
3d shift	8 × 9	72
Holiday pay	8 × 6	48
Total		$240

The reasoning of the consultant was that Gagne's work day of July 3 began at 8 A.M., the beginning of his regular shift, and did not end until 7:59 A.M., July 4. Hence he was entitled to only 1½ times his regular rate for the third shift, since it was technically on July 3 and not July 4. Had Gagne worked his regular shift on July 4, he would have been entitled to double pay. Since he did not work his regular shift, he was entitled to holiday pay for it.

What should the Company do in this situation, and why?

CASE 9-2

On the Thursday preceding Labor Day, 1975, the plant manager posted a notice that read, "There will be a scheduled work day *this Saturday* for all plant personnel." He was questioned by Union representatives as to whether this was indeed a *scheduled* work day, and on Friday put up another notice as follows: "You are required to work the day before and the day after a holiday to be eligible for holiday pay. *Saturday* is the scheduled work day before the Monday holiday. Anyone absent on Saturday or Tuesday must have a doctor's slip covering the reason for the absence. Any other absence will be unexcused and you will not receive holiday pay."

The contract provision to which he referred says, "Any employee failing to report for work the scheduled work day preceding the holiday and/or the scheduled work day following the holiday shall not receive holiday pay except in cases of excused absence or absence due to sickness or injury."

It is the practice in the plant to post a weekly schedule on the preceding Friday, and this was done on the Friday before these events, and it did not call for the Saturday work. However, unexpected developments led to the Saturday being added.

The grievants of this case worked on Friday, August 29, and on Tuesday, September 2, but did not work the overtime day of Saturday, August 30. The Company denied them holiday pay, and their grievance demands that it be paid.

The issue, of course, is whether the above Saturday overtime day is really a "scheduled work day preceding the holiday" and whether the grievants had to work that day to receive holiday pay. What are the proper answers to these questions?

Chapter 10

Selection, Promotion, and Compensation of Employees

As a general rule in this book, we have restricted each chapter to a single topic so that it may be dealt with more fully and completely. However, this is not always possible, because every topic in our field flows over into one or more others and hence cannot be treated in isolation. Even so, the one-chapter-one-topic plan introduces a degree of order and logic and is a good one. Nevertheless, in this chapter we cover three topics, and for at least two reasons. First, there is a limit to the degree to which one should fractionate a subject like supervisory management. We could have so many chapters, in other words, that we would run the risk of concentrating on the trees—the various parts or aspects of the subject—and actually lose sight of the forest itself, namely the overall essentials of supervision. And, second, the three topics of this chapter are closely related. People are hired and, if they stay with the firm, most are eventually promoted (or turned down for promotion), and all the while some determination must be made as to how and how much they will be paid for their services.

Even though the treatment of each of the three topics will have to be brief, we shall keep in mind our fundamental goal, namely to cover the topic from the point of view of the first-line supervisor. Concerning each, such a person really *needs* to know more than he or she is ordinarily expected to know; that is, one needs an understanding of the fundamental considerations relative to each topic. One likely cannot be an expert in any or all of them, but such expertise is usually present elsewhere in most organizations and clearly is not the supervisor's responsibility. But supervisors should be able to evaluate the assumptions and also to interpret and apply wisely the resulting rules and practices. Indeed the organization often must depend on them for essential parts of this important task. Additionally, supervisors ought to be an important source of input when it is necessary to evaluate and/or revise the relevant policies and procedures.

HIRING NEW EMPLOYEES

If one considers the history of personnel management, beginning as we often do about the time of World War I, it is evident that the selection of new employees has been the one topic most extensively examined by personnel specialists. The situation has changed somewhat in the last ten to twenty years as the fundamentals of organization, motivation, and decision making have begun to compete for center stage, but selection is still a topic of great interest, importance, and concern.[1]

The concern that both managers and personnel theorists already had for this topic was intensified by the Civil Rights Act of 1964, which prohibited for hiring, promotion, or compensation, any discrimination based on sex, creed, color, race, or national origin. (*Age* was added by the Age Discrimination in Employment Act of 1967.)

At this point it might be well to note a limitation we are placing on this chapter. We shall constantly have civil rights in mind as we consider its various aspects, but because of their complexity and far-reaching implications we have decided to deal with them separately (in Chapter 18). That chapter should be read carefully in connection with this one.

Tendency to Overemphasize Selection

No one would contend that selection of new persons to join the organization (or of present employees for promotion) is an insignificant matter. The filling of the jobs in a plant, store, or office with unsuitable people is certainly no favor to the firm nor in the long run, to most of those unsuitably selected.[2] At the same time, as pointed out above, we often have overemphasized the selection of new employees, at least insofar as this effort caused us to put less stress on other aspects of worker-manager relationships. Two factors underline this overemphasis.

Inadequacy of Hiring Decisions   Personnel specialists and other managers have difficulty in accepting one of these factors because it goes contrary to what they very much want to believe. It is that, after trying as hard as we can and using as many "scientific" methods as possible, we simply cannot do a very good job in selection. Our best selection devices, in other words, often yield misleading or inaccurate predictions concerning later job performance. On the whole, such selection devices have probably enabled us to do better than chance, but most likely not a great deal better.

The "Climate" after Hiring   The other limitation is our failure to realize that even more important than good selection is what happens to the person after he or she is hired. Potentially good employees, inadequately trained and supervised, are likely to be serious disappointments to themselves and the company, while relatively mediocre ones, well motivated, may well become quite effective. It is disappointing to see a business or a government agency that is having difficulty in getting its tasks accomplished spend most of its time and energy on new selection methods when the problem may lie far closer to home—in the day-to-day relationships between people on the job. We must make it clear that we are not against any reasonable effort to secure the right people for vacant positions, but we caution against the idea that doing so will solve most of our significant problems. Experience simply does not support such a conclusion.

Selection Procedures

Volumes have been written on the selection of people for initial hiring, for promotion, or for demotion when this becomes necessary, and almost every personnel management book deals with the subject.[3] Since our treatment of selection must be brief, some of these books may be well worth consulting.

Devices Used in the Selection Process   No doubt the most commonly used instrument for the selection of new employees is the *interview*. There was a time when many people were hired, especially for unskilled, blue-collar jobs, by the foreman's going to the plant gate and simply pointing out whom he wished. Today that would occur rarely if at all. Interviews may be held quite formally, often by persons who are assigned the task as their full-time job. At other times they may occur in informal settings with little or no advance preparation. But most employers want a chance to see and hear the prospect before adding him or her to the payroll. We shall have more to say about this selection device later in this chapter.

Another instrument that is quite common in this field is the *application blank*. Like the interview, it has not always been a part of the usual hiring program, but that situation has become increasingly unlikely. Application blanks often contain valuable information and should usually be consulted in hiring. However, in many instances they have grown unnecessarily long and even complicated. In others they serve as a sort of crutch for the interviewer, who may merely "rehash" the application blank and feel that an adequate interview job has been done.[4]

Another of the more recent selection devices is the *physical examination,* now widely required for blue-collar jobs. Potential claims arising under workmen's compensation have no doubt contributed to the use of this device. As to the results of the examination, it is important to note that the question the employer should ask about a prospect is not, Did he or she pass the physical examination? but rather, Is his or her physical condition such as to indicate appropriateness for *this* job?

It has become quite common these days to require applicants to furnish names of references, these being subsequently contacted in many cases by the employer. At one time considerable confidence was placed in the resulting *letters of reference.* We now realize, however, that they have serious limitations and are to be used with caution.

A selection device that, at least until recently, was gaining rapidly in use for employment purposes is the *psychological test.* While the use of tests has been challenged in some cases because of civil rights and other considerations there is nevertheless good reason to believe that they will continue to play a part in many selection programs.

Psychological tests cover a variety of fields.[5] They are used to measure intelligence, dexterity, personality characteristics, interests, aptitude (ability to learn along a particular line), and achievement (what one has learned) as well as other aspects of the person. Table 10-1 lists several kinds of tests.

It should be noted that a set of questions is not really a psychological test unless *norms* have been established for them and their *reliability* and *validity* have been determined. Norms refer to measures based on scores made by significant groups who have taken the test (for example, representative high school graduates or a random sample of qualified craftsmen). Validity and reliability are discussed below.

Usefulness of Selection Devices   The actual use of selection devices for hiring new employees (or for picking those for promotion) is considerably more complex than at first it appeared it would be. Why not, for example, just hire the person shown by letters of reference to be the outstanding applicant? And if intelligence and/or manual dexterity are

Table 10-1   Psychological Tests*

Kind	Attempts to Measure	Examples
Intelligence	General mental ability	Oral or written "IQ test"
Achievement	Accomplishment along a particular line	Knowledge of arithmetic, accounting, machineshop practice, or the like
Aptitude	Ability to learn along a particular line	Mechanical or musical or sales aptitude test
Dexterity	Motor ability and coordination	Hand-eye coordination, reaction time
"Personality"	Emotional adjustment	Personality questionnaire
Projective	Emotional adjustment	Rorschach ink-blot
Interest	What one enjoys or dislikes	Kuder or Strong interest schedules

*This list is incomplete, there being other sorts and indeed other classifications of tests. This table does not imply that each sort is as useful as any other in the work situation.

aspects of the job in question, why not simply select those who make the highest scores on tests of intelligence and manual dexterity?

A lot of considerations enter into the answers to these questions, but the fundamental one is that before we can afford to put much dependence on either letters of reference or psychological tests we must assure ourselves, to the extent that we can, that they actually pick the people who can and will do the jobs well and exclude those who either can not or will not. We know, of course, that this cannot be done perfectly but we want at least "a good batting average," an accuracy of selection above mere chance.

There are two principal ways in which we go about testing the accuracy of a selection device. One is to determine whether or not it measures consistently whatever it is that it measures. (This is known as its *reliability*.) Thus if we give the test again (or better still, an equivalent form of the test) to the same group we must have results that are in line with the first scores. (Another way to test reliability is to correlate scores on one-half of the items— for example, the even-numbered ones—against scores on the other half.)

The other thing we need to know about our instrument is the degree to which the various scores made on it are related to success on the job. Here we speak about correlating these scores against a *criterion*, that is in this case, a standard acknowledged to be a good indication of successful performance. If our device measures consistently and if results on it are closely related to later job success (its *validity*) we have a selection device of real value. The basic requirements for an instrument to be properly called a psychological test are set forth in Table 10-2 .

Before we conclude this topic, it is important that we recognize the difficulties involved. Satisfactory reliabilities are usually obtained fairly easily but satisfactory validities are obtained usually only with much time and effort and with professional assistance. Especially in view of the civil rights considerations, it is a matter to be dealt with carefully and wisely.

In connection with the determination of both reliability and validity the term correlation has been used. Figure 10-1 throws some light on this term. Each dot represents an individual who (a) has made a score and (b) has a production record (or [b] has made another score at another time on the test or a variant of it).

Table 10-2   Nature of the Psychological Test*

Characteristic	Based on	Comments
Norms	Scores made by a representative group	Must take into account (a) central tendency and (b) variability of scores
Reliability	Consistency in measurement	Based on test-retest or split-half correlation
Validity	Correspondence to job performance	Correlation against a reliable and valid standard of performance

*The table omits significant aspects of each subject, including some too complex for inclusion in a table.

The Supervisor's Role in Selection

Should the supervisor be "in on" selection decisions?   At one time personnel specialists urged that no one should be added to a work group without the supervisor's expressed approval. We now realize that while often it is desirable for the supervisor to be "in on" final hiring decisions, as a practical matter and for at least two reasons, this should not become a rigid requirement. For one thing, either through lack of knowledge or because he or she is not often involved in hiring, the supervisor may be able to make a small or even no contribution to the decision. For another, in many organizations people are shifted frequently from one work group to another (as supervisors often are), so the question of who the permanent supervisor of the employee is to be, if indeed there ever is one, is unanswerable at the time of employment.

What kinds of employees should be hired?   Here is an area where managers generally seemed to have failed to think through clearly the problems they face. It is easy to get the impression that for every job we want the most intelligent and capable person available.

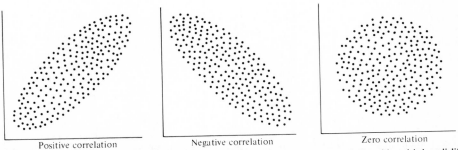

Positive correlation   Negative correlation   Zero correlation

Figure 10-1   The scattergram on the left represents high positive correlation (thus high validity or reliability, for example,), and the one on the right indicates no relationship at all between the two variables involved. The one in the center indicates as high correlation as the one on the left, except that high scores on one variable go with low ones on the other, and vice versa. *(From Sartain et al., op. cit., p. 391. Used by permission.)*

For some positions this is undoubtedly true, but for others it is not true at all. As a matter of fact, it is just as easy—and it may be easier—to overhire (selecting people who are "too capable" for the job) as to underhire. Generally one should recognize that two kinds of employees should be hired at least for the beginning jobs and other low status ones: One type is hired for what the people *are,* with the expectation that they will do this job or near to it for all of their employment, and the other for what they *may become.* The latter would be those who are counted on to be promoted to better positions.

While one can secure too few of the latter, an equally great but usually unrealized danger is to secure too many, to hire "too many chiefs and not enough Indians." This situation, when it obtains, can lead to serious difficulties for management.

Of course it must always be remembered that these two classes are not to be fixed and unchangeable. Some people we do not expect to be outstanding may turn out to be just that, and they should be promoted when the opportunity presents itself. Likewise, some in the "superior" group may fail to live up to the promise of their initial evaluation, and they should not be promoted. All this suggests that it is usually wise not to publicize the membership of each group. Not to make known the classifications usually allows management greater freedom of action.

Should one "sell" the job?   Especially in a tight labor market, management has another responsibility in connection with attempts at hiring, namely, persuading people to accept job offers that are made. Again two considerations are of consequence. One is that the supervisor should think through and carefully plan the "sales approach"; if practical, he or she should try it out in advance on some associates, and then adapt it to the particular individual.

Another is the danger of overemphasizing the good features of the job and playing down its limitations. To picture the job accurately, including its less desirable features, can introduce a note of challenge, not a bad basis for conditioning the attitudes of the new worker. Incidentally, it is easy to underestimate seriously the number of people who are more motivated by challenge than by pleasure and ease. Also it is considerably better for the newly hired employee to find the job even better than pictured rather than to find that it was misrepresented.

Can one improve interviewing skills?   Supervisors may be little involved with test scores and letters of reference and may even have only a minimum of contact with the application blank and the physical exam. However if they are "in on" hiring at all it is likely that they will interview the applicants. What suggestions can be made that might help them improve their interviewing skills?

First, advance planning of the interview can be most helpful. It has been suggested that a good outline for such planning would include (1) the *objectives* of the interview, (2) the *general strategy* to be followed, and (3) the *tactics* or minute-by-minute approach to certain aspects. It has been found that generally we give, to tactics especially, less attention than we should. Incidentally, advance perusal of all relevant and available information about the applicants is highly desirable.

Second, the supervisor's interview should be dovetailed with those of the personnel department and other managers. Few practices are more discouraging to a bright prospect than to see the company waste its time and his by "plowing the same ground over and over." What is to be dealt with by each interviewer should be determined in advance, though this should not be allowed to preclude the following of natural leads as they arise.

Third, while the supervisor will probably be most concerned to inquire into details of experience and job knowledge, it should never be forgotten that, while it requires real skill for its effective use, the indirect or nondirective interviewing method described in Chapter 12 has potential usefulness for this interview, not as the sole or only method, but to be employed as a part of it.

UPGRADING AND PROMOTION OF EMPLOYEES

As we turn now to the subject of upgrading and promotion, it is apparent that we are, in fact, still dealing with selection, since those who are promoted are chosen from an eligible group of people. Thus many of the remarks about initial selection apply here, but still the situations are not at all the same.

For one thing, the psychological aspects of the two situations differ a great deal. The to-be-promoted are typically not strangers to the organization, new application blanks are not usually required nor are new letters of reference or physical exams. Some promotion arrangements, particularly in civil service, do require promotion tests, and private firms occasionally require a test battery or a visit to an assessment center (see below). These arrangements are the exception rather than the rule, however. Thus our topic does deserve special treatment even though it is related to the preceding one.

This might be a good time to mention a subject that at least deserves notice in a book like this but that seldom involves the supervisor. It is the *assessment center,* best known for its use by the American Telephone and Telegraph Company. Those to be assessed are relieved from their duties for some days or weeks, are assigned to a central location, and are subjected to a variety of tests, inquiries, pressure situations, and the like. The use of such a center will probably be limited to a small number of highly placed persons and these typically in a large organization, but the evidence indicates it may have decided utility for them and the employer.[6] Assessment centers are discussed further in Chapter 13.

Definition of Relevant Terms

For clarity it probably would be wise to establish in the beginning what is meant, especially by the terms promotion and upgrading. We use *upgrading* to refer to a situation where an individual moves up in a family of closely related jobs. Thus if an employee is a Machinist C and is made a Machinist B, we often speak of an upgrade.

Promotion refers to assigning the individual to a job where he or she has more responsibility or encounters more hazard or difficulty. It is a "larger" job, one in which the employee has an opportunity to be of greater assistance to the organization in achieving its goals. It is likewise a position where one can make a bigger boo-boo, that is, where a mistake is potentially more costly.

There is a tendency to equate promotion with an increase in pay, but strictly speaking, there is no *necessary* connection between them. One can be upgraded or promoted (that is, given additional responsibilities) without change in compensation, although admittedly such action would be unwise except under unusual circumstances. But the fact is that not all increases in pay are promotions (for example, pay for long service or for cost of living) and not all promotions automatically bring about pay increases.

A related term which we shall use later in this section is *demotion,* which is the opposite of promotion; that is, it represents a decrease in responsibility and usually a decrease in pay. A demotion may come about for several reasons, of which two are most frequent. One is as a disciplinary penalty, and the other is the result of a reduction in force, at least in the job in question. Demotions as disciplinary penalties are discussed in Chapter 14. In this chapter we shall be concerned only with demotions arising from the second cause.

Another relevant term is *transfer,* which refers to a shift to another job with equal responsibility and usually equal pay. Transfer can also refer to disciplinary penalty, an undesirable transfer, for example, being used as a means of expressing disapproval. Again, when we discuss transfer in this chapter, we shall not be considering it as in any way a disciplinary sanction.

It will be noted that in the above discussion in each case we have used the term *job* and not *position*. The distinction is of no great consequence in this section, but it becomes so later in this chapter (see the section entitled "By Job Evaluation" below).

The Basis for Promotion

There are two general considerations that should be taken into account as one decides whom to select for a promotion or upgrading.

Promotion on the Basis of Merit   The basis for promotion spoken of most frequently and favorably by managers and management writers is *merit*. The argument goes that a desirable vacancy should always be awarded to the most capable of available persons, with secondary consideration, if any, given to such factors as age and length of service. On first inspection the position appears unassailable, but here, as is so often the case, things are not always what they seem.

For one thing, capability, ability, or merit is certainly not all that is involved in job success. As a matter of fact, actually *doing* what is needed is in many ways our fundamental concern. Thus we want the most capable, *best-motivated* employee and obviously not merely the one with greatest ability.

Besides in some cases, how contented an employee might be and how long he might be expected to remain in a position is a valid consideration. "Displaced" Ph.D.'s may be the most capable, best-motivated cab drivers (they also may *not* be!), but they likely are not, all things considered, the best persons to hire for or promote to the job. For one thing, they likely will leave it at the first opportunity.

Additionally we must recognize that merit is complicated and difficult to judge correctly. And even if one does judge it accurately there are likely to be others who disagree with the judgment. However, this point must not be overstressed. Managers are frequently in a position where they *must* make judgments as to merit, and they certainly should prepare to do so in the fairest and most accurate way. Perhaps the material on evaluation of employees as presented in Chapter 13 will prove useful here; certainly the cases of this chapter are relevant.

Merit should be considered when people are being evaluated for promotion. The authors are thoroughly convinced, however, that it is not the only proper consideration.

Promotion on the Basis of Seniority   Before we consider the role of seniority in promotion and upgrading we need to examine the concept more closely.

Kinds of seniority   Seniority is not as simple as it is often taken to be. For example, there is *company seniority, plant* (or store or office) *seniority, division seniority* (as in the maintenance or operations divisions), *department seniority* (as in a particular craft), and *unit* or *job seniority* (as among the operators on Unit A). There are other kinds also (for example, *shift seniority*). Obviously what usefulness seniority has or should have depends in part on what kind one has in mind.

And then there are *superseniority* and *synthetic seniority*. The former may be accorded to a leadperson, a local union official, or a particular group of machinists of unusual and vital skills. In case of a layoff, for example, they might be the last to go. Synthetic seniority, on the other hand, is the kind one accumulates when in wartime he is drafted from his job and spends, let us say, four years in the service. When he returns to his old job he then has whatever years of seniority he had when he left *plus four*. A leave for union business may lead to synthetic seniority as may an overseas assignment for the benefit of the purchaser of one of the company's turbines.

Other considerations enter into the determination of seniority. What if one is hired, works five years, is gone for a considerable time, and then is rehired? Or suppose an operator puts in five years in shift work, then serves as a foreman for five additional years, and then returns to shift work. Or a worker puts in a considerable period of time in another plant of a company and then returns to the original plant. It is evident that the determination of seniority is often quite complicated and should be governed by clear procedures and rules.

Seniority provisions in labor agreements An examination of the role of seniority in the usual labor contract may be useful for itself, but it also throws light on how substantial numbers of workers feel about the subject.

It should be noted in the beginning that it is a most unusual labor agreement indeed that permits management the freedom to promote or upgrade on merit alone. On the contrary, such agreements usually provide for one of three general ways of taking seniority into account in promotion situations. The most restrictive of these requires that the senior eligible bidder for a vacancy be given a *trial period* (perhaps of thirty days) to demonstrate his capability in the job. During this period management may disqualify him, but it has to have definite reasons for doing so. (It should be noted that not just any employee can bid on the particular opening, but only those who are *eligible,* a subject too broad for further discussion here.)

A second provision awards the opening to the senior *qualified* bidder. However, in this connection *qualified* clearly does not necessarily mean the best qualified. As a matter of fact it means *at least minimally qualified.* Under this provision the fact that a junior employee is much more capable than the one receiving the promotion is irrelevant.

From management's standpoint the best seniority arrangement it is likely to be able to negotiate is the "relatively equal" one. It provides that the opening is to go to the senior employee among all those whose skill and ability are "relatively equal." Translated into more common words, under this provision if management elects to promote other than the senior bidder it may have to show that the person selected is clearly superior to that senior bidder.[7]

Below are statements concerning the relation between promotion and seniority as these appear in different labor contracts:

Table 10-3 Promotion Provisions of Labor Agreements

"Promotion will be made on ability and efficiency with due regard to seniority. Determination of ability and efficiency is a Management responsibility" (a chemical plant).

"In all cases of promotion, demotion, layoff, recall, or transfer, seniority shall govern provided the employee has demonstrable ability" (a manufacturing plant).

"The Company will take into account the ability and efficiency of employees, and if the senior man is not capable of satisfactorily performing the duties...then the next man in the order of seniority capable of doing so shall be given the job" (a product-control laboratory).

"Promotions...shall be awarded on the basis of seniority. An employee awarded an open job shall have not more than thirty working days to demonstrate his ability, and progress" (a manufacturing plant).

"An employee ...trial period of not less than thirty days nor more than four months for the purpose of demonstrating he is qualified to perform the work" (a manufacturing company).

The attractiveness of seniority   There appear to be three reasons why employees, including many nonunionized ones, want an emphasis placed on seniority: In the first place, making decisions on the basis of something as objective as seniority is easier and also not so likely to cause disputes within the work group. Because decisions about merit can be and often are controversial, if a group must decide either formally or informally who is most meritorious, it may well encounter serious differences of opinion. In the local union, for example, it is usually more comfortable to back the top person on the appropriate seniority list and thus avoid a serious threat to morale. This point often applies also to cohesive work groups unaffiliated with any union.

In the second place, there is the feeling that all of us have, that long and faithful service should be rewarded. It is easy to approve the old expression (now in obvious violation of Title VII of the Civil Rights Act) about "the best *man* in every job" but no one really believes in it and wants to see it happen. Suppose, for example, the firm has an employee with twenty-five years of dedicated service and valuable experience, one who at the age of fifty is competent to step into a position he or she has long sought. But the firm has hired a youngster of twenty-two who now has one week or one month of experience but who is judged to be better qualified—not by much, but still in management's opinion better qualified. Very few of us really believe that the latter should be awarded the vacancy. And if the illustration is carried one step further and we suppose that hard luck has overtaken the firm, that only one position is left for these two and that hence one has to go, probably none of us really feel the younger person should be kept.

Thus it is easy to argue from a theoretical standpoint that merit should always govern. In practice it becomes apparent that such is not the case.

The third reason why employees stress seniority is simply that they do not trust management, if given a free hand, to make fair and proper decisions. One basis for this distrust goes to a lack of confidence in management's *competence.* Many times employees simply believe that management makes serious mistakes and picks the wrong person. The other basis is lack of confidence in management's *character* or *integrity.* People fear that, given a free hand, the managers would often select the worker who curries favor with management, who opposes and attempts to weaken the union, or who can generally be described as a "yes" person or a "politician."

There is no evidence that unions are about to weaken in their devotion to the significance of seniority, nor indeed is there any that indicates that employees generally want it downplayed in favor of a system basing promotion on merit alone or even nearly so.

Seniority in transfer and demotion   Employees insist on emphasizing seniority in desirable transfers in the same way they do in promotion and stress it even more heavily, as we have said, in reductions in force that lead to demotions for some and layoffs for others. In these latter situations the rule is almost universal in labor agreements: demotions and layoffs must involve those with least seniority, the more senior employees being the last to go. It is in this situation that we really see how deeply workers feel about seniority and why from a practical standpoint it is and will continue to be extremely difficult to make fundamental changes in these feelings.

The Supervisor's Role in Promotion

Being on the firing line, as we so frequently say, the supervisor has a direct stake in questions involving upgrading and promotion. What advice do the above considerations suggest for one in this position?

Avoidance of "The Easy Way Out"   In spite of what has just been said about seniority and the feelings of workers, supervisors must avoid always promoting on the basis of seniority, rewarding the person who is thought by the group to be most deserving, and especially promoting whether or not the employee is competent. Using his or her own best judgment in selecting or recommending for promotion and taking into account the above facts, the supervisor must pick the *most suitable* individual for any opening that is to be filled or concerning which a recommendation is made. And this may mean making an unpopular decision.

According Seniority the Benefit of the Doubt   All this discussion may have left the matter in some doubt, but what we are recommending is quite simple and should be generally acceptable: For a promotion the supervisor should consider both merit and seniority. If a certain employee is more meritorious than the others *beyond reasonable doubt* and if the supervisor is free to do so, the vacancy should ordinarily be awarded to this person. But if merit is equal or nearly so, that is, in cases where a junior employee is not superior *beyond a reasonable doubt,* the opening should go to the senior individual. This is obviously not the same as saying that seniority is more important than merit, and it certainly does not mean that seniority should always or nearly always be followed.

Striving to Objectify and Verify One's Judgment   It is obvious that decisions based on the actual facts of a situation rather than on one's feelings, fears, or prejudices are usually to be preferred. It is equally clear that we are not born with a tendency to make such judgments. Indeed it is much easier and in the short run often more pleasant to follow our feelings.

In this connection, three comments seem particularly appropriate for supervisors facing a promotion decision. First, they need to be careful not to be influenced by inconsequential and/or irrelevant factors. For example, in the great majority of jobs, race, religion, national origin, color, sex, and age (within certain limits) have nothing as such to do with job performance—and hence should not be considered. Neither do being the son or daughter of a fellow manager or having gone to the local high school or being "a great storyteller." In selecting for promotion, one considers three things principally: ability, character, and motivation to do the job well; seniority to the extent just described; and future prospects after some time in the new position. All else should usually be disregarded.

In the second place, they must have sufficient emotional security to accept the fact that for an employee to challenge their judgment is not an insult. It has been pointed out more than once already that an employee has at least the moral right to make such a challenge, and increasing numbers have acquired the legal right to do so.

Third, it is a good idea to check one's tentative choice, if feasible, with persons in whose judgment one has confidence. After all, in cases of promotions one almost inevitably knows other managers who know the individuals involved (and some may know helpful subordinates who can be trusted). Besides, there may be written procedures and/or precedents applicable to the situation. All these factors should be appraised to whatever extent they may be relevant to the decision in question.[8]

COMPENSATION OF EMPLOYEES

When two or more people are engaged in a common enterprise with an income flowing to the organization rather than to the individuals separately, they have a problem, namely, how to divide this income—or more properly, the income remaining after necessary expenses have been met—fairly and satisfactorily among themselves. This has obvious application to a partnership but applies also to the corporation, where at least the stockholders and the employees are entitled to, and in most cases must receive, some of the income. It also applies to the individual proprietorship if the owner has at least one person working for him in producing the income.

As we said, this can and often does become a serious problem. In this section of the chapter we want to look at one aspect of this problem, how wages and salaries are and should be determined. In many cases the supervisor has little to do directly with these matters, but wisdom suggests that an effort should nevertheless be made to become familiar with the principal facts.

Basis for Wage and Salary Determination

Much thought and attention have been given to the correct (or so-called scientific) basis for the determination of wages and salaries. A great many theories have been advanced for doing this fairly and accurately, but though most contain some elements of truth, none has been found to be applicable to all situations. We know that many factors influence wages, the most significant being prevailing rates, government edicts, worker productivity, the financial position of the firm, the supply of labor, and the tactics of groups of people such as labor unions. But when all is said and done, one conclusion stands out: There is no absolutely or scientifically correct way of determining wages and salaries.

The truth is that these amounts are determined by a sort of consensus. Many persons enter into their determination, but no one basis is the ultimately correct one. Thus the final price of product or labor results from many forces and depends on what the market will, and in fact does, bear. It is too bad that the price of labor, for example, cannot be set with precision on a sound, universally accepted basis, but such is not the case at present, and there is no reason to expect a fundamental change in this situation.

Determining Wages and Salaries[9]

Even though no universal or scientific grounds for setting wages have been found, they must still be determined. How is this task accomplished in practice? We shall discuss several methods.

By the Management of the Firm   At any time when management has considerable choice about whom to hire and no union or other agreement about wages is in effect, there is a likelihood that wage and salary rates will be set by the managers in charge. These rates are then advertised, either formally through newspapers or informally by word of mouth, and prospective employees are given the option of taking the jobs at the predetermined rates or refusing to do so.

This system of wage determination has historically been the most popular one. When large numbers of immigrants were being added to the work force, they were in no position to bargain about wages or conditions of work and frequently had no real choice but to accept the positions at the rates offered. The same conditions applied during later years when large numbers of farmers were leaving agricultural pursuits for jobs in the city.

It must not be supposed, of course, that managers were completely free in setting rates of pay. In most instances they were in competition with other employers, and if the proffered rates were seriously out of line they simply did not secure the needed workers. Furthermore, humanitarian motives, while not as prevalent then as they later became, were no doubt at times influential, and hence rates were not entirely arbitrary or necessarily at the level of bare subsistence. The point is, however, that so far as the individual worker was concerned, the rates were set by the employer and he individually could influence them but little or not at all.

By Individual Bargaining   At the same time that rates were being set unilaterally by the employer, there were job applicants who were in a position to bargain individually about their pay. This is always true for the person who is widely sought because of his own personal potential or when the skill he represents is in short supply. One illustration is the craftsman. If a contractor needs a bricklayer or a machinist and no surplus of such people is available, the individual applying for a job may be able to negotiate his rate with the employer. Likewise a person with considerable ability in football or engineering or management, to take other examples, can substantially influence his rate of pay. Of course as organizations become larger and more and more people are needed for particular job classifications, there is a tendency on the part of the employer to set up fixed rates for the jobs, and individual bargaining is less and less influential. But it is still a real factor in many cases, as it always will be.

By Collective Bargaining   One of the striking developments of the twentieth century has been the growth in, and extension of power of, labor unions. Unions serve other functions, but the truly significant one is to bargain with employers concerning wages, hours, and conditions of work. Such collective bargaining has resulted in thousands of labor contracts covering millions of workers.

The union philosophy of wage determination is certainly not accepted by all. As an example, it is frequently insisted that wages should be arrived at on the basis of some presumably objective measure of what the job is worth, but unions usually insist that rates be determined in collective bargaining between representatives of the worker and the management. Here it is not a matter of what the job is worth according to some management-selected or other standard, but rather what the parties decide on when other factors such as rates for other jobs, hours, shifts, working conditions, and fringe benefits are considered. These two ideas about wage determination represent a fundamental disagreement between most unions and most managements, a disagreement in philosophy that no amount of agreement in practice can eradicate.

As we have remarked earlier, millions of workers now have their wages and salaries set in collective-bargaining agreements; furthermore, these agreements have significant effect on many wages and salaries not covered by the agreements. The evidence is that collective bargaining will long remain an influential factor in wage and salary determination and administration. This subject is discussed further in Chapter 15.

By Job Evaluation   Most managers feel, and often with reason, that union demands are too high, but as we have just pointed out, their disagreements with unions go deeper than the demands as such. Management often believes that rates of pay should be set in terms of a device known as *job evaluation.*

Basis for Evaluation   It might be well to point out in the beginning that what is evaluated in job evaluation is *jobs* and *not positions.* The distinction here is that many persons may simultaneously occupy the same job, but a position may be held by only one person at a time. Thus all experienced, competent keypunch operators may occupy the same job (for example, Keypunch Operator A), but each person will have his or her own position.

Incidentally, not all Keypunch Operators A need be paid at the same rate, but under a program of job evaluation all would be paid within the same *rate range.* Thus the best one might receive $600 per month because she had received merit increases that put her at the top of the range, while the poorest or newest having received no merit raises, might draw only $450.

On what basis, according to the theory of job evaluation, should wage rates be set?

Two things are essential. In the first place, each job must be closely and carefully studied from the standpoint of duties, demands, experience and training, physical effort, responsibility, working conditions, and the like. The job occupants and their supervisors usually have a hand in supplying this information, and so does the job analyst, who specializes in this sort of work.

The second requirement is a job-evaluation committee, which takes this information and assesses its worth and significance. The composition of this committee varies considerably from firm to firm. At times a member of the nonmanagerial groups may be on the committee, as well as at least one person from executive management, along with other managers. The task of the committee is to arrange the various jobs in order of difficulty, responsibility, and so on, with proper regard for the distance (or difference in difficulty) between adjacent jobs. To put it another way, the committee is to arrive at a rational, objective basis for appraising the various jobs so that, among other things, rates of pay may be set fairly.

There are several ways in which the job-evaluation committee proceeds, but the most popular have in common the setting up of *factors* (or components of jobs) and assigning each job a given number of *points on each factor*. The total number of points (the sum of those assigned to each factor) is used as the basis for determining the rate of pay of the job.

Difficulties with Job Evaluation   As can easily be imagined, job-evaluation systems become very involved in large firms with many jobs. Whole sections or departments are designated to administer the plan or plans, and a great deal of time, energy, and money goes into the operation. It is easy to see why management is disappointed, therefore, when workers prove to be less than enthusiastic about it.

The source of the union's difficulty with job evaluation is not hard to locate. For one thing, job evaluation goes directly contrary to the union position that collective bargaining is the proper way to set wage rates. For another, job evaluation is viewed as a *management* device. It is not usually worked out in collaboration with workers; indeed the latter often understand little about how it operates. Thus, management is accused of using it to its advantage and to the detriment of the worker. This charge, probably false in the majority of cases at least so far as conscious planning goes, is no doubt true in certain instances, and only a few such occurrences are required to confirm an already-present suspicion.

It is probably apparent by now that the authors of this book do not favor one kind of wage determination over all others. It is doubtful whether a single one can be justified, even on theoretical grounds, as the exclusively correct or even clearly best one. All four ways of setting wages are in operation at present as they will continue to be in the foreseeable future. The job of the manager is to understand as fully as possible what is happening in this field, to use his or her best efforts to make the current plan operate well, and to lend influence to the discovery and implementation of any better plan that might be available.

Incentive Wages versus Time Wages

No doubt some workers have been "paid by the piece" or the amount of work done for a very long time, but it remained for the turn of this century to emphasize the advantages of incentive wages. *Scientific management,* mentioned earlier in this book, was the chief mover. Somehow, its proponents felt, if management gave the worker the best methods and equipment, provided the best conditions of work, furnished immediate and expert answers for his problems, and put him on incentive wages, a utopian situation for both management and the worker would be attained, or at least would be as near to being attained as possible in the world of work. It is easy to imagine their disappointment and disillusionment when things did not work out this way in practice.

Limitations of Incentive Wages   The Hawthorne studies, done a generation after the beginning of scientific management and discussed in Chapter 19, help us to see some of the difficulties. Restriction of output *should* be eliminated by incentive wages, but in fact it is not. Workers continue to fear a cutting of wage rates if they produce more. They also fear that through additional efforts they may work themselves or a fellow worker out of a job. Finally, esprit de corps and the concept of "a fair day's work" grow up. In many situations incentive wages are completely unable to overcome the combined effects of these factors.

Incentive wages also pose other problems. One is that the rate of pay per unit of production must somehow be determined, and this poses all the difficulties of setting wage rates on a time basis. (Incidentally, incentive rates may be determined in the same four ways as time rates.) Another problem is that quality of output may be of prime concern, as it would be in a firm attempting to make a truly superior product. There is much question about the appropriateness of incentive wages under these circumstances.

A third problem concerns the constant availability of work to be done. If the rate of work is not under the exclusive control of the worker, if production is subject to interruptions, if the backlog of work to be done fluctuates seriously, if there are frequent changes in the tasks of the average worker, if the components vary considerably in quality or pose uneven difficulties in handling—all these conditions make the use of incentive wages a problem.

In addition to these problems, it must be noted that some jobs (indeed, it is likely, the majority of all jobs) do not lend themselves to incentive standards. What sort of basis can be worked out so that we can "pay by the piece" the foreman or any other member of management, the secretary, the accountant, the college professor, the timekeeper, the football coach, the registrar, the title clerk, the personnel director, the inspector, and any one of thousands of others? Complicating this matter is the fact that the work done by many "service workers," for example, the janitor, goes up as production increases but not in a way that can be accurately quantified.

There is finally the fact that incentive wages may prove to be divisive of group spirit. In a very real sense, under incentive wages, "It's every man for himself," and a minimum of cooperation, especially of the spontaneous sort, is called for. The authors of this book are quite aware that group spirit may be and is often used to hold down production, and hence may be a serious liability. But they also believe that it has great possibilities for the wise manager and indeed is the only way in many cases by which outstanding performance can be attained. The point that we are making is not that incentive wages destroy or eliminate this feeling but only that they frequently put difficulties in its way. When this is true, the advantages of such methods of payment must be carefully weighed against its disadvantages.

Future of Incentive Wages   It should be made clear that the point of all this is not to condemn incentive wages. Two considerations stand out, however. In the first place, incentive wages do not represent *the* solution to wage and salary determination; they are not "the wave of the future." In the second place, like any other personnel device, they must be examined carefully, used wisely, and employed only where appropriate, considering both long- and short-term effects.

The Supervisor and Wage and Salary Administration

What we have been discussing thus far relates to the organization and its compensation problems and probably concerns the executive as much as or more than anyone else. It is hoped, however, that it furnishes a background of understanding for anyone having an interest in such problems. We need to turn to some suggestions for the supervisor concerning wage and salary administration.

The Effects of "Secret" Wages and Salaries   Before we do this, however, a word of caution to managers who adopt policies calculated to keep all salaries secret. Try as they may, they do not usually succeed in keeping all such information confidential. Additionally, the evidence indicates that when employees do not know the salaries of others but also know management does not want them to know, they tend to exaggerate them, especially the salaries of those who are higher than they in the organization, and thus minimize their own. Therefore they often become more unhappy than the facts warrant—and the final results are the opposite of what management desires, namely employee satisfaction with compensation procedures and practices.

Necessity for the Difficult Decision—and for Objectivity   The points made above concerning promotion apply equally to whatever discretion supervisors have concerning wages or salaries. They cannot always follow the popular course of action nor refuse to make proper distinctions between various individual employees. If they "duck" such decisions when they can, they may gain short-run approval but they almost certainly will not secure long-run respect. And it goes without explanation that so far as humanly possible they should make their decisions on the facts and not their feelings, "political" factors, or the like.

Finally, we mention again the usefulness of consultation with others, of checking the adequacy of one's conclusions. This, of course, has to be done with caution lest people feel that necessary confidences are not being observed and that their future depends on winning a popularity contest. But again the risk, to be guarded against in every reasonable way, is worth taking.

General Understanding of Fringe Benefits   One very important form of compensation, discussed in Chapter 8, is amounts paid to or set aside for employees, these amounts being over and above their usual wages and salaries. (Of course employees may make personal contribution to some of these.) These now represent 30 percent or more of the total compensation of large groups of employees and have become highly significant factors in employee compensation.

The supervisor, of course, has little or nothing to do with their formulation and usually has only minimum involvement with their administration. However, though he or she neither is nor can be expected to be an expert on them, the supervisor certainly should be a general source of information for the people and have dependable knowledge, at a minimum, about *where they can go* to get any facts they need. Hopefully the employer will help the supervisor secure this necessary knowledge, but the supervisor has heavy responsibility to get it on his or her own if necessary.

QUESTIONS

1   Why, in spite of our best efforts, are we usually unable to do a really good job of selecting a person for employment? To what extent is the same thing true of promotion?
2   In what ways may overemphasizing the effects of selection do damage to the organization?

3 Define (a) norms, (b) reliability, (c) validity. Do these apply to any selection device other than the psychological test? Explain.
4 What is wrong with promoting the best-qualified person in the case of every opening?
5 Why do workers (as well as most of the rest of us) often put very considerable stress on seniority in both promotion and demotion (including layoff)?
6 Explain and illustrate the three sorts of seniority provisions most often found in union-management agreements?
7 What are the principal (a) strengths and (b) weaknesses of *job evaluation* as a means of determining wages and salaries?
8 What are the principal (a) advantages and (b) disadvantages of incentive wages?

NOTES

1 For a century and more there has been a great deal of interest in the ways in which people vary from one another and in the significance of such variations. A recent, insightful treatment of the subject is Leona E. Tyler, *Individual Differences: Abilities and Motivational Directions* (New York: Appleton Century Crofts, 1974).
2 As examples of the decided interest in proper selection, in this case of potential managers, see Donna J. Rawls and James R. Rawls, "The Latent Manager: Identifying Him Early," *California Management Review,* vol. 14, no. 2, pp. 24–27, Winter 1971, and Allen I. Kraut, "Prediction of Managerial Success by Peer and Training-Staff Ratings," *Journal of Applied Psychology,* vol. 60, no. 1, pp. 14–19, February 1975. Incidentally in the second article it was found that while both were helpful, peer ratings did a better predictive job than did training-staff ones.
3 John B. Miner, *Personnel Psychology* (New York: MacMillan, 1969), chaps. 6,7; Paul Pigors and Charles A. Myers, *Personnel Administration: A Point of View and a Method,* 7th ed. (New York: McGraw-Hill, 1974), Chap. 15; and Wendell French, *The Personnel Management Process: Human Resources Administration,* 3d ed. (Boston: Houghton Mifflin, 1974), Chaps. 12–14.
4 Clemm C. Kessler III and Geo. J. Gibbs, "Getting the Most from Application Blanks and References," *Personnel,* vol. 52, no. 1, pp. 53–62, January-February 1975.
5 The references are again so numerous that only a small sample is cited: Michael Palmer, "The Application of Psychological Testing to Entrepreneurial Potential," *California Management Review,* vol. 13, no. 3, pp. 32–38, Spring 1971; Sidney Gael, Donald L. Grant, and Richard J. Ritchie, "Employment Test Validation for Minority and Nonminority Telephone Operators," *Journal of Applied Psychology,* vol. 60, no. 4, pp. 411–419, August 1975; Clifford H. Morgan and Richard A. King, *Introduction to Psychology,* 5th ed. (New York: McGraw-Hill, 1975).
6 Allen I. Kraut, "New Frontiers for Assessment Centers," *Personnel,* vol. 53, no. 4, pp. 30–38, July-August 1976.
7 An excellent discussion of this subject is *Labor Law Course,* 23d ed. (Chicago: Commerce Clearing House, 1976), pp. 2691 ff.
8 Books in personnel management usually furnish insights into the promotion process; see, for example, Pigors and Myers, op. cit., Chap. 17, and French, op. cit., Chap. 14.
9 The books listed immediately above also deal with wage and salary administration; see Pigors and Myers, Chaps. 20–21, and French, Chaps. 19–21. In addition wages in relation to labor contracts are discussed in Lloyd G. Reynolds, *Labor, Economics and Labor Relations,* 6th ed. (Boston: Houghton Mifflin, 1974), Chap. 22. David W. Belcher, *Compensation Administration* (Englewood Cliffs, N.J.: Prentice-Hall, 1974), deals more generally with the subject.

CASES

Both cases selected for this chapter concern promotion. In the first instance, to be promoted an employee had to be merely the *senior qualified* bidder, that is, he or she did not have to be the best qualified, and the question was simply, Is Ms. Gross minimally qualified without further training?

The shear operator and the crane operator of the second case faced a different situation. In order to become a Craftsman # 1, each had to have qualifications *equal to* (or of course, better than) those of any bidder with fewer years of seniority. Seniority governed, in other words, when qualifications were equal—but not when they were not.

The cases illustrate some of the difficulties in discovering—and in proving—that one employee is or is not better qualified than another.

CASE 10-1

Ms. Margaret Gross, who has been employed by the Company for nine months as a clerk-typist, has just bid on the job of General Ledger Bookkeeper B. In fact, she is the only bidder for the job.

The Standard Job Description for General Ledger Bookkeeper B reads as follows:

Under general direction from a professional accountant, posts to and maintains the
   general ledger.
Typical Duties:

1   Prepares, adjusts, and closes journal entries.
2   Prepares trial balance.
3   Compiles reports of receipts, expenditures, accounts payable and receivable, etc.
4   Performs similar or related clerical, typing, and bookkeeping duties as required.

Desirable Qualifications for Employment:

1   High school graduate.
2   Two years of bookkeeping experience with at least six months as full charge
     bookkeeper.
3   Good operating skills on adding machine, calculator, and typewriter.
4   Thorough knowledge of bookkeeping theory and practice.
5   Ability to perform a volume of detailed, complex numerical work involving arith-
     metic computations accurately with or without mechanical aid.

The labor contract between the Company and the Union requires that job openings go to the senior bidder if qualified and furthermore that "employees shall be expected to perform the work of the particular classification with the degree of efficiency required of the average incumbent working at a normal pace, without further training." The Company is to make the determination of qualifications in each case, but its decision is subject to the grievance procedure. The labor contract also permits the Company to hire from the outside if and when no qualified employee can be found among the present employees.

Ms. Gross has received the normal increases in salary during her employment and in addition has received one marked "merit." She is a high school graduate with about 1½ years of college (including one accounting course) and also a bookkeeping course in a business college. Since her high school graduation ten years ago she has had six employers, and job titles such as receptionist-bookkeeper, office head, posting clerk, payroll clerk, and accounts receivable clerk.

James Innes, the assistant controller and the supervisor of the vacant job, has questioned Ms. Gross carefully and in his own mind has determined that, while she has at least a fair knowledge of bookkeeping, she has neither the knowledge nor the experience necessary to post to the general ledger, prepare closing entries, arrive at correct trial balances, and prepare the necessary statements. According to her work history, she has kept accounts receivable and accounts payable ledgers and also payroll, but has gone beyond that only on rare occasions. Incidentally, the supervisor of the clerical pool has nothing but compliments for the way in which Ms. Gross has done her job since she has been with the Company.

What disposition should Mr. Innes make of this bid? Aside from his decision, what should he tell Ms. Gross? If he rejects Ms. Gross's bid, how successful will he be if the Union challenges his decision?

CASE 10-2

On February 27, 1976, the Company posted a job bid for "Craftsman #1. (3 Required; 2 for Warehouse [1 Electrical and 1 Mechanical] and 1 for Shop)." Among twenty others, the following signed the bid sheet: John Duke, whose seniority date was 4-11-68 and who was a shear operator, and James Willis, whose seniority date was 12-15-65 and who was a crane operator. Those selected for the openings were all classified as Craftsman #2 and were Messrs. Guthrie (seniority date 9-10-74), Lake (seniority date 6-4-74), and Mason (seniority date 6-1-74). Following selection of the latter, Duke and Willis filed a grievance protesting failure to choose them for two of the openings.

Duke had been a shear operator for six years, having previously worked in the paint department. During 1973 and 1974 he received several hundred (clock) hours of instruction in automobile repair and at the time of the grievance was taking college-credit courses at the local community college. Willis had been crane operator for some eight years, prior to which he had been a painter and painter's helper. He had taken a smaller number of hours in automobile repair, and at the time of the above bid had a bid pending for a Craftsman #2 (C-2) opening. The three persons selected for the openings were all originally hired as Craftsmen #2 and had occupied this position continuously since their employment.

The labor agreement provides that "where skill and qualification for the job classification are equal, seniority will govern." It also entitles an upgraded employee to a trial period of not less than thirty days or more than four months "for the purpose of demonstrating he is qualified to perform the work of the job classification into which he is upgraded." It is for admission to this trial period that Duke and Willis filed the above grievance.

The Union contends that the grievants were qualified by their background and experience for the C-1 openings. Not only their work experience, which brought them into contact with all sorts of mechanical devices, many of which they oiled and adjusted and often actively assisted in repairing, but also their outside training and education made them eligible for the trial period, during which they could improve decidedly on their present skills. (They admitted that they were not qualified for or bidding for the Electrical opening.) While the Company has historically required C-2 experience before promotion to C-1, that has not always been true, and besides even if it were, there is nowhere any contractual basis for such a requirement. Thus the grievants should at once be selected for C-1 positions and given a fair trial at meeting the qualifications of the job. The Union is convinced they already meet these qualifications, but has no doubt about the outcome following the trial period.

The Company contends that it was under no obligation to give the grievants a trial period unless "skill and qualification are equal," a condition that obviously did not obtain here. Certainly knowing how to repair a passenger car has little or nothing to do with the maintenance and repair of heavy equipment, tasks in which the C-1 is typically engaged and in which he leads and assists the less experienced C-2s. There is simply no way in which as shear and crane operators the grievants could have acquired the necessary skills and knowledge to be first-class craftsmen.

The Company did not contend that C-2 experience is necessary for the C-1 job, for it has hired people from the outside directly into the latter classification. However in promoting people within the plant from noncraft jobs it has always, as it legitimately should, required experience in the craft job that demands less skill before placing one in the C-1 position. The demands for the latter are very considerable, far more in fact than the grievants realize. Incidentally these grievants have for a long time had sufficient seniority to bid for C-2 openings but with the exception of Willis's recent and pending bid neither has seen fit to do so.

In spite of the fact that both grievants are black and the three C-2's selected for promotion are white, it holds that no discrimination was involved in the Company's action. (It should be noted that the Union has not charged that racial discrimination entered in it.) On the other hand, the Company holds that it made a reasonable, good-faith decision to the effect that the qualifications of those selected were beyond reasonable doubt superior to those of the grievants, and it should be sustained in its action.

What is the proper disposition of this grievance? If the Union had asserted Title-VII discrimination (see Chapter 17), how much and what kind of evidence would be required to establish it—or to refute it?

Chapter 11

Training and Development

THE NATURE OF TRAINING AND DEVELOPMENT

To what extent are supervisors responsible for the training and development of subordinates? This question is easily answered. Training and development is a *must;* it is inherent in the job of supervision. It is an essential ingredient in all the supervisory functions of planning, organizing, directing, and controlling. In performing all of these functions, whether they do it poorly or otherwise, supervisors are engaged in a training activity, although they frequently do not recognize it as such. Furthermore, regarding matters relating to productivity the supervisor has the ultimate authority for training his subordinates. If others do not do it, he *must.*

Everything that Happens Can Be Training

Almost everything that happens to employees after they join an organization serves as a training experience.[1] They learn at least in part by experience what is expected of them in each new situation. Those elements in an employee's repertoire of behavior that are rewarded and thus provide satisfaction tend to be repeated; those that are punished tend to be abandoned. Thus the acts that provoke discipline and/or approval tell them what is expected of them and what they can do with impunity. Good practices that are praised and slovenly work that goes uncriticized both serve as a source of training.

Training Can Happen by Default

There are many people within the organization who provide these rewards and punishments in addition to and sometimes to the detriment of supervisors. Informal work groups, with their clearly defined codes of behavior, can and do have a potent influence on their members. Formal groups like labor unions also can produce a strong effect. Similarly, the methods, short-cuts, and routines practiced by fellow employees all carry important meanings that are assimilated by novices as they learn their way in a new job situation.

The learning derived from all of these varied sources may be in sharp conflict with the prescribed ways of doing things. But it is those sources of information and advice that prove most consistent which will surely have the most profound effect on the employee.

The Values of Training

Of course, the values of training are not far to seek. Some of them are as follows: First, training can serve to improve employee skill, which in turn can increase the quantity and quality of output. Second, the relative amount of equipment and material required to produce a unit of output may be decreased. Third, supervisory effort may tend to shift from the disagreeable need of correcting mistakes to the more pleasant and mutually rewarding tasks of planning work and of encouraging good employees. Fourth, the various increases in productivity may well find a reflection in increased returns to employees. And last, the general tenor of relations between supervisors and employees, as well as their individual satisfaction, are likely to be more wholesome, resulting in more pleasant and satisfactory working conditions. Many of these benefits may be attained without adding to organization budgets. The money is being spent, so it may as well be spent wisely.

DEFINITION OF TRAINING AND DEVELOPMENT

Though it is admittedly arbitrary, we make an important distinction between the terms *training* and *development*.[2] *Training* includes some of what goes on on the job as well as formal courses or programs to facilitate learning and the establishment of good work habits. *Development* is much broader. Two aspects are (1) all the progress an individual makes in learning to move upward through an organization, including all experience and formal education or training courses, and (2) all the activities, including formal training courses and managerial and other (for example, staff) functions performed by an organization to facilitate early recognition of managerial and other talent, and to follow through systematically with meaningful experience, promotions, training and education courses, and encouragement to assure adequate growth and utilization of such talent.

Over the past year one of the authors has interviewed, in an eleven-state region, literally thousands of applicants for first- and higher-level managerial positions in a large organization. A question invariably asked each candidate, and one considered of first importance was: "What are your self-development plans?" People who have ambition and drive and know where they are going and what they are going to do to get there are a big step ahead of those who merely *want* to get ahead.

This suggests an important insight: In the last analysis, all development is self-development and we expect individuals who want to succeed to be so motivated. However, the problem of developing an elite work force and especially a fine management team also involves responsibilities on the part of the organization. Unless prevented by forces beyond their control, those organizations lacking such an overall employee-development program are as remiss as is the individual who merely dreams about the future.

SCOPE OF THE SUPERVISOR'S TRAINING AND DEVELOPMENT FUNCTION

All of the tasks and responsibilities of supervision discussed in this text should be viewed as having one element in common, the training and development of subordinates. Let us look at some examples.

Performance Rating

Performance rating, discussed in Chapter 13, is, or should be, a form of training. It can serve as a feedback mechanism. It should apprise subordinates of their superior performance, or of their failure to meet expectations, and thus serve as the sort of effective motivator discussed in Chapter 5. Hopefully, substandard performances can be viewed as learning opportunities and discussed constructively in such interviews with subordinates.

Disciplining

Similarly, the disciplining function, discussed in Chapter 14, can also often provide a valuable training opportunity. Discipline, like performance evaluation, is a means of providing subordinates with feedback concerning in this case failure in performance. Supervisors are, of course, obligated at least to recommend that penalties be given employees for persistent or serious performance failures, but these actions should follow every effort to train employees to improve their behavior.

Control Standards and Job Design

The function of job design, discussed in Chapter 17, is intimately related to the function of training. This is especially true when there are changes in existing jobs or when new jobs are developed. Changes in duties and responsibilities commonly mean changes in job standards. Subordinates clearly cannot be held accountable for new (or even existing!) performance standards which they have not been trained to meet.

At the other extreme, we often think of assigning subordinates to jobs (or designing jobs around them) solely in terms of their present capabilities for performing them. Generally overlooked is that the strongest motivation for employee development can occur when an individual has *not* mastered some of the responsibilities in a job. That is why the prescription of many supervisors and middle managers for the development of their subordinates during the coming year—"more seasoning in their present positions"—can easily represent a poor use of personnel. It is also why investigative, trouble-shooting, or training assignments can be among the most significant developmental experiences in an individual's career.

Jobs contribute to the development of their incumbents but only under certain conditions. It is to the advantage of supervisors to strive to create such conditions, for example, as the following: First, individuals have not yet mastered their jobs, and they know this. Second, mastery of the job is within their capabilities, and they have enough confidence, motivation, and drive to accept this. Third, achieving such mastery is more likely to lead to new learning opportunities than will long spells of practicing what was long ago mastered, especially if the individual knows this too.

Creating a motivating environment through providing such conditions calls, of course, for managerial skill and discretion. To design jobs for individuals so that the jobs are not fully mastered is to invite errors. On the other hand, long service in an essentially unchanged job may lead to thoughtlessness, blindness to new developments, and resistance to change. In the absence of the necessity to learn, people commonly simply stop learning. These and countless other variables involved indicate that creating a climate that motivates development is one place where the "professional" supervisor can be distinguished from the novice.

Job Enrichment

The concept of "job enrichment",[3] discussed in Chapter 5, holds that possibly the greatest motivator of all is providing individuals the opportunity for growth in their jobs. This involves, for example, allowing employees responsibility, and perhaps authority, for some of the planning, goal setting, and decision making which commonly reposes in the jobs of their superiors.

Regardless of the general applicability of the concept, it may be extremely helpful in individual situations. But it can founder in practice if employees are not provided the opportunity for training and development necessary for carrying out the decision-making or goal-setting responsibilities. When this happens, employees can become helplessly frustrated.

Management by Objectives

Management by Objectives, sometimes referred to as an example of vertical job enlargement (see Chapter 2), sometimes runs aground for a lack of training support. Tregoe describes it this way:[4]

> We install the MBO Program and then say to the employee, "Now you can set objectives." His situation may very well be analagous to the non-swimmer on the shore who sees someone drowning in a lake. But if he lacks the skills to go out there and reach the water, his frustration is intolerable.

Safety Training

All people, most likely, want to work safely. Unfortunately, most people also think they do work safely, just as most people consider themselves safe drivers. The truth is, that while some are not, most people are safety conscious. Yet studies show that it really is not so much a question of lack of concern but really more a question of poor training that causes people to develop unsafe working habits—or to work *unsafely*.

Not only is it desirable that the supervisor shoulder responsibility for training in safe methods, it must be recognized that it is now the law that he or she *must* do so. The Occupational Safety and Health Act (OSHA) of 1970 (see Chapter 16) requires that all work areas, conditions, sites, tools, and equipment comply with certain minimal standards. Furthermore, the law requires that the supervisor and the employee must cooperate in ensuring that those conditions are met and continue to exist. The law provides heavy fines and penalties for the employer if OSHA regulations and requirements are violated. It is up to supervisors not only to be safety conscious and to train their people in safe working practices, but also to insist on full cooperation from their employees to assure compliance with federal and state laws.

PRINCIPLES OF LEARNING

Supervisors have at their disposal, if they choose to use them, a great many principles (or laws) of learning developed over the years by social scientists. Their value, it must be recognized, lies in their use as generalizations. They describe the behavior of relatively large numbers of people in relatively large numbers of learning situations. Their application to a specific learning situation may be useful only if it is recognized that the principles of learning may require careful interpretation, adaptations, or modifications.

Too often, so-called principles of learning are couched in such academic jargon that they mean little to the supervisor. This is unfortunate since it so often leads either to indifference or misunderstanding.[5]

Four principles of learning are presented below as illustrative, rather than representative, of the large body of knowledge from which they are derived. They are (1) the principle of readiness, (2) the principle of exercise, (3) the principle of effect, and (4) the principle of operant conditioning. Stripped of their psychological terminology and stated simply, these principles present fundamentals of learning or habit formation. Each principle will be briefly defined and its usefulness to the supervisor will be analyzed in the next few paragraphs.

The Principle of Readiness

When any "conducting-unit" of the nervous system is ready to conduct, it is satisfying to the organism involved to do so; and vice versa, when any "conducting unit" of the nervous system is not ready to conduct, it is annoying for it to be forced to do so. Again, if the nervous system is ready to conduct but is not allowed to do so, the result is annoying. This explains why one must have attention and interest before starting to teach. The learners must be ready to learn, and their nervous system must be ready to function.

As he engages in the training and development of his people it is the supervisor's responsibility to get them into that condition before starting to teach. Perhaps more lessons do not get across because the supervisor has ignored this simple principle of readiness than from any other one cause. The application of the principle is so simple that a supervisor should never fail to make every effort to see that not only the class, but also the individual learner, is with him before he starts. Watching the expression on the faces of the learners as the lesson is started, asking questions of those who seem to be inattentive, changing pace, and other similar devices, may help the beginning supervisor-teacher develop skill in making the principle of readiness work.

In these classes, if interest has not been aroused, if it is not a challenge, if one has not made up his or her mind to get all one can out of it, the supervisor is not ready to begin. In other words, the law of readiness has not worked.

The Principle of Exercise

This principle is often said to contain two subprinciples, namely, the Law of Use and the Law of Disuse. The Law of Use, stated informally, says: when a connection between a situation and a response to that situation has once been made in the nervous system, that connection will be strengthened the oftener and the more intensely the connection is repeated. The Law of Disuse may be stated thus: when the connection is not repeated over a period of time, it will gradually become weaker. In other words, the oftener and more thoughtfully and vigorously a learner repeats an act, the easier and more nearly automatic the act becomes. "Practice makes perfect," but *only* if the practice is *thorough* and is done with *intent to improve*. The learner must give attention to the improvement of his or her work. Obviously, he or she should use the best method for the particular job at hand. Learning by a long, hard, slow method, when a short, easy one is available, is a waste of time. Learning wrong habits is often worse than learning none. Our "practice makes perfect" formula could well be written thus: "*thoughtful* practice with *intention to improve* makes perfect," or "intelligent repetition ensures mastery."

The Law of Disuse explains why we may lose our "touch" or "feel" and have to practice or review in order to revive a neglected skill, procedure, or item of learning. This practice or review period will be shortened in proportion to the degree that the skill or knowledge was mastered in the first place.

Obviously, a knowledge of the Law of Exercise and its sublaws of Use and Disuse is of value to everyone in the teaching field. However, thousands of teachers and hundreds of thousands of students, including many no longer in educational institutions, suffer every day in the year from lack of the proper application of the law.

The Principle of Effect

The Principle of Effect states that when a connection has been made in the nervous system between a situation and a response to that situation, with satisfying or pleasing results to the organism, that connection will be strengthened. It also states (negatively) that, if the results of a response are annoying or displeasing, that particular connection is not so likely to be used in the future, or in other words, it is weakened. This is perhaps the most neglected law of the three.

Supervisors who teach, in general, are all too prone to use the negative portion of the law, by punishing for *poor* results or misconduct, and rarely, if ever, rewarding for *good* results or conduct. They apparently assume that accomplishment is its own reward. Perhaps it is, but it should not be made to be its only reward.

Good work should not be taken for granted, and comments should not be made only on poor work. Indeed, much experimental work has led to the position that the negative portion of this law is of relatively less value than the positive one. Thus, the greater utility seems to lie in the reward side. A conclusion with wide applicability is: Students who work for grades usually really work for good grades, not to avoid poor ones. In the long run, motivation based on approval seems to be more effective than that based on censure. And most of life's worthwhile activities seem to be based upon striving for rewards of one kind or another, rather than striving to avoid punishment. This point can be overdone. Sanctions for poor conduct are at times very influential. But they should be used as infrequently as feasible.

The Principle of Operant Conditioning

Several closely related psychological concepts underlie a great many principles of learning. Among these are operant conditioning, reinforcement, discrimination, and behavior shaping. The term *operant* refers to the operation or behavior which is a desired goal or response. *Conditioning* refers to a behavior that has been changed from an initial behavior. This changed behavior has been brought about by a substitute or conditioned stimulus.[6]

An oversimplified example may indicate that, despite the formidable terminology used, these concepts may provide useful insights for supervisors in some training situations.

Operant Behavior + Stimulus = Immediate Reinforcement. Suppose you want to teach your dog to retrieve a ball out of the water. She runs to pick up a stick. She is responding to something, she is showing *operant behavior*. That is, her behavior operates on the environment. You immediately give her a bone. This is a *stimulus*. She is rewarded and tries again. You have given her *immediate reinforcement*.

It is important to note that your dog must be active. An important principle of learning is involved here. *You cannot reinforce her behavior unless she is busy doing something.*

Selective Reinforcement = Conditioned Discrimination. At this point introduce a ball and give her a reinforcing bone (stimulus) only when she picks up the ball. You are using *selective reinforcement* to make her react to the difference between ball and stick. The purpose of this is to bring about *conditioned discrimination*.

By designing a logical, systematic learning sequence, you can eventually train your dog step-by-step to retrieve the ball from the water. You are shaping her behavior. You are building a new skill. If you help her maintain this behavior, we can observe it and will conclude that she has learned.

Training the Human Animal

Animal trainers have practiced these basic principles of learning for centuries. It is hypothesized that these principles can be applied not only to laboratory training of children and adults, as in fact they have been, but also to training employees in general.

Research studies at the University of Michigan have resulted in the hypothesis that many or perhaps all supervisors are using operant conditioning right now, unwittingly, as a management technique. If supervisors have shaped employees' behavior by deliberately encouraging only desirable practices, they have used operant conditioning.

In operant conditioning, the *nature* of the stimulus which elicits the initial response is not as important as the *immediate presentation* of the reinforcer after the initial response is made. The presentation of reinforcement may be made in a variety of ways—verbally, affectively, (that is, emotionally), or physically. (The reinforcer is the specific content or means used—the phrase "very good," a smile, or a blue ribbon.)

Reinforcers, then, may be absent or present. If they are absent, a response may become extinct because the learning environment was not modified in any way following the response. Studies of animal behavior, on the other hand, have led to a belief that punishment weakens behavior on a temporary basis, unpredictably and undependably; that it is not constructive; and thus, that extinction may be a more desirable way to break habits than punishment. That these conclusions are often true of humans there can be no doubt. That they are always true is open to question. As we point out in Chapter 14 there still seems to be a legitimate place for punishment (discipline) in the work situation.

As an addition to obtaining practice and reinforcements of learning, learners as self-directing persons benefit from those opportunities that allow for their own sense of discovery and assessment of knowledge gained.

INDUCTION OR ORIENTATION OF THE NEW EMPLOYEE

We now turn from a summary of some fundamental principles of learning to a discussion of some procedures and practices related to training commonly found in the world of work. We first discuss the practice of inducting or orienting a new employee.

The process of induction, which we use as synonomous with the term orientation, is actually a pretraining process. It is the responsibility of supervisors to acquaint all new employees with their new jobs and to introduce them to fellow employees as well as their new environment. The way this is handled can have an important effect upon the employees' initial adjustment, subsequent progress, and perhaps eventual longevity of employment, since it can directly affect their attitude toward the entire concept of the organization.

The "Quaking Hours"

Most people starting a new job tend to feel at least a bit nervous, somewhat confused, anxious, and ill at ease. This is of course to be expected inasmuch as they are being introduced to a new milieu, as well as a new boss and a host of other people with whom they must function for half of their waking hours. With some truth, the break-in period has been called "the quaking hours."

The adjustment period should involve sound planning and a high degree of empathy on the part of the supervisor. Haphazard induction procedures are reflected in increased turnover figures, higher absenteeism, a greater proportion of disgruntled employees, and frequently in generally decreased productivity. To help new employees overcome the typical anxieties and fears of new employment, they should be informed about organization rules and policies, introduced to coworkers and those in adjacent areas, familiarized with the tasks they will be expected to perform, and given an understanding of the manner in which their job relates to the total operation of the organization.

Induction: A Self-examination for the Supervisor

Illustrative questions that might be included in a supervisor's self-examination of induction skills are: Have you personally welcomed new employees to the department? Have you checked their job training and made sure it is satisfactory? Have you introduced them to several of their fellow workers and, perhaps, arranged for someone to go to lunch with them (if you do not plan to do this yourself)? Have you checked their understanding of important rules, procedures, safety, benefit plans, and so on? Have you made them feel welcome, paid each a genuine compliment or at least expressed an interest in their families, outside interests, or the like? Have you encouraged their questions? Have you seen them personally at the *end of their first* day? Have you done your best to help make their first impressions good ones, so that when they get home they will have some favorable things to say about their first day at work?

To summarize, and to add an important question to those stated above, have you contributed one of the greatest and most lasting satisfactions to the employee and to yourself—your best efforts to give him or her a feeling of dignity and worth as an individual?

INDIVIDUAL, ON-THE-JOB TRAINING

Supervisors usually tend to think of training in terms of *group training* programs. We shall summarize characteristics of some of the more common types of group training methods later. First, however, we discuss on-the-job training. This is an *individual training* technique which is, or should be, a continuing responsibility of all supervisors.

Definition

The term "on-the-job training" indicates the place where training actually takes place rather than a type or method of training, for all sorts of training methods may be used in it. To be most effective it should be a continuous and systematic, organized program relating to a single individual. It should be designed to meet *definite objectives,* as contrasted with incidental, haphazard training or—as often happens—no training at all. (It may in this regard also be distinguished from much group training in which we engage.)

Purpose

The purpose of on-the-job training is to bring employees to the point where they can perform efficiently, safely, and in a minimum of time all of the steps and operations involved in the work to which they are assigned or will need to be assigned. It should aim to help employees to develop and maintain their greatest productive capacity. It should provide an environment in which subordinates may become motivated to achieve a sense of self-assurance, job satisfaction, and the capability for advancement to better jobs.

Essential Features

Some of the more important features of on-the-job training are (1) that it is given employees while they are at their work station; (2) the vehicle of instruction is the task to be performed, together with equipment, space, physical conditions, and other means necessary to the performance of the task; (3) it may be initial training for some employees, while for others it may be an addition or a supplement to other training, (4) it may be the sole training for some, and for others it may be a follow-through of off-the-job training. In any instance, it takes place in a personal supervisor-learner situation at the individual work station. It may be conducted in any of an almost countless number of areas of training, such as clerical, professional (for example, involving engineers, lawyers, accountants, operational research personnel), maintenance, security, craft, safety, and even orientation or induction.

When It Should Be Given

For some types of operations on-the-job training may be necessary for every employee as he or she comes to the job. In other cases it should be available to every new employee who shows weakness in the performance of any task, whose job is changed, or whose duties and responsibilities on the same job are changed. Too, the job induction phase of orientation of new employees may be most effective when it is part of their initial on-the-job training.

In addition, the performance of employees who have been on the payroll for some time should be carefully observed by the supervisor and their effectiveness appraised and most likely reviewed with them (see Chapter 13 on performance evaluation). For example, if an employee is not meeting quality, quantity, time, or cost standards, or not following safe and prescribed work methods, the causes should be studied to determine if, and what, training is needed.

An important principle bears repetition at this point. The causes of ineffective performance may not be the fault of subordinates. Hence supervisory self-examination should be a first consideration. The fault may lie in poor supervisory planning, organizing, directing, or controlling. Too, it may be due to poor management at higher levels, a factor over which the supervisor may have little or no control. For example, policies, procedures, and philosophies may be inadequate in meeting the current situation. When such conditions exist, the supervisor may be forced to live, at least in the short run, with the performance inefficiencies—in spite of textbook admonitions to the contrary.

A supervisory investigation (and often an admonition) is required if an employee continues at a low level of performance when the fault is that of the employee. Every effort should be made to develop such employees through training and counseling (see Chapter 12). When the best efforts fail, supervisors are obligated immediately to take other measures, such as disciplining, transfer, demotion or discharge. A failure to enforce promptly in an individual case the sorts of performance standards discussed in Chapter 4 can lead to a breakdown in supervisory control over an entire group. We previously referred to this principle as Gresham's Law of Control: bad controls can drive out all controls.

Supplementary Off-the-Job Training

On-the-job training by the supervisor is not always sufficient for several reasons. First, employees in some relatively complex and highly skilled jobs require a considerable amount of training that cannot be given advantageously on the job. Incumbents may need to know more than the "how" in performing their operations. There is often a considerable amount of basic job information that they must acquire along with a large amount of basic technical knowledge and related skills that would be useful. This situation may most adequately be handled by the supervisor or others in short-term, off-the-job training.

Second, even employees who come to the job with an adequate degree of experience and skill may be more profitably (to themselves and coworkers) trained in off-the-job situations in such matters as established operating procedures and methods of their particular activity and operating unit. Such training can help avoid mistakes caused by employees being left to pick up this information on the job.

Third, on-the-job training may not be enough for specific individuals who have ambition, drive, and potential, but are initially slow learners because of factors possibly beyond their control. Examples are employees who are unduly sensitive or aggressive, or whose behavior reflects previous "hard-core" environments. Frequently, we have found from experience, extra efforts to understand and train such types of individuals are more than repaid subsequently by their respect, loyalty, dedication to their jobs, and development of ambition, drive, and promotional skills and abilities. An added contribution is a feeling on the part of the supervisor of pride and accomplishment in having contributed to the worth and dignity of the individual. Such a feeling can be a lasting one, when all other details of a specific management assignment are forgotten.

Training the "Hard Core"

Supervisors in many organizations are involved today in various kinds of training programs for a group that comes under the category heading of "hard-core unemployables." These are workers, many unskilled, who just cannot keep (or have not kept) a job, for a variety of reasons. The objective is to rehabilitate these people and to make them productive members of the working force. At the supervisory level, on-the-job training programs are probably most common. The supervisor is obligated not only ethically but by policy to exercise a great deal of skill, tolerance, and understanding of human behavior in handling such situations. Trainees from disadvantaged cultural backgrounds often do not adapt easily to the world of work.

A variety of other training programs are conducted for the "hard core" and are commonly subsidized by the federal government. An example is training centers that offer vocational skill training as well as social training and discipline. Also there are some programs that attack the problem from a psychological standpoint by using "sensitivity training," encounter groups, transactional analysis, or similar less well-known methods. Finally, the problem is being approached from the other side by training the employers in supervision methods and motivation principles as well as improved training techniques.

Reports indicate that many of these training programs are working effectively, and many reformed "hard-core unemployables" are now holding steady jobs and have become productive members of society.

THE PROCESS OF GROUP TRAINING

Determining Training Needs

Just how do we go about developing and conducting formal programs of training *groups* of employees? Management should follow the basic approach to planning and decision making discussed in Chapter 2. The first step in the training process is to determine what, if any, problems exist that justify or necessitate training. It is important to note at this point that many problems that might carelessly be classified as needs for training may not properly belong in that classification at all. They may be problems of poor supervision, or poor organization policies, procedures, rules, and controls. A preliminary step, then, might be managerial self-examination.

A careful assessment of training needs of a group of individuals involves a careful evaluation of such things as their attitudes and performance on the job, their levels of aspiration, ambition, drive, educational and experience backgrounds, and even physical abilities (as strength, agility, health, sight, and hearing).

Gathering such data involves using all available recorded data, such as commendations, disciplinary actions, and other items in the personnel folder (as well perhaps as some outside of it). Frequently, however, the best source is the supervisor's personal observations of subordinates.

Although all employees should undergo training, all need not be trained to the same degree, and seldom can all be trained at the same time. An organization's facilities for training are rarely sufficient to undertake such a broad program even if desirable. Hence the guiding principle should be that of attacking training problems where the needs are greatest. After urgent needs are taken care of, those with lower priority should be served.

Determining Training Goals

Determination of the need for training provides us with a basis for determining training goals. In the authors' experiences this step in the process of training is too frequently slighted and sometimes even ignored. When this happens, trainees and at times even trainers have no idea during the training just what the learning goals are. This can be one good reason why a substantial number of organizational training programs go down the drain.

Following is an illustrative list of kinds of objectives of training. Supervisors or other trainers might well benefit by developing a comprehensive, specific checklist of their own: (1) to improve the performance of present employees on their present jobs, (2) to prepare present employees for newly developed or modified jobs, (3) to reduce accidents and increase safety and health, (4) to improve present employees' attitudes, (5) to orient new employees to their jobs, (6) to teach new or old employees about overall operations that extend beyond their jobs, (7) to train employees for promotions to specific jobs, (8) to train employees so they can help teach new employees in an expansion program.

Determining Subject Matter

Once the needs and training objectives have been developed, a decision must be made regarding specifically what should be taught in order to achieve the objective. Checklists of questions may be helpful here too. Following are some general questions designed to illustrate this point: (1) Can, and should, the job or training subject be broken down into steps or parts for training purposes? (2) Are there standards of quality, quantity, time, and cost that trainees should be taught? (3) Are there certain skills and techniques that should be learned? (4) Should trainees be taught about certain hazards and safety practices? (5) Should methods be taught regarding how employees may avoid or minimize waste and spoilage? (6) Should employees be taught how to operate computers and other kinds of equipment presently in use or planned for the future? (7) Are there attitudes that generally prevail that need improvement or modification?

After establishing the subject matter for a training course the next step may be the selection of a kind or method of training that best meets our present situation. Kinds of group training methods are illustrated next by a summary of some of the more important ones in practice.

GROUP TRAINING METHODS COMMONLY USED

The following summary of some of the more commonly used training methods is described in terms of the opportunity each offers for learner involvement in the training situation (see Figure 11-1.)

The Lecture Method

The lecture method is possibly the oldest and most widely used training method. It is teacher-oriented, not learner-oriented. The lecturer does the talking and trainees do the listening. It lies to the left in Figure 11-1. However, this method can have several advantages. It gives the lecturer a great deal of control over the subject matter. It can be organized and presented as seems best.

Training Methods

Lecture method	Modified lecture–dialogue	Conference method	Case	Incident method	Simulation method	Role play	Managerial grid	Sensitivity
Low			Degree of learner involvement					High

Figure 11-1 Some common training methods by degree of learner involvement inherent in each method.

The lecture method may also be useful in transmitting large amounts of information in short periods of time to a great many people. Thus the method may especially be useful in presenting factual and background information.

The lecture method may also be valuably applied when dealing with employees with little experience or in presenting general information on new policies, procedures, or methods.

In spite of all the advantages cited above, the lecture method is frequently condemned as being a poor training technique when used alone. It is commonly believed that its value, if any, lies in combining it with other techniques. For example, the lecture might be useful in summarizing the results of various kinds of group training sessions.

Probably the greatest limitation of the lecture approach is that over time it may create submissive and dependent tendencies on the part of learners. Worse, it may also sow the seeds of disinterest and apathy. Learners have little control over content and may find much of the preselected material of little use or irrelevant.

Modified Lecture or Dialogue Method

The modified lecture or dialogue approach is located to the right of the lecture method in Figure 11-1, a location that illustrates its relatively greater emphasis on learner involvement. This approach is often used by more skillful lecturers to engage learners in "round robin" discussions of and reactions to comments of the instructor. However, as compared to some other methods, it affords very little interaction opportunities for learners. This interaction is on a one-to-many basis and is limited by the skill of the instructor in handling learner comments. It is also limited by the learners' capacity for overcoming the barriers to self-exposure that exist in large groupings. Instructors often assume that the lecture-dialogue leads to effective learning, based on the assumption that as long as learners respond, learning is occurring. Learner control over, and involvement in, content may be still minimal, however.

The Conference Method

The conference method is one in which the leader commonly chairs discussion rather than acting as a lecturer. This method provides for more learner involvement, as shown in Figure 11-1. Effective use of this teaching method, however, is dependent upon meeting certain demands such as (1) good, stimulating leaders, (2) subjects with which a group of learners is familiar, (3) members who have similar backgrounds, and (4) members who are willing to participate actively. This method is frequently used in dealing with professional, scientific, and supervisory personnel where the training involves communication of ideas on subjects common to all.

Hopefully the participants learn by exchanging ideas. The leader typically is involved only in performing functions such as (1) rephrasing questions asked and submitting them to the learning groups for answers, (2) rephrasing statements made by trainees as necessary in order to clarify them so that all trainees have a common knowledge, (3) summarizing progress made at appropriate times during a discussion, (4) thinking along with a group to help it analyze and reach decisions, (5) adopting a permissive or accepting point of view that encourages trainees to express themselves without fear of censure or ridicule by the group, (6) exercising some control over the verbal output of the more talkative members and bringing out the more reserved ones, (7) developing sensitivity to the thoughts and feelings of individuals, and finally (8) obtaining general consensus on points without forcing agreement, or sidestepping disagreement.

The Case Method

The objective in the case method[7] is to sharpen the thinking of members, to increase their perception of the factors embraced, to improve their powers of analysis, and to enhance the ability to reach better decisions.

This approach to teaching-learning may be considered to lie to the right of the conference method, toward greater learner involvement, as shown in Figure 11-1. It incorporates many of the features of the preceding methods while adding a new one, intensive, small-group discussion. Discussions typically occur around case studies which may reflect actual situations that have occurred in industry or more appropriate settings (such as those presented in an abbreviated form in this book). Learners may and often do work in small groups which are required to analyze, diagnose, and recommend solutions to given problems. Small-group discussion is typically followed by discussion by the entire group. The instructor serves as both moderator and catalyst.

As compared with the lecture, lecture-dialogue, and conference methods, many of the barriers accruing from large groupings may be overcome and interaction rates increased significantly with the case method.

However, the case method makes heavy demands on the leader. It has suffered in practice from ill-prepared and poorly trained leaders and from groups that do not understand its objectives and potential. Like the conference method, it can degenerate into aimless discussion or can be monopolized by the more vocal members. When this happens, even sincere participants may become discouraged and wonder what they are deriving from the discussions.

The Incident Method

The incident method is shown in the above figure to the right of the case method, that is, toward greater learner involvement. It is related to, but is claimed to have a unique advantage over the case method. Whereas the case method is designed to aid trainees to work together in small groups in solving assigned problem situations, the incident method goes a step further and requires trainees to ask questions and to learn how to ask questions in order to find problems. These problems are then attacked on a case basis.

A group may be given only a sentence or two pertaining to a problem-incident. The group tries to obtain all of the information that it needs about this problem-incident by asking questions of the leader. Subsequently, the members interact with each other in small or large groupings, to discuss the problem-incident and arrive at a combined decision. A major value of this training method is that if trainees fail to gather enough information they will be unable to solve problems. Thus the importance of gathering adequate if not complete information is emphasized.

Simulation

Simulation training attempts to imitate real work situations. The use of this technique varies widely, however, and many times it employs elements seen also in other approaches. Simulation training goes all the way from business games in college or other training programs to various mechanical devices such as the Link trainer for pilot training. In the business game a simulated marketing, production, and/or financial situation is arranged while the students respond as if they really had to make decisions affecting the enterprise. Its purpose is to provide a challenging environment for students wherein they may be able to develop the skills that managers need. A premise is that the complex structuring of data and circumstances in the game allows for the acquisition of several abilities, among them the ability to set goals and to forecast and plan. Along with this, the game gives the opportunity to play the role of both generalist and specialist and to organize and use information from a complex environment. Not the least of the purported advantages is the additional chance to learn to work effectively with other people. The business game provides players, arranged in groups of five to ten, with 1000 to 2000 pieces of information for each "month" of play. The players are able, from this information, to make over 300 decisions each simulated month.

Role Playing

Role playing may be defined as a method of human interaction that involves practicing behavior in imaginary situations. As shown in Figure 11-1 it rates high in learner involvement, about on a par with the incident method. It is designed to aid individuals and groups in improving their effectiveness, not by discussing a problem, but by actually doing something about it. People play parts or roles (either their own or those of someone else) in a (usually) hypothetical situation.

Development of the technique of role playing dates back to the early nineteen hundreds. It can be credited to the Viennese psychiatrist Moreno. Historically, perhaps the most widespread use of the technique was in a program prepared under the direction of the War Manpower Commission (Training within Industry), which was a significant landmark in industrial training. The program, called Job Instruction Training (JIT), included sessions during which participants were asked to play their own role in teaching an industrial task to someone else. The basic purpose of these sessions was to increase supervisors' skills in on-the-job training. Thousands of supervisors were exposed to the method even though the label "role playing" was rarely used.

Today some form of role playing is included in most of the training programs that involve, for example, human relations, decision making, managerial skills, interviewing, and other situations where the goal is to increase the participants' effectiveness in dealing with others.

It has become, for example, an integral part of many sales programs. Salesmen practice handling objections, carrying out demonstrations, and "closing" through the use of role-playing techniques. Likewise, it is used in laboratory or sensitivity training. The most recent development in the use of role playing has been in business games, simulation, and problem-solving exercises. Students are often asked to play specific managerial roles to make a simulation or business game more realistic.

The basic training theory involved in this structured or preplanned role playing includes the following ingredients:

1 Learning by doing. Such training provides the opportunity for practice, experimentation, and trial-and-error learning.

2 Learning through imitation. Participants in these sessions can observe how others handle problems and imitate and adapt successful approaches and methods used by others.

3 Learning through observation and feedback. Participants not only act in a role-playing situation, but they have a chance to observe the actions of others and to react to the behavior of the role players. Since some group members identify with the actions of players, the feedback or critique session following a role-playing enactment frequently has meaning for everyone in the group, not just the people who are playing roles. Observations are discussed and clarified and provide a basis for changes in approach. Without feedback, role playing commonly becomes amusement or boredom. It is at the feedback stage and only there that the learning and behavior change will be effected. All else is designed to lead to this teaching point.

4 Learning through analysis and conceptualization. Observation and feedback activities may lead to a more careful analysis of the forces at work in a given training or real-life situation. It may be possible, after having observed a series of role-playing enactments, to begin to conceptualize principles of human behavior or management more systematically and more adequately. Maier says: "In order to test the adequacy of principles or points of view, one must go from conceptual thinking to a particular set of circumstances." The role playing itself provides the specific circumstances where ideas, skills, and viewpoints may be tested. When members of a group have carefully discussed a particular situation, it is hoped that they will be in a favorable condition to understand each other when an attempt is made to generalize the findings.

The Managerial Grid

The Managerial Grid,[8] discussed in Chapter 5, is a group training program designed to aid individuals in determining what present or potential leadership styles they possess. Ideally, individuals first describe in group sessions what their leadership styles are before they analyze them carefully for themselves.

At the end of the training program each of the individuals is rated by the rest of the group on what they *perceive* the individual's *actual* leadership type to be, this evaluation being based on the group's observation of each individual's behavior as the latter participates in solving group-assigned problems.

The Figure 11-2 shows five of the many leadership styles against which each individual is measured. We know that the kind of leadership style that should be used at any point in time depends on the situation. However, often the implication in this program is that the leadership style listed in the upper right-hand corner of the grid is generally the best. This is because it represents a high concern for both getting the work out (horizontal axis) and concern for people (vertical axis).

Sensitivity Training

The objective of sensitivity training, sometimes called T-group (T means training) training, is to aid the trainee in improving self-awareness and sensitivity to others. Further, it aims to develop leadership and teamwork behavior, and to facilitate changes in organization behavior. Sensitivity training is shown at the far right in Figure 11-1.

The forms that sensitivity training programs take vary widely. As Keith Davis states,

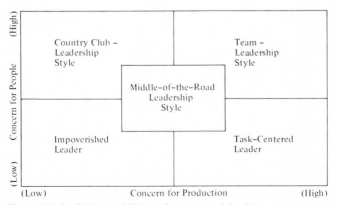

Figure 11-2 Blake and Mouton's managerial grid.

sensitivity training "as a group training method . . . may be routine, or it may employ intense, emotional group sessions which lay bare a person's psyche to the group."

Typically the role played by the leader in such training is minimal. Leaders may fade out of the group or remain unobtrusive, especially at early stages.

With no planned agenda, groups are thrown together for a substantial period of time in an environment so different that ordinary patterns of reacting and interacting in social situations are drastically affected. In these unstructured groups, members generally start with "small talk," move to intellectual exchange, gradually engage in guarded revelation of emotions and of themselves generally, and in some cases throw off defenses and become unrestrained in expression of feelings. The goal is a greater understanding of the interplay of emotion and intellect in people, a realization of difficulties encountered in ordinary daily communication, increased self-insight, and greater appreciation for the feelings of others.

Though its popularity has been great, it appears that an increasing number of critics question whether sensitivity training has much proven value in helping supervisors (or nonsupervisors) perform their jobs more effectively. Furthermore, some of them feel that even though it may be beneficial for participants to discover how others in a group may perceive them, such experiences can penetrate the defense mechanisms of individuals who lack self-confidence. Odiorne suggests that the sensitivity training lab is

> a great psychological nudist camp in which he (the participant) bares his pale, sensitive soul to the hard-nosed autocratic ruffians in his T-Group and gets roundly clobbered. He goes away with his sense of inferiority indelibly reinforced.

Herzberg is quoted as putting it more succinctly: "Some of his most acid remarks are aimed at advocates of sensitivity training and T-groups. He calls them 'touchie feelies' and asserts their sessions cannot truly help people to understand themselves and others: If analysts can't do it on a couch after six years, how can they do it in three days?"

Many authorities are of the opinion that Odiorne and Herzberg have overreacted to the negative features of sensitivity training, but the method obviously has shortcomings to go along with its real accomplishments.

QUESTIONS

1 Which of the training methods discussed in this chapter would you use in training (1) a group of credit clerks in a department store whose job has just been redesigned to include meeting the public regarding credit matters, (2) a group of recently hired (by a law firm) young lawyers who have just graduated from a university, (3) a clerk in an insurance firm whose skills have become obsolete? Why?

2 How should a supervisor go about handling this assignment: "Prepare a report on the training needs for people in your department."

3 All the basic functions of supervision include a responsibility and accountability for training. Is this true or not? Explain.

4 Describe the value of role playing as an asset in most kinds of group-training methods.

5 To what extent has the need for "hard knocks" type of experience been eliminated by individual and group-training techniques?

6 Describe the major factor that might be responsible for the incident method of training coming closer to reality than does the more commonly used case method.

7 Why is it important that an involvement in management training and development activities be started with top executives first?

8 Why would you think that many organizations with development programs have begun to critically reevaluate their programs?

NOTES

1　William Paul, Jr., Keith Robertson, and Frederick Herzberg, "Job Enrichment Pays Off," *Harvard Business Review,* **47**:61–78, March 1969.
2　For a psychological discussion see W. E. Scott and L. L. Cummings, *Readings in Organizational Behavior and Human Performance* (Homewood, Ill.: Irwin, 1973), pp. 29–42.
3　For a concise psychological discussion of learning theory see Edgar H. Schein, *Organizational Psychology,* 2d ed. (Englewood Cliffs, N.J.: Prentice-Hall, 1970), pp. 39–49.
4　Benjamin B. Tregoe, *Enrichment and Training in Business and Industry,* p. 22.
5　See Harold Frankel, "On the Job Training-Permanent Institution," *Training and Development Journal,* vol. 23, no. 3, p. 28, 1969.
6　Dimock, Hedley G.: "The Case Method in Teaching and Supervision," *Nursing Outlook,* vol. 6, no. 1, pp. 46–47, January 1958.
7　Greene, J. R. and R. L. Sisson, *Dynamic Management Decision Games* (New York: Wiley, 1959).
8　For a comprehensive discussion of the Managerial Grid see R. E. Blake and Jane S. Mouton, *The Managerial Grid* (Houston: Gulf, 1964).

CASES

As is usually true of these chapters, we do not have cases that relate to training and development alone. The Greenfield case certainly raises the question of the adequacy of the training the employee had received, including how well he has been advised by Management of his progress or lack thereof. Indeed it raises a question about the "climate" of the laboratory itself—in addition to the disciplinary decision faced by the lab director.

The other case raises at least one training issue: How far should an employer go—or be obligated to go—to provide training opportunities to "old-timers" who work in functions where a reduction-in-force is more likely? There is, of course, no simple answer to this question. On the other hand the answer to the grievance may not be so complex. What should the Company do in this situation?

CASE 11-1

Robert Greenfield is a Laboratory Technician A in the products laboratory of the Company. Along with other technicians, he runs samples taken from the product lines, records the results, and forwards them, in person, by telephone, or by messenger, to the process department involved, as well as to his own supervisor.

Greenfield has been with the Company for five years, all in this laboratory. He had two years of college prior to four years in the service, began work as a helper, was later made Technician B and has been Technician A for two years.

So far as the personnel records go, Greenfield has been a satisfactory employee. His absences are fewer than average, and he is nearly always on time. No formal records are kept of amount of work done, but Greenfield does his share of work in a group that is not, however, distinguished in output. On the other hand, its production is not low enough to have led to any disciplinary action.

From the beginning Greenfield has been active in the Union. For the last eighteen months he has been the grievance committee chairman for the laboratories, and about six months ago he was a vigorous and effective union witness in an arbitration case which the company lost. Fred Barratt, the supervisor of the products laboratory, was greatly irritated at this testimony, for it reflected directly on his judgment as a supervisor. Ed Robertson, the director of the entire laboratory, was also displeased, though not as strongly as Barratt.

The problem of this case arose from Greenfield's work of about a week previous. He was analyzing samples according to a new procedure which had just been adopted and in which he had been instructed for some time by Barratt and Robertson. On two successive samples he obtained, recorded, and reported values just half as large as were found when the product was meeting specifications. The obtained values were noticed at once by Barratt, who ordered another analysis and found the product to be satisfactory. The error was found in time to prevent any interruption of operations, though it could have been expensive if it had not been found early.

Barratt believes he knows what the trouble was. At one point Greenfield was supposed to use a 10-milliliter pipette to add a certain chemical to the sample and Barratt believes that for the two samples in question he used a 5-milliliter one instead. This would have led to the values obtained.

Barratt is really upset about this error. He has just recommended to Robertson that a notice of poor work be put in Greenfield's personnel folder and that he be given a three-day layoff for carelessness, poor work, and disobedience of written instructions. He contends that only carelessness and indifference could cause the error, unless indeed it was deliberate.

Robertson now has the problem of how to deal with the whole situation, including Barratt's recommendation.

CASE 11-2

The Company found it necessary to carry out a layoff of about 50 of its 250 Production employees. However, the maintenance department was not only fully occupied but was working overtime. It was therefore not reduced at all.

The most relevant contract provision is to the effect that "when work becomes slack the Corporation will either reduce the work week . . . or lay off a sufficient number of employees according to seniority in order to maintain . . . a forty-hour week." The Contract also says that the above seniority provisions apply "provided their application does not impair the efficiency of any plant operation."

Two Production employees with greater seniority than certain junior employees in Maintenance grieved to the effect that they should have been retained and two of the junior employees laid off. *The Union contends that* though not so classified they were qualified to do junior mechanic work and should have been so employed. *The Company contends that* it made a sound, good-faith decision; that to follow the principle supported by the grievance would have in many instances, including this one, impaired the efficiency of plant operations and hence was not contractually required. Even if the grievants were qualified—a conclusion the Company does not accept—their introduction would disturb the organization of the crew and inevitably cause a decrease in output.

Is the Union correct in its contentions? How about the Company? What "remedies" should be adopted if the grievance is sustained? (This question should *not* be read to imply that it should be.)

Chapter 12

Counseling Employees

In the chapter just concluded emphasis was placed on management opportunities to assist employees to become more responsible as persons and more productive as workers or managers. It was pointed out that while the organization cannot *develop* the employee, it can and should assist him or her in such development.

In this chapter the emphasis will shift a bit. Rather than stressing employee opportunities for personal growth and development, we shall discuss the problems that employees encounter—some in the area of development but many from other areas—and how the supervisor may assist in dealing with them primarily through counseling with the employee.[1]

In passing, however, it might be well to remember that counseling is not restricted to subordinates. The foreman's peers at times may come for help and so may persons who are not a part of line management (for example, staff people or workers reporting to another supervisor). Likewise the supervisor may also counsel the boss on occasions. These situations may be less frequent than those involving direct subordinates, but they can be significant nonetheless.

PERSONAL PROBLEMS OF EMPLOYEES

In a way it is artificial to divide the difficulties faced by an organization into two categories, those of the individual and those of the group or the organization, but at times it is profitable to do so nevertheless. (An example of the former would be increasing loss of hearing or of self-esteem—for example—by a certain employee, while an example of the latter would be the strains and challenges accompanying long and difficult labor negotiations.) In this chapter we shall concentrate on such problems as the former, whereas some other chapters deal primarily with things like the latter (see Chapter 15 in particular).

Inevitability of Personal Problems

From time to time virtually all employees, as well as virtually all managers, come face to face with personal problems. Many of these are work-connected, with job duties and responsibilities often involved in them. However, many of them do not concern work as such, though the nature of the problem and its solution or lack thereof may have real effects on performance. Perhaps an example or two would be in order.

Some of these problems may be connected with the worker's family. He or she may be faced with domestic difficulties such as incompatibility with a spouse, or a child who has become or is threatening to become delinquent. The problem may be basically financial and grow out of unwise use of money or a series of expensive illnesses or accidents. Health may be a problem, or crises may arise in connection with neighbors or others in the community.

Another group of difficulties may relate to the work situation. It could include outright rejection or real neglect by fellow workers. It may represent what is felt to be improper assignment to a certain job or improper pay for or classification of the job. It may also include feelings that he or she does not get a fair share of the easy tasks or the responsible ones, or that he or she is not properly represented by the union. And undoubtedly, the difficulties may involve the relationship with the supervisor, staff people, or other members of management.

Still other areas of conflict involve more directly and deeply the worker's inner-most feelings. The employee may gradually develop a sense of inadequacy or get the notion that he or she does not count as an individual but is just a number on the payroll, being valued only for what he or she can do. And of course the worker may become unduly worried without apparent reason, develop abnormal fears, or come to feel persecuted by some or all of his or her associates.

These are the kinds of problems that we want to consider in this chapter. Obviously, they are not always distinctly separated from other kinds of problems confronting the supervisor, for poor communication may be involved, disciplinary action may have to be considered or adopted, training methods may have to be used, and grievances that are filed may speedily bring the union into the picture. However, these situations will often involve personal counseling by the supervisor and will be well or poorly handled according to that person's skill in such counseling.

Bases for Personal Problems

When one looks over even a brief description of such problems as we have just mentioned, it can be seen that they tend to divide themselves into two sorts: first, those that concern the here-and-now, are tangible in their reference, and present a basis for analysis and diagnosis; and second, those that seem to reside more nearly "in the inner person" and are far from as easy to analyze.[2] Let us look at each in some detail.

"Factual" Problems As just indicated, some people encounter obstacles the nature of which is quite clear. A worker is just recovering from a heart attack, for example, and is restricted in the range of activities. Or another worker has taken a civil service promotion examination, only to make a low score on it. There are of course an almost limitless number of other examples.

The important point here is that these are factual problems in the sense that the worker (and often a number of other people) understands them well and probably can deal with them more or less calmly and rationally. This is not to say, of course, that the worker can never use help to "get his thoughts together." Indeed he or she may often need such help and perhaps even advice, and the supervisor, among others, may be one who might assist. To be of real assistance, of course, may be difficult or even at times impossible, but at least there is nothing deep or dark or hidden about the situation that the worker faces.

"Nonfactual" Problems   A term explained in some detail in Chapter 19 on the Hawthorne studies is "nonfact."[3] (Incidentally, that part of Chapter 19 that deals with the interviewing study furnishes especially valuable supplementary reading for this chapter.) For our purposes here, it is sufficient to say that it refers to a situation in which an individual accepts as his chief concern something that is really not his chief concern at all. Said differently, at the conscious level one item is seen as the real problem, whereas at the unconscious level it develops that the real problem is something else.

Here, for example, is an accounting clerk who detests her supervisor. She feels he is arbitrary and unfair as well as cold and distant. Suppose, however, that the problem is *in her* and not in him. She is anxious, thwarted, insecure—and takes her feelings out on her supervisor. Incidentally, if she did not have these thoughts and feelings about the supervisor, she might well find some other scapegoat for them.

Or here is an employee who feels discriminated against (in the Title VII sense—see Chapter 18) and that the organization has treated and is treating him or her most unfairly. Suppose, however, that the facts are just the opposite: that the company and the supervisor have gone out of their way to be fair and have made available not only the opportunities afforded to any other employees but many in addition. Obviously, the employee is not responding to the situation as it is, but as he or she sees it (and perhaps *needs* to see it).

This way of classifying the kinds of problems people have is set out in Table 12-1.

Symptoms of Mental Illness   There may be some question as to the appropriateness, in a volume of this sort, of a discussion of the most common symptoms of mental disorder, but a few words about them may not be out of place. However, three things must be kept in mind in reviewing such a list. One is that the uninitiated are not to diagnose or to decide whether or not a person has such an illness. This is often a difficult task for the expert and is certainly no place for amateurs. Another is that the *degree* of the symptom is fully as important as the symptom itself. In truth, virtually everyone, including normal, well-adjusted individuals, show many of these symptoms but not to the degree or with the persistence of the mentally ill.

Table 12-1 Nature of Personal Problems

Kind	Meaning	Examples
Factual	Real problem, well understood	Broken arm interferes with job performance
Nonfactual	Employee *mistakenly* believes problem is what he says it is	Self-deception as a means of preserving self-respect: "It's not what you know but *who* you know that counts in this company"

The third observation is that though this outline implies that mental illness stems from nonfactual causes, that may not always be true. This is a subject simply too complex for this volume, the causes of mental illness being many and varied. The important point for the supervisor is the one just made, that is, that his task is almost always one of *recognition* of symptoms (and efforts to find professional help) and not one of *treatment.*[4]

Mental illness is usually divided into two sorts, (1) *psychosis,* the more serious, and (2) *neurosis,* the less serious. One of the major groups of psychotics shows delusions of persecution or of grandeur. In the delusion of persecution the individual suspects that a person or a group of people or people in general "have it in for" him or her and are trying to harm or even kill him or her. In the delusion of grandeur the individual believes that he or she is a person of outstanding fame and competence. In both these cases the beliefs are held in spite of the complete lack of evidence for them and a great deal that shows them false.

The principal symptom of another group is withdrawal. In extreme cases the person may sit for hours apparently unaware of anything going on around, or he or she may repeatedly perform an action that has no relationship at all to the current situation. All this is done without the show of emotion; hence emotional detachment or withdrawal is exhibited.

Closely related is unusual, senseless, or even bizarre behavior. What the person does is often not only unrelated to the present situation but makes no sense in any circumstances. Endless repetition of words, all of which may be intelligible but which have no meaning when they are put together, serves to illustrate these symptoms. Another symptom shown by some psychotics is disorientation in time and space. The person may not know where he is, who he is, or what day or even what year it is.

Finally, another group of psychotics displays wide swings in emotion, especially those that vary from great happiness to extreme sadness or depression, and back again. It should be made clear here, as in the case of the other symptoms, that we are not talking about the somewhat unusual behavior normal people may show but a degree of deviation much more pronounced.

One symptom of psychoneurosis is extreme worry, worry that is unreasonable in view of the facts, and is persistent. Other symptoms include abnormal (or unreasonable) fears, especially if these are numerous or severe; compulsions, representing the individual's feeling that he or she must do certain things even if the person cannot explain why or even in spite of a wish not to do them; and obsessions, where compulsive ideas run through his or her head and cannot be avoided.

Disassociated behavior is also found. In it the person acts inconsistently, holding views, for example, that are contrary to each other but seeing no inconsistency, or developing the symptoms of disease (for example, stomach ulcer) when nothing at all is wrong with the organs involved. Undue fatigue characterizes some neurotics, while others have an unreasonable concern for the state of their health.[5]

Perhaps it should be repeated that supervisors are not, and cannot be expected to be, experts in this area. They are not to decide whether a person is or is not mentally disturbed and have absolutely no business trying to treat a person who has such problems. But they should be alert to the possibility of such developments in themselves and others and attempt a tentative recognition of the behavior if it appears. Obtaining assistance is then required.

The problem of classifying the various instances of mental illness and assigning the symptoms to each is a complex and controversial matter. Table 12-1 contains a very brief example of such classification.

Table 12-2 Nature of Mental Illness

Kind	Cause	Symptoms
Psychosis		
Organic	Injury to or disturbance of some system of the body	Many and varied, including most or all of those shown below
Functional	Poor use of good physical equipment — or unknown physical cause	
Schizophrenia		Bizarre behavior, stupor, excitement, delusion, disintegration of personality, etc.
Paranoia		Systematized delusion of persecution or grandeur
Manic-depressive		Wide swings in emotion
Psychoneurosis	Same as for functional psychosis	Obsession, compulsion, dissociation, anxiety, fatigue, hypochondria, symptoms of physical illness without physical cause

GROWTH OF THE COUNSELING MOVEMENT

Extent of Counseling

Counselors are now employed in a variety of places. Business and industry represent one of these, and this aspect of the subject will be discussed below. In addition, counselors are now found in many other groups.

The armed services are one example, as are community agencies like the mental hygiene or family service clinic, to say nothing of special institutes for the handicapped. Schools, and especially high schools, also do a great deal of counseling. The pastor has usually been available as a counselor to the members of the congregation, but in recent years seminaries and church administrators have placed particular emphasis on this activity.

Finally, there are the clinical psychologist and the psychiatrist, both representing occupations virtually unknown before 1900 and devoting their principal efforts to helping people with personal problems. While these counselors are likely to concentrate on people who have psychotic or neurotic symptoms, their work is not confined to such persons.

Thus we see that counseling has come to occupy an important place in our national life. Inevitably it has had its effect on the workplace and the supervisor's job.

Factors Influencing the Development of Counseling

A number of social movements and developments have played a part in the growth of this movement. The emphasis on the importance of the individual and the feeling that all people have certain rights, including the right to adequate self-development, have been influential. As a people, we have taken the democratic tradition seriously, and it is easy to see how this has led to the employment of experts to help with personal difficulties in many aspects of life.

A second development is increasing knowledge of human behavior and especially a recognition of the importance of the emotional patterns and development of the individual. Not the least of these insights has been the significance of unconscious attitudes and other feelings, for both the present situation and the future happiness and effectiveness of the person.

Growing to an extent out of the two developments just mentioned and also contributing decidedly to counseling have been certain historical movements, some of which are discussed later in this book and some of which have already been mentioned. *Scientific management* and *human relations* are examples of movements each stressing human factors in its own way, and each having an impact on counseling. And there are a significant number of other such movements (see especially Chapter 21), including Organizational Development.

COUNSELORS IN BUSINESS AND INDUSTRY

Before we look at the whole process of counseling in business and industry, however, let us look at the development of the full-time counselor, that is, the individual whose sole or at least chief responsibility is to help people to solve their personal problems. Such a person is concerned primarily with the kinds of problems discussed in the beginning of this chapter. He or she is not a supervisor, a disciplinarian, a conference leader, or a specialist in union matters, but, as we have said, one who works full time as a counselor in the plant, the store, or the office.

History of Industrial Counseling

It is hazardous to say when the first full-time counselor appeared (as it would be for the first job analyst or chemical engineer), but there is no doubt about when the movement to employ such people began. As was the case for so many personnel devices, it was the period just following World War I. By the mid-twenties quite a number of large (and some smaller) companies had employed such persons as had certain agencies of the government. These people came from a variety of backgrounds—teaching, personnel work, medicine, and the ministry among others—and functioned in many different ways.

The Depression slowed down this movement, but things were very different, in the late thirties and especially in World War II. Here large numbers of people were assembled, often in plants on sites that a few months before had been field, meadow, or prairie. Many of these people were inexperienced, some never having worked before, and others were making radical changes from prior occupations. Many were women with the extraordinary problems of absent husbands, preschool and school-age children, no previous work experience, and uncertain or difficult housing situations. And, of course, some were handicapped in one or more ways.

Under the circumstances it is not surprising that full-time counselors were employed in numbers far in excess of anything done previously. They were assigned all sorts of duties—arranging for housing or rides to and from work or for day nurseries; talking with employees, especially women, about personal difficulties; helping people who had complaints about rates or amount of pay, job assignments, shifts, and the like; visiting the ill and sometimes checking to see whether they were ill; and a variety of other activities. No doubt many of these counselors carried on valuable activities in critical times and made real contributions to the war effort.

During and just after the war, it was widely believed that a new profession had been born, namely, that of the industrial counselor. Colleges began to offer relevant courses, and students started preparing for this vocation. The expectations, however, proved to be unrealistic. Full-time counselors were not added in any numbers in the postwar years, and the extensive counseling efforts of the war years were often abandoned or distributed to others as part-time assignments. At present, while there are exceptions to the statement, full-time counselors are rare in business and industry, and the writers know of no evidence that they are likely to become more popular in the future. It seems safe to conclude that if there is to be much counseling in business and industry, the line managers, assisted no doubt by others, will play the significant part in it.

Difficulties of the Counselor

Three problems seemed especially to plague the full-time counselor. One was that he or she might easily interfere in the relationship between a supervisor and his or her employees. Thus the counselor who attempted to "straighten out" the worker (and especially the supervisor) courted the displeasure of both. And if that counselor bore tales to higher managers, there were real difficulties.

A second problem was the attitudes of unions and union members. Counselors were often thought of as attempting to prevent union organization or to restrict the growth and influence of the union. Naturally under these conditions prounion workers were not enthusiastic about counselors.

Finally, counselors faced a real dilemma with their clients, the employees. If they took an active part in employee concerns, advised them what to do, and helped them do it, they not only often came between the supervisor and the employees, but could easily give bad advice, create resentment, or build dependence. If, on the other hand, they tried only to encourage employees to solve their own problems and refused to say what they thought should be done, they were often accused of being "fence riders" or of wasting time.

Evidently, then, the full-time counselor is not the answer for most workers who need help with their personal problems. If most employees are going to be counseled, it is essential that managers at various levels and especially first-line supervisors be available for this function. Is it realistic to expect the supervisor to be or become an effective counselor?[6]

THE SUPERVISOR AS COUNSELOR

A point made earlier in this chapter is relevant here: Supervisors often have no choice in the matter of counseling. Some people, including some of their subordinates, come to them with problems of various sorts, and they cannot escape dealing with some of these even if they wish. Even courtesy demands under some circumstances that they listen to and try to help the other person. Furthermore, the emotional pressure behind some of these problems may cause the person almost literally to force himself or herself on the manager, welcome or not. The question is not, therefore, whether supervisors will serve as counselors. Rather it is to what extent and under what circumstances and by the use of what methods they are to do this part of their job.

Advantages of the Supervisor as Counselor

There are some things that work to the advantage of supervisors as counselors. One of these is the opportunity they have for becoming well acquainted with the person in question. They can learn his patterns of judging, valuing, thinking, feeling, and the like and not only anticipate many of his reactions but also understand to a considerable extent why he does what he does.

Not only may supervisors become familiar with a person, but they may also come to know quite thoroughly the person's associates, the work situation, and even the off-the-job activities and values of the worker. Needless to say, these may be quite influential in aiding in the solution of various kinds of problems.

Another favorable aspect of the situation, so far as supervisors are concerned, is the frequent and continuing contact they have with the worker. Some supervisors (for example, some sales managers) may see their subordinates infrequently, but this is the exception rather than the rule. Typically, supervisors see their subordinates at least once a day and sometimes much more often. This means that it is usually possible, periodically if not continuously, to see what is happening to the counselee, to see whether certain courses of action prove to be helpful, and to act quickly when necessary. In short, the factors favoring supervisors in their counseling relationships with their people grow out of the close and continuing relationships between them.

Disadvantages of the Supervisor as Counselor

It probably appears from what has been said that we are taking the position that supervisors are in an almost ideal position as counselors, but such is not the case. Indeed, as is not infrequently true in human affairs, the very advantages of a situation may also be among the disadvantages. To some extent this is true in this case.

The Effects of Familiarity   The close association between supervisors and their people can prove to be a handicap for several reasons. For one, there are inevitable irritations and misunderstandings that arise between people. These can prove to be serious limitations on the counseling relationship. For another, we hear it said that no prophet is without honor except in his own country, and surely supervisors are no exception. In other words, the ability of supervisors, in counseling and in other activities, may be outstanding, but their associates may and usually do tend to discount these. If they were outsiders and especially if they came with a mark of approval or competence (like a license, certificate, or title), their efforts would usually carry much more weight. Finally, the closeness of this relationship may appreciably lower the objectivity of supervisors. This does not necessarily mean that they come to like the employee to the extent of overvaluing him or her. It may be just the opposite, that they are irritated by or even disgusted with the worker to such an extent that they seriously underestimate the person. In any case, close association may not be an aid to the counseling relationship.

The Presence of Authority   On some sorts of problems the worker is unlikely to go to his supervisor for counseling. Among these are problems that clearly involve a serious violation of company rules or the standards of good conduct. Thus a person who has been stealing tools or merchandise from the company and who wants help in breaking the habit or making restitution is not likely to reveal all to a supervisor, especially if either supervisor or the company or both are known to be very strict about such matters. Much the same results are likely to follow for less serious shortcomings.

Actually, what has been said can be misinterpreted. Everyone who knows the supervisor-subordinate relationship knows that very often it is not one of fear and reluctance. Subordinates do go to their superiors with serious problems of the sort we have discussed, and either "throw themselves on the mercy of the court" or trust the supervisor to treat in confidence what has been revealed. These may be exceptional cases, but they are by no means so exceptional as to be called rare or astounding. People in authority do counsel those who come to them voluntarily after violation of rule or statute.

Here, however, is a very real problem for supervisors who have an ambition to be first-class counselors (and perhaps to many who do not): Employees may reveal to them information that can be embarrassing and difficult. Supervisors are then caught on the horns of a dilemma. If they reveal what they have learned, they betray confidences and may destroy a relationship helpful to all concerned. If they fail to reveal such information, they may be guilty of setting an unfortunate precedent, of condoning a wrong act, or even of aiding those who plan to do harm. Asking for the confidences of people is probably never a responsibility to be taken lightly, especially if one is in a position of authority.

One suggestion for dealing with this problem is to be on guard and to warn those about to reveal secrets of the circumstances under which they can be heard. There may be times, in other words, when employees should be told that they proceed at their own risk and perhaps had better not proceed. Another suggestion is the use of good judgment in handling information that one gets, confidentially or otherwise. After all, if the supervisor runs immediately to the boss with each tiny bit of new information, he or she is seen as a "tattletale" or "stool pigeon," so far as the workers are concerned. It requires judgment to determine what it is important to pass along to the boss, and how, where, and why.

The Influence of Status   Closely aligned to the matter of authority is the status or prestige of supervisors. All, or at least most of us, put some people on a pedestal, as we say. We may be reluctant to speak at length to these people, and when we do talk with them, we may be careful to use the title Mr. or Ms. or Doctor, to be guarded or reserved in our comments, and to defer to them regarding subject matter to be discussed, conclusions to be drawn, and the length of the conversation. Clearly this does not encourage free expression and elaboration of our own personal problems.

While the above statements are probably exaggerated in the usual supervisor-subordinate relationship, they not infrequently do apply to a degree. It is sometimes impossible, and it is seldom easy, for supervisors to overcome the status barrier and to bring their subordinates to speak with them freely about their problems or those of the organization.

However, one point should be emphasized: It is very easy, as pointed out above, to exaggerate the degree of formality in this relationship. True, it is sometimes distant, cool, formal, and "proper." It is, on the other hand and in many instances, warm, personal, friendly, and informal. In literally thousands of cases today supervisors and their subordinates come from the same background, have worked side by side for years, live close together in the same neighborhood, ride to and from work in the same car pool, belong to the same church, participate together in the same recreational activities, and even visit each other's homes. With the economic and educational progress of the working class (whatever that ambiguous term may mean),[7] these situations are becoming increasingly frequent, and now often involve not simply two levels in the organization, but three or more. Anyone who believes that most of American business and industry operates along caste lines or involves many clearly differentiated classes of people needs to make a careful study of these relationships as they actually exist. Status can interfere with good counseling relationships, but ordinarily it is not extensive enough to be fatal to it.

The Lack of Training   Another problem supervisors encounter in their counseling activities is lack of training for this sort of activity. For one thing, most have not had a course in counseling methods or philosophy or in interviewing techniques and objectives. For another, there is doubt whether, even if they have had such a course, they are made counselors thereby, for there is little real proof that training in counseling always makes good counselors or is essential to the activity. Finally and perhaps more significant than the other two points, typical supervisors do not typically come from "a counseling background," that is, they tend to be work-oriented, drilled in the logic of efficiency, and more inclined to give orders than to listen or be sensitive to the overtones of feelings expressed by subordinates. These things often handicap supervisors as counselors.

On the other hand, to be a good counselor one must study and practice counseling. Here mere information is not enough, for effective counseling represents a high order of skill, one that no one has without learning, indeed a skill that can be learned even reasonably well only after long and serious effort.

The Limitations of Counseling   One possibility that must be faced is that just as we have often been uncritical in our acceptance of counselors, so we may have been uncritical of the counseling process itself. Maybe we have expected miracles from counseling or at least much more than it really can be expected to deliver consistently.

There is some recent evidence that psychiatrists and psychologists have not been as successful in counseling (or psychotherapy, as they are more inclined to call it) as is often claimed or had been expected. Furthermore, all of us have seen many people who are "counseled" over and over and still have their irritating problems of absenteeism or uneven effort or alcoholism. All this is not to assert that counseling has no value. It is to say, however, that it is less effective than the uncritical suspect and may be less so than even the experts believe.

Counseling by the Supervisor

This discussion of the limitations of supervisors may very well have left the impression that they have no business in counseling, but such a conclusion is far from the one intended. Supervisors must be careful to use good judgment in these relationships as in others, and it is important that they recognize that they have significant limitations as counselors. But as we have already said, basically they have no choice in these matters: counsel they must, whether they choose to do so or not. They may do what they can to minimize the occasions for the activity and the time spent in them and thus succeed in keeping such time to a minimum. But people will inevitably bring their personal and other problems to them, and on occasion, they must do something with them. There is no question, then, whether supervisors should counsel. The significant questions are when, whom, where, and how they counsel.

METHODS OF COUNSELING

Counseling as Advice Giving

One of the conceptions of counseling, as we have just mentioned, is that it is essentially giving advice to one who needs it. This view assumes the superior wisdom of the counselor—the pastor, the psychiatrist, the personnel specialist, the vocational guidance expert, or the supervisor—and hence the limited understanding of the person being counseled. It furthermore suggests the obligation of the counselor to share his or her wisdom with the counselee.

Disadvantages of Advice Giving   This situation is much more complex than it appears to be on the surface. Appropriate as it is in some circumstances, advice giving often has two serious limitations. One is that the adviser may not know what advice to give or may give incorrect, inappropriate, or definitely harmful advice. The other is that the person being advised may be unable or unwilling to accept the advice, whether or not it would be ultimately sound or useful.

All counselors, regardless of experience, ability, or training, will encounter problems that they will not know how to solve. This would be true even if they could safely assume that other persons were like them and would respond as they would. It is especially so when the other persons are different (as they always are to a greater or less degree). After all, at least for many problems the individual who has the problem knows more about it in all its aspects than anyone else can, regardless of the competence of the counselor.

The other aspect of this situation is that counselors may not know, but may still think they know, what the other person should do. It is easy to be sure we know all about what should be done, and yet be wrong. One problem is that counselors may not know, and may know that they do not know. Another is that they may not know, and may not know that they do not know. If anything, the latter situation is more dangerous than the former. "Fools rush in where angels fear to tread" may be as true of amateur counselors as of any other group of human beings.

Limitations of the advice that is given may not be any more serious than those limitations posed by the inability of the counselee to accept and profit from the advice. All of us have been in situations that illustrate this point. We may have a strong suspicion that what the doctor, the minister, or a friend is advising us to do is what we should do, and yet we may fail to do it. This failure may come from a variety of reasons. Temptations to do the opposite may be too strong, self-respect in the form of self-determination may be involved in the refusal, dislike of the person giving advice may make it out of the question, or group pressure may prevent it. Parents of teenagers have little trouble finding illustrations. The young person is so intent on asserting and demonstrating independence and individuality that he or she frequently spurns good advice from parents or teachers, all the while unconsciously if not consciously recognizing the soundness of the advice.

It is not sufficient, then, for advice to be good from an objective standpoint; it must also be acceptable, at least at a minimum level, to the person who ultimately has the power to accept and act upon it, or to reject it.

Usefulness of Advice Giving   It may appear that we have said that advice giving is not a satisfactory form of counseling, but again that is not what is intended.[8] The real point here is our tendency to overvalue and to overuse advice and its effects. Like other good things, advice can be overdone, as it usually is by those who have not examined it and human behavior carefully. In counseling situations the best rule is to give *not giving advice* the benefit of the doubt; in other words, in case of genuine doubt, one does not advise.

Dealing with the "Mentally Ill" Employee   This may well be the best place to return to the situation where the supervisor has serious suspicion that one of his or her employees is beginning to show some of the symptoms of psychosis or psychoneurosis, mentioned above. (Especially noteworthy would be a condition in which the employee appears to be showing the symptoms more and more as time passes.) What should a supervisor do under these conditions?

The obvious answer is to try to find professional help for the affected person, but this is often far from easy. One of the professionals that is a likely referral is a psychiatrist, for example. How does one get a fellow worker to see a psychiatrist? Obviously even the suggestion that he or she do so may be insulting or at least unnerving in the extreme, especially if the worker is seriously maladjusted.

There is no easy answer to this question, but one that is found to work with some success is (1) to refer the employee to the company physician or possibly to his own physician and (2) in the meantime to alert the physician to one's fears concerning the employee and ask him to be alert for them. Hopefully if the supervisor's fears are at all grounded in fact the physician in turn will refer the employee to a psychiatrist. And the employee can take referral to a psychiatrist by his or her own physician better than when it is made directly by the boss.

Supervisors may have available others on whom they can depend for help. A member of the personnel department, the company nurse, a minister, priest, or rabbi known for his interest and skill in the area—all these are possible persons to whom the employee might be directed with good results.

Of course, at times it may be better to deal with such situations in a straightforward, factual manner; certainly, if it is appropriate, this course of action should be followed. But it is an area where caution is appropriate.

Nondirective Counseling

Another development in the counseling movement is that of *nondirective counseling,* which has been most frequently associated with the name of Carl R. Rogers.[9] This school of counseling is fully aware of the limitations of advising, suggesting, and otherwise persuading the counselee to do what the counselor thinks is best, and it warns against these procedures, especially when the counselee has personal problems that involve considerable feeling or emotion.

Basis for Nondirective Counseling

On the positive side, those who advocate nondirective interviewing believe they have clear evidence that in the great majority of personal emotional difficulties the person himself or herself is the best one to solve the problem and can do so provided he or she can bring his or her best reason to bear on the problem. In other words, I am usually in a better position to know all aspects of my difficulty than any other human being, and if I can bring myself, or can be brought, to a situation where I can think clearly about it, I can solve it best. (This "best" solution may not be the best from the standpoint of objective appraisal, but it may be best for me, for it will be one that I can both accept and apply.)

According to this theory, there is no serious question about what most frequently prevents a person from using this best reasoning and judgment: It is the presence of strong feeling, with its definitely upsetting effects. When under emotional pressure, the person is confused, distraught, inefficient, and ineffective. When emotional pressure is reduced, he or she is able to think more clearly, and the solution gradually appears. Nondirective interviewing and the attitudes and values that go with it represent a way to clear the emotion and aid the person in working a way through the problem.

Goal of Counseling If in a particular situation one is successful in using the nondirective method of counseling, three results hopefully will occur. For one thing, there will be a considerable degree of *emotional release.* No one quite understands why it is true, but it is true nevertheless: under conditions where one feels free to say whatever he or she thinks and feels, words do have *emotion-releasing value.* Said differently, after a considerable amount of such talking one feels better, and hopefully is then in better position to solve the problem.

A second possible result is a measure of *self-appraisal.* Feeling better, the person is usually able to think better and to appraise others—and himself—more accurately. Under these conditions, "You know, I may be partly at fault" is a not-unusual outcome.

The third possibility is the acceptance of the self-appraisal and the making of plans for *self-improvement.* By this time hopefully the interviewee has developed considerable insight into the situation and is bringing his or her best reason to bear on its improvement.

To what extent the above goals can be achieved in any given situation cannot be known in advance. Frequently, however, the strategy is worth trying. If it is successful, all concerned are likely to gain. If it does not work one can always fall back on advice giving, or even order giving and/or warning, should this appear to be necessary.

Method of Interviewing In a very real sense nondirective interviewing is not really a method of interviewing but a philosophy of human relationships and a way of feeling about and relating to people. There are, nevertheless, beliefs and techniques that are useful.

Certain Attitudes toward the Interviewee   First and fundamentally, there is the fact of the counselor's *permissiveness* in dealing with the counselee and the real acceptance of him or her. Unless the counselor is willing and even anxious for the client to say whatever he or she wants and needs to say[10]—all this in an atmosphere of acceptance for what the person is, with all his or her strengths and shortcomings—no method of interviewing, no matter how practiced, spontaneous, or clever, has usefulness here. Thus the invitation to the client to say whatever the person needs to say and genuine concern on the part of the counselor for him or her to do just that are the basis for and the heart of the method of nondirective counseling.

Practices to Be Avoided   In the second place, things that inhibit conversation are to be avoided. Thus the counselor does not interrupt, argue, disagree, reassure, praise, or blame. Here it might be well to note one point where this method differs from so-called common sense. The latter tends to believe that agreement with another person promotes discussion. The facts are the opposite. Agreement tends to inhibit discussion.

Likewise one needs to understand the prohibitions against disagreement and argument. It is not that they inhibit talk, for they typically do the opposite. It is that they encourage the *wrong kind* of talk. They tend to put the interviewee on the defensive, to encourage him or her to justify a position, to bring forth his or her best rationalizations for the position. This is just what the nondirective counselor does not want. Rather, he or she is trying to achieve the free and spontaneous expression of feelings, attitudes, repressions, and the like. These are typically inhibited by rationalizations.

Skill in Drawing the Other Person Out   Finally, there are useful strategies in getting the other person to talk. One is simply waiting until the interviewee does, but as we point out below, at least in the world of work that strategy has serious limitations. Another is the *neutral, generalized inquiry.* "Would you like to tell me about yourself?" and "How do people around here feel about these changes?" are examples of interviewer statements that invite and are usually followed by considerable talk.

Another is what we might call *signalling.* After the interviewee begins to show signs of "running down" on a topic, the interviewer can say, "Could you tell me more about that?" or "I'm not sure I quite understand," or "Would you run that by again?" These expressions of obvious interest and sincere efforts at understanding are often decidedly helpful.

And then there is the "I see" or "Uh-huh" technique. Naturally this is not the "I see" of praise or condemnation but rather the one that by implication says, "I'm here; I'm interested. I think I follow. Tell me more."

Finally there is *reflection,* that is, saying back to the employee what he or she has just said, hopefully in many fewer words, capturing at least the *feeling tone* of what has been said, and always putting a question mark on the end. "So you really feel you haven't gotten a square deal, do you?" is a possible example.

A Significant Misunderstanding   Here it might be well to point out a serious misconception that has arisen about nondirective interviewing. It is often referred to as "the listening method," a characterization that leads one to believe that there is not much to it beyond the self-restraint that keeps one from talking. This view is decidedly in error. The nondirective method of interviewing could just as properly be called "the talking method," for a considerable amount of expression on the part of the interviewer is required. Furthermore, though the counselor may talk for only one-fourth or even one-tenth of the time, he or she will nowhere be called upon to do more skillful and effective talking no matter what the undertaking. In other words, since the interviewer must talk and the results of his talking may be genuinely encouraging or seriously inhibiting to the other person, the quality of his or her conversation and the study and attention he or she gives it must be of the highest order of skill.

The nondirective method of counseling is far more difficult to learn than one who has not attempted it would be likely to believe. It is more than a matter of knowing what should be done and why, though of course such knowledge can be helpful. Nondirective interviewing is a skill, or a set of skills, and one of a high order of complexity and difficulty. In addition, it can operate effectively only on the basis of certain attitudes and values of the counselor. Learning to be even fairly good in these attitudes and the use of the method requires much laborious, dedicated practice.

Use of Nondirective Counseling   Supervisors have relatively few opportunities to use this sort of interviewing, at least in pure form. Furthermore, as previously noted, temperamentally and by virtue of their background and experience they are very often not disposed toward its use, though they are probably more so today than a generation ago. Besides, authority poses real problems. Thus this sort of interviewing has serious limitations in the work situation. Two comments, however, are in order.

In the first place, employees may at times be under great emotional pressure and need an opportunity to get emotional release and to talk their way through a problem. On occasion supervisors can be entirely nondirective, or at least almost so in dealing with these problems, even if it may be necessary later to discuss the problem with the employee on a much more directive basis. If the employee has a serious personal problem or if he or she "is really teed off" about something, this may be the best way to conduct the first interview—or the first part of the first interview—and possibly others.

In the second place, supervisors can learn from this method techniques of interviewing which they can apply from time to time in many situations. There is in this method a concern and respect for the other person not always found in other methods; there is a permissiveness strange to many work situations; and there are techniques of interviewing not common, to say the least, in the factory, the store, or the office. Supervisors who know about and have skill in such interviewing will find all these things useful from time to time and in many of their contacts with a variety of people.

What we are saying, therefore, is not that supervisors should become nondirective interviewers and do all their counseling that way. Rather, they should use the method whenever it is applicable, perhaps throughout a few unusual interviews and from time to time in some of the more usual kinds of counseling situations.

Other Counseling Methods

So far we have discussed a form of counseling in which the counselor takes the lead, tries to solve the employee's problem, and then gives advice on how to proceed, and also one in which the counselor "passes the ball" to the interviewee and tries to get the person to "run with it." In each case it has been noted that the method has advantages but that it also has limitations. Neither, then, is *the* way to counsel subordinates.

It is obvious that between the extremes of directive (or advice-giving) counseling and nondirective (or permissive) counseling there are all sorts of shades or degrees. Thus in a particular counseling session the interviewer may be mostly an advice giver but spend some effort and time in getting the interviewee to talk and in listening to him. In another he or she may be mostly a nondirective interviewer and yet at times take the lead in determining what will be discussed and spend some time in advice giving. Obviously there is an almost infinite variety in the degree to which this mixture may occur.

One interviewing method that might be worthy of special mention here is that in which the interviewer is directive, at least to a degree, in selecting the subject to be discussed, but nondirective in its development. To illustrate, after an interview has been going on for some time with the employee having done most or virtually all of the talking, the interviewer may say, "A while ago you said you don't think shift foremen get enough information in this plant. Just what did you have in mind?"

The interviewee is thus invited not only to develop his thoughts and conclusions about this situation but also to express his feelings. After he has said as much as he apparently wishes to, the interviewer having used silence, the "I see" technique, reflection, and the like, the interviewer may then say, "I'm not sure I understand fully what you mean. Could you tell me more?"

This method will be recognized as very similar to, if not the same as, the *indirect* method of the Hawthorne interviewing study. It is called the *controlled nondirective* method by some writers.[11] Its greatest advantage over nondirective interviewing is probably the saving of time, since the interviewer does not have to wait for the interviewee to bring up a particular subject.

This method requires good judgment on the part of supervisors to select the best counseling method or methods and considerable skill to use them wisely and effectively. This, however, is a necessary part of their counseling responsibilities.

Finally, attention needs to be called to the possibility of using the nondirective techniques in a manner quite different from the one described above. This is a procedure in which one uses the generalized inquiry, signaling, reflection, and "I see" not to induce the free expression of feeling but to put the individual on the spot. An investigative interview in which one is trying to discover unknown and possible damaging aspects of a situation is an example. One in which the interviewer is testing and even challenging the attitudes, beliefs, and values of another person is another. The first example is illustrated by an inquiry concerning a possible disciplinary infraction. The second might be demonstrated in an employment interview where the interviewer is testing how well an applicant responds to generalized inquiries concerning his or her reactions to a current social problem (reverse discrimination, right-to-work laws, or women as executives being possible topics).

This use of these strategies may be more appropriate in employment or discipline than in counseling, but there can arise counseling situations in which they might be useful.

A CONCLUDING STATEMENT

A subject that we have not attempted to cover in this discussion is what sort of information, if any, supervisors should give employees whom they counsel or what course of action they should recommend. This is often the critical part of the counseling situation, but obviously it is a matter that has to be dealt with in terms of the particular individual and set of circumstances involved. Here supervisors must draw on their training and experience and use their best judgment; there is no substitute for these and no way of doing a good job without them.

The real point of this chapter is that, like it or not, supervisors must counsel their people, at least on occasion. When they do so, it is important that they use the best methods available for the job and take their responsibilities in this area as seriously as they do those in any other phase of their job.

QUESTIONS

1 Distinguish between a factual and nonfactual statement or problem. (Use illustrations other than those in the book.) What is meant by saying "I must first sell myself on the (supposed) nature of my nonfactual problem"?

2 Distinguish between *psychosis* and *psychoneurosis*. What are the chief symptoms of each?

3 What are the responsibilities of the supervisor if he or she finds that an employee probably has a psychosis or a psychoneurosis?
4 Why have full-time counselors not worked out well in business and industry?
5 Discuss *pro* and *con* and state as specific a conclusion as possible: To what extent and in what ways should supervisors counsel their subordinates?
6 What are (a) the advantages and (b) the disadvantages of advice giving by the supervisor?
7 Set forth the fundamentals of nondirective interviewing or counseling.
8 Under what circumstances should a supervisor use nondirective counseling and when should he or she not do so? Is it feasible to combine the two methods in the same interview?

NOTES

1 Management writers are almost all aware of the supervisor's counseling responsibilities, but they may or may not deal with them as a separate topic. Thus complaints and grievances are discussed together in Chapter 13 of Paul Pigors and Charles A. Myers, *Personnel Administration: A Point of View and a Method,* 7th ed. (New York: McGraw-Hill, 1974). In the current chapter we are dealing with *complaints* but reserving the discussion of *grievances* to Chapter 15 of this book.
2 This distinction is elaborated in Fritz J. Roethlisberger and W. J. Dickson, *Management and the Worker* (Cambridge, Mass.: Harvard University Press, 1939), pp. 257ff and 373ff.
3 Ibid.
4 Abraham Zelznik, "Management of Disappointment," *Harvard Business Review,* vol. 45, no. 6, pp. 59–70, November-December 1967.
5 Jack R. Strange, *Abnormal Psychology* (New York: McGraw-Hill, 1965).
6 See Roethlisberger and Dickson, op. cit., and also William J. Dickson and Fritz J. Roethlisberger, *Counseling in an Organization* (Cambridge, Mass.: Harvard Graduate School of Business Administration, 1966).
7 To attempt to cover the sociology of blue-collar work and workers is beyond the scope of this discussion, but the following will be helpful: "Brutal, Mindless Labor Remains a Daily Reality for Millions in the U.S.," *The Wall Street Journal,* vol. 178, no. 11, pp. 1ff, July 16, 1971; Irving Howe, *The World of the Blue-Collar Worker* (New York: Quadrangle, 1972); and especially Edward J. Walsh, *Dirty Work, Race, and Self-Esteem* (Ann Arbor, Mich.: Institute of Labor and Industrial Relations, University of Michigan, 1975).
8 Two good discussions of the interview situations such as we are discussing are Pigors and Myers, op. cit., Chap. 10, and Robert L. Kahn and Chas. F. Cannell, *The Dynamics of Interviewing* (New York: Wiley, 1957).
9 Though it was published in 1942, one of the best discussions of nondirective interviewing is found in Carl R. Rogers, *Counseling and Psychotherapy* (Boston: Houghton Mifflin); see also Roethlisberger and Dickson, op. cit., Chap. 13.
10 Claudio R. Serafine, "Interviewer Listening," *Personnel Journal,* vol. 54, no. 7, pp. 398–399, July 1975.
11 See Kahn and Cannell, op. cit.

CASES

Unlike most other chapters, this one could include a large number of directly appropriate cases (since counseling enters into so many personnel problems), and the only problem was choosing which ones to include here. One that we have selected gives the second-level manager an opportunity to counsel with a good supervisor, Tom Moore. What do you say to an employee who is already "doing all right"?

The second case appears to be a counseling one exclusively. How do you get from a person with a problem the true nature and content of the problem? As a matter of fact, does a supervisor have any right to try to do so? If so, just what does he or she hope to accomplish, and *how?*

The third case affords an opportunity to examine the situation of an employee who is doing well but who has come to dislike and even distrust his boss. If you were the department head, how would you handle this one?

CASE 12-1

Tom Moore is an office supervisor for the Company, a medium-sized Midwestern firm that has written life insurance for nearly seventy-five years and has recently branched out into fire and casualty lines.

Tom is thirty-five years of age and has been with the Company for ten years. He has made good progress, starting as a clerk, holding other jobs of increasing responsibility, and being promoted to supervisor three years ago. Everyone who knows Tom well seems to feel that he has earned every promotion and has a fine future, all this in spite of the fact that, so far as formal education is concerned, his background included only high school graduation. However, he has made up for any deficiencies along this line by study and hard work.

One of Tom's greatest assets is his ability to get along with people. His subordinates all seem to like and respect him, and so do others with whom he has contacts, both inside and outside the Company. Though he is friendly and considerate of others, he knows how to be firm when the occasion arises. His work group is always more than satisfactory in its output.

Tom also knows the technical aspects of the jobs of his people and is able to be of real help to them. He has no college training in accounting, but he has done some correspondence work in it and has learned a great deal by careful observation and hard work. (He is planning some night-school courses as soon as the local college makes them available.) Even without formal training, however, Tom is an authority in certain phases of the work, for not only his people but also his fellow supervisors often come to him for help, partly because they feel he is likely to know the answers and partly because he is friendly and does a good job of listening to what they have to say and advising them on their problems.

There is a general feeling among those who know him well that Tom will be promoted rapidly and will eventually hold a much more responsible position in the Company, but this has not affected him in any way. Except through hard work he has not sought promotions, though he has taken any new assignment offered him and done it well. This is the attitude that he seems to have toward his present job.

Is there anything to be gained by holding a performance-review interview with Tom? If it is decided that one should be conducted or if company policy requires such interviews periodically, how should this one be conducted?

CASE 12-2

Jim Watson is an accounting clerk for the Company, which has twenty clerical employees, five salesmen, twenty-five warehouse employees and truck drivers, and a manufacturing division of three hundred employees.

Jim has been with the Company four years. He is forty years old, is married, and has two children. He has a high school diploma and six months of training in a business college. His work has been satisfactory but not outstanding in either speed or accuracy. Recently, Ralph Grey, his supervisor, has noticed that Jim has seemed less interested in his work than he formerly was; indeed, within the last two weeks the change has become pronounced. Jim seems to have "a chip on his shoulder," but though Ralph has given him opportunities to talk to him, Jim has not taken advantage of them.

Jim has just asked Ralph for permission to go to the personnel department, and Ralph has agreed. Ralph made an attempt to find out what the problem was, but Jim said something about not getting "the right amount of pay" last week, and Ralph decided not to press the matter.

Upon reaching the personnel department Jim asked for Tom White, the personnel director. The two men have known each other for a long time, but their associations have not been close. After the usual small talk, Jim started the conversation by reporting, "Payroll has really been fouling up my pay recently."

Jim's concern about his pay proved not to be serious. He had received a pay increase not long before and also had worked a good deal of overtime. The pay increase put him close to a higher bracket for withholding, and the overtime pushed him over. Jim suspected this already, and either simply wanted confirmation or was using this as an excuse.

Tom White found it easy to get Jim to talk, and his real problem began to unfold. It was a growing feeling that the world was going against him. For one thing he felt, deep down inside, that Ralph Grey either had it in for him or at best was hardly aware of him and that so far as Ralph was concerned, he "just didn't count." For another, he was losing his influence in his work group; or at any rate, it seemed that way to him. It used to be that everyone was friendly and people often asked him for advice, at least that is the way he remembers it. Now it seems to him that people just pass him by, and he does not count here either.

Jim also has his troubles at home. He and his wife have never gotten along too well, and within recent months their quarrels have become more frequent. He insists that she is disappointed at his low-status job and his rate of pay, and he is afraid she is plotting ways to get a divorce and to secure possession of their house, automobile, and savings.

Even their fourteen-year-old son, George, has become a problem. He used to be a fine boy and has always done well in school, but Jim suspects that he has been driving some of his friends' cars without a license and has also been smoking "pot" or worse. George has also talked back to Jim recently several times when some problem came up.

One of Jim's greatest joys is Nancy, his five-year-old daughter. They are devoted to each other, and Jim thinks she's the cutest and finest little girl in the world. However, even here Jim feels that he is "slipping" and that he and Nancy are not as close as they were.

What, if anything, does White do with the information he has received—and with or for Jim?

CASE 12-3

Jack Roebuck is a salesperson in a department store. He has been with the Company for three years and has a good record. He has been upgraded twice in this period and is generally thought of as one of the better salesmen.

Jack's immediate supervisor is an assistant buyer, Charlie Thompson, a man who knows selling and the technical aspects of merchandising, but one who has little regard for modern methods of supervision and shows it in his dealings with his workers. He is inclined to give orders without explaining the reasons for them and is often brusque in dealing with problems brought to him. On occasions he bawls people out for mistakes and is usually sparing with complimentary remarks.

There has been bad feeling between Jack and Charlie for quite a while, but things really come to a head when Jack learns by the grapevine that Charlie not only has refused to recommend him for promotion to assistant buyer in another department, but has advised management, "He just wouldn't do for a job like that. He's not buyer material."

For some time Jack has known Ed Blake, the buyer over this department and Charlie's boss. Yesterday afternoon he dropped by Ed's office to make an appointment to see Ed the first thing in the morning. It is now just after 8 A.M. Ed is in his office and Jack has just come in.

What sort of interviewing strategy should Ed use? For example, what should be his opening remarks? What specifically should he try to accomplish in this interview, and how should he proceed? What action should he take relative to Jack's promotion?

Chapter 13

Evaluation and Review of Employees and their Performance

Much attention has been given in recent years to the supervisor's appraisal of his or her subordinates and to a subsequent review of that evaluation with the individual employee. Such a program of evaluation and review is sometimes asserted to be the real foundation of a good personnel program, with every person in the organization having been informed as to where he or she stands with the company, what his or her strengths and weaknesses are, as well as his or her likely future. This point of view assumes that such a program is one that unquestionably produces a net gain for employers and employees alike.

Without at present either agreeing or disagreeing with this point of view, let us now summarize our approach to this problem: First, we shall *evaluate evaluation* carefully and critically, looking at current beliefs and practices, along with the underlying philosophies. Second, we shall examine what operating managers, that is, those on the "firing line," believe and what they do along this line. And third, we shall draw any conclusions that are relevant especially to the first-level manager.

One matter of semantics should be disposed of in the beginning. Two processes are involved here: One is the determination of the sort of individual the employee is and how adequately he or she performs, and the other is the passing along of relevant information to him or her. In a way it is arbitrary, but it will also make for clarity of meaning. In the following discussion, we shall use *evaluation* and/or *appraisal* to refer to the first of the above and the term *review* to refer to the second.

INEVITABILITY OF EVALUATION

At times discussion of the appraisal of workers takes the form of whether or not they should be evaluated. Actually, in that form the discussion is meaningless from a practical standpoint, for there is no question about whether such appraisal should and will go on. It does, in every work situation. Consequently, the only real questions are: when, by whom, how, for what purpose, and the like.

It must also be noted that this is a two-way street; that is, while supervisors are evaluating their people, the workers are evaluating them, often more thoroughly (because there are more of them) but in the same casual and informal way. They soon decide, for example, what sort of a person a supervisor really is—restrained, outgoing, dependable, punitive, self-centered, enthusiastic, or the like. Each worker arrives at his or her own conclusions, which are always subject to change and not infrequently do change; but there is usually also a group opinion, a consensus that is usually very real and very influential. Needless to say, the greater the amount of "we-feeling" in the group, the more weight the consensus usually carries, and the more nearly unanimous it is likely to be.

It can now be seen why the question of whether or not to evaluate subordinates is not really a meaningful or realistic one. Subordinates—and their supervisors and other bosses, too—will be evaluated. But a real question nevertheless remains: whether the evaluation should be entirely informal or should be carried out in part in a formal fashion.

FORMAL OR INFORMAL EVALUATION?

The question of formal or informal evaluation in the workplace has been widely discussed for the last fifty years and more. Should we depend on the usual activities of supervisors and their customary relations with people to take care of any evaluations needed, or should some sort of provision be made to encourage or even ensure appraisal in a systematic way and at certain times, with arrangements for a discussion of the results with the employee?

Table 13-1 compares and contrasts the two ways of evaluating and reviewing the performance (and perhaps also the characteristics) of employees.

Advantages of Informality

Those who favor informal evaluation point out that this is the normal or natural way to proceed. As we have already said, evaluation is constantly going on, and opponents of formal schemes hold that the time to evaluate employees is not necessarily December 31 or June 30, but whenever the circumstances suggest or even demand it. Likewise the

Table 13-1   Plans for Employee Evaluation

Kind	Perdetermined forms used?	When done?	Records originated?	Employee informed?
Informal	No	As needed—or "when the boss feels like it"	Only incidentally	At times
Formal	Yes	Every 3, 6, or 12 months	Yes	Yes—or at least he or she is supposed to be

proper communication with employees should not be discussing with them and/or showing them some sort of form, but rather whatever they need to hear about any current
situation. Thus, if a subordinate's performance is less than it might be or the employee is
failing to a degree in interpersonal relations, it is not only unnatural but unwise to wait
three months—or six or twelve—to talk about the situation.

Furthermore, if a formal scheme is provided, the tendency is to think in abstract
terms with less emphasis on day-to-day job performance, whereas informal evaluation,
these people urge, not only avoids most of the problems that center about discussion of
personality, traits, and character, but focuses the conversation where it should be, on how
well the tasks of the subordinate are now being accomplished.

Additionally, according to this point of view, much time and energy are saved, unnecessary records are avoided, topics on which discussion will accomplish nothing or even
create resentment are not brought up, and people can spend their time doing what they are
really supposed to be doing, actually turning out the work.

Advantages of a Formal Plan

It must be confessed that there is real point to the above position, but there is at the same
time another side to the story.[1] Those who advocate the adoption of a formal arrangement
in this area also have logic and relevant observations on their side. For one thing, they
point out that most opinion surveys, as well as the experience of most managers, indicate
that a large majority of workers say they wish to know where they stand with the boss.
(Evidently many feel they do not know under informal plans.) Whether they agree with
the boss's opinion is not the important point. If they do agree, their opinion is confirmed,
but if they do not, they at least know what the situation is, and can take whatever steps are
warranted. It is felt that a logical conclusion of this position is that the company should
take steps to see that subordinates periodically receive this desired and presumably useful
information.

Those who favor formal plans point out also that the company executives need this
sort of information too. After all, management constantly faces problems about who
should be promoted or upgraded, what transfers should be carried out, and what persons
are not doing their jobs well and should be demoted, disciplined, or discharged. Furthermore, and particularly so far as management people are concerned, there is the continuing
problem of replacement of important and even key individuals in the organization. Typically, decisions on these matters have been made informally and on the spur of the
moment, with harmful effects to all concerned. The contention is that the company needs
periodic appraisals and reliable records based on them so that it can do a systematic job
in wage and salary administration, promotion, discipline, and related areas.

Another and not inconsequential advantage claimed for formal plans is that, if carried out, employees at least are eventually evaluated and their performance reviewed with
them whereas in the absence of such a scheme one may go for years with no one ever
giving them even an indication of how they are doing. According to this point of view,
even a perfunctory review is better than none.

In appraisal of the advantages of both informality and formal plans, it must be
admitted that some of these arguments, both pro and con, are rather superficial. For one
thing, they often do not take into account important aspects of the situation, including the
degree to which the judgments are accurate and meaningful and are gotten into the record
in a useful fashion. For another, they may not consider realistically the possible effects on
the subordinates of both what and how they are told.

There is hardly any question about the position of the majority of management
authorities who are on record on this issue. Over the years they have favored and still
favor a formal plan over a merely informal one. Indeed, they frequently characterize the

latter as no plan at all and insist that a systematic, logical approach is obviously better than its opposite. Recently there has been some tendency to be more evaluative of the whole idea, but the majority still favor some sort of formal plan.[2]

Later in the chapter we shall raise this whole issue again and state some conclusions concerning it. Meantime we need to examine a particular plan for formal evaluation, namely, merit rating.

MERIT RATING AS A PLAN FOR FORMAL EVALUATION

There is no doubt what sort of formal evaluation has historically received most attention and has been most widely applied in practice, though perhaps less extensively today than formerly. It is a device known as merit rating.

Nature of Merit Rating

One matter on which we need to be careful is the meaning of the term *merit rating*. Not infrequently this term is used to mean the same thing as employee evaluation; when an author uses the term in this sense, anything discussed in the whole chapter belongs under that heading.

The present authors find it more useful, however, to use *merit rating* in a more restricted sense, as many other writers do. We shall use it to refer to a plan for periodic evaluation which employs a list of traits, qualities, habits, or reactions of employees, and requires the rater to indicate by check marks which of these are properly applied to the employee in question—or in some cases, to indicate by a check mark the *degree* to which the statement, phrase, or word properly describes the employee. Thus, "Is frequently late" may appear on one of these forms, and the rater typically either checks it to indicate that it properly applies to this particular worker or leaves it blank to indicate that it does not. Of course, there would be other statements on the form, and they would cover many aspects of the employee's work performance and personal habits and traits, with all, some, or in rare instances very few of which the rater might agree. Rating forms also frequently provide spaces for the rater's comments in addition to places to put his or her check marks. Depending on the situation, these comments may or may not be an important part of the evaluation.

Another feature of merit rating, typical of the system but not always employed, consists in giving each statement a numerical value. It then is easy to work out a total score for the individual who is being rated, and thus to compare his rating with those of others.

Attitudes toward Merit Rating

We have already indicated that managers, particularly personnel managers, were among the earlier supporters of formal evaluation, but those conclusions are not supported by certain other groups.

Union Attitudes Union pressures for a single rate for each job and for promotion policies placing heavy emphasis on seniority are well known. After all, if everyone in a job classification is paid at the same rate (or even the same rate adjusted for length of service), the company's opportunities to reward individual effort are seriously reduced, and places where merit ratings can have a real effect are equally restricted. And, of course, if promotions are based to a significant degree on seniority, this reduces the effective field for merit rating.

Raters' and Ratees' Attitudes So far as the attitudes of both raters and ratees are concerned, however, we have an unanticipated situation. Early advocates of merit rating felt that supervisors would welcome it as an effective tool for discharging many of their responsibilities and that workers would accept, if not be enthusiastic about, it, if for no other reason than because it enabled them to see where they stood in the organization.

In practice, however, it did not work that way. Workers are very frequently either indifferent or antagonistic to merit rating. Furthermore, they are not more deeply or openly so because in fact those who have administered rating plans have often merely gone through the motions and not seriously used the resulting ratings, and workers have come to realize this. And supervisors, for reasons which we shall discuss below, have usually been less than enthusiastic about the tasks imposed by the system. McGregor[3] wonders whether there is not an inherent wisdom here on the part of both raters and ratees, and the present authors are persuaded that there is real point to his observation.

Kinds of Merit-rating Forms

Descriptive-Adjective Rating Forms   One of the earliest kinds of rating forms was of the descriptive-adjective variety. It consists of about a hundred phrases such as "cooperative" or "ambitious," that is, phrases that collectively cover many phases of employee behavior, and the rater indicates by appropriate check marks those items that in his or her judgment really describe the individual being rated (the ratee). Often each phrase has a numerical value, and the sum of the values of those checked can easily be determined. The phrases are printed in a "jumbled" order, that is, favorable and unfavorable statements are included in random fashion.

A provision of the best-known scale of this sort is the presence of not one but three boxes to the left of each statement to receive the rater's check (if he wishes to place it there). The idea is for three different people (presumably the employee's supervisor and the two other bosses in line above him) to rate the employee and thus to furnish a check on the accuracy of the rating and also protection against prejudice or bias. Of course, putting all ratings on one sheet means that all managers except the first see how at least one other person has rated the employee, and this certainly influences the outcome.

We shall not attempt at this point to appraise this kind of rating form other than to say that it is not and never has been in widespread use. People are inclined to distrust its simplicity; most do not understand where the weights for each statement come from; and of course it cannot cover everything everyone might like.[4]

The following six phrases, in Figure 13-1, are arranged as they might be on this sort of form.

```
1    2    3

□    □    □    Is dependable

□    □    □    Often tardy

□    □    □    Works hard

□    □    □    Troublemaker

□    □    □    Limited mental ability

□    □    □    Outstanding employee
```

Figure 13-1   The descriptive-adjective form of merit rating. In actual practice, the phrases would be carefully selected after investigation, and there would probably be about a hundred of them. The three boxes to the left of each are for the use of (1) the immediate supervisor, (2) his boss, and (3) his boss's boss. In each case the manager checks any descriptive adjective that he or she judges to describe the employee.

Forced-Choice Rating Forms   The newest kind of rating system to receive wide attention is the *forced-choice*. It was worked out and widely used in the armed forces during World War II, and after the war was adopted by a number of firms; but it has not continued its early growth. Indeed its present use in the work situation is quite limited.

Nature of the Ratings   To present the details of the forced-choice system would require more space than we have available. It will probably be sufficient to say that it presents the rater with no fewer than twenty-five groups of four statements each, with each of the four statements having a different significance. Two are favorable, if checked, but only one of the two really distinguishes the better worker from the less successful. See Figure 13-2. The other two are unfavorable, but again only one applies to a less-than-satisfactory employee. The forced-choice system presents raters with scores of choices regarding the characteristics that by check marks they attribute to the ratees. However, of those they can choose, only half really characterize the good or poor worker and the others do not distinguish between them. Furthermore each rater is required to choose just half the available statements. Since the raters have no way of knowing which actually do differentiate, if they deliberately try to give a person a good rating (or a poor one) they have only a 50-50 chance of succeeding in their purpose; whereas if they honestly choose in each instance the phrases that fit the ratings, that result will be more accurate. Thus this system is designed to foil attempts by supervisors to give subordinates the ratings they want them to have rather than the ones that they actually deserve.

Problems of This Type of Rating   One problem with forced-choice rating is the time required. The forms used contain not less than 100 items, each of which must be examined for each ratee and a decision made as to whether it should be checked. If the supervisor has many employees, this becomes a time-consuming process.

And then there is the problem of the supervisors' not knowing which items really differentiate the good from the poor worker. The fact that this information is deliberately withheld from them has at least two seriously adverse effects: First, it is a vote of no-confidence in supervisors, who are thereby told that they cannot be trusted if they know what items discriminate; and second, there is the problem the supervisor faces when called upon to explain the resulting rating to subordinates. The truth of the matter is that he or she cannot really explain it, because the secrecy of the "key" makes it impossible for the rater to determine why the check marks resulted in the rating achieved.

Evaluation   The purpose of the forced-choice plan was admirable: to require supervisors to evaluate the worker as they actually saw him or her and to get away from the tendency to rate people the way they want to rate them. On this score, the evidence is that a considerable measure of success was attained. It is regrettable that the system also has these serious and overriding faults and has little or no place in the periodic evaluation of employees.

Graphic Rating Forms   The oldest and most widely used kind of merit-rating form is what is usually called the *graphic scale*. It is simple to explain and to use, though its accuracy and usefulness may be another matter. To begin with, one must determine how many and what traits, characteristics, behaviors, and the like are to be rated. Thus a form might evaluate a worker on job knowledge, dependability, cooperation, quantity of output, and quality of output. Each of these would be as carefully defined as feasible and each given a separate space on the rating form.

The Rating Form and Its Use   Underneath the name of the characteristic to be rated and its definition, a line would be drawn across the page, and just below the line there would be placed phrases describing this characteristic in varying degrees. For example,

Most Like	Least Like	
☐	☐	Is often late
☐	☐	A dependable worker
☐	☐	Gripes a lot
☐	☐	Has original ideas

Figure 13-2 A hypothetical example of a four-statement group from a forced-choice rating form. Let us suppose that the first two statements do not, but the third and fourth do discriminate between better and poorer workers. Then checking 1 or 2 counts neither for nor against the subordinate. On the other hand, checking "most like" opposite 3 or "least like" opposite 4 would be -1, and the reverse would be $+1$.

under one end of the line there might be a phrase describing the characteristic as favorably as practicable and thus indicating the maximum of the characteristic (for example, "Among the most dependable of employees"). At the other end of the line, there would then be a phrase that would indicate possession of the characteristic to a low degree or not at all (for example, "Can be depended upon seldom or never"). Below the middle of the line there would appear a phrase describing the characteristic of the employee to an average degree only, and an additional phrase might be placed between the average statement and the complimentary one and likewise one between the middle and the uncomplimentary phrases. Each of the other main characteristics or traits would be treated in the same way.

The instructions to the raters are quite simple. They are to write the name of the employee on the form and then to make one check mark on each line to indicate the degree to which they believe the employee possesses the trait or characteristic or shows the behavior being rated. Thus in any one case they may check at the left end, at the right end, in the middle, or at any other place on the line, including in-between descriptive phrases. Many companies have prepared a key that gives numerical value to the check wherever it is placed, and the sum of these values represents the employee's score for this particular rating. See Figure 13-3.

A variation of this sort of rating prints the characteristic and its definition and then the descriptive phrases but without the line. In this case the raters check one of the phrases (instead of being able to check somewhere between two if they wish). Theoretically this makes the rating less accurate; but in practice this theoretical conclusion does not seem to hold, for graphic rating with or without the line yields substantially the same results.

Evaluation This sort of rating plan avoids some of the limitations of the forced-choice plan. It is less time-consuming, the scoring system does not have to be secret, and the supervisor has a basis for discussing an employee's rating with him. However, it still presents a number of problems, as we shall see later.

Problems of Merit Rating

The Rating System A serious consideration is what system of merit rating should be adopted, if one has chosen to use this method of employee evaluation. We have already said enough to make clear that we would not choose either the descriptive-adjective or the forced-choice plan. However useful the latter may be for certain purposes (for example, as a "letter of reference") it is inadequate as a plan for continuing, periodic reviews, and for the reasons mentioned above.

Likewise the descriptive-adjective plan is inadequate for this purpose. It covers a largely disorganized collection of points, making it difficult if not impossible to find a

Directions: To indicate the degree of each quality possessed by the employee, place a
check mark (✓) on each horizontal line.

Job Knowledge

_____

Possesses this to the   Satisfactory   Needs great
highest degree   improvement

Dependability

_____

Always available   Above average   Thoroughly
when needed   undependable

Quantity of Output

_____

Unsatisfactory   Average for this plant   Outstanding

Figure 13-3 The graphic form, the most popular system of merit rating. As actually used, the
sheet would have a considerably larger number of traits, the descriptive phrases under each
line would be carefully determined, and there might well be four or five such phrases instead of
the three shown here in each case.

consistent pattern in the evaluation or to appraise the person as a whole. Also important
characteristics can be omitted from the form, and there is seldom any empirical basis for
the weights used to arrive at a total score. Again the plan may have its uses, but periodic
evaluation is not one of them.

This leaves us with the graphic system, and if one is to install a merit-rating plan this
is the most likely choice. However this plan, too, has its limitations, and they are numerous
and at times serious. They will be discussed in the major section following this one,
namely the one that relates to the accuracy of evaluators' judgments in general and also in
rating.

The Future of Merit Rating Before we cover that subject, however, a word about
the prospects for this form of employee evaluation. The authors of this book do not judge
the future of merit rating to be bright. Of course, evaluation of subordinates by supervisors
will continue (as will evaluation of supervisors by subordinates). Furthermore, there may
be some formal procedures accompanying the former, though they will probably differ in
important ways from traditional merit rating. It is doubtful whether such rating will have
a significant place among the personnel practices of the future.

However, two additional observations are in order. One is that when and if merit
ratings are obtained and seriously used in connection with employee evaluation, they
should be supplemented by other information. That is, when employees are being considered for promotion, all we know about them should be evaluated so far as feasible, and

this would mean considering, whenever available, work history, education, standing with their fellows, and their basic values and motivations, along with many similar factors— and certainly not the ratings alone. Used this way, ratings may have value. Used as *the* basis for personnel action, they are very questionable indeed.

The other observation concerns the circumstances under which merit rating, with all its limitations, has still been made to work quite satisfactorily. The most important aspects have already been mentioned: trust and confidence on the part of the workers in their supervisors and respect of the supervisors for, and security in, their role as evaluator. If managers *believe in* merit rating and employees *believe in the managers, merit rating can and does work, as the experience of some successful firms well demonstrates.*

THE RELIABILITY AND VALIDITY OF EVALUATORS' JUDGMENTS

Fundamental to any plan of employee evaluation, whether or not it includes merit rating, is the accuracy of the judgments made by those who do the evaluation. Here it is often useful to distinguish between the degree of agreement between such judgments (their consistency or *reliability*), and the degree to which they actually correspond to or reflect the characteristics of the person being evaluated, the latter being referred to as the *validity* of such judgments. What are the principal factors influencing the reliability and the validity of these judgments?[5]

The Qualities to Be Evaluated

There is little agreement as to what evaluators should evaluate. Some authorities hold that they should restrict such judgments to actual behavior, to tasks accomplished, while others would include character and personality traits as well. There is also no consensus as to how many such factors should be used, though it is clear that, at least for statistical purposes, a modest number usually leads to conclusions that are as accurate as those based on a multitude of aspects.

It is one thing to evaluate another person (or one aspect or trait of his) and quite another thing to get the evaluation on paper in reliable and valid form. Thus there is the fundamental problem of the meaning of words. Take fairness, for example. All of us can give a general definition of it, one that might provoke little, if any, comment or disagreement. But what does it mean in practice? Is a supervisor who bends every effort to please subordinates exemplifying what we mean? How about one who insists on enforcing the company rules just as they are written? More particularly, how fair is Foreman Jones or Supervisor Smith or Section Leader White? Needless to say, difficult questions can be asked about other such characteristics.

There is also the question of the precise meaning of the words or phrases indicating the degree of possession of the characteristic. For example, suppose productivity is to be rated as poor, fair, average, excellent, or outstanding. Just how good is *excellent?* How much better is *outstanding?* Does *average* mean the middle for this particular work group, for all workers similarly situated, for all workers in the United States, or for all people, whether workers or not? Does *fair* mean acceptable, barely acceptable, unacceptable, or something else? And how *poor* does a worker's productivity have to be before it is properly so rated?

Characteristics of Evaluators' Judgments

The Halo Effect   One thing that stands out in many of the judgments we make concerning subordinates (and bosses and other people too) is the *halo effect.* This refers to the tendency of the rater's overall impression of a person to influence his or her judgments on particular traits. Suppose, for example, a supervisor thinks of a particular worker as outstanding in productivity and cooperativeness, but suppose further that this worker is rather careless in his or her manner of dress and does not make a good first impression. Under these circumstances the supervisor is likely to rate the worker as above average in manner of dress and first impression, and thereby to evidence the halo effect. Or suppose that the supervisor has a poor impression of both the output and cooperativeness of another worker who, though he or she is inefficient, is quite friendly. The halo effect would probably manifest itself again, for the supervisor would be likely to rate this worker low in friendliness also. (It should be noted that the term applies to both favorable and unfavorable judgments, that negative halo is just as real and may be as frequent as positive halo.)

All this raises the question whether in fact we usually do judge people trait by trait and then arrive at a composite judgment, or rather get general impressions of a person and rate the various traits very largely in accordance therewith. Available evidence indicates that, while we do both to an extent, the *latter situation is by all odds the prevalent one.* Naturally such a finding does not contribute to our confidence in merit rating and other formal methods of employee evaluation.

Other Errors   Another limitation in such judgment is involved in what we often refer to as the *generosity error.* This represents a tendency to give people the benefit of the doubt and to evaluate them as higher than the facts warrant. For example, when terms like *poor, fair, average, excellent,* and *outstanding* are employed, it is commonplace for the majority of ratees to be put in the two "best" categories, and for virtually everyone else to be rated average. This is understandable if it happens in the case of some work groups, because we would expect some groups to be decidedly above average. But when it happens throughout an organization and the average person receives a rating definitely above average we know that, however useful the procedure, something is seriously amiss with the judgments as recorded.

A similar problem represents in a way an opposite tendency on the part of the evaluators. It is called the *average error* and leads the evaluator to evaluate unusual people—either the poor or the good—as closer to the average than they deserve. An interesting finding about human judgment is revealed by this tendency. While most of us who know the members of a group can agree fairly well on who the outstanding individuals are, we have a strong tendency to judge them as being less outstanding than they really are. Likewise, we have reasonably good agreement about who the poor performers are, but we also tend to underestimate how poor they really are and to rate them also as closer to the average than they deserve. Thus, while there is a tendency to judge people as higher than the facts warrant (the generosity error), there is also a tendency to compress the extremes, to fail to see the good as being as good as they are or the poor as being as poor (the average error).

When it comes to determining the accuracy of our judgments about employees, that is, the correspondence between them and the actual situation, the usual method employed is to correlate them with some sort of independent standard or criterion (for example, productivity figures). The results here have been discouraging, for while they at times relate to the criterion as a level too high to be accounted for by chance and hence have some validity, this is usually quite low.

The "Climate" of the Organization

A factor of major importance in the acceptance and effective utilization of evaluations of subordinates is, as pointed out above, how in general the participants feel about each other. If the subordinate usually sees the boss as a competent, well-meaning, "OK-kind-of-guy," almost any plan will have at least some success, and the total effect of an evaluation program may be decidedly positive. On the other hand, if either the competence or the character of the evaluator is in serious question among the subordinates, no formal system, no matter how elaborate, is likely to accomplish much. After all, if my boss really "doesn't know what the score is," no matter how kind or well-intentioned he may be, I am not likely to be much inspired (or even influenced) by what he says. And if he is somehow unworthy, a schemer known to be interested in himself and hardly at all in me or other people, even if he is competent, I will be influenced by him little or not at all.

OTHER PLANS FOR EVALUATION OF SUBORDINATES

The Evaluation Committee—and the Interrogator

Nature of the Plan A scheme for the evaluation of subordinates that gained some popularity a few years ago provides for a committee to carry out this activity. In theory one or more fellow workers of the person being evaluated could be on the committee, but in practice this does not seem to have worked out well. (Perhaps the American's feeling that this in the final analysis is the manager's responsibility and duty enter into this. And politics is likely to become rather decidedly involved.) The usual committee is made up of people who are on the organization chart above the person under scrutiny. Sometimes the committee members are the employee's boss and that boss's boss, with perhaps others from "up the line," in which case the membership of the committee will shift in composition as different people are appraised. At other times a department (or a whole organization, if small) may have a permanent committee on evaluation of employees. In either case the whole committee may, in addition to appraising the subordinate, also interview him or her for the review of performance, or it may designate one of its members, perhaps the employee's immediate supervisor, to do this job.

In the case of a particular government contractor, another feature was added to this scheme. For each person who was to be evaluated, a committee was set up consisting of his or her immediate supervisor, the supervisor's supervisor, and a third person of the supervisor's rank or higher. This third person was essentially a question-asker, or interrogator. It did not matter whether the third person knew well (or even knew at all) the person to be evaluated. His or her function was to help the other two find their areas of agreement and disagreement about the employee and to see whether in fact they had a substantial basis for their conclusions. In addition, the third person helped plan the strategy for conducting the interview with the employee. In one sense he or she was sort of counsel for the employee, seeing that the employee's case was well presented and that justice was done.

Evaluation This scheme has obvious advantages over the traditional sort of ratings. For one thing, if it is carried out well it assures deliberation and careful consideration of the strengths, weaknesses, and opportunities for the development of the employee. For another, it relieves the supervisor of the task of making an unaided or individual, and hence at times prejudiced, appraisal of the employee. Now he or she no longer has to say, "This is what *I* think," but can say, "This is what *we* concluded." Superficially this may appear to be a slight and inconsequential difference. In practice, it may change very decidedly the whole atmosphere of the appraisal and the interview.

However, the plan has at least two serious limitations. It does not encourage the employee either to appraise himself or to pay serious attention to means of self-improvement. After all, "the bosses" are going to tell him what is right and what is wrong with him, and this largely relieves him of both the burden and the opportunity for careful self-examination. The other disadvantage is the great amount of time required.

Mutual Determination of Objectives

A more recent plan is one proposed by Drucker, McGregor, and others and characteristically referred to as *Management by Objectives* (or simply MBO) and referred to in earlier chapters (see especially Chapter 3).[6] MBO requires that at the beginning of the period during which the employee is to be evaluated (for example, at the beginning of the year) he or she and the supervisor hold an interview or interviews for the purpose of determining the employee's proper objectives for the year ahead. Of course each may have to settle for less (or more) than he or she might actually wish. When agreement has been reached, it is reduced to writing and becomes the agenda for the performance review at the end of the year, as well as for any needed conferences during the period.

This plan is considerably more sophisticated than merit rating. Largely, if not wholly, it removes the supervisor from the role of "playing God." It demands of the employee careful self-examination as well as attention to means of self-development. It almost ensures that the supervisor will not do all the talking in the performance-review interview. Of course, it also has limitations, not the least of which is allowing managers an excuse to avoid "calling a spade a spade" when that might be the best course of action. There is also the problem of whether the objectives are really *shared* ones or only those forced (no matter how subtly) on the employee by the supervisor or higher levels of management. Additionally, it is clear that some workers do not want to share in setting their objectives and hence would not find this plan to be a challenging one.

Field Review

Some companies have found it desirable, in order to introduce a higher degree of uniformity, to select someone, usually from the personnel department, to meet with small groups of supervisors—or in some cases, with supervisors individually—for the purpose of going over their appraisals and helping to assure as far as possible uniform treatment for all employees. The scheme is an expensive one so far as time and effort are concerned, but it does often lead to improvement. Of course there is always the possibility of supervisory resentment.

The Assessment Center

A plan apparently feasible only for large organizations has been mentioned earlier, namely the assessment center, used primarily to appraise managers rather than workers and focusing on potential for development and future contribution. In such centers the individual spends several days, works both alone and in groups, is subjected to a number of testing situations, and is evaluated by a more or less permanent group of observers. There is evidence that such centers make more valid judgments about potential than persons outside of it do, but of course its expense is such that its use will doubtless be limited to relatively few employees.[7]

Peer Evaluation

There is a great deal of evidence to indicate that a person's peers know him or her better than immediate bosses do; hence if they could *feasibly* be brought into the evaluation (and possibly the review) their input would be significant. However, their use poses problems: What forms would be used to record their judgments? How would one get them filled out, especially in a way that would assure objectivity? How could "politics" be kept out of the scheme? How costly is the operation of the plan?

Such problems as these make it unlikely that this arrangement will be employed extensively even as a supplement to management conclusions (the only role it ought to play, as a general rule).

Appraisal by Essay

Particularly among professional employees, there has been some tendency to have the evaluation take the form of an essay written by the supervisor. And because an "open-end" essay might cover so much (or so little) and make comparisons between employees difficult or impossible, at times forms are prepared calling for essay answers to certain more or less general questions. This arrangement does, of course, introduce an element of uniformity into the process.

Aside from the question of how to interpret the essays and to compare the persons about whom they are written, there is still the fact that the sort of evaluation I as an employee receive may depend more on my boss's facility in writing than on my performance. Thus this plan may really evaluate bosses, at least to the extent of how well they write, more than it does subordinates.

Self-evaluation

The writers have never heard of a proposal to transfer the totality of evaluation from the manager to the worker and thus let the latter determine how he or she is doing. However, it is frequently suggested that it is desirable to let the subordinate evaluate himself or herself and then to have that evaluation compared with the boss's evaluation. There is no doubt that this procedure can be a useful one, though in practice and if universally used, it probably would not work out as well as theory suggests. Much depends on how comfortable the subordinate would be and, maybe more significant, how well the supervisor could deal with genuine differences of opinion in this, an area likely to be characterized by strong feeling. As a general rule, this is a practice that may be recommended, but it is usually unwise to require that all supervisors proceed in this fashion.

Peer Ranking

A relatively simple evaluation plan that may have more going for it than is usually recognized is a simple *ranking* (from *the best to the poorest*) of the members of a group. (This process should be carefully distinguished from *peer rating* or *peer evaluation,* discussed above.) In a large plant known to the authors, once each year each engineer is asked to select *all engineers of his rank and lower* whom he knows well enough to rank (not rate) and to proceed to put them in order of general value to the plant. By means of a statistical technique we do not have space to describe, the ranks accorded each engineer by all those who rank him (seldom fewer than eight) are combined in such fashion that a "master list" of rankings is compiled. The great majority of those ranked like the scheme, their principal justification being that "your future here does not depend on the judgment of any one individual."

The plan has obvious limitations. Like any other, it will not work in the absence of trust and confidence among the people. It gives little or no information for specific counseling of a subordinate, and furthermore, "politics" could enter into the rankings. But on the whole, it probably deserves more widespread use than it has received and might turn out to be more generally useful than we have expected up to the present.

THE FUNDAMENTAL PURPOSE OF EVALUATION AND REVIEW

One topic on which nothing has been said directly as yet is the fundamental reasons for employee evaluation and review. The easy reasons are: to get out more production, to make the firm more profitable, and in general to contribute to efficiency. However like most easy answers, these are in no sense complete.[8]

What this point of view tends to neglect is the welfare and inherent value of the evaluated employee. One certainly hopes that each such appraisal and review will contribute to making the firm more profitable (or the nonprofit organization more efficient); it is also to be hoped that it will, in addition, contribute to making the employee a better human being as well as a better producer. Put in realistic, everyday terms, the goal is to afford the employee an opportunity to improve and to give him or her help in doing so, all the while realizing that only *he or she* can really improve. (No human being can really *improve* another, at least not in the long run!)

It should now be apparent why in this chapter we have not felt it necessary to reach a final position about a proper form on which to record the conclusions, the correct period of time between evaluations, the exact information to be transmitted, and the like. All these have to do with the *mechanics* of a plan, whereas the larger concern should be with its actual utility. In reality the fundamental goal of any evaluation-review plan should be to inform those who need to be, and/or are entitled to be informed concerning what they need to be informed about. Furthermore such information should be afforded when it is needed or when it will be useful, when it can be employed by the individual as a factor contributing to actions he or she should take.

Obviously, getting information to people when they need and can use it is *so* much more important than the forms one fills out, whether appraisal-review should occur every six months, or whether one writes an essay, replies to a set of questions, or checks some phrases on a rating form.

So far we may have implied that the only significant factor is getting the information across, but that is not the whole story. A term which we develop in Chapter 14, namely *due process*, is of the greatest importance here, and one overlooks it at his peril. (The reader is urged, when he reads that section of Chapter 14, to remember that while due process can probably best be explained in connection with discipline, it also applies to other activities, including evaluation and review of performance.)

It is also essential that the supervisor be statesmanlike in what he does. Certainly he is not to run roughshod over the feelings of another; on the other hand, he is to do his best to select a reasonable and fair course of action.

One article of faith in what is written above: As a general rule when a supervisor does his best to help an employee to be a better employee and a better human being, he has also done his best, so far as his relations with that worker are concerned, in helping the company be a better, more efficient, more profitable employer.[9]

SOME GENERAL CONSIDERATIONS

While what has just been said may be the basis for effective appraisal-review, a number of other observations should be made on the subject.[10]

Building a Record

One important point, also much emphasized in the two chapters immediately following this one, is the significance of being able to prove the correctness of one's action if challenged. It is not enough, in other words, to *be right*. It is often desirable and sometimes necessary to *prove* that one is right. Just how this is to be done depends in part on personal ingenuity, but some suggestions are made in the chapters just mentioned.

Improving One's Skill in Appraisal-Review

A mistake that is easy to make is to assume that when one has the facts, how they are to be applied to the employee's situation becomes obvious; furthermore, it is easy to believe that when one has accurately and properly evaluated a subordinate, reviewing his or her record "comes naturally." These are serious misconceptions and for at least three reasons. One is that facts are not always evident. Indeed they often have to be sought out and then themselves appraised, sometimes under conditions of ambiguity. Another is that it is often both desirable and practicable to check one's conclusions with a fellow manager before making them final. Indeed where feasible one should avoid the unassisted, unchecked, unevaluated decision. Third, a good many firms insist on what is probably a good practice for most of us, namely, that from time to time we are required to take refresher training in appraisal-review. What form such training should take probably cannot be described in a fashion satisfactory to all, but even giving serious attention to the problem should be of assistance.

Right of Appeal

It is most important that once an appraisal is made the supervisor not take the position that any questioning of it or the basis for it is evidence of lack of either competence or loyalty. On the other hand, he must be willing to explore objectively any disagreement between himself and the employee and to correct any mistakes. And if the employee wishes to pursue what is judged to be the inaccuracy of the supervisor's conclusion, such action should ordinarily not merely be permitted; usually it should be encouraged, especially if the employee has strong feelings of having been wronged.

Empathy for the Evaluated Employee

So far in this chapter we have said little about how it feels to be evaluated and then told about the results (or for that matter, how it feels to have to evaluate). But people *do* have feelings about the process. Occasionally they are warm and responsive; sometimes they are indifferent and apathetic; on occasion they are resentful of anyone who would be so impertinent as to "play God" with the life and future of another human being. (Sometimes supervisors greatly prefer not to "play God" also.)

Whatever these feelings are, the supervisor needs to do his or her best to *empathize* (be careful not to read this as *sympathize*) with the evaluated employees, to come to understand what they are, and to appraise their causes as best he or she can. One then acts in accordance with the facts and not necessarily the feelings, though the latter is taken into account in the decisions.

Evaluation of the Supervisor

One point seldom made in discussions of evaluation, but a significant one nevertheless, concerns the subordinate's evaluation of the supervisor. As we pointed out earlier, such judgments are constantly being made, but most evaluation plans not only make no use of them but seem to pretend that they do not occur. What we are suggesting here is that, for the employee who is doing a satisfactory or outstanding job, this not only be permitted but even encouraged.

Furthermore, it is possible that the employee's evaluation of the supervisor could be quite significant to both of them and to the organization. After all, if a person is a problem employee, the supervisor could be the biggest problem. Here as elsewhere good judgment is essential, and the process will have to be used wisely and in some situations infrequently if at all. If an effort is made to get the employee to make such evaluation, some use of the nondirective interviewing methods discussed in the chapter on counseling might well be most appropriate for the supervisor.

It is at this point we suggest an addition to the MBO plan, discussed earlier. It is that there are times when such goal setting should have definite implications for the conduct of the supervisor as well as that of the employee. In other words, if a problem exists in the supervisor-subordinate relationship, it can frequently be talked over between the parties involved and plans can be made to resolve it. At times certainly this may call for a change in the supervisor's behavior or attitudes, and this change, along with the necessary changes in the employee, can be made a part of the goals for mutual accomplishment during the period.

Needless to say, this procedure must also be used with good judgment. Useful and appropriate items should be considered for both supervisor and subordinate, and every attempt at realism should be made. Neither the supervisor nor the subordinate should be required or expected to make known all innermost secrets, and many of the supervisor's duties may not concern the subordinate and not need to be discussed with the subordinate. But on many occasions aspects of supervisory behavior may properly be examined by both parties.

What we are really trying to say is that a fundamental goal of evaluation and the performance-review interview is the opportunity for people who are interested in helping each other actually to do so. This suggests that forms and records are secondary in importance and should be kept to a minimum. The important factor is the interaction between people and their success in being mutually helpful.

THE SUPERVISOR AND THE EVALUATION-REVIEW INTERVIEW

One of the difficulties in writing a book like this is, as has been mentioned before, that the same topic must be discussed in more than one context. We face that situation again. In Chapter 12, the immediately preceding one, we discussed at some length the interview and its use in employee counseling. Now we need to discuss the same topic as relates to the review of the employee and his performance.[11] In this discussion we are assuming that there are three methods of conducting such an interview, though obviously other methods might be suggested by someone. Furthermore two or even all three of these might be combined in the same interview.

The Telling Method

Perhaps because of the long association of performance review with merit rating and the stress of the latter on "letting him know where he stands," the opinion is widespread that performance review automatically involves *telling* the subordinate what the facts are. After all, he wants to know, does he not? Why should we not simply tell him? No small part of the disappointment connected with the whole field of formal performance review comes from the naive acceptance of this point of view.

Under some circumstances use of the telling method is not naive at all. As we pointed out earlier, if the subordinate has a large measure of confidence in both the ethics and the competence of his boss, telling can be very effective for both the long run and the short run. On the other hand, when the subordinate seriously questions either the accuracy of the evaluation, or the purposes for which it is used, the effects are seldom good, and they can be disruptive.

Another place where telling may be not only acceptable but decidedly desirable is in an interview in which the purpose is to warn the employee of the likelihood of quite unfavorable consequences unless a certain situation is remedied. This point is elaborated in Chapter 14, where the oral reprimand is discussed as an integral part of a successful disciplinary program.

The Nondirective Method

A second way of conducting the employee review is in some ways the opposite of the one just described. It involves "passing the ball to the interviewee and letting him run with it" and will be recognized as the nondirective method described in the preceding chapter on employee counseling.

What would one expect to come from such an interview? Maybe some emotional release for him or her (for we all have *some* negative feelings about our situation), maybe some self-evaluation, maybe some plans for improvement—who knows? It is possible that the interview might be quite satisfactory if conducted in a wholly nondirective fashion. On the other hand, these techniques might have to be supplemented by other methods in order to accomplish all of the needed review.

As has also been indicated earlier, the nondirective method might also be used—or at least may be the principal method—when one wants the employee to supply additional information and/or explain relationships and the like, even to the extent of literally "instructing himself" to a degree, that is, of discovering certain heretofore-obscure insights literally as he talks. It may also be utilized to put the employee on the spot, to inquire more and more deeply into beliefs, attitudes, values, and the like. We are certainly not saying that the review interview should always be or even usually be conducted nondirectively. We do say that nondirective procedures should always be available—and used where and to the extent needed.

The Shared-Responsibility Approach

What we have in mind in this connection is the modification of Management by Objectives discussed above. It consists in (a) mutual setting of goals by the two people involved, which goals will almost surely impose obligations upon each of them, and (b) an open, give-and-take discussion of such mutual goals as were agreed upon at the previous evaluation session. Wisely carried out, this activity could contribute directly to a good organizational climate.

QUESTIONS

1 What sort of reasoning has been used by those who recommend that every worker should be reviewed *formally* and *periodically?* Appraise.
2 Do subordinates evaluate supervisors? Should they? What use if any should the company make of these evaluations?
3 What is the principal difficulty (or difficulties) of making an appraisal on a *periodic* basis (for example, June 30 and December 31)? As a general rule, should a supervisor do this?
4 What are some of the difficulties in getting the evaluation of an employee on paper, that is, getting the written material to reflect the facts accurately?
5 Describe and point out the strengths and weaknesses of the *forced-choice* plan of merit rating.
6 Do the same for the *graphic* method.
7 Why has there not been agreement on the "qualities" or characteristics that should be rated in a merit-rating plan? What is your conclusion on this subject?
8 Explain (a) the halo effect, (b) the average error, (c) the generosity error, and (d) lack of validity as they affect merit ratings.

NOTES

1 The older or more traditional approach to this subject may be found in Dale Yoder et al., *Handbook of Personnel Management and Labor Relations* (New York: McGraw-Hill, 1959), pp. 15.1-15.35. The fact that this material was written some twenty years ago helps to explain why it differs decidedly from some of the more recent writings on the subject.
2 The older point of view, however, is not restricted to the fifties. See for example, Lawrence I. Bethel et al., *Essentials of Industrial Management,* 5th ed. (New York: McGraw-Hill, 1971).

3   Most or all of the above problems were anticipated in Douglas McGregor, "An Uneasy Look at Performance Appraisal," *Harvard Business Review,* vol. 35, no. 3, pp. 1-13, May-June 1957. This is an unusually significant and influential article.

4   A more complete description of these merit-rating forms, along with illustrations of each will be found in Aaron Q. Sartain et al., *Psychology: Understanding Human Behavior,* 4th ed. (New York: McGraw-Hill, 1973), Chap. 16.

5   Andrew J. DuBrin, *Fundamentals of Organizational Behavior* (New York: Pergamon, 1974), Chap. 8.

6   George S. Odiorne, *Management by Objectives: A System of Managerial Leadership* (New York: Pitman, 1965).

7   For an unusual use of an assessment center see James R. Huck and Douglas W. Bray, "Management Assessment Center Evaluations and Subsequent Job Performance of White and Black Females," *Personnel Psychology,* vol. 29, no. 1, pp. 13-30, Spring 1976.

8   A great many thoughtful articles on the nature and uses of the evaluation processes have begun to appear in recent years. See, for example, Harry Levinson, "Appraisal for What Performance?" *Harvard Business Review,* vol. 54, no. 4, pp. 30ff, July-August 1976; and George A. Rieder, "Performance Review—A Mixed Bag," *Harvard Business Review,* vol. 51, no. 4, pp. 61-67, July-August 1973.

9   See Harold Koontz, "Making Managerial Appraisal Effective," *California Management Review,* vol. 15, no. 2, pp. 46-55, Winter 1972; and Henry Tosi and Stephen J. Carroll, Jr., "Improving Management by Objectives," *California Management Review,* vol. 14, no. 1, pp. 57-66, Fall 1973.

10 A large number of empirical studies of performance evaluation and review have appeared in the literature, though many of them have little or no apparent application to day-to-day practice. Examples are Ronald J. Gray and David Kipnis, "Untangling the Performance Appraisal Dilemma: The Influence of Perceived Organizational Context on the Evaluation Process," *Journal of Applied Psychology,* vol. 61, no. 3, pp. 329-335, June 1976; Robert L. Taylor and Wm. D. Wilsted, "Capturing Judgment Policies in Performance Rating," *Industrial Relations,* vol. 15, no. 2, pp. 216-224, May 1976; and Walter C. Borman and Marvin D. Dunnette, "Behavior-Based Versus Trait-Oriented Performance Ratings: An Empirical Study," *Journal of Applied Psychology,* vol. 60, no. 5, pp. 561-564, October 1975.

11 A short but thoughtful and realistic treatment of personnel appraisal is found in Paul Pigors and Charles A. Myers, *Personnel Administration: A Point of View and a Method,* 7th ed. (New York: McGraw-Hill, 1974), Chap. 16.

CASES

As was true for the chapter on counseling, so for this one on appraisal: there are many appropriate and directly related cases. We have chosen three, two of which involve discipline and more particularly, discharge, and one of which involves appraisal of a leadman's duties.

The Westover case involves a black who talked back to his white supervisor, using what we would not call wild profanity (or maybe *no* profanity) but in the context of 1962 would be viewed as more insubordinate than it would be today. Feelings about blacks talking back to white bosses were also stronger then, and the 1964 Civil Rights Act was still two years away.

In the Ludwig case an important issue is involved: May a worker properly be discharged for absenteeism even if he does all he can to avoid it? In this situation there is also a question of whether the Company did all it might have done in the way of appraising and counseling the grievant and specifically warning him of the likely consequences of his attendance record.

The Gordon case raises an issue of whether there are any limits on how many leadmen a company can select if it has the freedom to choose them without consultation with the Union. Again the question of the proper appraisal and review of Gordon's performance is before us.

CASE 13-1

Bill Westover, thirty-five years old and a black, with a high school diploma and two years of college, is a Material Handler B for the Company. He has been in its employ for seven years, that is, since 1955, serving most of the time as laborer. When business is good, he usually moves to material handler (which pays.twenty-five cents per hour more), and then he is cut back to laborer as business falls off.

Bill has been an average, or perhaps a little better than average, employee during his seven years with the Company. His attendance record has been satisfactory, and his output (not measurable in any really objective way) could be improved if he had more interest in his job and would put forth more effort, but it is at least as good as that of the average person in his group.

The Company is a small manufacturer. Its principal products involve the use of sheet metal. Only forty people work for it, with a total of eighteen people in the shop.

Bill has been in trouble only once up to the present time. Three months ago he clocked in late (at 7:31 A.M. instead of 7:30). Instead of going to work at once, he sat in the lunchroom waiting until 7:45 to begin. (The company policy is the loss of fifteen minutes of pay for tardiness of even one minute.) Jim Handy, his foreman, shortly discovered the situation and ordered Bill to go to work. Bill refused, explaining that he would work only when he was paid for work.

Jim then asked, "Boy, why was you late?"

Bill refused to answer but began work promptly at 7:45. Later in the morning Bill apologized to Jim for lack of courtesy. He said nothing about his reason for tardiness or his refusal to go to work when ordered to do so.

This morning a truck came in with a coil of metal weighing about 300 pounds. It is Bill's job to unload the trucks, with the aid of power equipment and a laborer. Today no laborer was available to help Bill, but when this had happened before, Bill had gone ahead and unloaded the material. On this occasion, however, the metal was not tied through the middle (though it was strapped around the outside), and Bill did not feel it was safe for one person to attempt to handle it. (The principal risk was damage to the material, but there could be injury to Bill.) He reported the situation to Handy, who was quite busy, and went back to the truck to await a laborer.

After about twenty minutes of waiting, Westover again found Handy and asked him where to unload the metal and also for help. Jim said to put it over "where that machine is." Bill replied that there was no room to move the machine and besides it was not his job as material handler to move it. Jim then went and moved the machine himself with no help from Bill, and told Bill to unload the metal.

Bill again insisted that he would not move it without help since it was not properly tied.

Jim became angry and told him it was "tied OK," after which Bill said it was not, and then added, "Aw, hell, if you don't believe me, go look for yourself."

Jim then said, "Let's cut out the yelling," to which Bill replied, "I can yell anytime I want to."

"Bill," Jim said with obvious anger, "you're through at this plant. You're fired. Go to the office and get your time."

Instead of going to the payroll office Bill went at once to see George Smith, the plant superintendent and Handy's boss, and appealed to him to reverse Jim's decision. George Smith investigated the situation, including talking with Handy and inspecting the coil of metal. He found that the facts were as described above.

How should he handle this situation? The year, incidentally, is 1962.

CASE 13-2

The basic issue in this case is whether the Company had the right to discharge Laborer Ludwig for excessive absenteeism (including tardiness) regardless of whether the absences were justifiable and/or "excused." (The labor agreement contains the customary "just cause" clause.) A related question, if such a discharge is sustained, concerns the necessary procedures involved in warning the involved employee, in advance of discharge, of the seriousness of his situation.

John Ludwig had been an employee of the Company since February 1974, and was discharged on June 2, 1975, allegedly because of his excessively poor attendance record. That record is as follows, with tardiness and leaving early combined in the first column and full days missed in the second:

Time Period	Tardiness	Absences
March-May 1974	2	0
June-August 1974	4	0
September-November 1974	13	7
December 1974-February 1975	6	0
March-May 1975	12	6
	37	13

If one assumes that the total period included 280 working days not including any overtime assignments, Ludwig's 37 tardinesses thus represent 13 percent of the days involved and his 13 absences, 5 percent of the total. Cumulatively, therefore, he was absent, left early, or was tardy, 18 percent of the days he was supposed to work.

After the discharge, Ludwig filed a grievance alleging that the Company was without "just cause" in its action and asking for full back pay, fringe benefits, seniority, and so forth.

The Company contends that it can be expected to go, and can go, only so far with an individual who is very frequently absent from work. It does not contend that Ludwig misrepresented his reasons for nonattendance and admits that he usually notified his foreman when he was not coming in. But absences are costly to the Company, and the unpredictable, unexpected ones are much more so than continuing, predictable ones (for example, when an employee is recovering from a heart attack), for one can plan in advance for the latter. Furthermore in Ludwig's case there is no basis for optimism. His record suggests that the absences are increasing and will continue to do so.

The Company says it gave Ludwig ample warning. He was talked to a number of times, and in addition received two warning letters, one in April 1974, telling him he must improve, and one in October 1974, telling him this was a final warning and that discharge would follow if he did not markedly improve. Each letter was handed to him in a meeting attended by his department head, his foreman, a Union representative, and Ludwig. (Mr. Holt, the department head, conducted the meeting and signed the letters.)

The Union contends that (1) the burden of proof rested on the Company and it was unable to sustain it; (2) all reasons for Ludwig's absences and tardinesses were explained to the Company and accepted by it (were "excused" as justifiable); (3) these absences did not jeopardize the Company's work in any way, especially since the grievant was only a laborer; (4) when he was present, Ludwig's work was good, a point that the Company concedes; (4) Ludwig remembers being counseled by Holt, but he has no memory of any warning letters and indeed received none that he considered a warning; and (5) even the Company admits the Union was sent no copies of any such letters and hence the Company violated its agreed-to obligation to keep the Union informed of the disciplinary difficulties of employees.

Should the discharge of the grievant be allowed to stand? If he should be reinstated, what about seniority, back pay, and so forth?

CASE 13-3

The Company is an East Coast manufacturer of machine tools. It has a labor contract with an Independent Union representing its machinists. Though the Union has no ties with any other union, it is strong and at times belligerent. It has the support of the great majority of the hourly people and makes considerable use of the grievance procedures. An unusual percentage of its cases go to arbitration. In the arbitration hearing the Union cases are almost always well presented, and over the years about half of them have been decided in its favor.

In addition to machinist and a number of other similar jobs, the job descriptions included in the contract provide for leadmen. According to the contract, a leadman is to "carry out supervisor's orders and work instructions with a group of workers." Further, the leadman, who is an hourly employee and a member of the bargaining unit, is to have *superseniority,* that is, in case of a layoff even if he were junior to all the persons in his crew, he would be the last to be laid off. In fact, as long as he is a leadman, he is not on the regular seniority list of machinists.

Another contract provision, however, requires that he actually be a leadman. The company cannot, in other words, simply call a person a leadman and thus remove him from the seniority list and retain him instead of senior employees. On the other hand, he must be doing the work of a leadman in instructing workers about how to do their work and checking on how well they do it.

The case of Jack Gordon led to a grievance by the Union. For several years Jack has been a leadman, but recently the size of his crew has been reduced from the usual ten workers to three and then to two workers, and about a month ago to only one.

There had been a good many rumblings among the workers for several weeks, because of this situation and two additional facts. For one thing, a great many of them had seniority over Gordon (or at least they would have if he were returned to his prior position as machinist); and for another, business had fallen off sharply and a layoff seemed likely.

The Union grievance asserted that the Company was keeping Gordon as a leadman in order to protect his job security. It argued that he was not in fact doing leadman work but was actually simply a machinist, and hence that he was improperly classified. It also contended that since the contract referred to a "group of workers" in describing a leadman's job, Gordon could not be a leadman, since one worker does not make a group (and maybe even two or three do not).

Incidentally, while leadmen were paid by the hour and could (and most of them did) belong to the Union, the Company had a free hand in picking them and in returning them to the ranks.

Another relevant fact is that on the date of the grievance, two machinists were added to Gordon's crew. Union officials charge that this was done by design, to furnish a basis for answering the grievance.

How would you advise the Company to handle this grievance?

Chapter 14

Discipline in the Work Group

Every successful organization has to make some assignments of duties to its individual members, along with directions for carrying out these duties. At times such assignments may be highly informal, so much so that the people involved, though following them, could not put them into words. At other times they may be carefully written out and people's actions methodically checked against them. But they are present, or no coordination results.

Likewise there must be constraints that lead to performance that is in accord with them. Perfection is not demanded, but efficient work should be. These constraints may come from within the individual involved, or they may arise from outside and be forced on the participants.

SELF-DISCIPLINE VERSUS IMPOSED DISCIPLINE

While the two may at times overlap, it is useful to divide discipline into two kinds, closely related to the distinction just made. One kind is *positive discipline* or *self-discipline,* that which the individual accepts, imposes upon himself, and follows willingly, and the other is *negative discipline* or *imposed discipline.* For example, if a person really wants to help in attaining the objectives of the organization and strives voluntarily to do so, he is exhibiting self-discipline. On the other hand, if he does what he has to do because someone else is watching him and will punish him if he fails, the discipline that results arises from outside himself and is imposed on him.

Nature of Self-discipline

That self-discipline is the sort that is to be prized and sought goes without saying. Indeed, the ideal work situation would be one in which every member of the work group does what he should do in the way and at the time he should do it, because he wants to and not because someone is making him do it.

Increasing Self-discipline   Most of what has been written earlier in this book, as well as the remaining portions, is relevant to the subject of increasing self-discipline. Thus an understanding and the wise practice of effective planning, organizing, and controlling of work and workers are often critical in a well-run organization. Appreciation of the role of trust, confidence, wisdom, and empathy, along with generally useful supervisory techniques, may often produce fortunate outcomes, as may effective communication, selection, evaluation, training, and counseling. And topics to be discussed later, including unions, the history of the work relationship, and studies of various approaches to supervision can also be quite valuable. Interpreted in one way, the book might be thought of as just that—efforts to help workers and managers alike increase their own motivation and self-discipline.

Limitations of Self-discipline   Valuable as it is, however, the supervisor cannot afford to depend on self-discipline alone. For one thing, there may be inability or misunderstanding, and well-intentioned, well-motivated people may fail to do what they should (or may do what they should not). For another thing, people may be indifferent in spite of the very best efforts of the supervisor. People *should* be interested if we approach them correctly, but unfortunately some may not be.

Of course, there can also be genuine disagreement between supervisors and one or more of their subordinates. After all, as we have pointed out several times, two people can see the same set of facts and come to exactly opposite conclusions (and this can happen even if both are experienced, well-trained, capable, and sincere).

The conclusion is no doubt quite clear by now: Valuable as it is, self-discipline is not sufficient. The supervisor must be prepared, when circumstances warrant, to supplement the self-discipline of employees by discipline that he or she imposes upon them. Most of the remainder of this chapter will be devoted to the subject of imposed discipline.[1]

IMPOSED DISCIPLINE

When we assert that imposed discipline is inevitable in the work situation, we do not mean that every supervisor must constantly use it or else court failure. Rather, every supervisor should recognize that he or she may be called upon to take such action, and indeed that imposition of penalties is a normal and to-be-expected, though hopefully an infrequent, part of the supervisor's job.[2]

Reasons for Imposed Discipline

Like nearly every other subject involving people, the reasons for imposing penalties on members of one's group are more complex than they appear at first to be. Some of these reasons are laudable and proper, and others are improper.

Acceptable Reasons   It is fairly easy to state the only two proper reasons for imposing penalties on a guilty employee. One is to *reform* the offender, and the other is to *deter* others who may be influenced by what has happened. All imposed discipline, in other words, is to be valued in terms of its future effects on the people involved, offenders as well as observers, and such evaluation must involve calculations or appraisals about the likely results of the various penalties that may be available.

Thus the consideration facing the supervisor in the case of the imposition of a penalty is clear: What penalties are available and feasible? What would be the likely effects of Penalty A, Penalty B, and so forth, on the offender or offenders and on any who may be influenced by the infraction? When the effects have been estimated carefully, with both short- and long-range consequences considered, one selects the course of action calculated to be most effective. This may appear to be a cold, impersonal way to handle discipline. Actually, it need not be either cold or impersonal, but it should certainly be as objective and effective as can be attained.

Unacceptable Reasons　By now one unacceptable reason for imposed discipline should be quite clear, namely, decisions based primarily on emotion, on a strong feeling such as anger or revenge. This is a particular hazard of disciplinary situations, for frequently such infractions do cause such feelings. Sometimes this leads to efforts at revenge, but it must never be forgotten that revenge begets resentment, often of a deep and abiding character. It is not likely to bring about true reform, and its effects in deterrence will probably be transitory at best. Widely practiced in an organization, it typically leads to worse and worse relations between the parties involved, and makes genuine cooperation and teamwork virtually impossible.

Another "emotional" reason for discipline is *displaced aggression,* or *scapegoating.*[3] Here one takes out his feelings, not on the real culprit but on an innocent, or near-innocent, bystander. In other words, the supervisor is frustrated and resentful and since the real cause of the feeling cannot be located, a convenient scapegoat is found, and the supervisor takes it out on him. Needless to say, the effects of such action may be as serious as those growing out of direct revenge.

Here might be a good place to comment on a really difficult problem that faces the supervisor—the many minor infractions that become major because they are often repeated, many times after warning. Conspicuous violations of major rules (for example, drunkenness) are unpleasant and may take time, but they can usually be handled in a fairly straightforward manner. Thus an unprovoked physical attack or the theft of company property of considerable value is almost always the basis for serious penalty, and it is hard to argue to the contrary. But how many times does an employee have to be tardy before a disciplinary penalty should be imposed? Or how many days may one permit an employee's production to be a little below standard before taking action? And what of the "fence-rider" who knows just how far he or she can go without calling the wrath of the boss down upon his head, and who does this, tantalizingly, day after day? Most of us as supervisors have to admit that we are hardly up to handling such cases without great effort and planning. On the contrary, we usually go until we reach the breaking point, and then "let him have it." Needless to say, such action is emotional and not rational, and subject to all the imperfections of such actions.

The other unacceptable reason for punishment at first appears to have greater validity. Indeed it was once widely endorsed and still has its defenders. It is the theory of *retribution,* which holds that when a person has been guilty of an infraction, he or she owes the offended person or organization or society as a whole some penance simply because of the infraction. Thus, according to this theory, every violation should be followed by punishment appropriate to the violation, regardless of reform by the offender or effects on others. Thus the point is that such action must be taken *because of the sin* and not for its effects. This proves to be a fatal defect in the theory; the proper reason for discipline is to make the future more satisfactory, not to fulfill abstract justice.

Table 14-1 summarizes the reasons for imposing of penalties.

Table 14-1 Reasons for Disciplinary Sanctions

Motive or intention	Likely effects
Acceptable	
Reform	Improvement of offender
Deterrence	Prevention of violation by others
Unacceptable	
Revenge	Anger, provocation to more serious violation
Displaced aggression	Confusion, resentment
Retribution	Frustration, accusations of legalistic actions

Considerations in Its Use

The successful handling of imposed discipline is among the most demanding supervisory tasks. Properly used, such discipline can be valuable, building confidence and even morale among employees; improperly applied, it can have results that may be extremely adverse.

The point of all this may appear to be that the supervisor should be careful not to impose discipline unless forced to do so, and then to take such action after much delay. This conclusion does not follow, of course, in view of the necessity for such actions. However, the situation is such that at least three suggestions would ordinarily be in order.

Getting the Facts First, every reasonable effort should be made to see that the disciplinary decision is an informed one, that it is based on what actually took place (with account taken of the feelings of the participants) and not on false conclusions concerning the occurrences. The more serious the offense and the more severe the contemplated penalty, the more care is needed in ascertaining the true situation.

Keeping or Regaining Emotional Control Second, the disciplinary situation is usually an emotional one for the to-be-disciplined employee and for the supervisor. Infractions of rules and especially open defiance of them may arouse strong feelings in the supervisor, especially during the early years in his position. On the other hand, one of the hallmarks of emotional maturity is the ability to face such situations objectively and without loss of emotional balance.

Under the circumstances and assuming it is feasible, the course of action of the supervisor is clear: to take whatever time is required to cool off, to regain not only his composure, but his emotional control and his ability to reason logically and clearly.

On some occasions little time may be required, since emotional control may speedily return (or may not be lost); on other occasions considerable delay in a final decision may be advisable. Thus one may quite properly suspend an employee on the day of the offense, and wait until the following day, or at times until later, before deciding on a discharge or how long a layoff should be. Of course, there may be emergencies that make such delay inadvisable, but temporary suspension rather than discharge is often wise even in serious situations.

Choosing a Fair and Consistent Penalty Third, getting the facts and keeping emotional control are worth little, however, if an unfair or improper decision is ultimately made. It is important, therefore, before the supervisor makes a final decision relative to a disciplinary penalty that it be checked out carefully with trusted colleagues and other members of management in whose judgment the supervisor has confidence and who will assist in objectively evaluating what he or she contemplates doing. The supervisor must also make every feasible effort to find out how the contemplated penalty compares with those previously imposed in situations that are for all practical purposes the same. Widely varying penalties for the same offense imposed on people with the same background of production, disciplinary record, and the like are unjustifiable and morally, if not legally, wrong.

One objection to the points just made may be that, at least in large organizations, first-line supervisors are not really permitted to choose and impose serious disciplinary penalties on their subordinates; and hence the considerations do not apply to them. In truth, whether one likes it or not, this is a very common situation. Furthermore, as we shall attempt to make clear in the chapter immediately following, there is often very good reason for this policy, but correct or not, it is the policy the supervisor must live with until it is changed. In this case, the most he can expect is an opportunity to *recommend* concerning discipline, and the above considerations then apply fully to any such recommendation. In a later section of this chapter we shall discuss these points in some detail.

DISCIPLINARY PENALTIES

A number of sanctions against an employee are usually available to the supervisor. Some, however, are seldom or never used today (for example, physical punishment or the assessment of a fine), and hence we shall emphasize those often employed.

The Oral Reprimand

No doubt the most common punishment imposed on an employee is the oral reprimand, often not really thought of as a disciplinary penalty. This reprimand can vary, of course, from a mild expression of disapproval, in private and without undue feeling, to a public denunciation in strong terms. As time has passed, the latter sort of reprimand has diminished in frequency, but it would be a serious mistake to suppose that errant employees are no longer "chewed out" and that all reprimands are held in private.

Incidentally, if what we have said so far in this chapter is accepted, not all reprimands should be held in private. Indeed, a public expression of disapproval in unmistakable terms may at times be useful. After all, the real question here is, What will be the effects, on the offender and on others who may be influenced, of the mild, private reprimand and of the strong, public one? In the great majority of cases the former will be better, but in certain circumstances the latter might be. Only good judgment and a willingness to take the inevitable risk (no matter what one decides) will enable the supervisor to conclude whether to reprimand, and how.

A point made above in connection with nondirective interviewing should be emphasized in this connection: When an employee needs to be reprimanded, it is important that he realize before the interview is over that a reprimand is involved. There is real danger for the supervisor here; in his or her desire to practice good human relations and not hurt the feelings of the other person, he may first compliment clearly, then express mild disapproval which he immediately tempers, and close on a note of confidence in future performance. Not infrequently under these circumstances the person who is being disciplined may feel that he was not reprimanded but complimented, and who can say for sure that he is wrong?

Of course, the spirit in which the reprimand is carried out is usually as significant as the reprimand itself. More will be said on this point later.

The Written Reprimand

A penalty seldom employed a few generations ago but fairly common today, especially for blue-collar workers, is the written reprimand. This is just what would be expected from its name—a written expression of disapproval by the company, or its agent, of certain behavior on the part of an employee or employees. It may be general (though it can become too general) or specific; the behavior in question may relate to attendance, productivity, attitudes, or other reactions. It may definitely and explicitly include a warning; indeed it usually includes one by implication if not by direct statement. And of course it may or may not contain provisions putting the employee on probation, suggesting how the probation may be lifted (or the period of time after which the warning will no longer be held against its recipient), outlining likely penalties for future misconduct, and the like.

An additional comment or two about the written reprimand: if intended as a reprimand, it, too, must make this unmistakably clear. Generally, it should be written simply and to the point, and expression of definite disapproval is usually entirely appropriate. Ordinarily the original is sent to the employee, and copies are retained by the company. The union may also be informed of the action.

Of course, one must use such penalties wisely and sparingly. If the company develops the practice of sending them out frequently and for relatively mild offenses, they soon lose their effectiveness and may easily do more harm than good. Wisely used, however, they are real and often appropriate penalties.

The Layoff

A disciplinary penalty that is rather frequently used in dealing with manual workers is the layoff. It is usually for a few days or possibly a week, though longer periods are occasionally also used. During this period the employee typically loses his wages and the fringe benefits based directly on them, though his seniority is not usually interrupted or reduced.

Many contend that the layoff is most effective for the simple reason that it "hits the employee where it hurts most, in his pocketbook." Moreover, it is conspicuous because, while a person may receive a reprimand without its being known to his fellow workers, this is unlikely in the case of a layoff. Both of these points can be overdone, but an employee not infrequently greatly regrets the loss of wages, and a layoff will make a hero only in exceptional circumstances. They do caution us to realize, however, that there is no such thing as the perfect penalty for all offenses.

All this is not to condemn the layoff. When it is wisely employed and reserved for offenses of serious import, it can be effective, for there is reason to believe that in the great majority of cases employees find it real punishment, no matter how unconcerned they may appear to be about it. Incidentally, managers of clerical people who take the position that "if talking to them won't do it, there's nothing to do but let them go" should take another look at the possibilities of the wise and occasional use of the layoff.

It comes as a surprise to many people to realize that there may be another kind of layoff at least occasionally effective, namely, the layoff *with pay*. Many believe this would always be most unwise, for the person would simply enjoy himself, without any real penalty being imposed. We are certainly not advocating the widespread use of this disciplinary measure, but it must be remembered that under some conditions it can be effective in bringing the person to his senses. And especially if it is coupled with probation, it can be real punishment.

Such a layoff is most likely to be used in circumstances where the person has been derelict in his duties because of developments that are on the border between disciplinary situations and those not unmistakably the fault of the employee (for example, serious loss of emotional control or excessive drinking off the job). And it may be more effective with the professionally trained or management person than with the rank-and-file employee. Like any other sanction, it should be used only where the best deliberate judgment of management indicates its suitability.

The Demotion

A penalty that probably appears to the outsider as very effective but which is in fact used rarely is the demotion. Since it typically results in a definite loss of both pay and prestige, why is it not adopted more often?

Perhaps the best answer is its severity, for its direct effects may continue for many years and its indirect effects for the rest of the person's working life. Furthermore, its consequences for status and self-respect may be even greater than those for financial position. At any rate it is not a frequently encountered penalty, though of course it may be effective at times.

The Discharge

Within the last generation or two and in some quarters the notion seems to have grown that the discharge is old-fashioned, that its use is evidence not only of failure but also a lack of imagination, and that it should be abandoned as a disciplinary penalty. The facts are directly to the contrary on all these points.

As we have already said, there are times when management finds it necessary to take strong action. Sometimes, had all concerned been sufficiently wise, the outcome might have been avoidable, but no human is omniscient, and for a variety of reasons people do get out of hand. Thus the discharge is with us to stay, though it is no longer a penalty to be imposed without careful consideration.[4]

A significant factor in the use of discharge has been union pressures. Unions are as sensitive to disciplinary actions as to any actions of management—if in fact not more so— and this is especially true of the severe penalties. Many discharges, for example, even when the company is clearly within its rights and has acted wisely, are taken by the union to arbitration, and there is always the risk that the decision of the arbitrator will go against the company. It is understandable why supervisors and their bosses have been reluctant to invite a situation where a worker is discharged and later restored to his position by an arbitrator.

Actually, the anticipations in such situations are usually worse than the results. True, some discharged employees use their restoration to the work force to embarrass the company and create additional trouble. For others, however, the discharge, even if subsequently overruled by the arbitrator, still has a sobering effect, and the employee may very well become a quite different kind of worker. In addition, two other facts must be kept in mind. In the first place, the company has taken a stand on principle and has thus served notice of an intention to require employees to behave in a proper fashion. In the second place, an overruled discharge frequently serves as a warning to a troublesome employee and, if his conduct is repeated, makes his discharge for a second similar offense much easier to sustain.

One must, of course, be careful not to overstate the case for the discharge. It should never be undertaken lightly or on the spur of the moment, and except under most unusual circumstances should be a rare occurrence. When required, however, it should be imposed forthrightly and in the long-run interest of the organization.[5]

DUE PROCESS IN DISCIPLINARY DECISIONS

Recently a large intercollegiate athletic conference publicly declared ineligible certain members of an athletic team of a conference school because, it alleged, they had been illegally recruited. No details concerning the charges were made public, those "convicted" never saw their accusers nor knew the evidence against them, they were not represented by counsel, nor did they have any opportunity to defend themselves against the charges. There was really nothing unusual in this situation, assuming that it had been determined that a rules violation had occurred: Many times before, this conference had acted similarly and so had most or all other such conferences.

This time, however, the students and the university in question did not quietly acquiesce in the decision of the "conference fathers." They hired an attorney and took the matter to a federal court, not on the question of whether or not the parties were guilty as charged, but on the basis of the denial of *due process.* Their rights, they said, had been violated, and the judge agreed. He reinstated the players pending a second hearing in which due process was to be observed. The second hearing, presumably conducted in accordance with the court's instructions, arrived at substantially the same conclusion as the first, but those affected certainly then knew much better why the decision was made.

One present-day development of considerable significance must be noted: not only are people increasingly concerned with the decisions that affect them and their groups, but they are also often much interested in how the decisions are arrived at. After all, a fair and adequate procedure for arriving at a decision is one's best guarantee—or at least among the best—of its fairness and propriety.[6]

The Nature of Due Process

This term may be relatively new to many supervisors and hence some explanation is in order. Overall, the term refers to being sensitive to and respectful of the rights of the accused throughout the stages of investigation and decision making. This is not the place for a detailed or exhaustive explanation, but some of the most critical requirements deserve our attention.[7]

Just Cause For one thing, it implies *just cause* for the action taken. (Sometimes we speak of *good* or *sufficient* or *proper* cause, all these being equivalent terms.) Persons inexperienced in this field easily get the impression that the term really has no specific meaning, but is only what the judge or jury or arbitrator says it is. On the contrary, there is now substantial agreement concerning it among experienced persons. It means cause sufficient for and appropriate to the action taken, cause that is legally (and often morally) adequate to sustain the decision. The skeptic in this field should spend a few hours perusing opinions and awards of courts and/or arbitrators called upon to make decisions in the field. He will come away convinced that a real consensus has emerged as to the meaning of just cause in disciplinary situations in the area of work.

Table 14-2 below contains excerpts from four labor agreements:

Table 14-2　Disciplinary Clauses in Labor Agreements

"The Management of the Branch and the direction of the working forces, including but not limited to the right to hire, promote, suspend, or discharge for cause ... is vested exclusively in the Company, subject to ... such rights as are expressly provided in this agreement" (a packing plant).

"The Management of the plant and the direction of the workers, including but not limited to the right to ... suspend, discharge, or otherwise discipline employees for just cause ... is vested exclusively in the Company" (a construction company).

"The right to hire, reassign, demote, lay off and discharge employees for just and lawful cause ... shall rest solely ... in the Company" (a telephone company).

"The right of the Employer to discharge, suspend, or otherwise discipline in a fair and impartial manner for just and sufficient cause is hereby acknowledged" (a chemical plant).

Progressive Discipline   It was remarked earlier that some disciplinary infractions are so obviously wrong (and even illegal) that the employee may be presumed to know about them and their total impropriety, and hence they require no warning. Others, however, are far from as clear-cut, definite, or serious in themselves. It is especially to the latter situations that the concept of *progressive discipline* applies.

The essentials of this concept include the oral reprimand followed by the written one, followed by disciplinary layoff—all this before discharge is imposed. Put a bit more generally, progressive discipline means that before an employee is severely disciplined for a less-than-major offense he or she is entitled to be warned, thoroughly, convincingly, and usually more than once. (Thus the reprimands and also the layoff are forms of warning.) And it makes a lot of sense to suggest that the spirit of progressive discipline suggests *clear instructions as to requirements* as well as *counseling* even before the oral reprimand.

The point we are making, in other words, is that in today's society at least, people are morally if not always legally entitled to be dealt with respectfully, with dignity and equality—and thus entitled to be clearly informed of possible serious consequences before these become necessary. Thus poor production or unsatisfactory attendance may in some cases lead to discharge, but hopefully they will not, unless circumstances are exceptional, until after *due warning*.

The Presumption of Innocence   Historically the world of the law and that of work situation have been far apart on the matter of the innocence of one suspected of an offense. For centuries, our English common-law background has led us, so far as a criminal charge is concerned, to presume the person's innocence until proved guilty. In the world of work, on the other hand, the supervisor once could fire whom he chose whenever he wished, without any necessity for justifying his action. All this has changed in this century, however, at least for workers under labor agreements. When charged with an offense they are typically presumed innocent until and unless guilt is established. There is evidence to suggest that many nonunion workers are becoming increasingly aware of these circumstances and, unless afforded this presumption voluntarily, may take steps to secure it.

The Right to Be Heard   Another right that comes to no small degree from the same general background is that of accused people to make known their side of the story, to face their accusers, to know the evidence against them, and to confront their accusers. There is a lesson here that managers overlook at their peril: Employees are more and more demanding this right to be heard, and it is denied to them, when it is, only at increasing risk.

Another aspect of this subject is the right to be *represented*. In some cases this may involve the presence of an attorney for the accused, although admittedly this is rare at least in the early stages of a grievance procedure. But where there is a union and the employee is a member, *not necessarily of the union but of the bargaining unit* it represents, another situation arises. In this case it becomes clear that the employees are increasingly insisting on their right to have union representation, even in early phases of investigations, a right which a Supreme Court decision has recently strengthened. In general, management is well advised to be generous rather than reluctant in accepting such representation. Certainly its outright denial is fraught with serious risks.

Evenhanded Justice   One misconception of the uninitiated but well-meaning manager is likely to be that in disciplinary matters he or she is to "treat them all alike," that is, that all who commit the same offense are to be dealt with in the same way. While there is truth in the basic idea behind this belief, taken literally it is extremely misleading. To take an example: suppose that an employee has been tardy an excessive number of times and that he or she has been counseled with and subsequently warned, first orally and then in writing. A further unexcused tardiness certainly should lead to very different consequences from those of another employee similarly tardy but with years of unbroken attendance on the record.

Thus the principle is not "treat them all alike," simply because they are not all like. Rather the principle is—and it is a most significant one—"treat alike *all who are,* for all practical purposes, *alike.*" But one may and typically should treat differently those who are different.

It is in this connection that *past practice* comes to play a significant role. An instance in point is a company that had the right, clearly spelled out in the labor agreement, to discharge any employee reporting to work under the influence of alcohol. A certain employee, who incidentally was a strong union supporter and quite vociferous about his views concerning management, allegedly came to work "under the influence" and was promptly discharged. However out of some seven or eight similar instances the company was unable to produce a single case in which the offender had been discharged, the worst penalty having been a three-day layoff. Furthermore, there was no progressive pattern in the way in which the eight had been treated, one of the recent ones having been secreted in the mine by his foreman and even paid in full for the day! Under the circumstances the discharge of the affected employee would probably not be permitted to stand. The company might regain its negotiated right to discharge for this offense but only as a minimum after giving *due notice* to all who might be affected by the new policy.

Appeal   This brings us to what is probably the most difficult part of due process, namely, affording an appeal to a disciplinary decision. There are those, of course, who do not believe that such an appeal needs to be provided, but two considerations make that position difficult to sustain. The first is the feeling we all have that it is simply not right for a single individual to have, as it were, the unchallenged and unchallengeable power to "make or break" another person, and that regardless of how arbitrary, prejudicial, capricious, or unfair the decisions may be. The other is the increasing pressure from those affected. No longer are they, or at least many of them, the docile, compliant, resigned "lower class" of another day. Rather they demand their rights and often have ways of securing them. It is also evident that this willingness to challenge is in no sense restricted to the actions of managers. It also applies to physicians, professors, public school teachers, and even merchants and salespeople. Appeals we often simply must provide. The real question is how this should be done, in our case in the world of work.

The Arbitrator   If employees are under a labor contract, the chances are that they are covered by so-called voluntary arbitration. The arbitrator, who is nearly always selected by both the union and the employer, issues what is usually a *binding* award, and thus disposes of the case at issue. Arbitrators are, of course, only human and at times dispense only "rough justice." But arbitration gives the grievant "his day in court"; it is relatively speedy and inexpensive; and it has avoided countless wildcat strikes and other serious disturbances of the work. It does provide a genuine appeal, and is likely to be more extensively used in the future.

While labor arbitration is concentrated in firms and government agencies having unions, it need not be so. Employees and managers in nonunionized firms can also provide for arbitration of disputes involving personnel decisions, though relatively few have done so. It is not clear whether the number employing such provisions will increase in the future.

The Ombudsman   An appeals procedure with which managers in Sweden and some other countries have had considerable experience is the *ombudsman.* So far, however, it has been used but rarely in the United States, although the term (but not always the substance of the institution) appears with increasing frequency in U.S. organizations.

Ombudsmen are people who are highly placed in the organization but independent of it in that they are free to draw their own conclusions. They are selected because of their reputation, integrity, and objectivity. They have no authority over anyone in the organization and no power to enforce any sort of finding. On the other hand, they have virtually unlimited authority (a) to investigate the situation and (b) to publicize their findings. The assumption is—and it is not without considerable merit—that such revelations will lead to justice in decisions.

Just what the future of the ombudsman is in the United States is not clear. Finding appropriate persons would not be easy, but that could be accomplished. Providing for their true independence so that all would recognize it would be difficult, and perhaps impossible in many situations. And getting those involved to accept and properly act on the resulting findings might also be difficult. The ombudsman may or may not become a significant part of U.S. appeals procedure.

The Hearing Officer   A device that a number of firms have provided for their employees is what we are calling the *hearing officer.* Many firms, of course, allow a person who feels he or she has been wronged to confer with the boss's boss or even the boss's boss's boss, but this informal arrangement is not what we have in mind here. Rather we are discussing a formal arrangement whereby an employee may request a review of a personnel decision by a relatively high-level manager, usually from another location, or a different part of the company, and thus cause a hearing to be held in his or her case. This hearing officer does as the title implies: He or she conducts a hearing as to the facts in the case, investigates the situation thoroughly, arrives at what he or she finds to be the proper conclusions, and then makes recommendations to local management, though having no authority to enforce the decision. Obviously, however, it may be quite influential in the eventual disposition of the case.

Again, we are dealing with a practice that is in no sense widespread in the United States though more frequent than is generally realized. It has not been outstandingly successful, apparently for at least three reasons: In the first place, it is hard to be assured of the actual objectivity of the hearing officer. After all, he is a representative of the employer and not of the employee. And even if he is as fully objective as one can be, it may be difficult to convince subordinates of the situation.

The second problem relates to the acceptance by other managers of a manager who makes a recommendation contrary to their decisions. This situation may become critical, of course, if the hearing officer discovers a situation where a fellow manager is obviously and seriously in error. Furthermore, since the involved managers presumably will have to continue to work together, such findings may render it difficult or virtually impossible.

Finally, there are the forces operating on the hearing officer himself or herself. After all, it is usually far easier to go along with the findings of a fellow division head, for example, and it certainly requires courage to brand that person wrong when that is the decision demanded by the facts. There is also the additional question of whether executive management is mature enough to reward or at least not penalize the manager who has the courage to make an adverse finding relative to a prior management decision.

Informal Arrangements   Perhaps in the above we have not given enough attention to the usual, informal appeals procedures mentioned above, those in which one goes to higher levels of management in an effort to secure what one sees as justice. Such arrangements can and do work but only if (a) managers know that they are not perfect and acknowledge that they in fact make mistakes, sometimes serious ones; (b) managers want their mistakes corrected and restitution, if any is needed, made as quickly as feasible; and

(c) there are highly placed managers who are willing to call a decision an erroneous one when they find it to be. Effective as some of these arrangements are, it seems unlikely that they will continue indefinitely to be the only appeals available to a majority of American employees.

Thus we do not have a final answer or even a final recommendation as to the proper appeals mechanisms for the world of work. We are convinced that such appeals at times must be made available and that supervisors must often accept them and their consequences even though they see clearly the advantages of being able to make decisions that are final. Apparently, however, the days of the supervisor as autocrat are definitely numbered.

The Scope of Due Process

From our discussion thus far one could easily conclude that due process applies only to unpleasant situations, those in which the supervisor has taken action that will likely not be pleasing to the employee, and especially those involving some sort of discipline. Due process is nearly always significant in discharge or layoff or reprimand, but does it have application elsewhere?

The answer is clearly in the affirmative. Due process is just as significant and as applicable to promotion and/or upgrading as it is in conditions that call for censure. Except under unusual circumstances (for instance, a clear emergency) one should not discipline without unmistakably affording the to-be-disciplined employee the essentials mentioned above, but the same considerations apply to circumstances involving reward or other favorable action.

As a matter of fact we probably are not in actuality dealing with two different situations, favorable and unfavorable, for promotion typically means selecting from several or even many the one person most suitable; thus all the others are temporarily or permanently bypassed, and for them failure to be selected for an opening can be as disappointing as censure. Due process thus applies when a manager is picking from a group one person (or a small number) for favorable treatment.

Problems in Affording Due Process

Like the purported course of true love, affording due process to all who deserve it does not always run smoothly, certain situations making it more difficult. They are worth identifying.[8]

The Climate of the Organization   Undoubtedly one factor influencing the extent of due process in a particular work situation is the history of the organization and the attitudes, values, policies, procedures, and practices that have developed over the years. Some work climates are conducive to fair treatment, with conscientious attention to the feelings and the rights of all concerned, whereas others tend to be more efficiency-minded, "no-nonsense" operations. A wise supervisor who finds himself in the former sort usually has little difficulty. He is expected to treat his subordinates with consideration and dignity and usually finds it easy to do so.

What to do if one is a part of the second sort of organization has no easy answer. The moral obligation for fair treatment is of course present, no matter how much unattended or neglected, but supervisors usually have no feasible choice except to work within the framework of the management hierarchy and do as their superiors have determined. But they can do two things along the way: First, they can do whatever *they* can to afford *their* people due process; second, under some conditions, they can make their position known at the same time that they acknowledge the obligation to "go along."

Nevertheless one thing must not be overlooked in this connection: a person or group can become overly concerned with any good thing, including due process. After all, all work organizations exist primarily to get the job done, and not to serve as a forum or a debating society for those who suffer from felt wrongs. The organization, in other words, can spend so much time in interviews and hearings and meetings that it fails to "get the goods out the door." No one can tell an individual supervisor where lies the line between an underconcern and an overconcern for due process, but there is one, and he or she has to find it.[9]

The Ambiguous Situation   Closely related to the above is a set of circumstances in which there is genuine and plausible disagreement as to the proper decision, in other words, as to whether and to what extent due process has been or should be provided. Again no easy formula is available for such circumstances, and managers must fall back on their sense of fairness and their judgment as developed through study and experience. Certainly they need a familiarity with the relevant factors: the labor contract if one is in effect; arbitrators' awards, NLRB findings, court decisions, and the like; the firm's past practice in dealing with similar situations; practice within the industry; and other like matters. And then one does the best one can under the circumstances. More will be said on this point later, particularly in Chapter 18.

There is another important point as relates to due process: The intention to provide it is not enough; it is sufficient only when in fact it *is* provided. Thus doing their best, managers may still find their decisions questioned, either informally by griping and fault-finding or formally through the grievance procedure or a civil rights charge. Under these conditions they usually need to do one of two things, after thoroughly reviewing the decisions: either to change their decisions if they find them in error or vigorously defend them in the proper forum. All the while they must realize, however, that they are neither God nor an absolute monarch. If a challenge properly pursued through all proper channels finds that in fact they did not afford due process, they must attempt to profit from the experience and exert due diligence to see that future actions are above reproach.

Thus due process puts into a manager's job a dimension not known by the foreman of, say, the 1890s. It calls for a dedication to doing what is right, for careful evaluation, and for a degree of emotional maturity that the old-time boss did not have to provide.

The Basis for the Decision   A final point on our subject is that in many instances making known the basis for the decision is an integral part of due process. After all, assuming that my decision is entirely just and proper, if I refuse to disclose or discuss why I arrived at it, I will likely be accused of lack of fairness and/or wisdom and the decision will be challenged. Thus in the typical case I have little choice if I want to be judged as fair: I will have to reveal the basis for my action.

Again one has to be realistic: There are circumstances under which full, frank, and complete disclosure is not feasible. To engage in it might unduly invade the privacy of another; or trade secrets, or even state secrets, might be involved; or the disclosure might needlessly damage persons or institutions—to mention some examples. One must recognize, therefore, that he or she cannot always reveal why the decision was made. Usually, however, one can and should do so.

THE DISCIPLINARY INTERVIEW

Even though the subject of interviewing has been dealt with rather extensively in the two preceding chapters, a word or two about its use in the disciplinary situation would not be out of order.[10]

Planning the Interview

The points earlier made about planning the performance-review and counseling interviews apply here as well. One should not go into such a situation without as careful consideration as feasible of the *objectives,* the *strategy,* and the *tactics* of the interview.

Selecting the Approach

In general in an interview of this sort one may be indirect or diplomatic, or may decide to go "straight-from-the-shoulder." The diplomatic approach may lead the interviewee to suspect weakness or indecision on the part of the supervisor, and what would be worse, might lead to a suspicion of manipulation. But it does give the employee a chance to save face to a degree and the supervisor an opportunity to reassure and encourage.

The straight-from-the-shoulder approach seldom leaves any doubt about the seriousness of the situation and even management intentions, but it may do unnecessary damage to the employee's self-esteem. Furthermore counseling and reassurance, if needed, are rendered more difficult.

Clearly some circumstances call for one of the above and other circumstances for the other (and still others, for a combination). Again the supervisor's best judgment must be called into action.

Hearing the Employee Out

Ordinarily an employee has the right, as we have earlier said, to "say his say." Occasionally this may not be necessary. If the supervisor knows what the facts are and furthermore knows that the employee knows that the supervisor knows, hearing him or her out may be minimized or omitted. But hearing out should clearly be given the benefit of the doubt.

Other points about the disciplinary interview could be added, but the above will have to suffice. An interesting question is, to what extent and when, if ever, in a disciplinary interview, should one talk *with* (as opposed to *to*) the to-be-disciplined employee?

THE SUPERVISOR AND DISCIPLINE

There is probably no area in manager-subordinate relationships where the challenge to the supervisor is greater than in the field of discipline. On the one hand, discipline must be insisted upon and must be sustained before continued and cooperative efforts are possible; this becomes all the more necessary as work becomes more complicated and activities more interdependent. On the other hand, the growing sense of individual rights and freedom characteristic of today's worker often runs directly counter to the tendency of management toward unilateral action in this area. The challenge to management, including supervisors, is thus clear and direct: to maintain discipline while encouraging self-discipline, and to take the necessary actions in such fashion as, in the long run, not to threaten but to enhance the worker's sense of worth and real contribution.

QUESTIONS

1 Why is self-discipline seldom the only kind required in a work organization? What are its strengths and weaknesses?
2 What are some realistic methods of increasing the amount of self-discipline in workers?
3 What are (a) the acceptable and (b) the unacceptable reasons for imposing a disciplinary penalty on another person?
4 What are the most common disciplinary penalties? Which are used relatively frequently and which sparingly, and why?
5 Explain the general meaning of *due process* as it relates to discipline.

6 What are the nature and importance of (a) just cause, (b) progressive discipline, (c) evenhanded justice, (d) appeal, and (e) making known the basis for a disciplinary decision?

7 If a worker appeals a disciplinary decision, on whom (the worker or the employer) should the burden of proof lie? Just what does this mean, and what is its significance in employer-employee relations?

8 In the light of the discussion of the interview in Chapters 12 and 13, what are the most significant observations concerning the conduct of the disciplinary interview?

NOTES

1 General treatments of employee discipline are found in many texts in personnel management; for example, Wendell French, *The Personnel Management Process: Human Resources Administration,* 3d ed. (Boston: Houghton Mifflin 1974), Chap. 8; and Paul Pigors and Charles A. Myers, *Personnel Administration: A Point of View and a Method,* 7th ed. (New York: McGraw-Hill, 1974), Chap. 18.

2 Michael J. Jucius, *Personnel Management,* 8th ed. (Homewood, Ill.: Irwin, 1975).

3 Clifford T. Morgan and Richard A. King, *Introduction to Psychology,* 5th ed. (New York: McGraw Hill, 1975).

4 Neil W. Chamberlain and James N. Kuhn, *Collective Bargaining* (New York: McGraw-Hill, 1963), pp. 97-99, 362-367.

5 John M. Pfiffner and Marshall Fees, *The Supervision of Personnel,* 3d ed. (Englewood Cliffs, N.J.: Prentice-Hall, 1964), pp. 194-195.

6 The periodical literature in this field tends to avoid the presumably unpleasant subject of discipline, but that is not always true. See, for example, Hoyt N. Wheeler, "Punishment Theory and Industrial Discipline," *Industrial Relations,* vol. 15, no. 2, pp. 235-243, May 1976; Wallace Wohl Ring, "Effective Discipline in Employee Relations," *Personnel Journal,* vol. 54, no. 9, pp. 489-493, September 1975; and Benson Rosen and Thomas H. Jerdee, "Factors Influencing Disciplinary Judgments," *Journal of Applied Psychology,* vol. 59, no. 3, pp. 327-332, June 1974.

7 Background for this discussion can be found in Lloyd G. Reynolds, *Labor Economics and Labor Relations,* 6th ed. (Englewood Cliffs, N.J.: Prentice-Hall, 1974), Chap. 20; and in *Labor Law Course,* 23d ed. (Chicago: Commerce Clearing House, 1976), pp. 2581ff.

8 Maurice S. Trotta and Harry R. Gudenberg, "Resolving Personnel Problems in Non-union Plants," *Personnel,* vol. 53, no. 3, pp. 55-63, May-June 1976. This article calls attention to the greater training and sophistication one necessarily acquires in a unionized situation but typically misses when no union is present.

9 For an insightful article on the basis for disciplinary decisions see Dennis M. Sullivan, "Employee Discipline: Beware of the 'Company Position,' " *Personnel Journal,* vol. 53, no. 9, pp. 692-695, September 1974.

10 Deboral Meyers and Lee M. Abrahaurson, "Firing with Finesse: A Rationale for Outplacement," *Personnel Journal,* vol. 54, no. 8, pp. 432-434, August 1975.

CASES

Again we are in a situation where there is a multitude of cases relevant to the topic of the chapter. Indeed many cases assigned to other chapters would fit this one better or just as well.

The three disciplinary cases selected for this chapter include one, that of Ben Kelley, in which the employee made a serious error but not one serious enough, in the judgment of the Company, to justify discharge. It raises at least one important question: If the Company is not justified in punishing all who make errors, under what circumstances should such a penalty be imposed?

The Mathis case involves a driver who was discharged because the Company believed that it has clear evidence of theft. It is generally agreed that Management has the right to discharge for such acts (though there are times when it is better to select some lesser penalty), but one always faces the necessity to prove that stealing actually occurred.

The Sellers case raises the issue of whether an employee is ever justified in leaving the job without his supervisor's permission and/or in going home early without informing anyone in the Company. If there are such occasions when this may be done properly, was this one of them?

If it should be determined that discharge is too severe in both the Mathis and Sellers incidents, should a lesser disciplinary penalty be imposed?

CASE 14-1

Ben Kelley is a mechanic for the Company, which repairs and rebuilds airplane engines. He has worked for it for ten years and is considered an average mechanic.

A few days ago Ben made a serious error in his work. He was working on one of the rods in a customer's motor, and in installing the rod-bearing put about 1½ times as much torque on one of the bolts as the safety manual allowed. The error was caught by the inspection department and came to the attention of Ralph Harrison, Kelley's foreman.

Harrison was shocked by the error and its possible consequences. If the motor had been started on the test block with the extra tension on the bearing, the outcome could have been quite costly. The bearing might well have been ruined and most likely also the rod. Repairs to both of these would cost several hundred dollars and, worse still, would have delayed delivery of the customer's motor, which was going through the shop on a "red ticket," as a top-priority job. And if by any chance Inspection had missed the error and the motor had been put into service, an engine failure in the airplane would have been very likely. Incidentally, Inspection could easily have missed it, for detecting too much torque is more difficult than detecting too little.

The more Harrison thought about the situation, the more he was convinced that Kelley's error was due to carelessness of an inexcusable sort. This was the kind of error, he reasoned, that not even a mechanic's helper who paid any attention to his job would ever make, and it was inexcusable for a first-class mechanic.

Harrison made up his mind that failure to act would increase an indifferent attitude which he felt to be growing in his department, whereas strong action in this case would serve as a warning to both Kelley and the other employees. Consequently he recommended to his boss, Lawrence Mitchell, that Kelley be laid off for two weeks without pay.

Mitchell had misgivings about the severity of the penalty, but he nevertheless agreed to it. The labor relations department has just notified Mitchell of its reluctant approval, and Mitchell is about to pass this information on to Harrison.

How does Mitchell handle this case with Harrison? How do they (or does Harrison) handle it with Kelley? Is the Union likely to file a grievance in this case? If the grievance should go to arbitration, what would be the most likely ruling?

CASE 14-2

The Company is a manufacturer of storage batteries, many of which it delivers by trucks to stores within a 200-mile radius. Bob Mathis is a truck driver assigned to a regular route, a two-day trip going to four cities, in all of which he leaves new batteries and picks up trade-ins. In each instance he is required to leave an invoice signed by both the customer and himself, a copy of which he retains, for both the new and used batteries. He has driven for the Company for seven years, most of the time on this route.

From time to time the Company has found instances of theft of its batteries, and on occasion this theft has involved truck drivers. The plant manager recently became suspicious of Mathis, and he, the personnel director, and Mathis' foreman arranged to "salt" one of Mathis' loads.

The practice of "salting" a driver's load is common in the Company, at least to the extent that all drivers are told that on any occasion their loads might be salted. The process is simply putting on the load extra merchandise (in this case, nine batteries, each worth about $40), over and above those called for in the manifest given the driver as he begins his run. (The usual load is some 800 batteries.) Naturally salting depends on secrecy for its effectiveness, for if a driver knows that Management knows there are extra batteries on his load he presumably would not try to sell them on the side and pocket the difference.

Thus only the three men mentioned above knew of the salting of the Mathis load. So great was their concern for secrecy that in fact they did not take time to verify the exact number of batteries, including the number of each type, supposed to be on the truck.

Mathis was discharged because upon his return from this run he brought back only one extra battery, and it of a different type from any of the nine salted ones.

During the time Mathis had been a driver for the Company he had received three formal, written reprimands, one for too many accidents, one for reporting late to work, and one for refusing to drive on a trip he was ordered to run with a black assistant driver. The last of these occurred some eighteen months before his discharge.

What aroused the Company's suspicions about Mathis was his growing tendency to report "shortages" upon his return from his runs. (A "shortage" indicates that fewer batteries were loaded on the truck than were called for in the invoices.) While he occasionally reported "overages" also, the former outnumbered the latter by a ratio of 12 to 4 for the last several weeks.

Also relevant to the discharge was Mathis' report—on the salted trip—that he had picked up seventy-two used batteries from a customer, whereas it later developed that he had left a receipt for eighty-two. There is always a ready market for used batteries (at about $5 each). While the Company has never positively identified any of its used batteries in the hands of a "fence," it has found some of its new batteries in local pawnshops, though it has not been able to trace any directly to any Company employee.

The Company contends that any errors made in counting the batteries put on a truck are nearly always very small and that it is unreasonable to assume that Mathis' truck was underloaded by eight batteries. On the other hand, the reasonable conclusion is that Mathis pawned eight new batteries and also disposed of ten used ones somewhere on the trip. Needless to say, such conduct is intolerable and justifies immediate discharge.

The Company was careful, it maintains, in its preparations for apprehending Mathis, and also systematic in its efforts. For one thing, it had grounds for suspecting him, evidence on the point growing as it observed his conduct. For another, it used three responsible members of Management in the salting, all of whom verified the addition of the nine batteries. Actually, counting 800 batteries by three people was entirely infeasible, since unloading would have been required, and thus the Company's intentions would have become known. Likewise any extra counting as the batteries were loaded would have been obvious. Finally, if thirty or forty extra batteries had been salted, Mathis no doubt would have realized what was happening. Thus the Company's action was reasonable and proper under the circumstances, and hence the discharge should be upheld.

The Union contends that a discharge of this sort must not occur unless the Company can prove guilt "beyond the shadow of a doubt," and of course it did not succeed in doing so in this case. Company drivers know that fully half the loads leaving the Company docks have "overages" or "shortages," and these are by no means restricted to nine or fewer batteries. One driver recently, for example, had a shortage of sixty-two batteries; another had an overage of more than fifty. It is unthinkable that a seven-year employee would be fired because of a shortage of eight batteries, a discrepancy that could easily have occurred in loading his truck, and one that happened to be balanced by a like number of salted batteries. As a matter of fact, the Union asserts, Mathis stole nothing and converted nothing to his own use, and yet is about to be terminated under circumstances that may endanger his employability for the rest of his life.

The charge about the extra ten used batteries is a flimsy one, the Union says. It is true that Mathis left a receipt for eighty-two batteries and brought back only seventy-two, but everyone makes errors. Eighty-two was not the correct figure, as the customer later agreed. And of course a driver attempting to steal used batteries will not leave a signed receipt for eighty-two, sell ten and deliver seventy-two, for the customer obviously will eventually present the receipt to the Company. Successful thefts of this sort require incorrect receipts to the customer!

What is the proper disposition of the grievance that protests this discharge and asks for full back pay, seniority, and the like?

CASE 14-3

At the time of his discharge in March 1976, Duncan Sellers, an assembler, had been employed by the Company some sixteen months. During that time he had been absent twenty-six days and on numerous occasions had been tardy or had left work early. He had sustained two or three job-connected injuries, though none was serious enough to cause absences of more than a day or two. On the occasion of one of these injuries, he drove to the emergency room of a nearby hospital and then went directly home without returning to the plant or notifying his foreman. He received no warning, oral or written, concerning this matter.

As a result of his absences Sellers received a written warning in July 1975. In it his absences were characterized as "excessive" and his attendance record as "not improving." Two months later he was issued what was called a "final warning."

Sometime during the shift on the day he was discharged he stepped on a nail of 1⅛″ in length, and received first aid from the Company nurse, after which he returned to work. About an hour later he asked her for permission to go to the hospital emergency room for treatment, a request to which she finally agreed. He took a Company pickup for the trip, but before going called his wife to meet him at the hospital. After treatment he drove the Company car back to the plant, left it, and, without notifying anyone in the Company, got in the car driven by his wife and went home. This occurred about twenty minutes before the end of the shift.

The diagnosis of Sellers' injury, signed by a physician, reads as follows: "Clean, very small puncture wound over distal plantar [of left] foot. Foot elevation for 2 days, hot soaks. . . . Off work tonight, tomorrow if necessary." X-rays results were reported as negative, and the tetanus injection as "current."

The Company contends that discharge is the just and proper penalty. Sellers' failure to notify his foreman he was leaving the plant for the hospital was serious, especially in view of his attendance record, and subsequent failure to notify the foreman that he was leaving the job was inexcusable. Sellers' whole record "showed that he was . . . irresponsible, arrogant, and belligerent, and he *deserved* to be fired."

At one time during the investigation of the grievance protesting the discharge, the personnel manager heard a person who he is sure was Sellers refer to him under his breath as "an SOB." This removes any lingering doubt, if there is any, about the propriety of the discharge. Furthermore the state unemployment commission, after investigation, disqualified Sellers from benefits because of what it found to be a proper discharge. Additionally, at one point in the handling of the grievance, a Union representative attempted to get the grievant to resign in return for a favorable letter of reference. Thus it is evident that even the Union believes the penalty to be a just one.

The Union contends that after Sellers had worked for a while (after he stepped on the nail) the wound became quite painful, and besides he became quite concerned about the status of his tetanus innoculation. By that time he already knew he was in no position to continue work and hence the call to his wife.

There is not and never has been any posted requirement that an injured employee must notify his foreman before going to the hospital—or subsequently if he follows orders from the physician. As noted, Sellers had left the job once before under much the same circumstances and then had gone directly home, and no one in Management had expressed any disapproval.

Inasmuch as the Company did not discharge Sellers for absenteeism, the Union asserts that his prior record in this connection is irrelevant. And the attempt to show him guilty of profanity in relation to a Company official is uncorroborated; in fact the incident did not occur at all.

Certainly, according to the Union, the Company lacks just cause for Sellers' discharge. He should thus be restored to his job, his seniority connected, and he should be made whole for lost wages and benefits.

What is the proper disposition of this case? How much attention can properly be given to Sellers' past record?

Chapter 15

The Supervisor and the Union

Organized labor on a large scale is a fairly recent force in the work situation in the United States. While there were labor unions in this country even before 1776, they were very limited in membership and influence. Interest in labor organization really arose in this country after the Civil War, but even by 1900 only a small percentage of American workers belonged to unions, and these were largely in the skilled trades.[1]

Union membership has approximately doubled in the United States during three different periods of this century: World War I, 1935–1941, and World War II. (On the other hand, unions lost about half their members during the Depression.) Since World War II, union membership has grown about in proportion to the growth of the American labor force. Thus in 1946 unions represented approximately one worker in each four gainfully employed persons, a proportion that even to the present has not changed by more than 2 to 3 percent. The decline in the percentage of the hourly or blue-collar work force caused some decrease in membership especially in the fifties but by the sixties this trend was reversed, one factor being an Executive order signed by President Kennedy in 1962, one that significantly broadened the collective-bargaining rights of federal employees. This order was followed by large gains by unions among government workers, federal, state, county, and municipal.[2]

Needless to say, the coming of an influential labor movement has posed many problems for management. Even managers of nonunionized firms (and government agencies) cannot afford to be indifferent to unions and the "threat" (as they usually interpret it) they pose, and, of course, managers in unionized work situations have to consider the union and its position as they attempt to arrive at the best personnel policies, and furthermore must bargain with it. First-line supervisors find their actions subject to constant scrutiny and not infrequently have their decisions and even their orders challenged by their subordinates. Whether all this is bad or good, it is a far cry from conditions of a century ago.

COMMON MISCONCEPTIONS ABOUT UNIONS

In view of the strong feelings, pro and con, that people have about unions, it is not at all strange that there should be a number of misconceptions about their nature and development, misconceptions not nearly as widespread as they were some years ago but nevertheless definitely present and influential today.

That They Are Exclusively Economic in Aim

One view often encountered is that unions are simply devices by means of which workers attempt to get *more* for themselves. Furthermore, this *more* is held to be reducible to economic terms exclusively. Thus unions are thought to be devices for securing higher wages or salaries, more extensive benefits, shorter hours, and easier work. Many managers believe that behind every organizing drive and every labor-management dispute there is always a dollar sign.

It would be naïve to deny that economic considerations are important in union activities. Certainly all, or at least virtually all, of us want more money and hope that we will get more as time goes along. Much of union strategy is based on increasing wages, adding to retirement pay or vacations or holidays, or decreasing hours of work. But this is not the whole story.

For one thing, a union is a social organization. Union members typically like to be together and to engage in common activities. Especially for small groups of employees, the union may take on some aspects of a club, for example, sponsoring social events of many sorts. Furthermore, an esprit de corps or "we-feeling" often develops, and the people involved stick together, not only to increase their economic advantage and to resist outside pressure but for other endeavors as well. In an older day, when there was less organized and commercialized recreation as well as fewer means of securing what we now call "fringe benefits," these activities were considerably more important than they are in our urbanized society, but the common feeling on which these were based has by no means disappeared.

For another, union members, like virtually all other people, want to be treated with dignity and respect, and they spend at least part of their time and energy to see that this occurs. One form this endeavor takes is protection of union rights and the rights of individual members. These rights usually have their economic aspects, and these may loom large in any action undertaken, but this is not always so. In an arbitration hearing one often realizes that the particular point at issue involves the rights of the union or its members to take or refrain from taking certain actions where money, benefits, and job security are not in serious dispute, if in dispute at all. Often the union wants very much to win in order to vindicate its position and assert its rights.

Likewise, an employee may file a grievance not because of economic loss or damage, but to assert his independence, to "get even" with some member of management, or to preserve his sense of self-respect. Again, there may be no financial considerations involved.

In dealing with the union, therefore, the supervisor must realize that while labor organizations have significant economic goals and doubtless would not exist without them, they are also social organizations and furthermore at times become greatly concerned with the rights and dignity of the organization and its members.[3]

That They Appeal Primarily to the Underpaid

It is tempting to believe that labor unions chiefly involve the lowest-paid workers in the country and get their largest and most enthusiastic support from those most in need of increased income, but such is far from the fact. On the contrary, the typical union member is well paid, not poorly paid, as American workers go.

One reason for this situation is that it costs money to organize and support a labor union, and in general the poorer the worker's pay, the less likely he is to take on such obligations. Furthermore, the lowest-paid workers are more likely to work in small groups, and these are more difficult and also more expensive to organize and service. There are several other valid reasons here, including the background of such employees, but the fact remains that, in practice, labor unions are not bodies representing workers at or near subsistence levels of pay.

That They Are Essentially Socialistic

One charge made against American unions is that they are communistic; another is that they are socialistic. Admitting that there have been exceptions in the past, we can dispose of the first charge easily. The record will show that American unions not only are not communistic but that they are decidedly anticommunistic. Actions of the AFL-CIO (and of each organization separately before the 1955 merger) in removing Communist-dominated unions represent real evidence on this point.

On the other hand, when the charge is made that an organization is socialistic, some problems arise. One difficulty is the meaning of the term *socialistic*. Some use it to refer to being favorable to broadening the powers of government, and especially the federal government, in fields of social legislation. It is certainly true that most unions have supported this sort of activity more, for example, than has the National Association of Manufacturers or the United States Chamber of Commerce. At the same time, however, unions have often taken the lead in sponsoring the rights of the individual and also the right of the group to be free of government coercion.

Sometimes *socialistic* is taken to mean looking to the government for protection and even subsistence from the cradle to the grave. In this sense unions are not socialistic, nor are very many Americans. The American spirit and tradition of independence make most of us especially critical of "something for nothing."

If by *socialistic* is meant favoring government ownership and operation of the basic means of production and distribution, American labor unions are definitely not socialistic. On the contrary, they are committed to the market system, including the right of owners to own and profit from their business, and their right to organize workers and bargain collectively for them.

That They Are Basically Antimanagement

A similar charge against unions is that they are basically opposed to management and its right to manage. This is true of many unions in some parts of the world, but it is not true of those in the United States. Unions certainly oppose management on certain issues and on occasion challenge certain prerogatives of management, but all this is very different from opposing management as an institution or attacking management's right to make fundamental decisions for the operation of the business and to do so at a profit. True, the practices, including the demands, of labor leaders do not always appear to be consistent with this assertion nor indeed are they always consistent with it. But who among us fully lives up to his principles and professions? Union leaders and members are human too.

Of course there is another aspect to this matter. Union leaders do not conspire to abolish or destroy management's right to manage, but they very definitely do want to protect and advance the rights and interests of the worker. As long as management's decisions do not affect the worker, the union official keeps hands off. But thereby hangs the tale: The great majority of decisions of managers do in fact affect the interests of workers and hence frequently arouse union concern. The result is that union leaders often do interfere with management's freedom in decision making, not because they are opposed to management's having and exercising the right to make decisions, but to serve workers. This conflict, of course, often becomes very real and very serious, but it does not indicate a fundamental difference in economic philosophy.

It must not be overlooked, however, that it is easy to exaggerate the amount and degree of conflict in labor-management relations. Conflict is frequently present, but cooperation is frequently present too. Obviously the latter is seldom as newsworthy as the former. In fact, students of the subject have tended to concentrate on the conflict areas and to neglect the cooperative ones. The result is not infrequently a distorted public image of the relationship.

Unions are sometimes decidedly and vigorously opposed to management, but they sometimes work with management. And American unions are definitely not plotting the overthrow of management or the government so that they may take over.

That They Are Opposed to Change

A charge often made against workers, including their unions, is that by nature they are opposed to any and all change. This is obviously false with regard to people in general as well as to unions and union members. The truth is that at least by their formal statements unions do not oppose change, including automation or other more efficient labor-saving devices. (Again, their practices in particular situations, like yours and mine, may not always square with public statements.) They want to cushion workers against the effects of these developments and to protect, as far as they can, the worker's job security. But they do not oppose change as such.

Of course, union members, being human, are disturbed by changes which they do not understand or which they see as a threat. We Americans, including union members, often rush out to embrace change that is seen as really meaningful progress; we resist and try to neutralize change that poses a threat or harm.

That Goodwill and Sincerity Are Enough

One view that we encounter frequently is the notion that effective human relations is just good, sincere common sense. Many people, nearly all of them inexperienced, voice this opinion about the problems in labor-management relations. The view here is that if both management and union leaders were persons of goodwill, sincerity, and patience, they could sit down together and cooperatively solve their mutual problems. For example, many students in college courses in industrial relations feel that they could easily handle these problems if only their elders would step aside and give them free rein. Additionally some who profess to be experts, for example, in human relations and organizational arrangements hold that the proper use of confrontation, sensitivity, consensus, and the like would render the present win-lose strategy of labor relations immediately obsolete, with cooperation taking the place of bargaining.

Actually, relations between unions and management are complex and subtle to a degree not always understood even by practitioners in the field and not dreamed of by the novice. Goodwill and sincerity are assets in human relations, but here, as in other human affairs, they are not enough and, if unaided by wisdom, can easily do more damage than good.

IMPORTANT FACTS ABOUT UNIONS

An Adversary Relationship

In relation to the point just made about sincerity and goodwill, a consideration often overlooked is that present labor relations policies in the United States put unions and management in an *adversary* relationship. That is, the fundamental provision of the National Labor Relations Act of 1935 is the protection furnished by the government to workers who wish to organize for purposes of bargaining with their employer. Bargaining involves trying to get more for oneself and thus granting less to one's adversary in the bargaining.

Incidentally, one may regret the development of this situation, this creation of a sharp division within the employees of a firm, but it is the law of the land, one which is apparently approved of by the majority of Americans. It is easy to find fault with it on theoretical grounds, but the authors raise seriously the questions, Where is there a better and more practical plan? and What would be the essential provisions of a better plan? They do not deny that a better one may eventually be devised. They have serious doubts whether, with all the faults of our system, a better one has actually appeared as yet.[4]

Business Unionism

American labor unions are quite different from unions in many other parts of the world in that they have not taken basic reorganization of the economic, political, and social structure of the country as their fundamental goal. It is probably a sound generalization that both historically and at present and considering at least the free world, organized labor has typically been reform unionism or welfare unionism or a combination of the two.

Reform unionism refers to a fundamental effort to change at least the economic institutions of the country involved and typically takes the form of outright communism or some milder form of socialism. As earlier remarked, American labor, taken as a whole, has never been communistic, and any trend toward socialism (in the traditional or historical sense of the term), though present to a degree around 1900 and before, has now disappeared.

Welfare unionism, as the name implies, represents dedication to the uplifting of the poor, downtrodden masses. It conceives the owners and managers as exploiters and thinks of the union's duty as essentially one of protection. In theory this is close to reform unionism. In practice it is more likely to lead to an attempt to see that government and other powerful social institutions "carry the banner" for the poor and that the laboring classes secure more advantages. The movement is less an attempt to overthrow existing institutions than it is an endeavor to enlist their aid and support for the workingman's cause.

Certain aspects of reform and welfare unionism can be seen in some American unions and in some of the earlier union leaders, but neither has been a very significant influence in this country. Rather, American unions usually take the position that they have a commodity to sell—the labor of their members—and they make every effort to get a good price for the commodity, one as high as the market will bear. This position we refer to as *business unionism.* This point certainly ties in with one previously made, that unions are not basically antimanagement. One can hardly oppose management's right to manage and to make a profit at the same time that one insists on being free to drive the best attainable bargain for those represented.

Table 15-1 indicates three ways in which we often classify labor unions, and Table 15-2 describes some of the kinds of recognition accorded to American unions.

Table 15-1   Kinds of Labor Unions

As to affiliation	Description
Independent	Not part of AFL-CIO
Affiliated	Part of the AFL-CIO

As to organization	
International	The headquarters personnel plus the local unions
Local	The smallest part of the union; or an independent union in a particular plant, office, or locality

As to membership	
Industrial	May include the holders of all the jobs in the bargaining unit, from highly skilled to laborer
Craft	Restricted to a particular sort of skilled job

Variety in Unions

Another frequent error is to think of labor relations as though there were only one kind of union in the United States and as though all union members were essentially alike. This is far from an accurate conception. Some unions are very large, several having a membership of over a million; some are very small, consisting of a dozen or even fewer members. Some are relatively belligerent, occasionally employing force and violence and quick to resort to the strike; some are the opposite in these respects. Some are *affiliated* (with the AFL-CIO) and some are *independent* (not affiliated with the AFL-CIO). (The AFL-CIO represents some two-thirds of union membership in the United States.) Some show some inclination toward welfarism or reform while others are almost "strictly business." Some contain poorer and more poorly educated workers, others involve the trades or crafts, and some include only professional people. The truth is that the more than 20 million members of American labor unions make a motley crew, and the several hundred labor unions furnish many studies in contrast. Overlooking this variety and allowing oneself the luxury of stereotyped, simplified concepts and conclusions about all unions is dangerous to effective strategy for dealing with them.

A Philosophy of Opportunism or Expediency

We have frequently spoken in this chapter and earlier in this book about the tendency of all of us to profess a belief in a certain course of action while actually behaving in an opposite or at least a different fashion. Thus it is easy to say we are primarily concerned for the basic values of our society but to use our money or our influence for purely selfish pursuits. It is also easy to assert that we are dedicated to certain religious beliefs or practices while one who observes what we do (or sometimes fail to do) would not believe we really were committed to these values. Why do all humans show some of this sort of behavior?

Sometimes people who talk one way and act another are making deliberate efforts to mislead. They do not believe what they say and are merely trying to convince others of a falsehood.

On other occasions we do this sort of thing unconsciously. We are unaware of how much our conduct is inconsistent with our professions. Thus we can sincerely quote the Declaration of Independence about the equality of all people and at the same time believe that certain individuals or groups really should not have rights equal to ours. All this frequently happens through a process of *dissociation,* in which we simply do not permit

Table 15-2   Sorts of Union Recognition

	Description
Exclusive bargaining agent	Minimum degree of union recognition under U.S. labor law; union represents *all* in bargaining unit
Preferential shop	In hiring, union members are to be given preference
Union shop	Anyone may be hired, but all are required to join the union
Agency shop	Anyone may be hired, but all are required (1) to join the union or (2) to make payments to it in lieu of dues
Closed shop	Only union members in good standing may be hired; all must continue in union membership

inconsistent beliefs to come together and be consciously evaluated each in the light of the other.

Then there is the situation in which we practice *expediency* or *opportunism.* Here we take action to secure a short-term goal either regardless of, or more typically, without carefully considering its effects on, the long-term values we hold. Thus, I may "high-pressure" a customer into signing an order even at the risk of alienating him and losing his future business. Or as a candidate for public office, in the heat of a vigorous and close campaign, I may make extravagant promises to the voters either without giving thought to their feasibility or after convincing myself that a bit of misleading here and there can be more than balanced by the good I can do after I am elected. It is to be noted that I may or may not be consciously misrepresenting. Indeed, in most cases I am not. I am merely doing what I consider necessary to accomplish an immediate objective in which I am vitally interested.

When the matter is put this way, it is clear that all of us from time to time act expediently or in an opportunistic fashion, and hence no one should be surprised when it is said that unions and their leaders do this too. Recognition of this fact helps us understand some otherwise strange or inconsistent behavior on their part.

Here is the matter of automation, for example. At the level of theory or ideology unions are in favor of all real progress, including that connected with automation. At the local level and in the workplace, on the other hand, the union may vigorously oppose the introduction of *this* labor-saving device under *these* circumstances. (Of course, if *my* job is at stake, I can probably find a number of reasons why the action should not be taken.) Or here is the union doctrine that all workers should receive equal treatment and opportunity. At the working level the individual member may still find many arguments for excluding blacks from apprentice programs or oppose the company's hiring of women workers into jobs historically reserved for men.

An illustration involves management rights. I may be fully committed in theory to management's right to manage and to the fundamental values of private ownership and control of property. However, if as a union representative I see an opportunity to gain for myself or my fellow members at the expense (which I probably justify as slight and relatively unimportant) of those rights, I am likely to be weak enough to take advantage of the situation.

One trouble about opportunism, if it is successful in achieving the immediate objective, is its tendency to grow and to spread to other aspects of the situation. Thus the union may gain minor concessions relative to job assignments and promotions of workers. If these prove popular with the membership, next year there may be a drive for more, and this can continue until serious damage is done to the flexibility of the firm. It could, of course, go far enough to do serious damage to the whole system of free enterprise—as could continuing pressure for, and success in, getting more and more interference with the freedoms of management. One is reminded of the old story of the camel that got his nose under the tent. The danger is that eventually he may be completely inside it, or even throw over the tent, though he had no such intention in the beginning, or even as he went along.

Actually, we have just described what is probably the biggest threat of unions to our economic institutions. As we have said, union members are neither socialistic nor anti-American, nor are they plotting against our system. But the system could be destroyed through expediency. No one who looks calmly at the current American scene can fail to see dangers present in it.

Lest this seem unduly harsh as related to unions, let us make it clear that unions are not the only parties who practice opportunism or expediency. Time after time management people have engaged in such action. Price fixing in violation of the law is an example. Extravagant and unreasonable claims for a product or a service are another, and driving a hard, unjustifiable, or sly bargain with a customer or the union may be another. And management can be, and often is, just as guilty as union representatives of pushing for action by which it gains in the short run without at the same time a careful consideration of long-run adverse effects. Thus management, too, could destroy the free-enterprise system without intending to do so.

All this may seem far from the problems of the supervisor but there are two relevant observations. In the first place, there is real advantage in understanding what is happening. Indeed, if all supervisors in an organization are aware of what is going on, their combined influence may very well have a significant effect in encouraging or discouraging certain actions of executives and union officials in this important area. In the second place, the supervisor himself is not infrequently tempted to be opportunistic, to take action that may gain in the short run only to prove expensive in the long run. This, too, is regrettable when it occurs.

The Union Official as a Politician

As another important point, we need to be aware that the local union officials and the international officers are essentially political officeholders. In most cases they run for the office they hold. Not infrequently, they plan to run for another term, and even when they do not, they hope one of their "party" will succeed them. In many union matters, then, the president or the steward is thinking not only of the issue being discussed but of its longer-range political consequences.

Wise indeed is the supervisor who understands what this means. In presenting a grievance, for example, often the union official may not really be talking to the supervisor, though he may be addressing his words to him. Frequently he is talking to his fellow union members. (The grapevine is a great aid here, even if no member is present to hear.) Viewed in this light, many otherwise meaningless or even insulting speeches take on a different significance.

At the same time it must not be forgotten that the supervisor and other managers are frequently politicians too. In their case, the "electorate" is not usually the workers but rather their immediate bosses, or the big bosses, or New York headquarters. They too may make "political" speeches and take certain positions to "make brownie points with the powers that be."

At times the political nature of the union official's position is held to be a serious limitation of unionism in general, but this is a conclusion that must be carefully evaluated before being accepted. Ultimately, our government rests on the same sort of foundation, and the President of the United States, the congressmen, the governors, and even the sheriffs are in their respective positions by popular vote. (Of course in the eyes of some, considering the opinion they have of all politicians, this further condemns the union.) Fundamental values are at stake here, including some of those most basic to our way of life. Elected officials are often far from exemplary in their conduct and sometimes reflect discredit on the office and those who elect them. But nevertheless they render real service not only in representing their electorate but in bringing about the compromises that are essential to the operation of our system. It is easy to endorse a system that permits the selection of officials by a benevolent dictator rather than by voters, but Americans have historically been totally unwilling to adopt it, and they continue to be vigorously opposed.

In the last analysis, then, it is not a question of whether a person is a politician, for politicians we must have. It is really a question of what kind of a politician one is; there are politicians of all sorts both inside and outside labor unions, as well as in management positions.[5]

UNIONIZATION OF VARIOUS KINDS OF EMPLOYEES

One unusual development with regard to American labor unions is their very real success in organizing blue-collar workers and their much less fruitful accomplishments, at least until recently, with regard to workers in other sorts of jobs. While we do not have time to go into this subject exhaustively, it contains important insights into the nature of the American worker and the American labor movement, insights that everyone who deals with unions, including those who prefer to continue not having to deal with them, should understand.

Tables 15-3 and 15-4 give some data on union membership in the United States. Note that 1972 is the last year covered by them. The evidence indicates, however, that current figures would not differ greatly from these, there being evidence to indicate that in 1977 somewhat more than 22 million workers belong to labor unions and employee associations.

Union membership as a proportion of the nonagricultural labor force in the United States is shown in Table 15-5.

Table 15-3 Membership in U.S. Labor Unions*

	1940	1950	1960	1970	1972
Total (000s omitted)	8,994	15,000	18,117	20,752	20,894
Affiliated unions	7,872	12,400	15,072	15,978	16,507
Independent unions	1,072	2,600	3,045	4,773	4,386
Canadian members of U.S. unions	227	733	1,068	1,371	1,458

*Source: Adapted from U.S. Bureau of Labor Statistics, *Handbook of Labor Statistics*, annual; and *Directory of National Unions and Employee Associations*, 1973.

Table 15-4   The Largest U.S. Labor Unions (as of 1970)*

Union	Membership
Int'l. Brotherhood of Teamsters	1,829,000
United Auto Workers	1,486,000
United Steelworkers	1,410,000
Int'l. Brotherhood of Electrical Workers	922,000
United Brotherhood of Carpenters	820,000
Int'l. Ass'n. of Machinists	865,000
Retail Clerks Int'l. Ass'n.	605,000

Source: Same as for Table 15-3.

The Attraction of the Union for Blue-collar Workers

A great many factors have contributed to the unionization of blue-collar workers, some of them being obvious or nearly so. It was the blue-collar worker who bore the brunt of the dangerous, hard, exhausting work that followed the Industrial Revolution. Not surprisingly, he proved to be interested in anything that promised him better wages, hours, and conditions of work.

Furthermore, blue-collar workers were the sort first brought together in very large numbers. In recent years this situation has changed somewhat as thousands of white-collar workers are employed by one company or government agency in one place, but blue-collar employment continues to be mass-employment to a greater degree than is true for other sorts of workers. Size as such does not explain unionization, but extremely large groups of people make it difficult for management to be as close to its employees and to deal as effectively with their problems.

Another factor is the predominance of men in blue-collar groups. Furthermore, these men tend to come from what the sociologists call the lower socioeconomic class. One simply must recognize that historically and at present the value systems of men in our society are importantly different from those of women, and that those of the lower class (the term is used in the sociological sense without any presumption of inferiority) are different from those of the middle class, which has furnished the majority of white-collar and managerial workers.

Table 15-5   Union Memberships as a Proportion of the U.S. Nonagricultural Labor Force

Year	Total union membership (exclusive of Canada) (in thousands)	Total nonagri- cultural labor force	Percentage who are union members
1967	18,367	65,857	27.9
1968	18,916	67,951	27.8
1969	19,036	70,442	27.0
1970	19,381	70,920	27.3
1971	19,211	71,222	27.0
1972	19,435	73,714	26.4

Source: See Table 15-3.

The so-called lower-class values put less emphasis on the usual status symbols, on future achievement, on conformity to customary standards, and on the avoidance of confrontation and even violence. (The same can also be said to a degree of the values of men as opposed to those of women in our society.)

The result is that the American labor movement has traditionally been associated with strikes, picket lines, and threats of physical force, none of which white-collar workers in general and women in particular usually find appealing. As long as unionism carries this connotation, and is associated with the lower classes, its progress among white-collar workers is likely to be slow.[6]

An additional factor operates in the case of women, who make up a much larger percentage of white-collar workers. While more than 50 percent of all American women of working ages are now employed, and a majority of these will probably spend most of their adult lives as employees, they simply do not see themselves as permanently in the work force to the degree that is true of men. They are therefore less likely to be attracted to a movement that emphasizes long-run improvement in wages, hours, and conditions of work. We are not saying that women cannot be unionized, for they can be and are being brought into unions. But the predominance of women in many work groups inhibits their organization.

The Unionization of Supervisors

Before the Taft-Hartley Act was passed in 1947, foremen's unions were growing rapidly. This act made it unnecessary for the employer to recognize and bargain with such unions, and they have lost their influence. From time to time movements are started to repeal this provision of the act, but so far these have been without success. It is by no means certain that the present situation will continue indefinitely—in fact, unless middle and top management examines carefully the present status of the first-line supervisor and takes appropriate action, it may not—but it does not now appear that such unionization is likely in the near future.

The Unionization of Government Workers

A striking development of the sixties and seventies, as we have previously mentioned, was the large number of government workers who joined unions. While the 1962 Executive order was quite influential, it was by no means the only factor. For example, employees of state and municipal governments joined unions in large numbers, and they were not directly affected by the order. The present indications are that this trend will continue.

Government employees pose special problems in labor relations. There are still jurisdictions in which unionization is illegal, though this is no guarantee that there will not be unions. But even where unionization of government employees is permitted, two restrictions are usually placed on them: they are not permitted to bargain about rates of pay, and they are prohibited from striking to enforce their demands. Events of the last few years demonstrate that these prohibitions are often ineffective, and the pressure to have them removed will doubtless continue and may well grow in intensity. Involved here are important issues of public policy into which we do not have time to go.[7]

The Unionization of Professional Workers

An unexpected development of the past few years has been an obvious increase in union interest on the part of professional workers, especially those employed by various government agencies. For years managers as well as authorities in union-management matters had assumed that professionals would be the last groups to join unions, if they ever did, and that any success in organizing white-collar workers would begin with those "at the bottom," in sales and clerical positions. What accounts for this unusual set of affairs? Why have engineers, for example, to a degree, and especially teachers and nurses been more inclined than we had suspected to unionize?

Conditions of Work   Some of the factors that produced unionization in blue-collar workers have no doubt operated here. Organizations have increased greatly in size, and professional people, like all others, have been increasingly separated from top management. The "bullpens" of engineers (with scores in the same room doing essentially the same thing and furthermore, at times simply "busy work" or nonengineering activities) have certainly led to no increase in morale. The greatly increased size of the school system and the hospital and other health centers may have had a less obvious but probably no less decided effect.

Pay has also been influential, though it is difficult to make a factual appraisal of this situation. How much are engineers, or nurses, or teachers really worth in dollars per month? Has their rate of increase in pay kept up with that of blue-collar workers? As a matter of fact, should it not exceed that or any other rate of increase? And what of fringe benefits and their competitiveness?

As we have indicated these questions are very complicated and even if the needed hard economic data were available, definite answers would not be furnished thereby. After all, it is not whether people are paid equitably that really influences them. It is whether they *think* and *feel* they are. There is no doubt but that a concern over salaries and related items has been influential here.

Treatment as a Professional   It is easy to get the notion that we really already answered our question, that professional unions are simply devices to get more economic benefits for their members. Such, however, is far from the entire story, and it is probably not the most important part. An equally important factor relates to how these people feel that they are dealt with as professionals.

The authoritarian treatment of the nurse by the physician has been many times noted and certainly has not contributed to morale. What has hurt perhaps as much, however, is a failure of the nurse to fully achieve in the eyes of her associates (and maybe her own) the truly professional status to which she feels she is entitled. (Here hospital administrators and patients may be as much to blame as physicians.) Add to all that the pressures brought about by a shortage of nurses and the shift arrangements to which nurses must adjust, and unrest, especially among the RNs, is easily understood.

The public school teacher seems to have been treated in an equally unprofessional manner. Until a few years ago in large school systems and even today in some smaller ones, the teacher had to engage without any extra compensation in almost endless extracurricular activities; she was often forbidden on pain of the loss of her job, to patronize any bar or sometimes even to touch alcoholic beverages; her attendance at Sunday school and church was required; and any individual communication to any member of the school board was strictly forbidden. Had we been more perceptive, we might very well have anticipated the development of unions among teachers.[8]

THE FUTURE OF UNIONIZATION

Let us take a small amount of space to speculate about the future of the American labor movement. It must be recognized that interpreting what has happened and what is now happening, with all the limitations such activities involve, is easier than stating with confidence what will happen.

With regard to the blue-collar worker, the present evidence is that he will continue his favorable response to the union. Organized labor has not lost out and is not declining in influence among these workers, nor is there any support for a hope, often voiced by management, that younger workers are any less union-minded than are the older ones.

We have already remarked that government workers are showing a continuing interest in unionization, and we see no indication that this interest is about to decline. In a particular way we are all involved and have a stake in the conditions under which such unions operate, and it is shortsighted for the average citizen not to become informed and to exert his influence to secure what he thinks are proper, workable conditions for such employees.

At the professional level it is more difficult to make predictions. Engineers are apparently less interested than they once were in unionization, but it is not possible to say whether this is a temporary or permanent decrease in interest. So far as nurses and teachers are concerned, there is no evidence that their attraction to unions (or at least to "professional negotiations," as the teachers characterize it) is waning at all. Here unions (or at least unionlike activities) may shortly become the national pattern.

Finally, there is the large group of the relatively lower-paid white-collar workers in private business. Here the immediate past indicates that such employees have no particular interest in labor unions, and there is no tangible evidence at present that really substantial numbers of them are likely to give up their nonunion status. It must not be overlooked, however, that all of the media of public communication these days cover union activities in considerable detail. This includes not only the efforts of truckers, airline pilots, auto workers, and the like but the even-more-publicized negotiations by such groups as professional athletes. It seems a reasonable conclusion that such publicity has done unions more good than harm and may have helped to create a situation in which unionization will again grow at a rapid rate.[9]

THE SUPERVISOR AND THE UNION

So far in this chapter we have said little directly on the subject of the relations of the supervisor with the union. Rather the discussion has been, in a broad sense, on the nature and functioning of the labor union. We have tried to emphasize aspects of the subject that are somewhat subtle and not infrequently overlooked both by supervisors and by writers in this field. The assumption behind all this is that the supervisor is better able to deal with unions when he understands them better, and that understanding of their more intricate and less obvious aspects can be of great use.

Now let us turn to some of the more conventional aspects of union-management relations and discuss them from the standpoint of the supervisor. For this purpose we shall consider, first, the supervisor and his or her relationship to the negotiation of the labor contract; second, the supervisor and the administration of the contract; and, third, a topic logically belonging with the one just mentioned but sufficiently important to justify a separate heading, namely, the supervisor and day-to-day relationships with union members and union officials.

The Supervisor and Contract Negotiation

It is apparent, of course, that the first-line supervisor has little and often no direct involvement in the discussions and the bargaining that lead to a labor agreement. So far as the company or the plant, office, or store is concerned, these are carried on by executives, and even middle management seldom participates. This does not mean, however, that the supervisor is without influence in this important area.

For one thing, the company may hold meetings of managers at various levels of the company in preparation for these negotiations. The purpose here may be a dual one: to get ideas about what should be bargained for, including weaknesses in the present contract and difficulties that have arisen under it, and—less likely because of the danger of tipping management's hand in the forthcoming negotiations—to inform managers about the problems as seen by the company and its goals and objectives in bargaining. The larger the organization, of course, the less feasible it becomes to involve all members of management, but in any work situation a representative sample of the various levels may be called in if it is considered desirable.

Needless to say, supervisors who participate in this fashion have a real opportunity to influence the negotiations. Clearly, their status tends to make them timid in offering suggestions and to cause superiors not to seek their ideas actively or at least not to give them the consideration they may deserve. But the opportunity is present nevertheless, and the alert supervisor does not overlook this fact.

A similar opportunity presents itself, though in a different fashion, if supervisors are allowed to sit in on actual negotiations. Here they would usually be only observers, and the influence they might have would be almost wholly restricted to comments they might be able to make between sessions. These might at times be quite useful, however, and wise negotiators will not overlook the opportunities thus afforded.

However, a failure to include supervisors in negotiations in no sense proves or even indicates that they are without long-run influence here. Their actions, or lack of action, may be the basis for union demands; that is, the way they handle suggestions or grievances may greatly influence union strategy. Taken together, supervisory actions have a great deal to do with the issues in bargaining, a responsibility not to be taken lightly. This is something all supervisors need to take into account in the everyday execution of their duties.

Likewise, ideas concerning what should go into the agreement and ways of conducting the bargaining do not have to wait for a formal meeting or even for a direct request from management. These matters can be at the focus of attention of the supervisor, and suggestions can be made frequently and without solicitation.

The Supervisor and Contract Administration

There may be some question about the influence of the supervisor on the bargaining that leads to a labor contract, but there certainly is none about his or her very real influence on the way the contract is administered and applied.

Enforcement of the Contract   A consideration that must always be kept in mind is that, regardless of the words in it, a contract provision often becomes what the supervisors take it to mean, that is, what they require of employees under its provisions. For example, company negotiators may have succeeded in securing rather liberal rights for supervisors in such an area as transfer, duty assignments, or the like, but the supervisors may substantially give the provisions away by failing to exercise them. Similar illustrations can be found in supervisory actions relating to poor productivity or poor attendance. If company rights in these areas are neglected or unenforced they may be permanently lost or, at a minimum, regained only at considerable cost. Clearly the treatment of discipline found in the preceding chapter is relevant here.

Handling Grievances   One place where the supervisor undoubtedly becomes involved in union-management matters is in connection with the handling of grievances. While some contracts have provision for some types of grievances to go directly to a more highly placed member of management, the usual grievance starts with an oral presentation to the first level of management. How the grievance is handled here may easily become critical—for this grievance and often for other aspects of labor relations.

Familiarity with the Contract   One obvious suggestion about handling grievances is to be familiar with the contract. As just pointed out, this means a great deal more than simply what the words are and what they appear to mean. Handling grievances without a knowledge of company (and union) intentions, past and present practices, proposals made but not successfully negotiated in bargaining, and legal awards is dangerous business. The company should lend the supervisor every reasonable assistance here. Whether or not it does so, the obligation of the supervisor is clear: to get and assimilate this information in any fair and honorable way.

In this connection, one point that supervisors must be clear on is that they no longer have the luxury of simply acting for themselves. On the contrary, the law provides that when supervisors speak, the company has spoken. When they act, the company has taken action. This is a responsibility that must not be viewed lightly. On the other hand, since someone frequently has to speak for the company and supervisors are often so placed that they have to do it, they should neither dread nor shun the responsibility.

Action such as that we have been discussing is not to be taken in haste, unless one faces an emergency. Hence a suggestion made more than once earlier: One should *consult* before deciding. No one can know all about a complex labor contract (and virtually all have become complex these days). Labor relations people are often available and, where useful, should be used. One's boss and other managers may be quite helpful. And there may well be others with whom one may consult before one decides.

Building a Record   Another point of consequence, also discussed in the preceding chapter, arises from the fact that almost any grievance is possibly the basis for later arbitration. Hence the importance and even the necessity of "building a record" from the beginning. It is not sufficient for a supervisor to handle a grievance properly. He may well be called upon to *prove* he handled it properly. As a minimum this means foresight in the origin and disposition of relevant records and the location of necessary witnesses.

Recognizing One's Errors   Still another point relates to supervisors' attitudes toward a decision when it has been made. Here there is a strong tendency to demand that the company agree with what they have decided and back them up all the way. This position, however widely held, is completely in error and for reasons already made clear in preceding discussions.

This matter is of greater consequence than at first appears. Unless the supervisors, the labor relations specialists, and higher management understand it well, the organization can easily fall into one of two traps. The first trap is that a supervisor's decisions can be backed all the way to arbitration, with not infrequently unpleasant consequences, and the second is that a supervisor can develop the habit of checking all the way up the line before answering a grievance. Superficially, the latter may appear to be a desirable course of action, but it usually is not. Not only does it place a heavy burden on middle and especially top management, but it further encourages the supervisor to be a "messenger" for decisions he or she did not make, rather than to use his or her own good judgment. One can go too far either way on this matter, but in labor relations as in other things the supervisor needs "the right to be wrong," that is, to exercise his or her best judgment. Subsequently, the supervisor is not to be condemned if he or she turns out to be less than fully perfect.

Preparing for Hearings   And then there is the matter of preparation for hearings on the grievance at the second or higher steps and possibly before an arbitrator. Particularly in the latter situation, the supervisor is likely to appear merely as a witness. What suggestions are in order here?

One, of course, is familiarity with, and insofar as feasible, proof of, the facts. Likewise the position of the company and that of the union should be thoroughly studied and mastered. Every effort should be made to anticipate the questions one will be asked and the proper—meaning the truthful and, among other things, the most effective—answer to each. Here consultation with others can be most helpful. In general, the witness who gives the impression of being realistic while not having complete mastery of all facts concerning every detail is a more believable one than the witness who tries to appear perfect. But being a witness under these circumstances is not always easy. The supervisor's testimony may be damaging to one or more subordinates or even fellow managers and may lead to later difficulty. On occasions it may even not fully agree with the company's case. However, both morality and the long-run well-being of the parties involved dictate honesty and truthfulness in answers. One certainly must not encourage deceit in labor relations even where it appears that short-run gain may result.[10]

The Supervisor and Day-to-day Relations with the Union

It may be well to close this chapter with some remarks about the more ordinary relations between the supervisor and the union. Much of our early discussion, it is hoped, is also relevant to this topic.

Managers must always bear in mind that they are not candidates in a popularity contest and that the acceptance by subordinates of their decisions is not always a measure of their adequacy. They have management rights to protect, and this necessity may cause them to make unpopular decisions. That, however, is one of the limitations of the job. The feelings of subordinates should usually be considered. They need not and should not always be followed. It must be overlooked, however, that not infrequently one ultimately best earns the respect of others by demonstrating a willingness to do what is right even under adverse circumstances. The courageous supervisor is thus not necessarily condemned to being unpopular.

Furthermore, relations with union members and union officials need not be ones of perpetual conflict. Supervisors do work successfully and pleasantly with union officials, and not a few find in the union steward a strong helper on certain problems. Where proper respect and understanding are present, the supervisor may frequently consult with the steward and get his or her assistance in handling what might otherwise be a difficult situation. Under these conditions the steward must be allowed and encouraged to exercise independent judgment, but he or she may still be helpful. It goes without saying, however, that the supervisor must avoid here all substance or semblance of manipulation.

In some situations, of course, relations between managers and union representatives are poor indeed. There is probably no way in which the first level of management can avoid being influenced by this fact, but any such persons can make up their minds to do their best to see to it that *their* relations with workers are responsible and satisfactory. Such a resolve does not guarantee success but it often helps significantly.

Insofar as feasible, in union matters as in all others, the spirit rather than the letter of the law should be the guiding principle. Managers are not intent on getting the very last advantage to which they may be entitled legally, and they hope they do not have to rely on a technicality to gain an important point. However, we must be realistic here. One of the real disadvantages of having a union and a union contract is that *legalism* is to an extent inevitable. More than that, as contracts become more complex, as more and more efforts are made to anticipate every eventuality, and as decisions of government agencies and arbitrators become more numerous and more explicit, we shall probably have more and more of the letter of the law and less and less of its spirit. If this is inevitable, as the authors fear it is, supervisors can at least use their influence, insofar as good judgment will permit, to slow the process.

Our next point can perhaps be made best with an illustration. Some time ago a labor relations director for a large plant was in his office, attending to some details before going to a meeting with the workmen's committee of the local union. Shortly before the time for the meeting, the president of the local union dropped by, as he frequently did, and the two men chatted in a friendly fashion for a few minutes. Then they walked down the hall to the conference room where the committee had assembled.

As they came to the door, the union president said to the labor relations director, "Joe, if you don't mind, don't walk into the room with your arm around me!"

There is a wealth of wisdom in this situation, and particularly this remark, for the supervisor or any other member of management who deals with union representatives. That there should be friendly relations with these people and that they should be dealt with in an ethical fashion goes without saying. But as another union representative put it on another occasion, "It's the kiss of death to a union president to be too 'buddy-buddy' with management."

Herein lies one of the supervisors' biggest challenges in dealing with the steward, the business agent, the local president, or the international representative. On the one hand, they should be informal and even cordial at times, and they certainly may "shoot the breeze" and exchange stories with the union representative. But supervisors are wise not to put the latter in a position where it appears to the members that he or she is being "bought off" or that the company is attempting, through favors, to weaken the union's demands or lessen enthusiasm in working for them.

There is certainly no easy way to describe or to achieve an ideal situation here and no method, however well tested, which always succeeds. But it is most helpful if supervisors understand the situation and put forth their best effort to arrive at a fair and satisfactory method of operating under these conditions, involving as they do the adversary aspects mentioned earlier. Skill in this area goes a long way toward separating the amateur from the professional manager.

A CONCLUDING STATEMENT

In the matters discussed in this chapter, as for so many other topics of this book, there is no substitute for the supervisor's being—and being taken to be—the sort of person he or she ought to be. This certainly includes intelligence, understanding, and wisdom; emotional maturity; and ethical and moral character. In union-management matters perhaps even more than in some other areas, "It's not primarily what you *do;* it's primarily what you *are* that counts."

QUESTIONS

1 How important are the economic aims of unions? Do they have other aims? Explain.
2 Are American labor unions socialistic? What is business unionism? Explain.
3 What is meant by saying that in the United States labor unions and managements are in an adversary role? What are the advantages and disadvantages of this situation?
4 What is the nature and what are the strengths and weaknesses of *expediency* as a basis for action? How extensively do Americans practice expediency? What are its likely effects on labor-management relations?
5 In what sense is a union official a politician? What about a management official? What are the likely results if a supervisor attempts to become "buddy-buddy" with a local union official?
6 Why have blue-collar workers been easy to unionize? Why have salespersons, clerks, and claims adjusters (for example) been difficult to unionize?

7 What role does the supervisor usually have in (contract) negotiation? What role *should* he or she have?
8 Answer the same question for contract administration.

NOTES

1 Edward Pessen, "Labor from the Revolution to the Civil War," *Monthly Labor Review,* vol. 99, no. 6, pp. 17–24, June 1976.
2 "Union, Employee-Group Rolls Rose 4.8% to 24.2 Million between 1972 and 1974," *The Wall Street Journal,* vol. 56, no. 31, p. 10, Aug. 13, 1975.
3 It is well known that unions have arisen and grown in spite of what was often very strenuous efforts and not infrequently illegal actions to restrain them. For example, see a periodical known as *Worklife,* in recent numbers of which the following appeared: Kenneth Fiester, "A Labor Movement Begins to Stir," pp. 13–24, February 1976; "The Workingman's Party—A First in Labor Politics," pp. 23–26, March 1976; "The Workers' War for Economic Opportunity," pp. 12–20, April 1976; and Kenneth Fiester, "The Molly Maguires Were A Bloody Bunch," pp. 20–23, April 1976.
4 For a general understanding of union-management relations in the United States, see Sanford Cohen, *Labor in the United States,* 4th ed. (Columbus, Ohio: Merrill, 1975) and Arthur A. Sloane and Fred Whitney, *Labor Relations,* 2d ed. (Englewood Cliffs, N.J.: Prentice-Hall, 1972). Two other valuable references are the book by Reynolds and the *Labor Law Course,* both cited in an earlier chapter and in the footnotes below.
5 Though they emphasize primarily the legal and economic factors involved and pay less attention to social and historical considerations, as just noted, the following afford an excellent treatment of labor relations in the United States: Lloyd G. Reynolds, *Labor Economics and Labor Relations,* 6th ed. (Englewood Cliffs, N.J.: Prentice-Hall, 1974). Especially relevant are Chapter 15 on the history of unions, Chapter 16 on their organization and government, and Chapters 17 to 19 on the negotiation of labor contracts. See also the *Labor Law Course,* 23d ed. (Chicago: Commerce Clearing House, 1976), especially pp. 1001ff on the organization and operation of unions and pp. 3001ff on provisions of labor agreements.
6 John S. Greenbaum, "New Influences at the Bargaining Table: The Rebellious Rank and File," *Personnel,* vol. 49, no. 2, pp. 20–25, March–April 1972.
7 The *Labor Law Course,* cited above, discusses this subject at pp. 5901ff. See also Julius N. Draznin, "A New Approach to Grievance Handling in the Federal Sector," *Personnel Journal,* vol. 53, no. 11, pp. 822–824, November 1974; and Jonathan Kwitny, "Police, Other Officers in Some States Sign Up With Teamsters Union," *The Wall Street Journal,* vol. 5, no. 45, pp. 1ff, Mar. 5, 1976.
8 Everett Groseclose, "Teacher Strikes Rise as Local School Boards Tighten Purse Strings," *The Wall Street Journal,* vol. 57, no. 36, pp. 1ff, Feb. 23, 1976.
9 It is apparently not always recognized, but union officials, even including local ones, have not only a moral but a legal obligation to live up to the provisions of the contracts they sign. See, for example, "UMW Liability for Walkouts Is Set by Jury," *The Wall Street Journal,* vol. 57, no. 66, p. 4, Apr. 5, 1976. The award, incidentally, was for $736,000.
10 It would be hard to overstress the importance of the supervisor's understanding of the labor contract, its provisions and how they have been interpreted, and the resolution of disputes arising under it. In this connection Chapter 14 of this book is decidedly relevant. See also Frank Elkouri and Edna A. Elkouri, *How Arbitration Works,* 3d ed.

(New York: Bureau of National Affairs, 1973); and Byron E. Calaime, " 'Best Offer' Arbitration's Critics," *The Wall Street Journal,* vol. 179, no. 116, p. 10, June 14, 1972.

CASES

Again there is no shortage of cases for a chapter on union-management relations, a great many of those in this book involving that relationship to a considerable degree.

For this chapter we have chosen cases that directly involve interpretation of somewhat unusual contract provisions or at least unusual circumstances. In the Garner case, for example, the question is whether a newly designated representative of the workers is bound by prior promises and/or implications of promises made before the election in which the new Union was chosen.

The Quinn case is not concerned so much with the interpretation of the labor agreement itself as with a "side agreement" entered into by the parties, and the impact of this side agreement on Management's right to select produce managers at will. Finally the "right-to-work" case raises the issue of whether under the circumstances faced by these parties, employees could properly order the discontinuation of the deduction of their Union dues as soon as they resigned from the Union.

Each case illustrates what one very often finds in labor relations (and what also obtains but is not so clear in nonunion situations), that relationships between people often involve complexities that tax our best efforts to unravel and solve.

CASE 15-1

The events of this case occurred in late 1956 and early 1957 and grew out of an unusual set of circumstances. The Company is an integrated oil company with refineries in many parts of the country. One of these is located in Jonesville, a small city in one of the southeastern states.

To understand the situation that arose it is necessary to recall that in 1956 there was in effect a Department of Labor ruling relative to overtime pay for Saturday work. That year Christmas and New Year's Day were both on Tuesday, and the Department ruled that if Management wished *and if the employees agreed,* employees working a regular five-day week and subject to the overtime provisions of the Wage and Hour Act could work on the Saturday after (or before) each holiday and substitute this work for that which would have been done on the preceding (or following) Monday without making the company liable for time-and-a-half for overtime on Saturday. (The same arrangement could be made for Thanksgiving, with work on the Saturday preceding Thanksgiving substituted for that of the Friday following, again without overtime pay.)

In the Jonesville plant the employees worked on Saturday, November 24, and did not work on the Friday after Thanksgiving, which was November 19. Likewise they worked on Saturday, December 29, instead of on Monday, December 24, and on Saturday, January 5, instead of on Monday, December 31. In the case of all three Saturdays the Company paid (or at least planned to pay) for the work at straight-time rates.

Meanwhile, a complication had arisen. The employees at Jonesville had long been represented by an independent Union, but the contract with it had expired some months before, and the Company and the Union had been unable to agree on another. At this juncture the International Union petitioned for an election in which it would appear on the ballot (along with the independent Union and the option of *no union*). The National Labor Relations Board granted this petition and set the election for December 18. The election was held on that day, and the International Union received a clear majority. On December 26, it was certified as the bargaining agent for the employees covered.

The International Union had long had bargaining rights in most of the Company's other plants and had a master contract with the Company covering all local units of the Union. One provision in this contract was that if any independent Union in the company became a local unit of the International, provisions of the master contract applied to it at once.

The International Union had already made its position completely clear relative to the substitution of Saturday work for that of a day preceding or following a holiday. It refused to accept this arrangement without overtime pay, and the Jonesville plant was the only one in the Company where this substitution occurred that year.

The policy of the International Union on this matter was an issue in the election. Mason Garner, the representative of the International Union, tried to "soft-pedal" it and made statements that the Company interpreted as approving the arrangement for December 31 and January 5. (There was no question about December 24 and December 19, since all agreed that the International did not have jurisdiction until certified on December 26, and the Union agreed not to make an issue of the December 29 work.) At any rate, the company, relying heavily on Garner's statements, went ahead with the plan for December 31 and January 5.

On Tuesday, January 8, the Company received a grievance, signed by Garner and James Nance, who had been elected local Union president, asking for time and a half (instead of merely straight time) for all who had worked on January 5. About two hundred people were involved.

Officials of the Jonesville plant were surprised and definitely upset by the grievance. Nevertheless they now had three days in which to decide upon their course of action and their written answer to the grievance.

CASE 15-2

For six months there was a long and bitter strike between the Company and the Union involved in this case. The agreement settling the strike included this provision:

> The Employer agrees that all striking employees will be returned to their former positions as of April 3, 1975, without break in seniority, loss of pay or other benefits. . . . The Employer agrees that no striking employee will be discriminated against in any manner whatsoever . . . because of any act he/she engaged in during the course of this strike.

Prior to the strike George Quinn was produce manager (PM) of the 17th Street Supermarket of the Company. When he returned from the strike, however, he was made a food clerk (FC), a position he had filled before being promoted to PM. During the strike Harold Wrenn was promoted from FC to PM, and after the strike settlement the Company continued him as the PM. The grievance protests this action by the Company.

The Union contends that the continuation of Wrenn as PM was an open and flagrant violation of the agreement settling the strike. Furthermore it asserts that Quinn's work was satisfactory, there being, for example, no written evidence of any adverse sort contained in his personnel folder. Even though past practice may indicate the PMs had been appointed and removed at the pleasure of Management, any such removal under these circumstances must be for *cause* and not because of whim or prejudice. In this case it is clear why Quinn was demoted: it was because of his activities in connection with the strike. Hence the grievance should be sustained, Quinn should at once be returned to his rightful PM position, and he should be paid the difference between the FC rate and the PM rate from April 3, 1975, to the date when he is permitted to resume his duties as PM.

The Company contends that George Jonas, the 17th Street Store Manager, simply did on April 3 what he was about to do when the strike occurred. Quinn's work as PM had become unsatisfactory, and Jonas had told him so on more than one occasion. Furthermore, the achievements of Wrenn, as he ran the produce department during the strike, furnished positive proof of this conclusion. For example, profits of the department during the quarter in which Wrenn was in charge exceeded the departmental profits for the whole year before, when Quinn was PM. Additionally, what the strike settlement agreement referred to, the Company says, was the replacement of "scabs" hired during the strike. Inasmuch as Wrenn was a long-time employee who continued working, it did not apply to him. The grievance should therefore be denied.

Should the grievance be sustained or denied? If it is sustained what is the proper remedy? If Quinn is restored to his job under what circumstances, if any, may he be properly removed from the PM job? (The last two questions should not be taken to imply that the grievance necessarily should be sustained.)

CASE 15-3

The issue in this case is a quite unusual one. It took place in Texas, which is a "right-to-work" state. A "right-to-work" state is one that makes it illegal to require union membership as a condition of continuing employment, this form of compulsory union membership being referred to as a *union shop.* In a union shop, as opposed to a *closed shop,* one does not have to be a union member when hired, but he or she must become one within a certain number of days after his or her employment.

When the present contract between the Union and the Company was negotiated, it contained a so-called check-off authorization (COA) clause. This provision permitted any Union member who wished to do so to sign a COA form in which he authorized the Company to deduct Union dues from his regular pay and remit them to the Union. He also in this instance signed an agreement that read in part,

> This authorization shall be irrevocable for a period of one year from the date hereof. . . . Revocation of this authorization shall be effective only if I give written notice of such revocation to my Employer with a copy to the Local Union, not more than twenty (20) and not less than ten (10) days prior to the expiration of [the] period of one year.

In 1974 certain employees signed COA forms but within a matter of a few weeks or months sent both the Company and the Union a letter stating that since they had withdrawn from the Union, their COA forms were no longer to be honored. An example is Louis Dawson, who signed his COA form on August 6, 1974, and sent such a notice on August 16, 1974. Another is Susan Greathouse, who executed a COA on September 14, 1974, and sent her notice on July 13, 1975. In this case there were six other employees who were in a similar situation.

In every instance when the Company received the revocation notice it promptly stopped deducting and remitting the Union dues. The grievance of this case was filed on behalf of the local Union. It asked that the deducting and remitting of the dues be resumed and that the Company reimburse the Union for the amount of the dues which it "improperly and illegally" failed to withhold.

What is the proper disposition of the grievance, and why?

Chapter 16

The Supervisor's Responsibility
for Safety and Health:
The Man from OSHA

It is probably "old hat" to say that the supervisor is responsible to upper management for the health and safety of his or her subordinates. What is not "old hat" is the fact that today the supervisor may be confronted at any time and *always** without warning with the presence of a federal agent, possibly equipped with instruments for measuring factors in the workplace that may involve potential health and safety hazards. Further, the federal agent may converse at will with subordinates of the supervisor, subsequently report to top management what he or she has observed, and possibly recommend the issuance of citations for violation of a federal law.

This agent, whose formal title is Compliance Officer, is sometimes simply referred to as The Man From OSHA (the Occupational Safety and Health Administration). His mission is to enforce compliance by the supervisor, and all higher levels of management, with one of the most sweeping and powerful federal health and safety acts in the history of business and industry—the Occupational Safety and Health Act of 1970.

This chapter is devoted to a discussion of some of the major objectives, policies, procedures, and practices of the Occupational Safety and Health Administration (we shall use the acronym OSHA) as they relate to the supervisor and the supervisory job.

THE SUPERVISOR'S PLACE IN SAFETY AND HEALTH AND THE STATE
OF THE ART

The development and/or maintenance of safe and healthy working conditions for employees, who spend something like a third or more of their lives at their workplaces, is one of the most significant humanitarian or social responsibilities of the supervisor. Obviously, it

*See footnote on page 328 for further explanation.

is also one of the supervisor's most significant economic responsibilities because of its impact on his or her attainment of company goals. Injuries and illnesses can seriously disrupt supervisory productivity and carry with them sizeable costs.

The State of the Art

As we review the record of individual firms, we find that supervisory/management networks in many firms (especially some large manufacturing firms) have been relatively, exceptionally successful in providing and controlling safe and healthy working conditions for their employees. Many so-called blue-collar factory jobs are not only safer than a great many "white-collar" office or service jobs (where historically relatively little attention has been given to safety and health) but are in some cases even safer than the employees' homes.

Where results such as these have been achieved by some firms, they have been accomplished commonly by continuing efforts involving not only supervisors, but such staff personnel as human engineers, physicians, safety engineers, and behavioral scientists such as psychologists and sociologists working as a team. We discuss this subject in some detail in Chapter 17.

The View from Above

However, even spectacular results of many firms in providing safe and healthy working conditions for employees are not considered to be enough, when viewed from a macroeconomic vantage point—that is, a federal government viewpoint that must involve asking this question, "To what extent are we conserving our gainfully employed human resources *throughout the nation as a whole?*"

The answer is found in research data that reveal that each year hundreds of thousands of employees in the aggregate suffer injuries and death because of inadequate safety and health policies, procedures, work methods, and rules and/or inadequate enforcement by supervisors and higher-level managements. Monetary costs of such tragedies to employees, and employers as well, are counted in the billions of dollars. Noneconomic, human costs are of course incalculable.

The Centralization of Safety and Health Controls: The Birth of OSHA

The situation just described has led the federal government to hypothesize that decentralized controls of health and safety (that is, self-control by a firm, or even controls over individual firms by municipalities and even states) generally have been, presently are, and probably will continue to be, inadequate.

Based on the above hypothesis, the federal government created its own strong centralized controls, mentioned above, over business and industry (governmental agencies for some reasons evidently not widely known, are not affected) by passing the Occupational Safety and Health Act of 1970. The purpose of the Act is "to assure as far as possible every working man and woman[1] in the Nation safe and healthful working conditions and to preserve our human resources."[2] It is to be noted that the act limits enforcement of safety and health practices to the work environment as it affects employees. It does not cover safety and health practices in a community, for example.[3] This is the province of the Environmental Protection Agency.

This first all-embracing federal safety and health act is a labor-oriented law. It has been hailed as one that grants to workers the most extensive "Bill of Rights" in the history of labor legislation.

The Creation of OSHA

In order to administer and enforce the act a federal agency was created, with regional and area offices scattered throughout the United States. This agency was given the title, the Occupational Safety and Health Administration (as stated above, we shall use the acronym OSHA and hope that it will not be confused with the enabling act, the Occupational Safety and Health Act of 1970, which could carry the same acronym). OSHA is located in, and administratively responsible to, the United States Department of Labor.

THE OSHA CONTROL PROCESS: ITS IMPACT ON THE SUPERVISOR

We shall couch our discussion of the supervisor's relationship to the OSHA control process in terms of the major steps in any control process, discussed in Chapter 4: (1) establish standards, (2) compare performance with standards, and (3) take corrective action when performance deviates significantly from established standards.

OSHA Standards

OSHA develops health and safety standards in cooperation with another federal agency, the National Institute for Occupational Safety and Health (NIOSH), located in the Department of Health, Education, and Welfare. These OSHA standards are legally enforceable regulations aimed at making conditions in every workplace safe and healthful.

Standards that apply in general to most industries (see Table 16-1) as well as those applicable to specific industries are published by OSHA in pamphlets, loose-leaf brochures, and so on, that anyone can obtain free of charge. These standards are also published in the *Federal Register*. All amendments, corrections, insertions and deletions—and there are many—are also published in the *Federal Register*.

Table 16-1   Illustrative Summary of Selected General Industry Housekeeping and Sanitation Standards

All workplaces, including passageways and storage rooms, must be kept clean, orderly, and as dry as possible.

Workplaces must have aisles and passageways which are wide enough to permit easy, safe movement, and which are kept clear of obstructions and clearly marked.

Water which meets applicable federal, state, and/or local drinking water standards must be available at all workplaces for drinking, washing, food preparation, etc. Drinking fountains shall be constructed so as not to present a health hazard.

If shower facilities are required by the OSHA standard pertaining to that industry, one shower that includes hot and cold water must be provided for each ten employees, and clean towels must also be provided.

All workplaces must maintain a specified number of toilet facilities for employees of both sexes.

Where food service for employees is provided, all food handling activities shall be hygienic, and the food shall be wholesome and protected from contamination.

Fire alarm systems must meet rigid, detailed specifications.

Air shall be free of contaminents.

Noise levels must meet detailed specifications.

Specified electrical and illumination standards (for both safety and health) must be met.

A specified number of washing facilities must be maintained in a sanitary condition, with soap, towels (or other drying facilities), and hot and cold running water.

Supervisory/Management Obligations   Supervisors, as a part of the management network, are obliged to prominently display an OSHA poster (see Figure 16-1) and to keep their employees informed about any OSHA standards that apply to their workplaces. Failure can result in a citation to the form for noncompliance with OSHA standards.

Another major supervisory obligation, of course, is to see to it that the standards are complied with by subordinates. This obligation carries with it the responsibility for disciplining, as necessary, employees who do not continuously practice safety and treat it as an integral part of their jobs.

To illustrate this point a firm was cited for a violation of an OSHA safety standard, failure of an employee to wear a hard hat in a designated hard-hat area (a hatless employee was struck by a pipe falling from a hoist). Top management (the employer) appealed the citation stating that the firm had bought all employees hard hats, distributed payroll stuffers urging they be worn—and posted signs in hard-hat areas stating that they must be worn.

The citation was upheld by a Review Commission, discussed later, that stated *"the employer had not gone far enough. It should have taken disciplinary action* (including suspension and discharge) against workers who violated its hard-hat requirements."[4] This kind of situation puts the supervisor, of course, squarely on center stage.

Supervisors seldom, if ever, deal directly with representatives of OSHA, which recognizes only the employer-employee dichotomy (thus we shall refer to the employer as top management). However, supervisors may play an important role if requested, as advisers to top management in matters relating to safety and health standards. For example, top management has the right to apply to OSHA for a variance (exception) from a particular standard. If such an application is made, OSHA may grant a temporary variance if top management is unable to comply because of the unavailability of materials, equipment, or personnel to make changes within the required time.

Top management may even be granted a permanent variance if it can prove that facilities or methods of operation provide worker protection that is "at least as effective as" that required by the OSHA standard. However, if top management applies for either type of variance, it is required to notify its employees (through its supervisors, generally) that it has done so. Thus in each of the above illustrative situations the supervisor, who in day-to-day operations carries the major responsibility for employee health and safety, should ideally at least be an important part of the management team.

Employee Rights   Nonsupervisory employees have no obligation to OSHA (only to their supervisors) for complying with OSHA standards. However, employees have been legally granted an unprecedented right *to participate in the development* of OSHA standards, based on the reasoning that these standards have been developed for *their* protection and well-being. Employees having information, comments, or suggestions they wish to have considered regarding OSHA's issuing, modifying, or revoking a standard are encouraged (for example, through pamphlets mailed directly to them by OSHA) to submit them in writing to a nearby OSHA office.

Employees also have the right to request a public hearing on a standard under consideration for adoption, modification, or revocation. Finally, employees have the right to obtain copies of current OSHA standards from their employer or from the OSHA office nearest them. An effort by the supervisor/management hierarchy to deprive employees of rights such as these can result in the firm receiving a citation for noncompliance. If employees are discharged because of their demands for such rights, management may be required to rehire them and restore them to their positions with back pay.

job safety and health protection

The Occupational Safety and Health Act of 1970 provides job safety and health protection for workers through the promotion of safe and healthful working conditions throughout the Nation. Requirements of the Act include the following:

Employers: Each employer shall furnish to each of his employees employment and a place of employment free from recognized hazards that are causing or are likely to cause death or serious harm to his employees; and shall comply with occupational safety and health standards issued under the Act.

Employees: Each employee shall comply with all occupational safety and health standards, rules, regulations and orders issued under the Act that apply to his own actions and conduct on the job.

The Occupational Safety and Health Administration (OSHA) of the Department of Labor has the primary responsibility for administering the Act. OSHA issues occupational safety and health standards, and its Compliance Safety and Health Officers conduct jobsite inspections to ensure compliance with the Act.

Inspection: The Act requires that a representative of the employer and a representative authorized by the employees be given an opportunity to accompany the OSHA inspector for the purpose of aiding the inspection.

Where there is no authorized employee representative, the OSHA Compliance Officer must consult with a reasonable number of employees concerning safety and health conditions in the workplace.

Complaint: Employees or their representatives have the right to file a complaint with the nearest OSHA office requesting an inspection if they believe unsafe or unhealthful conditions exist in their workplace. OSHA will withhold, on request, names of employees complaining.

The Act provides that employees may not be discharged or discriminated against in any way for filing safety and health complaints or otherwise exercising their rights under the Act.

An employee who believes he has been discriminated against may file a complaint with the nearest OSHA office within 30 days of the alleged discrimination.

Citation: If upon inspection OSHA believes an employer has violated the Act, a citation alleging such violations will be issued to the employer. Each citation will specify a time period within which the alleged violation must be corrected.

The OSHA citation must be prominently displayed at or near the place of alleged violation for three days, or until it is corrected, whichever is later, to warn employees of dangers that may exist there.

Proposed Penalty: The Act provides for mandatory penalties against employers of up to $1,000 for each serious violation and for optional penalties of up to $1,000 for each nonserious violation. Penalties of up to $1,000 per day may be proposed for failure to correct violations within the proposed time period. Also, any employer who wilfully or repeatedly violates the Act may be assessed penalties of up to $10,000 for each such violation.

Criminal penalties are also provided for in the Act. Any wilful violation resulting in death of an employee, upon conviction, is punishable by a fine of not more than $10,000 or by imprisonment for not more than six months, or by both. Conviction of an employer after a first conviction doubles these maximum penalties.

Voluntary Activity: While providing penalties for violations, the Act also encourages efforts by labor and management, before an OSHA inspection, to reduce injuries and illnesses arising out of employment.

More Information: Additional information and copies of the Act, specific OSHA safety and health standards, and other applicable regulations may be obtained from the nearest OSHA Regional Office in the following locations:

Atlanta, Georgia

Boston, Massachusetts

Chicago, Illinois

Dallas, Texas

Denver, Colorado

Kansas City, Missouri

New York, New York

Philadelphia, Pennsylvania

San Francisco, California

Seattle, Washington

Telephone numbers for these offices, and additional Area Office locations, are listed in the telephone directory under the United States Department of Labor in the United States Government listing.

Washington, D.C.
1974
OSHA 2203

Peter J. Brennan
Secretary of Labor

U. S. Department of Labor
Occupational Safety and Health Administration

Figure 16-1 OSHA display poster.

The Ubiquitous Problem: Criteria for Standards   In some cases OSHA (and NIOSH, mentioned above) is the victim (as is the supervisor and indeed all of us concerned with developing or administering standards) of this problem, "What criteria can we develop that will enable us to create meaningful standards?"[5] Some kinds of hazards appear to defy the development of adequate criteria for establishing precise standards. To illustrate this point OSHA acknowledges a lack of definitive environmental data and medical technology concerning "safe" levels of exposure of employees to certain chemicals. Consequently, it recognizes that "feasibility" is a legitimate factor to be considered in the setting of occupational safety and health standards. Therefore, in setting standards for which no safe level of exposure can be shown, "OSHA's policy has been to set the standard at the lowest level feasible."[6]

Another somewhat related problem faced by OSHA is that precise standards governing every conceivable situation are not possible, of course. Therefore OSHA can in such instances only decree in very general terminology that management has a "general duty" to provide a workplace that is free from "recognized hazards."

The OSHA Inspection: Comparison of Performance with Standards

The OSHA inspection function, which can be of exceptional significance to the supervisor, consists of a series of well-defined steps which we shall now briefly describe. See Figure 16-2 for a simplified version of an OSHA inspection flowchart.

Step 1, Scheduling of Firms   The first step (one of three that are preliminary to the actual inspection tour) is that of scheduling, on a systematic basis, firms to be inspected. Obviously not all of several million establishments covered by the act can be inspected immediately. The worst situations need attention first. Therefore OSHA has established a system of inspection priorities. We shall list three of the most important.[7]

First priority is given to "imminent danger" situations where there is a reasonable certainty of death or serious physical harm occurring. Second priority is given to investigation of catastrophes, fatalities, and accidents resulting in hospitalization of five or more employees. Third priority is given to valid employee complaints of unsafe or unhealthful working conditions. Well down the list of priorities are random inspections conducted in firms of all sizes and types in all parts of the country.

Step 2, Familiarization with Characteristics of Firms Scheduled   A second preparatory step involves the compliance officer familiarizing himself or herself with as many relevant facts as possible about each workplace scheduled to be inspected, taking into account such things as the history of the establishment, the nature of the business, the particular standards most likely to apply and equipment necessary for analyzing noise levels, illumination, air content (such as fumes, gases, toxic substances), and so on.

Step 3, Entry of Establishment   A third step is the entry of a selected establishment. By law OSHA has the authority to enter, without delay and at reasonable times, and inspect virtually any place of business in the nation where work is performed by an employee of an employer.

The entry *must,* by law, *be unannounced,* with only rare exceptions. In fact, if anybody, including an OSHA compliance officer, alerts an employer in advance of an OSHA inspection he or she can receive a fine of up to $1,000 and/or be given a six-month jail term. If an employer refuses to admit an OSHA compliance officer, or attempts to interfere with the inspection, the employer by law is subject to appropriate legal action.

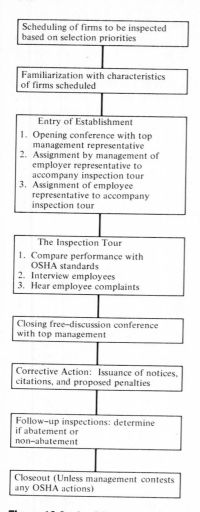

Figure 16-2 An OSHA inspection compliance operation flowchart.

Opening Conference After entering an establishment, the compliance officer asks to meet an appropriate top management representative. In a relatively rare type of situation, such as a construction worksite, the supervisor may be the only management representative on hand. In such a case the compliance officer deals with the supervisor.

The compliance officer then explains the purpose of the visit, the scope of the inspection, and the standards that apply. He will give the top management representative copies of applicable safety and health standards as well as a copy of any *employee complaint* that may be involved (the employee may or may not have filed a grievance with the supervisor; he may have sent his complaint directly to OSHA). If the employee making the complaint requests it, his or her name will not be revealed.

Selection of Employer Representative The employer will be asked to select an employer representative to accompany the compliance officer during the inspection.

Selection of an Employee Representative   Usually, an authorized representative of the employees also is given the opportunity to accompany the compliance officer. If the employees are represented by a recognized bargaining agent, the union ordinarily would designate the employee representative to accompany the compliance officer on the inspection. Similarly, if there is a plant safety committee, the employee members of that committee would ordinarily designate the employee representative.

Where neither employee groups exists, the employee representative may be selected by the employees themselves, if not by the compliance officer or top management representative. The law does not require that there be an employee representative for each inspection. However, where there is no authorized employee representative, the compliance officer *must consult with a reasonable number of employees* concerning safety and health matters in the workplace.

Step 4, The Inspection Tour   After the opening conference, the compliance officer and the representatives then proceed through the establishment, inspecting work areas for compliance with OSHA standards.

The route and duration of the inspection is determined by the compliance officer. While talking with employees, he or she makes every effort to minimize any work interruptions by avoiding peak operational time whenever possible.

The act prohibits discrimination in any way against any employee for making a complaint or for anything that an employee says or shows the compliance officer during the inspection.

Although the act gives the compliance officer full access and the right to take photos (for record purposes), make instrument readings, and examine records during the inspection, it forbids his revealing any trade secrets.

Any part or all of an establishment may be inspected, even if the inspection resulted from a specific complaint, fatality, or catastrophe.

The compliance officers inspect records of deaths, injuries, and illnesses that supervisor/managers are required to keep. They determine whether an annual summary has been posted and whether an OSHA poster is displayed. Required records of employee exposure to toxic substances and harmful physical agents are also checked.

Apparent violations may be found that can be corrected immediately. When they are corrected immediately, as is usually the case, the compliance officer records such corrections in order to help in judging management's good faith in compliance. Even though corrected, however, the apparent violations may be the basis for a citation and/or proposed penalty.

During the inspection, employees may bring to the compliance officer's attention, without receiving permission from their supervisors, any condition believed to be a violation of a standard.

Step 5, The Closing Conference   The closing conference is between the compliance officer and the top management of the firm. The Man from OSHA is charged with making this a time of free discussion of problems and needs in which frank questions and answers are encouraged. He discusses with top management what has been found during the inspection, including any apparent violations for which a citation may be issued or recommended. He does not indicate any proposed penalties. Only the OSHA area director has that authority, and only after receiving a full report.

Top management, on the other hand, may during the closing conference wish to provide information that may help OSHA determine how much time may be needed to abate (correct) an alleged violation.

Corrective Action by OSHA

After an inspection of a workplace, the OSHA area director determines what, if any, citations are to be issued to an employer and what penalties, if any, are to be proposed. Penalties can range greatly in severity. At one extreme is a simple notification (or *deminimus notice*), not a citation, that relatively slight deviations from standards exist, which would not directly affect the safety and health of employees.

At the other extreme of severity are citations for willful or repeated violations where the death of an employee is involved. For example, if top management of a firm is convicted of a willful violation that has resulted in the death of an employee, the offense is punishable by a fine of not more than $10,000 or by imprisonment for not more than six months, or by both. A second conviction for the same offense can double these penalties.

Management Responsibilities and Rights Regarding Corrective Action   Management has the right to contest a citation, abatement (correction of noncompliance) date, or proposed penalty. Cases contested by management are sent to The Independent Occupational Safety and Health Review Commission (not a part of the U.S. Department of Labor). If management is not satisfied with a ruling of that agency it may take its case through the courts, even to the U.S. Supreme Court, if it chooses. Though supervisors are usually only spectators of the top management-OSHA interface during contested citations, they may be inextricably involved, since they are located where the employee action is, and are often in a more knowledgeable position than higher levels of management.

Employee Rights Regarding Corrective Action   Employees have a great many more rights regarding OSHA noncompliance actions than we could possibly cover in this chapter. Thus we shall list only a few of the more important ones. First, employees may request an informal (anonymous if desired) conference with OSHA to discuss any issues raised by an inspection, citation, notice of proposed penalty, or notice of management's intention to contest.

Second, employees have the right to object in writing (to the OSHA area director) to the abatement time set in any citation issued to management. Third, if an inspection resulted from an employee complaint to OSHA, the employee has the right to request an informal review of any OSHA decision *not* to issue a citation. Fourth and finally, employees have the right to file a complaint with OSHA within a prescribed time if they believe they have been discriminated against, discharged, demoted, or otherwise penalized because they requested an inspection or because they exercised any other right under the act.

If OSHA determines that an employee's complaint is valid and that he or she has been discriminated against for exercising his or her rights under the act, the Secretary of Labor may bring legal action against management in the employee's behalf.

It is probably worth repeating that employees are not *responsible* to OSHA for any noncompliance or noncompliance-related infractions even though such infractions were the fault of the employees—through their own carelessness, insubordination, and similar reasons. When an employee-caused noncompliance occurs, OSHA reasons that supervisory and/or higher level management was negligent in not adequately disciplining or otherwise controlling its subordinates.

Follow-up Inspections and Closeout   The final phase of corrective action by OSHA (refer back to Figure 16-2) is a follow-up inspection of workplaces to determine whether abatement of conditions listed in notifications or citations has been accomplished, and a closeout if all required conditions have been complied with.

OSHA: OPPORTUNITIES AND PROBLEMS

Opportunities that can accrue from OSHA's administration of the provisions of the Occupational Health and Safety Act are infinite. As we discuss in the following chapter, Job Design, there is a compelling need in business and industry to more efficiently and effectively design (and maintain) equipment, work space, and lighting, air conditioning, sound, and other factors in the physical environment so that they *fit people*, rather than—as too often happens—designing such factors as hardware and then *fitting people* to the hardware, creating a potential source of safety and health hazards.

Most of the other chapters of this text are devoted to a discussion of another goal of OSHA, the efficient and effective management of subordinates' performance—including among other things their performances in practicing safety and health as an integral part of their jobs.

The *problems* faced by OSHA are also infinite. We can only briefly state that many of them are quite similar to those encountered by any new business, labor union, academic institution, or any other governmental agency that is in the birth stage of its life cycle: Lack of consumer knowledge (and interest); difficulties in securing adequate financing and budgeting (including perhaps coping with zero-based budgeting); relatively low productivity in terms of quality, quantity, time and cost; difficulties in developing efficient organization structures and in recruiting and training personnel, and so on.

Illustrations of specific major problems abound. For example, business and industry supports the social goals of OSHA but maintains that enforcement regulations are too tough (for example, freedom in making unannounced visits and in interviewing employees at random times).

Unions likewise support the goals of OSHA but maintain that enforcement is too lenient, that for example, the act provides to the employer too many phases of postponement of responsibility: employers can challenge and thus postpone enforcement of a citation through appeal in the courts, leaving the burden of possible exposure to hazards on the worker, as compared with a loss to the employer of interrupted production.

One of OSHA's greatest problems, in the experience of one of the authors, derives from the fact that much of business and industry has become far too large and complex to be understood and/or coped with by a single OSHA compliance officer making an inspection tour. Such size and complexity in organizations have brought about the need for diverse kinds of specialists working together in teams.

Where one OSHA compliance officer might be sent to analyze safety and health conditions and practices in a large, complex firm, a well-funded research program (such as has been directed by one of the authors) might provide for sending in an interdisciplinary team, comprised, for example, of a mechanical engineer, an acoustical engineer, a physician, a chemist or chemical engineer, and perhaps a psychologist and sociologist or other behavioral scientist (attitudes regarding noise, for example, are sometimes more compelling than actual db levels at higher frequencies) to make the same kind of analysis. This is discussed in the next chapter.

CONCLUSION: WHAT SHOULD THE SUPERVISOR DO ABOUT OSHA

Often the best—though sometimes the most difficult—thing the supervisor can do to get his or her house in order for OSHA is to bend with the winds of change. Generally speaking, managing people will never be the same as it has been in the past. Employees have more rights, and the supervisor has had added to his world a *new force—external to his firm*—the Man from OSHA with enforcement capabilities who can enter his workplace at will, interview his employees, and monitor his health and safety performance, as discussed above.

Another significant thing the supervisor can do is to recognize that his safety and health function is not something that is separate from his other duties. He cannot superimpose a crash OSHA-related safety and health program, for example, over a prevailing business-as-usual philosophy that has been insensitive to the health and safety needs of employees. Rather, the safety and health function is an integral part of the entire supervisory process of planning, organizing, directing, and controlling. Supervisors whose performance has generally been ineffective may have to start from scratch in order to be able to cope with the Man from OSHA.

The supervisor might well prepare his or her own specific and comprehensive checklist for assuring compliance with OSHA standards. The following brief and very general examples of considerations that might be useful in developing a supervisory self-quiz are couched in terms of the supervisory process.

Planning and Decision Making

Supervisors attempting to solve a problem may well get the habit of asking questions such as these: "Would this possible alternative solution to an existing problem be detrimental in meeting OSHA compliance regulations?" "Given that there is a question of compliance, would my superior approve (perhaps in writing) of my decision?" "Are my policies, work procedures, work methods, and rules of employee conduct as adequate as possible in helping me to meet OSHA standards?"

Organizing

In organizing his or her workforce the supervisor may ask, "Do I delegate authority and responsibility among employees so that it is clear, and without question, *who* is responsible for *what* OSHA safety and health standards?" "Are my jobs designed (this subject is discussed in the next chapter) with an eye toward meeting adequate safety and health requirements? For example, are performance requirements, equipment, work spaces, physical factors (for example, lighting, sound, and air conditioning) designed and/or maintained to the best of my ability so as to meet OSHA standards? Do I inform my supervisors (perhaps in writing, for ultimately I may be held responsible for doing so) of conditions beyond my control that I feel cannot meet OSHA standards?"

Directing

"Is my directing of employees such as to motivate them to communicate with me freely concerning safety and health standards—or might they be more likely to feel that they can gain more by communicating directly with OSHA, which protects their right to do so?"

"Do I praise good safety and health performance, counsel with and/or train employees who are poor performers, and discipline, transfer, demote, or discharge them as necessary (and if possible!) when my best motivational and training efforts do not pay off—recognizing that they are only responsible to me (not OSHA) and if they are guilty of noncompliance I am the one who will be held responsible?"

"Is my performance evaluation of subordinates based, among other things, on their safety and health attitude, effort, and performance?"

Controlling

"In controlling my employees do I ensure that OSHA standards and regulations are publicized (my firm will be advised by OSHA if I even fail to display an OSHA poster), known, understood, and within the power and capability of my employees to enforce them?"

"Do I have effective *means of comparing the performance* of my subordinates with health and safety standards, such as: standardized and random observations and inspections of their behavior; productive performance evaluation meetings; adequate training and/or retraining feedback data and so on?"

"Do I promptly and efficiently apply corrective action measures when performance of subordinates does not comply with OSHA regulations, as mentioned above, and keep *meaningful records* of counseling sessions, disciplinary measures, training and retraining, and so forth?" The personnel folders of employees commonly contain little information of any value whatsoever in helping the supervisor solve many kinds of significant problems such as: "What background data do I have to refer to when grievances are filed on me; when I must decide who deserves to fill a promotion opening; or when I must respond to my superiors who advise me that OSHA has filed a complaint involving safety and health in my department?"

In the experience of one of the authors involving interviewing thousands of employees for promotions over an eleven-state area, a lack of available, useful background and performance data regarding employees interviewed is one of the most frustrating and exasperating problems. An interview without written background data can sometimes be less than useless; often there is an inverse correlation between an employee's ability to sell himself or herself (or to verbally present a grievance) and his or her capability, dedication, and efficiency and effectiveness in performance.

QUESTIONS

1 An employee is deliberately insubordinate in violating a supervisor's specific and known safety rule, causing a serious safety and health hazard which also violates an OSHA standard. The firm receives a citation for this happening. To what extent is the employee responsible to OSHA for the noncompliance? To what extent is the supervisor responsible to OSHA for the noncompliance?

2 OSHA has been termed by some a labor-oriented law. Do you agree? Why or why not?

3 To what extent can subordinates of a supervisor go over his or her head and complain directly to OSHA of unsafe working conditions at their workplaces?

4 Do OSHA compliance officers have a legal right to enter a firm unannounced and proceed directly to a workplace and start interviewing employees? Explain.

5 To what extent can an employee file a complaint to OSHA that a compliance officer was wrong in reporting to management that the employee's workplace was safe?

6 What records concerning your subordinates would you consider important in developing and maintaining so as to aid you in better coping with any adverse report that an OSHA compliance officer might make concerning conditions and performances in your workplace?

NOTES

1 For a well-researched discussion of OSHA's concept of the rights of women in the work force, see "Women Workers and Job Health Hazards," reprinted from *Job Safety and Health Magazine,* U.S. Department of Labor Occupational Safety and Health Administration, vol. 3, no. 4, April 1975.

2 For more detail on the purpose of the act, see the act itself, *Public Law 91-596,* 91st Congress, S.2193, Dec. 29, 1970, (Washington, D.C.: U.S. Government Printing Office: 19730-522-085).

3 For a discussion of this and related subjects, see "Questions and Answers to Part

1910," (The OSHA General Industry Standards), Washington, D.C.: U.S. Department of Labor, Occupational Safety and Health Administration.

4 This is reported in *Man and Manager, Inc.,* OSHA Report, New York, N.Y., *Q-1231,* Apr. 1, 1977.

5 For a well-written discussion of this problem, see Richard E. Gallagher, "Setting Priorities for NIOSH Research," *Monthly Labor Review,* vol. 98/3, pp. 41–43, March 1975.

6 A discussion of "feasibility" as a criterion is included in "OSHA News Briefs Policy," *Job Safety and Health,* U.S. Department of Labor, Occupational Safety and Health Administration, February 1977.

7 For an excellent, well-written, comprehensive description of the OSHA inspection process see, "OSHA Inspections," U.S. Department of Labor, Occupational Safety and Health Administration, June 1975.

CASES

The first of the two cases for this chapter involves some aspects of the subject covered in this chapter. The questions at the end of the case raise some important and difficult considerations which one sometimes has to face in such instances.

The second case raises an issue dealt with in cases included elsewhere in this book, namely, "work" by foremen. In this instance, however, there are apparently repeated violations of the agreement. Management admits the errors and "counsels" the foremen involved, but the violations continue. What should the employees do now?

CASE 16-1

The Company manufactures and distributes ready-mixed concrete. A problem it encounters from time to time at its Springdale plant is the breaking of a conveyer belt to which large buckets are attached. This conveyer takes crushed stone from the ground level to a screen room about 80 feet off the ground. When the belt breaks, the two sides of the belt and their respective buckets fall in a heap at the bottom of the shaft. Getting the ends of the belt up to the top where they can be rejoined is not a minor undertaking. Fortunately, however, this operation has to be carried out only infrequently, perhaps on the average of once in eighteen months.

Ordinarily this task is accomplished by stationing two winch trucks some 50 feet from the building, attaching cables to the end of the belt to be lifted first, and running the cables over pulleys fastened to the roof of the room where the screens are located. When one end has been pulled up and secured, the other is then raised. In addition to the winch-truck drivers there are usually three employees on the ground level and three in the screen room who carry out these repairs.

Sidney Lynch is a mechanic who works for the Company at the Edgefield plant. (He formerly worked at Springdale.) He is a good, "all-round" workman with some five years with the Company and a good record as far as performance, attendance, discipline, etc. are concerned.

Lynch was asked on Friday if he would volunteer for overtime at Springdale on Saturday, and he agreed. Nothing was said to him about the broken conveyer.

When work began on Saturday morning, Lynch was assigned (along with Mechanic Granger and Laborer Yates) to the screen room. The workers on the ground had difficulty in getting the cables to stay attached to the first end of the belt they attemped to raise. Indeed they twice got it started up the shaft only to have the cables come loose and the belt and its buckets fall again to the floor. By 9:30 A.M., however, one end of the belt had been raised and attached to some holding clamps at the top.

Granger, however, did not return from the 9:30 break, having been given what Lynch was told was an "emergency assignment" in another plant. (Yates incidentally had been with the Company less than three months and had never seen the conveyer before.) Lynch had been a member of the ground crew the only previous time he helped repair the conveyer.

Lynch protested vigorously what he took to be the undermanning of the screen room, especially in view of Yates's inexperience. He and Foreman Brown had some rather sharp words, after which Brown ordered him back to the tower.

Raising the other half of the conveyer proved to be even more difficult. Not only did the clamps pull out of the belt once or twice, but as it was coming up the shaft it suddenly became stuck. In order to free it Lynch was required to look down into the shaft with his head just below the pulleys through which the cables ran to the winch trucks. He freed the belt once, only to find it stuck again almost immediately.

At this point Lynch felt (or at least said he felt) genuine fear, including the possibility of decapitation if one of the pulleys broke as he was looking into the shaft. Just as the belt became stuck the second time he happened to be looking toward the winch trucks and saw the rear wheels of one come off the ground (some 2 feet, he thought) and the other slide toward the tower a like amount, and he also felt the tower shake "real bad" [his words].

Lynch immediately "hit the stairs." Brown saw him as he reached the ground floor, dismissed his fears as not only groundless but actually faked, and again ordered him back to the tower. Lynch protested and asked for assignment to another job or at least for another mechanic, but Brown refused, warning him that failure to return to the tower would be insubordination. Lacking any other assignment, Lynch went home. He was suspended when he came to work on Monday and terminated on Tuesday.

The tower in question is about twenty years old. It is made of exposed structural steel, which has rusted a great deal. In the grievance hearings Lynch asserted he had for some time been afraid of the collapse of the tower. The Company dismissed all his fears as not only without merit but as being deliberate pretense.

Subsequent to his discharge Lynch requested an OSHA investigation of the entire operation including the condition of the tower. Accounts of the subsequent investigation differ, the Union asserting that immediately upon arrival the OSHA investigator was taken to lunch by the plant manager and the operating superintendent. It also asserts that the former had designated one of the older leadmen (who, while a long-time member of the bargaining unit, was not and never had been a member of the Union) as the workers' representative.

The Company asserts the investigator arrived at noon and that common courtesy suggested an invitation for him to eat lunch in the Company cafeteria. Furthermore it contended that there was no discussion of any safety matters during the meal, and that the investigator himself selected the leadman from a list of all the employees furnished him by the Personnel Department. Lynch, of course, was not in the plant; it later developed that he was out of the state on a lengthy trip. The investigator eventually concluded that the tools, machines, materials, and methods used in the conveyer repair were well within approved safety limits.

What should an arbitrator do with this case? Surely if Lynch was only faking his fears it would be unfortunate if he were restored to his job. On the other hand, an employer has no right to require an employee to put his safety in undue jeopardy. What should be the disposition of the case if Lynch erroneously but yet with complete sincerity believed he was in danger, especially in what he held to be an undermanned situation? (The Company also denied the need for anyone else in the tower, asserting that frequently it used only a mechanic and a helper in the screen room.)

CASE 16-2

The incidents of this case took place in the warehouse of the Company and involve little dispute as to the facts. While a crew of employees was procuring materials and preparing them for shipment, Elton Weber, the foreman, spent some time in "making" boxes, that is, in folding the sheet of corrugated paperboard from which each box is cut into proper form and gluing it. Both Management and the Union agree that making boxes is bargaining-unit work and that Weber's action was a violation of the labor contract, which prohibits managers from doing such work. Weber's testimony was that he spent ten to fifteen minutes in making fifteen to twenty boxes. Others thought the time involved was much longer, up to 1½ hours being cited by one person.

Sarah White, the job steward for the warehouse, filed a grievance for 1½ hours of pay at overtime rates, alleging that as the eligible packer, she should have been held over to do the work in question. The Company denied the grievance on the ground that (1) the amount of work—ten minutes—was minimal and of no consequence and (2) if Weber had not made the boxes someone in the crew would have done so by the end of the shift. It did, however, agree to instruct Weber to refrain from such activities in the future.

It turns out, however, that there have been a number of other similar incidents recently. Each time the Company has agreed to "speak to" the foreman involved but has denied any monetary remedy on the grounds mentioned above. Additionally, the Company points out that all foremen are "up from the ranks" and have trouble "keeping their hands off the work."

Ms. White is determined to put a stop to this activity, and at her urging the Union takes the grievance to arbitration, where it argues that because the foremen had formerly been workers they may be held all the more responsible when they do what they must know is bargaining-unit work.

What is the proper disposition of the case? If the arbitrator concludes that it is indeed unlikely that White or any other worker was deprived of overtime, might he or she fashion a remedy that awards some amount of money to the Union as opposed to any individual? How far can he or she go in giving orders to or disciplining a foreman? Or should the grievance be dismissed and the incident forgotten, at least until or unless a more serious breach of contract occurs?

·

*OSHA inspectors must now produce a search warrant if an employer refuses to consent to an inspection of a workplace.

The Supreme Court struck down that portion of the Occupational Safety and Health Act that permitted inspectors to conduct warrantless searches. It held that the constitution's protection against unreasonable searches applies to commercial property as well as homes.

However, just how serious the impact of this change may be on both employers and OSHA inspectors may not be known for a long time. For example, the court has also said that OSHA inspectors do not have to prove full "probable cause" before getting a search warrant, but only that the search is part of a general enforcement.

This subject is discussed in *U.S. News and World Report,* Vol. LXXXIV, #22, June 5, 1978.

Chapter 17

Job Design: Improving Job Content, Methods of Work, and the Work Environment

THE ROLE OF PEOPLE

People are the dominant, and often the most complex, element in job design. This is true in spite of the impact on jobs of great advances in computer and other facets of automation technology. Among the major problems in designing jobs for people are, first, that, as discussed in previous chapters, people have psychological, physiological, and sociological characteristics which define both their capabilities and their limitations in the work situation. Second, these characteristics are not fixed but vary from individual to individual, and from time to time with respect to each individual. Third, it is usually extremely difficult to determine whether the behavior of an individual at any particular time is due to physiological, psychological, or sociological stimuli.

The existence of problems such as these does not mean that we cannot make predictions about human behavior in order to aid us in designing jobs, but it does mean that there are difficulties (frequently formidable ones) in doing so, necessitating considerable expertise on the part of the supervisor.

We shall now discuss, first, the overall objectives of job design, followed by a discussion of some of the more important specific objectives.

OVERALL OBJECTIVES OF JOB DESIGN

The overall objectives of job design from a research viewpoint are frequently considered to be increased productivity and employee satisfaction.

Despite the importance of these two objectives to the success of the supervisor, however, a great many studies indicate that there may be little or no significant correlation between them (refer especially to Chapters 5, 19, and 20).

Productivity we define as a *ratio of acceptable output to input* or, in terms of our discussion, the acceptable output per person/hour (or person/minute, person/day, and so on) of input (acceptable output/input).

Productivity would be increased, for example, if an output of 20 units of work per 30 person-hours was increased to 30 units of work per 30 person-hours (20/30 increased to 30/30—a productivity increase of 33½ percent).

It is quite fallacious to think of productivity simply as the *amount* of output. An increase in output *could* decrease productivity—if, for example, an output of 20 units of work per 30 person-hours were increased to 30 units of work per 60 person-hours. Productivity would *decrease* by ⅙ or 16.6 percent (20/30 versus 30/60).

Output of any amount can be of zero productivity unless it is acceptable by higher level management. Four major factors involved in the acceptability of output are quality, quantity, time, and cost (see Chapter 4). It is important for the supervisor to remember that, first, all these factors must be considered in designing or redesigning jobs and, second, any one or more of them may be—by directives from higher management—predominant at any specific point in time. For example, it may seem highly desirable to increase constantly the quality of output of, say, electronic components. However, meeting extremely high criteria of *quality* of output may at some point disproportionately increase *costs,* both of labor and of machinery. Therefore the supervisor may be required simply to improve the quality of output the best he or she can within the limitations of prescribed allowable costs.

As another illustration, the amount of *time* allowed the supervisor to achieve a certain *quantity* of output may be predominant—for example, a customer *must* have a certain output by a certain time even though the supervisor may be forced to subordinate *quality* and *cost.*

SPECIFIC OBJECTIVES OF JOB DESIGN

Among the more important *specific* objectives of job design are to: (1) improve job content, (2) provide safe and healthy workplaces, (3) design equipment to *fit people,* (4) design an optimal work environment, and (5) design efficient and effective work methods.

The Content of Jobs

There is relatively little in the way of principles or guides to aid us in determining optimal job *content.* There are a number of general principles such as "tasks should be grouped into jobs on the basis of their similarity" (see Chapter 4 for other principles) which can be of value. However, we frequently do not even consciously design the *kinds* of work tasks that comprise jobs. Job content is frequently, rather, the result of limitations imposed by such things as product or service designs, machine designs, layouts, output quotas, pacing effects, and job evaluation and other efforts to make skill requirements uniform within jobs.

Safety and Health

Of the many and varied problems relating to persons working in business, industry, and the government, accidents and job-related illnesses are one of the most costly in terms of productivity and human well-being, as discussed in Chapter 16. Thus, the supervisor's goal of achieving and administering optimal working conditions and practices is economically as well as sociologically urgent.[1]

In recent years research and experience have repeatedly shown that both the skillful supervision of *people* as well as the skillful design of *things* such as equipment, layout, physical conditions, and work methods (all discussed below) can do much to eliminate or reduce accidents and unhealthy practices and working conditions.

However, looking realistically at the problem of safety and health, it is important for the supervisor to remember that the development and supervision of people and things to achieve safe and healthy work conditions may be limited by any one or more of the major factors involved in output discussed above—quality, quantity, time, and cost.

Designing work tasks that comprise jobs so that health and safety conditions are improved *may* increase *quality* and/or *quantity of output* (and also worker satisfaction). However, it can in some cases be exceptionally (even prohibitively) *costly.* The factor of cost (and time) especially is frequently overlooked in much of the literature on supervision that describes "how it should be done" and neglects to state "how it is."

The problems of safety and health are inherent in problems discussed—the design of equipment, the physical environment, and work methods.

The Design of Equipment

The supervisor has traditionally had little to do with the original design of equipment (and the work environment discussed next) even though the completed design is of critical importance to his or her performance. The design of equipment and of working conditions so that they will be most suitable for human beings assigned to perform work tasks is commonly the major responsibility of a group of professional staff personnel commonly called *human engineers.*

The term *human engineering,* however, does not include all the professions involved in performing this function. Not only various kinds of engineers, (for example, electrical, industrial, and mechanical) but psychologists and other professions such as medicine and physics contribute a body of important principles and practices.

For example, an interdisciplinary research contract directed by one of the authors to analyze the impact of incoming semiautomated equipment and the working environment on workers in a large organization included: two medical doctors (one an internationally known hearing specialist); an illumination engineer (analysis of lighting); a mechanical engineer (analysis of equipment design); an acoustical engineer (to design quieter environment); a chemical engineer (analyze air content for pollutants); and a psychologist and sociologist (analysis of attitudes).[2]

To illustrate the advantages of designing equipment to fit people, the improvement of the legibility and accessibility of dials and keyboards on machines operated by people might help increase reading accuracy and consequently reduce errors. The design of tools that better fit the contours of the hand might help increase the speed and precision with which they are used. To use an illustration in the field of public administration, the proper positioning of communication and other devices on the dashboard of a police squad car might increase the speed and accuracy of performing routine and emergency duties.

Design of the Work Environment

Can productivity be influenced by altering the work environment? It is logical to believe that people naturally prefer pleasant surroundings. This may or may not mean that to satisfy this preference is to ensure increases in productivity.

Exploratory research such as in the Hawthorne experiments (see Chapter 19) showed no definite relationship between changes in the work environment and productivity. However, the problem was not extensively studied at that time, and certainly the research done since provides no basis for dismissing working conditions as unimportant. Quite the contrary, extensive studies in the subsequent four decades by engineers, psychologists, physicians, and others in the United States and abroad indicate that the work environment may be very important to the health, safety satisfaction, and efficiency of workers.

Although much research remains to be done in this area, it is widely believed that deficiencies in physical conditions of work may significantly contribute to supervisory problems of recruitment, turnover, absenteeism, accidents, and lowered productivity.

For example, studies indicate that shop or office operations, when performed over extended time periods, may produce "psychological fatigue" with such effects as lapses of attention, lowering of work standards, and an increased probability of errors. Any stressing factors in environmental working conditions may tend to accelerate the onset of this psychological fatigue. Therefore, attention to improve the work environment may make it possible to reduce or exclude distracting features, contribute to worker comfort, and help to protect employees from health hazards caused by such environmental stresses.

We shall now briefly discuss three important factors in the work environment of supervisors and their workers: lighting, noise, and atmospheric conditions. It should be noted that a major criterion for evaluating working conditions is efficiency and effectiveness in task performance. Two other criteria instrumental in achieving task effectiveness are values in their own right: first, employees must experience acceptance and satisfaction in their work; and second, the physical and psychological health and welfare of employees must be provided for.

Lighting   In analyzing the lighting environment of the workplace, the first consideration is simple intensity of illumination. What criteria to use in measuring sufficient or "ideal" illumination has been the subject of controversy for many years. A procedure developed by Dr. H. R. Blackwell at Ohio State University, who has cooperated with one of the authors in illumination research, has received wide acceptance and has been adopted by the Illuminating Engineering Society (IES) as the basis for establishing illumination standards.[3] This procedure, which compares actual visual tasks with standard laboratory tasks through the use of various optical devices, facilitated the development of illumination standards for selected types of situations and tasks. For example, 100 footcandles (fc) is the recommended illumination for garage repair areas and for general office work; 30 fc for store circulation areas; and 1000 fc in extra-fine assembly areas. These recommended standards of the IES are now readily available to the public. Should the supervisor feel that poor lighting is an adverse factor in his section's performance, a simple comparison of the work-site illumination with the recommended standards should substantiate or refute his concern.

One study conducted by one of the authors relates to results of improved illumination in the Richmond, Virginia, post office. An 8 percent increase in mail-handling operations accompanied a general facility remodeling, including the replacement of incandescent fixtures (10 fc) with fluorescent fixtures (45 to 50 fc). This and companion and subsequent tests in other postal facilities were used as the basis for setting illumination standards in post offices throughout the country.

In addition to increased productivity, beneficial side effects may be generated by improved illumination. The Allis-Chalmers Manufacturing Company, for example, reported a 43 percent decrease in its accident rate after an illumination increase and painting (to get a more favorable brightness ratio) in an assembly shop.

These and other studies indicate that the supervisor may increase productivity and worker comfort and reduce accidents simply by improving the *intensity* of illumination at the workplace. It is equally important, however, to know that intensity is only a part of (and even sometimes not the most important part of) illumination. Other factors such as *glare, light distribution,* and *reflectants* have an extremely important effect on the adequacy of illumination for a particular task.

Noise   Noise is often regarded as a distractor (even as a "pollutant") and is therefore thought to interfere with work efficiency. The state of the knowledge of engineering, physiology, and other sciences is such that we know one thing with certainty regarding the effect of noise at the workplace, and this is of critical importance to supervisors: *Noises above certain levels and especially in the higher frequencies can, over extended periods of time, permanently damage hearing.* However, estimates of that critical level vary from a minimum "zero damage risk level" of 80 decibels (db), advocated by Dr. Aram Glorig,[4] up to, generally, 85 db. (It is to be emphasized at the outset that a db reading with a simple db meter is not a valid measure of sound. The db reading must be coupled with a reading of the sound frequency. Our discussion relates to db readings in the higher frequencies— which can be relatively harmful to people.)

A main problem is that *physical scientists have little or nothing to say about the effect of sound levels lower than this* on a worker's efficiency and satisfaction. We must look to contributions from behavioral scientists for theories regarding this subject because noise at various lower levels may or may not be fatiguing, for example, depending on the attitude of individuals and groups regarding such noise levels.

A pooling of knowledge by physical and social scientists has resulted in the development of sophisticated acoustical techniques for the sound-treating of work areas in order to reduce the irritating or dangerous effects of noise. A frequently heard cliché is, "A worker can be isolated from any unwanted noise if we have unlimited funds." This points up a recurring problem we have mentioned before. Many of our efforts to take affirmative action in contributing to the dignity and worth of individuals such as optimizing conditions at the workplace may be doomed because they cost too much (for example, a drop hammer room in a factory, or offices in airport sites).

Noise does not, of course, have the same effect on all workers and on all kinds of jobs. For example, a Defense Department study[5] concluded that noise will cause poorer performance when sustained effort is required and the task is not intrinsically challenging. Further, the study agrees with other studies that conclude that noise primarily affects higher mental processes.

Another study revealed that unpredictable noise results in a decrease in performance efficiency on the subsidiary task. Performance on the primary task, however, was unaffected by either predictable or unpredictable noise.[6]

Atmospheric Conditions   Our consideration of atmospheric conditions that may affect productivity will be limited primarily to temperature and humidity, with a brief mention of air circulation. These three factors are all involved in determining an *effective temperature.* The latter term is defined by the American Society of Heating, Refrigerating and Air Conditioning Engineers (ASHRAE) as "an arbitrary index which combines into a single value the effect of temperature, humidity, and air movement on the sensation of warmth or cold felt by the human body. The numerical value is that of the temperature of still, saturated air which would induce an identical sensation."[7] We are therefore concerned primarily with the impact of *effective* temperature on workers, rather than simply temperature. The latter is commonly and inadequately used as a sole measure of atmospheric conditions surrounding a workplace.

A major complicating problem in developing criteria for temperature at the workplace is that as temperatures vary, other conditions such as humidity do not remain constant. Therefore, closely controlled tests are required to isolate the particular factor being studied.

One study analyzed the importance of *humidity* in combination with high temperature as a factor limiting performance. For example, the task was found to be "relatively easy" with the existence of a 100 percent relative humidity (RH) and up to 92.5 degrees F.

However, at 30 to 40 percent RH, work continued on the "easy" scale with higher temperatures, up to 120 degrees F. In another manual task, 220 foot-pounds of work were accomplished at 80 degrees F. effective temperature. The amount of work was reduced to 60 foot-pounds when the effective temperature was raised to 100 degrees F.

Studies also indicate that highly skilled workers are not normally affected as much by high "effective temperatures" as unskilled workers (who require more effort to complete a given task). Also, high-pay incentives tend to retard the rate of output decrease in many cases studied.

Air circulation (as imagined by workers) was shown to be an important productivity factor in one study conducted by one of the authors.[8] While a post office building in Austin, Texas, had no windows, it was conditioned to control temperature, humidity, and air circulation. The ceiling height of 50 feet caused the air vents to be located far enough away from the workers to prevent them from feeling a breeze (ideally, air movement should be such that it is *not felt* by workers). Complaints persisted and productivity declined until tissue streamers were fastened to the ventilators so that the workers could *see* that the air was moving.

This study brings out a very important facet of environmental control and the larger subject of overall working conditions: Unless the workers *believe* that working conditions are favorable, management is usually "spinning its wheels" and wasting money on elaborate schemes to improve working conditions. Human feelings, despite almost overwhelming difficulties in analyzing them sometimes, can never be ignored in technical approaches to job improvement.[8]

The Environment as a System

A complicating situation for a supervisor is that workers are rarely exposed to merely a single environmental stress such as lighting, noise, or air conditioning. More typically, they are exposed to some combination of stresses, such as poor lighting against a background of noise. Therefore, no one environmental factor can successfully be considered as influencing work performance to the exclusion of all others. This leads us to a restatement of systems theory discussed at several points previously. The work environment may be thought of as a system composed of such subsystems as noise, illumination, and effective temperature. These subsystems are interrelated in such a way that the effect of any one of them on a worker can influence his or her conception of all the others. In other words, if the noise in a certain task area is especially severe, an employee may be much more sensitive, as a result, to inadequate lighting. On the other hand, if lighting and the effective temperature are adequate, the employee may withstand a much higher noise level without a significant increase in the degree of annoyance.

Human Adaptability

One factor seems to recur throughout most studies of the effects on workers of lighting, noise, and atmospheric conditions. People seem to be capable of adjusting in some instances with proper motivation, to almost unbelievably poor environmental conditions. This reinforces our discussion of the value of motivation as a supervisory skill. However, we must not overlook the point that this adaptability has a built-in danger. Employees may perform productively and even happily under illumination conditions that may damage their eyesight, noise conditions that may cost them normal hearing, and harmful atmospheric conditions that may subject them to serious disorders.

This social problem must be recognized by the supervisor. The economic aspects of the situation are also important because satisfied workers may actually find their productivity decreasing as their health is adversely affected by their work environment. Economic costs, in addition to decreased production, include medical costs, increased insurance rates, turnover, costs to train new employees, and so on.

In spite of the complexities of the situation, however, we must acknowledge the importance to productivity and worker satisfaction of work methods and the work environment. It must be remembered that the best kind of supervision may be of little or no value under intolerable methods and conditions of work.

Design of Work Methods: Role of Work Simplification

Having discussed the design of work content, equipment, and physical working conditions we now turn to a consideration of the problem of designing an effective method of accomplishing work. The method we have selected is referred to as *work simplification.* It is important to recognize that work simplification is more than a technique or set of how-to-do-its. It is also, and possibly more important, a philosophy or way of thinking, namely, that there is "always a better way."

To place the concept of work simplification in perspective, it can be said that there are two major ways of increasing productivity, or output per person-hour. First, it may be increased by *mechanization* or *automation,* typically a function of human engineers discussed above. However, the state of our knowledge is such that not all kinds of human activity can be duplicated by machines. Also, a great deal of work is of limited duration or intermittent in nature and may not justify the expense of installing machinery.

A second way may broadly be termed *methods improvement.* It consists simply of *improving the existing methods of work* employed by humans. Though far less publicized than the application of mechanization and automation, methods improvement has played and will continue to play a vital role in increasing productivity.

Methods improvement may be defined generally as any change made in the way work is accomplished that results in lower cost, better quality, or both. The process of methods improvement is known by many names and takes many forms, ranging from a relatively simple technique called *Job Methods Training* (discussed in Chapter 11) to the advanced techniques of a centralized industrial engineering staff. Techniques for improving methods go by such titles as *Job Methods Training, time and motion study, motion economy, operations analysis,* or *work simplification.*

Thus work simplification is a technique for identifying and eliminating the uneconomical employment of time, equipment, materials, space, or human effort. Professor Erwin H. Schell of the Massachusetts Institute of Technology is credited with coining the term to describe an improvement program, devised by Allan H. Mogensen, in which every member of a business organization can participate. It is not a new concept, but rather a new combination of concepts and principles. Mogensen's contribution was to simplify the complex technical field of industrial engineering, especially the technique of time and motion study, so that it could be applied to problems in a practical way by supervisors and employees without extensive technical training.

Work simplification differs from time and motion study basically in that it commonly does not involve the setting of performance standards by time study, does not involve the use of the motion picture camera to study human movements in slow motion (termed micromation study), and does not include work sampling or similar statistical or mathematical techniques that are used in time and motion studies. Another distinctive difference is that the responsibility for applying work-simplification techniques, due to their simplicity, can be decentralized to the supervisory and worker levels. The complexity of time and motion study, on the other hand, normally precludes its performance by any other than a centralized staff of industrial engineers or similar specialists.

The Problem of Introducing Change   An important problem of work simplification that the supervisor must cope with is that of making change more palatable to workers. A widely accepted hypothesis regarding human behavior is that workers can be expected to resist any change made in their customary work methods. However, contrary to this common management assumption, there is mounting evidence that people may like to change and may not mind criticism, especially if they make the changes and criticisms themselves and do not view them as especially threatening.

A conventional way of increasing the productivity of workers has been either for the supervisors personally to develop better work methods for their subordinates or, more commonly, for specialized staff experts, such as production or methods engineers, to perform this function. Both methods appear to be encountering increasing resistance from the worker of today because, among other things, they require him or her to play a passive role and thus to have little or no voice in making the changes.

Why do workers commonly resist change? One reason is that it is a comfortable feeling for the worker to be complacent, to feel that "all is right with the world." When he or she fears that this comfortable state of affairs may be disturbed or terminated, he is likely to act promptly to attempt to restore it. New ideas and methods often seem to pose a threat to this serenity. The individual's first reaction commonly is fear, fear that one may lose power, prestige, or face, that in the unknown future his needs will not be satisfied, or not satisfied as well as they were in the known past. Thus when our world is threatened, we develop behavior to cope with it.

Often this creates human problems that may exceed the technical problems involved in improving work methods, and if these problems are not solved, they can lead to failure for the undertaking. Furthermore, one problem that often appears when employees are subjected to a change is that they retaliate with considerable aggression. The person or persons responsible for the change may be attacked openly or covertly. Sometimes careless or sloppy work appears and steadily increases. Employees may simply display indifference or apathy, or they may restrict output or strike back more openly with absenteeism, tardiness, and turnover.

Such behavior often results from employees' efforts to satisfy needs that are important to them. These needs motivate them to behave in a way that will lead them to achieve their personal goals. If a person is interested *only* in attaining a personal goal which is important to him, he quickly determines the minimum that he has to do to attain it, and does just this, usually at the expense of achieving the organizational goal.

The *social group* of which the individual is a part also has an impact upon him when he is faced with a change in work methods. The change often affects established ways of doing things with the group. This causes the group to reinforce the feeling of insecurity of the individual and further complicates the supervisor's problem of introducing change.

One other explanation for the problem of introducing change in work methods needs to be examined. It is hypothesized by some that very few people are creative. To the extent that this is true it can present a double problem. First, few employees can be expected to recognize problems even when they are trained to do so. Second, even if creative solutions to problems are developed, the problem of securing acceptance of them by untrained, unimaginative, and uncreative persons may be insurmountable.

Acceptance of Work Changes   Work simplification is founded on a number of principles of successfully introducing changes in work methods. First, every effort should be made to provide employees with the reasons for any changes in their work methods. This information should come not from, or certainly not *only* from, informal channels of communications, which are frequently inaccurate, but from management itself. Second, the workers should know, if possible, that the change is good for them, or at least that it will not harm them. Third, it is important that the workers be sold on the change, because it generally requires new behavior on their part. Fourth, individuals and groups should participate in a change in their work methods, if at all feasible, so that it may be considered at least to an extent *their* change, one they will identify with and help make a success. When this happens, the change tends to become something they *do*, rather than something that *is done to them.*

In other words, work simplification is based on the concept that at least frequently everyone in an organization should participate in the process of improving methods of work, each to the extent of his ability. It recognizes that workers as well as supervisors and higher management have ideas for change. Day to day they run into problems and get ideas on how things can be improved. Some of these ideas are wild and some are sound, but all too often, nobody asks for their ideas. We know comments like this occur often: "Our supervisor thinks she's the only one with any ideas around here"; or often with good reason, "There's no use trying to do better work; our supervisor is only interested in his own advancement—he doesn't care about any contributions we can make to the success of the company"; or "I often wonder if things *have* to be done this way. It looks so wasteful. Doesn't anybody care?"

Some workers think their supervisors do not want things changed. They are afraid their supervisors will think subordinates are after their jobs, and therefore they will not make any constructive suggestions without being asked. Other workers do not open up at all, though they may do a great deal of talking among themselves.

What Should the Supervisor's Attitude Be?   Obviously, it would pay little dividends simply for the supervisor continuously to ask workers for ideas on how to improve things, or just occasionally putting on a "drive" to collect them. (Many cost-reduction "drives" fail because of this approach.) The supervisor can, however, help workers express their ideas naturally, little by little, day by day. The essential thing is to be sensitive to possibilities, approach problems by helping workers to solve them, and to be willing to listen to and seriously consider the ideas of their subordinates.

Of course, there are some situations in which workers won't seem interested in identifying and exploring problems. They won't come up with ideas for improvement. The work group may be so new and its individuals so green that they have no information or thinking to contribute; or they may be so insecure because of poor leadership in the past that they're afraid to stick out their necks in any direction. In such situations, a supervisor's best approach is to be gently but firmly directive in identifying the need for methods improvement. As supervisors initiate action, they will find small ways in which they can get creative expression from their workers. Gradually they will frequently be able to get them to identify and explore larger problems with them. Such an approach may not only reveal better ways of doing things, but also build teamwork. As supervisors gradually get their workers to work together on such problems, they will tend to relate to each other more and feel that the work they do is more worthwhile and purposeful.

We now turn to a discussion of (1) the basic steps in work simplification, (2) analysis of work process, (3) analysis of work flow, and (4) analysis of work methods.

The Basic Steps in Work Simplification

Approached from one point of view, work simplification may be described as consisting of a sequence of steps. It is to be noted that a body of knowledge exists to support a systematic approach to the performance of each step. The steps are: (1) select a job to improve, (2) record the details of the present method, (3) analyze the present method, and (4) develop a better way.

Select a Job to Improve   It is easy to see that deciding what operation, process, or task needs to be improved can be the hardest part of work simplification. The things that need improvement are not always apparent. It is easy to walk by the same bad situation day after day without seeing it. Paradoxically, work methods that need to be improved are often overlooked simply because employees are too familiar with their work and are accustomed to seeing it performed improperly.

A realistic approach as discussed above is to recognize that *most* processes or tasks or procedures can be improved. Some can be studied over and over, with significant improvements resulting each time. It must also be recognized that all factors in any situation are constantly changing. People change with training, age, composition of their work groups, and many other factors. New tools, accounting systems, materials, and machines are constantly being developed. Supervisors who close their eyes to the forces that are obsoleting their jobs and those of subordinates are courting obsolescence of their own work skills.

Thus this first step involves the development of creative thinking by supervisors and their subordinates. Creative thinking is usually described as a process that enables one to achieve imaginative answers. Sometimes it refers simply to the application of ingenuity. Nearly everyone can be more creative than is generally acknowledged, but our traditional preoccupation with the practical side of life, with its stern demands for conformity at every turn, all too frequently stifles the development of ideas.

There are many clues to inefficient work methods. Basically the job to work on, from a work-simplification viewpoint, is the one where work is repetitive, where too much time is spent in performing simple work, where there are bottlenecks and backlogs of unfinished work, and where an undue amount of time and effort is spent gathering and organizing paper work, tools, materials, and other work needs. Tasks involving many employees may also offer work-simplification possibilities. The more often a particular kind of work is performed, the greater the possibilities of savings from improvements. That is, any savings that are made can be multiplied by the number of times the work is done each day, week, or month.

Record the Details of Work   A second step is to determine and record every detail of the operation, process, or task in the sequence in which it occurs. This step is fundamental to all efforts to improve any kind of work. It is essential that a determination be made of the way work is being done to provide a point of departure for determining what improvements may be possible.

In describing the way work is being performed it is helpful to remember that there are three phases to every job. In work-simplification terminology, there must be, first, a *make-ready phase.* This entails assembling materials, setting up equipment, or arranging for personnel to do the job. Second, there must be a *do operation,* which is the actual accomplishment of the work to be done. Third, there must be a *put-away* or *clean-up phase.*

An analysis of the make-ready, do, and put-away parts of a job may facilitate the questioning of details that may affect the total process. The amount of detail needed will vary with the kind of work to be analyzed. However, an important point to remember is that seemingly trivial details are often of critical importance in developing an improved method.

Analyze the Details   A third step in the process of work simplification is to analyze the details of work. This step is based on the premise that a systematic exploration of the best way is more dependable than past or present practice, haphazard inventiveness, or cleverness.

In analyzing the details of work it is helpful to remember that an immediate improvement will result if the make-ready and put-away time and effort are reduced. Thus, concentration on these aspects first might be most immediately productive. A moment's reflection by almost anyone will serve to provide an illustration of this point from past experience. For example, students are likely to spend an excessive amount of time *making ready* to study for an assignment. By the time a workplace is cleared and writing and reference materials are located, assembled, and positioned, perhaps little time is left for the *do* part of work before an interruption such as a coffee break occurs.

Perhaps some *put-away* is required, even though work will be resumed later. When work is resumed, some degree of *make-ready* will again be required depending upon the length of the interruption. Probably the same thing—spending more time on *make-ready* and *put-away* than the *do* part of work—happens in thousands of shops and offices daily as executives, clerks, and others struggle with the complex problem of most effectively planning their personal time.

Each detail of work may be analyzed by asking these six questions: Why is it necessary? What is its purpose? Where should it be performed and why? When should it be done and why? Who should do it and why? How should it be accomplished and why?

Develop a Better Way   A final step is to develop a better way. Clues to finding a better way often result from answers to the six questions listed above. A formula recommended for systematically processing such answers is as follows: First, attention should always be directed toward the possibilities of *eliminating* unnecessary tasks or portions of a job. Second, unnecessary hand movements, transportation of materials or supplies, and poor utilization of equipment and layout can often be avoided by *combining* all related details in a process. Third, time and transportation distances may be reduced by *rearranging* the sequence of details in an operation. Finally, a better way may be found by merely *simplifying* the way work is being done.

Analysis of Work Process

Logically, an analysis of the details of present methods of performing work tasks should begin with a study of the *overall work process* of which specific tasks are a part. Often the overall work process or procedure contains useless operations, nonproductive tasks, unnecessary travel, excess movement or handling of materials, or delays, that can be completely *eliminated.*

Nonproductive, worthless operations and activities creep into almost all procedures and work processes in the office as well as in the factory. They develop because of poor planning, and because workers improvise to take care of special situations and then forget to eliminate the extra work when things get back to normal. Once such habits are established in a work pattern, workers and supervisors commonly accept them as necessary. No one is really conscious of how wasteful they are.

That is why it is so important that supervisors constantly be alert to worker feelings and reactions. When a worker makes a remark about something being a waste of time, for example, it may pay dividends to encourage him to talk about it. As problems are identified by subordinates, discussions with them may be made in an orderly and systematic fashion by taking them through the stages of problem solving discussed in Chapter 2: identify the problem, explore it, and find possible solutions, select the best solution, and start action.

Several techniques of work simplification can be used in conducting such a discussion with one or a group of workers. For instance, a supervisor may notice that workers show irritation when they perform some tasks. They make remarks like, "I don't see why we have to do this," or, "I sure wear myself out hauling stuff back and forth around this place." Or they may just show their frustration by a lack of enthusiasm.

When supervisors hear such comments they should give them their attention and encourage workers to voice their ideas for improvements in work processes, procedures, and methods.

The Work Process Chart   One useful approach the supervisor can employ as a first step in ferreting out work problems is to prepare a work flow-process chart. The flow-process chart is used in analyzing an entire process for the purpose of eliminating unnecessary steps or operations, combining operations, and reducing transportations. The importance of charting the process as a whole before analyzing a work task lies in its value in analyzing separately the effectiveness of each step in an entire sequence of work, rather than evaluating the sequence as a whole.

Often a process that appears efficient as a whole turns out to be inefficient when it is broken down so that each of its parts can be examined independently and in terms of its contribution to the whole. The work process chart is used to classify all activities of a job as constituting either operations, transportations, inspections, or storages (delays may also be identified). In examining charts of work activities classified in this manner, the supervisor keeps in mind that *operations* are productive, but *transportations, inspections,* and *storages* are unproductive and costly and should be reduced to a minimum. This is sometimes referred to as the O-T-I-S principle. The relatively undesirable activities—transportation, inspection, and storage—can usually be more easily spotted when charted. Also, various characteristics of each kind of activity can be graphically included on the charts, such as distance traveled, time elapsed, and so on. In addition to other values, the improved work method, when charted, may provide a sales appeal when the time comes for the supervisor to get action from his superior.

As the supervisor begins to talk about a process or procedure with a worker who indicates that some operations or activities might not be necessary, a process chart can help both think systematically. The subordinate might be encouraged to help make a *list* of all the operations and activities that take place in the process, in the sequence in which they are performed. This list should not only contain the names of the productive *do* operations, but it should also identify all nonproductive operations or events such as travel of the worker, transportation of tools and/or materials, inspection or checking of work, filing of documents, storage of materials, delay of work in process. Such nonproductive operations usually occur *between* the *do* operations.

As a supervisor makes this list he or she can draw one of five symbols in front of the name of each operation, to classify each one so that he will be able to see at a glance whether it's productive or nonproductive: He should use a large circle for *do* or handling operations; an arrow for travel or transportation activities; a large *D* for delays; a triangle for filing or storage operations; a square for inspection or checking operations.

Examples of charts resulting from use of the above symbols might look like Figures 17-1 and 17-2.

Analysis of Work Flow

As the supervisor and subordinates analyze the work flow they may see that delays, storage operations, or filing of documents can be eliminated completely by redistributing or rerouting work. Often it will help to visualize such possibilities by drawing a picture of the *flow* of work. This picture can be done by making a *work flow diagram,* which can be a crude sketch or finely drawn diagram—approximately to scale—of the work area, showing the location of machines, desks, benches, storage cabinets, and other major pieces of furniture or equipment. Then a line (or several kinds of lines—solid, dotted, or colored) can be drawn to show the flow of work, the traveling the worker does, or the transportation of materials or materials-in-process through the department. Two such work flow diagrams are Figures 17-3 and 17-4.

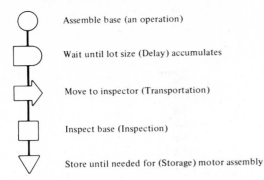

Assemble base (an operation)

Wait until lot size (Delay) accumulates

Move to inspector (Transportation)

Inspect base (Inspection)

Store until needed for (Storage) motor assembly

Figure 17-1   An example of a process chart from a shop operation.

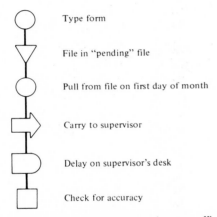

Type form

File in "pending" file

Pull from file on first day of month

Carry to supervisor

Delay on supervisor's desk

Check for accuracy

Figure 17-2   A similar chart from an office situation.

A completed process chart will, usually, contain many operations. But once the supervisor and the worker have listed every operation in the process, they can identify the problem spots. The supervisor has a basis on which to explore the necessity for each operation and to think about whether operations can be eliminated, combined, or changed in sequence to simplify the process.

A supervisor should explore the situation thoroughly with the worker by going through the entire list of operations, questioning him or her. The supervisor should ask, "Why do we do this?" "Is this necessary?" "How worthwhile is this operation?" Let the worker give you his or her ideas. Listen. The employee has been doing the work, and his or her reactions are probably more accurate than anyone else's.

Then possible improvements can be discussed. An employee may, at first, have only vague notions about what might be done, even though his or her complaints may have been loud. The supervisor needs to help the worker think and make ideas specific.

Creativity may be stimulated by asking subordinates questions such as: "What are some alternative ways we could do this?" "Could we combine any of these operations and perform them at one work station to save setup time?" or, "How could we change the sequence of operations, to save work, travel, or handling of materials?"

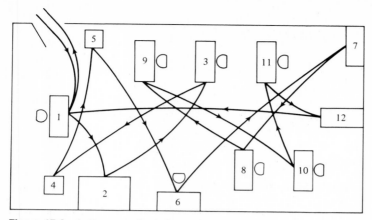

Figure 17-3 A diagram of existing work flow.

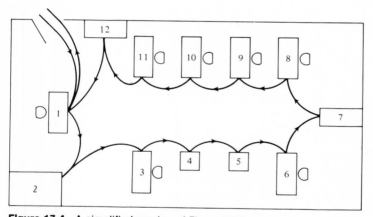

Figure 17-4 A simplified version of Figure 17-3.

Once the supervisor and the subordinates are satisfied, however, that each operation is necessary, they may find that it is also worthwhile to study whether the work *method* for each operation can be improved or simplified. One approach to such a study is a critical analysis of the present established procedure (written or not) for performing the operation. The supervisor may go through the procedure with subordinates, identifying unnecessary steps, exploring problems encountered at each step, and questioning every step. Ideas on steps that might be eliminated, changed, or combined may be jotted down. No matter how good the supervisor thinks a procedure for accomplishing a task was when it was established, it can always be improved. Almost every worker, as he or she performs a task many times, is likely to find short cuts and ways of simplifying such tasks.

A work flow diagram can be a useful supplement to the process chart described previously. It shows at a glance whether work and workers travel by short, efficient routes, or whether there is excess movement and backtracking. It can make it easy to explore the possibilities of different arrangements of desks, machines, and storage places.

Workers should be encouraged to suggest ideas for better arrangement or location of furniture, supplies, and equipment, and new diagrams can be drawn by the supervisor as discussions occur. Drawing and redrawing such diagrams can help in developing possibilities for combining, rearranging, simplifying, or eliminating operations as well as possibilities for shortening the flow of work. It is commonly necessary to try several times before a worthwhile improvement emerges. Good ideas usually come gradually.

Sometimes startling improvements can result from the application of imagination and expertise of a work group. On processes and procedures that have not been studied before, a 30 to 50 percent reduction is often possible in such elements as time required to perform the process, distance traveled by the workers and materials, or the number of times work is handled.

When a new flow of work is determined to be feasible, supervisors are then generally faced with the task of determining if and how changes may affect other departments. (An improvement that speeds the flow of work in one department but that results only in creating a backlog of work in another department where further processing is necessary can have little or no—or even negative—value.)

If it is determined finally that a new flow of work is valuable to all concerned, the supervisor then must usually sell the change to his or her superior.

Prompt attention by the supervisor to all phases described above of analyzing work flow problems can be of great importance, especially to the morale of employees who have participated in the analysis. Immediate improvements—no matter how small—can be especially effective. Finally, the supervisor of course must continuously follow up on changes proposed and/or made and give credit to ideas contributed by subordinates.

Analysis of Work Methods

We now discuss the approach to analyzing the details of work methods. Supervisors may have just as many good ideas for improvement of work methods as they do about simplification of the work process and flow.

Arrangement of Workplace   Many problems of work methods—from worker to chief executive—are due to poor arrangement or layout of the individual's workplace and of the larger physical area surrounding it. Of course, we know that the physical layout of a workplace, or of a larger segment of an office or shop, is usually a compromise among a number of factors. An ideal layout may be impossible to achieve because there are limitations in the space and equipment available to work with. However, in addition to the environmental considerations mentioned earlier, almost any layout may be improved through a systematic application of elementary concepts.

It may be useful for the supervisor to draw a workplace layout—a picture of a desktop or benchtop, for example—to help visualize the reaches the worker makes while performing his or her operations. The worker may be asked to show where he or she positions materials or supplies, how the worker reaches for them, where and how he or she looks at the work.

The present layout of the supervisor's workplace may be as represented in Figure 17-5.

Then the supervisor can evaluate the present layout in terms of the principles of comfortable layout, some of which we now summarize.

The workplace should be so arranged that the nonproductive motions that are so easy for a worker to make are eliminated as far as possible. An obvious point is that an orderly workplace where everything is within easy reach is of first importance. However, a point that often escapes notice is that commonly a workplace such as a bench or ma-

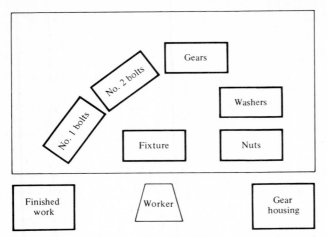

Figure 17-5 Existing workplace layout.

chine, or office desk or reception table, is laid out with supplies or materials or tools placed in straight lines. Where this occurs, the possibility of an immediate improvement is suggested, for we know that a person naturally works in areas bounded by lines which are arcs of circles.

An illustration of an efficient, circular layout of a workplace is the console of an organ. The keyboard is commonly laid out in circular form for ease of playing. We should visualize an ideal workplace as being of similar design, that is, the circular areas should break down into what are usually called a "normal" working area and a "maximum" working area. These two terms are concerned with a fundamental point, that insofar as possible all efforts should be devoted to seeing that *all work possible should be done within the normal working area, and none beyond the maximum working area.*

First, we shall describe the normal working area. On a horizontal plane, such as a desk or table or bench, there is a definite and limited area that can be used by a worker without undue fatigue. To be more specific, there is a *normal working area* for the right hand and one for the left hand, each working separately. In addition, there is a normal working area for both hands working together. We can very generally determine our normal working area at a desk, for example, by holding our elbows against our sides and swinging each forearm in an arc across our desk.

By doing as much work as possible within the normal working area, we stand a good chance of increasing productivity with less fatigue. Where one cannot work within the normal area, every effort should be made to perform work at least within the *maximum working area.* We can very generally determine our maximum working area at a desk by extending our arms completely and swinging each in an arc across our desk. Figures 17-6 and 17-7 show standard and revised workplace layouts.

Mechanical Holding and Moving Devices

Prominent also in the theory of layout are principles dealing with *mechanical holding and moving devices.* A concept long practiced in production shops is that all tools and materials that can be held or moved mechanically should be so held or moved. This approach has increasingly been taken in office layout studies with telling effects. A major objective is to free the workers' hands for useful activity and productive motions. For example, foot

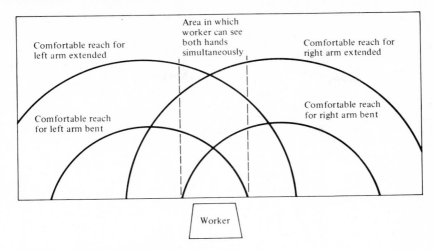

Figure 17-6 Standard guide to comfortable layout.

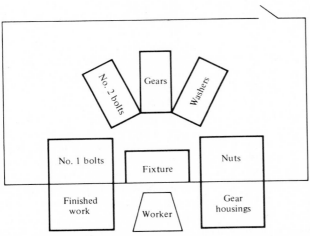

Figure 17-7 Revised workplace layout. (Compare with Figure 17-5.)

pedals have long been attached to factory equipment to help in the operation of the equipment and to free workers' hands for other activities. Only relatively recently has this concept been applied in the office to any marked degree. The use of foot pedals to help operate dictation machines is an illustration.

It is especially significant to recognize that the hand is the poorest holding device. It is also very expensive. Often relatively inexpensive devices can be used to hold work in order to free both hands for productive work. A rack for holding pages of a manuscript to be assembled is an illustration. Better still, a box with slots for each page, placed in front of a seated worker, facilitates the free use of both hands, and if properly designed makes possible rhythmic movements of both hands. Also good layout requires that care be taken to assure that finished work disposed of by hand should be moved the shortest possible distance. Further, if the same hand is used for disposal and for picking up the next item to be processed, the point of disposal should be close to, or in the path of travel to, the point where the next piece is picked up.

A fundamental concept of disposing of anything is that the quickest way is to drop it. This principle is frequently applied in shops and offices where desks or other workplaces have openings through which finished work may be dropped into a delivery chute by simply releasing it in the position in which it is completed, without having to move to dispose of it. Such chutes may feed into a conveyor that delivers shop parts or office papers to the next work station in the process. The time saved in moving the finished work to its destination is not as important as the fact that both hands are free so that they may proceed simultaneously in unbroken rhythm.

Importance of Pre-positioning   A fundamental principle of layout concerns *pre-positioning*. It is easy to see that an incalculable amount of time and fatigue may be saved if everything one needs in order to get out the work is placed in a fixed position within a worker's maximum working area. Probably less obvious than the time saved by doing this is the saving in eye fatigue, which can be much more serious than many people realize. Pre-positioning eliminates shifting the eye from work that is being done to search for a pen, pencil, or working tools. A fountain pen desk set is a simple illustration of pre-positioning. This eliminates the waste of time and motion required to search for and remove the cap from a pocket pen.

Comfort in Layout   Finally, one of the most important considerations in layout analysis is the *physical comfort* of the worker. Fortunately, as discussed in the first part of this chapter, scientific research has provided us with a number of clearly defined, ideal standards. For example, we know that standards of lighting intensity and glare for all kinds of work are easily available. We know too that when visual perception is involved, the direction of vision should be confined to a sector of not over 30 degrees and that the need for frequent change in the focal distance of vision should be avoided. To illustrate, a typist when typing copy or notes should not move her eyes back and forth over a wide angle to look alternately at her copy and her work. The sheet being typed and the notes being copied should be located at approximately equal distances from her eyes.

We also know the importance of proper posture not only for comfort but also for health. Good layout comprises worktables, desks, benches, and chairs of proper height to permit an individual to work confortably while maintaining proper posture. We also know that, if the work permits, fatigue may be lessened by providing for the worker to sit and stand alternately at work.

Proper color of workplace and tools and equipment, good ventilation, and reduction of noise and other disturbances or interruption all contribute to the comfort of the worker. Another factor that bears mention is that psychological studies have revealed that while a worker under either mental or physical tension, due to outside stimulus, may perform at top speed for considerable periods, the duration of such performances must be limited. All factors in a layout must contribute to make the operator mentally and physically at ease, if we wish to secure a continuously high level of performance.

In analyzing work methods it must be remembered, as was the case in analyzing *process* and *flow,* that subordinates should be active participants. Supervisors should help workers identify uncomfortable reaches, unnecessary bending and stooping, awkward ways in which they may be watching the work. These have a bearing on how tired they get; if they can be eliminated, workers may find the work easier, more comfortable, and more satisfying. Subordinates should be encouraged to come up with their own ideas for improving placement of materials and work, improvement of lighting, use of fixtures or jigs, positioning of tools, changes in height of bench, to make the work more comfortable. Questions such as these may be asked: "How can we position these pans to make your reaches as short as possible?" "Where could you put these supplies so you don't have to bend over to pick them up?"

Subordinates should not, if possible, be pushed or rushed. By recognizing their ideas and attempting to understand them, by listening instead of threatening immediate change, and by giving them the experience of looking for easier ways of working, the supervisor may help them *want* to make changes. Alternative workplace layouts may be prepared as the worker comes up with ideas.

Table 17-1 summarizes some ways of making the work smoother and easier.

Finally, it is to be repeated, the supervisor should not forget a follow-up step: Give praise where due, take action as promptly as possible, sell feasible change to his or her superior, and constantly evaluate changes made.

Table 17-1 Ways of "Working Smarter, Not Harder"

Minimize the number of motions by eliminating unnecessary movements.

Minimize the length of motions by reducing reaching distances to tools, supplies, and machine operations.

Distribute action among the used members of the body in accordance with the inherent capacities of members.

The hands should begin and end their activity in a cycle at the same time and should work simultaneously with duplicate parts in opposite and symmetrical directions.

The hands should not have idle or hold time; but if it becomes necessary for this to happen, the hands should not have idle or hold time occurring at the same time.

The hands should not do work that can be assigned to other body members through the use of foot pedals, etc., as long as the hands have other work to perform.

The tools and parts should be pre-positioned in a definite location and so located that the hands travel the least distance and perform the fewest activities.

The workplace should be arranged to permit smooth, continuous motions with a natural rhythm.

The classification of body members (muscle groupings) used should be kept to the lowest feasible for the work. (Fingers are the lowest, progressing through wrist, elbow, full arm, and body.)

The motions of the hands should be arranged to take advantage of body-member momentum through either previous motions or ballistic activity.

The number of eye fixations required in an operation method should be reduced to a minimum. (No eye fixations is the proper goal.)

When eye-hand coordination is required for grasping, positioning, assembling, etc., parts in a simultaneous, symmetrical hand pattern, the points at which the simultaneous activity takes place should be as close together as possible.

The workplace height should be arranged to permit the elbows of a worker to be above the table or desk.

A CRITICISM OF WORK SIMPLIFICATION

It is well for the supervisor to know that there has been, and is, criticism of the use of work simplification. As seems to be true of all methods of increasing productivity by improvements in machines or methods, there is the social objection that when productivity is increased, unemployment will result. There is certainly an element of truth in this argument, especially in the short run and where improvements are extensive, widespread, and revolutionary in nature. It must be recognized, however, that if constant attempts had not been made to increase productivity in the manufacture of such products as automobiles, clothing, and refrigerators, their costs would be so high that few people could afford them, and the number of people employed in making them would be only a small fraction of what it is now. It must also be pointed out that to a great extent workers displaced by increased productivity in one area are absorbed in other areas, even within the same company.

There are also psychological objections. For example, it is objected that an attempt to establish a standard group of motions which any or all employees are required to use violates the principle of individual differences. Some proponents of work simplification answer that no one would object to an operator working differently if by doing so he could get better results. Others answer that this is a matter of employee selection.

There are also objections that work simplification may cause the employee to work too fast. A rebuttal may be that, on the contrary, excessive speeds are frowned upon. A principle of motion economy may be cited that if a motion is too fast, more energy will be required to stop this motion than can be gained by high speed. Also, the answer sometimes is in the form of a *definition of a fair standard time*. It is *that rate at which employees, properly selected and trained, can best work, at a normal pace that they can maintain throughout the day without undue strain or fatigue.*

Proponents of work simplification emphasize that it is not a "speed-up" program, a charge leveled at early time and motion studies by workers and unions. In other words, it is not designed to make employees work faster and harder for the same pay (nor, in fact, was early time and motion study ideally designed to do this). On the contrary, its objective is to help employees to produce more with the same or less effort. It is hoped that, in the process, it will increase employee satisfaction and morale.

Disciples of a school of thought referred to as *job enlargement* often criticize work simplification because it concentrates on reducing the skills required for any one job. It is argued that the result is jobs that are simple, frequently boring and monotonous, and that produce no worker satisfactions. The concept of job enlargement, on the contrary, is that the individual should be given more activities to perform, which usually requires a greater variety of skills and a longer time cycle. Such jobs are claimed to possess the advantage of keeping the individual more involved in his work by requiring more of his attention.

It can be argued, on the other hand, that there must be a balance between the techniques of job subdivision and job enlargement. To illustrate this point of view, it can be shown that even automation becomes feasible only after work has been subdivided, for whereas the old-fashioned cobbler could not have been automated, the modern shoe factory with its subdivided jobs can be. While job enlargement may correct some excesses of subdivision of work, it cannot be an entire program.

Another criticism centers on the assumption in work simplification that the person on the job knows best how his job is performed and is thus better qualified to improve it than a centralized staff of specialists. Critics concede that the worker may best be able to subdivide his work and to suggest changes in his *present* work methods. They argue, however, that the knowledge a worker has about his *present* way of doing work may actually limit and crystallize his thinking and may make almost any significant change in work methods more difficult to get across to him.

THE ADMINISTRATION OF WORK SIMPLIFICATION

We have described work simplification as a philosophy and as a technique. It also requires skillful management on the part of the supervisor. To summarize, it is a philosophy that maintains there is always a better way to perform any kind of work. It is a technique, or collection of techniques, designed to be applied by individuals at the supervisory and worker levels of management. This enables workers to participate in improving their own jobs, and helps to make the supervisor a "key person" in the improvement of methods. As is true of all other aspects of the supervisory job, however, successful work simplification involves many supervisory skills. A few of the more important ones deal with the management of departmental objectives, rewarding employees for suggestions, appraising the efficiency of *existing* work methods, balancing the realities of today with the uncertainties of the future, and selling work simplification.

Importance of Departmental Objectives

First, it is important for the supervisor to recognize that work simplification and resulting work improvement are a continuing and fundamental part of the departmental objectives. It is not enough to wait for problems or trouble to appear before applying work simplification. Each and every kind of work performed in the department should be viewed as a problem. Constant attempts should be made either to eliminate the problem or to simplify it. The major problem areas that demand the constant attention of the supervisor are outlined in the short- and long-range departmental objectives. Wherever work is performed, in offices or shops, such objectives are given the supervisor by management as goals in running his department. They are his or her reason for existence. Some of these objectives refer to problem situations and others to normal situations where continuing progress is expected.

Need for Rewards

Second, one of the most complicated aspects of administering work simplification may not be to develop improved methods. It may be to reward employees personally for their efforts in striving for, and contributing to, productivity increases. Unless this is done, the possibilities of securing the cooperation of employees may be very limited. This problem is complicated by the fact that the supervisor usually has little, if any, control over financial rewards. Decisions of this kind are usually reserved for higher management. For example, management may establish a policy of providing a lump-sum payment or a small wage increase to an individual who suggests an improvement. Sometimes a group bonus is awarded when several workers are involved in improving work methods. In other cases, more general and indirect incentives are provided, such as a share in company profits or annual productivity wage increases. Neither of the latter, strictly speaking, may be considered an incentive for individual suggestions. Both violate a fundamental principle that *reward should follow accomplishment as soon as possible.*

Thus the supervisor must rely to a great extent on the use of nonfinancial incentives, such as conferring status, in order to motivate workers personally. As discussed throughout this book, this requires more than a separate and uncoordinated effort to influence workers, used only when the supervisor desperately needs help. Rather, motivating employees to accept and accomplish work simplification must derive, as in all other cases requiring motivation, from the supervisor's way of life and philosophy of work, and must involve a continuous dedication to achieving good human relations with his or her employees.

The constantly recurring perplexities of motivation may be illustrated by a problem frequently posed when a subordinate suggests an improvement in his or her work methods which is considered not quite as good as one developed by the supervisor. Using the employee's method may be more efficient and effective than using the supervisor's technically superior method. In other words, a well-motivated employee using his or her own, though possibly inferior, method may operate at a higher level of productivity than the poorly motivated worker using what the supervisor considers a better method. Later it may be possible for the supervisor to make a change without causing the employee to lose a feeling of status and self-fulfillment.

Short-run versus Long-run Considerations

A point repeatedly stressed in the work-simplification literature is that the supervisor should strive always to develop better ways of getting optimum performance from *present* personnel, equipment, and layout. However, very often efforts to develop something entirely new could better be devoted to improving that which already exists. For example, a supervisor may find that the present people, equipment, and layout are utilized at only 50 percent of capacity or potential. Improving such a condition may be much more opportune than attempting to create a new situation.

The truth of this statement should not lead to the misconception that the supervisor, in visualizing possible work-methods improvements, should limit himself or herself entirely to the existing capabilities of present workers. Such a philosophy could be destructive to the growth of both the supervisor and the organization as a whole. Obviously, the limitations of existing personnel may, in the immediate present, make it more opportune to install one method of work rather than a better method that would require special training of the work force or hiring new workers with greater potential. However, the possibilities of improved methods of work that might be feasible after present personnel are trained in new techniques should always be kept in mind. Also, the supervisor should remember that a normal turnover may make it possible to hire workers with a higher capability for using new and improved methods of work.

In the same way, the limitations of present equipment and layout may dictate the installation of a certain method rather than a better one requiring new equipment. However, it must be emphasized that supervisors who wish to excel should be alert to new developments in equipment in their fields of specialization that might profitably replace existing equipment, and perhaps even justify a revolution in the present methods of work. In other words, it may be of value for supervisors to visualize an *ideally* operating department. This visualization should be kept constantly updated to incorporate the newest selection and training techniques, the newest equipment applicable to their specialized areas, and the newest approaches to material handling and layout. This may provide them with the basis for comparing their existing situation with innovations that are constantly developed in our competitive world of business and industry. Such comparisons are apt to provide valuable clues to creative improvements in work methods.

Constant Selling of Work Simplification

Another supervisory problem is that work improvements do not necessarily sell themselves. Selling work improvements involves, of course, fundamental sales principles. For example, many good ideas for improved work methods are never used because the psychological lift and excitement have decreased after a new method has been found. This psychological letdown obviously should be overcome, and it is the supervisor's responsibility to make a determined effort to see that worthy suggestions, with proper credit given to the employees, are sold to his or her superior. Often this is indeed a formidable barrier. The superior certainly cannot be considered an isolated entity, always ready to accept and appreciate good ideas. He or she should be regarded as basically much the same as the supervisor or the employee, a human being possessing fears, opinions, and habits that frequently must be changed before something new can be adopted. It may be necessary for the supervisor to attempt to change these habits and erase these fears if the superior is to understand a suggested method and accept it.

Most people tend to respond favorably to well-organized information and to be impressed also by an efficient presentation. A neat, orderly report and an efficient presentation may convey a feeling of confidence. A fundamental point in selling creative suggestions is to start with the known and proceed into the unknown, in order to take advantage of this feeling of confidence. Thus, supervisors may best prepare themselves to sell their departments' output of work simplification by, first, anticipating and preparing themselves to meet a negative attitude. They may also effectively apply creativity in designing schemes for presenting work improvement suggestions effectively. Finally, they should carefully figure out the benefits, substituting facts for opinions insofar as possible. For example, what are the specific improvements in terms of quality, quantity, time, and cost? What is the level of acceptance of the employees involved in the change? It must be recognized by supervisors that it is sometimes necessary to use every possible and unusual idea to win over superiors and all others concerned with a suggested improvement.

In summary, we have research evidence that a supervisor's careful attention to workers' physical surroundings and development of better and easier ways to work can go far to increase productivity. By now, the reader has recognized that human engineering and work simplification constitute only two facets or specialized approaches to increasing productivity and worker satisfaction. By themselves, they accomplish little or nothing, as the Hawthorne studies indicated. For one thing, workers must be convinced that the better and easier way is *really* better and easier. Certainly the best way to do a job is not the best way unless workers think it is. They will not usually accept it unless they are sold by the person who developed the new method, or unless they participate in developing the better and easier way. But it can be sold, and it often pays large dividends.

QUESTIONS

1 The noise levels during rock musical performances often reach 140 decibels. What would be the relevance to the workers' well-being if this level of noise (at higher frequencies, of course) occurred on the job?

2 What social and economic problems in jobs may be present and correctable by job simplification even though the jobs are being performed with a high degree of productivity and employee morale?

3 It is often said, "No one really knows more about a job than the person who performs it." Would this make the worker the best person for redesigning his or her job? List the advantages and disadvantages.

4 What are the advantages of using the flow-process chart and the flow diagram prior to attempting to improve specific work methods?

5 Why is a "fair standard" as defined in this chapter almost impossible to apply to an entire group in some situations?

6 How can you tell a poor work layout when you see one?

7 Compare and contrast automation with methods improvement as a technique for increasing the efficiency of production.

8 One of the arguments advanced in favor of automation is that it removes the drudgery

of repetitive work from human operators. Is this a determining factor when a company is considering installing automated equipment?

NOTES

1 For a more detailed discussion of this subject, see Walter Van Dyke, *Industrial Psychology* (New York: McGraw-Hill, 1966).
2 Alton Wesley Baker, Director, *Exploratory Study of Environmental Conditions [In Large] Postal Installations,* 2 vols. (Washington, D.C.: Office of Postmaster General, 1970).
3 For a good discussion of illumination intensity, see Ernest J. McCormick, *Human Factors Engineering,* 3d ed. (New York: McGraw-Hill, 1970), pp. 451–453.
4 Aram Glorig (an international authority on hearing) was one of the consultants who worked as a member of an interdisciplinary research project conducted by one of the authors involving extensive laboratory and workplace studies of the effect of noise on work.
5 H. J. Jerison, "Effects of Noise on Human Performance," *Journal of Applied Psychology,* vol. 43, no. 2, pp. 96–101, 1959.
6 J. M. Finkleman and D. C. Gloss, "Reappraisal of the Relationship Between Noise and Human Performance by Means of a Subsidiary Task Measure," *Journal of Applied Psychology,* vol. 54, no. 3, pp. 211–213, 1970.
7 ASHRAE, *Guide and Data Book, Fundamentals and Equipment,* p. 852, 1961.
8 Alton W. Baker, Director, *Exploratory Study of Selected Factors Which May Influence Fatigue and Monotony Associated With the Letter Sorting Task* (Washington, D.C.: Office of the Postmaster General, 1967).

CASES

The first two cases of this chapter involve the question of the proper (or improper) assignment of job duties to certain individuals. The Bellows case raises the issue of whether a better qualified (by virtue of his experiences of the last two weeks) employee may be retained out of line of seniority and a more senior person otherwise eligible for the work continued on layoff. And that can get complicated!

The second case involves the peculiarity of employees not wanting overtime and then grieving when it is given to outsiders. In addition to deciding the proper outcome of the resulting grievance, a student of this case will want to look into the psychological and other factors that led these people to respond as they did.

The third case involves a disagreement with regard to the application of a negotiated incentive-wage provision. Certainly, as pointed out in Chapter 10, pay-by-the-piece does not resolve all disagreements and misunderstandings concerning wages.

CASE 17-1

The Company assembles room air conditioners. It employs more than a hundred people in assembly and warehousing work. The plant has long followed a policy customary in the Company in that it shuts down for two weeks in August, and virtually all employees take their vacations at this time. A few have to work in spite of this policy; guards are on duty around the clock, though the guard force is reduced, and from time to time other jobs have to be done during the shutdown. The fact that the plant has followed this custom for years and that there are no protests against it indicates that employees are not opposed to it.

Some employees have more than two weeks for vacations, and the additional weeks are scheduled at other times.

The vacation season just past gave rise to the problem of this case. Arthur Bellows was a material handler with relatively little seniority. When Frank Gibson, the foreman, found that he would need a material handler for the two weeks of shutdown, he started at the top of the seniority list and gave each man an opportunity to work. (It was not certain at the time whether the man would be paid for his work or whether he would schedule his vacation at another time.) Everyone had refused it when it came to Arthur Bellows, who accepted cheerfully and quickly.

The first week and a half went by without event, but on Wednesday of the second week local Management was notified by the Company that the plant would be shut down for an additional week due to a surplus of assembled air conditioners in the warehouses and in the hands of dealers. The people who did not work during the third week of shutdown would, of course, not be paid for that week.

This development posed a real problem for Frank Gibson. Bellows had done good work during the almost two weeks since the shutdown. Furthermore much of what he had done consisted in unloading and stacking parts in a large warehouse. He was the only one who knew for sure where each of the various parts was stacked, and Gibson had counted on him to instruct fork-lift operators when they started moving the parts to their storage bins, which had been overhauled.

The difficulty lay in the five material handlers who had seniority over Bellows. If Bellows worked for the third week and they did not, they would probably feel that Bellows was doing work to which the senior man was entitled. If he was laid off and the senior man brought on the job, without Gibson to help in locating the particular parts in each stack, several hours and perhaps a day or two of work would be lost.

Gibson decided to continue Bellows on the job, for the third week. Early in the week, however, he received a grievance from Henry Jones, the senior material handler, who asserted that the work of the third week was improperly assigned to Bellows and asked full pay for himself for all work done by Bellows until the plant was started again or until he was recalled to work.

The labor contract contains a provision that in case of layoff, the senior employee shall be the last to go and the first to be recalled if he is qualified to do the work. It also assigns overtime on the basis of seniority.

How should Gibson handle this grievance?

CASE 17-2

The Company operates a processing plant for catfood and other types of animal feed. In the department in question, the catfood is placed in bags, in some of which there is placed a coupon entitling the purchaser to a discount on his next purchase. Some of the bags in which coupons are placed are "flagged," that is, a notice on the outside of the bag calls attention to the coupon within.

On some of the packing machines there is an attachment for coupon-dropping (CD). However, the CD machine is unreliable, and by the spring of 1975 the Company was receiving many protests from customers who bought "flagged" bags but did not find the promised coupon inside. As the number of such instances increased, the Company became concerned, and decided that the CD machine should be constantly monitored to assure 100 percent accuracy.

For some time the plant had been on a seven-day-per-week schedule, one that required much overtime. (Overtime was mandatory in the plant in that one could *decline* if asked but if all declined and a certain employee was the low person on the overtime list he was *required* to work it or face disciplinary sanction.) Warning letters concerning required (but not worked) overtime were issued to thirteen employees in 1974 but to thirty-five in 1975, many of the latter relating to refusal of overtime to monitor the CD machine.

At this point the Company decided to contract the monitoring of CD. A firm called Temporaries Inc. (TI) was contacted and each day sent to the plant the number of people needed. These people never became employees of the Company. Rather it paid for their services through invoices submitted by TI, the invoices including labor charges and all deductions for income tax, withholding, Social Security, and so forth, as well as overhead for TI. These people were able to reduce the errors in CD to almost zero.

Past practice with regard to subcontracting included the Company's bringing in con-tractors for construction of new facilities, for handling emergencies, and for skills not available in the work force.

The grievance of this case protests the bringing in of these TI people. It also asks for overtime payments for employees losing overtime on account of the TI arrangements.

Should the grievance be sustained? If so, what is the remedy? One provision of the labor agreement says that the recognition clause defines "the scope of the employees in the bargaining unit, not the work."

CASE 17-3

The contract between the Company and the Union includes the usual management-rights and union-recognition clauses. It also describes in some detail the wage-incentive plan that has long been in operation in the plant. This part of the contract contains these provisions, among others: (1) that Management "at its discretion may establish new incentive stan-dards to cover new jobs . . . on the basis of accepted engineering practices"; (2) that once established, a rate will not be changed "unless new or changed conditions" lead to the change; (3) that in the event of a change the old rate is to continue in effect until the new one is fully established, at which time the employee's pay will be retroactively adjusted; and (4) that any new rates are subject to the grievance procedure of the labor contract.

The Company in question manufactures golfing equipment, one of its principal prod-ucts being golf clubs. It was in connection with a certain type of driver that this grievance arose. For some time the Company had produced two forms or styles of this particular driver. For one the head was made of laminated wood, which was stained (and not painted) (SLW). The other was made of solid persimmon wood, which was painted a glossy black (PPW). Different rates had been established for these clubs, the PPW requir-ing more time and skill principally because the paint had to be uniformly and smoothly applied, whereas less care was needed for the stain. (For the paint to be properly applied, for example, the wood had to be filed somewhat more smoothly than was required for the stain.)

Some time in 1974 the PPW driver was discontinued in favor of one still made of persimmon wood stained instead of painted (SPW). The Company at once applied the SLW rate to the SPW club.

The grievance alleges two contract violations: (1) that the PPW rate should have been applied to the SPW club until a new rate for the latter, based on careful engineering studies, could be determined; and (2) that as a matter of fact, no rate other than the PPW one would be acceptable, and it should therefore be established as the SPW rate.

The Union contends that there was a *persimmon-wood* rate in effect at the time of discontinuation of this club and it continued to apply to all persimmon-head drivers, that the difficulty and skill involved rest far more on the type of wood employed than on its finish, and therefore that the affected employees should henceforth be paid at the PPW rate and made whole for payments lost after they were put on the SPW rate.

The Company contends that there is nowhere in either past practice or the labor agreement a requirement or even a suggestion that the wood and not the finish properly determines the rate of pay; that in this instance, contrary to Union contentions, the wood as such makes no difference, but the lesser amount of care required in both filing and staining does lead to a reduced rate; that in fact, it conducted engineering studies immediately after starting production of the SPW club, studies that revealed that producing SPW clubs was slightly faster than producing SLW clubs, this difference, however, being less than the 3 percent difference required by the contract before a new rate can be set up; that paying employees the SLW rate for producing SPW heads is thus proper and contractual; and that paying the PPW rate for SPW clubs would therefore be out of line with the payment rates established in this and the other departments of the plant.

How should this dispute be resolved?

Chapter 18

The Supervisor and Civil Rights

As developments in the world of work go, the civil rights movement is new. Prior to the mid-sixties many and perhaps most of us discriminated against so-called minorities or the disadvantaged, often without a twinge of conscience and many times without even stopping to realize what we had done or the consequences of our acts. Thus if one happened to be a black, a Chicano, or a woman—to mention only three of such groups—he or she very often had a hard time in the world of work, getting only the jobs that paid less and led to less in the way of status or advancement, but which often required more in the way of effort, hours, or boredom. To get ahead with one of these handicaps the employee had to be considerably more lucky or more capable than his or her Anglo male counterpart— and needless to say, a majority of such people did not "make it," at least not to very satisfactory positions.

Some years ago *Psychology Today* carried an article that helped explain the role of women in employment. It was entitled, "How Nursery Schools Teach Girls to Shut Up."[1] There might also have been articles on how nursery schools (or public schools or other significant institutions) teach blacks or Puerto Ricans or American Indians to shut up too.

We still practice discrimination against these groups but hopefully not to the degree we did. It was not easy to realize, from the vantage point of fifteen or twenty years, how discriminatory we were. We may also overlook how much the situation has changed—in jobs, in education, in public accommodations, and in general acceptance. No doubt from the standpoint of the "disadvantaged" progress has been painfully slow—some would say it has been hardly more than tokenism—but the forties and the fifties and even the sixties are gone and will not return. There has been at least some progress.

Partly because interest in our subject is relatively new and also because its implications are so extensive we have decided to devote an entire chaper to it and to emphasize its significance to the supervisor. However, it is not possible to discuss some other subjects without reference to this one, and the reader is reminded that there is other material on it elsewhere in this book (see especially Chapters 7, 10, and 22).

It would be interesting, if time and space permitted, to discuss the various psychological and sociological forces—joined no doubt by political and economic ones—that brought about the awakened conscience and changed behavior of the recent past, but that is beyond the scope of this treatment. Rather we have chosen to stay with the more tangible legal aspects of the subject and to discuss the genesis of these changes under three headings: congressional acts and executive orders, decisions of the U.S. Supreme Court, and attempts to enforce the resulting civil rights provisions. If the reader has a feeling that these three headings will lead to technicalities beyond the interests of the supervisor, and indeed beyond anything that can be of use to a person in that position, the proper comment is that the opposite is true. It is a failure on the part of managers, including supervisors, to understand where we are and how we got that way that accounts for some of the unfortunate developments in the area. The topics covered may seem to be "theoretical." As a matter of fact, they concern the rules and regulations under which we operate, and of course we need to be familiar with them and the spirit in which they are promulgated.

FEDERAL LEGISLATION AND CIVIL RIGHTS

Any history of our subject would have to include certain congressional acts as well as constitutional amendments of the period immediately following the Civil War. Of these, the Civil Rights Act of 1866 and the Fourteenth Amendment are most frequently cited, and each of these, along with others, is definitely a part of the modern story. The more contemporary part of it, however, probably began with President Franklin D. Roosevelt's Executive order of the early part of World War II, one in which he authorized the Fair Employment Practices Commission (FEPC), whose task was to stamp out what we now call discriminatory behavior on the part of federal contractors. Every President since Roosevelt has endorsed the idea and taken steps to implement it, the Office of Federal Contract Compliance (OFCC) being a more modern version of the FEPC. The term federal contractor now typically includes a host of different kinds of "businesses," embracing universities and municipalities, for example, if they receive federal funds; and the OFCC has become a force that many, including almost all large employers, must be prepared to work with.

The Civil Rights Act (1964)

The Civil Rights Act of 1964 applies to employers in interstate commerce (and not to federal contractors only). It was signed into law by President Lyndon Johnson on July 2, 1964, and is designated as Public Law 88-352. It consists of ten titles, of which *Title VII* is our main concern. Section 703 of Title VII makes it illegal

> to fail or refuse to hire or to discharge any individual or otherwise discriminate against any individual with respect to his compensation, terms, conditions, or privileges of employment because of such individual's race, color, religion, sex, or national origin or to limit, segregate, or classify employees in any way which would deprive or tend to deprive any individual of employment opportunities or otherwise adversely affect his status as an employee because of such individual's race, color, religion, sex, or national origin.

The above language is foreboding and would fare badly on the readability test described in Chapter 9. To comprehend it fully, one needs to *study* it, and that is exactly what every supervisor should do (preferably by reading the act in the original and thus viewing the above quotation in context). One should especially note that it is *illegal to discriminate* concerning pay for or conditions of work and *illegal to deprive* anyone of employment opportunities or status if such discrimination or deprivation is based on (a) race or (b) color or (c) religion or (d) sex or (e) national origin. The act evidently means to include recruitment, screening, hiring, promotion, demotion, disciplining, compensation, laying off, or transferring—when such actions affect a person adversely and are based on any one of the prohibited characteristics.

It should also be observed that to violate the law it is not necessary to do any of these things fully or completely. To "tend to" do them seems to be sufficient.

The act, of course, has other provisions: It specifically applies to unions and employment agencies as well as to employers. It provides that one may legally discriminate on the basis of the prohibited characteristic where the latter "is a bona fide occupational qualification reasonably necessary to the normal operation of that particular business or enterprise." (Thus it would apparently be legal for a Baptist church—if it were covered by the act—to require a person to be a Baptist before being hired as a minister!)

The act also allows the use of "professionally developed ability tests" provided they are not "designed, intended, or used to discriminate." It does not require the favoring of a particular group on the basis of the percentage of such a group in the population. It makes it illegal to discriminate against anyone who opposes any practice made illegal by the act. Finally—because we do not have space to summarize all the act—it sets up the Equal Employment Opportunity Commission to enforce the act.

Again we emphasize that supervisors who function under the Civil Rights Act of 1964—as the great majority of supervisors do—need to be familiar with the act and of course with its subsequent interpretations.

Equal Employment Opportunity Act (1972)

It is not surprising that on the part of many employers (as well as of unions and employment agencies) there was much concern about the provisions and enforcement of the 1964 act and many protests in regard to both. It might be anticipated, therefore, that when Congress saw fit to examine and modify its provisions, the more radical ones might well be softened and their inclusiveness restricted somewhat. However, that anticipation was not borne out by the actual events.

In 1972 the Congress passed what is known as the Equal Employment Opportunity Act (Public Law 92-261) of that year. It did not weaken the provisions of the prior act so far as force and intention were concerned, but it did make substantial alterations in the coverage and enforcement and these in the opposite way from what employers wished! For one thing, it broadened the coverage to include certain government agencies and other employers exempt under the earlier law. For another, it gave the EEOC the power to file charges under the act. (The 1964 Civil Rights Act merely gave the EEOC the right to request the Department of Justice to file such charges.) It took steps to expedite the hearing of charges under the act, provided for a hearing under certain conditions before the contract of a federal contractor could be cancelled for civil rights violations, and spelled out the circumstances under which the employer is required to respect the religious observances of employees. (If he does not do so, he must be able to "demonstrate that he is unable to reasonably accommodate [such practices] without undue hardship on the conduct of [his] business.")

Anyone who is unsympathetic with the provisions of the Civil Rights Act of 1964 finds nothing in the 1972 act to furnish any comfort!

The Equal Rights Amendment

Another congressional action of this period was the passage of the Equal Rights Amend-ment (ERA). It was known as Joint Resolution 208 and was adopted on March 23, 1972, by an 84-8 vote of the Senate. It was not a statute, as the above were, but a proposed amendment to the Constitution of the United States. Its text was quite short:

> Section 1. Equality of rights under the law shall not be denied or abridged by the United States or by any State on account of sex.
>
> Section 2. The Congress shall have the power to enforce, by appropriate legislation, the provisions of this article.
>
> Section 3. This amendment shall take effect two years after the date of ratification.

Initial reaction to the proposed amendment was most favorable. Within two hours after its final passage by the Congress, the state of Hawaii became the first of the thirty-eight states required for its approval (within seven years). Other states quickly followed suit until thirty, and finally by 1977, thirty-five states have ratified it. At this point, how-ever, it seemed to "become stuck on dead center." At least four states that had not taken affirmative action considered it in 1977, and turned it down. Whether the needed number of states will be secured by March 1979 is at this writing in genuine doubt.

Opposition to the measure seems to stem from three principal sources. One is a religious and/or philosophical one. There are people who sincerely believe in the inferiori-ty (or perhaps better, in the subservience in certain areas) of women to men and find a scriptural or other similar basis for such belief. This point of view is closely related to the antiabortion, Pro-Life movement. A second is a fear that the amendment would be ex-tremely upsetting not only to established practices but especially to state laws designed for, and proponents of this view maintain, very effective in, protection and advancement of genuine rights for women. (Senator Sam Ervin of North Carolina led the Senate opposi-tion to the bill and used this as his principal basis for his position.)

A third factor is a fear of extreme results that might follow if the provisions were interpreted and applied as broadly as possible. "Coeducational" restrooms are an exam-ple. The conscription of women for combat assignments in the armed service is another. And the legalization and approval of all sorts of sexual arrangements and behavior are another.

Proponents often find such opposition almost unthinkable. The provisions are held to be nothing more than an additional step in the long and difficult struggle of women to free themselves from demeaning and very often harmful restrictions they have faced for centuries, and therefore to be heartily and speedily approved.

As an aside, it might be pointed out that the slowing down in adoptions by state legislatures has apparently come not so much from a shift in national sentiment toward the amendment as from the fact that the more "progressive" or "liberal" states have approved it, whereas those that have not done so tend to be the historically more conser-vative ones, especially when judged in terms of receptivity to social change.

The ERA has generated a great deal of feeling on both sides and led some propo-nents to feel that the whole future of the civil rights movement is at stake in its adoption. At the same time, some opponents seem to feel that the future of the whole country hangs in the balance. Neither position appears to be sound, however. Without attempting to minimize its possible effects one must note that regardless of whether the ERA is finally adopted, events have occurred and are occurring that will accomplish most or perhaps all of what it intends. The above civil rights acts, along with some mentioned below, are examples of what we have in mind. Other examples are certain already-existing provisions of the Constitution, including notably its "equal protection" and "due process" clauses.

Another relevant fact is that the movement for equal rights for women has now gained such acceptance and brought about such changes as likely to be irreversible, regardless of the fate of the ERA. In other words, there are now literally millions of Americans, only some of whom are women, who have become convinced that it is morally, even when not legally, wrong to deny or abridge the rights of women because they are women, and this point of view is likely not only to persist but to grow in both strength and numbers in the years ahead.

Other Civil Rights Acts

One could make a case for saying that many laws of the thirties were in actuality civil rights statutes even though they are not usually viewed as such. These would include the Social Security Act, the Wage and Hour Act, the public contracts acts, and perhaps even the basic labor laws (and especially the National Labor Relations Act).

Regardless of whether one so classifies the above, other laws, all unquestionably civil rights legislation, should be noted: the Equal Pay Act of 1963, the Age Discrimination in Employment Act of 1967, and the Civil Rights Act of 1968. (The last of these dealt primarily with affairs involving American Indians, with no substantial change in earlier civil rights provision.) The first of the above made it illegal to discriminate (in 1964 CRA terms) with regard to pay for men as opposed to women, and the second extended the antidiscrimination provisions to include *age* (when the person was between forty and sixty-five). Enforcement of the age provisions was lodged with the Department of Labor, however, rather than with the EEOC.

In all of the above, one important aspect of the civil rights movement has been entirely neglected. It is that in addition to relevant legislative enactments by the Congress and decisions by the Supreme Court of the United States, there have been such actions on the part of state legislatures and state courts. These, however, are an important fact of life for the manager in a particular state and are overlooked only at one's own peril. Such acts and decisions are, however, too diverse and complicated for treatment in a book of this sort.

Our subject turns out to be an almost-inexhaustible one. Thus under some conditions it is illegal to discriminate against veterans and also handicapped persons. And one cannot exclude from the sort of laws we are discussing voting rights and open-housing legislation, among others. Evidently the mid- and late-sixties and the seventies comprised a period of unequalled interest in civil rights in the United States!

THE SUPREME COURT AND CIVIL RIGHTS

The Congress is not the only American institution that has dealt with civil rights considerations in the recent past. Another is the Supreme Court.

Tables 18-1 and 18-2 summarize the material on legislative and judicial actions in the civil rights field.

Court Decision Relative to Segregation in Education

One evidence that the antidiscrimination movement actually began considerably before the mid-sixties is to be found in certain decisions of the Supreme Court of the United States. One of these of considerable historical interest is *Plessy v. Ferguson,* which was decided in 1896 and related to accommodations on a passenger train. In it the Court decided that "separate but equal" is nevertheless equal and enunciated a doctrine that prevailed for fifty or more years, until challenged particularly in the field of tax-supported education.

Table 18-1 Some Antidiscrimination Acts (U.S. Congress)

Legislation	Description
Civil Rights Act (1866)	Passed just after the Civil War
Equal Pay Act (1963)	Men and women to be paid same for same work
Civil Rights Act (1964)	Among other provisions, contains Title VII
Age Discrimination in Employment Act (1967)	Protects employees 40-65 years of age
Equal Employment Opportunities Act (1972)	Extended coverage of 1964 Act and powers of EEOC

Table 18-2 Important Civil Rights Decisions of the U.S. Supreme Court

Style of case	Date	Brief description
Missouri ex rel Gaines	12/12/38	Unlawful not to provide legal education to blacks
Sipuel v. Board of Regents	1/12/48	Same
McLaurin v. Oklahoma State Regents	6/5/50	Illegal to separate black student in classroom or cafeteria
Sweatt v. Painter	6/5/50	Illegal to prohibit black from entering white law school
Brown v. Topeka Board of Education	5/17/54	Prohibited racial discrimination in public education
Griggs v. Duke Power Co.	3/8/71	Ruled to be illegal certain tests and education requirements for promotion
Alexander v. Gardner Denver	2/19/74	Disadvantaged individual not precluded from filing EEOC charges because of losing in arbitration
Albermarle Paper Co. v. Moody	6/25/75	Even if professionally developed, tests must *not* discriminate
Franks v. Bowman Transportation Co.	3/24/76	Retroactivity seniority awarded to an employee illegally denied earlier employment
McDonald v. Santa Fe Trails Co.	6/25/76	White males illegally discharged when a similarly situated worker was kept because he was black

Decisions Involving Colleges and Public Schools A decision handed down by the Court as early as 1938 is in point. The state of Missouri had set up a law school for whites but none for blacks, rather providing for the latter that legal education could be secured in another state with Missouri making payment toward such education. The Court held that such an arrangement was not sufficient, that it violated the U.S. Constitution.[2] A decision ten years later in a case arising in Oklahoma required that legal education be provided for blacks, since the state was already so providing for whites.[3]

Finally, in two cases decided on the same day in 1950, the Court decided that (1) a black admitted to graduate training could not be required to sit in a certain classroom or library seat or to eat in a place or at a time reserved only for him; and (2) a state which had set up a law school for blacks but which law school was inferior in size, variety of courses, library, and certain qualities "incapable of objective assessment but which make for greatness in a law school," could not deny a qualified black admission to the white school.[4] The direction in which the Court was moving was becoming increasingly clear. Any lingering doubt was removed by the next decision we wish to discuss. One of the best-known decisions *(Brown v. Topeka Board of Education)* is the 1954 one that struck down public school segregation when based on race.[5] In this case the Court noted that it had been established that facilities were equal in the white and black schools and hence it was being forced to face again the issue involved in *Plessy v. Ferguson,* namely, whether being separate by law *in itself* leads to inequality. Here the Court basically disagreed with the previous decision and found that when mandated by law separate but equal is *unequal.* It pointed out that such separate facilities "generate a feeling of inferiority" and hence that "separate but equal" has no proper place in public education.

The effects of this decision have, of course, been far-reaching, and the decision itself has been controversial. However, in the intervening years neither the Congress nor the Court has substantially altered the fundamental conclusions of this case. Of course there have been a host of other cases relating to the integration of public (as well as in some instances private) education, but we do not have the space to discuss them.

The point of discussing the above decisions of the Supreme Court is probably apparent by now: Civil rights is not a brand-new idea in the United States. In both Court decisions and legislation, activities having to do with the actual achievement of such rights go back at least to the thirties and have continued at an undiminished if not an increasing pace throughout the period. In general, the role of the supervisor of a work group in such activities is not spelled out, but these Court and legislative actions have undoubtedly had a marked influence on the human relationships in all areas of employment.

Court Decisions Relative to Discrimination in Employment

The number of Supreme Court decisions relative to civil rights in the world of work is, of course, smaller than in public education, if for no other reason than that they hardly began until 1964. We have chosen to discuss two in particular, to establish the importance of the Court in this critical area and also to throw light on how the CRA (1964) and the EEOA (1972) are being interpreted and applied.

Civil Rights and Requirements for Promotion   The plaintiffs in the best-known case *(Griggs et al. v. Duke Power Co.)* relative to the meaning and application of Title VII of the Civil Rights Act of 1964 were thirteen employees of the Dan River Steam Station of the Duke Power Company in North Carolina.[6] Earlier, blacks had been employed exclusively in the Company's labor department, where the highest rate of pay was less than the lowest rate in the operating departments, where only whites were employed. With the *effective* date of the CRA, namely July 2, 1965, however, the policy was changed to permit blacks to bid into some of the latter jobs, but only if they had a high school diploma, or alternatively, could reach or exceed the national mean score of high school graduates on the Wonderlic *Personnel Test* and the Bennett *Test of Mechanical Comprehension.* A number of whites were performing satisfactorily in these jobs without either high school graduation or required test scores. Evidence was presented to the Court to the effect that only one-third as many blacks as whites were high school graduates, and that more than half of the whites could pass the tests whereas only 6 percent of the blacks could do so.

The Court struck down these job requirements and in connection with this action made a number of interesting points: (1) Congress intended the 1964 act to achieve equality of opportunity and to remove any artificial barriers for persons such as the plaintiffs. (2) The act prohibits practices that are "fair in form but discriminatory in operation"—as it found both the education and the test requirements to be. (3) Good intentions, including the absence of intention to discriminate, are by no means enough. The real question is whether in fact the practice *does* discriminate. (4) It is unlawful to freeze existing inequities, even though no discriminatory motive may be present. (5) The educational requirement and the level of test score required are "artificial, arbitrary, and unnecessary barriers" because there is no evidence of any relationship between these requirements on the one hand and job performance on the other. And since they discriminate on the basis of race, they are therefore improper. (6) The real question to ask concerning any such requirement is, Can it be justified by "hard evidence," that is, by "business necessity"? If so, its use is permissible even if it does discriminate on any or all of the Title VII characteristics. And (7) tests as such are not prohibited, but they must be professionally developed and must not discriminate in the above sense. In other words, "What Congress has forbidden is giving these devices and mechanisms controlling force unless they are demonstrably a reasonable measure of job performance."

Needless to say, this decision was an epoch-making one. It challenged a great many stereotyped beliefs widely held by managers (among others) and called into question psychological tests and similar devices at least as they were then being used. Overlooked, however, in much of the criticism of the Court was the freedom of the employer, within wide limits, to hire, promote, demote, and so on, "according to business necessity," though admittedly such business necessity would, if challenged, have to be *demonstrated* in order to justify an existing practice. Even though later cases have elaborated and explained it to a considerable degree, in a very real sense this is the controlling Court decision as to the meaning of Title VII.

Civil Rights and Arbitration of a "Discrimination" Grievance   Many labor contracts of today contain a provision prohibiting discrimination against employees either for union activities or on the basis of race, color, religion, sex, national origin, or age. The first of these prohibitions has customarily appeared in labor contracts for years, whereas the second is usually as new as or newer than the CRA (1964). (Incidentally, since it is *illegal* to discriminate in both ways, is not such a prohibition already in every labor agreement *by implication* even when not in so many words?)

Though stated in different words in different contracts, many if not most labor agreements now contain civil rights provisions. Table 18-3 contains three examples.

At any rate, in the case *(Alexander v. Gardner Denver)* we now have under consideration[7] a black machinist who was discharged by his employer because of "too many defective parts that had to be scrapped." He grieved that he had been unjustly discharged (with no reference to his race or color), but just before the arbitration of his grievance a charge of such unlawful discrimination was made. Also before the arbitration of the grievance Alexander filed a discrimination charge with the EEOC.

The arbitrator found the discharge to be proper and furthermore found the charge of racial discrimination to be without foundation. In its later defense against the EEOC charge, the Company contended that the arbitrator had disposed of it as well. However, the Supreme Court disagreed. It held that the arbitrator's decision did not prevent the employee from filing and pursuing through the appropriate channels a charge of Title VII violation. The decision was greeted with surprise in view of the fact that in 1960 the Court had given arbitrators broad powers toward making final and binding awards. However,

Table 18-3   Nondiscrimination Clauses in Labor Agreements

"Neither the Company nor the Union shall discriminate against any person because of race, creed, color, national origin, sex or age, or Union membership or nonmembership in the Union" (a manufacturing plant).

"The Union and the Corporation affirm the intention that the provisions of this Agreement will be applied without discrimination because of race, creed, color, sex, national origin, or union affiliation of the employee" (a manufacturing plant).

"The Agency and the Union agree to cooperate in providing equal opportunity for all qualified persons to prohibit discrimination because of age, sex, race, religion, color, or national origin....The Union agrees to become a positive force in this endeavor" (a large government agency).

when charges of Title VII violation were involved, the situation was found to be different and hence the arbitrator was more easily overturned. In common language, under these circumstances the employee "gets two bites at the apple," an allegedly unusual development in American labor relations.

Other Relevant Cases   In a case about a year after the Alexander one, the Court put additional stringent requirements on an employer who develops and uses a psychological test that discriminates against blacks.[8] The fact that a psychologist was used in its development was not sufficient. A significant correlation, the Court held, must be demonstrated between test scores and job performance; furthermore, supervisory ratings are not a sufficient indication of the latter, at least as gathered and used in this instance.

The Court again held that one may violate the law even when acting in good faith, and also that the seniority system was too narrowly conceived. Under certain conditions plant seniority, rather than job seniority, was to govern in the future.

The above cases dealt with alleged racial discrimination, but it must not be overlooked that other disadvantaged groups are also protected by implication, if not direct statement. For example, in 1974 in a case involving Corning Glass, the Court determined that it was illegal to pay women less for doing certain work on days than men were being paid for the same work at night. (The pay differential was of long standing, women once being denied opportunity to work at night.) The Court recognized the propriety of a reasonable shift differential; this decision spoke to higher pay—beyond that differential—to men as compared with women.[9]

The reader is aware, of course, that the above cases at best represent a sampling of those dealt with by the Court and available for our examination. However the limitation of space and a recognition that we are in no sense attempting to make our readers experts in the law suggest that we permit these cases to stand for the many others that could be included.

It must also be noted that in all the above, including the legislative acts described, we have said only a minimum about how the several provisions have been interpreted and applied by the various governmental agencies. Naturally this topic involves additional court decisions, including some from the Supreme Court, but in discussing them we will be centering on how they and other related activities have affected day-to-day operations.

ADMINISTRATION OF CIVIL RIGHTS PROVISIONS

If the above legislative acts and Supreme Court decisions appear to be involved and complicated, one can imagine how much more so is their application to the actual workplace. It is one thing to pass a law and to interpret it and any relevant constitutional provisions, but it is something else again to apply all these. Laws can be high-sounding and idealistic and allowed to lie idle in government documents with little or no effect on those toward whom they are directed. On the other hand, they can be implemented with vigor and applied to countless situations that may arise in employer-employee relationships. There is no question about where recent civil rights enforcement is found. However wise or misguided, reasonable or arbitrary, such efforts have been frequent and forceful, especially since the late sixties.

Means of Enforcement

We have already indicated that two agencies are directly involved in the enforcement of civil rights provisions in the employment relationship, the Office of Federal Contract Compliance and the Equal Employment Opportunity Commission. While these organizations are independent of each other, efforts have been made to coordinate their activities and requirements. At the same time, a very large number of charges have been filed and are awaiting action (for the EEOC, 130,000 at one time in 1976) even though other agencies of the federal government have been enlisted to assist in administering and enforcing the provisions.

In general when a person believes that he or she has been a victim of illegal discrimination, a charge to that effect may be filed with, let us say, the EEOC. This body investigates and attempts to resolve the situation before making the matter any more formal. (If there is a state agency designated to perform this function, the EEOC must defer to it and its efforts at settlement for sixty days.) If no resolution can be effected, the EEOC proceeds with its investigation and arrives at a finding, which finding may be accepted by the parties, or it may be challenged in federal district court. Of course it may then be pursued through the circuit court and to the Supreme Court under certain circumstances.

Penalties for violation may be quite large. Back pay from the date of filing charges and for up to two years prior is not unusual. Attorneys' fees may also be awarded and, in addition, under certain conditions compensation for damages other than loss of pay may be involved.

One development, not at all restricted to civil rights cases but still often found in connection with them, is the *class-action* suit. The action may be initiated in this form, that is, to cover the aggrieved employee and all others similarly situated, or it may be broadened, at the time of filing or later, to include such persons, even though they were not a part of the original action (and for that matter may never take any direct part therein). The Supreme Court has put some restrictions on how and how extensively a proceeding may be broadened along this line, but such restrictions have in no sense removed the possibilities in such actions.

Affirmative Action Programs

A device of real significance in this area has been the requirement that the employer in whose place of employment there is evidence of present discrimination or the effects of prior discrimination file with the appropriate enforcing agency an *Affirmative Action Program* (AAP). This consists in about what one would guess from its name: It is an agreement to take positive steps ("affirmative action") to improve an undesirable situation, for example, to increase the number and proportion of black employees or to see to it that more women are promoted to positions of higher pay and greater responsibility. These affirmative action programs are for a definite time period; that is, the employer pledges to make good-faith effort to achieve an agreed-upon amount of progress by a specified time. And the appropriate agency will likely revisit the firm or agency on or near that date to see what progress has been made; and if the goals have not been achieved, why not? At this time, of course, another AAP may be drawn up for the months ahead.

AAPs, like other activities in connection with civil rights, have been subjected to criticism, some of it no doubt deserved, but they continue to be developed and implemented. No small part of the criticism has revolved around "quotas"—that is, proportions of the total employment properly represented by a certain disadvantaged group or groups.[10] Another has turned on so-called reverse discrimination, to be discussed below.

Significant Developments in Civil Rights Enforcement

Cases Involving Prominent Employers Naturally with as many employers as there are in the country and with the degree of enforcement of the various provisions, a great many parties have either been found guilty of discrimination (in pay, status, promotion, demotion, or other activities) or else have pleaded *no contest* when faced with the charges. Typically these cases have involved a monetary settlement at least in the form of back wages and often upgrading to women and/or minorities. Occasionally both the money and the number of people involved have been quite large.

Before presenting some of these instances—obviously there is no way in which all or even most can even be mentioned—it should be borne in mind that discrimination in the employment relationship was a way of life for so long that no one should expect an overnight correction of all those practices that became illegal in 1965 (a year after passage of the 1964 CRA). Hence mention of a firm or government agency or union in this connection should certainly not lead one to assume that it is among the poorest or least responsible. Indeed it will be evident that the list includes some very good and likely even some of the best so far as equality of treatment goes.

A case that received a great deal of publicity involved AT&T and about 15,000 women and black employees. The Company agreed to pay them some $15 million in back wages and to award some $23 million in raises to people as they were moved to new jobs. There was also a promise to attempt to increase the percentage of minorities and women in jobs theretofore filled exclusively or almost so by men. AT&T was later involved in similar actions relative to disadvantaged employees in other parts of the Company.[11]

Another finding concerned significant parts of the steel industry, where $30 million in back wages was involved and $25 million in raises to some 40,000 people. Also craft jobs formerly closed to minorities and/or women were opened to them with percentage goals set for the numbers to be promoted to them.

Another company was American Brands. Here the emphasis was on standards and criteria for admission to certain jobs, with the Company agreeing to try to achieve a proper proportion in various jobs in the light of the composition of the Richmond work force. In some instances the disadvantaged were given the right to tour the work areas and pick out jobs, though in each case they had to be able to meet reasonable job standards set by the Company and could be removed if they could not do the work properly "following a reasonable time."

In the case of Bank of America a judge ordered it to place in trust $3,750,000 to be used to upgrade the management skills of 1000 women employed for five years or more. There was some evidence that some women used some of the money unwisely; consequently educational grants and outside advisers were instituted later.

An instance of a different sort involved Standard Oil Company of California. Here the employer was ordered to pay $2 million to 160 employees who were over forty years of age and who had been laid off, in many instances as early retirees. In this decision it was concluded that the burden rested on the Company to prove that persons forty and over could not do the job well.

As we mentioned, there are many other cases that could be cited on the above and other aspects of these provisions. (Indeed the three Supreme Court cases of the section preceding this could be included here, for all three involved settlements that favored the complaining employees.) However we shall have to let these represent the larger group.

Obligations of Labor Unions   It has been mentioned previously that the CRA (1964) applied to labor unions as well as to employers. A great many instances can be cited involving charges and/or threats to file charges of illegal discrimination against unions. Indeed in more than one of the cases cited above, the union was charged right along with the employer.

Typical civil rights problems of labor unions have involved admission to apprentice programs, though this by no means the only one. Apprenticeships have often been almost "handed down from father to son" and it has been difficult for any outsider to be selected. It is thus easy to see the obstacles that might face an applicant who was a woman or a minority-group member. The now-famous "Philadelphia Plan" was designed to open more jobs to the disadvantaged; it was followed by other "plans" in various parts of the country. But just as not all civil rights practices of all employers are above suspicion, the same is apparently still true of unions.[12]

Two Important, but Unresolved Issues   Naturally when a greatly altered point of view appears suddenly—or nearly so—and laws are made and other decisions taken to implement it, there are uncertainties that arise and unanticipated issues that must be resolved. Hopefully after a time these are settled, along with the mistakes and inefficiencies that inevitably accompany such changes. These developments have occurred and are likely to continue to occur in the field of our present interest.

Among the unanswered questions in this area of the world of work, two have received considerable publicity. For each, there are strong considerations on each side—or maybe there are more than merely two sides—and no final course of action has either been agreed upon nor is one clear to those who are familiar with the field. One of these is the role of seniority when illegal discrimination is found to exist or even to have existed in the recent past, and the other is so-called reverse discrimination.

Seniority and Discrimination   A moment's consideration leads one to see that conflict is likely to arise when the usual seniority provisions or practices are examined in the light of illegal discrimination—in selection, transfer, promotion, discipline, and the like. For one thing, nearly always in union agreements (and usually where there is no union) we have followed the practice of "last in, first out" if a reduction-in-force is necessary. Most people find this to be a just or fair practice; but suppose some or all of the "last in" are the illegally discriminated blacks, or women, or Chicanos. Then are they to be laid off and the white males, at least some of whom presumably should not have been in these places, retained? What if some of the white males have been hired since July 2, 1965? "Business necessity" or at the very least good business judgment says one should reward long and faithful service and also keep the more experienced workers. But the CRA (1964) and related laws say directly that certain kinds of discrimination are illegal and furthermore are interpreted as providing for the wiping out of the effects of past illegal discrimination.

An additional troublesome issue concerns the effects of *job seniority, department seniority, plant seniority,* and the like. Thus if one is promoted on the basis of craft-department seniority and a black person has spent a longer time in the labor department, his or her seniority for transferring into or moving up in the craft department is *zero*. Clearly such situations can raise many troublesome questions.

Cases involving this and related issues have been dealt with frequently by the courts, though it is agreed that the Supreme Court has not yet (in 1977) spoken definitely on the subject. Let us look at a few developments in this area, some coming from proceedings before the EEOC and some from lower-court decisions. In one such case, Bethlehem Steel was ordered to substitute plant seniority for department seniority for purposes of transferring out of a department, and to take plant seniority into account "in all job comparisons." In a Continental Can Company case it was determined that the Company violated the CRA (1964) when it used seniority as the sole criterion in determining who should be laid off, since the low seniority of blacks resulted from the previous failure to hire blacks. A public utility in New Jersey also found itself "caught between a collective bargaining agreement and the EEOC," as other employers also have.[13]

In a recent Supreme Court case, two black plaintiffs were awarded retroactive seniority (*synthetic seniority* in terms of Chapter 10) based on the fact that they had previously applied for but had been illegally refused employment with the company. They were later hired and began the action that eventually led to their lengthened seniority.[14] This case, however, does not deal with circumstances that no doubt involve many more people than the ones described, namely, what should be done when persons are denied jobs to which, except for Title VII discrimination, they would have been appointed, but are not hired later? Is synthetic seniority proper here? If so, shall it be year-for-year or on what other basis? And how does one compensate for the years of experience that some will have been denied? These questions have not as yet been clearly answered but they probably will have to be in the not too distant future—by Congress or the Supreme Court or both.

If one needs any evidence that the world of the supervisor is undergoing changes and that the ground rules of yesterday may or may not be those of tomorrow, he or she need look no further than the civil rights field for proof!

"Reverse Discrimination"   The other issue is equally as troublesome as that involving seniority. It concerns the standing of white males under Title VII of the CRA.

It is clear of course that the hiring—or promotion or retention—of a black, a woman, a Puerto Rican, or other disadvantaged sometimes occurs at the expense of a white male, that is, if the former were not hired or promoted, the latter probably would be. And making places for more women managers and executives is likely to mean that there will at times be fewer places for men.

It might be wise at this point to recognize that while it is common to refer to this situation as one involving reverse discrimination, there are those who object to the term, maintaining that reverse discrimination does not really occur but rather that the disadvantaged are only getting a measure of what they morally and legally deserve. It is furthermore held that white males use the term to justify holding on to their often-illegal advantages.

That many alleged instances of so-called reverse discrimination are not truly so is quickly admitted. However true reverse discrimination can occur and has occurred; that is, on some occasions—the writers do not know how frequently—better-qualified white males have been turned down, and less qualified members of disadvantaged groups selected on racial or similar grounds. When we use *reverse discrimination,* we shall mean by this term only those situations in which this actually occurs.

A case of a few years ago illustrates the point, though it comes from education rather than employment. The applicant, a white male, for a certain law school had a better grade-point average and better test scores than some disadvantaged who were selected in preference to him. He sued on the ground of illegal discrimination, alleging that he was denied admission because of his race and/or sex. The case made its way to the Supreme Court, which eventually decided not to rule, since the applicant had meantime secured a lower-court order that enabled him to enter and by that time virtually to complete law school. And no Supreme Court case since that time has settled this issue.

A recent case from Texas may throw some additional light on this matter, though it is admittedly not definitive. In it the Court held, when three men were clearly involved in fighting and the company fired the two who were white and kept the one who was black, allegedly on racial grounds, that the civil rights of the two whites had been violated.[15] But this case in no sense disposes of the larger question (for example, when no discipline is involved).

The authors of this book do not know, of course, how this issue will be resolved and furthermore, are not at all sure they know how it *should* be. While there can not really be any argument about whether white males have a standing under Title VII (they do!), we are hazarding a guess that the most likely resolution by the Court will be to affirm this fact and award the white man the vacancy—to take an example—when he is beyond reasonable doubt better qualified, but under at least some existing conditions to give the disadvantaged the benefit of any reasonable doubt. If adopted, this may not be the most equitable solution, and it certainly will not please all who are involved. What we are all hoping for in any case is for the day, clearly some time in the future, when the vast majority of us will really and truly make the significant personnel decisions without regard to race, color, religion, sex, national origin, or age!

CIVIL RIGHTS RESPONSIBILITIES OF THE SUPERVISOR

Even after this long discussion of civil rights in the United States we still have said nothing directly about what must be the major concern of a chapter like this in a book like this, namely, what should the first-line supervisor do about civil rights? It is to that question that we devote this last section of this chapter.

Keeping Up with "What the Score Is"

One obligation resting on every line manager, and on many staff ones as well, is to be sure he or she has a good general idea of "what's going on" in civil rights. Here as in so many other aspects of our lives, "a little learning is a dangerous thing." On the other hand, if one must act with regard to a certain issue, then by all means he or she needs to be informed concerning it. For civil rights, it may appear that the material so far presented in this chapter is all that is needed, but such is not the case. For one thing, there is much more to the subject than we have been able to present, a fact that will be evident if some of the references cited in the notes at the end of the chapter are followed through. And second, the subject is constantly changing, and from time to time momentous events occur. One certainly needs to keep up-to-date concerning areas in which he or she must take actions.

Avoiding the Extremes

A useful bit of advice at this point is avoid going to the extremes on any aspect of the subject. It is unlikely, for example, but one could be so enamored of equality in civil rights that he or she subordinates all other concerns to it. The authors of this book wish such rights could become universally recognized and practiced in the world of work—and elsewhere—and hope our efforts help to bring that condition about. But meanwhile there are payrolls to be met, unions to deal with, and goods to get out the door. One can "go to seed on civil rights," as might be true for virtually any other good thing.

And then there is the possibility of being against the whole movement whenever it appears. Such attitudes may spring from deep feelings of white (or male) superiority (or other kinds!) and the present movements may constitute a direct challenge to these feelings. Or one may have had a series of unpleasant experiences in the area or even believe on religious or other grounds that the movement is wrong. Again two words of caution: First, Title VII and associated provisions are now the law of the land; many are heartily in favor of them; they will apparently become stronger rather than weaker; and one is likely to spend the rest of his or her career working with (and for) people who believe in them. The choice under these conditions seems to be to go along or become a martyr to a cause. This, of course, is a choice that each person has to make for himself or herself.

Second, since the cited provisions are the law of the land, managers, including supervisors, must abide by and enforce them whatever their feelings. Furthermore, it must never be forgotten that under these circumstances when the supervisors speak the company has spoken. In other words, they become directly responsible, and so does the company, for their actions. Inability to go along with requirements here certainly indicates that such persons should leave the job to those who can.

In addition to being overenthusiastic or underenthusiastic about civil rights, it is possible to develop another set of attitudes, namely one of complete discouragement and resignation to what it seems is the inevitable or even misdirected and ultimately disastrous. How many of us, for example, have been in management sessions where someone, with obvious pessimism, expresses the belief that as relates to an inefficient member of a disadvantaged group, "There's nothing you can do about it"—or, "We're stuck with this so-and-so without any hope of relief." Actually, of course, this is not the case at all. After all there is always hope that through training, counseling, warning, or otherwise apprising the individual of the situation, things might change for the better. Besides, if this does not work there *is* something one can do about it. The *Griggs v. Duke Power* case cited above makes it clear that one does not have to put up indefinitely with an employee who can be proved to seriously interfere with "business necessity." Before one undertakes serious adverse action, however, he may want to look closely at the material in the chapter on discipline (see Chapter 14) and on some that follows in this chapter.

Improving One's Attitudes and Behavior

It is easy to throw responsibility for civil rights on to the shoulders of the company executives and to feel that the supervisors are only "hired hands," doing as they are told. If that were true, they would need to concern themselves very little about the subject and even conclude that their influence is of no consequence. Such obviously is not the case, since every one of us helps shape every environment of which we are all a part.

Cleaning Up One's Language   We often give offense to an individual or group of individuals by the expressions we use. Words can and at times do "put people down," reflect on them adversely, hold them up to ridicule, or in other ways deal with them in a derogatory manner. Sometimes these effects are intended; frequently they are engaged in unintentionally or even unconsciously. But their effects are not cancelled thereby.

Supervisors can accomplish much in this area. They can monitor and revise their words and sentences and the jokes they tell and encourage, and thus go quite a way toward creating a favorable civil rights climate among their people. And as a fortunate fall-out, the recognition that such a climate exists may be quite helpful in the event that discrimination charges are made against them.

Setting an Example   Perhaps this is just a way of saying again what has just been said; but the fact remains that in this area, as in many others, the attitudes and values of supervisors, as these are manifested in day-to-day conduct, often become critical to the attainment of proper goals. Supervisors *can* be unbiased—or at least they can *try* to be. They *can* refuse to discriminate on the prohibited grounds. They *can* treat every individual fairly, all circumstances considered, and live by the spirit as well as the letter of the law— or again, at least they can do their best. No one can expect more, and no supervisor should be content with less!

A Willingness to Decide   This area, like a number of others, is a good one for procrastination. One may see a situation, for example, where a woman is not getting the breaks to which she is entitled, but the supervisor may fail to act, for inaction is often far easier. Or here is a case where a Spanish-surnamed American is simply not "putting out," his or her attendance is irregular, and others have to do a considerable amount of extra work. These situations call for careful analysis and consultation, followed by a resolve to act. Just what action should be taken and when, is a matter we cannot decide here, but the point is that such decisions are called for, now or eventually. One measure of a supervisor's competence is a willingness to act when action is called for, along with the ability to decide wisely when such a time has come.

Due Process

Here is a place where substantial parts of the treatment of discipline (Chapter 14 above) could be copied with only minor changes in phraseology, and the discussion would fit precisely. It seems unwise to repeat that material here, at least in detail. But it is probably not unwise to mention the most salient points: *Just cause* for one's actions; *provable* just cause, since as in discipline so in civil rights, the burden usually rests on the employer; *evenhanded justice,* which is just what the civil rights provisions aim to bring about; *progressive discipline* to whatever extent adverse action is involved, and *effective counseling* and tutoring as needed; and the opportunity for *appeal* already provided by the law for all discriminated individuals but hopefully made openly available in-house to those who wish to take advantage of it. Many times provisions for a genuine appeal within the organization will convince the individual that an outside one will not be needed.

A Willingness to Reconsider—And to Live with a Reversal   An appeal, as the term is used just above, asks an individual or the organization to reconsider an accomplished or a contemplated action. As we have said more than once previously, within reasonable limits one should always be willing to do this and to have it done by others in position to sit in judgment on and take steps to correct the decision. This point of view obviously is relevant to civil rights matters.

In a very real sense doing what is right with regard to civil rights is the same as doing what is right in other human relationships.

QUESTIONS

1   What are some illustrations, other than those in the book, of the ways in which we may "put down" women or members of minority groups? When we do this, do most of us most of the time do it intentionally or unconsciously? Explain.

2   What are the chief provisions of (a) the 1964 Civil Rights Act? (b) the 1972 Equal Employment Opportunity Act? How much effect have they had on the employment (or work) relationship in the United States?

3   What is the significance for today's supervisor of (a) Supreme Court cases having to do with segregation in college education and (b) *the* case involving public school segregation *(Brown v. Topeka Board of Education)?*

4   Answer the same question for the Supreme Court case involving (a) promotion *(Griggs v. Duke Power)* and (b) arbitration of discrimination charges *(Alexander v. Gardner Denver).*

5   What efforts have been made to enforce civil rights, what have been the principal results, and what do you think the future holds along this line?

6   What are the civil rights problems involved in an emphasis on seniority as an important factor in personnel decisions?

7   What is the meaning of *reverse discrimination* as used in this chapter? What problems does it present for civil rights policies and enforcement? How should this situation be resolved?

8 What should be the most important civil rights considerations of the first-line supervisor?

NOTES

1 Lisa A. Serbin and K. Daniel O'Leary, "How Nursery Schools Teach Girls to Shut Up," *Psychology Today,* vol. 9, no. 7, pp. 56–58, 102–103, December 1975; see also June Kronholz, "Lagging Behind: Though More Women Work, Job Equality Fails to Materialize," *The Wall Street Journal,* vol. 58, no. 3, p. 1, July 6, 1976.

2 *Missouri ex rel Lloyd Gaines v. S.W. Canada,* 305 U.S. 337 (Dec. 12, 1938).

3 *Sipuel v. Board of Regents,* 332 U.S. 631 (Jan. 12, 1948).

4 *McLaurin v. Oklahoma State Regents,* 339 U.S. 637; *Sweatt v. Painter,* 339 U.S. 629 (June 5, 1950).

5 *Brown v. Board of Education of Topeka,* 347 U.S. 483 (May 17, 1954).

6 *Griggs et al. v. Duke Power Co.,* 401 U.S. 474 (Mar. 8, 1971).

7 *Alexander v. Gardner Denver Co.,* 415 U.S. 36 (Feb. 19, 1974).

8 *Albemarle Paper Co. et al. v. Joseph P. Moody,* 422 U.S. 405 (June 25, 197?).

9 "Several More Slaps at Bias in Business," *Business Week,* no. 2334, p. 28, June 8, 1974.

10 "Affirmative Action: The Negative Side," *Time,* vol. 104, no. 3, p. 86, July 15, 1974.

11 At the time of occurrence, the cases of this section received a great deal of publicity in the daily press, the newsweeklies, business periodicals, etc. The following are some of the relevant references: "Ma Bell Agrees to Pay Reparations," *Newsweek,* vol. 81, no. 5, p. 53, Jan. 29, 1973; "Steel Pays Up," *Newsweek,* vol. 83, no. 16, p. 88, Apr. 22, 1974; "A Sweeping Remedy for Job Discrimination," *Business Week,* no. 2366, p. 21, Feb. 3, 1975; "A New Bias Blueprint at B of A," *Business Week,* no. 2377, pp. 27–29, Aug. 18, 1975; and "Several More Slaps at Bias in Business," *Business Week,* no. 2334, p. 28, June 8, 1974.

12 "Construction Union Ordered to Halt Bias Against Minorities," *The Wall Street Journal,* vol. 58, no. 44, p. 8, Sept. 2, 1976; and H. Hammerman and M. Rogoff, "Unions and Title VII of the Civil Rights Act of 1964," *Monthly Labor Review,* vol. 99, no. 4, pp. 34–37, April 1976.

13 "The Fight Against Bias in Seniority," *Business Week,* no. 2231, p. 166, Mar. 9, 1974; "Who Gets the Pink Slip?" *Time,* vol. 105, no. 5, p. 58, Feb. 3, 1975.

14 "Justices Uphold Giving Seniority Retroactivity," *The Wall Street Journal,* vol. 57, no. 60, p. 4, Mar. 25, 1976; "More Seniority for the Victims," *Time,* vol. 107, no. 14, p. 65, Apr. 5, 1976.

15 "Reverse Discrimination: Has It Gone Too Far?" *U.S. News and World Report,* vol. 80, no. 13, pp. 26–29, Mar. 29, 1976; "Court Turning Against Reverse Discrimination?" *U.S. News and World Report,* vol. 81, no. 2, pp. 63–64, July 12, 1976; "Job Bias Ruling in Favor of White Males," *Business Week,* no. 2240, pp. 30–31, July 12, 1976.

CASES

As just pointed out, labor contracts now usually contain a provision in which Management and the Union agree not to discriminate on the basis of race, color, religion, sex, national origin, or age (limits of forty to sixty-five years being included) and hence matters of discrimination may and not infrequently do become the subject—or one of the subjects—of arbitration hearings. The cases of this chapter all fall into that category.

The first two involve discharge, in one instance because of what Management decided was theft and aiding another employee to commit the crime, and in the other for an admittedly brutal attack upon the employee's supervisor. In each case there is the question of whether the discharge should be sustained, but there is also the allegation of illegal discrimination on the basis of national origin and/or race. This allegation may well complicate Management's handling of the case.

The third case involves a woman who was disqualified as group leader during a negotiated trial period. She strongly felt that she in no way deserved to be removed from the job, having performed it conscientiously and satisfactorily, she believed. Actually, she asserted, her situation was due to the obvious prejudices of the male managers against a woman being allowed to take what might turn out to be the first step toward a manager's position.

How should these grievances be handled?

CASE 18-1

This is a case in which the question is whether the Company had "just cause" for the discharge of Food Clerk Carlos Ortega, and if not what the remedy should be. The contract provided that "the Employer shall have the right to discharge any employee for just cause." It also stated that "pilferage or theft of company property . . . shall be cause for discharge."

Ortega had been with the Company almost three years, starting as a courtesy clerk and being promoted to food clerk about a year later. His work was satisfactory or better, there being no evidence of adverse actions on his personnel folder.

On the day of his discharge, Ortega was working with a crew in cleaning and stocking the store after the doors closed for the day at 9 P.M. At 10 P.M. the assistant manager left and put Ortega in charge of the crew of some six persons.

During that day Bill Stephens, the district manager, had received an anonymous phone call alleging that employees on the cleaning shift were stealing groceries from the Company. Consequently he parked in his car in a dark part of the parking lot, but in a place where he could see into the store and also see who came and went. Shortly before midnight Ricardo Garcia left with a big bag of groceries after being checked out by Ortega. Stephens stopped him outside the store, found merchandise worth $6.98 and a cash register receipt for $1. Garcia, who was subsequently discharged, insisted that he had told Ortega he had "a dollar's worth of merchandise" and that the latter "took his word for it" and rang up the $1 he was given.

Inside the store Stephens found two other bags of groceries that had been checked by Ortega, one for another employee and one for himself. Upon investigation he found that both had been checked without error or discrepancy.

Ortega was discharged for violating one of the posted store rules: "Selling merchandise to fellow employees . . . for less than market . . . price shall be construed as theft and cause for discharge."

Ortega insists that he did not know that Garcia had merchandise worth more than $1, that he had always before found him honest, and had no reason to suspect him this time. The Union makes much of the point that had Ortega been guilty of theft (or aiding in stealing) he would hardly have checked out his own groceries correctly when he had no reason to suspect that anyone would check on him. It also alleges that he would not have been fired if he had been an Anglo instead of a Spanish-surnamed American (SSA).

Should the discharge be sustained? If not, was Ortega guilty of a lesser offense for which he deserves some punishment short of discharge? If he is restored to his position, what of back pay, and so forth? (The last two questions should not be read as intending to imply a negative answer to the first one.)

CASE 18-2

Robert Bryan, a black and a folder operator, had worked for the Company for ten years prior to his discharge in March 1976. The first three years he spent as a porter; the last seven he has been in the production department of this printing establishment. His work, while not outstanding, has been satisfactory, his attendance record is average or above, and his personnel record shows no instance of any previous serious disciplinary infraction.

On the day in question, Bryan operated a one-fold machine until about 11 A.M., at which time his foreman transferred him to a 16-fold machine, on which he worked until 11:45 A.M. In his opinion, though he had some difficulty with the improper functioning of both machines, his production on both was average and satisfactory, although Richard Hines, his foreman, felt the four hours on the one-fold were distinctly unsatisfactory and that during the forty-five minutes on the 16-fold he did virtually nothing at all.

At any rate Hines ordered a leadman to go to Bryan's machine at 12:30 P.M., when the lunchbreak was over, to monitor Bryan's work and assist him with it. At this point Bryan made an otherwise-unprovoked physical attack on Hines, hitting him a number of times with his fists and at least twice with a 2″ × 4″ about 10 inches long. Seven stitches were required to close Hines' wounds, and he lost the remainder of that day and all the next from work.

The Company promptly discharged Bryan, and a grievance was filed to protest the discharge.

The Company contends that (1) Bryan was not provoked in any way by Hines, who was simply doing what his job required of him; (2) no provocation, however severe, could possibly justify such an attack; (3) Bryan had an adequate remedy, if he had been wronged, through the grievance procedure; and (4) if the Company is not upheld in this discharge, which was clearly for just cause, all discipline in the plant may break down.

The Union contends that (1) the Company in general and Hines in particular have long been highly discriminatory in the way they administer discipline, severely punishing employees who are disliked and taking no action against "favorites"; (2) supervisors disobey rules (for example, concerning alcohol) with impunity while insisting that employees follow them; (3) Bryan had been provoked and "ridden" by Hines in an unmerciful and grossly unfair manner for days, and while the Union does not condone violence, it is understandable why Bryan reacted as he did: (4) while some form of discipline might be justified, discharge is obviously too severe; and (5) the real reason for harassment of Bryan was that he was (a) a black and (b) a strong and persistent Union representative.

Should Bryan be put back to work? If so, under what conditions (for example, as regards back pay)? Should the fact that he is black and also a very active Union member play any part in this decision? If the discharge is allowed to stand, what would be the justification for such a decision?

CASE 18-3

Ms. Ruth Payton is an assembler in an electronics firm. She has ten years of Company service, nearly all of it in her present job and department.

The latter part of last year an opening was posted for group leader—assembly and Ms. Payton bid on and was awarded the job. There is a provision for the senior eligible individual to be awarded a job vacancy and to be given up to thirty days "to demonstrate his ability, and progress; otherwise he is disqualified."

Some fifteen days after beginning her trial period Ms. Payton received a Notice of Disciplinary Action for "negligence—too many errors," and about a week later another warning and a two-day layoff, the latter being in connection with a serious production error on the part of one of the workers whom she was "leading." Shortly afterwards she was disqualified as group leader and returned to her job as assembler.

Jim Jones, Ms. Payton's foreman, kept a daily log of her activities, and it showed numerous instances where she allegedly spent too much time "working instead of leading or failed to assign and/or subsequently check on work tasks of crew members." She herself said she never told people what to do. Being grown and experienced, she said, they already knew, and she always helped them when she could.

Ms. Payton subsequently filed two grievances, one protesting the two-day layoff and the other the demotion. It is her position that she was unjustly laid off in the first instance and unjustly demoted in the second. She also asserts that the Company's treatment of her was based on (1) discriminatory treatment because she is a woman and (2) the preference of Jones for a man who was number 2 on the seniority list, was a close personal friend, and was awarded the group leader job when she was disqualified.

What facts and what factors should be considered in the Company's reply to this grievance? How should it be decided?

Part Four

Background Factors in the Supervisor's Job

In many ways, the following was the hardest part of this book to write—because there is so much that might and should be covered and so little space. One theme running through the book is that it is *essential* in many instances for the supervisor to understand the history and/or background of a development if it is to be dealt with intelligently and effectively. Examples are almost limitless: To deal with today's American worker one must know something about "the melting pot," the frontier, and a sense of "manifest destiny" for the United States; to evaluate a wage-and-salary program, one must have an appreciation of the motivations actually operating in a work force; to understand labor unions, it is essential to know the history of work in the West, including attitudes toward it, conditions under which it has been done, the effect of general economic conditions upon it, and the influences of Adam Smith, Karl Marx, and other moral and economic philosophers. We remark in one of the chapters of this part that those ignorant of history are bound to repeat its mistakes. This view has its limitations, but it contains a powerful insight.

In this part we have been able to cover some important developments but have been forced to omit others (and to include some others as a passing reference only). Among those omitted—or barely mentioned—are the views of philosphers through the ages, notably Plato, Aristotle, Augustine, Aquinas, Hobbes, in addition to Locke, Smith, Marx, Darwin, Spencer, and Freud—to mention only a few; the Industrial Revolution and its effects; the genesis, development, and fundamental alterations in the puritan ethic; the doctrine of the survival of the fittest; industrial development in America, particularly from

1865 to 1941; political movements having an impact on the workplace; and international events and developments.

There are a lot of areas that the student of this subject might profitably investigate after finishing this book.

Chapter 19

The Hawthorne Studies:
Worker Attitudes and Productivity

From time to time in the chapters preceding this one and in the management literature generally, tribute has been paid to "scientific" studies of supervisor and worker behavior. While they have made significant contributions to our conclusions, knowledge about supervision comes from many sources, including actual observation of "real-life" work situations as these occur under many different circumstances. The most important of these studies are, however, quite worth our examination and in this and the succeeding chapter they will be our chief topic of concern. In Chapter 21 additional ones are presented, along with some other material.

BACKGROUND OF THE HAWTHORNE STUDIES

The Hawthorne studies are so called because they were carried out in the Hawthorne plant of the Western Electric Company near Chicago. Not counting some preliminary investigations into which we do not have space to go, there were three of them, each beginning in 1927 or 1928 and continuing until 1932.

The first of these studies consisted in placing a group of five relay assemblers in a separate room, with the purpose of investigating the effects of rest periods on output. A second study involved a group of nine wiremen, three solderers, and two inspectors who were in a room where the effects of group solidarity could be studied. A third was an interviewing procedure which eventually involved more than 21,000 nonsupervisory employees in the plant. To an extent each of these studies was separate from the others and complete in itself, but an attempt was made, in interpreting and reporting the results, to combine them all into a meaningful program of motivation for workers.[1]

THE RELAY ASSEMBLY INVESTIGATION

One of the problems of considerable concern to the Hawthorne management was the effect of repetitive work on the attitudes and output of workers. This problem had previously been investigated somewhat from the standpoint of both fatigue and monotony, and the results indicated that repetitive work had a pronounced and unfavorable effect in both areas. In this first Hawthorne study the problem was further investigated by introducing rest periods with the expectation of reducing both fatigue and monotony.[2]

Background of the Study

The task selected was the assembling of relays. It involved putting together in proper relationship, and securing, thirty or more small parts. However, methods of assembly had been carefully studied and tools and jigs provided so that the entire operation required about a minute. Since there was a large and continuing need for these relays, there was always a backlog of work awaiting any worker, and hence the whole day could be spent in uninterrupted, definitely repetitive work.

At the beginning of the experiment about 100 women were engaged in relay assembly. Five of these were selected to leave the main floor where the 100 worked and to constitute the Relay Assembly group. These operators were studied in the main work area for some weeks in order to establish a base rate of output and then, after explanation about the purpose of the experiment, were moved into the Relay Assembly Test Room.

It is important to note that in choosing the girls to go into this room care was taken to select only experienced operators, so that any improvement that might occur could not reasonably be attributed to learning the job. Also the experimenters were careful not to select either the outstandingly good or the unusually poor workers. Rather it was thought best to find competent, interested, and typical operators.

Finally, the girls were requested to hold their motivation level constant so far as possible. After all, the purpose was to examine the relationship between rest periods on the one hand and fatigue and monotony on the other, and significant changes in level of interest and determination would introduce variables that might seriously affect the outcome of the investigation.

One other change in the work situation might also be mentioned: The girls were paid a bonus on the basis of the output of the group of five rather than, as on the main floor, on the basis of the output of the much larger group. It should be noted, however, that the rate per piece was not changed at all.

After some time for the operators to become adjusted to working in the Relay Assembly Test Room and to the new way of computing earnings, rest periods were introduced into the work schedule. The first such periods were only five minutes in length, one in the morning and one in the afternoon. Later this was extended to rest periods of ten minutes in duration. Still later, six 5-minute rest periods were provided, three in the morning and three in the afternoon. Finally, a fifteen-minute period in the morning (with light refreshments furnished by the company) and a ten-minute period in the afternoon became the work pattern and was continued with some variations for about eighteen months.

Some other changes were introduced into the above arrangement, that is, the workday with the two rest periods: during one part of the study the girls were allowed to leave work thirty minutes early each day; afterwards they were permitted to leave an hour early; still later they were not required to work on Saturday morning; finally, in the last part of the experiment a full workweek was required, the fifteen- and ten-minute rest periods being provided, but without anything furnished by the company.

In about the middle of the investigation, however, another important variation was introduced: for almost three months the girls returned to the original conditions of the test room, with no rest periods, no time off from work, and no refreshments. Thus, we have a situation where rest periods and time off from work were introduced and expanded, then the arrangement was modified to eliminate all of these, and finally the fifteen- and ten-minute rest periods were restored and continued for a number of months, to the conclusion of the study. What were the results of the investigation?

Results of the Study

Naturally, the investigators were much interested in the outcomes of the investigation. If rest periods do relieve fatigue and monotony, they may hold the key to large increases in productivity.[3]

Initial findings from the Relay Assembly Test Room strongly indicated the helpful effects of rest periods. With few exceptions, an increase in time spent in rest periods was followed by an increase in hourly output by the workers. Furthermore, this was not simply a temporary result, for each period lasted for a considerable time and the increased output was sustained during the period. Likewise, the longer rest periods were usually followed by a greater increase in output. Giving considerable time off from work in the afternoon or on Saturday did not lead to reduction in hourly output.

At this point, however, it seemed wise to investigate the possibility that something other than rest periods or time off might be operating; hence the decision to return to the original conditions of the experiment, with no rest periods, no refreshments, and no time off.

In some ways the results here are what might have been expected. Hourly output during this period did not go up, as it had in most other periods. On the contrary, it showed a slight downward trend. There are two noteworthy observations at this point, however. In the first place, the decline was in no sense a steady and prolonged one. As a matter of fact, two of the operators showed a slight gain and the other three declined only a small amount, so that the net effect was hardly more than a "leveling off." In the second place, the productivity was higher by about 50 percent than it was in the beginning of the Relay Assembly investigation and showed no sign that it would ever decline to the earlier level. Thus the interesting fact is that while the operators were experienced (and the results were therefore not explainable in terms of learning) and made a conscious effort not to try harder, output was in fact decidedly higher than it had previously been under similar conditions. And in the last period, with the return of the rest pauses, significant gains in productivity again occurred.

Table 19-1 shows the output of the five relay assemblers during *the last week* of each of the three periods. (It should be noted that these are not mean figures, these not being easily available. Furthermore, they are extrapolated from a table and hence are subject to some error.) It is noteworthy (1) how much production increased by the end of thirteen months and (2) how little it apparently declined when rest periods were removed. (As a matter of fact, if mean figures were available they would probably indicate no decrease and possibly a small increase.)

Explanations of the Results

At least five explanations of the findings were critically examined by the investigators. Two of these, that the results could be attributed to relief from fatigue or monotony, had been considered from the beginning of the study. Three more were later added for examination: first, that the overall increase in output was due to the new way of calculating wages and bonus payments; second, that it was to be explained in terms of the fact that the girls were working in a different sort of environment or work situation; and, third, that there had been a change in the kind of supervision the girls received.

Table 19-1 Hourly Output by Selected Periods (Relay Assembly Rm)*

	At beginning (no rest periods)	Just before elimination of rest periods (13 months later)	At end of 3 months with no rest periods
Operator 1	50	64	63
2	52	66	65
3	53	62	59
4	52	62	60
5	49	59	57

*Source: Roethlisberger and Dickson, *Management and the Worker*, Harvard University Press, 1939, p. 76.

The Fatigue Hypothesis On the surface, the assumption that the results of the studies were due to the rest which the operators obtained from the rest periods appeared to be quite attractive. After all, rest periods did generally accompany increased output, and it is quite logical to give the former credit for the latter. But disturbing questions could also be asked about this conclusion.

For one thing, the increase in output was not proportional to the amount of rest. In the phase of the study where six 5-minute pauses were provided, for example, the girls were not pleased with the large number of interruptions and did not perform as well as might be expected. Also, shortening the workday and the workweek did not produce corresponding increases in *total* productivity.

In the second place, the hour-by-hour production pattern was not fundamentally altered. Production continued to be low in the early morning and lowest in the late afternoon, and in spite of any pattern of rest periods the peak of production continued to be in the middle of the morning and in the early afternoon.

What is perhaps even more significant along this line is that the girls did not report an accumulation of fatigue and did not see the rest periods as noticeably relieving feelings of fatigue. Furthermore, they had reserves of energy on which they could and did call, for on occasions when one girl had to leave work early, the others made up for her absence by additional efforts and without complaints about being tired.

Most discrediting to this explanation, however, were the results obtained when the rest pauses were removed. If rest caused the greater output, its removal should have been followed by a rather rapid drop to the levels of productivity of the beginning of the experiment. The fact that this result was not obtained calls into question the whole idea that relief from fatigue was the principal factor operating in the situation.

Thus we are forced to conclude that the greater productivity obtained in the study came principally if not wholly from causes other than relief from fatigue.

The Monotony Hypothesis It proved to be impossible to test the monotony hypothesis in any final sense. After all, monotony is largely a subjective thing, a state of feeling within the individual, and it certainly arises as much from how a person feels about his work, his fellow workers, his supervisor, and the like as it does from the character of the work itself. If a large part of the explanation from the results of the experiment is to be found in the sentiments or attitudes of the workers, monotony cannot be ruled out. More fundamental than monotony as such, however, might be more basic feelings of workers and the reasons for such feelings.

In this situation monotony did not appear to be an important factor. Most of us would think that it would be, for if we had to assemble hundreds of relays per day, day in and day out, we might very well be decidedly bored. But the girls in the test rooms made no report of feelings of monotony and did not appear to suffer from such feelings. Thus there was no evidence of relief from monotony as the study progressed.

The Wage Hypothesis   Another possibility was that the results of the investigation could best be explained by the different method of compensation adopted for the operators, that is, by figuring their "percentage" (or bonus) on the basis of a group of 5 rather than of 100 operators. After all, in the smaller group one can have more direct influence on the amount received than in the larger one, and if one can persuade the others to cooperate, the results can be immediate and decided.

This attractive hypothesis proved to be fairly easy to test. A second group of five relay assemblers was selected. They were given substantially the same instructions as the first group and were the same sort of operators. They, too, were studied during a period in which average output was determined, were then put into a compensation system which involved payment on the basis of five operators instead of the larger group, but *were left on the main floor* to do their work. If wages were the controlling factor, the second relay assembly group should have achieved results comparable to those of the first group.

This did not prove to be the case. While there was some improvement in output, it was by no means as large and continuing as in the Relay Assembly Test Room. Payment on the basis of five people may have had something to do with the results obtained in the room, but the effects were minor or at least not nearly great enough to match the results of the previous group.

Even if the outcome had been the same in both cases, the wage hypothesis would not have been proved. The explanation could lie in the attention the girls received and its effect on their attitudes. Hence, the wage theory must be rejected as the main cause of the results obtained.

The Work-Environment Hypothesis   It will be recalled that another explanation of the results was that they were due to the effect of merely being placed in the test room. Certainly this was an environment quite different from being on the main floor, especially when one considers how word about the study spread and how carefully records were kept.

This hypothesis was also subjected to a test. A group of operators whose income was calculated on an individual-incentive (rather than a group-incentive) rate was selected on the same basis as other operators (not the best or the worst and only if they were experienced workers), given the same sort of instructions, observed in their usual work situation, and then moved into a special, separate room. If the work environment was the critical factor, they should have responded as did the girls in the Relay Assembly Test Room.

As was true for the second group of relay assemblers, these operators showed some favorable response to the changes. But also, as was true for the second group of assemblers, they showed nothing like the same amount of increased, sustained output. The conclusion, therefore, has to be the same: The work environment was not the *principal* factor operating in the situation.

The Supervision Hypothesis   Another theory was that the increased and sustained productivity arose primarily from a changed supervisory situation in the test room. Certainly this had changed, though perhaps as much without planning as otherwise. On the main floor the girls were under the constant (or potentially constant) surveillance of the group chief, the section chief, the assistant foreman, and even the foreman. Furthermore, some restrictive rules of conduct were enforced; an example is talking with fellow workers, an activity the girls were required to keep at a minimum. Though a careful record was to be kept of what went on in the test room, restrictions on conversation were never announced or enforced. The girls were cautious along this line at first, but as time went by they became less so.

In addition, the actual amount of supervision in the test room diminished as the experiment developed. Thus the group chief and section chief spent less and less time in the room, and the assistant foreman and foreman came by infrequently. Undoubtedly the girls came to be freer in their activities and to have less feeling of being watched. In fact they sometimes remarked, "We don't have a supervisor in this room."

It is one thing, however, to say that increased productivity *followed* more relaxed supervision and quite another to prove that the latter is *responsible* for the former. It is not impossible, for example, that increased productivity may have caused supervisors to watch the operators less closely. Indeed, it may be that the critical factor here was not the relaxed supervision but the development on the part of the workers of attitudes that led them to feel that they were being trusted more, were being dealt with in an adult fashion, and were making a real contribution to the company and perhaps to society in general.

The Operators as a Social Group A consideration that has been implied, though not expressly discussed thus far, is the relations among the girls who constituted the work group. Certainly they could hardly have gone through all these changes and worked together as they did for many months without their feelings toward each other having undergone some alterations.

The fact is that the girls developed a great deal of group spirit. They were friendly enough from the first, but as time went by they became a closely knit, cooperative group. Formerly they went their own way after work. This gradually changed and most of them became close personal friends off the job. In addition, their willingness to help each other on the job, especially if one was ill, became a very pronounced development. Also their group goals went higher and higher and so did their output. The development of esprit de corps was undeniably influential.

Changed Attitudes toward Work Growing out of this situation but also doubtless contributing to it were basic changes in attitudes toward the work and the work situation. No longer were they merely cogs in a machine, simply numbers or names among scores of others. They were now engaged in at least a mildly exciting, new adventure. Furthermore, they became persons in whom increasing numbers of people had an interest, for as word of the study spread people from many parts of the plant and from outside of it became interested in them.

All this raises the question of how well the operators followed their instructions not to put more effort into their work. The evidence indicates that they did attempt to work in the way in which they had always done. In other words, they did not consciously try harder, and they were often quite surprised at how high their productivity had gone.

This situation suggests an important observation: If a worker finds his job boring, lacking in challenge, and carrying no sense of accomplishment, the work is likely to seem difficult, unpleasant, and monotonous. On the other hand, if there is challenge and purpose in the tasks, hard jobs may seem easy and monotonous tasks may seem interesting. This is apparently what happened here; the girls did not consciously try harder but their attitudes toward the work made it seem easier, and they accomplished more.

In summary it might be well to point out the three hypotheses that Mayo and his collaborators concluded were most significant. One was the relaxed supervision in the room. It is easy to observe in many work groups that close or "tight" supervision dampens enthusiasm. A second was the growing group spirit, increased morale, and "we-feeling." The third was the growing sense of the girls that they "really counted," that they were not held to be merely a means of production but had significance as individuals. The study does not give us sufficient evidence to demonstrate the degree or order of importance of these conclusions.[4]

THE BANK WIRING STUDY

One phenomenon observed by those in charge of the Hawthorne investigations was restriction of output on the part of employees. There were times, in other words, when employees could have produced more than they did and that in spite of the fact that management very much wanted the additional output. To study this condition more carefully, it was decided to use a group of men engaged in the wiring of banks of switches used in telephone equipment.

Background of the Study

Bank wiring seemed to be a suitable activity for a number of reasons. For one, it involved cooperation of at least three different kinds of workers, wiremen, solderers, and inspectors. For another, the output of each worker could be accurately expressed in numerical terms. Finally, the compensation of the workers was so arranged that their efforts largely determined their income.

The job of the wireman was to insert a wire in each of the 100 to 200 holes already made in the part being worked upon. These parts were put together in multiples in such fashion that a completed equipment usually involved either 3000 or 3300 connections. After the wireman had completed his task, a solderer took over and finished the operation by the application of solder to the inserted wires. An inspector was then responsible for "buying" or rejecting the complete part.

Ordinarily it was possible to solder connections about three times as rapidly as the wireman could make them. Hence one solderer was usually assigned to each group of three wiremen. Furthermore, an inspector could inspect about 50 percent more connections than a solderer could complete. Hence, it was decided to put in a separate room a group of fourteen workers, as follows: nine wiremen, three solderers, and two inspectors.

The manner in which the employees were compensated for their work needs to be examined in some detail. (Incidentally, it was not changed in any basic respect when the men were moved into the room.) They were paid on the basis of an incentive plan based on the output of the entire group. Each employee had a base rate of pay per hour, this rate being set, insofar as practicable, in accordance with his continuing productivity. In addition to the pay they earned on an hourly basis, they were also paid a "percentage" equal to the amount by which the group exceeded a predetermined and fairly easily attained output.

Results of the Study

One point worth noting is that at least during the first part of the study there was an almost unlimited backlog of work to be done, and the company wanted all that the group could put out. Furthermore, the company had a uniformly good record insofar as maintaining rates was concerned, in that it simply did not reduce them once they had been set, unless substantial changes were made in production methods.

Amount of Output Careful study had set the "bogey" (or work standard) for the wireman's job at approximately 7300 per day, but virtually none of the workers produced that much, none in fact on a sustained basis. Rather, the typical output was between 6000 and 6600 units per day. Workers would occasionally exceed these figures, just as at times they did not produce this much, but no worker consistently exceeded them by any great amount. At the same time the workers were earning an appreciable "percentage," since the *base rate* was considerably below 6000 units.

A significant fact in this connection was the ability of nearly all the workers to do substantially better than they were doing. Indeed, none occupied themselves all day in sustained, vigorous work, and none reported or appeared to be suffering from any decided amount of fatigue.

Reported versus Actual Output   The wiremen were required to report each day on how much they had produced. These reports were not the basis for computing weekly pay, for this was determined by the actual output of the entire group for each week. Rather the purpose of the reported figures was to furnish a basis for rating each man on his proper hourly rate of pay. Some observations about these reports are noteworthy.

The first fact to notice concerns the reported figures considered on a weekly basis. Here the surprising thing was how accurate they turned out to be. A man might report today that he produced more than in fact he did, but some time during the week he would likely report less than he had done and by about the amount necessary to compensate for the former exaggeration. In fact, it was surprising how accurately the men reported their actual weekly output in spite of the fact that *daily* reports were inaccurate; furthermore they did not appear to keep records for their own purposes. However, it is clear that they were going to considerable effort to report "straight-line" output.

An additional comment: while it is true that reported and actual figures were close when considered over a longer period of time, there was a slight tendency to exaggerate them. Specifically, two of the nine wiremen reported slightly less than they actually did, five reported slightly more, and two substantially more.

Table 19-2 gives some output data from the Bank Wiring Room. The real point is that reported output and actual output were very close (except for Wiremen 7 and 9) when averaged for the whole period. Daily reports and daily output, however, varied decidedly. Incidentally, if certain daywork allowances are made (a subject too complex to discuss here) Wireman 6 (as well as Wireman 3) reported less than he actually did and the other seven reported more.

Table 19-2   Reported vs. Actual Hourly Outcome (Bank Wiring)*

Wireman	Reported	Actual	Percentage of deviation
1	740	724	− 2.2
2	877	860	− 2.0
3	821	823	+ 0.01
4	769	757	− 1.6
5	812	804	− 1.0
6	824	822	− 0.01
7	711	651	− 9.2
8	741	710	− 4.3
9	468	416	− 12.5

*Source: Roethlisberger and Dickson, *Management and The Worker*, Harvard University Press, 1939, p. 434.

Reasons for Restriction of Output   Why was it that though these people had the ability and the opportunity to earn more money, they consistently refused to do so? Why did they report a greater uniformity in daily productivity than they actually achieved? The investigators examined a number of possibilities, no one of which they considered fully adequate to explain the situation.

One possibility was the fear of working themselves, or at least some members of the group, out of a job. This assumption may have been logical as the Depression deepened, but as already stated, it was not realistic in the early part of the experiment. Another possibility was the fear of rate cutting, but in view of the announced policy of the company and its past practice, there is little to recommend this hypothesis.

A third possible reason was that the 6000 to 6600 units made a "natural" day's work. After all, this represented the completion of two units of equipment and may have represented a logical stopping point. But they did not start each day on a brand-new equipment, and besides, why should just two units (and not, for example, two and a half) be a "natural" work load?

While none of these hypotheses was considered sufficient to explain what was discovered about output, it may well be that each had some effect, and, taken together, they may largely explain the situation. At any rate, one thing seems certain: from some source the employees had adopted the standard of 6000 to 6600 units per day, and this standard came to have real significance for them. Most of them showed no inclination to exceed it. Furthermore, in order to give it a reality and a stability which it did not in fact have, they adopted the habit of reporting output near to (though seldom exactly the same as) these amounts, whether actual production fell below or exceeded them. Actually, their production standard seems to have acquired an ethical basis: *It was not right* either to exceed or to produce under it by any great amount.

Group Enforcement of Output Standards   One important finding of the study was the concern the men had with seeing that their standard of output was observed. In fact, they used various means, usually with decided success, to prevent serious deviations from it. As is true for many groups one or two of them did not accept the standard, though it must be emphasized that the majority did so without apparent reservation and even with some enthusiasm and determination.

One way to deal with the offender who deviated from this rule of the group was physical punishment. The custom of "binging" consisted of hitting a person, with varying degrees of intensity and vigor, on the upper arm just below the shoulder. This practice had a number of uses, including the settling of minor disputes, and might even be used to express regard for another. One of its uses, however, was to control the behavior of group members who deviated from group norms. It was so used on numerous occasions for the person who deviated from group standards for output.

Another form of punishment was ridicule and sarcasm. A number of choice names were invented for those who consistently exceeded the output standards of the group, and these, along with other forms of sarcasm and ridicule, were often used with telling effect.

A third method of accomplishment of group purposes was isolation. Particularly since the entire group formed itself into two or more subgroups, the worker who did not follow group standards could be excluded from group activities and conversation and also prevented from becoming a part of either subgroup.

With few exceptions, these methods proved to be effective, and the group got approximately what it wanted from each member, both in actual and reported output.[5]

THE INTERVIEWING STUDY

The first two of the Western Electric experiments involved small and definite numbers of employees in particular locations, and in each case the problem was at least fairly straightforward and direct. Not so the third, or interviewing, inquiry. The problem was hardly as clear-cut, and the thousands of employees involved came from all over the plant.

Background of the Study

Before the interviewing investigation was begun in 1928, the company had been engaged for some years in training supervisors and other managers. This was done principally by using as a leader a person who attempted to keep the group "on the track" and to make progress, though he did not supply answers to the problems discussed. This method worked quite well as long as production methods and modifications were being considered, but the situation was different for the human relations problems. Here in many instances there was nothing like complete agreement on the facts; the sentiments of the workers as well as those of the supervisors were mixed up with whatever facts there were; and proposed solutions, even when advanced by experienced, capable managers, were often poles apart.

At this point it was decided that reliable knowledge about what workers thought and how they felt would be valuable, and hence the plan to interview a considerable group of them to discover their attitudes toward their supervisors, their pay, their working conditions, and the like.

Initial Phases   The Inspection Branch of the plant was picked as the place to carry out the investigation. Inspectors were present in large numbers (about 1600 in the plant). Scattered throughout the factory, they were also probably somewhat older and more experienced employees on the average, and this might well contribute to the usefulness of the information they supplied.

Three men and two women were selected to be the interviewers, representing about the proportion of male and female employees in the branch. These interviewers were without formal training and experience in interviewing, but they knew the Inspection Branch and its work quite well and were judged to have the personality characteristics needed for the task they were undertaking. They were then given considerable training in the objectives of the program and the proper methods for conducting the interviews.

The interviewers started the study with questions to which they wanted the answers, and after putting the interviewees at ease they began asking these questions. They had been instructed to take notes in spite of a fear that proved to be groundless, namely, that note taking would make the interviewing difficult. On the contrary, once the employees were convinced that what they said would be treated in confidence and nothing they revealed would be linked to them individually, they talked freely and in apparent disregard of the note taking.

Unexpected Outcomes   There were, however, unanticipated developments. For one thing, people who were not interviewed at first indicated their approval that others had been interviewed earlier, and those initially interviewed often expressed their satisfaction when they later had informal contacts with the interviewers. Not only that, but people frequently indicated that, after one or two members of a work group had been interviewed, real improvements occurred. For example, they said that supervisors had improved in their conduct or that complained-of situations had been corrected. This puzzled the interviewers, for they had not revealed any of their findings to anyone.

Another development involved the supervisors. There was some fear, as we have said, that employees might resent being interviewed, though it was not anticipated that this would be very serious. On the other hand, there was genuine concern that supervisors would dislike and oppose the program. This concern also proved to be groundless. Most supervisors cooperated with the program, and a majority expressed a desire to be included in it. While this was not done at that time, a couple of years later almost five hundred managers were interviewed.

The most unexpected development of all, however, was a certain reaction that characterized most of the early conversations. The interviewer would ask a question and get a serious, relevant answer, after which the employee would begin to talk about a topic bearing no logical relationship to the question. Somewhat puzzled, the interviewer would get the conversation back to what he considered important by asking another question. However, after one or two more questions, the employee would return to the topic he had earlier introduced and again talk about it at some length. This continued in some cases throughout the interview.

By now it was apparent to the interviewers that the employees were reacting to forces which the interviewers did not anticipate or understand, and it was decided to reexamine the program and in particular the interviewing procedure.

Change in Method Interviewing   Out of this situation a new way of conducting interviews emerged. As before, the interviewer was to be sure the interviewee was put at ease and brought to understand the general purpose of the interviews. He or she was to be guaranteed that although notes were to be taken his statements were confidential. Also as before, the interviewer was not to argue with the employee, not to try to convince him of the incorrectness of his position, and not to defend the company. Now, however, instead of asking questions, the interviewer was to encourage the employee to talk about whatever was of concern to him and to keep on talking until he decided that all matters of consequence had been covered.

The effects of the new method became apparent at once. The average time per interview had been thirty minutes. With the new method it increased to ninety minutes. Those interviewed seemed pleased with the first interviews and the method employed, but with the new method they seemed even more so. In fact, so well was the program received among the remaining members of the Inspection Branch and so valuable did management consider both the effects of the program and the information that was gained that it was decided to interview virtually all nonsupervisory people in the plant. The 1600 inspectors were interviewed in 1928; over 10,000 people in the Operating Branch were interviewed in 1929; the remainder were brought in in 1930, until a total of 21,126 employees (not including the supervisors and managers later interviewed) had been involved. This is probably the largest program of its kind ever undertaken.

Results of the Study

Naturally a study involving this number of people and their attitudes and feelings is too complex to present here in detail, but some of the findings were of considerable significance to the supervisor.

The Informal Organization   This investigation was one of the earliest to call attention to a phenomenon now widely accepted and recognized as of great significance in dealing with people. It is, as pointed out in Chapter 3 in particular, that alongside the formal organization with its job descriptions, work standards, and organization charts there exists another set of relationships between people. These are based not on how the organization should work but how it does, not primarily on the intellectual relationships and understandings but on the feelings of people.

Good examples from the present investigation are (1) the greater prestige or status of the white-collar (as opposed to the blue-collar) worker, (2) the increased acceptance that goes with seniority and experience, and (3) the "psychological distance" between successive levels in an organization. Thus in this study the psychological (or social) distance between the group chief and the section chief, the lowest levels of supervision, was relatively small, whereas it was quite large between them and the assistant foreman and particularly the foremen.

Analysis of Comments   Another significant finding came directly from the contents of the conversations. One way to analyze the interview comments would be in the context in which they appeared. Instead, it was decided to set up a set of topics and subtopics, about eighty in all, and to place each comment under the proper heading. Also each comment was to be judged as favorable or unfavorable (or, perhaps better, pleasant or unpleasant in feeling tone). When these decisions had been made, it was possible to determine two things for each topic: first, the frequency with which, in comparison to other topics, it was commented upon by the workers; and, second, the degree of favorableness with which it was viewed (determined by the percentage of comments that were favorable). It was thus possible to see what people were most concerned about and, for each aspect studied, whether they were favorably or unfavorably disposed toward it.

Naturally some topics were mentioned quite frequently and others but rarely. Likewise some were commented upon very favorably and some unfavorably. Of course there were some that were intermediate in both frequency and favorableness.

One way to get at the meaning of the results is to ask what *kinds* of topics were discussed in highly unfavorable terms and what sort in favorable ones. For example, what kind of topic do workers comment upon favorably 90 percent or more of the time (to pick a purely arbitrary percentage) and what kind do they see favorably only 10 percent or less of the time? The following topics among others, appear in the favorable list: stock-purchase plan, vacations, benefit plans, company placement, thrift, general club activities, ready-money plan, life insurance, and legal service. The unfavorable group, again among others, contains lockers, spitting, tools, time clocks, aisles, trucks, pans, quality of materials, elevators, and fans.

The problem of what all these findings mean remains, and we shall now turn to that topic.

Interpretation of Findings   One way to begin our task of interpretation is to look at the kinds of complaints (or unfavorable comments) people made.

Kinds of Complaints   Generally, these were found to be easily classifiable in one of three groups, called Class A, Class B, and Class C. A Class A complaint was one that could be definitely located, that involved objects that could be seen and touched, and that referred to operations easily defined. Examples were, "The tool is dull" and "The doorknob is broken." A Class B complaint was less definite. The terms involved in this sort of complaint usually concerned experiences other than sight and touch, for at least some part of the complaint, and also referred to an operation not easy to define clearly and unambiguously. Examples were, "The work is dirty," "The lockers are unsanitary," and "The room is hot." The last term in each of these could certainly be defined differently by different people, and while the work, the lockers, and the room can be seen and touched, the same cannot be said for "dirty," "unsanitary," and "hot."

Class C complaints seemed to deal very largely with the hopes and fears of the employees. Any reference to sensory experience was general and vague, the terms of the complaint being so broad that it was difficult and even at times impossible to determine the objective fact, if any, that was being discussed. For example, if a person says, "The rates are too low," it is difficult to determine whose rates are referred to. Is it all, most, or some? Besides, how low is "too low," and to what standard is "low" relative? Likewise, if an employee says, "Ability just doesn't count in this company," he does not specify what sort of ability or whose ability he has in mind, and it is open to question just what he means by "count." Actually, the statement is so sweeping in scope as to overstate the situation even in the worst condition one is likely to encounter.

At first this division of complaints may appear to be without any real significance to the manager. However, there is more here than meets the eye: While some complaints refer to what the employee is unhappy about and state the actual situation with regard to that thing, some do not. Included in those that do not reflect the true situation may from time to time be those in which the employee is deliberately trying to mislead. For example, he may be saying that "ability doesn't count in this company" when he knows full well it does count and he is simply misrepresenting. But Class B and Class C complaints were numerous, not scarce or rare, and it requires little investigation to demonstrate that much more than deliberate deception is involved.

The fact is that it was in connection with this distinction that one of the most meaningful findings of this study emerged. It is that when people *need* to complain, they most likely *will* (and almost certainly will if they have the opportunity to do so and are not penalized for it). However, what they complain about may bear no logical relationship to what they are unhappy about. The complaint, in other words, often is not an expression of fact or truth as such. It is an expression of feeling. This point leads us directly to two closely related, indeed almost identical, sets of concepts arising from the study.

Manifest versus Latent Complaints One way to approach the distinction we were making above and the one we have in mind here is to follow some of the teachings of Freud. This pioneer investigator of human emotions arrived at the conclusion that behind what we say to others (called the *manifest*) there frequently lie feelings, attitudes, thoughts, and conclusions of which we are not aware but which cause us to select a certain proposition that well expresses our particular feeling state (the *latent*). Thus, "Ability does not count in this company" may have little reference to who is selected for promotion or the basis for such selection. The statement may actually be a way the person has of expressing his disappointment or even resentment at his own lack of attainment. (Unconsciously he may realize that his lack of progress may be due to his own ineptness or lack of effort, though relatively few of us are able to admit this at the conscious level.) In this illustration, "Ability does not count in this company" is the manifest complaint. The *latent* is the frustrations of the person about his slow progress and his own feelings of unworthiness.

It cannot be emphasized too strongly that in these circumstances the person who complains is often the one who least understands the situation. He is not trying to fool anyone (unless he is trying to mislead himself) and he very definitely is not lying. He is expressing his feelings and at the moment accepts the truth of what he has said, though a moment later, upon reflection, he may be at least partially aware of what is happening. The manifest, then, is stated as the truth and intended as such. The latent comes out of unconscious states and is an expression, in the most accurate and appropriate terms the person can find, of his underlying emotion.

Fact, Falsehood, and Nonfact Another distinction that throws some light on our problem is that between *fact, falsehood, and nonfact*. While there could be argument about the definition of fact and the meaning of falsehood, in the main these present no great problem. A factual statement attempts to reflect the situation as it is, and a false statement tries to distort the situation or mislead the hearer or reader.

What those in charge of the Hawthorne studies introduced at this point was the notion of the *nonfact*. A nonfactual statement is one which is neither true nor false but nonfactual, that is, a statement giving expression to some underlying feelings and attitudes of the person. As such and at the unconscious level, it is not designed to tell the truth or to mislead; it is designed to secure emotional release.

Herein lies one of our most important discoveries about human behavior: Human thought and its expression in speech or writing serves not one but two distinct functions for the individual. One of these is the well-known one of conveying ideas (or truth or information). A person thinks about or investigates a situation and arrives at what seems to him to be the correct conclusions. These he formulates in proper and accurate words, and he transmits them to others by writing or speaking these words. From this point of view, every statement is either true or false; it is either a statement of fact or it is not. Frequently the important thing is to detect those statements that are not factual and get them corrected speedily.

Without denying that language deals with ideas and that statements may be either true or false, the point of view here being described insists that language (and thinking) has another and equally important function: to convey and especially to release feeling. Perhaps the most significant aspect of this situation is to demonstrate that words do have emotion-releasing value.

This is easy to do. Everyone has at one time or another experienced the relief that comes from "getting if off his chest." Many of his expressions may be literally and completely factual, just as some may be false, but if we stop there we miss the most important point of all, namely, that many of these statements are as such neither true nor false but nonfactual.

The attitudes that workers express toward the employee cafeteria often are a case in point. The food may be tasteful, nutritious, and economical, but people need a scapegoat; food in the cafeteria often provides a convenient one. Similarly, expressions such as "It's not what you know but who you know in this company that really counts" are in a majority of cases nonfactual rather than being serious attempts at an objective analysis of the situation. Indeed, all sweeping generalizations about conditions in the work situation, black workers, women supervisors, and a host of related items should be suspect from the beginning. Allowance may be made for the possibility that they represent serious, non-emotional attempts to portray the situation as it is, but the presumption should be that they are nonfactual. In the great majority of cases they are just that.[6]

Figure 19-1 presents one of the most interesting findings from the Hawthorne investigations.

The Interviewing Method

It remains to say something about the method of interviewing used in the study. For one thing, it is obvious that one does not treat everything that is said as having the same psychological or other meaning. What is said must be seen in the larger context and the meaning, if any, that lies behind the words must be sought.

Basically the method is designed to get the individual to speak freely and express himself on a number of topics. The interviewer is to be friendly without being sentimental. He is to show no authority, nor is he to "pass moral judgment" on what has been said. He asks questions, not to put the interviewee on the spot nor to further his point of view, but to get more expression from the other person and, at times, to introduce or reintroduce different topics. When questioned, the interviewer may explain the assumptions of the

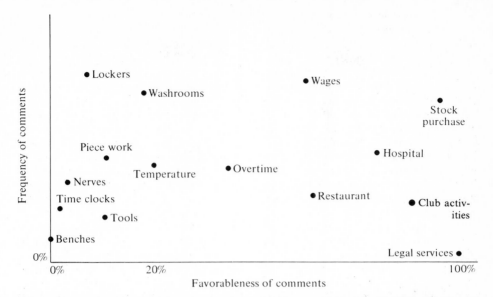

Figure 19-1 The above is not drawn to scale, but it does not seriously distort the location of any topics shown (about one-fourth of the total of eighty-three, the others omitted because of space). Note that topics relating to (physical) working conditions are commented upon favorably no more than one time in five. In view of the fact that working conditions at the Hawthorne plant were in no sense poor, we are evidently dealing here with *nonfacts* (or *manifest* complaints which have underlying causes [*latent* complaints]). *(Adapted from Roethlisberger and Dickson,* Management and the Worker, *Harvard University Press, 1939, pp. 232–239.)*

method, including the wish for free expression and the hope that, through expression, insight will be thrown on particular existing problems and that the interviewee will be the better for having been interviewed.[7]

   The Hawthorne Studies and Nondirective Interviewing   It is obvious, of course, that this method of interviewing has much in common with the nondirective method described in some detail in Chapter 12 and referred to in other chapters in this book. True it grew out of a different background—the workplace rather than a counseling center—and was used, not for psychotherapy but to understand and deal with employee attitudes, values, hopes, and disappointments. For purposes of the supervisor, however, these distinctions are not important. What is quite significant is the fact that the two approaches led to highly similar conclusions and have furnished managers who use it wisely with one of their most effective personnel techniques.

THE SUPERVISOR AND THE HAWTHORNE STUDIES

One way to conclude this chapter, coming as it does late in this book, would be to summarize the above findings and attempt to show how a great many of them either were the basis for conclusions drawn in previous chapters or at least are consistent with and reenforce such conclusions. Much of this is apparent without express statement, however, and can be done by anyone who is interested. We have decided to close this chapter by raising some questions that grow directly out of the Hawthorne studies, questions without definite, generalized answers but still matters worth considering, especially in particular supervisory situations, long after one has finished reading this book.[8]

One question is the degree to which the group-centeredness of a work-crew pays off in higher production. In the Relay Assembly study it did, and in the Bank Wiring one it did not. To what extent should a supervisor cultivate such feelings and how can he see that they contribute to the good of the organization?[9]

Another question relates to the kind or quality of supervision. How far may one go in believing in and practicing "relaxed" supervision? Can it be carried too far? Does the average manager of today make more mistakes by overdoing or underdoing this? To what extent is "relaxed" supervision related to self-confidence on the part of the supervisor?

Still another concern involves "using" people. In what sense and under what circumstances do people seek, permit, discourage, or rebel against being "used"? Did *scientific management* give this point proper consideration? Do most of us? Are there important ethical issues here?

And then there is the matter of restriction of output. Just how widespread is it? Are blue-collar workers the only ones who practice it? Is it ever present, consciously or not, in engineering organizations? among faculty members? in college students? on athletic teams? Are the only ethical aspects of this phenomenon that the worker may be cheating the company by doing less than his best? Do work groups have serious ethical standards?

The interviewing study raises a host of inquiries. How common is scapegoating among workers? among managers? How does one distinguish between a genuine, well-founded objection and scapegoating? May a worker grieve about one thing when his real problem is something else—and all the time be unaware himself of the true situation?

Finally, there is the informal organization, how it operates, and how, if at all, the supervisor might make use of it.[10]

It is apparent that all of the above are fundamental questions for today's supervisor. One of the greatest contributions of the Hawthorne studies is that they originally raised or gave added impetus to the above questions—and a great many others like them.

QUESTIONS

1 Describe the work situation in which the Hawthorne studies took place and the numbers and kinds of workers involved in each of the three studies.
2 On what basis were the workers of the Relay Assembly Room selected? What changes were made in the work situation as compared to the main floor (a) at first and (b) as the study progressed?
3 What were the chief results of the Relay Assembly investigation?
4 What was the relation between reported output and actual output in the Bank Wiring Room? How do you account for these discrepancies?
5 How well did the Bank Wiring employees conform in comparison to what they could have done? How is this situation to be accounted for?
6 What were (a) the kinds and numbers of people interviewed (in the Interview study) and (b) the chief results obtained? How do you account for the unusual or unexpected results?
7 How widespread is restriction of output? Why do people engage in it? Mention examples that you have personally observed.
8 Distinguish between *fact, falsehood,* and *nonfact,* and indicate the significance of this distinction for the supervisor.

NOTES

1 Prior to this time emphasis in supervision and motivation had been placed on economic and technological factors. For example, *scientific management* was at the height of or just past its greatest acceptance. On the other hand, little or no attention was given to such influences as are spelled out today in a book like Elliot Aronson, *The Social Animal,* 2d ed. (San Francisco: Freeman, 1976) or in an article like R. L. Payne, S. Fineman, and T. D. Wall, "Organizational Climate and Job Satisfaction: A Conceptual Synthesis," *Organizational Behavior and Human Performance,* vol. 16, no. 1, pp. 45–62, January 1976.

2 The earliest report on the Hawthorne studies is probably Elton Mayo, *The Human Problems of an Industrial Civilization* (New York: Macmillan, 1933).

3 An unusually meaningful interpretation of the Hawthorne studies and their implications for managers is Fritz J. Roethlisberger and William J. Dickson, *Management and the Worker* (Cambridge, Mass.: Harvard University Press, 1939). The Relay Assembly investigation is described and interpreted on pp. 19–186.

4 Naturally these conclusions drew much attention. See, for example, George C. Homans, *Fatigue of Workers* (New York: Reinhold, 1941), especially pp. 56–65.

5 The description and interpretation of the Bank Wiring investigation are covered in Roethlisberger and Dickson, op. cit., pp. 379–550.

6 The relevant reference in Roethlisberger and Dickson, op. cit., is pp. 255–378.

7 In addition to Roethlisberger and Dickson, op. cit., see Carl Rogers, *Counseling and Psychotherapy* (Boston: Houghton Mifflin, 1942); and William J. Dickson and Fritz J. Roethlisberger, *Counseling in an Organization* (Cambridge, Mass.: Harvard Graduate School of Business Administration, 1966).

8 One of the most stimulating books on modern management is Elton Mayo, *The Social Problems of An Industrial Civilization* (Boston: Harvard Graduate School of Business Administration, 1945). Contrasting points of view are found in Henry A. Landsberger, *Hawthorne Revisited* (Ithaca, N.Y.: Cornell, 1958), and Donald R. Schoen, "Human Relations: Boon or Bogle?" *Harvard Business Review,* vol. 45, no. 6, pp. 91–97, December 1967.

9 William A. Ruch, James C. Hershauer, and Robert G. Wright, "Toward Solving the Productivity Problem: Worker Correlates to Performance," *Human Resource Management,* vol. 15, no. 1, pp. 2–6, Spring 1976.

10 Roethlisberger and Dickson, op. cit., discusses application of the Hawthorne results on pp. 551–604.

CASES

The two cases selected for this chapter both involve the imposition of discipline upon employees. Furthermore the penalties are by no means light or token ones, ten working days in the first and discharge in the second.

The Janes case raises some issues concerning who should be assigned to do unpleasant work and more particularly the appropriateness of assigning the same dirty job to the same employee year after year. In this case Janes has not alleged illegal (Title VII) discrimination, but he still might. In any case do his actions, when considered in the light of his past record, justify a layoff of two weeks? Why?

Issues in the Flanagan case include (a) the fairness of the "bumping down" procedure, which was a matter for bargaining between the Company and the Union, (b) the extent to which Flanagan was really insubordinate, and (c) the "firmness" of Cason's original statement (as well as the later one) concerning Flanagan's continued driving. Under the circumstances was discharge the most suitable penalty? Why?

CASE 19-1

Wesley Janes, a black, is an operator in a small plant of the Company. The term operator is used to cover a variety of duties, especially during the two-month period in the summer when the plant either does not operate at all or does so infrequently.

For the last several days, during this shut-down period, Janes has been assigned a tough job. With a foreman, R. T. Leinbach, he has been painting the inside of a tower that is about four stories tall. Janes works inside the tower, applying a paintlike substance as Leinbach prepares it and hands it in. Janes draws this assignment every summer. In fact he is about the only employee who has the nerve to work so high off the ground and the only one willing to do the very hot, dirty work involved.

This morning Janes and Leinbach were doing some work outside the tower when Leinbach asked Janes to go downstairs and get the "mop," a term for a 6-inch brush which Janes knew Leinbach was going to substitute for the 3-inch brush Janes had been using.

Janes had had experience with the mop before. Not only did it make the work harder, but it was not possible to use it without getting the paint all over his face and clothes. In fact, earlier in the summer he had ruined a set of work clothes this way, and though he protested that the Company should reimburse him for the loss, his demands had not been met.

Janes protested that it was not his job to get tools but only to use them. Leinbach insisted, however, and Janes went down the three flights of stairs, at the bottom of which he saw the mop lying on a shelf in plain view. However, instead of picking it up Janes went directly out of the building. Just outside he found Arnold Noel, the foreman for whom he usually works, and told Noel he was exhausted and was "going in for the rest of the day." (The hour was about 11 A.M. and less than half the shift was completed.) He proceeded to leave the plant without notifying or speaking to anyone else.

There are two additional factors involved in the case. First, some two years ago Janes received a five-day suspension for leaving the plant under similar circumstances; and, second, Leinbach's situation is unlike that of other foremen. He is a skilled mechanic and spends some days as a machinist while on other days he serves as a foreman. (There is no formal way, however, in which the men are informed on any particular day in which job Leinbach is working.) Even when he is a foreman he is permitted to do "production" work. The other foremen seldom do this.

Leinbach has just reported to Superintendent A. R. Pope what has happened and has been asked for his recommendation as to how to handle the case. He has recommended a ten-day suspension (without pay) for insubordination.

What should Pope do with this recommendation?

CASE 19-2

The events of this case took place in a warehouse of the Company, a manufacturer and distributor of oil-field tools. Some twenty-five people were employed in the warehouse, with hourly jobs ranging from laborer to shipping clerk. Included among several other jobs was that of fork-lift driver, a position intermediate in rate of pay.

The hourly people in the warehouse were covered by a labor contract which also covered the plant employees. The contract applied only to the plant in question, although the Company had similar agreements with other locals in its other plants.

One provision of the contract was that if a worker successfully bid on a job in a higher classification and then left it, he could not voluntarily return to his immediately prior job until after a period of six months. Thus if a fork-lift driver was made a shipping clerk and by his own choice relinquished the job, for whatever remained of a six-month period following his bid he had to serve as a laborer and could not become a fork-lift driver. Provisions concerning Management's right to assign people in emergencies were included in the contract.

Richard Flanagan was in just this situation. He had been with the Company five years and had a satisfactory record. Four months before, while a fork-lift driver, he had bid on a shipping clerk's job and was assigned to it. He found the work taxing and distasteful, however, and by no means worth the additional pay he received over what he had been getting as a fork-lift driver. He therefore requested permission to become a laborer, figuring that shortly after the six months were up a vacancy would occur on the fork lifts and he could return to his old job and rate.

On the afternoon in question, about a month after Richard went to the labor gang, George Douglas, the fork-lift driver, was injured and had to be replaced for the remainder of the shift. Lou Cason, the warehouse foreman, instructed Larry Michaels, a Material Handler A, to operate the truck for the rest of the afternoon. Flanagan protested, claiming that this was an emergency and that he should drive the truck (and have the rate for driving it) rather than Michaels, who had never been classified as a driver. Flanagan happened to be standing closer to the truck than was Michaels, and he promptly got into the seat of the truck.

Michaels protested weakly. Cason also protested Flanagan's action and said, "Dick, I don't want you to drive. You're not eligible."

Flanagan refused to move, however, and shortly began to operate the fork lift. About fifteen minutes later, Cason encountered him again and said, "Dick, I wish you wouldn't do it. I can't pay you (the extra rate) for it."

Flanagan drove the truck for the remaining two hours of the shift.

At the end of the shift Cason reported the incident to John Wilson, the warehouse manager, who decided that Flanagan had been insubordinate and decided upon his discharge. This action was taken after he had questioned Cason carefully about what had happened, but had not consulted with him about the penalty.

Cason has just learned of the decision of Wilson and the Company and is sure that neither Flanagan nor any of the other employees know about it as yet. What does he do now? What does he do after the decision becomes known? What does he say if called as a witness in an arbitration hearing (if the action is protested and carried that far)? Would an arbitrator sustain the Company's action or restore Flanagan his job?

Chapter 20

The Michigan Studies:
The Successful versus The Less
Successful Supervisor

When one becomes familiar with a great many studies of a particular subject it is often difficult to choose from them the one or two that are most significant. So far as empirical studies of supervision go, however, the authors do not face that problem. In our opinion, especially when considering influence on subsequent developments in the field, two sets of investigations stand out above the others. They are the Hawthorne studies, discussed in the previous chapter, and what we are here referring to as the Michigan studies, to be evaluated in this one.

The latter studies were done by a part of The University of Michigan known as the Survey Research Center, which in turn is a part of the Institute for Social Research. They were begun in 1947 (thus some twenty years after Hawthorne) and were repeated in different organizations over a period of years. Thus a number of separate investigations make up the Michigan studies.

The plan for this chapter is to present the first investigation in some detail, then to look less thoroughly at the second and subsequent ones, then to examine the general findings from the several studies, and finally to comment on their significance for the supervisor in today's world.

THE PRUDENTIAL STUDY

The Setting

The first of these studies was carried out from 1947 to 1949 in the offices of the Prudential Insurance Company in Newark, New Jersey.[1] The company employed about 10,000 people in the offices at the time. About 9500 of them could be classified as clerical in the broad sense, and about 500 were administrative. Approximately 6000 of the employees were women.

Much of the work was routine and repetitive. While there were many old-timers in the group, the average age of employees was lower than the national average, and the educational level was higher. Girls who had graduated from high school or college frequently sought jobs at Prudential as they worked between education and marriage. In fact, this was "fashionable" to a considerable degree. Except for marriage, pregnancy, death, and retirement, labor turnover was low.

Employees in the lower-level jobs were typically organized into groups of fifteen to twenty and reported to a first-line supervisor known as a section leader. These supervisors varied rather widely in age, background, and education and included both men and women.

Rates of pay for both employees and supervisors were in line with the going rates in the community for such work, but fringe benefits were outstanding. As an example, the workweek was five days of seven hours each, with a lunch furnished by the company. As part of the fringe benefits an extensive social and recreational program was maintained.

The Design of the Study

The fundamental question underlying the investigation was this: In what ways do the behavior, attitudes, values, and the like, of the more effective supervisor differ from those of the less effective? A related question concerned differences between the people in the more and the less effective work groups.

The company had long kept production records by sections, though not by individual workers. Thus it was possible to find for any work groups doing the same work which was the best and where the others stood relative to it. What those in charge of the study decided to do was to find *pairs* of work groups, alike in every variable they could check *but differing significantly in productivity.* Suppose, for example, we consider Groups A and A', both doing the same kind of work. To be left in the study as a matched pair of groups, the first requirement was that A and A' must differ in productivity too much for the difference to be attributed to chance. In this case an eight-month period was involved and three different checks were made. If A and A' did not differ in this way and to this extent, they were omitted from the study, no matter what else might be true about them.

Groups were kept in the study as a matched pair, however, only if they were alike in all the other variables examined. Thus, within the limits of a chance difference, there were the same number of men and the same number of women in each pair of groups; the average age was the same, and so were education, years of experience, and salary grades. Psychological tests were given and average scores on them also had to be the same, and the average distance from home to work was not allowed to vary significantly between a pair of groups. It was possible to find twelve such pairs of work groups, composed of 419 employees and, of course, supervised by 24 section leaders.

Table 20-1 may make the plan of the investigations somewhat clearer.

The main question for the study was now easy to state: Why is it, if age, salary, education, experience, ability, and so forth are alike for each of two groups, that one consistently and significantly outproduces the other, and to what extent will the same findings obtain for most if not all pairs of groups? Obviously this is a question of first-rate importance.

While there were production records on all the groups, there were no records that revealed attitudes, values, perceptiveness, and practices of either supervisors or employees, and it was necessary to secure information on these. There were at least two possibilities. One was to send observers into each work group, as was done in the Hawthorne studies,

Table 20-1 Differences* in Characteristics of Matched Work Groups (Prudential Study)

Groups	Number of men and women	Work done	Age	Test scores	Educa-tion	Salary	Productivity	Supervisor's demographic characteristics
A vs. A'	No	No	No	No	No	No	Yes	Not considered†
B vs. B'	No	No	No	No	No	No	Yes	Not considered†
L vs. L'	No	No	No	No	No	No	Yes	Not considered†

*No indicates no difference or one probably accounted for by chance. (Other factors also showed no difference.) *Yes* means a difference that was statistically significant.

†No attention was paid to demographic characteristics of supervisors in setting up the matched groups; they were not investigated until after completion of interviewing.

and let them make observations over a considerable period. This might very well be the more accurate method, but it was expensive and time-consuming, and besides, the presence of the observer would introduce another variable. The second was to have experienced interviewers contact and interview each supervisor and each nonsupervisory employee. This was the method that was chosen.

The interviewing method had some characteristics of the one used in the Hawthorne study. In this case, however, the interviewer had questions to which he or she wanted the answers, and if they were not answered voluntarily or spontaneously by the interviewee, the questions were asked. People were not reluctant to talk; indeed they talked freely. The average interview with the supervisors lasted 2½ hours, and the average with the nonsupervisory employees lasted 1½ hours.

Results Obtained [2]

Demographic Characteristics of Supervisors One possibility is that supervisors of high-producing groups differed from those of low-producing groups in some such factors as age, education, experience, salary, or the like. Thus, supervisors of high-producing groups might be better educated and better paid, or might have been in their jobs longer than their counterparts in the low-producing groups. (Such characteristics of supervisors were not taken into account in the original matching of the groups, though they were balanced out for the employees who were not supervisors.)

The facts did not support these conclusions or any similar ones. Considering these two groups of twelve supervisors each (those supervising high-producing groups versus those supervising low-producing groups), not a single trait of this sort differentiated between them. This says that "high" supervisors (section leaders of the more productive groups) are not older or younger, better educated, better paid, or more experienced than "low" supervisors (section leaders of the low-producing groups). This was also true of women supervisors. About a third of the twenty-four section leaders were women, and about a third of the high and a third of the low section leaders were women. In other words, the sex of the supervisor had nothing to do with the adequacy of the job he or she did.

To many these are surprising and even disappointing conclusions. Psychologists and others have long looked for the traits of the successful versus those of the less successful leader, and it cannot be denied that such information would be valuable.

One can always object that only twelve pairs of leaders are involved in this study and hence care should be exercised in drawing conclusions. This is of course true, but it must be confessed that at least up to now little evidence for the "trait" theory of supervision is to be found anywhere.

Of course we cannot deny that another possible conclusion is that good and poor supervisors simply do not differ from each other in any way that is useful and dependable, and hence that the study of supervision as such is a barren one. If the authors of this book accepted that theory, they would not have undertaken the book, but the reader may want to keep this possible conclusion in mind and determine for himself whether the material presented in this book refutes it.

Differences between the Work Groups   If the demographic characteristics of supervisors do not cause or are not even related to the greater productivity of the high-production sections (hereafter referred to as the *high groups*), where else should we look for an explanation? The next possibility we need to explore is differences between the employees (excluding the supervisors) who make up the groups.

The design of the study is such, of course, that we are not going to find differences in age, education, sex, and so on, since these were controlled in selecting the groups. An important difference which was found, however, had to do with *pride in the work group*. Here the high groups usually exceeded the low ones. Members of the high groups, in other words, generally thought that they and their fellows were capable and efficient and that they did their work well. Members of the low groups typically were not sure on these points.

It is not immediately apparent whether we are dealing here with a cause or an effect. (Since the finding was a statistically significant one, we can with reasonable assurance rule out the possibility that it was only an accidental or chance one.) After all, members of the high groups may have looked at the low groups and simply recognized that they were better. In this case, of course, we would be dealing with an effect rather than a cause.

While this possibility cannot be denied outright, the evidence is against it. For one thing, the production records were not generally known, and so it is not likely that the people could have been so sure that they were better or worse than their counterparts. For another, the actual differences, while significant, were not large ones, seldom exceeding 10 percent. It is not likely, therefore, that these differences would be immediately evident to the people involved. Finally, it must not be forgotten that when 9500 employees are divided into sections of 15 to 20 each, a large number of sections will result. Since the group members were not told with which particular section they were being compared, if indeed they were told that they were being compared with any group, the likelihood of the conclusion about recognized superiority becomes even less.

It is interesting to look at some areas in which differences were not found between the high and low sections. Three of these are particularly worth examining, since a good deal of what is believed about effective leadership today would predict that there should be significant variation. One of these has to do with a liking for the actual work done, another relates to suggestions made through the formal suggestion system of the company, and the third is concerned with participation by workers in the social and recreational system of the company. In not a single one of these areas were there significant variations between high and low groups. The failure to find such differences needs to be carefully borne in mind.

Members of high and low groups differed from each other in other ways, particularly in how they perceived their supervisor and his attitudes and behavior. Since, however, these related to supervision, it will be more convenient to discuss them under the next heading, where they can be treated in connection with results obtained from the supervisors themselves.

Differences between Supervisors   The most meaningful findings of the study came from this area. In fact, the number of significant differences between high and low supervisors was surprisingly large considering the small number of supervisors involved. Let us look at several of these.

General Supervision and Time Spent in It   In the first place, high supervisors typically supervised in a general fashion, while low ones supervised closely or tightly. For the latter, it was typically a matter of "breathing down the necks" of their people, "looking over their shoulders," or "bird-dogging." (Virtually every experienced worker is sensitive to this difference in supervision, and blue-collar workers in particular have all sorts of quaint and expressive ways of describing it.) This was a finding not only from what employees said about the section leaders but also from what the interviewers judged to be true of the leaders. (Incidentally, in no case did an interviewer know whether he or she was interviewing a member of a high or low group or a high or low supervisor. It is easy to see how important it was to control this variable, for otherwise interviewers might have unconsciously or unintentionally found what they expected to find.)

In the second place, it was the low and not the high supervisors who gave the greater amount of instruction to their workers. This is a surprising conclusion to those who have great faith in employee training and particularly to those who believe that at all times a worker should know exactly what he should do, just how he should do it, and the level of both quantity and quality of output expected. However, if general supervision is usually better than close supervision, this is just what we would expect to find, because, as we have said previously, overinstruction is one of the easiest ways in which to oversupervise.

In the third place, while high supervisors usually supervised generally and instructed less rather than more, they still reported that they spent more time in supervision. For example, when high supervisors were asked how much of their time went to supervision as opposed to all the other things they did (including "production" work, in which they were free to and expected to engage), nine of the twelve replied 50 percent or more, while the corresponding figure for low supervisors was only four of twelve. What can account for this peculiar or at least unexpected situation?

One real possibility is that high supervisors spent more time in talking *with* their people than low supervisors did for theirs. At various points in this book we emphasize the great psychological difference between talking *to* and talking *with* another person. Perhaps consciously or unconsciously the high supervisors appreciated something of this difference and reflected it in their behavior.

Another difference between high and low supervisors was related to their attitudes toward the separate dining rooms for supervisory and nonsupervisory people. When they were questioned about this, high supervisors expressed disapproval. They would have preferred to eat in the same dining room with their people. Low supervisors, on the other hand, usually approved the arrangement or thought that it did not make any difference.

Recommendations for Promotion   A fifth finding had to do with the practices of supervisors about recommending employees for a promotion, a salary increase, or other favorable personnel action. Here it was the low supervisor and not the high who characteristically made the larger number of such recommendations. This finding too may run contrary to "common sense," for it is usually assumed that the effective supervisor is "more interested in people" and is constantly trying to do more for them. Again, we are confronted with the task of trying to explain an unexpected result.

One explanation is that there is genuine doubt about whether one really helps a person by promoting him, or recommending him for promotion, when there is real uncertainty about whether he is prepared for or deserves it. A second is that while a supervisor has obligations to his people, he also has obligations to his employer, and though some idealists are reluctant to admit it, these two not infrequently come into conflict. The third is that it often requires courage on the part of the supervisor to say no when no is what needs to be said. After all, the emotionally insecure supervisor can "get the employee off his neck" by recommending a raise or promotion for him even if the supervisor is not thoroughly convinced of the propriety of the action. If the recommendation is turned down, he or she can always say to the employee, "I'm sorry, Joe, I tried." It takes a more courageous and emotionally secure person to refuse to make the recommendation initially.

As a part of this same finding, it was discovered that though high supervisors make fewer such recommendations, a larger percentage of them were acted upon favorably. This, of course, is to be expected, since by the design of the experiment people in the high and low groups had been with the company on the average the same length of time and were in the same average salary grade. Of course the high supervisors' being more careful in their recommendations might well lead to greater confidence on the part of top management in the supervisors in question and hence to their better "batting average."

Attitudes toward the Company   In the sixth place, high supervisors were more critical, including more critical of the company, than low supervisors were. It is important to recognize that we use the word "critical" in at least two different ways in the English language. One meaning is being more perceptive, more insightful, and more *evaluative,* and the other is being more inclined to find fault. In this study high supervisors were probably more critical in both senses of the term; undoubtedly they did criticize the company more.

Person-centeredness   The final result which we shall mention relates to what supervisors talked about when they were free to select the topic for discussion. It might be well to remember that there were many such occasions, particularly since the interviews lasted 2½ hours and the method of interviewing encouraged people to talk freely. One of the striking findings of the experiment is that high supervisors characteristically talked about *their people,* while low supervisors usually talked about *the work.* In other words, the former discussed the hopes, aspirations, attainments, problems, and shortcomings of their employees, while the latter talked about quotas, deadlines, efficiency, costs, and generally "getting the goods out the door." The experimenters say that the high supervisors were "employee-centered" or "person-centered" and the low ones were "work-centered." It must not be forgotten, however, that it was the former who supervised workers who "got more goods out the door" at less cost. That is the one and only reason why we call them high supervisors.

Again, we are at a point where it is hardly appropriate to try to make a final interpretation of the finding, for it too will be discussed later. However, a few remarks are again in order. It certainly would not be reasonable, in view of the records of their sections, to conclude that high supervisors simply liked people more and cared little about their output. There is nothing, indeed, in all the investigations of supervision to support such a conclusion.

A number of other possibilities suggest themselves. Perhaps high supervisors had more genuine respect for their people and interest in their problems and saw them less as production machines and more as real people like themselves. Maybe they were unwilling merely to "use" people in order to make a record. Or they may have felt more comfortable in the presence of their employees, more free to talk when in their presence, and more concerned to talk with and about them generally. One thing is apparent: Good supervision is not the simple thing that many who write about it and many others who practice it tell themselves and others it is.

Some General Observations It is important to keep in mind that so far we have been presenting the results of a single investigation involving in all fewer than 450 people. Basically, clerical work was the type of work that was done. Furthermore, the majority of the people were women, and they were on the average both younger and better educated than most American workers. Salaries were at least average, benefits were unusually good, and no union or union activities were involved. All these limitations must be kept in mind as one attempts to draw from this study any final conclusions or even lessons to be applied extensively.

Another limitation of the study has to do with the fact that it was a study of groups and not of individuals as such. The very composition of the groups is relevant here. Undoubtedly in many if not all of the low groups there were employees who consistently outproduced some (and perhaps in some cases, all) of the members of the high groups. We are not contending that this is a serious fault of the study or asserting that, wherever feasible, individuals rather than groups should be studied. What we are pointing out is that individuals were not the main focus of attention and that to get the complete story they should be carefully evaluated in some studies.

Generalizations, Not Universals Finally, not a single conclusion from the study was true without exception. Thus there were, for particular pairs of sections, low groups with more group pride than their counterparts. There were high supervisors who supervised closely and low ones who supervised generally. Some low section heads were employee-centered, just as some disliked the separate dining room, were more critical of the company, made fewer recommendations for promotion, spent more time in supervision, and instructed less completely. Certainly no *principles* of supervision emerge from the investigation, if one uses the term *principle* to signify a carefully formulated generalization that has been tried many times by many capable people under a variety of circumstances and to which no important exception has yet been discovered.

The truth is, as we have pointed out several times in this book, that our knowledge of supervision is at present quite incomplete. We may and often do make generalizations that have a high "batting average," that is, are of such nature that they "work," hypotheses about how we should act in a given set of circumstances unless we see good reason for doing otherwise. But ironclad rules for supervising cannot be furnished at present (or perhaps ever) from this or any other study or from all of them together. Managers at every level in business are wise if they understand the limitations of knowledge and expect neither the unlikely nor the impossible.

OTHER MATCHED-GROUP STUDIES

No one was any more aware upon the completion of the Prudential study of its limitations than those responsible for it, and they began even before its completion to do others designed to supplement the results obtained from the original. We shall look briefly at the second in this series of experiments and then mention some still later ones.

The Railroad Study

The next investigation by the Survey Research Center involved employees quite unlike those in the Prudential study.[3] These differences were in the age and educational attainments of the workers, the type of work done, the physical surroundings of the work, and the geographical location involved.

The Setting The company involved in this study was the Chesapeake and Ohio Railroad and more specifically, the Père Marquette division, running through Michigan and southern Canada. The employees were all men and were all involved in the maintenance of the track. They worked in small groups, often referred to as *section gangs,* with only four or five employees in a crew. Their job was to keep the track of the railroad and its surroundings in good shape. While some were stationed in or near cities, most worked in rural areas. It was customary for an employee to live a few miles away and to drive to the place where the crew assembled each morning.

The men thus typically came from a rural environment. They were usually unskilled, and their average education was little if any beyond grammar school. Aside from their foreman they rarely saw members of management. Besides, except for a few times during a year, each group worked by itself without direct contact with other employees in similar gangs.

Design of the Study   To a large extent the railroad investigation duplicated the Prudential study. From the large number of gangs involved, forty pairs were selected. These were pairs that could be equated on factors like age and education and also on whether they were urban or rural and whether the track on which they worked ran through swampy land, level terrain, or hills. In addition the kind of track, including the weight of rails and type of ballast, was taken into account.

For each of the forty pairs, maintenance-of-way managers were asked to pick the better and the poorer so far as productivity was concerned. They were unable to agree in the case of four pairs, and hence the study finally involved only thirty-six pairs or a total of seventy-two gangs.

As was true in the Prudential study, each member of each gang, including the foreman, was interviewed privately. The same method of interviewing was used. The men were encouraged to talk freely, but the interviewers had questions to which they secured the answers if these were not discussed otherwise. Here again the interviewers did not know in any case whether a man belonged to a high or a low group.

Results Obtained   We do not have space to go into this experiment as fully as we did into the Prudential one, but some pertinent observations should be included.

In the main, the results of the two investigations were much the same, though naturally some of the findings could not be checked. In this work situation there were no separate dining rooms, for example, and of course there were other ways in which comparison would be meaningless. Many of the conclusions, however, were the same. The high groups showed the same kind of group pride, and men in the high groups liked the work itself *less well* than did men in the low groups (a finding that was statistically significant in this case). Supervisors of high groups supervised more generally and spent more of their time in supervision. They too were somewhat more critical and were essentially more employee-centered.

The only way in which high and low foremen differed demographically was that low supervisors had worked in other than railroad jobs to a greater extent than had high ones. The investigation also revealed that the high supervisors spent more of their time in planning the work than was true for the counterparts. Finally, the evidence was quite clear that high and low supervisors perceived their roles and their duties somewhat differently. For instance, the low foreman was likely to see himself first as a worker and to try to put more of his day into the actual physical work of the gang. High supervisors, on the other hand, seemed to see themselves primarily as supervisors and only secondly as workers, for they actually did considerably less of the work. It is noteworthy, however, that the efforts of the low sections, even when the greater amount of work done by the foreman was added in, did not in the opinion of management produce as good results as the efforts of the high gangs.

Additional Investigations

Unfortunately, we do not possess the same amount of detail on subsequent ones as on the clerical and railroad studies, but we do know that most of them were carried out in the same way, that is, they involved the matched-work-group technique followed by extensive interviews with each member of each work group, including the supervisor. We also know that some of the industries in which investigations have been carried out were: automobiles, chemicals, delivery service, petroleum, public utilities, heavy machinery, electrical appliances, electronics, and paper. Studies have also been made in hospitals and government agencies. Fortunately, Rensis Likert, then director of the Institute for Social Research and the person chiefly responsible for the studies in the first place, has made available some summaries of the findings from these many investigations, and has also suggested a theory of what these results mean. We shall devote the rest of this chapter to that topic.

Table 20-2 summarizes some of the principal findings of the group of studies.

GENERAL FINDINGS FROM THE INVESTIGATIONS

Since for three decades the Survey Research Center has been actively investigating effective leadership in the work situation, and since it has in the course of that period made a great many studies and dealt with a large number of people, a great many data have been accumulated. Any attempt to summarize all these data would be an undertaking beyond the scope of this book. Rather what we shall do is attempt to present the most important findings and especially those that go beyond the results of the two studies summarized earlier in the chapter.[4]

It would probably be well at this point to call the reader's attention to the fact that in this section, as well as in preceding parts of this chapter, the authors of this book have included some of their own ideas. What follows, therefore, relates to what the Survey Research Center found, but at times it includes our own interpretations of or comments on these findings.

Table 20-2 Some Characteristics of "High" Supervisors*

Influence with upper management
Influence with subordinates
General supervision
Supportive behavior
Consideration
Being more critical
Talking *with* associates ("visiting")
Time spent in supervision
Friendliness
Warmth
Acceptance
(Fewer) recommendations for promotion
Dislike of supervisory dining room

*Differences in the above were statistically significant in one or more of the studies. The list is incomplete, no effort having been made to prepare an exhaustive one. What sort of person appears to emerge from this list? Is he/she best described in terms of (1) the practice of System 4 or (2) trust, emotional maturity, and wisdom?

Self-perception versus Perception by Subordinates

Though most of the Center's conclusions have been based on the contrast between high and low supervisors, in the course of the studies there have been opportunities to study the differences between the way in which managers think of and evaluate themselves and the way in which they are seen by their subordinates. The finding here is that there are decided differences and that supervisors generally see themselves in a more favorable light than that in which they are perceived by those whom they supervise. Some examples will help make this point.

In one study, 90 percent of the bosses of foremen said that these foremen felt very free to discuss important things with them, whereas only 67 percent of the foremen said they did. In turn, 85 percent of the foremen said their employees felt very free to discuss important matters with them, but only 51 percent of the workers said they did. In another study, 90 percent of the general foremen said they understood the foremen's problems well, but only 51 percent of the foremen agreed. When the foremen described themselves, 95 percent said they understood the workers' problems well, but only 34 percent of the workers thought they did. Finally, 70 percent of the foremen's bosses said they always or almost always got their foremen's ideas before deciding, whereas only 52 percent of the foremen concurred. On the other hand, 73 percent of the foremen said they always or nearly always got the workers' ideas, but only 16 percent of the workers agreed with this.

Attitude toward Routine Work

A finding of consequence concerned the way employees felt about highly repetitive, routine jobs, the sort of job often found in mass-production factories and large clerical pools. Here subsequent studies confirmed what the Prudential and railroad studies suggested: that those in high-producing groups doing this kind of work actually liked the work less well than did those in the matched low-producing groups.

Why should this be the situation? Presumably the better a person likes his work the better he or she will do it, and, conversely, dislike of work is usually thought to go with poor performance. There are two likely reasons for these contrary findings. One is that such work is most closely associated with pressure to get the job done. After all, it is in situations like this where time-study has been applied most widely, incentive wages have been set, and close supervision is likely to be employed. It is easy to see how more capable, more ambitious people might resent these more than less capable, less ambitious ones.

The other point is that, after all, there is little challenge in such work. It can usually be learned quickly, there is little or no way in which the way of doing it may be varied, and one can hardly feel that he is growing and developing as he does it. Again, it is not surprising that the high employee found it less satisfying than the low. It should be noted in this connection that the opposite conclusion was obtained from studies of more varied and complex work. This is particularly true of the professionally trained person. Here the high employees did like the work better.

Employee Meetings

Another opinion held by many of those who emphasize the importance of human factors in an organization is that there should be a great many meetings with employees. In these meetings participation is to be encouraged, according to this theory, and of course such meetings are supposed to give opportunity for management to communicate with the workers. It is clear, however, that the matter is not quite as simple as this.

For one thing, especially in a plant, store, or office where many meetings are held, they frequently become the object of criticism and even ridicule. It is interesting how high in the chain of command this feeling often goes. Committees are often thought to be devices to delay or postpone decisions and to avoid individual responsibility for decisions. On the other hand, a "good" meeting is well received by nearly everyone.

The findings of the Survey Research Center go along with this. As a general rule, the better supervisors hold more employee meetings and such meetings are generally helpful. For example, where people feel a sense of genuine participation, they readily approve of frequent meetings. By contrast, where they feel that nothing is really accomplished by the meetings, the overall effect appears to be negative. This general conclusion was confirmed by a study that Likert reports in another volume on leadership.[5] Work groups where the men and the management felt that meetings were worthwhile and made a real contribution were typically high-producing groups. Those where either the men or the managers, and particularly the former, felt the meetings were a waste of time were typically low producers. Those where few or no meetings were held were in between in productivity, being superior to groups that met frequently but accomplished nothing in the meetings, and being below the many-meetings, feeling-of-participation groups.

Influence with Upper Management

A conclusion that is a bit surprising at first but perhaps makes more sense when studied further has to do with how much real influence a supervisor has with his boss and the bosses on up the line. Here the finding was clear: The high supervisors were judged by their people to have more such influence. In fact, this feeling did not stop with the first level of supervision. The managers at the second and third levels were also judged to have more influence with their supervisors. A similar finding concerns the relation between the pressure a supervisor puts on his people and their judgment of his influence with the bosses. Here, if the pressure is felt to be unreasonable, the more pressure the supervisor brings to bear, the less influence he is thought to have "upstairs."

Again, these findings make sense when we reflect upon them. After all, employees are not simply pleasure-driven, money-hungry robots. They often work best in a spirit of respect and for a person who is thought to be capable, worthy, and efficient. If they see him as "pushed around" by his own bosses, the image that results is not likely to be favorable. Certainly pressure which employees consider unreasonable can hardly have any other effect than that of undermining this respect.

Attitudes toward Subordinates

It is readily apparent by now that growing out of these situations—and perhaps also causing some of them—is a set of attitudes on the part of supervisors toward subordinates.[6] High supervisors tend to feel about people in one way, and low ones in at least a somewhat different way. The employee-centeredness of the Prudential and railroad studies is certainly in point. Attitudes toward the separate dining room in the clerical situation probably are also. But let us look at some of Likert's other findings.

One interesting result is that employees did not report great differences between high and low supervisors in such things as arranging work, supplying tools and materials, and enforcing rules, partly, it may be surmised, because even poor supervisors usually did most of these. But there were areas where the more effective supervisor was judged to be better than a less effective one and by a decided margin. Among them were keeping the workers informed, thinking of them as human beings rather than a means of production, taking an interest in them, creating an atmosphere that helped the employee feel free to discuss important things with his boss, and wanting the subordinates' ideas and trying to do something about them. In another study, life-insurance agency managers were involved. High managers were said by their agents to be more unselfish in dealing with agents, and to be more cooperative, sympathetic, democratic, and sincere.

One real possibility here is that we are dealing with the "halo" effect discussed in Chapter 13, that is, the tendency we all experience to let our overall impression of a person influence our judgments about his particular traits or characteristics. Thus, if I am very favorably impressed by a person, I am likely to see him as courageous, sincere, unselfish, and handsome. Likewise, if I have a poor opinion of him, I am likely to think of him as deficient in these and other desirable areas. The same forces may be operating here. Supervisors seen as good in general may tend to be seen as good in particular, and the reverse may well be true also. However, even though we thus discount the finding somewhat, this is not enough to cast doubt on Likert's main conclusion: that more effective supervisors do have attitudes that differ from those of less effective ones. At times and even perhaps characteristically, these differences may be of degree rather than of kind, but they are real and influential nevertheless.[7]

Supportive Behavior

This point also may overlap with the one just discussed, but it does seem sufficiently important to deserve separate treatment. It is that in their relations with their subordinates, high supervisors tend to be helpful and supportive; low supervisors by contrast either lack these traits or show them to a smaller degree.

Perhaps general as opposed to close supervision is a good illustration. After all, if one supervises generally, he helps the subordinate see what the objectives of the job are and the guidelines for attaining these objectives and, to whatever degree it is feasible, leaves the subordinate free to accomplish his tasks in his own way. Close supervision, on the other hand, is likely to be perceived as being, and is likely actually to be, a vote of no confidence and no genuine support.

Another example of supportive behavior is the supervisor's treatment of mistakes. Generally, they can be handled in either of two ways: as an occasion for a general expression of displeasure, a reprimand, and even severe discipline; or as a learning opportunity for the one who made the error. High supervisors characteristically saw mistakes in the second light, and low ones saw them primarily in the first.

Another example of supportive behavior is the supervisor's willingness "to go to bat" for his people. After all, sooner or later a supervisor is likely to find himself in a situation where he is convinced that his employees are right and his bosses have made a mistake. This can be a delicate matter, of course, but the findings of the Survey Research Center are clear: High supervisors are seen by their subordinates as being (and they probably are) considerably more willing to stand by their people and to defend them against criticism. Again, we may be dealing with differences in degree, but differences that are real and significant.

Another finding of the center is that high supervisors characteristically are seen as "pulling for the company and the workers" and not simply as "pulling for the company." When supervisors do "pull for the company and the workers," they go against advice they are sometimes given by management, namely, that when they are upgraded from a worker's to a supervisor's job, they join another team and are no longer to identify with the workers. Rather, it is urged, their loyalty and identification must be directed toward the employer. Apparently, there is nothing wrong with identifying with the goals of the work organization: indeed this is highly desirable. The problem comes in turning one's back on the workers. This is seldom wise.

Thus the ability of the supervisor to furnish support to his subordinates, to stand by them if he believes they are correct, and to identify with their goals and values seems to be quite important. Like other good things it can be overdone. However, one wonders whether the limitations of the typical manager are not more likely to go in the opposite direction.

Figures 20-1 and 20-2 illustrate other significant conclusions.

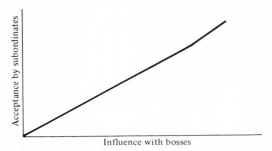

Figure 20-1 While the straight line is in error in implying a one-to-one relationship between the two variables, there is no doubt about a significant positive correlation between (1) the esteem in which a supervisor is held by his/her boss and the "big bosses" and (2) that accorded him/her by subordinates.

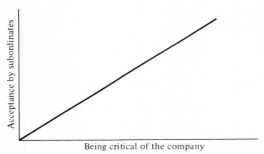

Figure 20-2 The straight-line relationship is again an overstatement, but it is clear that the supervisor who is more critical, including being more critical of the company, is usually better regarded by the workers. Is there a causal connection here, that is, does being critical cause more acceptance or is there a common cause for both factors?

TWO THEORIES OF MANAGEMENT

In Likert's judgment two systems of management have grown up in America and are functioning side by side at the present time. One of these he calls the *job-organization* system and the other the *cooperative-motivation* system.[8]

Nature of the Theories

The job-organization system is used extensively in work situations involving a great deal of repetitive work. It organizes jobs thoroughly after breaking the larger processes up into tasks, often simple and highly repetitive ones, assigned to individual workers. The arrangement of the work, the machines, and the tools is carefully studied and, where advisable, changed in the interest of efficiency. Standards of output are determined and expected if not demanded of workers, supervision is close or tight, and wages are often on an incentive (or pay-by-the-piece) basis. Indeed, this system depends primarily on the motivating force of wages, salaries, and fringe benefits. It tells people just what to do and expects them to do it. All this may not be very challenging, but the workers are paid to do it. If it is unpleasant and otherwise unrewarding, the pay should make it bearable and even desirable.

The cooperative-motivation system is found primarily in organizations where the work shifts in character and varies in amount rather frequently. Instead of using the standards of *scientific management* and studying and rearranging jobs carefully, as well as putting on pressure to meet certain management-determined standards of output, it makes much use of what are sometimes referred to as the *ego motives*. These include a desire to cooperate with one's fellows, to be accepted by them, and to find a sense of challenge in one's work. Economic motives are still appealed to, of course, but the appeal is now supplemented by other types of motivation.

Results of the Theories

From the standpoint of history and tradition, American managers tend more to job organization than to cooperative motivation. After all, *scientific management* has been with us for seventy-five and more years, and some elements of the job-organization system antedate even that. Today's managers have largely "grown up on" the system, and those who do not use it are likely to be apologetic to themselves as well as to others and to be tempted to adopt it (or perhaps to readopt it).

Furthermore, results from the job-organization system usually develop rapidly and are seen readily. The cooperative-motivation system, on the other hand, tends to be a slow starter as people without so many explicit directions attempt to find the most satisfactory methods and pace of work. In fact, there is evidence to the effect that after a few months the job-organization system may show considerably more in the way of improved output than the other system does. However, this increased output is bought at considerable psychological cost, and studies of employee attitudes reveal an increasingly unsatisfactory situation. By contrast, in the second system output goes up slowly at first, but a reservoir of cooperation and goodwill is being built up which will be likely to lead not only to greater output but also to more challenging situations and may very well be of great help to the company in adversity.

Incidentally, Likert feels, as we have already indicated, that the fact that repetitive work is disliked by the more efficient employees while more varied work is accepted favorably is at least to a considerable degree due to the practice of managers of using the cooperative-motivation system much more widely for that sort of work.[9]

THE SUPERVISOR AND THE MICHIGAN STUDIES

At this point we find ourselves in the same situation we faced at the end of the chapter just before this one. As was true for the Hawthorne results, those of the studies discussed in this chapter could be repeated and applied to the supervisor's job, but again we have elected not to do so. After all they have been presented, and the reader can reexamine them if he wishes.

What we have chosen to do, on the contrary, is what we did at the end of Chapter 19, namely to raise some questions to be pondered even after this book has been laid aside.

There is, for example, the question raised immediately above. To what extent is participation, or letting the group decide, a feasible tactic today? As a general rule, have American managers used it more or less than is optimum? Is there reason to believe its use either will or should increase until it becomes the standard and predominant way of supervising? Or is the emphasis on participation a sort of fad or fashion that will soon run its course? We shall speak specifically to this point in the chapter following this one.

A second inquiry relates to the sorts of workers who are superior. Do they produce more because they are naturally better or because of the way in which they are supervised? Are most of the better workers really more critical of the company than are the less effective ones? Is this also true of supervisors? If it is true, why is it true? Does being better make them more critical, or being more critical make them better? Or do both characteristics arise from deeper causes?

A third question: What does all this say as regards the supervisor's loyalty to the company? Is dissent among supervisors to be encouraged by executives? Is disagreement a form of disloyalty? How far can one realistically expect a supervisor to go in expressing disapproval of company action? How far should executives go in permitting—or even tolerating—such disapproval?

Finally, what does it really mean to be "employee-centered" or "person-centered"? Is this as a matter of fact simply "high-level manipulation," that is, is the supervisor interested in people because he has found he can get more out of them this way? If this is not the whole story, is it a part of the story? Why should a supervisor be interested in his people?

We make no pretense, of course, that either the Michigan studies or this book answers these questions with any finality. But they are important questions, and the supervisor who disregards them runs considerable risk to himself and his organization.[10]

QUESTIONS

1 Explain the basic design of the Prudential investigation and subsequent studies conducted in the same fashion.
2 In the above, why were no differences in age, education, experience, intelligence (as measured by tests), and so on, found between (a) workers in high- and low-producing groups? (b) "high" and "low" supervisors? (If you do not know the answer to (b), what would be your "best guess"?)
3 In what areas were differences found between the high and low groups? How do you explain them?
4 What were the principal differences between high and low supervisors? (Consider the studies as a whole and not merely the Prudential one.)
5 How do you account for the differences (see Question 4)?
6 What is the relationship between (a) the number and kind of organization meetings and (b) the satisfaction and productivity of work groups?
7 Why are employees more influenced by supervisors who (a) are thought to have greater influence with upper management? (b) see themselves and their influence about as their subordinates do (instead of holding themselves to be much better than the latter think they are)?
8 What are the three or four most important lessons a supervisor can learn from the matched-work-group studies?

NOTES

1 Daniel Katz et al., *Productivity, Supervision, and Morale in An Office Situation* (Ann Arbor: The University of Michigan Press, 1950).
2 A study as unusual as this led at once to a great many comments. See, for example, Donald C. Pelz, "Influence: A Key to Effective Leadership in the First-line Supervisor," *Personnel,* vol. 29, pp. 209–217, 1952.
3 Daniel Katz et al., *Productivity, Supervision, and Morale in a Railroad Situation* (Ann Arbor: The University of Michigan Press, 1951).

4   The Director of the Institute for Social Research made one of the first systematic presentations of results from the matched work groups. See Rensis Likert, *New Patterns of Management* (New York: McGraw-Hill, 1961), especially pp. 46–60.

5   This point is elaborated in Rensis Likert, "An Emergent Theory of Organization, Leadership, and Management," in Luigi Petrullo and Bernard M. Bass, *Leadership and Interpersonal Behavior* (New York: Holt, 1961).

6   For a point of view that relates to these attitudes as well as to the influence of one's peers, see Lyman W. Porter, Edward E. Lawler III, and J. Richard Hackman, *Behavior in Organizations* (New York: McGraw-Hill, 1975), especially Chaps. 13 and 14.

7   As we have mentioned earlier, the theory of management by *participation* has become popular among behavioral scientists. The theory owes much to the Michigan studies. For more on it see Alfred Jay Morrow, David G. Bowers, and Stanley E. Seashore, *Management by Participation: Creating a Climate for Personnel and Organizational Development* (New York: Harper, 1967).

8   In 1968 Likert further elaborated on the implications of the Michigan studies and presented his interpretation of their meaning for the supervisor. See *The Human Organization* (New York: McGraw-Hill, 1968).

9   See also Likert's most recent book in this area: *New Ways of Managing Conflict* (New York: McGraw-Hill, 1976).

10 David G. Bowers, *Systems of Organization: Management of the Human Resource* (Ann Arbor: The University of Michigan Press, 1976).

CASES

Two of the cases of this chapter involve discharge, in one on charges of fighting and in another for absence from work and deliberate misrepresentation of the reason therefor. In each instance the employer is faced with (a) proving that the alleged events took place and (b), if (a) is demonstrated, showing the appropriateness of discharge (that the Company had the right to impose it and furthermore that it was the most suitable penalty). As you study each case you will need to determine whether the Company succeeded at both points.

The third case involves an admittedly illegal strike which resulted in overtime advantages to bargaining-unit members—very likely in some instances, Union members—who did not support the strike. Should they be permitted to keep advantages gained under such circumstances?

CASE 20-1

Jim Buhler is thirty-five years of age. He is an over-the-road driver for the Company. During the six years he has driven for it he has not had a chargeable accident, that is, one for which he has been found responsible. He makes excellent time on the road and handles his truck and his freight with care. His errors in delivery to customers are considerably fewer than those of the average driver, and there have been no complaints about the service he renders. In fact Bill Glad, his supervisor, has heard a number of favorable comments about Jim and his work from customers of the Company.

Jim seems to get along well everywhere except on the loading docks in the terminals. Here he has the reputation of being quick-tempered and irritable, and he uses profanity considerably more than the other drivers and the freight handlers. He has many arguments, in some of which he becomes loud and threatening, and is quite unpopular with many fellow workers. He accuses most workers and particularly freight handlers of being "goldbricks" or "goof-offs," and they in turn believe him to be hot-headed and unreasonable in his demands on them.

About a year ago matters reached a climax. Jim and a freight handler named Linus Morrison became involved in an argument that ended in Morrison's cursing Buhler and Buhler's bodily attacking Morrison. Morrison was knocked down before he even had a chance to strike Buhler, and the two men were immediately separated. A trip to First Aid revealed that Morrison, though in considerable pain for a time, was not seriously hurt and suffered no long-run injuries.

The Company policy had long been to discharge an employee who fought under these circumstances, and Buhler was immediately suspended for the rest of the day and was discharged the next day. It was realized that provocation was present, but the Company felt that no verbal provocation could justify bodily attack since other means of recourse, for example, the grievance procedure, were available to the one who was provoked. It reasoned that many of the workers came from a background that did not view fighting as a very serious offense and that consequently it must make every effort to prevent fighting from becoming an accepted practice.

The Union immediately filed a grievance concerning the discharge, and since the Company was unwilling to relent, the grievance went to arbitration. The arbitrator found for the Union on the ground of undue provocation and restored Buhler to his job without, however, any pay for time lost.

When Jim first returned to work, things went quite smoothly, but after some weeks his belligerence began to appear again. Matters came to a head a second time when another freight handler, Frank Crutchfield, cursed Buhler. He, too, was knocked down, and several stitches were required to close a wound on his cheek.

Buhler was again discharged by the Company. As before, the Union filed a grievance, alleging that the penalty was too severe in view of the provocation and citing the prior arbitration award. Bill Glad and his superiors now have the problem of answering this grievance and deciding on their strategy if the Union continues to push it, even possibly to another arbitration hearing.

Does the Company have just cause for discharge this time, even though it has been determined that it did not in the earlier case?

CASE 20-2

The Company is an automobile manufacturer with an assembly plant in the Midwest. Hazel Keith is a departmental clerk in this plant. She works in an office on the manufacturing floor, and though she is salaried, she is eligible to join and in fact does belong to the Union. Her husband is also employed in the plant and is active in the Union.

On Monday, August 26, Ms. Keith did not report for work, nor did she appear on Tuesday or Wednesday. She came back to work on Thursday about noon.

On the Monday in question Ms. Keith's son called the personnel department of the Company and reported that his mother had gone to see a doctor and would not be at work that day. Similar calls were received on Tuesday and Wednesday.

When Ms. Keith appeared for work at noon on Thursday, she had a signed statement from a local physician, which read: "Mrs. Keith is under my medical care, and studies are being made for a chronic genito-urinary condition, including x-rays and laboratory tests."

Meanwhile Dwight Rowland, Ms. Keith's foreman, and John Tatum, the industrial relations director, had suspected that the matter was not as simple as it might appear to be. Hazel had asked Rowland almost a month before for a vacation beginning on August 26, but her request had been denied because of the press of work in the department. Tatum, remembering that she had protested this decision to him and also to others, checked on the vacation dates of her husband and found that his vacation began on Monday, August 26.

Now thoroughly suspicious, Rowland and Tatum decided to visit the Keiths on Monday afternoon. They found no one at home, but on Tuesday when they made another visit the son was there. When asked about his mother, he said at first that she had gone to see the doctor but later revealed that she was on an out-of-town trip with her husband. Further inquiry, including conversations with neighbors, revealed that the Keiths had left the prior Saturday morning on an automobile trip to a resort area in an adjoining state. Tatum left word with the son that his mother was to call at the earliest possible moment, but he received no call. In the meantime, he suspected, the son had called his mother and told her of the visit of Rowland and Tatum. This information, he thought, caused the Keiths to cut short their vacation and return on Wednesday night. Since the doctor's statement was dated Thursday, the morning.was probably spent in seeing him and getting the statement.

Rowland was uncertain what action to take, but Tatum was not. He recommended discharge on the grounds of misrepresentation, falsification of information, and insubordination so far as her foreman's orders about her vacation were concerned. Rowland agreed, and the discharge was cleared "up the line." Ms. Keith was notified of her discharge on Friday, and on Monday filed a grievance alleging that she was fired "without just cause."

Did the Company handle this case properly? Did Tatum take too active a part in it?

CASE 20-3

There is no disagreement between the parties as to the essential facts in this case. In August 1975, a "wildcat" strike, an illegal one that undoubtedly violated the no-strike provision of the labor agreement, occurred at the plant, its duration being five working days. Between 85 percent and 90 percent of the bargaining-unit employees failed to report for work during that period. The plant continued its operations, however, being staffed by management personnel and those bargaining-unit employees who continued to work. Naturally, the latter had opportunity for as much overtime as they wished and all accumulated a significant number (in no case less than twenty-five) of hours of overtime.

There is a long-standing practice in the plant of attempting to equalize overtime opportunities. While not done exactly the same way in all departments, the general arrangement is to offer the overtime opening to the appropriate employee, that is, the one having the smallest number of overtime hours worked and/or charged. (It is the established practice that when an employee is offered and refuses overtime it is charged against him just as though he had worked it.)

When the strike was over, the above 10 to 15 percent of the employees, having accumulated much overtime, would by the usual rules go to (or toward) the bottom of the overtime lists (there being different lists in the different departments), and the strikers would rise to (or toward) the top.

In assigning overtime after the conclusion of the strike, however, the Company chose to disregard the overtime earned by the nonstrikers during the strike and to assign overtime on the basis of the list in effect before the strike began. The grievance of this case protests this Company action and asks that overtime worked during the strike be included in the subsequent overtime lists. It also asks for monetary damages to any employees wrongfully deprived of overtime since the strike.

How should this dispute be decided, and why?

Chapter 21

Other Studies:
Three Theories
of Supervision

As we indicated at the beginning of this part of the book, we are making no effort to survey all the empirical studies of the supervisory process nor even all of the significant ones. Rather, we have devoted a chapter to each of the two that appear to us to have been the most influential and insightful; then in this chapter we present three additional investigations that have also had a considerable influence on the conclusions that management theorists have drawn.

The choosing of just these five studies and the exclusion of many others is admittedly an arbitrary choice, one biased furthermore in the direction of the older studies, since naturally it requires time for an investigation to become well known and influential. But familiarity with these does bring the reader an acquaintance with the field as it is known to those who write and speak on subjects related to supervision. Besides, the studies are valuable in themselves since they raise meaningful questions and contain significant insights.

One other thing we do in this chapter: During this century there have developed at least three distinct and influential theories about the nature of supervision, theories growing largely out of empirical research on the subject. They have been referred to at least indirectly a number of times in this book, but this is a good place for a summary and a critique of each.

ADDITIONAL STUDIES OF SUPERVISION

Styles of Leadership

One of the influential persons in shaping our thinking about worker motivation was Kurt Lewin, who migrated to the United States from Germany in the thirties. We shall mention him later in connection with the third theory of supervision, discussed below. Here we are concerned with a well-known experiment he did in the late thirties. He assumed there were three styles or kinds of leadership and proceeded to investigate them empirically. He called these *authoritarian, democratic,* and *laissez faire.*[1]

Background of the Study This research was carried out with four groups of ten-year-old boys, there being five boys to each group. The boys were grouped so as to be about equally distributed relative to interpersonal relationships, intellectual and physical abilities, and socioeconomic status. They were voluntary groups, meeting after school to engage in hobbies.

Four men were selected as leaders and thoroughly trained in each of the three leadership styles. They were shifted to a new club every six weeks, and each changed his style of leadership as he made these shifts. The situation was arranged so that each group experienced each kind of leadership method under each leader.

The reactions of the boys and the leaders were carefully observed in each meeting. Later the boys and their parents were interviewed, with the purpose, among others, of discovering how the boys reacted to the different styles of leadership.

Description of Styles The various styles of leadership may be described in terms of what the three sorts of leaders did. There is, for instance, the matter of giving orders. Authoritarian leaders did this many times more than either democratic or laissez faire leaders. Similarly, authoritarian leaders gave many more disrupting or upsetting commands.

A somewhat less obvious difference has to do with criticism and praise. These were not at all unusual in both authoritarian and democratic situations, but there was an important difference. In the former both praise and criticism were typically of a personal, nonobjective sort, whereas in the latter both tended to be more objective and to grow out of the demands of the situation. Guiding suggestions were characteristic of democratic leaders, these guiding suggestions being designed to stimulate self-direction and often succeeding in doing just that.

Democratic leaders were essentially equalitarian (or egalitarian) leaders; that is, they tried to put themselves on the same level as the boys and to become functioning members of the group. They tried to pass decisions to the group, whereas the authoritarian leader made the decisions himself and the laissez faire one simply left them unmade. Democratic leaders were more jovial in dealing with the boys and more inclined to confide in them.

Thus, the authoritarian leader was one who made decisions, chiefly without consultation, and who put pressure on the boys to do what he determined that they should. The laissez faire leader left the boys alone very largely. He did not directly concern himself with either directing the group or giving information to it, and he participated only when asked. Finally, the democratic leader attempted to build group spirit, group cohesiveness, group determination of goals, and cooperativeness in achieving the common goals.

Principal Results One way in which the results can be presented is in terms of the personal satisfactions and success of the leaders, but this is hardly an important consideration here. In this book we are primarily concerned with the effects on the boys of the three styles. In a number of areas these were rather decided.

One finding was that the boys played most, did least work, and did their poorest work in the laissez faire situation. Democratic and authoritarian leadership were close together in amount accomplished, each being clearly superior to laissez faire leadership.

Democratic leadership, as we have just said, produced as much as authoritarian, but it left a far better feeling on the part of the boys. Indeed, one characteristic of authoritarian leadership was more hostility and aggression, typically directed toward another group member but often toward a scapegoat or the leader. In this type of situation, hostility and aggression continued after the meeting was over; some of this did not become evident nor was it observable during the actual meetings.

Still another finding was the greater dependence on the leader, and hence less individuality, in the autocratic situation. This contrasted sharply with the findings in the democratically led groups, where friendliness and independence were much more common. For example, democratic groups continued to work while the leader was away. This was not true for the authoritarian ones.

Thus we see that the democratic groups were friendly, productive, enjoyable, and cohesive; the authoritarian ones were productive, leader-dependent, aggressive toward members and outsiders, and individualistic; and the laissez faire ones were lethargic, unproductive, and disinterested. It must not be forgotten, however, that all groups received all three kinds of leadership and the behavior of the group shifted according to leadership. Thus each of the four groups showed all or virtually all these characteristics depending on its leader at the time.

Evaluation of the Study   We have earlier indicated that the investigation was an early and quite influential one; indeed it actually had an influence out of proportion to its real contributions. One limitation clearly is that it was done in a country and in a climate where democracy is esteemed and by one who was a refugee from Hitler's Germany. Thus one would be surprised if democratic leadership did not win out. The leaders themselves no doubt initially believed that democratic leadership was the best kind, a fact that may have helped them so conclude.

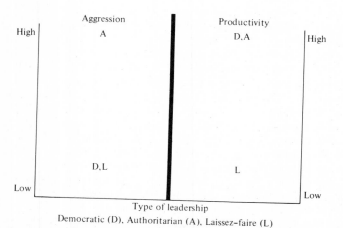

Figure 21-1 Lewin's study indicates that democratic leaders get high productivity without inducing aggression, that authoritarian ones also get high productivity but create much aggression, and that laissez faire leaders engender little aggression but also little or no output.

Besides, one has to be careful how much he generalizes from the research itself. These were ten-year-old boys and there were only twenty of them. We are not sure the results would be the same if the study were repeated. We are even more unsure about the extent to which the conclusions fit adults in the usual world of work. The investigation, in other words, does not *prove* that the democratic style is always best.

At the same time the study is significant. For one thing, it turned attention to the question of leadership styles and suggested that more study of them might be productive. It also served as a starting point for a movement known as *group dynamics,* an institution called the National Training Laboratory, and a type of training known as *sensitivity* training. More will be said of these in the last part of this chapter.

Participation and Productivity

It has been pointed out several times earlier (see particularly Chapter 8) that among the important concepts recently added to directions for effective supervision is that of *participation* by workers in decision making. This notion has been investigated by a number of researchers, with the study we are here reporting being one of the early and influential ones.[2]

Nature of the Study   This research was carried out in the late forties in a clothing factory in Virginia. Four groups of employees were investigated in the main part of the experiment. In each case the group was changed from its usual work to a new or modified task. These tasks were not introduced for experimental reasons, but were a necessary part of the ongoing activities of the factory. The groups were approximately equal with regard to such factors as prior productivity, the degree of change involved in the new situation, and the amount of cohesiveness in the groups. The employees were principally women and were paid on an incentive basis.

One group consisting of eighteen hand-pressers was used as a control. After the nature of and necessity for modifications were explained to the group, the changes were simply introduced and carried out. The second group, thirteen pajama folders, likewise heard an explanation of their new situation. They approved the changes and selected from the group a small number of operators who had an opportunity to make suggestions, were given special training in the new methods, and then trained the other folders. The third and fourth groups, consisting of eight and seven pajama inspectors, respectively, went through the same routine except that all the operators were trained, having opportunities to make suggestions and help carry them out. The groups may be described as a *no-participation group* (Group 1), a *participation-through-representatives group* (Group 2), and *participation groups* (Groups 3 and 4).

Principal Results   The results were evaluated by noting speed of attaining the proper rate, expressions of satisfaction and dissatisfaction, aggressive acts toward supervision, and the "quit" rate. The findings were that Group 1 was clearly inferior in all measures, Group 2 was intermediate, and Groups 3 and 4 were decidedly superior in all respects.

Two months later the remaining members of Group 1 were transferred to another job, and this time the techniques used originally for Groups 3 and 4 were employed. The results were little short of dramatic. Behavior that had previously been displayed by Groups 3 and 4 (rapid adaptation and attainment of and even surpassing the accepted standards, expressions of satisfaction, and no aggressive behavior and no quits) quickly came to characterize this group as well.

Figure 21-2 relates to the study concerning the participation of workers in determining how the work is to be done.

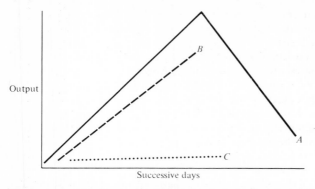

Figure 21-2 The Coch and French Study indicates that if (1) the group as a whole makes decisions as to how to do its work, productivity will rise decidedly but it will go down again when the group no longer is allowed to decide (*A* above); (2) a group participates in decision making but only through a limited number of representatives, it will improve in output but much less than *A* (*B* above); and (3) a group is simply "told what to do" it makes no progress and may even decline in productivity.

Interpretation of the Study   The researchers interpret their results as clear evidence of the superiority of participation as a means of motivating increased productivity and seem to conclude that such participation is to be viewed as "the wave of the future." We have already expressed some reservations about this supposedly all-powerful effect of participation,[3] and more will be said on the subject in the last part of the chapter.

Initiating Structure and Consideration

Since 1946 some important investigations of leadership have been carried on at Ohio State University.[4] Often leaders in other situations than business and industry have been studied (for example, in the armed services or in government), and stress has been placed on the executive rather than on the supervisor. Some of the findings are not directly relevant to our interests, therefore, especially since top management not only has a different set of duties from those of the first-line supervisor but, as we have said earlier, has other functions than simply supervising those who report to it directly. Nevertheless, these studies have considerable significance for us.

Basic Requirements of the Leader   One result that has stood out clearly in the Ohio State studies is that there are competing and often inconsistent demands on the leader. In these studies two factors in particular are identified: they are called *initiating structure* and *consideration*.

The first of these refers to the necessity for "getting the job done." It includes those things a manager does to see that the principal functions of the work group are accomplished, namely, the production of goods or the rendering of services. The other factor, consideration, refers to a concern for the feelings of people and in particular those of subordinates. In this connection one may refrain from putting pressure on people or making demands upon them. The tendency is to be warm, personal, and friendly and to avoid unpleasantness in one's relations with his associates.

The presence of both these tendencies in virtually every work situation leads to important consequences for supervisors. One is the conflict that exists between these tendencies. In some cases this conflict may be avoided entirely and in many others it may appear fairly infrequently, but in some it is constantly present. Supervisors must see that the jobs are done, and yet they do not want to be considered cold and demanding. However, if they emphasize, and especially unduly emphasize getting the jobs done, it is likely that subordinates will so consider them. In spite of the manager's best efforts, this conflict is inevitable in many work situations, and supervisors have to learn to live with and adjust to it.

Figure 21-3 relates directly to the Ohio State studies.

Theory and Practice in Organizations   In accord with many others who have examined the field, Shartle and his associates at Ohio State have found that much of what we tell ourselves about how an organization functions is not borne out when the facts are assembled and evaluated. A good example is the informal organization. Shartle has found, as the Hawthorne investigators did, that a person's place on the organization chart may reveal only a little about how great or how small his or her influence is. A great many instances of lateral influence (rather than merely up or down in the chain of command) and of the effects of personal liking and disliking of a certain individual were apparent, as were numerous cliques among managers and in work groups.

A second finding concerned the proper type of motivation or supervision. Here one fact stood out: There is no such thing as the perfect way or even the outstandingly good one. In other words, techniques that work well for one manager might not work for another. While communication and participation are associated with higher motivation and productivity, it is not at all clear that there is a causal relationship here. (Some underlying factors may account for and cause this association.) Differences between work groups and leaders, whether productive or not, are subtle and complex and not reducible at this time to clear and unequivocal statements of principle. One thing is apparent, however: There is no evidence to support the belief that workers who are contented and approve of their jobs and surroundings are more productive than their less "happy" counterparts.

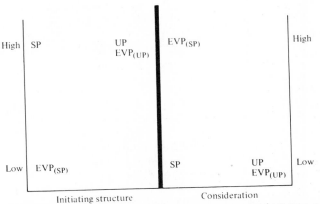

Figure 21-3 Suppose two presidents who are relatively high in Initiating Structure and relatively low in Consideration are each selecting a new Executive Vice President. Furthermore, suppose one President is relatively successful (SP) and the other is relatively unsuccessful (UP). The Ohio State evidence indicates that the UP is likely to pick a subordinate *like* himself and the SP one *unlike* himself. The same logic applies to persons high in Consideration and low in Initiating Structure.

An interesting conclusion, reminiscent of the Michigan studies of the preceding chapter, has to do with the manager's perception of himself or herself, especially in relationship to associates. For one thing, managers tend to see themselves quite differently from the way subordinates see them—and, as a general rule, more favorably. In other words, they typically see themselves as doing a better job than subordinates see them as doing. For another, their superiors came closer to agreeing with the subordinates than they do with the managers.

Let us mention two other findings of the Ohio State studies: First, the *trait* approach to leadership has proved to be less satisfactory than the *performance* approach. In other words, it is usually less useful to know that a person is extroverted or unusually intelligent than it is to understand how he or she behaves in relations with subordinates. Correlations between any trait, or combination of traits, and supervisory success are low at best.

Second, we need to be humble or even skeptical about our abilities to do a good job of selecting workers and especially managers and executives. Actually, we know so little as yet about what most jobs require, and usually so little more about how to measure or otherwise appraise these requirements, that we have to recognize our very serious limitations in this area. Select we must and will, but we can seldom afford to be dogmatic about our choices.

In this connection a good deal is made of the patterns of work required of the new executive and the importance of selecting someone likely to fit into the expected or required patterns. Thus, if a manager who is strong on initiating structure replaces one who emphasizes consideration, difficulties most likely lie ahead. (Of course the reverse is also true.) As managers, we all have a tendency to pick assistants much like ourselves. For example, if we are strong in initiating structure, we tend to pick as subordinates people who are similarly disposed. The evidence indicates that the reverse is usually better, that one typically should select a subordinate unlike oneself, but of course this is not easy to do.

Suggestions Concerning Leadership   A number of suggestions about the effective motivation of subordinates have come out of these studies. Some are contained, either openly or implicitly, in what we have already discussed. There are also a few others.

One temptation for the knowledgeable manager is to take advantage of other people, and particularly subordinates, through his or her superior knowledge and understanding. Thus, one might use one's human relations skills to inveigle workers into doing what they would not do if they understood the situation fully. To this sort of manipulation Shartle is opposed, as are the authors of this book.

Another tendency is generally to stress *who is right* or wrong and not *what is needed* in the present circumstances. Here is a place where the manager often errs. When a mistake has been made or a calculation has gone awry, it is easy and tempting to begin by asking: "Who is to blame? Who made this serious mistake?" Granted that at times these may be appropriate or even necessary questions, it is frequently the case that much more is gained if one focuses on the future rather than on the past. At least in many cases, "Who is to blame?" is far less significant than "What must we do now?"

Still another suggestion concerns how to handle the consistent objector. There is a tendency to argue with him or even to "beat him down." Again, some of these courses of action may be required by particular circumstances. However, another technique, useful at times, is to put the objector on a committee to study the situation. Even when the majority does not agree with him, he still has a chance to express his ideas and may indeed feel that he has real influence on the outcome. At any rate he may take the decision more gracefully than he otherwise would.

Evaluation of the Study The Ohio State leadership studies have proved to be interesting and valuable. There is question here, as there always is in such investigations, about how many of their findings were original or new and how many had been anticipated and accepted. But if the idea is useful, this is a small consideration.

Favorable Aspects The initiating structure-consideration concept is a case in point. This may not have been altogether new or original (in one way Lewin came close to saying the same), but it is a valuable notion nevertheless, and emphasis on it has to be ranked as a real contribution of the Ohio State studies.

A second contribution is the finding that no one pattern or method of leadership is necessarily—or even likely to be—the best. Traditionally, as we have said, the authoritarian has been stressed, and more recently the democratic, but apparently either may succeed and either may fail. Of course, Shartle has not said that there are no differences between the more and the less effective leader. What he has said, correctly, is that these differences are more subtle and difficult to understand than is usually believed.

The Ohio State investigators also deserve credit for reaffirming through their investigations what the Hawthorne studies had earlier revealed, that alongside the formal organization there exists an informal one; and for reaffirming the Michigan conclusions concerning the perceptions of the supervisor by his fellow workers and by himself. It has been a valuable set of investigations.

Unfavorable Factors In this study considerable use is made of questionnaires, rating scales, and the like. There is, of course, nothing wrong with using such instruments; but as pointed out earlier, we like better those researches in which people "get their feet wet," that is, when they proceed principally by observing people at work rather than by questioning them about work. The Hawthorne and Michigan studies in particular come off well on this score.

A secondary tendency, by no means unique to the Ohio State investigations, is the attempt to stay very close to the actual observations themselves, to let these observations "speak for themselves" to whatever extent they will and can. This tendency is understandable. Certainly throughout human history people have made more mistakes by getting too far away from the observed facts than they have by sticking too closely to them, but one can go too far either way. One of the real gains of Hawthorne is the willingness to speculate and then to draw conclusions about the hopes, the disappointments, the feelings, the values of relay assemblers, bank wiremen, and workers in general. One of the limitations of the Michigan studies is that they did relatively little of this. And the Ohio State studies are in this respect more like Michigan and less like Hawthorne.

THREE THEORIES OF SUPERVISION

In the concluding section of this chapter we are presenting three theories of supervisory leadership—or maybe it would be better to say, three approaches to supervision—which are relatively modern ones and which grew in large part out of the empirical rather than a "philosophical" approach. These are not the only theories that can be discussed, but taken together they represent fairly well the thinking of the principal theorists in the field.

The theories will be presented in chronological order of appearance, first, because that seems to be a logical way to do it, but second and more important, because the first influenced the second and the second (and also to an extent, the first) influenced the third.

The "Hard-Nosed" or Formal Theory

History   Strictly speaking, it is incorrect to place the beginning of formal management theory within the confines of the twentieth century, for as earlier mentioned, it had its beginnings at least as long ago as the Prussian army and the hierarchy of the Roman Catholic Church. However the previously discussed movement known as *scientific management* is a product of the very last part of the 1800s and of the early 1900s, and it certainly refined and sharpened the theory.[5] Hence we shall include formal management theory as a modern approach.

It is clear, of course, that formal theory did not disappear with Taylor's death. Just as it had its adherents pre-Taylor, so it continued to have advocates long after—and it still does, for that matter. Indeed a case can be made for the proposition that the average working manager (as opposed to the management theorist) of today accepts and practices it to a larger extent than he or she does any other. Hence it is very much with us and continues to be a force of real consequence.

Concerns   The fundamentals of this theory or approach have been covered in earlier chapters of this book and deserve only a brief reference at this point. First, however, a word of explanation for the term "hard-nosed," which we have chosen to apply to it.

The explanation is easy: Proponents of the formal theory believe that management *has a right to manage* and that it should do just that. The theory does not demand autocracy or unilateral decisions—unless the situation does! But when such actions are called for, they are exactly the ones to be taken. Thus management is to decide to *manage,* and however much it may consult with workers or delegate to them, it always has and retains the right to give orders and require that they be obeyed. Needless to say, this easily leads to a "hard-nosed" attitude.

In view of these assumptions, management's concerns are what one would expect: a clearly defined chain of (management) command, short spans of control, careful delegation of authority, defined line-and-staff responsibilities, accurate descriptions of job duties, an unambiguous organization chart, and the like. Stress is put on seeing to it that each individual knows exactly what is expected of him or her, that from time to time he or she is evaluated as to performance, and informed, especially of shortcomings. To say that its fundamental concern is for the subordinate to "shape up or ship out" might be a bit extreme—but not much.

Additionally it should not be overlooked that not only is *productivity* the single goal of the organization, but that there is for every task a *one best way* to perform it. Wherever feasible, that one best way should be discovered and made known to workers, and they in turn should be paid in accordance with their use of it in achieving output and not simply the time they have put in. Obviously, in such situations, promotion should depend on merit and not seniority.

Additionally it is by now obvious that *scientific management* strongly insists on leaving decision making to management. The time involved in making decisions is clearly (and correctly) recognized, and provisions are made to relieve the worker of all responsibility along this line. Thus workers are to have within easy access an expert for whatever kind of problem they might encounter—and problems are to be taken at once to the appropriate specialist while the workers get on with the business of continuing to produce.

Evaluation   At this point we refer back to Chapters 2, 3, and 4, and remind the reader that the authors of this book have a great deal of respect for formal management theory. We, too, believe management has—and should continue to have—the right to manage. Most Americans agree, and yet sometimes in our concern for the rights and/or feelings of workers we may lose sight of the fact that the business of the world of work is serious business, namely productivity in the broadest sense, and not the entertainment and/or amusement of workers.

Furthermore it must be made clear that by its failure to exercise its rights—or its unwise exercise thereof—management may lose some or all of them. Chapter 15, for example, pointed out that the labor agreement may literally become not what is written in a contract but what the managers *do* or *do not* enforce.

At the same time we must remember that this is not the Middle Ages! After all, people, including workers, do have rights and no one, not even the sole owner of a business, can take them away. Certain rights of workers, in other words, had better be observed voluntarily by management, because if it does not do so voluntarily, it will do so involuntarily.

Besides, workers have feelings, and if one seriously offends or does violence to these feelings he runs the risk of inefficiency, disruption, or failure. If authoritarian actions by management turn people off, as we often say, output is likely to be lowered, not increased. And of course a type of organization or a set of policies or orders that repeatedly offend might ultimately lead to management's loss of certain rights—or even the right to manage.

Thus much as we might wish to return to the "good old days" when the manager was really the manager and everyone knew it, there is no indication that we are about to reenter that era. Management, it is hoped, will continue to have the right to manage, but it must do so wisely, empathically, and ethically.

The "Sentimental" or "Happiness" Theory

It has been pointed out earlier that management did not give serious attention to the sentiments of workers until approximately fifty years ago. It was not so much that management did not care. It was rather that workers were taken for granted. It was assumed that they worked primarily for money (for which incidentally they appeared to have an unlimited appetite and concerning which their demands for more must constantly be thwarted or at least restrained), little or no thought being given to their feelings or the notion that such feelings importantly influenced output.

Concerns   But workers do have feelings, as Mayo pointed out at Hawthorne and elsewhere. Furthermore these feelings are significant, for they often lead to the informal organization, to "we-feelings," to restriction of output, or to an outpouring of nonfactual statements. And of course it is widely assumed that disappointment leads to diminished effort and lowered output.

It was but a step further to the widespread emphasis on selection of new employees. "The square peg in the round hole" was pictured as an imminent risk and, when it occurred, as a great tragedy. One thus tried to find just the right person for each job—or else altered the job so that disappointment would not be the outcome.

One additional step led us to the *happiness philosophy*. Indeed supervisors of and just after World War II were often openly told that "the happy worker is the productive worker" and exhorted to "keep 'em happy" in every reasonable way—and sometimes in ways not so reasonable!

This feeling added impetus to the growing movement toward fringe benefits. After all, recreation activities, company teams, holidays, coffee breaks, vacations, employee clubs, medical insurance—these and a dozen or more additional provisions were aimed at building a happy, contented work force. We never achieved such a work force, of course, but for a long time that in no way diminished efforts to do so.

Again a next step: It was a short distance from the *happiness philosophy* to *manipula-*

tion, that is, to doing things for workers not because you loved them but because you could get more that way. Thus the supervisor was exhorted to *demonstrate* an interest in his people. He was to call them by name, to praise in public, to reward suggestions for improvement (indeed he was to "plant" such suggestions and when they were "returned" by the worker to greet them as original to the worker and as of truly outstanding merit). It is hard to say whether the flood of "human relations" or "how-to-do-it" books of the thirties, forties, and fifties caused these developments or were caused by them. The chances are that the books fed on the happenings, which in turn were reenforced by the books.[6] To say the least it is not a *happy* chapter in the history of the worker-manager relations in the United States.

Evaluation The proper conclusion with regard to this theory is not unlike that for the "hard-nosed" one, namely, that it contains quite significant insights but can easily be overdone. The sentiments of people are important. They do construct an informal organization, and it can lead to most serious restriction of output—or under fortunate circumstances to an output greater than we believed possible. People do prosper under sincere, deserved recognition, and fringe benefits can be motivating. (Many of them should be provided even if not directly motivating.)

But as we have repeatedly said earlier in this book, the critics of the *happiness philosophy* ultimately must triumph. Man is not simply a bundle of desires palpitatingly seeking fulfillment. Most people are mature adults recognizing something of the seriousness of life, its disappointments, its obligations, and hopefully its rewards. At times it is not apparent that managers and management theorists recognized these simple facts.

Manipulation was the crowning blow to, as well as the mortal sin of, the naive practitioners of this philosophy. Through their shortsightedness they have seriously—some believe irreparably—damaged worker-manager relationships in the United States, even to the extent that today in many cases proper and considerate actions by management are greeted with the question of "How in the hell are they trying to get to us now?"

The writers of this book believe that the situation, while serious, especially among blue-collar workers, is not beyond repair. In our opinion, however, the time is short. Management needs basic understanding of the fundamental nature of the problem and then the character and determination necessary to ban such unprincipled manipulation from the world of work.[7]

Before we leave this approach to supervision we must make clear that the extremes of this view, as just set forth, are in no sense what Mayo and his associates in the Hawthorne studies and the *human relations* movement had in mind nor what they advocated and practiced. Perhaps they were not as careful as they might have been to warn and guard against the happiness philosophy and manipulation, but responsibility for these excesses must be placed where it belongs, namely, on certain of those who adopted, advocated, and naively implemented these views, and not on the founders.

Incidentally something of the same can be said relative to Taylor and the "hard-nosed" approach. Many followers of the movement tried to "out-Taylor" Taylor and no doubt carried formal management theory to an extreme of which perceptive advocates of the theory would have disapproved. There is one historical note here, however, that is relevant: Taylor did have a low opinion of the worker of his day and was not hesitant to make this opinion known to all involved. Thus he may well have done more to set the stage for the abuses of his theory than Mayo did for those who were influenced by him.

The "Sensitivity" or "Sweetness-and-Light" Theory

It is not surprising, in view of the unfortunate turns often taken by the above two theories, that people tried hard to develop a new and more satisfactory one. It is an approach that has come to be associated with a certain use of the term *organizational development* and has been quite prominent for the last ten or more years, especially in graduate schools of business.

History There is not much question about who the first advocate, or at least the most important spiritual ancestor, of the approach was. It was Kurt Lewin, mentioned early in this chapter and at least by implication at other points in this book. As we said, Lewin was strong for democratic leadership and in addition put much stress on the development both of sensitivity and skill in interpersonal (especially small-group) relations. The National Training Laboratory of Bethel, Maine, founded principally by Lewin more than thirty years ago, has supplied relevant training to thousands of persons.

Lewin's interest in group dynamics also led directly or indirectly to the founding of the Survey Research Center (or equivalent), which emphasized real-life empirical research in group behavior, often in the world of work. Thus the Michigan studies of Chapter 20 are indirectly attributable to him, though he had died about the time they were begun.

Also related are such investigations as the *participation* study (Number 2 in the first section of this chapter) as well as efforts of persons like Maslow, Herzberg, McGregor, and some other behavioral scientists (see especially Chapter 5).[8]

Concerns This OD (for *organizational development*) theory holds that a major limitation of people and their effectiveness in group relations is a lack of sensitivity to the feelings of others (and perhaps to one's own) and undue concern when adverse opinions about one are known to be held and especially when they are expressed by another person. One way in which the needed sensitivity is to be acquired is in T-group (for *training-group*) sessions, where there are no leader and no agenda, and people literally flounder for hours as they make efforts to find and pursue meaningful activities. The process is too involved for analysis here. It will have to suffice to say that persons occasionally find T-group experiences quite traumatic, but most who persist come out with increased self-understanding and awareness of themselves and their groups, and with an ability not only to "take it" when disagreement and even hostility are expressed, but with an actual desire to have such feelings openly expressed, along with skills in encouraging such expression. It is easy to see why T-groups are controversial.

As the OD procedures have been applied in business and government agencies the T-group procedures have been made less threatening and abrasive, principally under the guidance of an OD consultant. Eventually it is hoped, people will learn to avoid win-lose situations, the assessing of *who* is to blame, the resort of punitive actions and other disturbing behavior, and will come to depend on continuing discussion, encounter, confrontation, open expression, and the like, until *consensus* as to the proper action emerges. When the group can wholeheartedly bend its best efforts to accomplishing mutually determined goals, the result will be a great increase in efficiency of effort.

The OD theorists have also made much of the importance of *change* in an organization. Somehow they have come to see the ordinary individual as a "stand-patter," one who does not want to "rock the boat" and can be counted upon to resist innovations. (How wrong they can be is evidenced by the many changes the Auto Workers, to take an example, have brought about in virtually each new contract with the Big Three. They seem to have been especially interested in changing wages and fringe benefits, in making overtime optional, and in new arrangements to protect job security.) Thus the OD consultant becomes a "change-agent" for the organization, and through his or her efforts and the efforts of the assisting group, others are also oriented toward change.

In all this it must be noted that if *sensitivity* is the chief characteristic that people strive to develop, then *participation* in decision making becomes a prevailing management strategy. The OD people are not naive: this is not the old "industrial democracy" of the early 1900s where the employees comprised, as it were, an old-fashioned New England town meeting, and by majority made all the important decisions of the organization. (The authors do not know of any firm that for any long period actually operated successfully in this fashion.) Rather the OD theorists want the people who are to implement a decision (which they may have had little or nothing to do with making) to be the ones who decide *how it is to be carried out* (and by consensus, not by a win-lose vote). Thus we as a work group are not to make *your* decisions if you are an executive, but we are to make *our* decisions with parameters laid down possibly by executives, engineers, inspectors, and others. And our supervisor, instead of being the "decider" as to how we are to do our work and when and how much, becomes a "linking-pin," or a connector between our group and the appropriate higher group and other groups in the organization.

Thus in summary, stress is placed on mutual trust, on a free exchange of ideas and feelings, on easy communication throughout the organization, and on what is called *action research,* a process by which the people involved are constantly studying their own reactions and improving them as they learn through their successes and their failures.

Evaluation   It is hard to tell when one reads OD theory or even accounts of OD as applied in particular firms just how fully it is intended to be used and how extensively it really has been. There is no question about it: Certain firms and government agencies have used it to a greater or less extent, but it is seldom clear how extensively. In any case the present authors have many reservations about its becoming "the wave of the future" in the field of personnel relations, reservations based in part on management theory and in part on more mundane, everyday considerations.

So far as the latter are concerned, it is an unavoidable fact that people often find themselves in situations involving disagreements that no amount of sensitivity or confrontation or additional conversation can resolve. There simply have to be other methods for conflict resolution, for genuine conflicts not amenable to the proposed ones are inevitable. Besides, we are at times in situations where our position is supported by a great deal of feeling as opposed to reason. Theoretically OD procedures should diminish such feelings on all sides, but in fact they often fail completely. It is also significant that conflict may involve ethical or moral issues where the person feels that any compromise is immoral (and it might be). These are troublesome situations for all people; they are especially so for any who somehow believe that sincerity and goodwill ("sweetness and light") are adequate if only people are sufficiently able and try hard enough.

Earlier in this book (see Chapter 7) we challenged the belief that man is fundamentally a rational creature. We now add the serious reservation that in general he is not sufficiently rational to make the OD approach the one to which we must all eventually come. Additionally, there is the *adversary* relationship that characterizes many important activities in American life. The union-management relationship is a prime example. However much OD people might want to alter this relationship, it is here to stay for the foreseeable future. While OD tactics no doubt are at times useful in collective bargaining they will not and cannot occupy "center stage."

Finally, it is simply a fact of life that while cooperation is valuable in a society, so, very often, is *competition* (and even at times at least moderately abrasive competition). It is not at all certain that a wage package or a production schedule or a personnel program arrived at by sensitive people on the basis of consensus is necessarily the best. The present authors have a lot of confidence in the give-and-take that characterizes our free enterprise economic system—where various groups, including more than simply workers and managers, are in competition with each other, and where undoubtedly on occasion it has achieved very satisfactory results. Too much competition may be destructive. At times everyone loses from a win-lose situation. But both competition and win-lose situations *may* produce better outcomes than any other.

Thus the sensitivity approach is a well-motivated, sophisticated endeavor emphasizing some important insights into the work situation and producing a great many satisfactory outcomes. But that is far from saying that it is the proper approach to supervision.[9]

Table 21-1 is an attempt to summarize briefly the three approaches to the supervision or motivation of employees.

THE SUPERVISOR AND *HIS* PHILOSOPHY OF SUPERVISION

This book is close to its end and yet we have not as yet told interested supervisors just what they should believe nor have we given them "the last word" on the nature of people, including their subordinates, or on the supervisory process. Why have we delayed so long on these matters?

There is here, of course, no deep strategy to keep the reader's interest high or to save the best to the last. We have not done this thing because we cannot, nor can anyone else. (It is true that some may claim this for their views but they are unintentionally or deliberately misleading those whom they "instruct.") By now it must be apparent that no one research study, and no group of studies, has supplied us with all or even nearly all of the answers, and similarly that no one theory about supervision is *the* proper one. Thus one can learn from the Michigan and Hawthorne studies, and some of the resulting insights may be almost brand new. And one can see advantages in *scientific management* and *human relations* and *organizational development*. Indeed each contains important truths for our field, truths which one should appropriate and use. But each also is in error or at least limited at certain places and no one of them can be accepted at the expense of giving up the insights furnished by the other.

There may, however, be one philosophy that the supervisor can accept, and that is his

Table 21-1   Approaches to Supervision

Approach	Associated with or growing out of	Characteristic reliefs	Contributions	Distortions or limitations
"Hard-nose"	Scientific management	One best way; incentive wages	Methods for improving efficiency	Neglect of employee aspirations and self-esteem
"Keep 'em happy"	Human relations	Informal organization; sentiments as motivators; restriction of output	Feelings as influential in work behavior and organizations	Shallow hedonism; encouragement of manipulation
"Sweetness and light"	Organizational development	Importance of openness, confrontation, empathy, consensus, cooperation	Many problems have an avoidable emotional base; possibilities in intrinsic motivation and identification	Idealistic, impractical in many situations; overlooks gains sometimes resulting from competitive and win-lose situations

own, no matter of what elements it is composed. Such a philosophy should be *eclectic,* composed of the best parts of available theories; *tentative,* subject to examination, review, and improvement as developments warrant; and *ethical* or *moral,* used in the best interests of the supervisor, subordinates, and the enterprise of which all are part.

QUESTIONS

1 Describe and evaluate the study on the three styles of leadership.
2 Did the study of participation and productivity *prove* that participation is the only or at least the best way to ensure productivity? Why do you say so?
3 What is so important about the Ohio State distinction between initiating structure and consideration?
4 To what extent are the findings from the Ohio State studies of leadership consistent with what has been concluded elsewhere in this book? Explain.
5 Describe and evaluate *scientific management* and the theory of supervision that grew out of it.
6 Do the same for the *human relations* movement.
7 Do the same for the movement known as *organizational development.*
8 The last part of the chapter discusses some characteristics of the sort of supervisory theory one should develop for managing in today's world. Evaluate them.

NOTES

1 Ronald O. Lippitt, "An Experimental Study of the Effect of Democratic and Authoritarian Group Atmosphere," *University of Iowa Studies in Child Welfare,* no. 16, pp. 43–195, 1940.
2 Lester Coch and John R. P. French, Jr., "Overcoming Resistance to Change," *Human Relations,* vol. 1, pp. 512–532, 1948.
3 The literature on this subject is extensive. See, for example, the following articles: William Brown, "From Strikes to Participation: *A Sociologist's Eye View," Personnel Management,* vol. 8, no. 6, pp. 29–31, June 1976; Nancy Foy and Herman Gadow, "Worker Participation: Contrasts in Three Countries," *Harvard Business Review,* vol. 54, no. 3, pp. 71ff, May-June 1976; and Johannes Schregle, "Workers' Participation in Decisions Within Organizations," *International Labour Review,* vol. 113, no. 1, pp. 1–15, January-February 1976.
4 Carroll L. Shartle, *Executive Performance and Leadership* (Englewood Cliffs, N.J.: Prentice-Hall, 1956).
5 An early, relevant article is Frank T. Carlton, "Scientific Management and the Wage Earner," *Journal of Political Economy,* vol. 20, pp. 726–733, 1913. A recent (and complementary) one is H. Jack Shapiro and Mahmoud A. Wahba, "Frederick W. Taylor—62 Years Later," *Personnel Journal,* vol. 53, no. 8, pp. 574–578, August 1974.
6 A controversial book of the period was Dale Carnegie, *How to Win Friends and Influence People* (New York: Simon & Schuster, 1936). Carnegie's admirers see it as valuable advice in human relations; some detractors have seen it as an invitation to manipulation.
7 "Job enrichment" has also grown to a considerable degree out of this approach. See, for example, Denis D. Umstat, Cecil H. Bell, Jr., and Terence R. Mitchell, "Effects of Job Enrichment and Task Goals on Satisfaction and Productivity," *Journal of Applied Psychology,* vol. 61, no. 4, pp. 379–394; and Greg R. Oldham, J. Richard Hockman, and Jane L. Pearce, "Conditions Under Which Employees Respond to Enriched Work"—from the same journal, pp. 395–403.

8 Another stress of the OD movement is on conflict-resolution and the avoidance of win-lose situations. See Alan C. Filley, *Interpersonal Conflict Resolution* (Glenview, Ill.: Scott, Foresman, 1975); and Lyman W. Porter, Edward E. Lawler, and J. Richard Hockman, *Behavior in Organizations* (New York: McGraw-Hill, 1975), especially Chaps. 16 and 17.

9 While criticism of the OD point of view has been in the minority, there has been some. See, for example, W. R. Nord (ed.), *Concepts and Controversy in Organizational Behavior* (Pacific Palisades, Calif.: Goodyear, 1972); and Thomas J. Cottle, "Let's Keep a Few Secrets: Our Soul-Baring Orgy Destroys the Private Self," *Psychology Today,* vol. 75, no. 9, pp. 22ff, October 1975.

CASES

The three cases of this chapter have one thing in common: each involves an out-of-the-ordinary application or interpretation of a labor-contract provision. Furthermore this interpretation may appear to be, and may in fact be, legalistic, unfair, and injurious to one or more employees.

The larger question is how to deal with such provisions. Must they be enforced as written, or is Management entitled to reinterpret them to achieve fairness and justice? If the answer to this question is yes, how far may it properly go along this line? Must Martha McBain be laid off even though she is the senior employee and fully qualified? Must Ronald Cravens and W. H. Elliott be content with one week of vacation while a more-recently-hired worker gets two? And is Dick Mantle to be demoted because of an obvious and admitted error on the part of the Company? The answer to all these questions poses real difficulties for the people involved.

CASE 21-1

The Company operates a motor repair and rebuilding shop on the West Coast. Most of the work is on diesel engines from the motor trucks, but other kinds of motors are also accepted. Typically, mechanics remove, rebuild, and replace motors in trucks brought to the plant.

Among the departments in the shop are the radio department and the instrument department. These are small departments as compared to most of the others, but according to the labor contract with the International Union, each constitutes a seniority unit. In this connection, the contract provides that "the last person hired shall be the first laid off within a department," the only reservation being that the person retained must be able to do the job. No provision is made, in other words, for the exercise of anything other than departmental seniority in case of a layoff.

For some time the amount of work to be done on radios and instruments has been declining. This is due primarily to the fact that more and more engines are shipped in for rebuilding and then shipped back to the owner rather than being installed in the truck. For these units radio work is eliminated and instrument work greatly curtailed.

The instrument and radio departments each have one person who serves as departmental clerk: Martha McBain in Radio and Ruth Fairfax in Instrument. Both are good workers, capable of keeping accurate records, taking dictation, writing letters, and doing stockroom work. Martha, however, has ten years of seniority and Ruth only two.

The situation recently came to a climax with a further sharp decline in radio business. Indeed the work declined so much that Martha could do her job in two hours each day, and hence efforts were made to find special projects on which she could work. Finally it was decided that her position must be abolished.

Herbert Anderson, foreman over both departments, now had a real problem. Martha is fully as efficient as Ruth Fairfax and is extremely popular with her fellow workers. Furthermore, her husband is a mechanic in the shop and an officer in the local Union. She can very quickly learn whatever she does not already know about Ruth's work, and Ruth could be laid off. On the other hand, the Union contract contains the provisions referred to above.

Anderson has reluctantly decided that Martha, rather than Ruth, must be laid off. Do you agree? Why or why not?

CASE 21-2

Ronald Cravens and W. H. Elliott are assemblers who work for the Company. They were hired on January 17, 1968, and have been continuously employed since that time. Jack Green is also an assembler for the Company. He was hired on April 30, 1968.

Later in 1968 the International Union won the bargaining rights to represent a number of Company workers, including assemblers, and shortly after negotiated an agreement with the Company. Among its provisions was one that gave employees one week of paid vacation after one year and two weeks after three years.

When the 1968–1969 contract expired, considerable difficulty was encountered in negotiating a new one. In fact it was April 8, 1970, when it was finally signed. The new contract provided for two weeks of vacation after two (instead of three) years of service.

As of April 8, no one of these three men had taken his 1970 vacation, and a question arose as to how much each was entitled to take. The Company decided as follows: that Cravens and Elliott were entitled to only one week, since on their anniversary date (January 17, 1970) they had only two years of service and the contract then in effect provided only one week until *three* years of service. (The Company contended that the 1968–1969 contract remained in effect until replaced by a new one, and that its provisions must therefore govern until April 8, 1970.) On the other hand, Green was conceded to be due two weeks of vacation since he had completed two years of work after the new contract was signed.

Do Cravens and Elliott have a basis for a grievance in this situation? How should it be answered if they file one?

CASE 21-3

The Company is a public utility supplying electric power to a New England town of 25,000 people and a considerable surrounding territory. For some time the Company has been concerned about the competence of its power-plant operators. Without exception these employees started with the Company years ago and became operators by progression through lower-rated jobs. Thus the youngest operator has thirteen years of Company service, though he has been an operator for just the last year. The contract requires that the operators be "qualified to perform the duties of the job," but no formal training or testing of competence has been provided, and very few if any employees have been refused the job of operator because of inability to discharge its duties. Recognizing the growing complexity of modern machines and procedures, the Company has for several years encouraged operators to take training (typically through correspondence courses) in power-plant operation. Only a few of them have taken advantage of the training even though the Company pays all the costs.

More than a year ago John Thomas, manager of the plant, made up his mind that something must be done about the situation. He persuaded Management that the next labor contract must contain provisions requiring correspondence training for everyone in the power-plant operator classification. The Union resisted strongly. There was a good deal of talk about a strike, and bargaining continued for much longer than usual. Finally the Union gave in on the point.

The particular provision that Management won required that after an employee became a power-plant operator he would have six months in which to complete five units in a specified correspondence course, and eighteen months in which to complete the whole course, consisting of eighteen units or lessons. If he failed to meet either the six-months or the eighteen-months deadline, he was to revert to his former classification, and another person was to be selected as operator.

The first person to become operator after the provision became effective was Dick Mantle. At the time, Dick was forty years of age and had been with the Company for more than twelve years. He had always been considered a satisfactory, but in no sense an outstanding, employee.

By some oversight that no one could satisfactorily explain, the personnel department failed to order the correspondence course in power-plant operation for Dick. Six months and one day following his appointment to the job the Union filed a grievance alleging that the Company was in violation of the contract since it continued to classify Dick as power-plant operator in spite of the fact that he had not made satisfactory progress in training. Indeed, the grievance asserted correctly that he had not completed a single lesson. The Union asked that Dick be disqualified and that Jim Brown, Union president and the next man on the seniority list, be made power-plant operator in his place.

What action should the Company take? If it denies the grievance, on what grounds should it base the denial? If it grants it, what explanation should be made to Dick Mantle?

Part Five

The Supervisor of the Future

Predicting the future is always hazardous business, and for at least two reasons: One is that the trends on which a prediction is based may be incorrectly appraised. Thus an assumption of this book is that the great majority of Americans are in favor of civil rights and want to see them achieved by people generally. We could be wrong on either or both counts. Maybe they are not really in favor of them; or maybe they want them in theory but not in practice.

Another conclusion drawn in earlier parts of this book is that Americans are basically committed to the fundamental assumptions of the market economy, not in the pure form of that economy, but nevertheless to a large degree. Again we may be wrong. Most Americans may be socialists at heart and secretly at work to bring about a socialist society. In both the cases we think we are right, that the facts are as we have stated, but of course we could be incorrect in our appraisals here and elsewhere.

A second place for error in prediction is that trends, even if correctly appraised, may change abruptly or gradually. If it is reasonable now to conclude that the future is at least relatively safe for civil rights and the market economy, that may not be true tomorrow or next month or next year or in the next decade. Some changes in beliefs and feelings we can anticipate and take them into account in projecting trends. Some are unpredictable at least at the particular time and under the circumstances.

The reader needs to keep these facts in mind as he or she reads the last chapter in this book. In it we make predictions and in some instances suggest some courses of action. These may be correct, or they may be in error, totally or partially. In addition, the reader may have to come to different conclusions. All we can ask at this point is a careful consideration of the ideas of this chapter—and then a conclusion by the reader based on his or her own judgment arrived at in the light of what is judged to be the best information available.

Chapter 22

The Supervisor of the 1980s: Challenges and Opportunities

A point made earlier in this book, more than once, in fact, is that supervisors, like the rest of us, almost inevitably pay most attention to the day-to-day problems they confront and then attempt their short-run solution. Thus they have little time to devote to the theoretical aspects of the world or their jobs. And since they are so involved in short-run issues, little of their attention goes to discovering and appraising long-run developments, including the trends even in areas that may eventually have a direct effect on their jobs.

In theory at least, this is undesirable, since the wise individual tries to become familiar with his or her entire situation, including developments and trends, and is prepared for events as they occur. In practice, of course, one has only so much time and energy and furthermore is often required to spend that on immediate matters rather than on events that may happen weeks or months or years from now. Thus it is easy to understand why the supervisor is not an expert on cultural values nor an outstanding authority on what is likely to happen in the world of work in the 1980s.

While, as we have just acknowledged, the average front-line member of management should not be expected to be a scholar in these fields, it is unfortunate if he or she is entirely ignorant with regard to them. Maybe a study of them is like the frosting on a cake; however, cakes may be rescued from mediocrity by a first-class frosting.[1]

We make no apology, therefore, for closing this book with a chapter on basic values and developments in the world in which we find ourselves, and in particular, a discussion of such factors as seem to lie ahead of the supervisor in connection with his or her work and how it is to be done.

UNIQUENESS OF CULTURAL VALUES

One conclusion with which no one would argue these days is the great variety of customs, practices, beliefs, and the like that are exhibited by people in different parts of the world. We may be interested in the manner of dress, the language or dialect spoken, the marriage practices, or even fundamental religious beliefs and habits as these have appeared in society. All these may, and they frequently do, vary to a degree that people would not have believed until travel became possible and a knowledge of what was happening worldwide became available.

When we look further into this matter, however, we characteristically find two things: First, the customs do not seem strange to those who have long followed them. On the contrary, they usually seem natural, normal, highly desirable, and even necessary. One measure of their emotional base is the fact that any fundamental change in them is likely to be stoutly resisted. And second, these *values*—for that is what they usually are—tend to form a *whole*, a characteristic and basic way of thinking, feeling, and acting that sets these people off from others. Each culture, in other words, has its own pattern of habits and values, and to understand the culture one must understand these and the resultant *milieu* or social climate. To attempt to deal with that culture without a knowledge of these values and this climate is to run the risk of serious error.

It turns out that the United States is no exception to the above remarks. While it is certainly true that our values are not unique in the sense that no other people in the world share any of them, the fact remains that there are characteristically *American* values, some of which values we may share with certain countries most like ourselves (for example, Great Britain) but which are predominant in our thinking and feeling. Being familiar with them is necessary to understand the American scene, including the work scene, and to that subject we are devoting the next section of this chapter. The supervisor does not have to be a student of these values to be successful, but such an understanding is likely to contribute to his or her success in the long run.

FUNDAMENTAL AMERICAN BELIEFS AND VALUES

One difficulty we face in discussing fundamental beliefs and values in the United States is that there are many of them; however, we find ourselves where we shall have to pick and choose, for there is not sufficient space to examine all, even if we knew all about them. In this instance we have chosen four, hopefully the most influential four, of them.[2]

A Pessimistic View of Human Nature

A fundamental part of our heritage is an essentially pessimistic view of the nature of the average person or the "common man." This belief goes all the way back to the Acropolis of ancient Greece; it also became embedded in the orthodox Christian views that have influenced the United States so much.

As developed by the Greeks, this view we have in mind is often called *rationalism*. It holds that the essential element in being human is man's ability to reason and that man is man to the extent that he does engage in true and objective reasoning. Indeed, according to Plato, the state was to be governed by the wise men (this was before Title VII days!) and the rest of the people were to do as they were assigned and were to "stay in their places." However, Plato's idea was not one of forceful repression but rather grew out of his belief that those who were not wise would recognize and willingly accept their proper place in the state. Plato's views were more extreme than the Athenian practice of the time, but contrary to a widely held American belief, the Athenians were *elitists*, with high status and power given to a few and no status or authority accorded to women, slaves, barbarians, and most common people.

In addition to the unrealism and oversimplification of these views, they carry a most serious implication for our world. It is that man always falls short of this rational ideal, and most of us fall seriously short of it. Thus man—and especially the common man—must be recognized for the inferior person he in fact is, and will, of course, have to be dealt with accordingly. It follows that a person should acknowledge and must accept his or her inferiority and the superiority of the king or the priest—or the manager?—or other capable persons. One must then fulfill one's role in accordance with their dictates. But man in himself is certainly not an admirable sort of being.

This point of view has particular implication for workers and the work scene generally. The most worthy activity of Athens was that of the philosopher-king or the wise ruler. The next most worthy was that of the soldier, capable of a vigorous and stout-hearted defense of the state. And the least worthy and admirable was that of the worker, who represented a sort of necessary evil and in no sense an admirable activity or position in society.

It is hard to estimate the tragic effects in the intervening 2500 years of this rationalist view of mankind. It not only condemned the common person to a role of inferiority but branded work—including the economic activities essential to mankind's survival—as somehow to be shunned wherever possible and in any case relegated to those who were second-class. In our own society the blue-collar worker has received the full brunt of this unfortunate attitude. Somehow white-collar jobs were never thought as inferior in the sense that "work with one's hands" was, and hence they escaped the low esteem in which the latter was held. Thus a full understanding of the blue-collar worker's preference for labor unions has to take into consideration that it was in part a defensive reaction to an element in our Greek heritage.

It might appear that with the coming of Christianity all this would have changed, but nothing of that sort took place. The Church made much of the doctrine of *original sin,* itself to a considerable extent a continuation of certain aspects of this rationalist view but one that added a divine sanction to man's inferiority and unworthiness. One might have anticipated that the Church would put itself firmly on the side of the dignity of work and extol its virtues, but that was not what happened. On the contrary, the lot of the common person and ordinary worker has been a hard one, right down to the twentieth century. Even today, while the economic position of workers has markedly improved, the intelligentsia still deny them equal esteem and frequently discourage developments that contribute to an increase in especially the blue-collar worker's self-respect and self-esteem.

No doubt to many it seems unfortunate that relations between workers and employers are often far from cordial and optimistic. One who knows our history, however, could hardly expect anything else, especially when the above developments are seen in the light of a certain economic philosophy of a couple of centuries ago, one to which we now turn.

The Pursuit of Self-Interest

It is probably only an historical coincidence that the same year that witnessed the Declaration of Independence in the United States also saw the publication in Great Britain of Adam Smith's *The Wealth of Nations.* In it the author promulgated a philosophy known as *laissez faire,* which has been very influential especially on business thinking in the United States. Its influence has included a decided effect on worker-management relations.

One problem man has confronted, no doubt since the beginning of human history, has been what to do when one's own interests seemed to run contrary to the good of the group. Societies often emphasize the virtues of self-sacrifice for the common good, such a point of view, for example, having been a prominent part of Christianity from its beginning.

It was thus quite a shock when Smith asserted what seemed to be an opposite view, namely, that *insofar as economic matters are concerned* one not only may but *should* uniformly and always pursue his or her long-run best interests. Smith asserted, in other words, that if each person would attempt to get for himself or herself, the "invisible hand" (or competition) would assure that the result would be the greatest economic gain for the greatest number of people. Thus economic gain was no longer unworthy. On the contrary, it was desirable, including one's own personal gain.

Regardless of the merits (or lack thereof) of Smith's philosophy in itself, it was accompanied by at least two incidental developments that seriously detracted from its widespread acceptance among workers. One was the so-called iron law of wages, which held that the natural laws of economics were such that ultimately labor's share of society's income is fixed and cannot really be increased; the other was the *commodity conception of labor,* which maintained that labor was a commodity to be bought as cheaply as possible, with as much profit as possible to be made on its production. Thus the employer had no moral obligation—and usually no economic incentive—to be kind to workers, to increase their pay, to ease their drudgery, or to provide for decent housing or even safe conditions of work. When these two views are put alongside the desperate economic position of workers of 150 to 200 years ago, it can easily be seen that Smith's views did not strongly commend themselves to those workers who came to know about them. Furthermore, it should be emphasized that all three views—striving for self-interest, the iron law, and the commodity conception—in themselves inevitably lead to pessimism, and thus they added, in the world of work, to the gloom already induced by the views discussed in the preceding section.[3]

Thus again one can profit from historical perspective: In view of the unfavorable attitudes toward work and workers as these developed in the Western world, including the United States, it is in a way remarkable that modern labor relations are as good as they are. Evidently other forces were operating to keep American workers from developing more radical tendencies than they have developed.

A point made earlier in this book (see especially Chapter 6), namely that we are typically suspicious of people who put self-interest above the common good (to whatever extent Smith's followers do—or are believed to), still applies, and undoubtedly puts before the American business of today its greatest philosophical challenge.

The Virtues of Hard Work

In a very real sense the two values just discussed have to a greater or less extent been an impediment to the development of good worker-manager-owner relationships in the United States. The one now to be considered and the other covered in this section, however, on the whole may have had the opposite effect.

The movement which we now have in mind is frequently known as the *puritan ethic.* Its proponent was John Calvin, and its birthplace was Geneva, Switzerland. And it preceded Smith's laissez faire by a couple of centuries.

To put Calvin and his views in perspective, one must remember the *elitism* that characterized his time, especially as relates to work and economic activity generally. Thus the desirable occupations were clerical and professional (though being of the nobility and not having to work was also approved), and the best use that could be made of any economic surplus was to turn it over to the Church for its use in bringing salvation to those souls otherwise eternally lost.

Calvin had a different view. To him there was nothing unworthy in honest hard work. Indeed if done "to the Lord" it was noble and ennobling. Furthermore, one evidence of how favorably a person was esteemed by God was found in the degree to which his work prospered. Thus each individual was encouraged to thrift and frugality—and to the investment of his resources in assets that would *produce additional resources* (for example, the capital goods of the economist). It is far more than a mere coincidence that the American colonies and later the young American nation (1) accepted and practiced the puritan ethic with enthusiasm and dedication, and (2) prospered as few people ever did before.

Years have passed and much of the theological underpinnings (for example, predestination) with which Calvin bolstered his views have disappeared (indeed many of these theological doctrines were never generally accepted in the United States). The heart of the puritan ethic is still amongst us, however. There is question about how extensively Americans now accept it and how deeply they are committed to it, but there is no question about this: It is still an important part of the American scene, and one who is ignorant of it is destined to misinterpret significant aspects of what he encounters.

The Equality of All People

One of the most celebrated and doubtless most noteworthy of American values is that of *equality.* Virtually all Americans know (or have heard) that "all men are created equal" and are "endowed by their Creator with certain unalienable rights." We may disagree somewhat as to what these rights really are and about what equality means, but there is no doubt that at least at the conscious or "talking level" we are committed to the view.

At the same time, however, some Americans maintain that this is a thoroughly idealistic view with no chance to be realized and that no one is really in favor of it. They point to the obvious differences among people—in intelligence, in "looks," in status, and in countless other characteristics—and assert that we neither are, nor can, nor want to be equal. Furthermore true equality, if ever achieved, they say, would last only a little while, until the strong again come to dominate the weak. It must also be confessed that there are Americans who are not sure they favor equality anyway, for they suspect that the judgment of superior people—among whom they nearly always consider themselves—should carry much more weight than that of ordinary people.

All this, however, is not typical. Americans generally believe in equality and wish to see it realized. At the same time, however, the notion has been slow in coming; it has been interpreted and practiced at times with great ambivalence; and it has been applied in what was often totally inconsistent forms. At first, for example, in some of the newly formed states of the Union, a person could not vote unless he was a male and a member of the established religion, and it was fifty years after the founding of the country before the ownership of real property was dropped as a prerequisite for voting. Blacks were outside the sphere of acceptance, counting originally for only a fraction of a human being and even then only for restricted purposes. Women were totally disenfranchised for the first century and a half of the country's life, and for years before and after the Twenty-first Amendment various restrictive devices were used systematically to exclude large groups of Americans from real citizenship in the country. Even today "one man, one vote" (no doubt another Title VII expression) is imperfectly realized in voting, and people are discriminated against unfairly in many other aspects of life.

But we have made progress (or at least we have moved in a certain definite direction). The above changes are relevant. So are numerous decisions of the Supreme Court, including those discussed above in Chapter 18, and many acts of the U.S. Congress as well as of state legislatures and city councils.

Democratic egalitarianism, as the movement is called, has thus developed extensively, though *elitism* dies slowly in the United States, as it does all over the world. But again the current American scene would be unintelligible if a student of it did not understand the long-standing, basic dedication of Americans to the notion that "all men (now including women) are created equal" and are at least morally entitled to treatment with dignity and respect.

Effects of the theories discussed above are shown in Table 22-1.

Table 22-1   Effects of Theories about the Nature of Human Beings and of Work

Theory	Essential beliefs	Results
Rationalism	Man is by nature rational but most men are far short of rational ideal	Censure of especially "the working class"; lack of dignity in work; introjected attitudes of inferiority on the part of workers; elitism; pessimism
Laissez faire	Because of competition, pursuit of self-interest will produce the greatest good	Dynamic to work and especially to investment and risk; exploitation of workers; no provision for safety, sanitation, etc.; worker-owner antipathy
Iron law	Natural laws of economics put a low and unchangeable ceiling on wages (income of labor)	Opposition to efforts to better the lot of workers; resignation to poverty, accidents, disease; pessimism and distrust
Commodity conception	Labor is only a commodity to be exploited for owner's benefit	Exploitation, low wages, "sweat shops"; resistance to efforts at improvement
Puritan ethic	Work is worthy; accumulation of world's goods is a sign of God's favor; one should constantly strive to do better	Dynamic to hard work, to investment, including risk taking; emphasis on *material* well-being; dignity of work
Democratic egalitarianism	All men are created equal and are endowed with inalienable rights	Entitlement of all to treatment with dignity, respect, and equality; increase in self-esteem and ego-strength on the part of "the common man"; increased willingness to challenge "the system"; civil rights; litigious tendencies; opposition to elitism

TRENDS IN AMERICAN BELIEFS AND VALUES

Thus far we have spoken as though values are merely handed to us or otherwise simply appear and then become a functioning, unchanging part of our culture. Such is not the case, of course. Values come and go, though our most significant ones nearly always change slowly. But change they do, and it is possible to detect trends in them as they undergo alterations.

Increased Dignity of Work

There is now evidence from the late sixties and the seventies that American attitudes toward work (particularly blue-collar or hourly activity or "work with one's hands") are beginning to be altered. There is, for example, some indication of a decrease in the percentage of high school graduates going on to college, with a not insignificant and an increasing portion of such persons turning toward "manual" jobs. The spread of vocational training, notably in community colleges, is one of the striking educational developments of the last decade or two, and vocational curricula in high schools and elsewhere are far more common than formerly.

If this does prove to be a genuine trend, it is one long overdue. For far too long in the United States we have been "educating" our brightest young people in colleges, especially the so-called liberal arts colleges, where not only is the practical and/or vocational not emphasized but is often held in low regard if not in contempt. (This of course represents the values of Plato and Aristotle made incarnate and moving among us.) The result is untold numbers of persons who are presumably well educated but are unable to make their full contribution to the world's activities, as well as being almost totally ignorant in such vital fields as finance, personnel relations, technology, and even the law.[4]

A point of great significance in this connection is the tendency of our society both to underestimate the demands (intellectual and otherwise) made on blue-collar workers, and especially skilled ones, and to undervalue to a conspicuous degree the contributions they make to the world in which we live. It is too much to hope that in this generation such persons will actually receive the status and respect which they are due, but any tendency in that direction is a hopeful sign.

Changing Moral and Other Standards

Contrary to what is often believed, neither are moral standards fixed and immutable, this statement being true whether the term is used in the narrow sense of sexual behavior or the broader one that includes conduct and motives relating to the social benefit or public good. In fact such standards are altered through time, as other standards are. And sometimes the alterations occur with unexpected speed.

The present happens to be such a time. To consider sexual behavior first, in recent years we saw—or should have seen—these basic changes coming in the ever-increasing divorce rate, along with the far greater acceptability of divorce and remarriage. More recently, living together "without benefit of clergy" has become a widely accepted practice, and when marriage is contracted it is often not for "as long as ye both shall *live*" but rather for "as long as ye both shall *love*." Couples may be as dedicated to each other as ever—there is as yet no showing of a radical increase in promiscuity—but such devotion is now typically "for time and not for eternity." In retrospect, it is hard to believe that so drastic a transformation has occurred so swiftly.

But other standards are also being called into question. Particularly among younger people, there is increasing question as to whether *status, pay,* and *promotion* are the only proper or most significant goals of life, and making a career is often far less attractive than it was to earlier generations. Companies encounter increasing difficulty in getting even management people to move to a new location when and where some executive decides.

Nothing manifests this point more than the style of dress, particularly among the young: long hair and full beards for men, blue jeans, or even overalls, and T-shirts for women—these are but illustrations of profound changes in the teenagers and young adults of today when they are compared with their counterparts of the early sixties and before.[5]

A point that also relates to changing standards is attitudes now being manifested toward work. In recent years there have been articles (and even television documentaries) about the boredom of the assembly line and the meaningless demands of repetitive work. It has also been asserted that assemblers do everything possible to escape the monotony in which they are entrapped, but for most of them the efforts prove to be unsuccessful.

It is not all clear how much substance is found in this point of view. Certainly if work is now more boring and monotonous than ever before, much of this feeling resides in the new model of worker, for clearly working conditions on the assembly line are better now in most respects than they were in the twenties and thirties, for example. In truth this belief in boredom may well come principally from *students* of the work (with their greater education and middle-class backgrounds but no assembly-line experience) rather than from the workers themselves. It is interesting that in collective bargaining monotony is not usually a substantial issue, whereas voluntary overtime, greater rest periods, increased supplementary unemployment benefits (SUB) funds, greater job security, more "free" days, and the like are main concerns. Monotonous work is not fun, but to a great extent "monotony is in the eye of the beholder"—or the observer. No doubt there are problems here, but they are probably less serious than they are usually thought to be.

Obviously, the moral concerns we are discussing in this section go far beyond what we have so far mentioned. We shall say more of some of this in the following section of this chapter, but let us mention here questions about the quality of the environment (and of life!), the fairness of profits received by certain groups, the responsibility or lack thereof of large corporations (as well as politicians and others), and the whole set of beliefs based on growth, efficiency, productivity, and the like. Our point is not the approval or disapproval of any or all of these beliefs. Rather we emphasize the necessity for the supervisor to arrive at an understanding of what is happening—and why!

A Reconsideration of Laissez Faire

We have earlier remarked concerning how we continue to talk in terms of individual profit and freedom from government interference even though our conduct is not always consistent with our statements. For example, in certain business publications it has become almost a ritual, whatever the problem being discussed, for the editorial writer to assert that the solution lies in the direction of reduced taxes, more competition, balanced budgets, and no—or at least less—regulation.

But we do not always mean it! At times we accept government regulation; we take advantage of deficit financing; we plead for government guarantees if things go badly— and all the while there are a whole host of sophisticated observers who are either puzzled by what they see and hear—or more recently, increasingly turned off by it.

Again we are not opposing the operation of the free enterprise or market economy where appropriate, but there are things better done by government than by business. Many economies (for example, Japan and West Germany) have done a better job of recognizing and handling this problem, including its philosophical foundations, than we have, and their solutions do not always follow the government-hands-off position. One wonders how much time we have left to work out our own philosophies concerning the competing forces herein involved.[6]

Civil Rights—An Idea Whose Time Has Come!

Earlier in this chapter we spoke about democratic egalitarianism as a basic American value and used the civil rights movement as a concrete illustration of it. Here we simply again call attention to the movement and point out that it is a very definite trend in America today. Civil rights decisions of the Supreme Court are often unanimous ones, and this includes many of those made after the Nixon appointees joined the Court. Legislative acts in this field, when they are revised, are usually strengthened rather than weakened. Pro-segregation candidates have all but disappeared from the scene, even in the South. Those who oppose civil rights changes almost never do so any more on philosophical grounds but rather on the ground that "they're trying to go too fast" or that regulation is "nit-picking" and/or unduly costly and time-consuming. We may have yielded on busing as a means of achieving school integration, and it is not apparent at this writing where reverse discrimination may take us, but the trend toward increasing emphasis on civil rights is clearly supported and unmistakable.

ISSUES IN THE WORLD OF WORK

By now it has become apparent that we are not always successful in maintaining a distinction between the three major sections of this chapter—the basic values, the trends, and the current issues. At times they flow into one another, and it may not be clear where the value stops and the trend begins or where the issue ceases and becomes a trend.

But that is not really important anyway, is it? We are emphasizing certain facts about American life, facts that directly or indirectly are quite likely to have an impact on the supervisor. Under the circumstances, whether each topic fits in its own proper category or overlaps into others does not seem to be of great significance.

In this section we want to look at some of the unanswered questions in the world of the supervisor and to emphasize certain issues that directly or indirectly most managers, including first-level ones, will face whether or not they are now fully aware of them.

The Individual versus the Group

It has historically been a pleasant and intriguing notion that ultimately there can be no genuine conflict between the welfare of the individual and that of any meaningful, legitimate group of which he is a member. (This was a belief embraced by Socrates, for example.) Actually, of course, the view is untenable, and those who hold it are fine examples of wishful thinking. The young man called upon to risk (and perhaps forfeit) his life on the battlefields of Germany or Iwo Jima or Korea or Vietnam made a genuine (for him) sacrifice for what society (that is, *our* society) judged to be the greater good, and no logic can really refute this conclusion. Likewise the mother who exposes herself to contagion and engages in hard work and unpleasant activities for a desperately sick child often runs risks greater than any *likely* personal gains from her actions. To be called upon to give up something in order that another—or others—may have more is an occasional (and maybe even a frequent) demand of every society.

The supervisor certainly faces this problem. Shall he "play it safe" and accumulate all the "brownie points" he can or should he speak out resolutely for what he thinks is right? Shall he acquiesce in his boss's incorrect and possibly unfair appraisal of one or more of his subordinates, or shall he "stick his neck out" for the offended persons? Or put more realistically, when and under what circumstances if ever, should he risk his future for his friends—and for what is right?

In reality we do not have an answer to this question. However, we know two things: First, most supervisors will inevitably face such problems at least on occasion; and second, how supervisors handle these problems may well determine where they stand and will stand in the organization. Additionally, we need to make one point clear: It is not *always* right and proper "to go to bat" for another person, nor is it always right to uphold a boss who has made a mistake. Thus on this issue the supervisor has a problem—or more accurately, potentially he has many problems, problems that only he can resolve.

This topic is closely related to one of the most critical issues facing business today, namely, that of its social responsibility. The subject is obviously too complex to explore here in detail, but the above considerations are relevant to this issue too. Regardless of what Mr. Wilson of General Motors did or did not say—and of whoever else did or did not say it—what's good for General Motors is *not* always good for the United States (nor is the reverse true!). Furthermore, business must be seen as accepting and attempting to discharge its moral obligations, or else it will continue to occupy one of the lower rungs of the ladder of social esteem! ˜

Economic Gain versus the Quality of Life

A problem which as recently as fifteen to twenty years ago most of us did not know we had is how far we are willing to go in an effort to increase the GNP and/or make economic gain if in so doing we overpopulate the planet, damage the environment, render the earth less habitable, and/or detract from the quality of life of countless individuals. The problem may sound contrived, but it is very real. Furthermore competent, conscientious individuals, including experts in the involved fields, have sometimes the widest differences of opinion.[7]

Illustrations are legion. They range from the Concorde and/or the American SST, through the Trans-Alaska pipeline, to the snail darter, an endangered species inhabiting a particular part of the Little Tennessee River. They include the leading business, scientific, and professional people of the country (not all on the same side of every issue), and public-interest advocates like Ralph Nader, Paul Ehrlich, and Rachel Carson. Scores of legislative enactments (not all on the same side, either) have resulted, and public as well as private debates on the subjects appear to be never-ending.

Again even if they are involved only as interested citizens, supervisors must face the problems. Is bigger always better? Is *more* profit the always-to-be-desired goal? Is a larger GNP superior to a smaller one? Are people and their needs and desires the only important standard for determining actions? Are leisure and more purchasing power the true measures of how well one lives? These questions represent issues, real ones that must be faced. They simply will not go away.[8]

The Locus of Organizational Control

One problem that we believed until recently we had behind us is who is to own and manage and control business. Few if any dissenting voices were formerly heard, at least in the United States: it was management, the directors, the stockholders. The company was theirs to do with as they pleased, at least within wide limits; and they permitted other groups (suppliers, employees, customers, and so on) a place in it only because it was advantageous for the firm to do this. The clear and overriding goal of the business was profit for stockholders.

This, however, was a situation that did not last. For one thing, there was the labor union, with its demands for bargaining concerning wages, hours, and conditions of work. And then there was the government with its insistence that certain things be done certain ways—and certain other things not be done at all! More recently management has had to deal with consumer groups, ecologists, social-responsibility advocates, and others, including those making serious proposals that corporations be governed entirely by outside directors. Additionally, much has been said and written about the desirability—some say, the inevitability—of worker participation in corporate decisions.

If all this seems disturbing to the old-line managers, he or she should remember that it is only part of a worldwide trend. For example, the spread of communism over a third of the globe was shocking to many, and the success of a milder form of socialism, particularly in countries like Great Britain, Italy, and Mexico, was hardly less surprising. In addition there is *codetermination* in Germany and *workers' management* in Yugoslavia. All these represent a trend to open up the work situation and give the ordinary worker a substantial voice in matters that affect that worker most. It is important that we avoid interpreting American happenings without being aware that they do not typically happen in isolation.[9]

Since the supervisor is "right on the firing line" where workers and managers meet, he or she cannot afford to be indifferent to the question raised by these developments: How far should workers go—or be permitted to go—in corporate control? To whatever extent they are involved, what form should their influence take? We have indicated earlier that we believe that (1) collective bargaining is here to stay and (2) worker participation (at least in the form advocated by OD) is not the wave of the future. But this leaves the supervisor with some serious homework to do. What should be the nature of control in the world of work and who (and in each case to what extent) should exercise it? These questions may not be earthshaking in the short run for the supervisor. In the long run they might be.

The Permanence of Employment

Another worldwide development that as yet has had relatively little influence in the United States is various efforts to assure the continuity of employment for the workers of the firm or agency. This movement has gone quite far in some parts of the world, with Japan perhaps receiving the greatest publicity. There, for a significant portion of the work force up to age fifty-five, the normal retirement age, when one secures a job with a firm, he has virtually a lifetime job. Firms keep their permanent employees, in other words, through bad times as well as good, and job security is therefore well assured.

While the arrangements vary from country to country, (virtually) guaranteed employment is an actuality or a serious concern in many other parts of the world. Various parts of Latin America can be cited, as can some of the Scandinavian countries. Indeed there are few places in the more advanced nations where the matter is not being seriously considered. (Parenthetically one might remark that the United States has firms with long-standing commitments along this line. The best known is Procter and Gamble, which has had guaranteed employment—subject, of course, to certain conditions—since 1923.) It should also be remembered that especially in the fifties the guaranteed annual wage was a live bargaining issue and that in the latter part of the seventies similar efforts were renewed in negotiations.

Historically, U.S. firms have looked upon the layoff as a proper and effective means of either increasing profit or reducing loss, and their right so to act has seldom been questioned. However, concern about such decisions has arisen in a good many quarters, and employers of the future may or may not continue to have along this line the freedom that they have previously enjoyed.

At the same time it should not be overlooked that we have already taken steps that limit this freedom of the employer. Unemployment compensation is an example and perhaps workmen's compensation is also in a way. Supplementary unemployment benefits (SUB) are now provided to hundreds of thousands of workers, and various programs of providing jobs for the unemployed are now a part of the work scene. Interest in the federal government as "the employer of last resort" must not be taken lightly, and the negative income tax (or some other form of guaranteed income) has been seriously advocated by representatives of both political parties and by conservatives as well as liberals.[10]

It may not be directly relevant to guaranteed employment, but attention nevertheless needs to be directed to an arrangement of recent internal revenue legislation that may eventually have a profound effect on the ownership of American business by transferring what may become a significant portion of it from present stockholders to employees. This plan operates by means of a certain investment tax credit and typically to the gain of both the firm and the employees. It is referred to as the Employee Stock Ownership Plan (ESOP) and is often called the *Kelso* plan. Legislatively, the principal sponsor has been Senator Russell Long of Louisiana. It is too early to tell what its ultimate outcome may be, but if employees become employers also, the old order may be significantly modified.[11]

Meanwhile the supervision has another more-than-simply-academic question to ponder: How far should employers be allowed to go in separating workers from their payrolls?

Job Enlargement or Enrichment

Earlier in this chapter we spoke about the boredom and lack of a sense of purpose and accomplishment thought to accompany much work in the United States. Various proposals have been made to overcome this situation, a situation which, as pointed out above, some writers view as a great misfortune. One of these is *job enlargement*, a process by which the worker's tasks are increased in number so that he or she does not have as much repetition of the same small operation. Another has been a frequent topic in earlier chapters of this book. It is *job enrichment*, which consists in adding more challenge to the job and giving the worker an opportunity to exercise judgment, initiative, and the like. An example of either or both might be to let a person complete a whole operation rather than being responsible for interminable repetition of a small part of it.

While there is no doubt that much work is boring and without challenge and perhaps at times unnecessarily so, we have earlier expressed some doubt about the logic of job enrichment and similar plans. They seem like intellectual or white-collar or middle-class approaches to what is typically a blue-collar situation. It is not certain, for example, that every task that appears boring to an observer also is boring to the one who is responsible for doing it. Nor is it clear that workers are consumed with a desire for greater creativity, initiative, or sense of contribution in or to their work. Job enrichment has worked quite well in some situations, of that there can be no doubt, but there is question as to how far it should go or how far workers want it to go. After all, the feelings that workers develop as to *why* managers attempt to enlarge or enrich jobs may be far more influential than the enlargement or enrichment itself. In any case the supervisor has another issue to ponder: How successful have these plans been and what are their prospects for the future? Should he or she attempt actions calculated to reduce boredom, monotony, and pointlessness among subordinates? If so, how should the supervisor proceed?

The Unionization of Supervisors

One way in which American labor law differs significantly from that of many other Western nations is in its virtual prohibition of any collective-bargaining activities by managers, or even on their behalf. More specifically, as pointed out earlier, the Taft-Hartley Act of 1947 relieved the employer of any obligation to bargain collectively with any union representing members of management, beginning with the first-level supervisor. (For the purposes of the act, a manager is anyone who has the authority to take certain personnel actions or to "effectively recommend" such actions.) Already by 1947 foremen's unions had been organized and had achieved considerable strength in certain industries, but with the passage of the Taft-Hartley Act, for all practical purposes they disappeared. Incidentally, it should be noted that the act did not make collective bargaining with supervisors illegal. Rather it did not *require* it. Thus an executive can with impunity fire a foreman for union activity as such, though he or she may also legally bargain with such a union if he or she chooses.

So far as interest in collective bargaining for themselves is concerned, foremen and other managers appear to have been decidedly (or maybe even remarkably) quiescent for the last thirty and more years. The reason for this situation is not apparent. Certainly it is not because of the outstanding ways in which first-line supervisors in particular and other managers in general have been treated (as regards independence of judgment, pay, job security, overtime, and the like), but nevertheless the foreman's union movement was effectively muted. One cannot be sure whether this is a permanent situation or only the calm before a storm. Most likely, the facts are somewhere in between these extremes. Thus another issue is, Will there be supervisory unions? and if so, what will they be like?

THE SUPERVISOR OF THE FUTURE

By now it should be clear why we made the point early in this book as well as at other points in it that American managers, including supervisors, have usually been *technique-minded* to an undesirable degree. Somehow there has been a feeling that there is a way to supervise and that certain methods, and only those, are really successful. This, however, is not borne out in experience. On the other hand, the supervisor's techniques, instead of being critical, are typically only one factor—and usually not the most important—in success. In other words, assuming that they are not definitely offensive or illegal, the techniques have their greatest significance in the light they throw on what sort of person the supervisor is.[12]

Thus success does not consist primarily in what supervisors do, nor even, important as it is, in why they do it. Success in supervision is most frequently a matter of why their subordinates—and often their bosses—*think* and *feel* supervisors do whatever they do. The techniques are thus often taken to reveal the *character* of the boss, and this has more influence on how we evaluate him than any other factor does. Somehow we just are not inspired by people whose motives are open to serious question.

At the same time, character alone is not enough. In order to get cooperation on a continuing basis, bosses have to show a certain measure of *competence*. They must be realistic, for example. They may not (and should not be expected to) know all the details of every job, but they should know what each job is all about. Furthermore, when they cannot help us in our jobs, they need to know where the help may be found, and to do whatever is reasonable to see that we secure it when needed.

They are also to be competent in their personal relations. Regardless of whether they have ever been one, they still must know what it is like to be a janitor or a sheet-metal worker or an accountant. And when they deal with a worker they make use of this knowledge (plus what they have learned about the hopes, aspirations, and frustrations of the particular individual) in dealing with him or her.

They also do their level best to be *fair*, guarding against favoring people they like just because they like them and also against discriminating against people they like less well. They also try to keep things that are merely incidental and of no real significance to the job (for example, sex, race, and so on) from influencing their actions about it. At the same time they are *firm*, knowing full well that the ultimate good of all depends on developing and adhering to certain standards of conduct and performance and being unwilling to sacrifice the long-run gain of the organization and its members by trying to be popular through "winking at" conduct which should not be approved.

They are also *alert*. They have a feel for "what is going on in the world" and more particularly in the world of work and in the firm, plant, store, or office. They have a lively interest not only in what has happened and is happening, but also in what is likely to happen; and they make mistakes, including some big ones. But in general they know where they and their people are going, and they enlist their people's cooperation in achieving these goals. Theirs is one of the most challenging of jobs.

QUESTIONS

1 Is the book correct in saying that in general we have a pessimistic view of human nature as well as of the nature of workers and of work? Why is this true? What philosophical developments lie behind whatever pessimistic views are found?

2 In what ways did (a) the puritan ethic and (b) democratic egalitarianism tend to counter the pessimistic views mentioned in Question 1?

3 What evidence is there that the Western world, including the United States, has historically accepted the view that work is unworthy or at least largely lacking in dignity and challenge?

4 What is *your* view of the proper relationship between private enterprise on the one hand and the government (including but not restricted to the federal one) on the other? (If you are not sure what yours is or how correct it is, many of us share your feelings. That fact is not sufficient for us to fail to try to formulate such a view.)

5 Does the text say or imply that there might be times when a firm should forego certain profits in order to discharge obligations of citizenship? Do you believe there are such times? Why?

6 In what ways has an interest in the "quality of life" affected business firms and government agencies in the last twenty years?

7 How far should a firm (or an agency) go in assuring continuing work for its (permanent) work force? Have we generally gone too far along this line in the United States? not far enough? Why do you say so?

8 What is the present situation with regard to the unionization of supervisors and other managers in private business in the United States? Will this situation continue for the foreseeable future? Why? Do you approve of it?

NOTES

1 Peter Drucker, *Management* (New York: Harper & Row, 1974).

2 Keith Davis, *Human Behavior at Work: Human Relations and Organizational Behavior,* 4th ed. (New York: McGraw-Hill, 1972).

3 Elton Mayo, *The Social Problems of An Industrial Civilization* (Cambridge, Mass.: Harvard Graduate School of Business Administration, 1945). See especially Chap. 2.

4 Walter Guzzardi, "Education for the World of Work," *Fortune,* vol. 92, no. 4, pp. 124–129, 184–193, October 1975; and Charles E. Burck, "Schools Where Students Learn Paying Jobs," *Fortune,* vol. 92, no. 6, pp. 124–130, December 1975.

5 A great deal has been written on the student protests of the late sixties and early seventies. As examples, see Daniel Seligman, "A Special Kind of Rebellion," *Fortune,* vol. 79, no. 1, pp. 67–71, 172–181, January 1969; Seymour Martin Lipsit, "American Student Activism in Comparative Perspective," *American Psychologist,* vol. 25, no. 8, pp. 675–693, August 1970; and "ACE Study on Campus Unrest: Questions for Behavioral Scientists," *Science,* vol. 165, no. 3889, pp. 157–161, July 11, 1969.

6 If one finds this notion a bit strange or even radical, it might be worthwhile to study a recent article by the president of Atlantic Richfield; see Thornton Bradshaw, "My Case for National Planning," *Fortune,* vol. 95, no. 2, pp. 100–105, February 1977.

7 Again the available material is almost unlimited. See for example, "Price of Pollution: The Fight to Clean Up Lake Erie Is Proving to Be Long and Costly," *The Wall Street Journal,* vol 58, no. 47, pp. 1ff, Sept. 9, 1976; Joseph J. Spengler, "Population Problem: In Search of a Solution," *Science,* vol. 166, no. 3910, pp. 1234–1238, December 5, 1969; and Wayne R. Bartz, "While Psychologists Doze On," *American Psychologist,* vol. 25, no. 6, pp. 500–503, June 1970.

8 "The Law's Delay: Huge Plant's Demise Signals Trouble Ahead for Energy Expansion," *The Wall Street Journal,* vol. 58, no. 47, pp. 1ff, Sept. 9, 1976.

9 George W. England and Raymond Lee, "The Relationship between Managerial Values and Management Success in the United States, Japan, India, and Australia," *Journal of Applied Psychology,* vol. 59, no. 4, pp. 411–419, August 1974; and Michael Osbaldiston, "Skandia Insurance Group: Restructuring the Work and Enriching the Job," *Management International Review,* vol. 16, no. 2, pp. 9–22, 1976.

10 Apparently interest in this subject is becoming widespread. See, for example, David Ignatius, "A Bitter Election Over, Steel Union Turns to Negotiating a 'Lifetime Security Plan,' " *The Wall Street Journal,* vol. 59, no. 30, p. 26, Feb. 11, 1977. A not-unrelated article is "Solidarity Forever—Forty Years On," *The Wall Street Journal,* vol. 59, no. 32, p. 20, Feb. 15, 1977.

11 Charles G. Burck, "There's More to ESOP Than Meets the Eye," *Fortune,* vol. 93, no. 3, pp. 128–133, 170–172, March 1976; and W. Robert Reum and Sherry Milliken Reum, "Employee Stock Ownership Plans: Plusses and Minusses," *Harvard Business Review,* vol. 54, no. 4, pp. 133ff, July-August 1976.

12 Lyman W. Porter, Edward E. Lawler, III, and J. Richard Hockman, *Behavior in Organizations* (New York: McGraw-Hill, 1975), especially Chap. 17.

CASES

In the preceding chapter we encountered cases that involved either unusual personnel policies or an unusual set of circumstances or both. That is also true of the two cases of this chapter.

In the Hart case, a vacation policy was agreed to at some point during the several years that the grievant was working in another plant of the same Company. When he returned to the Houston plant, he felt that it should also cover him as a former employee of that plant and an uninterrupted employee of the Company.

The Evanston case involves the extent to which Management can make and enforce rules relative to the return of an employee from a legitimate sick leave. Certainly the Company had the right to make rules that enabled it to treat such employees fairly and uniformly (insofar as their situations were the same). The question in this case is whether the action relative to Ms. Evanston represented a proper exercise of such Management rights or whether the Company was arbitrary in its action toward her.

CASE 22-1

Since December 6, 1951, John D. Hart has worked for the Company in various production or bargaining-unit jobs. From 1951 to 1966, he was employed at the Houston plant of the Company, but when it became necessary to lay off employees, he was given an opportunity to transfer to the Des Moines plant instead of taking a layoff, and this he did. When he left Houston he was paid in full, and at Des Moines went under a separate labor agreement with a different local Union, occupied a different job classification, and was paid at the Des Moines rate for that and all his subsequent jobs.

In 1975 Hart was given an opportunity to return to the Houston plant, though in doing so he had to pay his own moving expenses. The Company did agree to give him his original seniority date (1951), and the Union concurred. This date was effective, however, only for layoff purposes and for calculating retirement benefits; he was to use the date of his return to Houston for vacation bidding, overtime, promotion, and other purposes.

For many years the Houston plant had an incentive-wage plan, under which the average yearly earnings figured in determining the employee's rate of pay for his annual vacation. In 1970, the Company and the Union agreed to abolish the incentive-wage system, but as a concession to the persons then on the payroll decided that henceforth each would receive each year his or her regular vacation pay plus a bonus of twelve hours of pay per week for each week of vacation. To be eligible for this bonus, an employee had to be "on the payroll as of April 4, 1970."

When Hart returned to Houston, he contended that he was eligible for this vacation bonus since he was "on the payroll as of April 4, 1970." True, he admitted, he was working in Des Moines, but it was the same Company. Furthermore he had been a Company employee uninterruptedly since 1951, as evidenced by the Company's recognition of his 1951 seniority date.

The Company's position is that the agreement about the vacation bonus was intended for and applied to only those regular, full-time employees who were on the payroll *in Houston* on the date in question.

How sound are Hart's contentions?

CASE 22-2

Ms. Rachel Evanston is a roll packer for the Bakery. She works the evening shift, starting at 6:00 P.M. each day except Friday and Sunday. Ms. Evanston became ill in late January 1970, and lost a week or more of work. On Friday, February 6, 1970, at about 11:00 A.M. she secured a release from her physician, such a document being required by the company before she could return to work. At once she called Alvin Granville, her foreman, and told him she would report to work at 6:00 P.M. the next day. (Friday was one of her days off.)

Granville hesitated for a moment and then informed Ms. Evanston that she could not come back on Saturday but would have to wait till 6:00 P.M. on Monday (Sunday being her other day off). The basis for his decision was a notice that for some months had been on the department's bulletin board. It was signed by the plant manager and read as follows:

> In the event of an emergency, when an employee *must* be off, it will be necessary that you call one of the Superintendents to advise him of your *not* being available for work.
> The Superintendent will schedule a replacement to work in your place until such time as you are able to return to work.
> When you are ready to return to work, it will be necessary that you call one of the Superintendents and give him notice of your availability for work no later than the end of the shift on which your replacement is working.
> If you call after the designated time, you will be scheduled for work on the next available schedule.

Ms. Evanston was quite upset by this ruling. It meant that though she was giving the Company thirty-one hours of notice, she still would lose pay for an extra day. Besides needing the money, she felt the Company's action was arbitrary and unfair, especially in view of the fact that the Company maintained a list of so-called jobbers, who received more than the regular rate for the job when they worked but to whom no guarantee of work was made. Ms. Evanston knew that she was being replaced by one of these jobbers.

Incidentally, another posted Company rule required that an employee who found he could not come to work had to give his supervisor at least two hours of notice. Ms. Evanston was struck by the discrepancy between this two-hour period and the unacceptability to the Company of her thirty-one-hour notice.

Considering all the facts, did Granville handle this situation correctly? Actually, did he have any other choice in view of the posted notice? Did the plant manager have the right to make, post, and enforce the rules contained in the notice?

For Those Who Wish
to Explore More Fully

Especially in view of the wide variety of subjects discussed in this book, there is virtually an unlimited number of sources where one can find materials for additional investigation. These are usually found in books and periodicals, though posters, bulletins, and pamphlets may be useful.

The location of relevant sources is not at all difficult if one has access to a large or medium-size library. The card catalog is easily available and knowing either the title or the author usually makes the book easy to find. Books may be located by general subject matter as well.

Finding relevant articles in current or bound periodicals, however, is a bit more complicated, especially when one is investigating a topic without previous knowledge of specific articles, authors, or even the most closely related periodicals. Here the indexes or abstracts of such materials are invaluable.

For topics covered in this book two such publications are ordinarily most useful. One is the *Business Periodicals Index*, published annually by H. W. Wilson Co., and the other is the *Readers Guide to Periodical Literature*, also published annually by Wilson. Additional ones are the *Social Sciences Index,* the *Psychological Abstracts,* and *Personnel Management Abstracts*. Librarians are always willing to assist one in using these guides and in locating the needed volumes of periodicals. (Books are also cited in some of the above, and hence they may be located in this fashion as well as by use of the card catalog.)

Such periodicals as the following are likely to contain articles relating to the topics discussed in this book: *Harvard Business Review, Fortune, The Wall Street Journal, Personnel, The Personnel Journal, Personnel Management, Public Personnel Management, California Management Review, Business Week,* and *Supervisory Management.* In addition there are hundreds of interesting and valuable articles in more generalized publications (e.g., *Time* and *Newsweek*) and in journals devoted to a particular profession or specialized activity (e.g., steel manufacturing, sales management, or dentistry).

Another source of personnel information that often proves valuable is the loose-leaf services (updated biweekly or more often) of both Prentice-Hall and the Bureau of National Affairs. The former contains volumes with titles such as (1) *Personnel Management,* (2) *Industrial Relations Guide,* and (3) *Labor Relations.* The latter has volumes covering *OSHA Cases, FER Cases, Guidebook to Labor Law, Basic Patterns in Union Contracts,* and others.

Labor arbitration awards are published by the Bureau of National Affairs (cited as, for example, *59LA 12*), the Commerce Clearing House (cited as, for example, *76 ARB 28*), and the American Arbitration Association (cited as, for example, *216AAA56* or *LAIG1844* or *90-AIS-5* and appearing in summary forms). The awards often make interesting and valuable reading and, like the loose-leaf services cited above, can be located quickly by the reference librarian in any library that has them.

An area in which some readers might have an interest is the acts of the Congress or decisions by the U.S. Supreme Court or the National Labor Relations Board. Relevant materials are in the library of any law school and again the reference librarian can help in their location. Such documents are often much less involved and more interesting than the average person suspects and frequently prove to be quite enlightening.

The list below represents a few of the most significant books in areas covered by this text. It could obviously be extended to many times its present length:

Chris Argyris, *The Application of Organization Sociology.* Cambridge, 1974.
Elliott Aronson, *The Human Animal* (2d ed.), Freeman, 1976.
Wayne Bennis, *Changing Organizations.* McGraw-Hill, 1966.
Robert Blake and Jane Mouton, *The Managerial Grid.* Gulf, 1964.
Lemuel R. Boulware, *The Truth about Boulwarism.* BNA, 1969.
David G. Bowers, *Systems of Organization.* U. of Michigan Press, 1976.
Keith Davis, *Human Behavior at Work* (4th ed.). McGraw-Hill, 1972.
Peter Drucker, *The Concept of the Corporation,* John Day, 1972.
Peter Drucker, *Management.* Harper, 1974.
Andrew DuBrin, *Fundamentals of Organizational Behavior.* Pergamon, 1974.
Frank and Edna Elkouri, *How Arbitration Works* (3d ed.). BNA, 1973.
Saul Gellerman, *Management of Human Resources.* Holt, 1966.
Robt. T. Heilbroner, *The Worldly Philosophers* (4th ed.). Simon and Schuster, 1972.
Robt. T. Heilbroner, *The Making of Economic Society* (2d ed.). Prentice-Hall, 1968.
Paul Hersey and Kenneth H. Blanchard, *Management of Organizational Behavior* (2d ed.).
    Prentice-Hall, 1969.
Paul T. Heyne, *Private Keepers of the Public Interest.* McGraw-Hill, 1967.
Frederick Herzberg, *Work and the Nature of Man.* No. Am. Library, 1973.
Robert L. Kahn and Chas. F. Caunell, *The Dynamics of Interviewing.* Wiley, 1957.
Labor Law Course (a new edition each year). Commerce Clearing House.
Rensis Likert, *The Human Organization.* McGraw-Hill, 1967.
Rensis Likert, *New Ways of Managing Conflict.* McGraw-Hill, 1976.
David C. McClelland, *The Achieving Society.* Van Nostrand, 1961.

Douglas McGregor, *The Professional Manager*. McGraw-Hill, 1967.

Alfred J. Marrow, David G. Bowers, and Stanley E. Seashore, *Management by Participation*. Harper, 1967.

Abraham Maslow, *Eupsychian Management*. McGraw-Hill, 1960.

Abraham Maslow, *Motivation and Personality*. Harper, 1954.

Elton Mayo, *The Social Problems of an Industrial Civilization*. Graduate School of Business, Harvard, 1945.

Chas. R. Milton, *Ethics and Expediency in Personnel Management*. U. of South Carolina Press, 1970.

C. N. Parkinson, *Parkinson's Law*. Houghton Mifflin, 1957.

Lawrence J. Peter and Peter Hull, *The Peter Principle*. Bantam, 1970.

Riva Poor, *4 Days, 40 Hours*. Bursk and Poor, 1970.

Lloyd G. Reynolds, *Labor Economics and Labor Relations* (6th ed.). Houghton Mifflin, 1974.

Fritz J. Roethlisberger and William J. Dickson, *Management and the Worker*. Harvard, 1939.

Carl Rogers, *Counseling and Psychotherapy*. Houghton Mifflin, 1942.

A. Q. Sartain, A. J. North, J. R. Strange, and H. M. Chapman, *Psychology: Understanding Human Behavior,* (4th ed.). McGraw-Hill, 1973.

Carroll L. Shartle, *Executive Performance and Leadership*. Prentice-Hall, 1956.

Studs Terkel, *Working*. Avon, 1974.

Robert Townsend, *Up the Organization*. Fawcett, 1971.

Edward J. Walsh, *Dirty Work, Race, and Self-Esteem*. Inst. of Labor and Ind. Rel., U. of Michigan, 1975.

Wm. F. Whyte, Jr., *Is Anybody Listening?* Simon & Schuster, 1951.

Wm. F. Whyte, Jr., *The Organization Man*. Clarion, 1956.

Index

INDEX